HOTEL

Untold Stories

Rene D. Egle

Llumina Press

ISBN: 978-1-59526-918-8 (PB)
     978-1-59526-919-5 (HC)
     978-1-59526-920-1 (Ebook)

Printed in the United States of America by Llumina Press

Library of Congress Control Number: 2007910329

"I was a banquet waiter at the Beverly Hilton hotel. You learn a lot when you're in the service industry-the jerks of the world really come to the fore. It's a valuable learning experience to be in the position where you're of service to someone who sometimes doesn't even know you're there."

Andy Garcia,
Actor, Director, Producer

Chapter 1: *The Black Forest Grand Hotel*

The foggy morning mist still lingered above the grey surface of Lake Talasee and the sun had just begun clearing the picturesque treetops of the surrounding forest. Early birds were already singing away and from deep inside the forest the unmistakable cries of a lonely cuckoo echoed across the lake; this would be a glorious late summer day indeed. For me, of course, it was the beginning of real life and I was nervous, very nervous. I was about to embark on something completely new and very different from that sleepy little town that had been my goldfish bowl for so long.

The first night I had not slept at all and the following morning I deeply regretted my decision of having chosen a career in the hotel business. It suddenly occurred to me that being so far away from home and surrounded by strangers was not actually what I had in mind when I came back from Talasee that day with my father boasting proudly to everyone that I would be working at the famous Black Forest Grand Hotel. It now dawned on me that a one-day practical training session is one thing, having to work for a living is something completely different. This would be the first but unfortunately not the last time in my career that I would make decisions out of momentary enthusiasm without considering the possible consequences. However, that was me.

After my shower that morning, I had to force myself into my brand-new traditional black and white waiter's outfit. The—in my opinion—funny-looking outfit consisted of a pair of black trousers, which I had bought a few days earlier with my mother, a white shirt and a black bow tie. The most important piece of this uniform, and the only one provided by the hotel, was the black vest. Standing in front of the mirror, I closed the last of three large buttons on my vest, which looked as if it had been worn by generations of waiters before me. I briefly wondered what stories it could tell if it could talk. I shook my head. Satisfied that all was in order I switched off the lights in my room, locked the door and left for my first day in real life. When I stepped out of the staff building, I was greeted by a warm and beautiful summer morning. I hoped this would be a good sign for things to come.

As I walked across the large and spacious car park, I noticed more luxurious cars than I had ever seen in my hometown. I wondered what the owners of these cars would be like, probably very rich and very demanding. These thoughts did not help, of course, to make me feel any better—quite on the contrary. I was intimidated and became even more nervous.

For a moment I considered turning back, getting changed and driving off to more familiar territory. This certainly would have been the easiest way to handle this but only cowards do things like that. Not wanting anyone to call me a coward, I continued walking towards the hotel. As I walked, I saw my reflection in the car windows and I became painfully aware of my funny black and white waiter's outfit. I entered the hotel via the main entrance, which was forbidden for all employees, but at the time I didn't know that and walked across the deserted hotel lobby trying to find my way to the restaurant.

"Aah, the new guy," someone suddenly called from behind. I turned around and before me stood a young man dressed in the same black and white waiter's outfit as I. With a smile, he walked towards me and shook my hand.

"Welcome to the Black Forest Grand Hotel, Rotstift." I must have looked silly standing there shaking his hand, wondering *who* or rather *what* a Rotstift was.

Johnny Pokwa was one of the senior trainees whereas I had just become the most junior trainee, called "Rotstift." The title of Rotstift, or "Red Trainee," was assigned only to the newest and youngest trainees joining the hotel fresh from school. There was a strict hierarchy amongst trainees and in this hierarchy, the Rotstift ranked the lowest. The color red simply implied that this person was very fresh like a piece of raw meat.

Johnny had a very cheerful and outgoing personality, which was exactly what I needed considering the fragile state I was in. He immediately took me on a tour of the hotel. His relaxed and confident demeanor impressed me immensely, especially the way he talked with literally everyone we met. The tour was amazing; I was lost soon after we started. Absolutely everything was a "first" for me—the many rooms, the swimming pool, the huge kitchen where someone announced guests' orders via microphone and busy waiters dashing in and out of the kitchen. It was impressive and scary at the same time.

Johnny then went on to introduce me to the boss, Mr. Hanter. Mr. Hanter was in his early fifties, he was tall and had a set of very large ears on which rested a pair of glasses with some very thick lenses. He was dressed like us except that his vest was green. Despite his somewhat funny looks, he radiated leadership. I always thought that if he walked into a room, it would have not mattered how he was dressed; people would know that he is the boss. His welcome speech was short and to the point.

"Ah, the new one," he murmured. "You will follow Mr. Pokwa for the next few days," he said with a deep booming voice and that was it. He looked at Johnny and then walked off leaving us standing there. I was impressed by this brief encounter even though the thought of his funny looks left a smile on my face.

The Black Forest with its pleasant mild climate in August drew many tourists from all over Germany, Austria, Switzerland and other parts of Europe. To sit on a garden terrace overlooking the lake on one of these beautiful days was the very reason why people came here in the first place. The Black Forest Grand Hotel had the largest garden terrace on Lake Talasee. Divided into the upper and the lower terrace, both combined contained over 100 tables with close to 500 seats, each terrace divided into four-to-five sections with forty-to-fifty seats per section. The size of a section was determined by the capability of the waiter assigned to it. The capability of a waiter was determined by how much he needed the gratuities or, as we professionals call it, "tip"!

In addition, tip was good on the terrace for a capable waiter. The day I started, Johnny was assigned to the garden terrace. It was a perfect day with plenty of sunshine and a clear blue cloudless sky. The terrace teemed with life; there were tourists in their thousands, families with screaming children, couples having ice cream and people looking for tables. At that moment, I became painfully aware once again that I was wearing a waiter's uniform. I froze instantly. I felt as if the entire terrace was staring at my funny black and white outfit and me.

There is a difference in walking through a restaurant in front of guests wearing civilian clothes and doing so dressed as a waiter. Especially for a first-time waiter who had never been a waiter before. In my case, I was a waiter who had never even been served by a waiter before.

Johnny explained to me that being a waiter is not much different from being an actor; both earn their living on a stage and in front of an

3

audience. Whilst for the actor, the stage is that of a theater, for the waiter it is the restaurant floor. The actor performs for his audience; the waiter performs for his customers. Both the actor and the waiter will never be able to let personal tragedies or unhappy experiences in their lives influence their performance. They strive to please their audience and both know the audience can be cruel, but whatever happens they will always have to hide their true feelings.

Hiding *my* true feelings was absolutely impossible. I somehow felt as if everybody on the terrace and from the hotel windows and all fellow employees were watching me. I had stage fright and hardly noticed Johnny telling me that I would spend my first day with someone called Ingrid. Strangely enough, he introduced Ingrid as "Kiki," a nickname by which she was commonly known. Judging by her less-than- pleasant response, she did not like being called Kiki and, judging by the way she measured me up, she did not like *me*, either. She was not very pleased having to baby-sit the new guy—me. Johnny left, laughing.

I just stood there, lost and waiting for instructions from Kiki as to what to do next. I did not have to wait long and the instructions came in the same impolite manner she showed during the introduction. Kiki growled, asking me what I was waiting for; the tables would not clear themselves.

One should think that clearing tables is a pretty simple and straightforward task. Just walk up to a table, pick up as many dishes as you can and then take them back to your service station. Having never cleared a table before, I was left approaching this task without any prior experience. Obviously, I did not waste time contemplating a strategy or some sort of plan to master something so incredibly simple. I know now, of course, that this was the very reason why I was only able to remove two items clumsily.

I picked up one cup and one saucer and wondered what to do next. My instinct and common sense urged me to bring both to a dishwasher. So far so good, except it now occurred to me that I did not actually know where the dishwasher was. Since I did all this contemplating in the midst of a busy garden operation and without any sense of urgency, another verbal slap in the face from Kiki was inevitable.

She suddenly stopped what she was doing and looked at me as I stood there with one cup and one saucer in my hands. Her face turned sour and she asked if I had never done this before. Of course, I had not.

She stared at me, clearly upset, and obviously assuming that every human being is blessed with the skill of table-clearing from the moment of birth. She asked me where I intended to go with the cup and saucer and why I was not using a tray.

I got the feeling that Kiki expected me to have some sort of basic knowledge in waiting tables; maybe she was not aware that this was my first day. So I decided to point this small but important detail out to her. This made her even angrier, asking me whether I thought this was funny, which for me, of course, it was not. It took her a while to realize that my level of expertise—for her, just simple common sense—was little more than nonexistent.

I just stood there and stared at her. At that moment, she must have realized that if she wanted any results from me, she would have to explain each task to me in at least some basic detail.

During the days and weeks that followed, I was confronted almost daily with expressions, abbreviations and tools which I had never heard or seen before. I had to ask for explanations or instructions in almost every conversation. They talked about "front of house," and "back of house." I didn't have a clue what that meant until Johnny explained that front of house is all those areas which are meant exclusively for customers—lobby, restaurants, reception and so on—whereas back of house is all areas which are not accessible to customers—laundry, kitchen, pantry, etc. Whenever I was assigned to work with Kiki, I pretended to know exactly what she was talking about. I was too scared to ask.

One day, for example, she ordered me to pick up one "OJ," two "AJ" and one "Irish." I remained calm, said yes and dashed off to the kitchen. Once I was in the kitchen, I would look for Johnny who would translate "AJ" into apple juice and "OJ" into orange juice for me. I still got slapped for being slow but at least I managed to bring her the right items.

During these first weeks, I interacted daily with many different people but mostly my fellow waiters, the chefs and, to some extent, the customers—*if* Kiki let me, that was. Interacting with such diverse groups and characters of people in a very dynamic environment was something I had to get used to. A busy food and beverage operation is a *very* dynamic and hectic working environment involving waiters, chefs and, of course, customers. During peak periods the kitchen can easily be compared with a battlefield. Chefs are shouting at waiters and waiters shouting at chefs, the banging of pots and pans, the intense heat, confusion, angry voices, swearing and all other side effects associated with war were all present.

The day I was exposed to this environment for the first time, I was literally shell-shocked. Facing a fuzzy customer after a heavy confrontation with an angry chef in the kitchen and still having to be friendly and polite is not a gift but a skill that has to be learned and, more importantly, practiced. I needed a lot of practice in this and pretty much everything else associated with serving guests.

I spent the coming weeks mostly with Kiki and was faced almost daily with new impressions and experiences. I felt as if I was in a different world. This new and luxurious world of elegance and style included also my fellow colleagues. The coolness with which they handled their guests and each other impressed me immensely.

There was Anita, for example, a girl of stunning beauty and, as I soon found out, Johnny's girlfriend. Anita was straw-blond and hailed from northern Germany. I have never met many people from outside my hometown and definitely not from as far away as northern Germany. She had a light Friesian accent and the most beautiful holes in her cheeks when she smiled.

Then there was Ralf Black, who happened to be straw-blond, too. Ralf had already completed two out of the three years apprentice-ship. Over time, I would grow quite fond of him. He was very organized and seemed to have planned out every step of his future down to the last detail, be it in his personal or professional life. More amazingly, Ralf had traveled through Japan on a bicycle. At first, I did not believe him, but when he produced the pictures as proof, I was in his spell.

Ralf talked a lot about his trip to a point that I started to hear the same stories over and over again. I remember when he told us that the Japanese constantly bow when meeting each other, which to me sounded a bit farfetched. Maybe it was true, but Japan for me was a place which was simply too far away and too alien. I had my doubts but I listened patiently. He was also fluent in English, which was of great help to all of us as we were not exactly masters of this language.

Another unique character was Antonio Barrollo and, as the name already implied, he had some Italian ancestry that was probably the reason for his high-strung temper. Antonio was the most senior and the wildest amongst the trainees. Antonio hailed from a town called Blumberg, only about thirty minutes from my own hometown. We both shared the same passion and that was motorbikes. Motorbikes is actually an overstatement; they were more mopeds than motorbikes.

On his day off, he would put on his leather jacket and take his bike for a spin. We always called him by his family name Barrollo and he liked his beer, had his share of girlfriends and was a kind of free spirit. Although he was a hard worker and usually had to run the busiest stations, he wasn't liked by Mr. Hanter. This was a fact that would eventually lead to his dismissal after taking things a little too far. He was frequently late for work, sometimes did not show up at all and always seemed to be in some sort of trouble. In many ways, he did not fit the profile of a waiter at all. Despite this, there were a number of things that I learned from him.

There were many more people and amongst them, some girls. Ulrike or Maja, as we called her, were girls that made an incredible impression on me and I ended up with a big crush on her. Then there was Petra Mueller, who was the fashion-model type. Tall and slim with long blond hair, she was the best-looking girl in the hotel. Her beauty was only marred by her loud squeaky voice. She was a little naïve, which made her a natural target for many practical jokes.

Besides us trainees, there were a number of regular employees from various countries: Angelo from Italy, Mohamed and Abi from Tunisia and the bartender Uzli from Turkey. Mr. Hanter was the restaurant manager and acted also as food-and-beverage manager. He was responsible for the organization of events, functions and promotions. Mr. Hanter was not the most handsome man with his thick glasses, protruding ears and skinny stature but he was one of the few people who left a lifelong impression on me.

As I have mentioned before, Mr. Hanter radiated leadership even without using his deep commanding voice. He would never scream or shout but chose his words carefully. On the few occasions when he disciplined me, it was his careful choice of words that stung more than a severe dressing down. Mr. Hanter reminded me much of a German U-boat captain in movies; he never showed his feelings to the crew, was always optimistic and in control. The only person he shared his concerns or feelings with, if he ever had any, was Hendrick, the senior headwaiter. If we really had been on a U-boat, Hendrick would have been the first officer. Mr. Hanter never talked much with us trainees, which by no means meant that he did not care; quite the opposite, we knew that he cared a great deal.

Mr. Hanter's right-hand man, Hendrick, was the only true professional in the team. He always seemed to roll his eyes at everything we did, be it on the job or in our free time. To work with Hendrick meant learning the finer details and the essence of our profession. Working with the other waiters, such as Angelo, Abi, and Mohamed, taught us the operational skills, speed and coordination—in short, the rougher parts of our profession.

Hendrick was the one who taught us the skill of opening wines professionally, filleting fish on the table, how to properly cut Chateaubriand at the table and much more. If he felt that we might not have understood what he had attempted to teach us, he would explain it again and again until we could do the job or answer all his questions. In my case, he realized quite early on that a lot of the basic requirements were lacking and, three days into my job, he patiently taught me how to present myself a little more elegantly, how to walk straight and essentially how not to look like a farmer. And Hendrick was gay.

Mr. Hanter had another right-hand man and that was Mr. Megan. Mr. Megan had one problem: He did not like customers. For him, customers were like unwanted intruders, funny creatures that deserved not more than sarcastic comments about their body features, the clothes they wore or the way they walked. For him, there was nothing likable in a customer. Customers had the unpleasant habit of appearing at the most inconvenient of times, which for Megan was pretty much all the time.

The executive chef, Mr. Karl, was the embodiment of a chef. His rough manners, round and oversized body with big arms and incredibly large hands made him the absolute and unchallenged ruler of the kitchen. He had a natural dislike for everything and everyone that moved outside his kitchen, waiters in particular. He looked after his chefs like a hawk and let nothing and nobody come over them. Punishment of chefs was conducted exclusively by him and only in his kitchen. He did not like having to leave the kitchen to see customers, not even for compliments. He felt very uncomfortable and vulnerable outside of his natural environment.

Slowly, I got to know them all, started to remember their names and made friends. My initial responsibility was not too big but nevertheless very important: the preparation of mise en place for all restaurants. Mise en place is a French term for the pre-service preparation of all equipment and condiments that may be required during the service. Mise en place includes the cleaning of ménages, polishing of cutlery, polishing of plates, folding of napkins and more. This had to be done daily.

I would start in the morning by collecting all ménage trays from the different stations (one such tray consisted of sugar bowl, mustard pot, toothpick holder, salt and pepper mill, ketchup bottle and parmesan container). I emptied mustard pots, ketchup bottles and the salt and pepper mills. Then I cleaned them thoroughly and refilled all with the respective contents. The mustard pots in particular left a lasting impression on my taste buds. Even today the smell of mustard reminds me of those days when I had to refill countless ménage pots, day in and day out.

Once I had completed the mise en place, I would distribute the trays back to the service stations in the different restaurants and continue with folding the napkins. By the time I finished all this, breakfast service was nearly over and the breakfast cutlery had to be washed and then polished. Once I had done the cutlery, I assisted the station waiters in setting up the individual sections of the restaurant for lunch.

Having achieved proficiency in mise en place, meaning being able to finish before breakfast was over, I was assigned to a breakfast station to help the station waiter with the service. I had not actually served any guest until then. My main task was more like that of a runner—picking up coffee, tea and other items from the kitchen and the bar as instructed by the station waiter.

Since I had mastered mise en place and was able to find my way to and from the kitchen without getting lost, Johnny and Barrollo decided that it was time for my initiation by playing their first practical joke on me. One sunny Thursday morning, we were in the midst of breakfast service when Johnny approached, telling me that I would witness my first gourmet dinner on Saturday night.

"What is a 'gourmet' dinner?" I asked innocently.

The word *gourmet* sounded remotely French to me and French was not a language I spoke, but then again, I did not speak any other language. Johnny passionately described the menu in a manner in which other people would describe a new motorbike, a brand new sports car or something else exciting. Up to that point, I had never thought of a menu as being something exciting or even interesting, but the way Johnny described the dishes made them sound very interesting indeed and, at least to me, a little mysterious.

Live lobster was one of the dishes that left me puzzled. Having never seen a lobster in my life, I wondered how one could possibly eat a live lobster since it was certain that the doomed creature would try to defend itself. My puzzled expression made him laugh. Authentic Russian caviar was another dish that got him very excited. When he quoted me the price for one 50-gram tin, I was sure he must have been wrong, but with him being the senior trainee, I decided not to tell him that. I thought I had tasted caviar before from our local supermarket and if I could get it in my hometown, why was it so special? Johnny laughed, saying that *that* caviar was not the real thing. I wondered what the real thing would look like. Therefore, Johnny explained the entire menu, saying that if I had to pay for this dinner, one year's salary would not be enough. Needless to say, I didn't believe him. *Why would someone want to spend so much money on food?*

Johnny finished by giving me a detailed explanation of the wines that would be served and their prices. It struck me again, as it had many times in the past three weeks, just how different this world was from the goldfish bowl I had left behind. Money did not seem to matter to these people.

We finished the breakfast service, cleared and cleaned the tables in our station and prepared everything for lunch. The weather outside was glorious. It would be a busy day for the people in the garden since there was not a single cloud in the sky and the terrace was blessed with a cooling breeze.

Shortly before lunch, I was just in midst of setting up a table when Barrollo came to my station telling me that the chef wanted to see me in the kitchen at once. I was shocked; it was difficult for me to believe that the almighty chef would request me, especially since, due to my rock-bottom rank, he had never shown any interest in communicating with me before. This excluded, of course, his occasional angry shouts when I would pick up the wrong dish or did not carry a plate straight, turning his carefully arranged food presentation into little more than, as he called it, "a railway station meal." What could he possibly want from me, *had I done anything wrong?*

Since Barrollo was the most senior waiter in the hotel, I did not dare to ask him whether he was sure about that and therefore went straight to the kitchen. I greeted the chef politely and when he saw me, he moaned indescribably and looked at me with pity in his eyes. His eyes reflected the pity of a man who clearly did not expect me to last longer than three months in this hotel. Without greeting, he yelled "Go and get the lobster gun from the Berg Hotel" so loudly that everyone in the kitchen could hear it. All eyes were on me.

My ears rang and the words lobster gun, trolley and Berg Hotel were all I remembered from his order. I stammered away trying to figure out what to do next. I left the kitchen with my head down, avoiding the looks of the girls behind the service bar. I went to see Barrollo. I found him in the restaurant and recounted my encounter with the chef. He patiently listened to my plight and explained to me, step by step, what I had to do and how I had to do it.

He explained that the lobster gun was needed for a gourmet dinner on Saturday night. I still had no clue what the word "gourmet" meant, except that it was French and maybe stood for dinner, and that they would serve the poor live lobster. The lobster gun was a delicate piece of equipment, Barrollo lectured, and since the lobster is a very expensive creature, it has to be killed without damaging the outer shell. The lobster gun was specially designed for this purpose and it too was very expensive. This gun was a complicated piece of equipment and since the hotel did not own one, we had to borrow one from the Berg Hotel. The chef had assigned this task to me.

Barrollo then went on to explain that the lobster gun was heavy and, to some extent, fragile. Therefore, I had to proceed with utmost care when transporting the device back to the hotel. I was eternally grateful to Barrollo who, in my mind, had saved my life. I would never have dared to go back to the kitchen to ask the chef to explain the task again. I was convinced he would have terminated my life there and then.

Barrollo accompanied me to the basement to organize a trolley, which turned out to be very large, old and rusty. But it was the only one that would support the weight of the gun I was supposed to pick up. Barrollo explained to me how to get to the Berg and who to ask for once I got there. It now dawned on me that the chef had entrusted me with quite an important task. I felt proud. The lobster gun was expensive, fragile and for our Saturday-night dinner of vital importance. To find the way to the Berg Hotel was no problem for me; I knew it from my walks around town during my afternoon breaks. My problem was that I felt somewhat out of place walking through town in my waiter's uniform and with a rather large and rusty old trolley, which happened to be much heavier than expected.

Talasee was a very small town packed with countless souvenir shops, street cafes, restaurants and all of them were crowded with tourists. They all looked in amusement, seeing me pushing and pulling the rusty trolley through the crowds of tourists. They, of course, were oblivious to the important task I was given and all they saw was a waiter with an old trolley.

I arrived at the Berg Hotel about twenty minutes after leaving the Black Forest Grand Hotel. By now I was covered in sweat all over and had already taken much longer than expected. Reaching the delivery entrance of the hotel, I asked to speak with the chef. To my surprise, the chef of the Berg Hotel was a much more accommodating and pleasant person than the one I had to put up with every day. He informed me in an apologetic manner that the gun is not actually at the Berg Hotel since they had lent it to the Roessle Restaurant in the morning.

I knew the Roessle restaurant very well, since it happened to be just opposite my hotel! Without showing my disappointment, I thanked the chef, explaining that I would just go back and pick it up at the Roessle. In a way, I was quite grateful and relieved to not have to manhandle this trolley, with even more weight on it, all the way back to the hotel. I was just about to thank him for his help when he asked me not to forget the tripod for the lobster gun and some other parts which we would need in order to operate the weapon.

I waited for a few minutes, then two chefs with a rather large and heavy cardboard box appeared. The two chefs carried the heavily taped box to my trolley. There was a loud metallic *bang* when the chefs placed the box, with considerable physical effort, on the trolley. They told me that the actual gun is at the Roessle and with a strange grin, they wished me good luck.

The trolley was, or rather used to be, a kitchen trolley that was made for transportation of food in kitchens with tiled floors. It was

12

never meant for the transportation of heavy goods on streets. The lobster gun equipment they had placed in my care was heavy, very heavy. Not only was it a very difficult task to move the trolley, it was an even bigger challenge to keep it going straight once it was in motion.

I pushed, dragged and pulled the trolley as best as I could in the general direction of the Roessle. Initially the going was manageable as long as I kept up the momentum. The slight downhill slope in front of the Berg Hotel helped but in the city center, the street leveled out and things were a bit more difficult. The crowds got thicker and many of the tourists stopped, laughed and probably thought this was some kind of show. Some people kindly helped when I struggled to push my trolley from the main road onto the pavement.

When I did eventually arrive at the Roessle, I was exhausted, drenched in sweat and had one of my trouser legs ripped, which happened when I tried to stop the trolley on a slope just in front of the Roessle. I had to rest for a while to gather my thoughts. I felt terrible. I was a funny attraction for passing tourists. I was frustrated and contemplated getting help, but then again, the chef had entrusted *me* with this important task, which meant that he must have had at least some faith in me. A more self-confident person would probably have already gone back to the hotel and angrily demanded help, but this was not me. The fear of the chef's wrath, which I could expect coming back empty- handed, gave me new strength.

I went to the kitchen of the Roessle and asked to see the chef. They told me that the chef was out but thankfully, one of the cooks had expected me. He greeted me and, with a sad expression, told me that just an hour earlier, two chefs from the Marten Hotel had picked up the lobster gun for an urgent dinner the same evening.

My heart and shoulders dropped when I heard the name Marten Hotel; that was another kilometer down the road. The thought of pushing this trolley once more through town made me sick. My trousers were ripped, I was soaked in sweat and I still had not had lunch. In addition, as if all this was not enough, the Roessle chef topped it all off by placing another box on the trolley. Apparently, these were the "lobster bolts" which the Berg people had forgotten.

I began to wonder what this gun looked like if all this additional equipment was already so big and heavy. The only good news was that the way to the Marten Hotel was mostly downhill. At this point, I did not ponder much about how I would get back up that hill. I looked at my watch, realizing in horror that nearly two hours had passed since I had left the hotel. It would take me at least another forty-five minutes to get to the Marten Hotel. My heart was beating fast and adrenaline began pumping through my veins. I had to get going.

I reached the Marten Hotel completely exhausted and disillusioned. Suddenly a scary thought crossed my mind. What if the Marten had given the gun to someone else? All my efforts would have been in vain. I cursed myself for not asking the Roessle chefs to call them first.

I reached the back entrance of the hotel where two impatient chefs were waiting for me. They were definitely not very happy because of my delay; I had spoiled their lunch break. They showed me a very large, heavy-looking cardboard box which, according to them, was the dreaded lobster gun. Now I was worried about the size of my trolley; the only way to accommodate the gun and its equipment was to rearrange the boxes. We unloaded all of them and, with the help of the two growling chefs, I finally managed to fit all on the rusty trolley.

Now the trolley was so heavy that I began to doubt it would survive the journey home. The chefs hurried away without saying a word and I was standing there staring at the old rusty kitchen trolley loaded with three scruffy-looking boxes, one heavier than the other. I felt overwhelmed by the task ahead.

Even at this point, I did not doubt the content of the containers, nor was I upset or harbored miserable feelings towards my hotel. All I had in my mind was to complete the job and not to make a mistake in doing so. I took a deep breath and began to manhandle my trolley towards the hotel.

With all the weight placed on it, the trolley was nearly impossible to move, and if it weren't for the kind help of various tourists, I would have never made it back to the hotel. I eventually reached the hotel over five hours after I had left. I was completely oblivious to the excited screams and laughter coming from the canteen window as I approached the hotel. All I had on my mind was to get the lobster gun to the kitchen and the chef as fast as humanly possible. Only when I had reached the delivery entrance of the hotel did I look up at the window of the canteen and that's when I saw most of my fellow colleagues, Johnny, Barrollo and several chefs all killing themselves laughing at the miserable sight of me.

I must have presented a truly sad picture with my torn trousers and a rusty trolley full of cardboard boxes which resembled the last possessions of a homeless man. Not even at this point did I doubt the purpose of my mission; I was just proud to have made it.

My colleagues stormed down from the canteen to the street and welcomed me, laughing back to the hotel. They ripped open the boxes, which were filled with scrap metal of some sort or other. It had all been just a joke.

Every hotel I visited had done their best to contribute whatever they could, the heavier the better. It turned out that my entire journey from start to end was watched by staff members from three different hotels, each reporting their hilarious observations back to my fellow colleagues. Only now did it dawn on me that I was the latest victim of an ancient tradition of practical jokes exclusively reserved for Rotstifts. Although I was slowly becoming a full member of the team, it would be another six months before I was in a position to hand over the title of Rotstift to my successor. Until then, I still had a lot to learn.

Improving my skills as a waiter in the shortest time possible was in everybody's interest. The quicker I could run a station, the easier life would be for the more senior guys. The senior guys, namely Johnny and Barrollo, were consistently assigned to the largest and busiest stations. These stations could have as much as twenty tables, providing seats for over one hundred guests. These stations were also quite far away from the kitchens and therefore they had runners assigned to them. My task for the coming weeks was that of a runner in the garden restaurant.

On a typical summer day, one station on the garden terrace would serve over six hundred and, on weekends, up to nine hundred guests between lunch and dinner. On such days, the garden literally resembled an ant's nest with a continuous coming and going of people, screaming kids, people asking for their bills, chasing their orders or simply waiting for their change. It was wild and it was a complete mystery to me how Johnny kept an overview on what was, in my mind, a complete chaos.

But Johnny was fully in control and he always seemed to know exactly what was going on. The way he handled two or three different tasks at the same time was amazing. He would ask me, for example, to pick up things in the kitchen whilst standing at a customer's table taking an order and reminding me at the same time which tables needed clearing. How did he do this, I wondered? He would send me off to the kitchen with three or four orders, always reminding me "do not leave our station empty-handed."

This was easier said than done, considering that all soiled crockery was placed on a large rectangular tray. I lifted the heavy tray onto my shoulder and, carefully holding it with both my hands, I headed as fast as I could to the kitchen. In the beginning, this was quite an awkward undertaking but as time went on, I began to get the hang of it. Soon I managed to balance the tray single-handedly and hold some more plates in the other hand.

Once I reached the kitchen, I would drop the tray at the dishwasher and dash to the cash till where I punched my orders, printing a docket. I would rush with the dockets to the coffee station, shouting orders as I approached, and then to the cake station, dropping off the cake orders. I would immediately double back to the coffee station to prepare the tray— milk, sugar, etc., for coffee orders, and straws, ice cubes, etc., for beverage orders. Then again back to the cake station, picking up the cakes and in the meantime, my coffee and beverage order would be ready. I would quickly check that all was there and off I would go back to my station in the garden were Johnny would be waiting for me already.

The loads we carried on busy days were truly astonishing—seven or eight plates of cakes, three to four pots of coffee, some beverages and some ice cream sundaes. In order to carry such substantial quantities, we always used large rectangular trays which we usually carried in our left hand with the tray resting on the left shoulder. This would leave the right hand to carry another four to five plates of cakes. As I have been blessed with rather large hands and reasonably long legs, I was getting the hang of the runner job in a relatively short time and I even began to enjoy it.

Over time, I was becoming quite a strong and popular runner, which reflected in the stations I was assigned to. It came to a point where Barrollo and I were getting into competitions to see who could carry the largest number of plates at the fastest speed. Day in day out, we ran the garden business, my confidence in wearing my funny uniform grew and I became slowly more comfortable in the hospitality environment. All this reflected positively in the tip that I was earning from my station waiters.

After a busy day, the tip could sometimes be as high as a third of my monthly salary. Tip was what we all lived for. However, as I found out after a while, it was not always the fairest share we runners received from the different station waiters. It was therefore not surprising that I began to yearn to get my own station. I felt I was ready.

As runner, I was following orders to clear tables and to pick up orders but my communication with the actual customer was kept at a minimum for obvious reasons. Slowly, Johnny and the others trusted me with more and more responsibility and the day finally came when they thought that I was ready to take my first order from a customer. Of course, I had taken orders before but since my main job was that of a runner and the orders I was confronted with were always just silly things like requests for more whipped cream or more sauce, I had never taken a full order. Taking an order sounds much easier than it is and, mind you, it does take some preparation. As for me, when the day came, I was not prepared whatsoever.

I do remember this day very well, simply because it was a traumatic experience. Johnny asked me to go and take an order from a table of six customers. As I approached, I suddenly became very conscious of my funny uniform, just as on my first day. As if this was not enough, when I asked them what they would like to order, all heads turned and suddenly I had six complete strangers staring at me, full of expectations. My heart stopped and I had the strong urge to leave the table and run away. In my hand I held an order pad but I was unable to write; everybody seemed to be talking to me at the same time and I froze.

They were all talking at me from left to right. I heard the words coffee, cake, and all of a sudden someone asked a question. The question was clearly directed at me. I was electrified and do not remember what I answered but what I do remember is that I left the table with an empty note pad, went to my service station and stood there completely lost. I put down the notepad and started writing down some of the few items I remembered. Most of what I wrote were blind guesses and of course when I delivered the orders, I had too much of this and not enough of that. It was a disaster from which I had to be rescued by Johnny. He quickly and skillfully turned the disaster into something funny for my guests. For me, it had been hell.

That evening, I was depressed and wondered how I could ever run a station like Johnny if I could not even take a simple order. I did not sleep that night until late and did not look forward to go to work the next day. Despite this, I did go to work the next day and the day after that and slowly, with Johnny's help, I began to develop a concept of taking orders. The problem for me was not the order itself but the talking and acting in front of guests. Slowly, the more time I spent talking with guests at the table, the more comfortable I became.

I learned the hard way that customers tend to ask questions about the dishes on the menu and therefore as a waiter, I should know the menu inside out. What does this cake taste like? What is this dish made of? Where does this fruit come from? But that was not all; they would ask all sorts of questions about everything from the weather forecast for the coming day all the way to my personal life. I learned that it is easier to talk to strangers if you know what you are talking about. Therefore, in order to avoid looking silly in front of customers in the future, I took all the hotel's menus to my room and began to study them. I got to know the menus and over time was able to describe every single dish, its taste, content and presentation.

My level of expertise in the order-taking process grew and slowly my focus shifted from trying to get an order right to guiding the customer into ordering the things I wanted him to. The reason for this was simple because for me, the waiter, it was much easier and more convenient to take an order for six cheesecakes and six coffees rather than six different cakes and six different beverages. Such orders were difficult to control and even more difficult to carry. Since customers normally do not have a habit of considering this aspect, they have to be guided by the waiter. Johnny and Barrollo were highly skilled in this respect and I watched them with eagle eyes and I learned.

The skill is to make things up as you go along. If one particular dish was not convenient to me, the waiter, I would simply make a negative comment about the dish pretending to quote a customer "who had tried this cake before," or say, "The steak doesn't look nice today." This method was surprisingly successful since both had the potential to end with the customer having to listen to "I told you so" from the waiter. As this can be quite humiliating, most people tried to avoid this. If I did not like a particular dish, it was simply sold out. All this and more I learned from Johnny and Barrollo.

Of course, these tactics could only be applied in the busy garden operation and we rarely used it in the restaurant except in emergencies. If one wanted to avoid an unpleasant encounter with the chef, it was advisable not to end up with a large number of different dishes.

In the weeks that followed, I became more and more comfortable in running a station in the garden. Suddenly there were occasions where I found myself standing idle at my station waiting for customers to finish their meals instead of customers waiting for me to get my act together. Taking orders had become a routine, and now it was I standing at the table waiting for guests to make up their minds as to what they wanted to order. I had more time to study the different types of customers I encountered.

There were the romantic young couples who just wanted to relax, hold hands and enjoy the beautiful view. There were elderly couples trying to enjoy the peaceful surroundings, which was not always possible because on the table next to them would be one of the many couples trying very hard to keep their kids under control. It was interesting watching all these different characters. Then, of course, we had plenty of foreigners.

Due to our close proximity to France, Switzerland and Austria, we had many customers from these neighboring countries. We liked them because they paid their bills in foreign currency, which was an additional source of income for us waiters. In terms of currency exchange, we had adopted a "take it or leave it" attitude towards the Swiss and French francs when it came to accepting their currencies. We knew they had no choice and we could only win. If the exchange rate quoted by us was accepted—one for one for Swiss francs and a similarly staggering rate for French francs—then we made a small profit on the exchange rate in addition to the tip. They would usually ask before placing an order and if they were not happy with the exchange rate quoted, then they would just get up and leave, meaning less work for us.

A rather unpleasant customer type was the boys from the bowling clubs on a weekend outing. We had many of them in Talasee. If they were not already drunk on arrival, they certainly would be by the time they left. Between arrival and departure, their target, if no girls were around, was the waiter. For me, the most difficult types to handle at that time were groups of guys my age trying to make me look silly. Over time, I learned how to get back at them with a vengeance and without them ever knowing.

Groups of girls were always welcome but they presented another challenge in terms of me trying to concentrate on taking an order or serving the right dish to the right girl. The reasons for this were bikini tops and girls not wearing bras under their tank tops.

We had all types of guests and in summer, the garden would resemble a giant beehive. There were customers fighting each other for tables, couples fighting with each other, elderly gentlemen with very young girlfriends and very young gentlemen with elderly girlfriends. It was a little bit of everything and no day was the same.

The types of customers in the garden and in the restaurants were of a completely different caliber and they had to be, considering the prices we charged. They were normally of an advanced age, wealthy, and generally used to more elegant and exclusive surroundings. Based on that, for me, they were the crème de la crème of customers. However, I did learn over time not to judge books by their covers.

Whilst I was busy studying the different types of customers, I also learned to recognize the importance of meteorology in a garden restaurant operation. Running a garden restaurant, the weather was of course always a major concern for us. It was a concern because many clouds meant rain and rain meant no garden restaurant. No garden restaurant for us meant day off.

If I was assigned to the garden restaurant and the weather turned bad, it would mean I would be off for the rest of the day. If the weather was good, it meant a busy day and lots of work. This is not to say that we were lazy, but an additional day off due to bad weather was always a welcome break. After a couple of months, I had developed into a strong station waiter and was frequently assigned large stations in the garden. There, I had plenty of time to study the weather and soon I became quite proficient in meteorology.

Johnny and Barrollo taught me the names and meanings of the different cloud formations, which we would carefully observe every evening in order to predict the weather for the next day. I learned that a red sky at sunset was a certain harbinger of rain for the next day and so were sheep-like cloud formations in the evening. Cumulus clouds in the morning meant thunderstorm later in the day.

The weather report in the evening news was a must for all garden waiters and if rain was predicted for the next day, then this important message had to be relayed to everybody immediately. Unfortunately, our own weather forecasting based on manual observations of the sky were off the mark most of the time. It did not rain when we were convinced it would, and it rained when we least expected it.

If the sky was darkening in the afternoon and it looked as if it would rain at any moment, we despised every customer who dared to take a seat in our station. At that moment, the guest was an intruder whilst we were ready to close the operation at a moment's notice. As soon as we observed the first tiny droplet of rain falling from the sky, we would urge Mr. Hanter to close the garden restaurant. Mr. Hanter would only authorize the closure after a personal inspection of the meteorological situation outside and in seven out of ten cases, he would let the operation continue. However, if he *did* give us green light to close, we still had to deal with those customers who had dared to sit under the sun umbrellas. We then advised them that the umbrellas were made to provide shelter from the sun and not to protect during rain. We would immediately advise them that, in order not to damage the umbrellas, we had to remove them. In most cases this worked quite well; the customers left and we closed down. All this had to happen as a matter of utmost urgency since there was always the danger of a sudden change in weather for the better.

Watching the daily weather forecast became a habit for all of us. We usually checked two or three different channels for better accuracy. Unfortunately, meteorology at that time was technically not as advanced as it is today and, judging by the outcome of our predictions, I soon realized that the study of cloud formations was far from accurate and applying old farmers' wisdom produced better results.

In those days, I would get up in the morning, open the curtains and look out of the window only to be disappointed with a beautiful cloudless sky. Even during my morning shower, I would pray that once I got out, the weather had changed. Wrapped in a towel, I would look at the sky and if it was still blue, then another wonderful day for our beloved tourists and a busy, hectic day for me the waiter. What had happened to the bad weather that the news had forecasted the previous night? Even on my short walk to the hotel, my eyes would frequently scan the sky in hope of detecting some clouds but most of the time it remained bright blue.

During breakfast, we would discuss the weather forecast, trying to guess when the first cloud would appear. The weather in the Black Forest can change fast without much notice and it was on these grounds

21

that we tried to convince Mr. Hanter not to open the garden. Many times the sky would darken in a matter of hours and we would be certain that there would be no more sunshine for the rest of the day. But, once the rain had started and the garden was closed, it would already begin to brighten up somewhere on the horizon and Mr. Hanter would give us cleaning jobs to do until the bad weather had blown over. Once again, we waiters were the losers in this gruesome game of nature.

The more we studied the weather, the more we realized that we could not actually predict it. I accepted my fate and rather than hoping desperately for bad weather, I turned to look forward to a sunny and busy day with lots of tips. If the weather happened to be bad and I got an additional day off then that was a pleasant surprise.

As I grew more and more comfortable in my job, I began to discover some of the more pleasant side effects of working twelve kilometers away from home. One of them was independence. For the first time, I had complete freedom in planning my leisure time, which included the late evenings, and what I would do on my weekly two days off. At first, it felt strange to be completely without the protection of mother's watching eye but as time went by, I began to enjoy this part immensely. Of course, as with all new things, it was only a matter of time before I would find out that freedom had its price and that was responsibility!

In addition of having the freedom to determine how long I stayed out, I also had the freedom to choose *where* I spent my time. For the first time in my so far relatively uneventful life, the "where," included the hotel's girl's quarters.

One day, Ralf and I received an invitation from two of our female colleagues. They had invited us to visit them after work in their quarters, which we gladly accepted.

We could not have chosen a worse venue.

The male and female employee accommodations at the Black Forest Grand Hotel were clearly separated. All female employees lived on the top floor of the hotel and all male employees stayed in a separate building located opposite the hotel. The female employees occupied one floor in the hotel just underneath the roof which, in typical Black Forest houses, normally served as the attic.

The rooms on this floor were very basic, to say the least. There were eight twin rooms in total. Each room was equipped with two beds, one sink and a small window. Since all rooms were located just underneath the un-insulated roof, temperatures frequently dropped to zero in winter and produced a tropical climate in summer. There was a multitude of insects living on this floor and they, too, changed with the seasons. Whilst in summer ants, spiders, beetles, flies and the occasional cockroach shared the girls' habitat, in winter the insects gave way to small rodents such as mice. All eight rooms shared a number of small bathrooms at the end of the corridor. During high season when this floor accommodated up to sixteen girls, there was a tightly controlled timetable for the use of the bathroom, with thirty-minute slots per room. All girls, both apprentices and full-time employees, were assigned to this floor.

It was for this reason that this floor held a special attraction for us. Male employees and male visitors were not permitted on this floor. For males to get to this floor was difficult and hazardous—but not impossible.

In order to reach this floor, one first had to cross the hotel lobby and then use either the elevator or the adjacent wooden staircase. The staircase, covered with a thick carpet, was made of wood and was over one hundred years old. After midnight, the staircase was the only access to the guest floors since the elevator was shut down after midnight. This procedure ensured that any nightly visitor had to pass by the reception desk.

Based at the reception desk was the night manager, at the time a ghastly man called Salah. He hailed from Morocco and was born without the ability to smile. His whole demeanor reminded me of the Hunchback of Notre Dame, with a long curved nose and thick glasses. From midnight to six in the morning, he considered the hotel his personal kingdom.

Nobody liked Salah because he was different and strange, which was probably the reason why he only worked at night. Dealing with customers was not one of his strongest points. As matter of fact, if it had been up to him, then no customer would have been allowed to return to the hotel, or move about in the hotel, after eleven in the evening. For us employees, he had little or no regard and in his mind, we presented an unavoidable nuisance. He detested days when the hotel had large functions that stretched late into the night with customers and employees mingling freely in his kingdom.

All this didn't change the fact that we had an invitation from the two girls and our strategy was simple—we had to reach the girls' room in the early evening, wait until they both had finished work, have drinks and fun and leave before Salah came on duty at eleven. Such adventures were not really in my nature but the confident and determined manner in which Ralf had planned everything left no doubt in my naïve mind that it was a safe undertaking. One thing was for sure: Salah never came on duty earlier than he had to and as long as we entered and exited before eleven, we would be safe. It was a good plan.

When the time came, we leisurely strolled through the lobby, took the elevator to the third floor and from there we sneaked up a wooden staircase to the female floor. So far so good, we thought, once we had reached the girls' room undetected. The girls had not finished work yet so we sneaked into the room and got comfortable on the sofa.

Whilst we sat there waiting, we talked and let our fantasy run wild as to what would happen once the girls came back. Up to that point, my sexual experience had not yet gone beyond touching a girl's bra. Not like Ralf. The way he talked gave me the impression that he had gone "all the way" once or twice before and that made me nervous. As we waited, my initial excitement turned into fear and the longer we waited the more nervous I got. What if they offered to go further than the bra? I had no idea what I would do.

Finally, the girls came home, they changed and we started chatting and drinking bottles of Rothaus beer. Ralf and his bicycle adventure through Japan dominated the conversation and as he went on, I began to wonder what Ralf would have had to talk about if he had never done this trip. Maybe he only took the trip in order to have something to talk about.

In any case, it was obvious that the girls had heard Ralf's stories before since they did not really listen. But this was no problem for Ralf; he went on and on. To my disappointment, neither of the girls made a move on Ralf or me. Gone was the dream of going beyond the bra. We talked, laughed, drank, had fun and...forgot about the time. By the time one of us eventually checked the clock, it was already far too late.

"Shit! It's eleven-thirty!" Ralf blurted out and jumped up.

I was shocked. How could this have happened? The girls found it funny and laughed. I felt panic creeping up inside my stomach and had only one thought on my mind: We have to leave. But the girls cautioned us. They argued that if we left now, Salah would most certainly catch us. We argued for about half an hour and finally we agreed that as long as the elevator worked, we had a chance to get down to the ground floor and sneak out via the staff entrance. This was a good and workable plan, offering the best chance of success.

The plan, as many good plans before, had only one flaw—it came too late. By the time we agreed, it was already several minutes past twelve and knowing Salah, the elevator was turned off already as soon as the large antique cuckoo clock in the lobby had noisily announced midnight. Our only escape route was now blocked. The old staircase was out of the question as it made lots of screeching noises when people walked on it. In the middle of the night, these noises would be amplified manifold. I knew it there and then that we were trapped.

The next and probably most sensible suggestion came from the girls, urging us to stay until six in the morning and leave once Salah had gone. This was another good and workable plan. This certainly would have been the most sensible thing to do and would have had the best chance of success. However, we were convinced that if caught in the morning, the management would know that we had spent the night in the hotel, which of course was not permitted. To spend the night on the girls' floor was reason for termination. Therefore, leaving in the morning was not an option; instead, we assumed that Salah, being Moroccan, would certainly take a nap in his office at one point during the night and we guessed that this would be around four o'clock in the morning. How we came up with this I do not really know. We decided that this would be the time for us to escape. The girls, with their much more advanced and better developed common sense, tried hard to make us see the overwhelming flaws of our plan. We stood our ground like men and decided to go ahead with our plan of escape.

I could not really enjoy the rest of the evening because I was constantly checking my watch. At around three-thirty, tired of waiting, we couldn't stand it any longer and we made our move. We left the girls' room and quietly made our way down the old staircase to the third floor. However, the moment we took the first step, we realized just how old the stairs were. Every step we took was answered by a loud screeching noise from the wood under our feet. We continued unperturbed in the knowledge that the noises simply could not travel down from the third to the ground floor.

We reached the third floor, which was a guest floor. From now on, the floor and staircase were covered with a thick carpet which effectively absorbed any unwanted noises—or so we thought. We slowly worked our way down to the second floor, from there to the first floor and then we had to tiptoe step by step, trying to move ultra quietly. We now reached the most dangerous part of our mission—the last flight of stairs leading into the lobby. Suddenly, the stairs screeched in protest. We looked at each other in horror but Ralf motioned for me to continue.

We had nearly reached the ground floor when suddenly the entire lobby around us came to light. My heart stopped! We froze. Right in front of us stood Salah, with his arms crossed over his chest and a most sadistic smile on his face.

"Welcome, gentlemen," he barked, waving his fat little sausage fingers at us. He seemed sadistically excited by having caught us. We descended the remaining few steps and hesitantly walked over to the reception desk. Waving a pen in his fingers, he asked for our names and department. Ralf tried to persuade him to give us another chance which Salah, of course, denied. The tone in his voice clearly indicated that the whole spectacle satisfied him intensely.

I just stood there in shock. I felt as if I was caught stealing red-handed by the police. I was scared like never before in my life and felt nauseated. Salah took down our names and kept repeating the hotel rules concerning access to guest floors after midnight. He also reminded us that we were in deep trouble because he would report us to the management. He finished his sentence with the smile of a crazy maniac.

When he had noted everything down, he shoved us in front of the automatic glass doors, which opened instantly. We stepped outside into a chilly but beautiful clear night, and walked slowly towards the staff accommodation. Ralf suddenly started laughing. I looked at him and began to laugh, too, and together we let out all the tension of the last few hours. I was happy that it was finally over.

I got up a few hours later and had completely forgotten about the incident of the previous night. Unfortunately, during my morning shower, things suddenly started to come back and I became seriously worried.

At one point during breakfast service, the personnel director summoned me to his office. For some reason, I was nervous but not afraid. I went to his office where he confronted me with Salah's report, asking me if it was correct. I admitted everything, upon which he issued me a final written warning. He informed me that any further incident, no matter how small, would result in my immediate dismissal. I signed the warning with a shaking hand and handed the sheet of paper back to him. I was free to go. I apologized one more time and left the office.

I stood outside the personnel office for a moment, holding the copy of my final written warning. I took a deep breath thinking, Only halfway through my probation and already on a final warning. The more I thought about our nightly escapade, the more certain I was that this would be the last warning in my career that I would ever get.

News traveled fast and everyone heard about our nightly adventure, which was the talk of the day. Nevertheless, we had survived and soon the incident was ancient history. The days and months went by and slowly but surely I became a seasoned waiter. The stations assigned to me by the end of the summer included the largest garden station, which in itself was a compliment for me. Towards the end of September the weather became colder and the flow of tourists began to ebb away. Our weather studies turned from predicting rain and sunshine to studying the temperatures. The end of the summer garden operation neared.

A clear sign was the three large pine trees, standing at one end of the terrace, which now began to shed their needles into our customers' soups and coffees. Soon it was simply too cold for guests to sit outside. Then, one day, Mr. Hanter announced the closure of the garden operation. Although we did not show it, we all were happy that another busy summer season was over; from now on business would slow down substantially.

But first, we had to clear the garden terrace, which meant for us to thoroughly clean all tables, chairs and umbrellas and prepare them for winter storage. We deep-cleaned the service stations before we wrapped them tightly in heavy sheets of canvas. The terrace without all those tables, chairs and sun umbrellas looked now rather small and it was difficult to imagine that on a busy summer's day, up to two hundred people mingled here. The terrace was ready to receive its first snow.

Autumn in Talasee had nothing pleasant to offer but cold, gray and windy autumn days. The last summer tourists had left and it was still too early for the winter tourists. The first snow was still several weeks away and until then the town would be empty. Most hotels in Talasee used this period to close down, sending their employees on leave. The Black Forest Grand Hotel was no exception and closed its doors from mid-October to the end of November. However, before any of us could go on leave, the hotel had to be prepared for its nearly two-month hibernation.

One week before the closure, all of us in the food and beverage department were busy transferring all operating equipment to the ballroom. This was, of course, the best opportunity for the account department to conduct their annual operating equipment count. For several days, we were busy emptying side stations, cabinets, cupboards, shelves, bars, refrigerators and other storage areas. Everything was moved into the ballroom, where all equipment would be neatly laid out on tables. We were kept busy with counting all crockery, flatware and hollowware, and once we had completed counting, we handed the sheets over to finance. Then the girls from the finance department carefully counted all again, cross-checked their numbers with ours and entered them into their inventory lists. Whilst finance cross-checked our numbers, we had not much to do and this was the time when we honed our skills in "plate acrobatics."

The ballroom with its massive row of windows commanded a beautiful view over Lake Talasee. Only one wall of the ballroom was solid; the rest were windows. Plate acrobatics was something we could only do when none of our managers was around since it sometimes involved the breaking of plates. Plate acrobatics was not more than throwing plates, pretty much like a Frisbee, from one person to another. At one point, we had started to have them rotate in flight by one or two revolutions. I had come a long way, from throwing a plate so that it rotated only once to achieving the skill of five to six revolutions. I did this by using only my right hand.

Ralf and I started off by simply throwing plates at each other like a Frisbee. Since chinaware plates are heavier than and not as aerodynamic as a Frisbee, the first few attempts were atrocious, resulting in several crash landings on the floor. Ralf had the habit of throwing plates too fast, causing me several times to abandon my position out of fear of being hit by the missile-like projectile. In this case, the plate would end up crashing to the floor. The heavy ballroom carpet proved to be a lifesaver for numerous plates. However, once we realized that the carpet did quite a good job in cushioning crash landings, we became more daring in the type of acrobatics we performed.

I remember one particular experiment where the goal was for the plate to achieve the highest possible number of mid-air revolutions. In order to achieve this, we had to stand as far away from each other as possible. Space was not a problem since we were conducting this experiment in the ballroom. However, on this occasion, Ralf had already reached the far end of the ballroom and, due to the distance between us, he had to apply far more thrust in order for the plate to reach me at the other side of the room.

Ralf got ready, his upper body slowly swayed from left to right, getting into the momentum. Then he suddenly recoiled, putting all his strengths into the launch and the plate shot out of his hand. It accelerated much faster than Ralf had intended and shot towards me like a missile. It did not take me long to realize that there was no way I would be able to catch that plate without getting hurt and instantly dove to the floor cushioned by the thick carpet. I saw in slow motion, from one corner of my eye, the plate crossing at a phenomenal speed over the space where I had stood only moments ago. The fact that I was standing in front of a large glass panel before I dropped to the floor was confirmed immediately by a loud shattering bang and the unmistakable noise of disintegrating porcelain.

The plate had hit the window hard, causing it to crack before the plate itself disintegrated into a thousand tiny pieces. I was still lying on the floor when we both broke into a relieved laughter; we were happy that no one got hurt. When we saw the long crack in the window, we fell silent; the fun was over. Ralf came over and we both just stood there looking at the damage. It did not take us long to realize that there was no way to hide this damage; the only choice we had was to get rid of any possible evidence linking this damage to us.

We agreed that we would act completely surprised and innocent should the crack be discovered whilst we were still around. This was a good plan. Within minutes, the last trace of the broken plate had gone and we went about our business, taking stock of the surviving chinaware. The crack was only discovered on the day when we all returned from our holiday. By then, of course, there was no doubt that the damage had been caused during the closure of the hotel, *possibly due to the extremely cold temperatures that winter.*

In the meantime, we continued with the closing of the hotel. Overall, we enjoyed this time immensely when we had the hotel completely to ourselves. The restaurants, bars and the lobby, normally teeming with guests, were all deserted. Even the large car park in front of the hotel was completely empty. Throughout the hotel, all non-essential lights had been switched off, which added to the deserted atmosphere. There was absolutely no one around other than us employees.

I loved these few days in October when we were able to roam around the hotel in jeans and jumpers. Outside the weather was chilly and the town was empty, and we knew that in a few days we all would depart for a month of well-deserved holiday. Yes, I liked this time of year a lot. We eventually completed our closing duties and the hotel shut down. We went for one final farewell dinner, had fun and then we said our goodbyes and everybody went off in different directions to enjoy a peaceful one and half month's holiday.

It was good to get back to my hometown for a while after all the excitement and experiences over the past months. I was looking forward to spending some time with my friends at home, as I had not seen much of them since I had started my career in the hotel business. To see my friends again was exciting; we went to neighboring towns where live bands performed in town halls on weekends. We would get there by motorbike or with one of my older friends who already had a driving license and a car. I much preferred going there by motorbike since my older friends usually felt they had to prove their manhood by driving either unreasonably fast or by overtaking other cars in a completely suicidal manner.

Arriving at the venue had to be done in the coolest possible manner, especially when girls were around. We would drive towards the main entrance at high speed and then pull the breaks, which would bring the car to a screaming halt with smoking tires. We then casually opened the doors and, without a smile, stepped out of the car feeling really cool.

I can only guess what those girls must have thought seeing us arriving in this rather unsophisticated manner, realizing that we were immensely proud of ourselves. In the absence of discotheques in our area, I have always quite enjoyed these weekend concerts where local bands performed popular pop and rock music. We all were dressed in jeans, leather jackets and a sleeveless jean jacket featuring an embroidered "Fire Devil" logo on the back, just like the Hell's Angels.

The similarity between the Fire Devils and the American Hell's Angels ended there. Whilst the Hell's Angels' mode of transportation consisted exclusively of Harley Davidson bikes with engines sporting up to 1300cc, the Fire Devils' bikes consisted of Zuendapps, Hercules and Puchs and none of them exceeded 80cc. The difference of 1220cc between the Hell's Angels and us was due to our age, which legally did not permit us to ride anything faster then 80km/h. Another substantial difference between the Hell's Angels and us was that if a weekend concert venue was too far away from our town, one of our members' parents would drive us there and pick us up again. It was all quite embarrassing.

There were other such gangs just like us from other towns in the area but unlike us, they took this gang business far more seriously. We found that out the hard way. There was a substantial rivalry between the different gangs and it was not unusual that these rivalries ended in gang fights if two gangs happened to be at the same time in the same place. Again, we learned all this the hard way and in order not to end up with black eyes and bruises, we started to send scouts into a potential venue before we entered. If our scout reported another gang was present, we left our jackets somewhere outside.

This was pretty much what a typical weekend looked like before I joined the hotel business. We drank beer and tried to impress the local girls by making fools of ourselves. Although I enjoyed being with my friends, after months of wearing my waiter's outfit, mingling with the sophisticated customers of the hotel, it did take me some time to get back into my "Fire Devil" mode. Strangely enough, I was very polite to the waitress serving us. I watched her dashing from table to table and suddenly I missed my newfound friends from work.

The time at home passed by quickly and before I knew it, I had to return to Talasee. I arrived there on a typical cold late November afternoon and went straight up to my room. The room had not changed but it was in desperate need of a deep cleaning. My room was large but very sparsely furnished. I had set up my "bed," consisting of not more than a mattress on the floor, located just underneath the window—something I would later regret once winter had arrived in all its glory. There was also an old wooden cabinet with one door missing; other than that, I had a couple of empty wine crates which served as book shelves.

There was one bathroom on each floor with only one shower cubicle and washbasins for about fifteen souls. The entire bathroom was in a deplorable state; the sinks were made of stone and the one shower stall was cleaned only once a week by the hotel's housekeeping department. I made myself as comfortable as I possibly could and then went to see if Ralf had already arrived. He had, in fact, arrived already one day earlier and, after a joyful reunion, he updated me on who was already there and who was still missing. We talked and then went out for dinner.

The next morning, we all met and joked about who had put on the most weight during the long holiday. We checked out all the newcomers, especially the girls. There were plenty. The following two days were filled with dusting of cabinets and other cleaning jobs. The chefs were preparing the kitchens for operation, the maids were busy cleaning rooms and we prepared our restaurants.

On the third day, a Friday, we were ready to welcome our first customers. After over four weeks of wearing jeans, cowboy boots and leather jackets, it felt a little strange to be back in that funny waiter outfit. It didn't take me long to get used to it again and slowly things fell back into the same routine as it had been before my holiday.

The weather not only got colder but it also started to freeze overnight and then one day, the first snow fell. I had already regretted the location of my bed since it was freezing cold every night. Then, one morning, I got up as usual and opened the curtains, which did not make any difference since it was pitch black outside. And there it was—the first snow. Glimmering in the light of the street lanterns, everything was white; it had snowed throughout the night and even the cars were covered in a thick blanket of snow. Seeing this, my mood changed from autumn to winter. Ever since I was a child, I loved these mornings when I got up and outside everything was white. I immediately was in a good mood, ignored the freezing cold in my room and the adjoining bathroom. On my way to the hotel, I had to walk through knee-deep snow. Everything was covered in snow—streets, cars, and the hotel. There was also the familiar crackling sound under my feet when I walked through the frozen white. This would be a beautiful day! I checked my watch; it was six-thirty in the morning when I entered the hotel.

The first duty for us trainees in the morning was to say good morning to Mr. Hanter, who was sitting, as usual, in the upper part of the restaurant having his coffee and reading the newspaper. This was an absolute must! There was no way that anyone could start his day without passing by Mr. Hanter's table and not wishing him a good morning. It was our equivalent of clocking in.

This was also Mr. Hanter's way of checking on the arrival times of his people. Anyone arriving after six-thirty was late and in addition to the good morning, an apology was required. Mr. Hanter usually answered the "good morning" with a grumble, which presumably meant "good morning," too. In response to an apology for a delay of a few minutes, one would get the same grumble. If, however, a delay exceeded more than ten minutes, an explanation, in addition to the apology *and* the "good morning," was required. In response, Mr. Hanter would offer another grumble which meant, "Don't do it again," and the person was registered in his mind and, mind you, Mr. Hanter had an excellent memory.

The very worst case was to be so late that Mr. Hanter would already be finished with his coffee, which usually was about seven o'clock. Then you were in trouble. I remember very well when that happened to me for the first time. I was very late one morning and secretly hoped that he might not realize that I was the last one, but I could not have been more wrong. About one hour passed before I met him and the reaction when he saw me later was typical. He would just look at me (and he must have seen the absolute horror in my eyes) with a hardly detectable smile and before I could utter "good morning" with an apology and explanation, he would just walk off. The penalties came in different shapes and sizes but they all had one thing in common: They came when we least expected it. In my case, I was lucky since it was that time of the year when Mr. Hanter was really busy with the preparation for Christmas. The penalty never came. That time, I got away lightly.

The atmosphere in the hotel after the re-opening was different from that of summer; gone were the tourists in shorts and t-shirts, families and screaming kids. The customers we had now seemed more sophisticated and slightly more advanced in age. They looked very distinguished, with ladies in fur coats and gentlemen in expensive-looking winter coats. The restaurants felt much more "fine dining" than before and, strangely enough, we waiters acted differently, too—a little more esteemed.

The service was much more focused and attention to detail was the order of the day. This was a new sensation for me and, surprisingly, I enjoyed it. As we came closer to Christmas, the occupancy level of the hotel began to rise. By mid-December, the hotel was fully booked and we were busy for breakfast, lunch and dinner. Many of the tasks I was afraid of three months earlier had become routine. I had already been allowed to run my own station for breakfast whenever one of the station waiters was late or off sick.

During lunch and dinner, I was assigned as commis de rang to station waiters and I realized then that I was still far away from running my own station at these meal periods. Now I experienced for the first time what real service was all about. This was different from what I had experienced on the garden terrace during the summer. The customers were different, the menus were different and so were the prices. The entire service process from taking the order to serving the actual meal was much more detailed and sophisticated. And it had to be, considering the prices we charged.

Having passed my probation, Mr. Hanter decided that it was time to begin with my training in earnest and for this, he assigned me to Hendrick's station. Hendrick was technically the most competent waiter and it was his job to teach us the finer details of service, which included the opening of wines, filleting of fish at the table and other service-related tasks. Hendrick had a lot of what was needed in order to deal with inexperienced waiters like me and that was patience!

I vividly remember my first day with Hendrick. First, he gave me a long lecture about how we would be working together; he physically led me through the station and made me remember the table numbers. Our station consisted of two rows of tables, four tables to the right and two to the left. On the right side, the table numbers ran from one to four and on the left side were tables eleven and twelve. The reason for this was the shape of the restaurant—it was rectangular. The tables on the window, due to its excellent view, were very popular whilst the tables to the right were the cause for many complaints and unhappy people. Our station could accommodate up to sixteen guests—not too bad, or so I thought, remembering the comparatively huge stations out on the terrace in summer.

Once I had a grasp on the table numbers, Hendrick began to familiarize me with the menu. He made me read the individual dishes and then I had to describe them in detail. This was not easy; the menu was written in a different language, or so it seemed. It contained dishes with alien-sounding names such as "Entrecote," "Chateaubriand," and "Meuniere." I had no clue what any of that meant.

Until I became more familiar with the menu and its dishes, Hendrick restricted my duties to that of a runner. The service style in the restaurant was "Gueridon service," meaning the food was portioned on silver platters by the chef, covered with a lid called cloche and then served by the waiter from a side table, the gueridon. I wondered why everything had to be in French.

As a runner, I took the order from Hendrick, entered the different dishes with its prices in the cash till, dropped the drinks dockets at the service bar and the food dockets I handed politely over to the announcer at the pass. Here, I had to explain how the dishes were communicated to the chef. The dishes for all restaurants came from one kitchen. Until today, I have to admire the organization of that kitchen considering that it served four restaurants, the ballroom and one private room, each with its own menu. The organization of the kitchen was tight and clearly divided into Gardemanger, Saucier, Entremetier, Patissier and so forth. The executive chef controlled incoming and outgoing orders and conducted the quality check of each dish before releasing it into the care of the waiter. The most important task, however, was that of the announcer.

With so many restaurants and different menus, it was important to have one person who kept an overview of the big picture and this was the one and only job of the announcer. The announcer was the person who communicated every order via microphone and loudspeaker to the kitchen. The announcer decided what dishes would be prepared when and which dish would be released next. A member of the owner's family always held the position of announcer. The announcer sat on a raised platform overlooking the pickup point called the "pass." The pass was the place where the waiters picked up the dishes—always under the eagle eye of the announcer. Different announcers had different strengths, weaknesses and habits. I was afraid of all of them.

There was, for example, Mrs. Meier. She was an auntie of the owner and with her 65 years, she was a very experienced announcer.

She did not like it when waiters at the pass checked dishes by lifting up covers to take a peek. She expected us waiters to trust her when she pointed to a plate telling us that this was steak, for example.

Since it *had* happened before that she had sent people off with the wrong dish, I always tried to take a peek when she was busy with other things. More often than not, she would see me and bark from the top of her voice, "Take your hands off that cloche!" Since she always had the microphone right in front of her, the whole kitchen could hear her screaming at me. Just like the chefs acknowledged each dish she announced, so did they acknowledge each dressing down by shouting in unison, "Take your hands off that cloche!" and the kitchen would roar with laughter.

Another well-known announcer was the owner's sister, Mrs. Messer. She was our favorite announcer since she had a lot of patience and a little more understanding for the plight of a waiter in the chef's territory. I personally appreciated the fact that whenever she spoke with one of us waiters, she covered the microphone with her hand so the chefs could not hear her.

At the pass, I would carefully place each dish on my tray and rush back to our station where Hendrick was already waiting. If I also had a beverage order, I would pick it up from the service bar on my way out. I had learned quite fast to balance the large rectangular tray on my left hand whilst carrying a small tray with beverages on the right. "Always carry the tray with your left hand and use your right hand to open doors or carry small items like salads, ice cream or beverage trays," Hendrick had "hammered," this sentence into my head day by day every time I left the station. It took me a while and some training to carry anything with my left hand but after a while, it worked rather well, quite possibly because I just wanted him to stop saying that tiring sentence.

After a while, the sentence did stop because I never carried the tray with the wrong hand and I never left the restaurant empty-handed. The award for my rapid progress came in the form of more responsibility. Hendrick put me in charge of serving side dishes. Sounds simple enough, but to do this in the middle of the restaurant with people staring at me was something that I had to get used to. There was also a very specific order in which the different food items had to be portioned from the platter onto the plate. The hotel logo on the plate had to be in the twelve o'clock position with meat or fish placed in the

36

six o'clock position. Vegetables were always placed above the meat or fish, vegetables to the right and potatoes to the left.

I remember that at one time, the chef was hooked on baby vegetables, which were miniature versions of the real thing. I was asked to place the vegetables individually and in a fan shape onto the plate instead of in clusters. Doing this nicely put immense pressure on me and because of that, many times my hands would tremble, especially in the early stages. As time went by, the trembling stopped and I became more comfortable working on the table in front of guests. There were even occasions where I talked with the customers whilst serving the food; for me, that was a big step.

Over time I started to serve entire menus by myself if Hendrick was busy taking orders from other tables. He still did not allow me to take orders by myself since my menu knowledge was far below his expectation. I didn't know the composition or the method of preparation of many of the dishes. Therefore, I took a sample of each menu and the wine list to my room. I read them daily and made notes of words or descriptions I did not understand. The next day, Hendrick would patiently explain to me the meaning of them.

Towards the end of December, business began picking up and the streets of Talasee were crowded again. Three days before Christmas, the hotel was fully booked and we were very busy. Winter had finally arrived in all its glory, leaving Talasee covered in a thick blanket of snow. The lake had frozen over with hundreds of people walking across the icy surface. The town itself looked like something out of a fairy tale. Houses, streets and trees covered in snow and brightly lit Christmas trees lined the streets. In the center of Talasee stood a large, brightly illuminated Christmas tree and it looked truly beautiful.

For us waiters, things now got really busy. We had full restaurants for breakfast, lunch and dinner. The time we had for preparatory work between meal periods shrank to merely minutes. The first guests for lunch sometimes sat next to guests still having their breakfast. During those busy days, we usually went without lunch because we simply did not have the time for it.

Mr. Hanter was busy preparing table plans for Christmas Eve, a task that made the few hairs he had left turn grey. The restaurants of the Black Forest Grand Hotel were popular venues for festive dinners and from mid-December, the telephone didn't stop ringing from guests trying to make reservations. Tables changed from two to four and the next day back to two and everyone wanted a window table, which was difficult for me to understand since in winter it got dark very early and it would be pitch black outside. The real reason, of course, was that the restaurant only had eight window tables and in order to get one, a person had to be either a very regular customer or a friend of the Messer family. To sit at one of these tables was more a status symbol than anything else. At that time, I did not fully understand all that and, in any case, my priorities lay elsewhere.

On the morning of Christmas Eve, the first guests approached Mr. Hanter, asking to see their table for the evening. This was not something Mr. Hanter appreciated that early in the day, but he patiently led them to their table and, if the table was not good enough, he agreed, with grinding teeth, to assign a "nicer" table. He spent most of the day with the table plan, shifting guests from one end of the restaurant to the other. Every so often, he went into a restaurant, scanning the table arrangements to see if there was any way to squeeze in another table for two. By three o'clock, he reached a point where he did not accept any more changes, much less reservations.

After lunch, we started setting up and decorating the restaurants for Christmas Eve dinner. We were busy setting up tables, folding napkins, polishing champagne glasses, preparing festive menus, setting up candles and polishing cutlery and glasses. We trainees did all this whilst the senior waiters and Mr. Hanter spent the afternoon with their families.

The absence of the management was a great opportunity for some plate-throwing exercises. The damage that afternoon was not too severe, but one of my plates, impossible for Ralf to catch, crash landed into one of Johnny's tables, destroying a couple of champagne glasses and a flower vase. The damage was cleaned up before Johnny realized it ever happened.

By five, we had set up and decorated all stations, which left us just enough time to take a shower and change into our tuxedos provided by the hotel. Having never worn a tuxedo in my life, I once again felt like a clown. I was rather tall, a fact which showed clearly in the size of my tuxedo trousers—they were far too short. The same applied to the sleeves of the jacket. I looked at myself in the mirror, shaking my head; I really looked like a clown. Back in the hotel, I found that the others looked not much better; none of the other tuxedos was made to measure.

"You look good," Hendrick said when he saw me. I noticed a slight grin on his face and decided that he was not serious. Our own "festive," dinner in the staff canteen was hurried and far from festive and at six-thirty sharp, we all were on standby in our stations waiting for customers to arrive.

This was the only time for us to really enjoy Christmas, with all the snow outside, the festive decoration in the restaurants and the wonderful-looking tables with shining silver, polished glasses and beautiful Christmas bouquets. The candles on the large Christmas wreath, suspended from the center of the restaurant ceiling, were lit and gave the entire restaurant a festive touch. Hendrick told me that the service would be easier than usual since everybody would get the same menu.

From seven o'clock onwards, things slowly gained momentum as guests began arriving and the restaurants started to fill. The service went very smoothly, almost leisurely, as all guests had the same festive menu. It consisted of six courses, and we served only the main course from the gueridon. Throughout the Christmas dinner, most of our time was spent observing the tables in our station, waiting for customers to finish their dishes so we could clear them and move on to the next one.

I spent the time discreetly observing the guests on the tables in our station. On table one, there was a couple, probably in their forties, hardly talking to each other. I remember the woman very well because she had a thick, expensive-looking fur coat flung over her shoulders and heavy gold bracelets on her wrists. I remember thinking that she must have been pretty hot under that fur coat since the restaurant was comfortably warm with the freezing cold outside. She did not look very happy and her husband looked even grimmer. I realized that they were annoyed by the noise coming from the table next to theirs, where two young couples had a good time laughing and chatting. Since table one was located right in front of our side station, I was able to overhear the frustrated comments from the unhappy couple.

"Do they have to be that noisy?" the wife grumbled to her husband, who just sat there shaking his head. It seemed to me that they were unhappy people by nature. But it was more likely that, since the wife was wearing a fur coat in a well-heated restaurant and him with his golden watch and rather large golden rings, they just lacked attention. The only attention they got at that moment was mine. "They could become a problem for us," Hendrick whispered to me.

The two couples on table two couldn't care less and had fun. Table three was occupied by another young couple who was just holding hands, looking into each other's eyes and whispering to each other rather than talking. They did not seem to notice much about the world around them—easy customers for us. Table four was a challenge since the customers at this table had an urge to talk to us waiters every time we passed their table. If they managed to get one of us entangled in a conversation, it was quite a challenge to get away without having to offend them. At this stage of my career, I was not very comfortable talking to such sophisticated people and tried to avoid this at all costs. Therefore, I did my best not to get too close to table four unless one of my colleagues was caught at the table, tied into a conversation and there was no danger for me. Other than that, I pretended to be busy observing other tables, not noticing them.

So-called "passive," customers occupied table eleven and twelve. Passive customers, for me, were those who came to the restaurant, placed their order, ate, paid and left. Conversations with such customers were normally limited to standard greetings and polite comments and only seldomly did they engage in long conversations or complain. It is unfortunate that these were the customers who were sometimes forgotten by the waiter due to their passiveness. That was when things normally went wrong. If they did complain, they usually apologized at the same time for the fact that they had complained in the first place and were embarrassed for having done so. Passive customers are the losers in a busy restaurant. Standing at my service station, I watched with interest the different characters at the different tables.

"Don't stare at the customers," Hendrick said, bringing me back to reality. Our problem was clearly table one, and Hendrick had already realized that if the lady did not get some sort of attention soon, she would shift her attention from her neighbors to the service or the food. If that happened, we would be in trouble. I did not see this with my limited experience but Hendrick was about to change this situation to our advantage.

He went up to the table and opened the conversation with, "That is a lovely coat you are wearing, madam," followed by, "Did you enjoy your starter?" The comment about her coat had done the trick. She did not know what to say at first but then her face changed and she answered with the sweetest voice, "Thank you, and yes, the food was lovely, too."

Yack, I thought, how could he do this? She looked ridiculous in that fur coat in a comfortably warm restaurant and he knew it. When Hendrick returned to the service station, I had to ask him, "Don't you think she looks funny with the coat draped over her shoulder?"

"Of course she does," he replied and walked off. I was standing there, left to ponder. What I did not realize, of course, was that he just saved our tip from this table. During the evening, he dropped a couple more flattering comments that made me chuckle but he had brought table one back in line.

Everybody was in a festive mood, including us waiters; we joked when we passed each other with fully laden trays and made jokes with the chefs in the kitchen. The only one who did not appreciate the fact that he had to work on Christmas Eve was Johnny. He was also angry because a customer had asked him if he had this intense festive feeling. When he told us in the kitchen that he wanted to answer the customer with, "My festive feeling is running down the center of my a** in form of sweat," we killed ourselves laughing. Barrollo reckoned he had a chance with the daughter of one of his customers and kept us updated on the progress whenever we met in the kitchen.

The timing of the dishes was organized in a way so that all main courses would be "fired," at the same time. One hour into the service, we began to assemble in the kitchen, lining up in front of the pass to pick up our main courses. Only when the last waiter had arrived would Karl start firing. All the previous courses were pre-plated and had been issued pretty fast, but the main course, which was the highlight of the festive menu, had to be prepared "a la minute," and therefore it was now the kitchen's turn to be busy. It was our turn to tease the chefs.

"Shut up, you bunch of sissies," Karl screamed from the kitchen when we sarcastically inquired on the whereabouts of our food. Barrollo was the last one to join the queue.

"Six mains, fast!" he shouted from the end of the queue.

"Oh shut up, Barrollo," was the thundering reply from behind the chef who was sweating all over.

"Hey guys, I've got it," Barrollo said with a big grin on his face, waving a piece of paper with his victim's telephone number. I wondered how the hell he was able to extract a telephone number from a girl sitting at a Christmas dinner with her parents.

"I will meet her at the Pferdestall tonight!"

I was impressed; he not only had the number but also a date! Then it was my turn to pick up my dishes and with an angry remark from Karl—"Make a move, sissy"—I packed those onto my tray and off I went. On my way out of the kitchen, I passed by the service bar and noticed the new bar girl—"the frog," as we called her, due to her frog-like eyes. Her name was Helen and her looks made her the target of quite a few nasty comments from us.

We served the main courses in one go and went back to our standby position at our service station. Hendrick asked me to prepare mise en place for dessert, coffee and tea service. We cleared the main course about twenty minutes later and served dessert. Coffee was served from silver coffeepots that we had to pick up at the coffee station in the kitchen. Once again, most of us waited in line at the coffee station for our orders.

"If table twenty does not shut up about festive feelings, I will pour hot coffee all over this idiot," Johnny grumbled whilst waiting for his silver pots of steaming hot coffee. No, for him this was not a happy Christmas; having to work and serve other people on Christmas Eve was not his idea of a festive season and definitely not an occasion to be overwhelmed by festive feelings. We laughed and continued with the job at hand.

After coffee and dessert was served, our two passive tables asked for the check, paid and left. The couple at table one had grown quite fond of Hendrick who, in my opinion, had gone a bit overboard with his compliments and he now paid the price by having to listen to the stories of their lives. I was just in the process of clearing the already abandoned tables when the lady from table four, the one who didn't stop talking, approached me and pressed ten marks into my right hand. I thought she wanted to shake hands; she said, "Thank you and Merry Christmas," and left. I looked at my open palm with the bank note sitting there. Wow, I thought, incredible. Ten marks! I quickly stuffed it into my trouser pocket. My first Christmas tip; the couple had not been so bad after all.

The days after Christmas Eve passed quickly and soon New Year's Eve arrived. New Year's Eve followed pretty much the same pattern as Christmas Eve; we did all the preparation in the afternoon whilst the management spent the afternoon with their families. We spent our afternoons practicing our plate-throwing skills. We got better and better at it and none of the plates ended up on tables. The loss was kept at a minimum.

I was assigned to a waiter by the name of Peter, a veteran with over thirty years of experience. His style of service was completely different from that of Hendrick; he was a worker rather than a fine dining waiter. This was also the reason why his station was much larger. When I saw the number of tables in our station, first I wondered how we would possibly manage to serve nearly forty customers between the two of us. Now my experience from the garden in summer and working with Hendrick on the terrace came in handy and I learned from Peter how to combine the two perfectly. Working with him kept me in a state of constant laughter since he had absolutely no respect for anything and anybody. He had a sarcastic comment about every one of our customers and if he wanted them to hear it, he made sure they did.

"Didn't you forget something?" he would say if I was about to leave our station without taking a tray of soiled plates, glasses or something else with me. "Starters, table twenty and twenty one, and second course, table nineteen," he called out and I rushed to the kitchen, repeating the order in my mind five times on the way. I did this in order not to forget.

"Starters, twenty and twenty one, second course, nineteen," I called out once I reached Meier. She repeated the order through the microphone while I waited.

"Get back to your station," she barked at me, sending me back into the restaurant. "Don't waste time. I call you when your order is ready."

At each side station, there was a small red light, which, when lit up, meant that our order was ready. Meier activated the light from a master panel next to her seat, listing all station numbers. The light went on and I took off towards the kitchen.

"Aren't you forgetting something?" Peter called out behind me, making me realize that I had once again forgotten to take something with me. Throughout the evening, I was running and Peter was talking. He hardly moved out of the restaurant at all, relying completely on me.

Pick up this, take out that and do not forget the other. He ordered and I would run; it worked perfectly. His intention, as always, was to be the first in the main-course queue, something which had no meaning at all for Hendrick. For Peter, it was all just a question of getting it over and done with as quickly as possible and then get out and off to the pub. Whenever I worked with Peter I was the first to finish for the night. The service we delivered was not the most sophisticated and it was not unusual that he would send me for the soup when customers had not even begun to eat their starter. The soup would then sit on a plate warmer in our service station until the customers finished their starter.

"They should have eaten their starter faster" was his only comment when customers pointed out that the soup was not hot enough. To change the soup was out of the question, since this would completely upset his time schedule. If one customer at a table insisted to have his soup changed, Peter would change the soup for a new one but he still would continue to keep up the same momentum for the other customers at the table. To drive his point home, he would serve the main course to all but the soup guy. The soup guy's main course would be waiting for him on the plate warmer. Against Peter, the customer was always the loser. By the time we served the desert, the other waiters had only started clearing their main-course plates. I served coffee and tea whilst Peter sat in our employee dining room having a cigarette.

"Call me when one of them wants to pay," he would instruct me and the evening would once again be over and done with for him. An evening with Peter normally left me soaked in sweat at the end of the night.

Perspiring was another problem. Having never used deodorant before, something only women used where I came from, left me smelling not at my best after a busy meal period. Johnny, to whom I am still grateful to this day, pointed out this fact to me once. From that day on, I was so conscious of my body odor that for a while, out of fear, I kept on smelling my armpits, another fact that drew Johnny's attention and it was once again him who made me aware of it. And, as usual, my fellow waiters, who, whenever they saw me, put their heads into their armpits with laughter.

Following this, I sometimes used too much deodorant, which made me again the subject of sarcastic remarks from my colleagues. I then got into the habit of taking showers in the morning and before I started my evening duty. This in turn earned me sarcastic comments from my father once he found out and he reminded me that when he was my age, showers or baths were only taken once a week, on Saturdays. In his opinion, this was also the reason for their good health because they did not kill with soap all the body's natural bacteria, which, according to him, protects us from disease. I have to add that this was a long time ago and even my father now takes daily showers. But to this day, I get intensely irritated by people ignorant of the odor they produce, especially if I have to serve them

At midnight, we all toasted to a "Happy New Year" and I was impressed by the fact that the owner went through the entire hotel and toasted with each and every employee, trying very hard to remember their names. As I expected, he didn't remember mine but at least he asked and nervously I told him, "My name is Andre," and from then onwards he remembered. New Year's Eve ended late and by the time I got home it was five o'clock in the morning. I had a shower and went to bed. I vividly remember lying there and thinking, This is the real beginning of my hotel career. My first year begins.

Chapter 2

The first year of my hotel career began pretty much the same way as the last one had ended—we were busy every day. Our customers were still relaxed and I learned. By mid-January, business started to slow down again, mostly in food and beverage. For restaurants and banqueting, this was one of the slowest months of the year. In order for us not to get bored, Mr. Hanter had us cleaning the restaurants from top to bottom. We cleared out cupboards and cabinets, cleaned the inside, filled them up again and moved on to the next one. Once we had run out of cupboards and cabinets to clean, we were instructed to take on the silverware.

Polishing silver cutlery, pots and other equipment was always a big and smelly job. Silver equipment has the unpleasant habit of corroding after a certain time of intensive usage. We normally cleaned small patches of corrosion with a special silver cream when needed but every three to four month, we had to "bomb" or burnish them. For this process, we had a silver burnishing machine, which consisted of a rotating drum filled with small steel balls. The items to be burnished would be placed in the drum, a foul-smelling cleaning substance would be added and the drum would be closed and switched on. The drum was left rotating for one to two hours, after which the items would be removed and placed in cold water. After another hour or so, the items would be removed and then had to be polished. After a thorough polishing job, the silver equipment would look as new.

Much of the actual work was left to the most junior trainees, which happened to be Ralf and me. Johnny and Barrollo, in the meantime, would sit in the employee dining room, smoking and having coffee. We were of course under strict orders to inform them immediately if Mr. Hanter, Megan or Hendrick approached the stewarding area. Having been at the hotel now for over four months, I was trained in how to detect an approaching superior by using various methods. There was the visual monitoring of the entrance, whereby we made use of the reflections on the stainless steel doors of the kitchen refrigerators.

These refrigerators, due to their positioning, offered an excellent view from all the way back in the stewarding area to the entrance of the kitchen. If visual monitoring was not possible, we used our "sonar."

Ralf had taught me to recognize the specific sound signatures of approaching superiors such as Hendrick, Megan and so on. One shuffled, one yawned, and the next coughed so every one of them had a different habit that gave them away. Both the visual and the audio detection methods gave us plenty of time to warn Johnny or Barrollo of an incoming supervisor. The employee dining room adjoined the stewarding part of the kitchen and therefore we were always under close supervision. We would either whistle or call and Johnny and Barrollo would get up, rush out of the dining room, grab two towels and by the time the supervisor entered the stewarding area, four of us would be standing there busy polishing freshly burnished silverware. We cleaned and polished forks, knives, spoons, oyster forks, lobster forks, butter bowls, salt and pepper shakers, candle holders, napkin rings, you name it—we cleaned and polished them all.

The silver got cleaner and I got dirtier and smellier. My self-consciousness about perspiring and the odor that comes with it had by now developed into paranoia and I smelled my armpits constantly, to the delight of Ralf.

After all was spotlessly clean, we wrapped every item individually into clingfilm and off it went to the stewarding storeroom. Having completed the task, we got ready for inspection by Johnny, the most senior trainee. Johnny loved these inspections and he behaved as if he was a drill instructor in the army. He took the silver bowls, held them under the light, pretending to know silver cleaning inside out and pointing out nearly invisible water stains. "This is not good enough. I want all bowls cleaned again," Johnny said and, like a drill instructor, he marched out of the room.

We knew this part of the show all too well and, unlike the first time, the last thing we had in mind was to clean, burnish and polish again. Standing in front of three or four bowls, Ralf and I spent the next hour pretending to busy ourselves with cleaning and polishing whilst the burnishing machine rotated away—with the same bowl—whilst we chatted instead of polished. By now, Barrollo and Johnny were not paying any attention to us whatsoever so we took it easy. Once we ran out of things to talk about, we wrapped up the bowl, which by now looked like new, and then called Johnny.

He grabbed the first bowl like an expert. It was the bowl we had polished for one hour and strategically placed in front of him. He checked the bowl and, as expected, had nothing to say; the bowl was shinning brightly in the light. "Okay, now it's clean. That's it," he grumbled and left. We smiled at each other.

Between this assignment and the next one, we used the time productively to practice plate acrobatics; six revolutions with a dinner plate was easy by now. Mr. Hanter was busy finding new things for us to do and we were busy finding new ways to do them in the shortest possible time or not at all, without him ever realizing. We hoped that by doing this, he might be forced to send us home since there were not many customers around. Unable to find any more cleaning jobs—not surprising after three days of cleaning and polishing—he resorted to having us clear snow around the hotel. After all snow had been cleared, he resorted to training. Whilst Johnny and Barrollo were given the task of taking inventory of the beverage store, Ralf was asked to introduce me to room service.

Unlike in larger hotels where a dedicated room service department handled all orders going up to guest rooms, every morning we had one waiter assigned to handle room service orders. Since we never had more than two or three room service orders per day, the assigned waiter usually helped with breakfast in the restaurant until such an order came in. The room service telephone, red in color, was located at the service bar. If that phone rang, the girls at the service bar answered with, "Room service." Ralf was the dedicated room service waiter and because of this, he was selected to train me. I still remember his introduction: "Room service is where you make the real tip!"

He taught me how to prepare a tray and where I would find the different plates, cutlery and condiments. And, typical for Ralf, he gave me a typed checklist, which I had to complete before delivering a tray. Besides telephone orders, customers also had the choice of filling in a breakfast order form in the evening which they would hang on the doorknob. Ralf and I would patrol the corridors several times in the evenings to collect these order forms. We would prepare the trays the evening before, ready for delivery the next morning. During the night, Salah, the miserable, non-smiling night manager, would collect late orders, which we would then prepare in the morning.

In the beginning, I just followed Ralf and waited at the door when he delivered a breakfast. I watched him set up the breakfast table in the room. I soon started to dislike rooms which had not been aired yet by their occupants. These experiences in the morning did not help much to heal my developing perspiration paranoia. After my first few room service deliveries, I made a point of opening my own window daily immediately after getting up in the morning.

We worked as a team for the first couple of days and I appreciated the fact that I was able to stop at the door whilst Ralf had to work his way through the stale and smelly room, but I knew that my time would come. As for the tip, the collection of it happened usually inside the room and I had to rely on Ralf's honesty as to what amount was collected.

Room service was a new and amazing experience for me. Guests being served in the room are different than guests in the restaurant. They were never rude or aggressive to the room service waiter; quite the opposite, they were almost always very polite. Maybe this was because a room service waiter enters the very private sphere of the customer and it is in both parties' interest to make this encounter as short as possible. It did not happen very often that I was asked to set up the breakfast table in the room. Most guests wanted their privacy and asked us to leave the moment the room service trolley was parked in the room. Nevertheless, the room service waiter always looks around the room, noticing all sorts of details like clothes, lingerie and other very personal items. If the tip is good, these observations would never leave the room. If the waiter leaves the room without tip, rest assured that the waiter's observations, whatever they might be, would be disseminated to his colleagues. Most guests would then be surprised when employees with knowing smiles greet them throughout the hotel.

Ever since those early days, I make a point of keeping my room clean and tidy whenever I travel, because some of the things I have seen in guest rooms are truly amazing. For example, it was not uncommon for rooms to look as if suitcases had exploded with the splattered remains of clothing everywhere. More than once, customers noticed me observing their room, offering an apologetic "Sorry, I haven't had the time to clean up." And, more than once, the apologetic remark was accompanied by a handsome tip. Some customers traveled with framed pictures of their dogs, all nicely set up in the room, and others had expensive-looking jewelry lying around and not-so-expensive-looking underwear.

49

Many times, the moment I entered the room, wives would disappear half-naked into bathrooms and sometimes they remained in the room, just standing there with a bathrobe wrapped loosely—very, very loosely around their body. This happened so frequently that I began to wonder if they did this on purpose. Far less attractive was the range of odors we encountered in rooms, especially in the mornings, ranging from expensive perfumes to odors resembling that of decomposing cadavers.

I served my first room service breakfast on a day when Ralf was off. It went fine and I got five marks tip. Ralf had taught me to listen at the door first before knocking, which turned out to be an interesting experience. Guest room doors are normally not soundproof, making it easy for a waiter to hear what is going on inside. I know for a fact that some of my breakfast deliveries interfered with people's morning pleasures and I always timed my interference accordingly.

As I gained proficiency in room service, I had more and more time to observe the inside of the rooms more closely whilst customers searched in their wallets for my tip. The room service customer profile was mostly younger couples and only seldom elderly guests and this, of course, made room service that much more interesting.

One beautiful Saturday morning in January, I received a really interesting breakfast order because it included a bottle of champagne! This was a first for me. *Champagne for breakfast; they must have money!* I thought. Most of our customers were German upper class, and for them, the alcoholic beverage of choice was German Sekt rather then French champagne. Top brands of German sparkling wines normally entered the price range of champagne at the lower end. Therefore, champagne was still considered a beverage for the wealthy. And here I was, preparing a bottle of champagne for breakfast.

I had never actually opened a bottle of champagne before and that made me nervous. What if the cork popped and I spilled half of the champagne? What if I dropped the bottle, or what if I did not get it open? Suddenly a rush of panic came over me, hoping that maybe the guests would want to open the bottle by themselves. I finished setting the trolley and ran once more through Ralf's checklist. Ice bucket, champagne, champagne glasses, opener—all was there. I took a deep breath and off I went to the room.

Having reached the guest room door, I made final preparations. I carefully removed clingfilm from fruits, straightened cutlery and, spitting on one of the coffee spoons, I removed a lonely water stain using an edge of my jacket. One last check and, satisfied that all was there, I put my ear on the door. I could not hear a thing so I knocked. Nothing happened. I waited for a moment and knocked again.

Then I heard some shuffling in the room. The shuffling stopped and somebody glanced through the peephole to see who was there and then the door swung open.

"Good mor—" I tried to say, but when I saw the lady standing before me, I nearly swallowed my tongue with my heart missing a beat. She was tall with blond, shoulder- length hair. But that was not the reason why my heart jumped; it was because she was half-naked! All she wore was some sort of very thin, silky transparent scarf that was so transparent, she might as well have stood there stark naked. I was momentarily thrown off my tracks and I just stood there trying to make sense of the image in front of me. *Is this for real?* The beautiful young lady stood there half-exposed with a gigantic tattooed eagle on her chest, holding the door open. I stared at the eagle with its head and body tattooed around her navel, stretching its wings across her breasts all the way up to her neck.

"Good morning, please come in," she said.

Although I clearly heard her asking me to come in, I was not able to move. I had never seen a naked woman in my life except on TV. I was in tatters.

"Good…good…morning," I mumbled.

I pushed the trolley into the room, placed it near the open window and tried hard to concentrate on opening the champagne.

"Would you like me to open the champagne?" I asked, hoping she would say no. To my great relief, she declined my half-hearted offer. I prepared the breakfast table. She watched me and lit a cigarette, waiting for me to finish my setup. I had just asked her if I should pour the coffee when another girl's voice, coming from the bed said, "Give him some tip, Julie."

My heart jumped; there was another girl curled up in bed but this one wore no clothes at all. I had not paid any attention to the bed when I entered the room and completely overlooked that there was another couple in bed. The girl sat up.

"Take it from my wallet," she said, pointing at a small leather bag. The moment she sat up, the bed sheet slipped and exposed her upper

51

body completely. I immediately turned my head and was deeply embarrassed because she had seen me starring at her. As if this was not enough, my eyes ended up on Julie's behind. She bent down right in front of me picking up the leather bag to retrieve the other girl's wallet. It only took split seconds for me to see that Julie was not wearing any underwear. I immediately took my eyes off her, only to end up on the other girl's exposed breasts. She just smiled at me and I had the urge to apologize. I was in a mess. *This is not going well,* I thought.

"Here, this is for you," said Julie, the girl with the eagle, and she passed me the tip. I took it, not knowing what to do with my eyes. I concentrated hard to look into her eyes, thanked her and turned towards the door.

"Thank you," Julie, the eagle girl, said and with a cheeky smile, she closed the door behind me. I walked two steps and stopped, my heart pounding. I needed a few minutes to recover. On my way back to the kitchen, I tried to figure out what had just happened. Being my innocent self, I made a bit a fool of myself when I told Johnny about my breakfast experience. Whilst I seriously thought that the couple in bed had probably invited another couple for breakfast, Johnny came up with a more realistic theory based on facts such as the girl's tattoos and the fact that they were only lightly dressed. As we later found out, the guest was a strip club owner from Switzerland who was here for the weekend with two of his employees.

Soon, I was appointed the dedicated room service waiter and Ralf moved on to a more responsible position. I was proud because I knew that Mr. Hanter would not have done this unless he really trusted me. I was determined not to disappoint him. Every day I prepared my trays diligently and determined to deliver all breakfasts within five minutes of the requested delivery time. I got more confident and the handsome tips I generated by now paid for the petrol for my motorbike.

Ralf had shared a few tricks with me during the final handover, such as memorizing guests' preferences. According to him, this was a good way of securing tip. One customer, for example, mentioned that he normally only takes brown sugar and since we did not have it in the hotel, Ralf suggested I go out and buy it in the supermarket. The next morning when I served his breakfast, I pointed out the brown sugar, which, needless to say, surprised him and boosted my tip considerably. Ralf was right in his theory that the tip would by far exceed the cost of the sugar. I developed a habit of listening to guests, which, although inspired by financial considerations, would be a great asset in my future career.

The relatively large number of single lady guests at our hotel is difficult to explain, but I guess it was due to the fact that Talasee as a summer and winter resort was ideal for rest and recreation from the hectic life in large cities, especially for businesswomen. I met some of them during my time in room service. One such lady stayed with us for two weeks. I noticed her first at the front desk when she checked in. She was in her early thirties, wore a long fur coat and a fur hat. Her luggage looked expensive and, considering our poor porter was already in his sixties, it was very heavy. I saw her again the next morning when I delivered her breakfast at eight o'clock. She opened the door with a warm and friendly smile.

"Good morning." I entered the room and asked where she would like me to put her breakfast.

"Just leave it on the table over there," she said, pointing at the coffee table outside on the balcony.

"May I set up the table?" I asked.

"Yes, please," she replied. I placed a pink tablecloth on the coffee table and folded her napkin.

"How long have you been working here?" she suddenly asked, standing behind me whilst I was just putting down the cutlery.

"Six months," I answered and was surprised at her interest in my personal life. I finished the table setup and asked if there was anything else I could do for her. Throughout our brief conversation, she kept on looking straight into my eyes, which made me feel a little uncomfortable.

"That will be all," she replied and squeezed a banknote into my hand as if she wanted to break my fingers. I thanked her, opened the door and I was just about to leave when she asked me for my name and I told her.

"See you tomorrow then, Andre," she said and closed the door. I was impressed that such an elegant lady, traveling alone and obviously holding a very high position or possibly running her own company, wanted to know so much about me. On the way back to the kitchen, I opened my hand and discovered to my surprise a twenty-mark note.

Complete privacy was granted.

The twenty marks became a daily occurrence and only slowly did I realize that the time I spent with her in the mornings caught in lengthy conversations got longer and longer. We talked about many things but her questions were mostly about me. Johnny started to make sarcastic comments about the time I spent in that particular room, which I easily explained with having to set up the breakfast on the balcony. Even though it was the truth, he didn't quite believe me.

"Breakfast on the balcony in January?" he would ask suspiciously, but once he saw the lady, he was convinced that the last thing on *her* mind was the room service waiter and he stopped harassing me on the subject with a sarcastic "in your dreams." She stayed for two weeks, and during this time we became something like friends, even though I would have never dared to call it that way. For me, she was always a customer and I was the waiter, the room service waiter, to be precise. She left and I never figured out what our meetings in the morning were all about and why she had asked me so many questions. Indeed, as Johnny said, what interest could such an elegant and obviously successful lady have in a room service waiter called Andre?

With breakfast completely in my control, Ralf also gave me more responsibility during lunch and dinner service. Occupancy began picking up in late March and from then on I was fully occupied with room service. During this time I had grown quite close to the girls at the service bar because my room service telephone was located there. Opposite the service bar was the coffee station, which also was run entirely by girls. The girls liked me. I guess they liked me only because of my innocence and the fact that I got embarrassed at their constant jokes.

Since my near dismissal during my probation, I had set my mind on proving that I took this job seriously. I tried to run room service without needing the help of the guys from the restaurant. I could only achieve this by being as organized and disciplined as possible. And, although I did joke a lot with the girls in the kitchen, for some time to come, I would not accept any invitation to their floor again. The relentless self-discipline of mine was made a little easier by the fact that none of them was a stunning beauty.

Room service had other advantages, such as being able to taste the food being delivered to the rooms and getting to know the female room attendants. Many of our room attendants were trainees and amongst them, there *were* real beauties. We normally had not much contact with the maids because, sad to say, they were confined to the guest rooms and corridors.

Carrying trays with my left hand had become second nature during my time in room service. This left my right hand free to pick up and taste whatever food I had on my tray. Ralf had taught me right from the start that if a dish was ordered which he personally liked, he would request a large portion from the kitchen "as requested by the guest." He would then, between the kitchen and the guest room, reduce the requested large portion to regular size by eating some of it on the way. French fries, mushrooms, strawberries, raspberries, small medallions of veal or pork, potatoes, chocolates—you name it, I've tried them all in the deserted guest room corridors. I would run room service for the next four months until I handed over to my successor. In the meantime, my training intensified.

I had now completed nearly six months and during that time I had learned a lot. Not everything I learned was part of the official training plan. Part of this "unofficial training" was taking revenge on customers. So it happened that one day I witnessed Johnny taking revenge on one particular nasty guest. I learned that many unpleasant things can, will and do happen to food between the kitchen and the guest room or restaurant, *if* a guest is particularly nasty to the waiter. Whilst the majority of guests are pleasant and accommodating, there are the occasional individuals who can drive waiters to a point where they see themselves forced to take revenge. The same applies to chefs when their dishes were returned unjustly for no reason other than to humiliate or insult the chef's culinary skills. The revenge of a waiter or chef comes in many different shapes and sizes, ranging from being funny to utterly unpleasant for the guest.

Revenge on customers in the food and beverage industry can fill chapters of books and are rarely discussed in public. But it does happen and it happens on a daily basis. It happens in fast food restaurants, five-star hotels and Michelin-star restaurants—it happens everywhere. What can a customer do to prevent it? Treat the waiter with respect and be objective about the food. This is really all about respect.

Conflicts between restaurant employees and customers in many cases turn personal, with the employee being in the disadvantage. Whilst a customer is free to choose whatever language he desires to humiliate a waiter, the waiter is bound by the "customer is king" principle which expects him to ignore unpleasant and insulting comments. The offending customer is well aware of this and instinctively knows that in a verbal conflict he cannot lose; the employee has to take whatever abuses are being thrown at him with only one possible reply and that is an apology. Some customers thrive on the knowledge of complete dominance, sometimes to a point where the encounter can get out of control. If the employee loses his temper and decides to retaliate, it can quite possibly be the end of his or her career.

Therefore, the ability to stay calm in such situations is one of the most important skills a young hospitality employee has to learn. Verbal abuse in public is taken to the highest extremes in food and beverage. There are two different types of abuses: justified complaints and unjustified complaints. Needless to say, if a serious mistake was made concerning a customer's order or damages were caused to a customer's property, the customer has all the right to bring this to the attention of the employee in charge. If serious damage was done, then the employee would most certainly be aware of the mistake and would be understanding to the customer's reaction, even if verbal abuse is severe.

It is not unusual for customers to use restaurant employees as an outlet for accumulated tension or stress that is normally completely unrelated to the dining experience. As mentioned before, due to the "customer is king" principle, the customer is fully aware that his potential victim—the waiter—cannot defend himself and has to take whatever abuse is thrown at him. The waiter, while taking the abuse, is momentarily defenseless and will take his reprisal in form of discreet revenge. A waiter's revenge is completely invisible, undetectable and without a trace. A sudden burst of politeness towards a previously abusing customer as well as a nearly undetectable satisfied smile on the waiter's face are the only indication of a waiter having taken revenge. The first revenge I witnessed was the chef who lost his temper with a guest about a schnitzel that was returned to the kitchen three times. I remember that incident well.

That day, a customer had ordered a "Wiener Schnitzel," a dish that was not listed on our regular menu. As this was an easy dish to prepare, Barrollo had accepted the order. This particular customer happened to be from

Austria, which also happens to be the home country of the Wiener Schnitzel. These so-called "out of menu" orders were not very popular with the chefs and normally would be given the lowest priority in a busy kitchen. The chef did this to punish the waiter for accepting the order and the customer for having the audacity to ask for it in the first place.

By the time the schnitzel was ready, the customer had already chased Barrollo twice for his meal. Barrollo eventually got his schnitzel and served it to the impatient guest.

"Please be careful, the plate is hot," he said with a smile, but the customer cut him off before he had finished the sentence.

"This is supposed to be a Wiener Schnitzel? Where are the lemons and the capers?" the customer shouted, looking angry at a bunch of parsley that proudly crowned the schnitzel. Barrollo offered to get some lemon and capers, but the angry Austrian passed Barrollo the plate, asking him to have it changed. Barrollo apologetically took the plate and rushed back to the kitchen. In the kitchen, the chef listened impatiently to Barrollo's request, picked up the schnitzel and slammed it under the Salamander, a sort of double-sided grill. Once the lemon and capers were ready, he grabbed the schnitzel, slammed it onto a new plate and topped it with a lemon and the capers.

"Barrollooooo!" he screamed. "Pick up your damn schnitzel."

Barrollo hurried to the kitchen, picked up the schnitzel and rushed back to the restaurant. He served the dish with a polite smile, saying, "Enjoy your Schnitzel," and placing the dish in front of the unhappy Austrian. I watched the Austrian as he observed the dish Barrollo had placed in front of him. He shook his head and after a few minutes, he called Barrollo back to the table.

"The batter of this schnitzel is not right; it's too soft. Doesn't your chef know how to make a simple schnitzel?" he blurted out. "Get me a new one."

Barrollo stood at the table with a confused look on his face.

"I am sorry," Barrollo mumbled, took the plate and headed back to the kitchen. I remember thinking, *I do not want to be in Barrollo's shoes right now.*

The chef was not impressed.

"He says the batter is not right, eh? I don't believe this!" the chef shouted. "I have made more schnitzels in my life than he will ever be able to eat. No problem, I make a new one for the sissy," he shouted and threw the schnitzel, together with the plate, into a nearby bin. He was very angry.

He growled and swore as he picked up a raw schnitzel that had not been battered yet. Barrollo and I stood in front of the pass trying to avoid the angry chef.

"Do you guys know how I make a proper schnitzel? Here, I show you hussies. " He suddenly took the schnitzel and shoved it down the back of his pants.

"Aw, yack!" I cried and Barrollo laughed. The chef rubbed the schnitzel several times up and down his sweaty bum. I could not believe my eyes.

He finally took it out and threw it into the same batter as he had used before. He turned it a couple of times and slammed it into the hot frying pan.

"This one is a special for my Austrian friend," he growled again and we burst out in laughter. When the chef finished the schnitzel, he slammed it onto the red-hot plate.

"That looks truly delicious, chef," Barrollo joked.

"Piss off and serve this damn piece of …"

At the table, Barrollo was hardly able to keep a straight face when he said to the Austrian guest, "Enjoy your Schnitzel." The Austrian looked skeptically at the new schnitzel and finally said, "It's not perfect but at least it begins to look like a schnitzel."

"Would you like me to change it again?" Barrollo asked with a bittersweet voice.

"I don't want to spend the entire day here," the Austrian growled and picked up his knife and fork. Johnny, Barrollo and I stood at the service station watching the Austrian gulp down a schnitzel that only moments ago had come face to face with the chef's backside. After he had finished, Barrollo went back to the table and asked if he had enjoyed his schnitzel.

"Was okay," the Austrian grumbled. When Barrollo came back to the service station with the empty plate in his hand and looked at us with a smile, we burst out into laughter. The Austrian would never know.

Waiters take revenge on chefs, chefs take revenge on waiters and chefs and waiters take revenge on customers. The next time, the chef would take revenge on me.

With my skills improving, my confidence grew proportionately and I became cockier when dealing with chefs. Whilst only months ago the chefs had been chasing *me* to pick up my dishes, now I was chasing the chefs to finish my dishes. During busy periods, the waiting time at the pass was longer and as we waited, we made all sorts of nasty remarks at the chefs in order to speed things up.

On this particular day, it must have been my cocky "Come on, guys, not sleeping…cooking!" remark which made the chef decide to teach me a lesson. I was at the pass waiting for one Black Forest Game Ragout with mushrooms, green vegetables and potato croquettes. This was one of our seasonal specialties, typical for the winter season. I was second in a line of five impatiently waiting waiters. I had just made a rather rude remark about Chef Karl when he asked me to shut up and pick up my dish.

The game ragout was a culinary masterpiece, which also happened to be my favorite dish. I quickly set up my tray, collected the croquettes and off I went to the restaurant. When I arrived at my service station, Hendrick had already prepared the gueridon next to the table occupied by a young couple. Since Hendrick was nowhere to be seen, I served the meal by myself. I placed the covered platters on the gueridon and neatly served the ragout onto two plates, followed by the vegetables and croquettes. Satisfied with the presentation, I served the lady first then the gentleman, wishing them an enjoyable meal.

After a while I could see that the gentleman seemed to have difficulties with his food. It looked as if he was trying to cut something without success. *Better go and take a look,* I thought, and walked over to the table.

"Do you enjoy the game ragout?" I asked.

"I think there is something wrong with your croquettes," he said and picked up a half-cut croquette. He passed the fork and the croquette to me.

"Take a look at this," the guest said, smiling. I took the fork and looked at the troublesome piece of deep-fried potato. I could not believe my eyes when I saw what was stuck on that fork. I was dumbstruck. Instead of a potato croquette, I was looking at a deep-fried piece of cork which once crowned a bottle of Ihringer Muller Thurgau wine.

"I…I am so sorry," I stammered. "I will change this immediately."

I cleared the two plates with shaking hands. On the way to the kitchen, I checked the other croquettes, which all turned out to be fried corks. Naïve as I was, I thought, *The chef will be very angry at the poor sod who messed this one up.*

Chef Karl was expecting me and before I could say anything, he barked, "Where the hell have you been? Here is your bloody game, pick it up and get out of my kitchen!" he screamed. He had already prepared two new dishes. I stood in front of him with the two plates in my hands. Half of the kitchen brigade had gathered at the pass, laughing. "Go on, move it, big mouth!" Chef Karl barked whilst I dropped the old plates in the stewarding section. I picked up the dishes and hurried back into the restaurant.

"Let me know how they like their croquettes" was the last thing I heard before leaving the kitchen. I apologized once again to the laughing couple who carefully tested the new croquettes right in front of me to see what I had served them this time. This time, they had real croquettes made out of real potatoes. I was lucky with my customers because they had a sense of humor, but the chefs had managed to make me look pretty stupid in front of my guests. Nevertheless, feeling a bit sorry for me, the couple left a nice tip to make up for it.

If the croquettes were meant as a warning, it had failed to get the message miserably. I was angry and decided to check carefully each and every item coming out of the kitchen. This, of course, did not go unnoticed by the chefs and they secretly decided that heavier ammunition was required in order to shut me up. I had no problem in checking each and every item as long as Mrs. Meier was not around.

"This *is* a chicken or don't you trust me?" she would shout at me. If on occasion she would give me the wrong dish, it was of course my fault. This too did not go unnoticed by our ever-watchful chefs.

Two weeks later, it was a Saturday evening; Mr. Hanter had assigned me to work with Hendrick, who was kind enough to let me have my first try at filleting a trout in front of a customer. I did not like working in front of customers; it somehow terrified me and I had difficulties performing even the simplest tasks. Hendrick must have felt sorry for the trout when he saw me starting to work on it and quickly decided to take over.

"You have to cut off the tail fin first," he told me later, already for the second time. I had actually heard him the first time, but once I stood at the guests' table, I was completely paralyzed and could not remember anything, much less what part of the dead fish I had to cut off first.

"Don't worry, you will learn," he said patiently, but something in his voice told me he was not too sure. I, for one, had no hope at all.

He ordered me to the kitchen to pick up two trout for another table. *Damn trouts again*, I swore to myself on the way to the kitchen. I was never a great fish eater myself and hated to bite or, god-forbid, swallow a fishbone. I was frequently watching customers sitting at their tables trying hard to make conversation whilst digging fish bones out of their teeth.

In the kitchen, a very unhappy-looking Mrs. Meier asked me, "What do you want?"

"Two trout, table three," I answered humbly and as always, I was completely intimidated by her.

"Are you blind?" the chef suddenly screamed, pointing at a platter covered with a cloche. I shuddered the second I heard the voice; it was Karl himself and I hadn't seen him standing behind the pass.

"Ah, no, sorry," I stammered. Mrs. Meier barked, "Go on, move it before it gets cold."

I nervously loaded the platter with the trout and side dishes onto my tray and went back to my station, glad to be out of the kitchen. As I arrived, I was upset, telling Hendrick that Karl had screamed at me for not seeing the platter.

"Don't worry, let him scream. That's the only thing he is doing well, screaming and shouting!" Hendrick said, waving his left hand in the air like a woman, which at least made me laugh. "You put the platter on the rechaud and I will do the filleting, and this time WATCH!"

I was relieved, since I was really not in a mood to try my luck on another trout. I prepared the rechaud on the gueridon, took the hot platter carefully with a service cloth and placed it on the rechaud. The couple looked at the platter, full of expectation. *They must be tourists*, I thought, and lifted the cloche, expecting the usual "Ahh" and "Ooh." This couple, however, remained quiet, and instead, the couple's expression of expectation suddenly changed to something resembling horrified surprise that left me puzzled for a second. When I looked down to see what had caused this strange reaction, I found myself staring at a very big, very rotten and very old carrot, neatly garnished with parsley and lemons. The carrot had already started decomposing. My heard stopped; I could not believe my eyes. What sick mind could possibly come up with something like this, in front of customers? The couple looked at me and, seeing the horror in my face, they started laughing.

I carefully placed the cloche back onto the platter and mumbled, "Ah, um, I am sorry, I will change this for you." Hendrick had watched everything from the service station and was laughing.

"Go and get the trout," he said. "I will talk to them."

I dreaded going back to the kitchen and as I approached the pass, Karl was standing there, arms crossed with a big grin on his face.

"Serving old carrots, eh? Here, you monkey, pick up your trout and get out of my kitchen," he screamed, with his voice getting progressively louder towards the end of the sentence. I hurried back to Hendrick, happy to be out of that hell hole. This was a warning that came from the chef on behalf of all the cooks.

The "warning" worked for the first couple of hours, during which I seriously considered being a little nicer to the chefs in the future. Of course, it didn't take long for Johnny and Barrollo to hear of the incident and they immediately urged me to seek revenge. According to them, the sheer atrocity of the "foul carrot incident" called for a major revenge on the kitchen. We didn't know quite how, where and when, but we knew our time would come.

One day in February, it was cold and snowy outside, which led Mr. Hanter to believe that it would be a quiet day for lunch in our restaurants. With this in mind, Mr. Hanter decided to send my boss, Peter, home. This left me in charge of the "Woodpecker Restaurant," which seated about forty-five guests. I was hoping to get at least one or two tables, the tips from which would have been a blessing for the damaged rear light of my motorbike.

There was not much to do for me once Peter had gone; the restaurant was empty. There were also not many cleaning jobs left; everything was spic and span. I strolled leisurely to the kitchen, chatting away with the girls at the service bar. As usual, I wasn't doing any of the talking; it was the girls who were teasing me and me being shy about it. I knew that the girls liked me because of my innocence and the fact that there was nothing to fear from me. I was no playboy, never made advances and they just liked to play with me. The girls were just in the middle of making fun of me when Mr. Hanter came storming into the kitchen.

"Andre, to your station immediately!" he shouted as he was passing me and, with large steps, continued on to the kitchen. I dashed off to the restaurant, only to find it already half-full. I was shocked; five tables were occupied and Hendrick's station was already completely full. Where did all those guests come from? All heads turned when I entered the restaurant and several guests began waving their hands at me. I rushed to the first table, only to be welcomed with an angry "Do we get a menu here?"

"Yes, of course," I stammered and returned to my service station. I felt a mild panic creeping up inside me, *five tables, two already angry and I am alone.* I looked around the station, counting about eighteen guests, realizing that none of them had menus and that they had all arrived at the same time. I grabbed a stack of menus and went from table to table handing them out. Several guests stopped me, trying frantically to order their beverages, which I answered with a friendly "I will be back in a moment." I got my order pad and, going from table to table, began taking beverage orders, all eighteen of them at once.

I dashed to the kitchen, shouting out orders to the girls as I punched them into the cash till. The cash till confirmed every order with a ring of a bell, after which it printed the dockets. The bell kept ringing, leaving me with a very long roll of printed dockets. I dropped them all at the service bar and prepared baskets with bread at the bread station.

Back in the restaurant, my guests were very impatient now. First, they had to wait for the menus and now they had to wait for their drinks. Out of the corner of my eye, I saw Hendrick in a similar state, dashing back and forth in his station. Having dropped bread and butter on each table, I dashed back to the kitchen and picked up a large tray with beverages. I served them as quickly as I could, skipped the pouring of the beers, and readied myself for the food orders.

Although I slowly gained control of the situation, the sarcastic comments from my guests weakened my spirit considerably. They had no mercy with me whatsoever. The next logical step should have been to sell as many of the same dishes as possible in order to make things easier for the kitchen and of course for me, but I was too rattled to make any kind of sensible recommendation. The result of me being rattled was that I involuntarily allowed them to order anything and everything. By the time I realized that the first order I had taken consisted not only of all different starters and main courses but also lots of different side dishes, it was too late.

I moved on to the next table where the host stopped my half-hearted recommendations dead in its tracks. The attention of all guests in the restaurant was now on me. Somehow, they all had but one goal in mind and that was to humiliate me. Already the first table had left no opportunity out to make sarcastic remarks whenever possible. For the benefit of the other guests in the restaurant, these sarcastic comments were thrown at me in a very loud and rude manner. I felt like a swimmer in a raging river trying to save myself from drowning but without luck; in my case, I was drowning physically and mentally. Once I had completed the order from the last table, I was relieved that this part was over.

I returned to my service station to rewrite the orders. When I looked at them, I thought, *What a disaster, the chef will kill me.* My five tables had managed to order between them pretty much each and every dish on the menu and, as if this was not enough, they had changed most of the side dishes, too. I cannot repeat the exact words the chef threw at me when he looked at my orders but needless to say, they were no words of praise. I had made him and his team my mortal enemies. The workload, which I bestowed on the chef and his team, was tremendous, not only in quantity but also logistically.

"Chicken ragout without onions and instead of rice the potatoes from the daily special but no parsley," "Beef Stroganoff with cucumbers on the side, slightly smaller portion beef but more sauce and noodles"—the order was a nightmare. I was dead meat. For the kitchen, the last fifteen minutes had already been a nightmare without me. I was not the only one placing orders for five tables at once; so were the others. The only difference was that the others had managed to streamline their orders a little better than me. The kitchen once again seemed like a battlefield, with orders echoing through loudspeakers, chefs screaming their acknowledgments and, louder than anybody else, Karl's thundering voice screaming at us waiters. His hatred for us was written all over his face. The clattering of plates, glasses and cutlery provided the necessary background noises. Whilst the chef was screaming in the kitchen, wishing for my immediate demise, my guests grew more and more impatient. The tables seemed to be competing as to who could be the most sarcastic and who would eventually manage to break the waiter. The waiter, of course, was me and, although I was severely in the shit, so to speak, I did not break. I was too busy.

Finally, one by one, the dishes started coming. "Starters, table thirty, soups, table thirty-one, soups and starters, table thirty-five," Karl shouted as he pushed platter after platter onto the pass. The sheer quantity and speed with which the kitchen prepared the dishes by far exceeded my capacity to carry them. I packed whatever I could onto my tray and dashed back to the restaurant to feed my hungry guests. I deeply regretted not having sold at least some set menus that would have made my life much easier. I dumped the tray in my service station and began serving my guests, who by now resembled a pack of hungry wolves. Then Mr. Hanter appeared in the restaurant, carrying a large tray in his left hand and three salad platters in his right. He dumped all in my service station and went back to the kitchen without saying a word. I wasn't sure if this was good news or bad news but I was grateful for his help. I hadn't even had time to thank him but now was not the time for pleasantries; I had to concentrate on my guests and their meals.

Unfortunately, I didn't concentrate enough and so I began mixing up tables, serving the wrong soup to the wrong guest and by doing so, giving them plenty of ammunition for more unwarranted sarcasm. Things were not getting better when I served the main courses. "I did not order this!" complained one lady, only to be answered by the next table with, "I am looking for a trout. Do you want my quail?" If they did not complain about having received the wrong dishes, then the food was cold. It was a mess. I offered to change the dishes, praying that they would decline since I really did not want to face the chef again with such unpleasant news. I was right. My guests continued complaining. "You want to change it so that you can let me wait even longer? I'd rather eat it cold," or "I will never be back to this place again" were the unanimous answers from my guests. Everybody had a comment to make; it was as if sharks had gone crazy after having tasted blood and I was their victim. Finally, they all got what they had ordered and the restaurant suddenly went quiet. The sharks were feeding.

I stood at my service station soaked in sweat, not so much from physical labor but from the mental stress I had gone through in the last hour. It was really a mess and so was I; the day suddenly had turned into a nightmare. I looked at my five tables, five tables of people who had never met each other. Judging by their accent, they were locals who would normally not interact with each other and definitely not in a restaurant unless they felt it was absolutely necessary. But in this case, not only had they joined together, they actually had made it a competition of who could be the most sarcastic or rudest in trying to wear down and then finish off the waiter—me.

Once all guests had finished their meals, I cleared the tables. I did not dare to ask my usual question, "Did you enjoy your meal?" Nor did I dare to make eye contact with any of them, so I just cleared. With their stomachs full, they at least quieted down a little and I was even rewarded with a "thank you" here and there. Some of the women seemed to feel sorry for me and they even tried to award me with a smile. But it was too late for that—my mood was gone. After what I had gone through during the last hour, I was too suspicious to smile and expected comments that were more sarcastic. I just wanted them all out of my restaurant.

I served coffee and desserts and began preparing the bills. At last, one by one, they paid and one by one, they left. Suddenly, the restaurant was empty and quiet. The entire episode had lasted only a little over an hour and now, standing in the deserted restaurant, I wondered what had happened just now. I looked at the terrace and it was pretty much the same picture. The battle was finally over.

Mr. Hanter entered the restaurant, looked around and, with only a trace of a smile, he said, "Come on, let's clean up." And with that, he left. I cleaned up my station, prepared all tables for dinner and at three o'clock, I went on my break. Back in my room, I crashed into my bed. I was exhausted, both physically and mentally. Since I had begun my training back in August, I was blessed with mostly positive experiences with regards to my colleagues and guests. Today, however, was different. My self-confidence had been seriously damaged. I asked myself if I was actually up to the job. *Today I had been hopelessly lost during the horrible luncheon,* I thought, and then I fell asleep.

In the evening when I met the others, I heard that I was not the only one who had a hard time at lunch. Johnny actually got so upset with a guest that he added a dash of saliva to a dish for one of his most troublesome guests on the way from the kitchen to the restaurant. Whilst we all laughed, I could not actually believe that Johnny would do something like that. I was wrong.

Over the coming weeks, I was assigned mostly to Hendrick and, having shared my experience of that day with him, he concentrated on sharpening my organizational skills.

"Never leave the restaurant empty-handed," he hammered this sentence into my head almost daily. It came to a point where I felt guilty walking to the kitchen or into the restaurant without carrying anything. Watching Hendrick carefully, I started to adopt a more systematic approach to my job. I began to combine different service tasks until they turned into habits. Leaving the restaurant and going to the kitchen, I would take soiled plates, glasses, napkins, orders or anything else I could find, and on the way would make mental notes of what I had to bring back from the kitchen. I hated those occasions where I would arrive back at the restaurant only to realize that I had forgotten or overlooked something.

Whilst my service skills made progress, my social skills with guests were lagging far behind. Once I was in front of a guest, especially Hendrick's caliber of guests, I was lost. I watched Hendrick with eagle eyes but this was not something one could learn by memorizing. He just had such a unique and sophisticated way of dealing with guests that seemed far beyond my own capabilities. I was intimidated by it. Much of it had to do with the fact that he communicated in pure refined German whilst I struggled with my strong south German accent. On those few occasions where I did make an effort to talk with guests, my words came out inaudible and I was asked to repeat myself. If I then did make an effort to speak high German, my guests still had a good laugh because my sentences were grammatically wrong. These were challenging times for me, sending my self-confidence onto a roller coaster ride.

Having spent four months with Hendrick, Mr. Hanter decided it was time for me to get back into a busier operation and so he assigned me to Angelo. Angelo was on permanent assignment in the "Mountaindew" restaurant, which was used mainly for groups and as overflow outlet when Hendrick's or Peter's station were fully booked. Overall, the guest profile in the Mountaindew was different from that of Hendrick's on the terrace. I also observed that Mr. Hanter selected guests for the different restaurants based on their presentation and looks. The Mountaindew struck me as a venue for the middle class whilst the upper class wined and dined on the terrace. The Mountaindew was also unpredictable when

67

it came to business levels; one day the restaurant would be packed and the next day it would be dead quiet.

The Mountaindew fell under the jurisdiction of Mr. Megan, officially Mr. Hanter's right hand man. Both Megan and Angelo were most suited for this outlet since they had much in common with the guests seated there. Angelo was Italian, easily recognizable by his heavy Italian accent. Angelo had been working in the hotel for many years. The only challenge we had with him was the fact that he was born without any sense of urgency. There was absolutely nothing that could make Angelo lose his relaxed and easygoing temper. Even if the restaurant was full to the last table with impatient guests asking for their orders, Angelo would stroll leisurely to their table and tell them with a big smile, "Donta worry, your food is cominga" and walk off, smiling.

He also talked a lot. Often he would get stuck at a table talking for up to an hour, completely oblivious to the happenings around him. This left me to run the station. Once Angelo had started talking to guests, it was virtually impossible to get him away, even when guests were eating. The only person who was then able to drag him away was Megan. He would come up with all sorts of weird things to say to Angelo, some of them bordering on the bizarre. He would go up to the table and with a very serious face he would say, "Angelo, the hospital is on the phone, your wife is having her baby now," or, with panic in his face, "Angelo, your service station is on fire."

Mr. Megan did not like guests. He did not like them because he had to be nice to them and they were not always nice to him. It was clear that over the years, he had lost patience for guests who were rude or impolite to him. This showed quite clearly in the way he handled complaints. For Megan, a complaining guest was simply seeking attention and in his mind, the only way to handle such guests was to give them a little more attention than they could handle.

I remember the first time I witnessed him handling a customer who had just asked to see the manager because he felt he had to wait too long for his chicken. The guest had complained several times by raising his voice at Angelo. The first thing Megan did was to stand at one end of the restaurant and stared at the table. He stood there and stared. When he was sure that the guest had noticed him, he straightened his jacket and then walked with large determined steps towards the complaining guest. Megan started addressing the guest when he was only halfway across the restaurant. He did this with such a loud voice that everyone in the restaurant suddenly looked up.

"Sir, I understand that you still have not received your chicken?" he bellowed. Reaching the table, he leaned with both hands on the table's edge and continued in the most patronizing manner. "I am so sorry, sir, this is unbelievable and unacceptable, and I can assure you that this has never happened before. Allow me to go to the kitchen right now and give the chef a piece of my mind, sir!"

He did not bother to wait for the guest's response. Instead, he stormed out of the restaurant. Of course, he didn't go to the kitchen and definitely not to see the chef. Instead, he waited outside the restaurant. After a minute or two, he returned to the restaurant, walking up to the table in the same stern manner as he had left.

"I am so sorry, sir," he said as loudly as possible and when he reached the table, his voice got even louder. "I have spoken with the chef and he is very sorry for the delay. He is now preparing your chicken, sir." And again, without waiting for the guest's response, he dashed off. The guest was left with everyone in the restaurant staring at him. Throughout the encounter, the guest had not said a single word nor had Megan given him a chance to do so. This performance worked every time on complaining guests, effectively shutting them up for the rest of the meal.

Megan spent most of his time smoking cigarettes and reading the papers in the back office. Once in a while, he would come into the restaurant, greet every table in his usual patronizing manner and, after making funny comments about the different guests, he would return to the back office.

I reported for duty with Angelo on a Monday morning. Angelo was small, even for an Italian, maybe because he was from Sicily. In fact, he was so small that I always made an effort to not stand too close to him so he would not have to look up to me. He was a cheerful character and on that Monday morning, he greeted me with a big smile.

"Ah, Andre, welcoma to da Mountaindewa. Firsta, we ava to teach you how to walka," he said in his terribly accented German. I had absolutely no clue what he was trying to tell me so I looked puzzled.

"How to walk?" I asked.

"Yes, how to walka because you walka lika farma," he grinned. He was trying to tell me that I slouched forward and my steps were too large when I walked. "You hava to walka straighta." I was even more puzzled. Was he trying to tell me that I had to learn how to walk?

He stood behind me and pushed with his fists against my back, making me stand straight. Then he asked me to walk in this pose up and down the restaurant, watching me with eagle eyes. I felt like an idiot.

"No, no, no," he said when I returned from the other end of the restaurant. "You walka too fasta." He demonstrated with a few short funny steps what he meant and asked me to try again. *Easy for you with your short legs*, I thought, but I tried again.

This time he was satisfied. Of course, I was not able to keep this posture up for long before falling back into my large steps. Angelo was not happy. I was naive enough to think that Angelo had finally given up on me, but I was wrong. In the late afternoon, when I was just clearing up his service station, he suddenly grabbed me from behind and, pulling my shirt out of my pants, he pushed a long broomstick underneath my shirt so that it exited at the collar. I straightened instantly and nearly strangled myself in the process. Only when I stood perfectly straight was I able to breathe. Megan and Johnny witnessed the spectacle and roared with laughter. Angelo looked at me, satisfied that he had made his point. Because of this silly exercise, I became very conscious of the way I walked and whenever I passed by a window or a mirror, I glanced at myself and straightened up almost immediately.

I learned a lot from Mr. Megan and Angelo, both good and bad. From Angelo I learned how not to panic, a word that did not seem to exist for him, especially when things got really busy. The only thing I learned from Megan was how not to respect guests. Respect was a word that did not exist for him. Of course, it was not in my nature to accept such teachings, but in fact, there were guests who needed such treatment.

As matter of fact, Megan did not respect anybody. He was about fifty years of age and wore glasses. Whenever he had to look a bit further into the distance, he would lower his head, peer over the rim of his glasses, looking like a bull ready to attack. He usually did this when his eyes caught sight of an attractive woman or a guest walking into the restaurant shortly before closing time. He would then make sarcastic comments about the attractive woman or the late-arriving guests. He hated guests who dared to ask for a table shortly before we closed. If that happened, the guest would be in for a ride.

When that happened, Megan would take the order personally and, using his years of experience, he would ensure that they did not order more than one dish. The main course would be served in no time and before they had finished their meal, he would already ask if he could clear the plate. Once everything was cleared, he would order us to stand as near as possible by the table and make them feel as uncomfortable as possible so that they would eventually pay their bill and leave. No coffee or dessert would be offered. This was not the most discreet and pleasant way of getting the message across and I don't necessarily approve of it, but I finished every lunch and dinner before any of my fellow colleagues so of course I never complained about that.

Working with both of them was a lot of fun but also hard work because Angelo talked, Megan smoked and I had to do all the work. The way Megan talked about customers right in front of them never ceased to amaze me. If we had guests who did not speak German, he would make all sorts of funny comments in front of them. This was particularly true for the French guests whom Megan did not like at all.

"There you go, my French friend, gulp it down and don't choke on it," he would say to them in German with a sugar sweet voice and a friendly smile on his face. Our French guests would innocently reply with their customary "Merci, messieurs." The first time I witnessed this, I was shocked and wanted to sink into the ground, so embarrassed I was.

As for me, I only did this once in my four years at the Black Forest Grand Hotel and was shocked when the guest answered, in perfect German, "Sorry, I did not understand." At the time, I had not realized that they came from Alsace, where they spoke a German dialect. Lucky for me they did not understand and I got away with it. I never tried again. Megan was different. If he encountered a couple with an attractive lady, he would smile at them and say to me something like, "Hey, look at the girl. She has a nice bum."

I was usually embarrassed, could hardly keep a straight face and had to get away from the table as quickly as possible. He also had the habit of assigning funny names to guests like "Mickey Mouse," for the gentlemen with the "large ears." When we served the food, he would whisper, "The steak is for Mickey Mouse." Once again, I would struggle to keep a straight face. The amazing thing was that he actually remembered all the nicknames he had given to different guests on

71

different tables—"Mickey Mouse," on table twelve, "Long Nose," on table thirteen, "Captain Fantastic" on table two and *the bill, please,* for "Madam Butterfly" on table one. I am sure that some of our guests must have heard him calling them those names, but for some reason we never got a single complaint from any of our guests.

Whilst my female colleagues thought of him as "creepy," we guys found him cool and had lots of fun with him. But there was also the moody Megan and when he was in that mood, it was best to stay away from him. This was at least true for us trainees; Angelo could not be bothered less. The moody Megan also did not care much about whether guests were in the restaurant or not. Quite the opposite, I think he actually thrived on the fact that he had the opportunity to vent his frustration at us, or worse, guests. With his mood, the nicknames also changed.

"The hunchback on table fifteen still hasn't got his bloody dessert and he is getting itchy," he would shout through the restaurant to make sure table fifteen understood that he was following up. He would shout at us right in front of the guest when a dish was delayed or forgotten. The moment moody Megan got stuck on a table to take a complaint, we immediately evacuated the restaurant. Since Angelo was hardly in the kitchen and always could be found talking to some unlucky guest in the restaurant, normally he took the full force of Megan's bad temper.

After two months with this duo, the weather began to turn milder and it was time to prepare the garden restaurant once again. It was still too cold in the mornings and evenings but during the day, it was pleasantly warm. We only set up a small number of tables, as Mr. Hanter did not want open full stations in the garden yet. Over the coming weeks, we gradually expanded the garden operation and by early June the garden was fully open. In order for us to cope with the expected crowds, Mr. Hanter needed some additional manpower. For this we used seasonal workers who helped us in the garden during the busiest periods of the year.

That summer, our season worker was Italian and his name was Rafaele Vangese. Rafaele could not have been more Italian. He was in his early twenties and blessed with good looks and a very charming and outgoing personality. He was a hard worker and he and I would frequently operate the largest stations in the garden. He could carry the largest trays with incredible amounts of dishes. We soon started to compete as to who could carry the largest number of dishes and whisk them at the highest speed from the garden to the kitchen and vise versa. Balancing such large rectangular trays on one hand whilst running in between crowded tables, dashing up steps and opening doors took considerable skill. Rafaele and I became true masters of it. These daily competitions turned us into the best and fastest waiters when it came to carrying trays over great distances at the highest possible speed.

After some time I outperformed Rafaele with the tray, thanks to my long legs, but I was no match for him when it came to communicating with guests. With his great sense of humor, his outgoing personality and of course his much admired Italian accent, he was an expert in making conversations with guests. To watch him dealing with guests was just as entertaining for us waiters as it was for other customers.

There was no dish on the menu he could not sell. He would make guests feel overjoyed if they accepted his recommendations and he would make them feel bad if they hadn't. He also had a way with girls. When he took the order from a table full of girls, he would leave them giggling, awaiting eagerly his return. More often than not, he ended up dating one of the girls the same evening, the juicy details of which he would share with me the next day.

In this respect, compared to Rafaele, I was a disaster. Even though I was now nearly one year on the job, I still had not overcome my fear of guests and girls in particular. I was so afraid of not being able to answer a guest's question that I frequently lost my cool in front of them. The ease with which Rafaele handled his guests was intimidating for me. I was still very conscious of my accent, the way I talked and the way I walked. Rafaele hardly ever lost his temper, but when he did, then he lost it badly. So it happened one morning when both of us were assigned to the garden terrace for breakfast. I liked serving breakfast on the terrace in the mornings, especially early mornings when it was still pleasant and cool with the sun just appearing on the horizon over the tree line. There was the smell of freshly brewed coffee lingering in the air throughout the hotel and even on the terrace. That's when our guests were most relaxed and most pleasant.

That morning when Rafaele lost his temper, it was particularly *un*pleasant. I woke up early that day and was the first one to report for duty. Mr. Hanter, with a surprised look, greeted me with a pleasant "Good morning, Andre." I felt honored by the fact that he addressed me by my first name, which did not happen very often. I stepped outside onto the garden terrace and began to prepare the station. By the time Rafaele arrived with a cheerful "Bon Giorno," I had already finished the mise en place.

"You gotta upa early today?" he asked, visibly pleased with all the work I had done already. There was not much more to do so we took our breakfast in the employee dining room. We finished a leisurely breakfast and returned to the garden just in time to greet our first guests.

As always, the terrace filled up quickly and soon only two tables were left. I had just returned from the kitchen with a tray full of freshly baked rolls and coffee when I saw Rafaele dealing with a guest who obviously was not happy with the table he had been given. By the time I arrived at the station, the guest, by the name of Staufen, had accepted the table but Rafaele's face had changed. Gone was his cheerful mood, replaced by tension. I served coffee and rolls to my guests and met him at the service station. He finished taking his order and together we went to the kitchen. Rafaele was swearing in Italian all the way. As he told me later, Mr. Staufen had been quite rude to him, calling him "spaghetti," a very rude nickname for Italians at the time.

"Take it easy," I said. "Maybe he got up on the wrong side of bed." I tried to cheer him up but Rafaele's theory about the guest's behavior was different and slightly more adventurous, involving Staufen's wife and his possible performance or rather non-performance the evening before.

We picked up coffee and rolls, loaded all onto our trays and returned to the terrace. After we had served coffee, we both stood at our service station and had a moment to relax. Then Rafaele was suddenly called back to Staufen's table, only to be told that the cold milk he had just served was not cold. Rafaele offered apologetically to change it for fresh milk and rushed back to the kitchen.

Meanwhile, I watched the Staufen couple. It was obvious that they had some sort of disagreement and by the looks of it, Mrs. Staufen was the one who was not pleased with something. *Maybe Rafaele's speculation regarding their disagreement was correct*, I thought. She kept on talking with him with a subdued voice but her facial expressions showed obvious anger. It was also obvious that Mr. Staufen used Rafaele as an outlet for *his* anger. Rafaele returned with a fresh glass of milk, which was so cold that the glass was covered in condensation.

I just stood there at the station observing quietly, thinking, *That milk is cold,* and I was sure that now he would be happy. But he was not. Rafaele served the milk and before he had made it back to the station, Mr. Staufen shouted his name.

"Waiter, I asked for COLD milk," he said angrily. "If your hotel has no cold milk then put some damn ice cubes in it." Rafaele froze and I could see him boiling. He grabbed the glass without a word but he was grumbling.

"Ice-ah cubes he wants, eh? Ice-ah cubes, I will give him ice-ah cubes," Rafaele grumbled. He was really pissed off now. "Let's go we get him some ice-ah cubes."

We left for the kitchen and whilst Rafaele was still swearing in Italian, I couldn't stop laughing. I did not understand what he was saying but it was certainly nothing pleasant by the sound of it. In the kitchen, we went straight to the ice machine.

"Let's getta some nice tasty ice-ah for Mr. Staufa."

Rafaele suddenly shoved both his hands down the front of his pants. He rubbed his testicles and all the while he was swearing in Italian. Then he took out the hands, grabbed a handful of ice cubes, and dumped them in the glass of milk. He then stirred the milk with his finger. He put down the glass, washed his hands and grabbed more ice cubes. He quickly put them in his mouth gargled and then spat them together with a good portion of saliva into the milk.

"Rafaele, what on earth are you doing?" I said laughing.

With a big grin, he held the glass in front of my nose.

"He asked for ice-ah colda milka, I give him his milka, Italy style," he said. I was in tears.

I followed Rafaele to our station and watched him as he approached Staufen's table.

"Hera isa your milka, Signore Staufen," he said, turned around and came back to the station. He winked at me with a sarcastic smile, crossed his arms and we both watched Mr. Staufen gulp down his ice cold milk "Italy style."

"Bon appetito," Rafaele whispered to me and I burst out laughing.

Rafaele and I became friends. Up to that point I had never had foreigners as friends and although there were several Italian families living in my hometown, we never had much contact with them. I grew very fond of Rafaele; he talked much about his family and his hometown in Italy. Sometimes I detected some homesickness in his voice when he talked about his mother and his brother who at the time served in the Italian Army. I was able to relate to his homesickness since I too was far away from home—over twelve kilometers to be precise.

For him, it was not the first time living and working outside of Italy. The previous summer he had worked in a hotel in Geneva, Switzerland at the beautiful Lake Geneva. He told me much about his experiences working in all these places and I always listened to him patiently. On my off days, I would go back home and tell my family, full of pride, about Rafaele and the places he had visited. The only thing I didn't tell them was what we did to customers if they made us upset; I felt it was too early for that and I did not want to spoil my parents' image of the elegant and sophisticated place I worked.

I admired Rafaele and liked him as a friend; everything seemed so easy for him and he seemed so confident in everything he did. This was not the case with me and I knew it. I had worked in the hotel now for just over nine months and was still in the process of settling in, whilst he had only been at the hotel for a little over four weeks and seemed to know everything. Rafaele was also incredibly confident with girls. He had no qualms whatsoever talking to single girls and he would almost always make them laugh. Watching him was for me like watching TV. I enjoyed the show and I knew that I could never be like him. I was afraid of girls full stop—or was it simply some sort of anxiety?

I was not very confident about my looks or the way I presented myself. This lack of self-confidence was so strong that on the few occasions when a girl did show some interest in me, I did not even realize it. I even went so far to believe that girls were only nice to me or tried to talk with me because I was doing a good job as waiter. Even when female colleagues made advances, I simply didn't get it.

Rafaele, on the other hand, knew all the right lines and I knew nothing. Whilst he was busy chatting up girls before and after taking their orders, I was busy focusing on getting the orders right. When he got stuck on a table with girls, I got stuck running his station *and* mine. Sometimes the girls he was talking to would look at me giggling and I knew they were talking about me, but instead of going there to join the fun, I shyly turned away, pretending not to have noticed. In this regard I was hopeless and I still had much to learn.

I had much to learn about everything in life, including living in a world away from the shelter called home. I always like to believe that I grew up in what I would call a perfect home. My parents never fought or argued and if they did then at least not in front of us children. There were no scandals in our family nor did anyone ever seem to get divorced. Such unpleasant things always happened to others but not to us—that much I knew. I knew I was very lucky. Throughout most of my upbringing, my parents had successfully kept us children away from such unpleasant experiences. Whilst all this was very nice, it had left me a little unprepared for the experiences I would face during my time in the hotel business. The first of these experiences was about to hit me and hit me hard. The Black Forest Grand was a family-owned hotel and at the time of my training, the owner's son managed it.

We knew him only by his nickname "Jimbo." I don't know how he got that name but that's what everybody called him. Besides looking after the hotel, he was into different types of sports such as sailing, golf and paragliding. He was of muscular build and carried a permanent suntan. He was a clever businessman as well as a good hotelier. Jimbo never hesitated to help out in the restaurant and kitchen when things got busy. Even though we appreciated this gesture, we all preferred not to have him around because Jimbo normally caused more confusion than he was actually helping. For example, he would pick up any tray from the pass if it *looked* ready to him. He would carry it to any station he *assumed* was the right one. Whenever we saw Jimbo in the operation, we knew that if dishes or drinks were missing, we would almost certainly find them in somebody else's station. He also had the tendency of becoming a little panicky when things got too busy. Needless to say that the chaos he created during such times did nothing to make things run more smoothly—quite the contrary.

Jimbo's wife was an attractive woman with a suntan that outdid his by far. Whilst his tan was from holidays in sunny places, hers was created mainly by the only sunny place in Talasee—the tanning bed in our fitness center. Because she went daily to bake under the artificial sun, her skin had a very leathery appearance like the dried skin of a mummy. Overall, her short blonde hair with the dark leathery skin made her an eye catcher wherever she appeared. We considered her friendly but not kind. She hailed from Bavaria and her family owned one of the most prestigious breweries in Munich. Members of her family made constant appearances in social gossip magazines shoulder-to-shoulder with Europe's royalty and aristocracy. She had an arrogant air around her and for a long time I felt that she did not consider me worth of a friendly word or even a glance. When one day she finally did call me by my name, only because I had forgotten something in the kitchen, I was surprised that she actually knew who I was. All in all, Jimbo Messer and his wife were an attractive and loving couple, judging by the fact that they always held hands when walking through the hotel. I liked and respected them.

One Saturday morning, she came for breakfast together with a middle-aged gentleman. As usual, she just passed by me, ignoring me completely. I recognized her guest as the windsurfing instructor from the lake. With his dark tan and the matching arrogance, they made a nice couple. She headed straight for table three on the terrace and, although she saw that I was already on the way to her table, she still had to call out "Waiter!"

I smiled politely and took her order, which she placed as usual without looking at me. After I had served them their breakfast, I observed them discreetly from my service station, just in case she needed anything else. Then Johnny joined me at the station. He looked at the terrace and noticed Mrs. Messer. "Ah, the boss's wife with her boyfriend," he said, squinting his eyes to get a better look at them.

I innocently said, "Come on, don't talk like this."

"What do you mean, don't talk like this?" Johnny said. "Jimbo is out of town and she buggers off with the windsurfer because he is her boyfriend."

I didn't like the way Johnny talked about her, never mind her bad attitude; at the end of the day she was still Jimbo's wife. There was no doubt in my mind that I was right. There was simply no way that Mrs. Messer would go out with anybody else whilst Jimbo was out of town and she definitely would not sit with a boyfriend having breakfast right in front of us employees. Johnny just made one of his silly jokes.

"So, Andre, tell me, if that's not her boyfriend, why is she stroking his hand?" he said, motioning his head at her table.

I discreetly glanced at Mrs. Messer and suddenly noticed her hand gently stroking his, for all of us to see! I was shocked and couldn't believe my eyes. How could she do that? She was still the boss's wife;

how could she possibly do that? Of course, there was still the possibility that she was comforting him because something tragic had happened to him or someone he knew.

"Andre, don't be so bloody naïve. That is her boyfriend," Johnny whispered impatiently.

I stood there staring at the couple and tried hard to convince myself that there was nothing between Mrs. Messer and the windsurfing instructor. Unfortunately, the only proof I found proved Johnny right. The windsurfer did not look as if something tragic had happened in his life but rather as if something very nice had happened...the night before. I still hoped that whatever happened had not happened with Mrs. Messer. But the way it looked, it did. Mrs. Messer had a boyfriend. I could not stop thinking about this, even when I went home. The next day I started to get worried what would happen when Mr. Messer came back. What if someone told him?

"So what?" Johnny said. "What do you think *he* is doing on his short holiday?" I did not dare to ask what exactly he *thought* Jimbo was doing. I did not dare because I knew he would prove me wrong again. For me, this was like being in a movie. Something like this could never happen in my hometown, but then again, my hometown was small and unimportant compared to the cosmopolitan city of Talasee. It was just another incredible story to tell back at home on my next day off.

When Mr. Messer returned, I was not able to look him in the eyes. I felt that if I did, he would certainly see that I was holding back on something. I knew something about his wife that had to remain a secret. This whole episode had gotten to me and if Mr. Messer had started a conversation with me, I am sure I would have told him all I knew about his wife's indiscretion. I would have told him because I was sure he knew that I knew. The same accounted for his wife; I could not look into her eyes. In her case, that was not too difficult since she never looked at me anyway. But at least now I knew why. I wondered what my mother would think when I tell her all this.

In early July, temperatures began to rise and by the end of the month the weather was at its hottest. In summer, we spent most of our afternoons down by the lake on the beach. This small strip of pebble beach was reserved exclusively for hotel guests and was separated from the public by a high fence.

We, the staff, normally swam to a floating raft which was made of wood and anchored close to the beach. On this raft we would either sunbathe or practice jumping as artistically as possible into the lake. Whilst we were playing like little children on the raft, Jimbo practiced his sailing skills on the lake. He had managed to get accepted as part of the crew of the German boat participating in the America's Cup. In order to hone his skills, he and some friends had brought a stunning sailing catamaran to Lake Talasee.

One Saturday afternoon, Johnny, Barrollo, Ralf and I were sitting at the beach watching Jimbo and his friends on their catamaran. The twin-hulled sailing boat was by far the largest boat around. The others' vessels were mostly smaller sailing boats, dinghies and some lonely windsurfers. They all had one thing in common: They had no wind.

The windsurfers and the catamaran hardly moved, with their sails just hanging flat on their masts, leisurely flapping in the hardly noticeable breeze. Looking at the prevailing weather conditions, it was doubtful that the wind would pick up soon and Jimbo and his crew decided to stir the boat back to the beach. We watched with interest as the boat drew nearer. Amongst Jimbo's crew were three young attractive ladies in their bikinis standing on deck laughing and giggling. The boat ran aground on our small pebble beach. One of the young men jumped off the boat and tied the anchor line to a steel pole near the changing rooms. We watched with interest as two of the crew assisted the young ladies in tiny bikinis in getting off the boat. They were very attractive indeed. I wasn't quite sure but I felt that one of the girls had been staring at me for some time. *Why should I be that lucky?!* I brushed that thought aside. When all had disembarked, they stood in a group with Jimbo in its center.

All of a sudden, the girl who I thought had been staring at me left the group, walked towards me, and then stopped right in front of me. *Oh my god, this is it, I knew it, she is going for it. What is Jimbo going to think?* She stared right into my eyes and began to speak.

"Hey, Andre, is that you? What are you doing here?" she said.

All my friends' eyes turned on me and I didn't know what to say. *How the hell did she know my name?* I didn't know what to say.

"What a surprise to see you here. What are you doing?" she asked.

"Ah, uh…I am working here," I stammered, trying to remember who she was.

80

"That's excellent. Please give my regards to your parents. I am Mary from Carlsbach." And with that, she walked off.

Who is Mary from Carlsbach? What was that all about?

"Hey, Andre, great taste you have. Who was that?" Johnny asked.

I had no clue who she was and so I just kept quiet.

Johnny didn't let go. "Tell me, who was that gorgeous little creature?" he said, rolling his eyes mockingly.

"Johnny, I swear I don't know who she is, I have no idea."

"Look at this, our Rotstift is a little Casanova. Who would have thought?" he laughed and clapped me with his hand on my bare shoulder.

Who is this Mary and why did she know me? I was confused; she could not have mistaken me for someone else because she knew my name, but who the hell was Mary? The guys were looking at me with knowing smiles and for all that it was worth, for them I was a hero.

That same evening I called my mother telling her about my day at the beach and Mary from Carlsbach. My mother suddenly laughed.

"Mum," I said. "Do you have any idea who this Mary is?" But my mother kept quiet. After a few minutes she answered.

"Well, I know who she is, although I have only met her on a few occasions."

I was stunned. Carlsbach was a small town close to my hometown and I knew most people living there. As far as I knew, we never had any relatives there.

"Mary is your cousin," my mother said.

"She is my cousin?" I cried in disbelief. *How could she be my cousin and I didn't know anything about her*?

"She is my cousin?" I asked again, not sure if I had misheard.

"I think it is time to give you some insights into your family," she laughed. "Mary is a daughter of your Uncle William."

William was one of my father's older brothers and he lived with us at home. William was not married and always had a reputation of being a sort of countryside playboy. I have heard many stories about him, but I never thought that they would be based on facts. For me, Uncle William was always my Uncle William. He was well known in my hometown for his addiction to sport; in summer he would go swimming and hiking and in winter he took to the skis. He was president or member of pretty much every sports club in town and everybody knew him; he was a personality. It was only because of him that I have tried my luck in pretty much all sports known to man but I really enjoyed only a few. He was the one who taught me how to swim, ski and how to ride a bicycle. He was never the fatherly type and therefore his teaching methods were strictly authoritarian. Just do it. I had never seen him intimate with women and somehow, it didn't suit him, either. He was just my Uncle William whom I had known since I was born.

"Uncle William is the father of Mary?" I asked in innocent disbelief. "She is really my cousin?"

"Yes," my mother said. "Don't be so surprised. Your uncle was quite a Casanova in his days."

I detected a hint of disapproval in her voice but I didn't say anything.

"I can't believe it. Uncle William has a daughter and I have a cousin I've never met," I said.

My mother then went on to explain to me the whole story of Uncle William and Mary in detail and, for good measure, dropped another two bombshells on me along the way. Each shell came in the form of another cousin I had never met. And as if this was not enough, I actually knew them. She finished by telling me that my three cousins had three different mothers. Not even in TV soap operas could they come up with such tacky stories. Today I know that my Uncle William may have been an extreme example but not one that was unheard of in our small town. The issue was that birth control in those days was not as advanced as it is today, and therefore the chances of pregnancies were naturally much higher. In Uncle William's case, three times higher to be precise.

"There you have it," my mother said. "Think about it, Andre. At least Mrs. Messer is still married to her husband or better, she got married to him in the first place. William never managed to do even that." She asked me not to think too much about it and soon after that we finished the call.

That evening, I lay in bed thinking. My Uncle William had tarnished the impeccable impression I had of our family for the last eighteen years. He had fathered three children from three different mothers. Little did I know that my mom had more in store for me.

I celebrated the first anniversary of my hospitality career on August 15th of the following year. That day I was so busy that the occasion passed unnoticed and unfortunately it would not be the last time that I missed special occasions because of work. I did not realize it at the time, but the hotel had begun to transform me. I had become much more conscious of the way I dressed and I had even started to dress according to the occasion. Before joining the hotel, my standard clothing consisted of jeans, leather cowboy boots and preferably a T-shirt. Now, I was willing to trade the jeans for linen pants, the T-shirt for an elegant silk shirt but I still insisted on the same old cowboy boots. I also had begun to make an effort to speak High German rather than my dialect and I used deodorant! All these changes had not gone unnoticed by family and friends during my weekly trips home.

I realized that my daily experiences in a luxury hotel were quite different from those of my friends back home. They talked about technical subjects related to their jobs such as electricians, carpenters and other crafts, whilst I told them all about the different people and characters I met and how rich they all were. They talked about wild weekends with lots of beer; I talked about gala dinners and champagne. All this led to increased teasing since it looked as if I just wanted to show off.

Then, one evening with my friends at home, while we were drinking beer and just hanging out, I realized to my surprise that I was bored. In order to avoid the teasing, I soon stopped talking about my experiences in the hotel. I was bored and caught myself longing for my newfound friends at the hotel. They where probably out for a nice meal together. I had grown accustomed to a world of wealth, expensive cars, gala dinners and gala balls; I had been exposed to the exciting world of a luxury hotel. And whilst I was still able to understand the world I came from, my friends were not able to understand the one I was heading into. Our interests had changed.

The summer drew to a close and it was time for me to attend my first semester at hotel school. I left in early October and the timing was perfect since it meant that I would not have to work on Christmas and New Year's Eve. Little did I know that for the next twenty years, this would be the last time for me not having to work during festive season.

The school was located in Munster, a city with a population of about thirty thousand. The school complex consisted of five buildings that included classrooms, show kitchens, restaurants, and one ballroom. One building was reserved as dormitory to accommodate us students.

The accommodation building had about one hundred and fifty rooms with four students per room. As expected, male and female students were strictly separated. I was not looking forward to this part of my apprenticeship because I had never enjoyed school.

However, this school would be different, very different, and the reason for this was a teacher by the name of Mr. Kapferer. It was because of him that I would pay attention in class and I would do something that I had never done back in school—I did my homework. I even studied during my free time, something that I would have definitely never done in school.

I remember the first day when we all sat quietly in the classroom awaiting the arrival of our teacher. The classroom was completely silent because we were all strangers. Suddenly the door flung open and a bear of a man stormed into the classroom. His briefcase landed with a loud bang on the teacher's desk. Without greeting us, he introduced himself

"My name is Kapferer, and I am telling you right here and now that anyone not paying attention or disturbs my class will be dismissed immediately." He paused and looked around the classroom. Everyone was quiet. "Good. I see we understand each other."

It didn't take long for Kapferer to set his first example by throwing out a student who kept on talking to his classmate. From that day onwards, we all paid attention. Kapferer was tough, fair and we respected him a lot. We knew that if someone got told off by Kapferer, he deserved it. Kapferer would never do it out of spite or because he didn't like someone; this was not his style. We respected him not so much for his authoritarian leadership style but his in-depth knowledge of our business and the sincere interest he had in teaching us. We admired him for his professionalism.

During the first semester, we got introduced to the hospitality industry and its intricacies in detail, economics, cost control, accounting and many other subjects important to our trade. We studied day in, day out. If we did not study, we had examinations and tests. We worked in the mock-up restaurants and in the show kitchens, always under the eagle eyes of our teachers. We served and we cooked, we got served and we tested the dishes prepared by our fellow colleagues. When our first semester came to an end after three months, he was the only teacher we invited for our leaving party.

When I arrived back in Talasee, the city was covered in a thick white blanket of snow and the lake was frozen over. Business in the hotel was still slow and only on the weekends did our occupancy pick up.

I was assigned to Hendrick as it was normal for trainees returning from school. I guess this was done to ensure that we put into practice what we had learned. Hendrick made me re-count everything I had learned and he even wanted to see my books and other materials. Hendrick was the only one who would follow up on all points from school down to the last detail whilst the other supervisors couldn't have cared less. They would not change established operational standards just because some hotel school taught otherwise.

Based on what I had learnt in school, Hendrick began to prepare me to take on more responsibility, such as running a station on the terrace and being in charge of functions. He paid much more attention to detail and things which he would have ignored before school were now pointed out to me as mistakes. Overall, I was now treated much more as a senior employee than I had been before hotel school.

I was now in my second year and had lost the title of "Rotstift." Things would not be the same anymore after school. Then one morning I found my name on the daily roster listed as being in charge of the VIP room. This came as a surprise.

The VIP room was the only private room in the hotel and it was normally reserved for our VIP guests. In order to reserve this room, guests had to be prepared to spend a small fortune. It was an elegantly furnished room just big enough to accommodate up to twenty guests seated at its massive dining table. The room with its large window offered a stunning view over the lake, and just next to that window in a corner was the real attraction of the venue—a beautiful old wood-fired oven covered in richly decorated white tiles. The oven was truly unique, ancient and without doubt priceless. This was the venue which Mr. Hanter had assigned me to.

I still could not quite believe it and, hoping that this was all a mistake, I decided to ask Mr. Hanter. The answer was short and to the point.

"No, you are in charge," he said with a smile. "There are only eighteen, no big deal."

He was correct; it was only a party of eighteen but the host happened to be a very demanding lady who normally dined exclusively at Hendrick's station. I had never done any function by myself before.

Why would they leave me alone with such an important guest? I was nervous. I had to talk with Hendrick; something had to be done.

"Don't worry," Hendrick said laughing. "I will be around. Just do what you always do and you will be fine."

What was happening here? We had several waiters who were far more suited for this assignment than I; what was going on? I had no choice other than to get ready for the evening ahead.

The lady host arrived at six o'clock sharp, ahead of her invited guests. I had gone out of my way to ensure that absolutely everything was perfect and nothing was missing. I had set up one long rectangular table with white tablecloth, white napkins, silver cutlery and one beautiful six-arm silver candelabra which I had polished myself for over half an hour. Around the candelabra, Mrs. Messer had placed white and red rose petals which, surrounded by all the silver, looked very elegant. I had to admit she had great taste in decorating tables.

Once the setup was finished, I had prepared, checked and double-checked the mise en place. Everything was ready to serve the three-course menu, which the chef would prepare personally. This, of course, put additional pressure on me and so I checked my mise en place for the sixth time: service cutlery, ashtrays, condiments, ice cubes and cooler for the sparkling wine. Yes, everything seemed fine but still, I was nervous.

"Good evening, Mrs. Suter," I said as friendly as I could when I met her outside the VIP room. She ignored my greeting and charged into the room.

"Is everything ready?" she barked. "And who is in charge?"

"That would be me, Mrs. Suter," I answered nervously.

"You? And who are you? I have never seen you here before," she grumbled.

This is not a good start, I thought. My lack of self-confidence kicked in, trying to convince me that she didn't like me. All of a sudden, I had a very bad feeling about this evening.

"My name is Andre and…"

She cut me off. "Where is Hendrick?" she asked very impatiently.

"Mrs. Suter, how nice to see you." Hendrick's voice suddenly appeared out of nowhere and there he was, standing casually at the door, waving his hands gaily in the air.

I was relieved. Mrs. Suter's face lit up when she saw him.

Hendrick looked at her and with mock admiration, he continued. "Where did you get this lovely dress?" he said, taking her hands, looking at her. "It is absolutely stunning!"

I hadn't paid any attention to her dress and as far as I was concerned, there was nothing stunning about it; it was full of unrecognizable little flowers of some sort. As matter of fact, it looked very much like something my Auntie Klara would wear at home.

Mrs. Suter practically bathed in Hendrick's compliments. "Oh, Hendrick," she beamed. "Stop it! It's nothing special."

There you go; this is exactly what *I* thought!

"I am not lying when I say that this dress makes you look much, much younger," Hendrick continued.

Jesus, what was wrong with him?

"And, by the way, let me introduce you to Andre, who will be looking after you tonight."

So much for my hopes, wishes and prayers that maybe Hendrick would stay for the service tonight since they seemed to be good friends.

"Good evening, again," I said nervously and tried to shake her hand, which Hendrick first had to release since he was still holding onto her. Or was she holding him?

"Andre is your name. I see. Well, I hope you understand that my guests tonight are very important and I want to impress them."

Now it was Hendrick's turn. "Don't worry, Mrs. Suter, Andre is one of our best waiters," he said, winking at me.

Did he mean that or did he just say it to calm her down? I wondered. I should say something, but what? My head was completely empty. *Just say something, but quick,* I thought.

"No problem," I blurted out with a voice that suddenly sounded like a bird being strangled. The moment I had finished my sentence, I thought, *What a stupid thing to say—no problem. No problem what?* God, I felt silly.

"Well, I hope so," Mrs. Suter answered icily. By the tone of her voice it was clear that she only accepted me because of Hendrick. But deep down she was not convinced.

"Well, I have to go back to my station," Hendrick said. "Mrs. Suter, I hope you have a lovely evening. I will be coming by once in a while to see how everything is going." And with that, he left the room, but not without winking at me once more.

I just stood there looking at Mrs. Suter then at the table and again at Mrs. Suter. For a moment I was lost and didn't know what to do next.

"The table looks nice and elegant, soo typical of Hendrick," she mused. "Now, about the service tonight," she said to me with a commanding voice. "You will always serve the oldest lady, Mrs. Von Schleicher first, then the other ladies and then the remaining guests. I will be served last, do you understand?"

"Yes, Mrs. Suter," I replied.

"I will taste all wines and I will tell you when to serve the white wine and when to begin serving the red wine. I will taste all new bottles before you serve them."

"Of course, Mrs. Suter. "

"I always like to be able to call the waiter when I need him, so make sure you are always around."

"I will be here, Mrs. Suter. "

"My guests may order whatever they wish and make sure you add all additional items to *my* bill."

"Yes, Mrs. Suter. "

"I will wait outside for my guests now. Make sure you have the sparkling wine ready on a tray when they arrive but not too early or it will be flat," she said with a stern face, then turned and left to welcome her guests.

"Not too early, yes, Mrs. Suter, " I answered, but she had already gone.

I was very nervous now and had difficulties deciding what to do first. The first thing I would need was the sparkling wine. I went to the bar to get two bottles and placed them in a cooler with ice. I proactively removed the foil around the top of both bottles. All I had to do now was to open them and pour several glasses once I saw the first guests approaching. I took a silver tray with eight glasses and placed them next to the cooler. I was ready.

Just at that moment, Mr. Hanter entered the room without saying a word and in his usual silent manner. He always seemed to float rather than walk when he moved through the operation and it was due to this ultra quiet way of walking that he continuously caught us off guard. Not that we continuously did things wrong but we did have idle chats here and there during times when we should have been working. I guess generations of naughty trainees like us have forced him to develop such stealthy capabilities.

He looked around, picked up a glass, held it into the light to check for water stains and then put it down again. He then stopped in front of my mise en place, observed it for a few moments and left the room without saying a word. This was typical for Mr. Hanter; I had no idea whether or not he was happy with my set up and mise en place. I assumed that if something had been wrong he would have told me so.

Mr. Hanter had a very brief conversation with Mrs. Suter and then moved on to the restaurants. Mr. Hanter never entered into long conversations with guests; he restricted his interaction with them purely to ensure their satisfaction with the food and service they had received. If he *did* talk to guests for longer periods then we knew it was somebody important. He sometimes would even laugh with guests but this happened only on few occasions. Mrs. Suter was waiting outside the VIP room, nervously checking her watch.

"Darling!" somebody suddenly called. "How very nice to see you." The first couple had arrived.

I frantically opened the first bottle of sparkling wine and was just about to pour when I suddenly remembered her instruction of letting her try all wines first. But this was not wine, it was *sparkling* wine and, remembering my training where I had learned to let guests try champagne first, I made the fatal mistake of asking her.

"*Not* the sparkling wines, for God's sake, now get on with it," was her angry answer. She looked at her guests and I heard her saying, "He is new."

I quickly opened the bottle, poured two glasses and served her guests. Soon the remaining guests arrived. The good news was that four guests had excused themselves and that had reduced the total number of guests to fourteen. Whilst my guests were enjoying their sparkling wine, I re-arranged the table. When this was done I informed Mrs. Suter.

"Thank you, my...dear," she said, realizing her mistake of calling me "my dear," a title that I clearly had not yet earned.

There were "ooh's" and "aah's" as her guests entered the room complementing the table setup. Mrs. Suter got several compliments on the room and table decoration, which made her soar.

"My darling Hendrick has done all this just for me," she said and went on explaining who Hendrick was. Although I felt a little hurt by the fact that he got all the credit, I was quite happy not to get all the attention. Whilst she was assigning seats to her guests, I opened the first bottle of white wine and left it in the cooler. I then rushed to the kitchen to pick up bread and butter. I approached Mrs. Suter, offering her to taste the first bottle of wine.

"Britzinger Gutedel, QBA 1980," I announced as I presented her the label. She glanced at the bottle and then nodded.

"Yes, thank you my…" she said, and I poured just a little for her to taste. Contrary to my expectations, she accepted the wine and I continued pouring for the others, serving Mrs. Von Schleicher first and Mrs. Suter last. Having successfully completed this task, it was time for me to fire the first course. I went to the kitchen and called up the starter consisting of a dish of smoked salmon trout with the chef's own homemade horseradish sauce. As it was a cold starter, it would be individually plated. I went back to the VIP room. I checked the table and to my surprise I noticed that Mrs. Von Schleicher had finished her first glass of wine already. I refilled her glass immediately and checked the rest of the table. When I was satisfied that everybody had wine, I positioned myself in a corner where Mrs. Suter could see me. A short while later, Mr. Hanter peeked into the room and nodded at me.

"Your first course is ready," he said and left.

His words "*your* first course," made me painfully aware of just how much responsibility I carried. I quickly went to the kitchen to pick up *my* fourteen plates of salmon trout. Mr. Hanter had already started to place six plates on a tray and placed another two in my right hand.

"Let's go," he said. "I will bring the rest."

And off I went. Back in the VIP room, I began to serve the dishes, starting with Mrs. Von Schleicher. In the meantime, Mr. Hanter brought the remaining salmon and left it on my service station. After the service, I managed a shy "Enjoy your dinner," which nobody seemed to have noticed since I did not get an answer. So far so good; everything went well. I just wanted to return to my holding position in front of Mrs. Suter when I realized that there where four plates left. *Oh, shit.* I forgot to inform the kitchen of the reduced number of guests. I took the plates and went back to the kitchen.

As expected, the chef was furious. "You are a completely useless monkey! All of you waiters are completely useless monkeys!" he screamed. While he was screaming, he carefully, almost religiously, removed slice by slice his precious salmon from each plate and placed it in a small plastic container. "How many are they now, monkey?" he barked at me.

"Fourteen. All in all, there are fourteen," I answered nervously.

"Are you sure, you monkey?"

"I am sure."

"How about the main course—can we fire?" the chef asked.

"In five minutes, chef."

"How many main courses?" he wanted to know.

"Fourteen, chef," I said again.

"Are you sure, you monkey?" he growled without looking at me.

"Yes, chef, fourteen," I said and left the kitchen.

Mrs. Suter and her guests had a good time, aided of course by the Britzinger Gutedel, which I poured again, especially for Mrs. Von Schleicher, who looked relieved when she saw me coming back with the bottle.

"Excuse me, Mrs. Suter, may I open the red wine now?" I asked after I had cleared all starter plates.

"Yes, please, and do not forget to let me try it first," she said in a much friendlier tone than before.

"Oberbergener Bassgeige, QBA 1978," I said, presenting her the label. "Excellent," she said and I poured a little for her to taste. "A little bit too chilly but otherwise excellent. You may serve," she said, waving her hand like a sultan ordering his servants.

Not only did I serve Mrs. Von Schleicher first but I also filled her glass up to the rim with the *excellent* Oberbergener. This made *her* very happy and saved *me* from having to refill her glass constantly.

Mrs. Suter was now giving a speech and I prepared my gueridon for the main course. I placed rechauds, service cutlery and napkins neatly on the gueridon near Mrs. Suter so she could supervise the service. Now it was time for me to face the dreaded chef once again in order to pick up the main course.

I had just entered the kitchen when I heard him already screaming, "Somebody call that monkey. His food is ready!"

"I am here, I am here," I shouted as I approached the pass.

91

"Come on, monkey, move it. My food is getting cold!" he screamed. Several cooks were standing next to him with grins on there faces. The main course the chef had chosen consisted of a selection of fine Black Forest game with red champagne cabbage, potato croquettes, traditional spaetzle and a red wine sauce. There were four large silver platters on the pass, one for each dish.

Looking suspiciously at all the chefs behind the pass, I had no intention of getting ambushed with an old carrot again and quickly lifted the cover. Everything was in order. However, the chef's patience was running low.

"What the hell are you doing fussing around like this? Do I have to tell you again?" he yelled. "GET THIS MAIN COURSE OUT OF HERE!" He screamed so loudly that everybody in the kitchen looked at the pass and me.

I packed three platters onto the tray and carried another one with my right hand back to the VIP room. Judging by the noise level in the room, Mrs. Suter and her friends must have been having a good time.

Mr. Hanter suddenly appeared as usual out of nowhere just in time when I needed help. I placed all the platters carefully on the gueridon just as Hendrick had taught me: meat platter to the left, hot plates in the middle and side dishes on the right. Mr. Hanter carefully served the meat and I served the side dishes.

"Change the ashtrays," Mr. Hanter suddenly whispered whilst serving a piece of wild boar. I looked at the table and to my surprise, nearly all four ashtrays were full of cigarette buds. *Why had I not seen this?* I asked myself. I quickly changed them all.

We had just finished the last plate when Mr. Hanter whispered again, as always without actually looking at me, "Wine, wine."

As expected, Mrs. Von Schleicher's glass was empty. I had to open two more bottles in order to refill them all. Mrs. Suter readily approved each bottle without realizing that, when I asked her to taste the third bottle, she actually tasted her previous wine and not the one from the new bottle.

"Excellent, my dear."

Since everybody was busy chatting away, I just continued to pour. I felt more relaxed now; the main course was served and that meant the worst was over. For the next half-hour, all I had to do was to serve second helpings and refill my guest's wineglasses. They ate, drank, laughed and generally enjoyed themselves. By the time I started to clear the tables, Mrs. Suter's mood had changed completely.

She called me "my dear" now every time she wanted something and on top of this, she suddenly couldn't thank me enough for removing the plates, cutlery, ashtrays and other items. The Oberbergener seemed to do its job. After I cleared the salt and pepper only, the wineglasses remained on the table.

I started to crumb the table in front of each guest, which was a rather difficult task since they were getting very close when talking to each other, again courtesy of the Oberbergener. When I reached Mrs. Von Schleicher, she grabbed my arm with her right hand, stared into my eyes and, with her long and dark red painted fingernails of her left hand, kept on tapping on the wineglass. I got the message. She still looked at me and, with a knowing smile, blinked her right eye. Minutes later, I had blessed her with Oberbergener up to the rim.

It was time to set the table for dessert. I placed the silver dessert forks and spoons neatly to the right and left in front of each guest, after which I went to the kitchen to pick up more of chef's masterpieces.

The dessert the chef had chosen was a specialty of the house, our famous Black Forest Coupe. It consisted of three scoops vanilla ice cream, sour cherries, champagne sabayon, chocolate chips and a dash of the finest cherry schnapps. The crystal cup in which it was served was reminiscent of the Holy Grail and was about the same size.

"Fourteen BFCs," I screamed into the kitchen as I entered.

"Shut up, monkey," came the immediate reply from somewhere behind a stainless steel screen in the kitchen. Well, at least they heard me. It was a quarter to ten in the evening and most of the hot kitchen chefs had left, including Karl, the man who hated me so much. Only two chefs had stayed behind for the desserts. Just as the chef handed over the finished BFCs, I had an idea.

"Please give me one with more cherry schnapps," I told the chef.

"You couldn't tell me that before, monkey?" asked the chef angrily.

"Sorry, I forgot," I apologized without the slightest trace of remorse.

A few minutes later I had loaded all fourteen BLCs, plus one with plenty of cherry schnapps, onto my tray and rushed back to Mrs. Suter and her guests.

I served the desserts one by one. My specially enriched dessert, distinguishable from the others by two cherries instead of one, I served to Mrs. von Schleicher. "This one is special, Mrs. von Schleicher," I said with a friendly smile.

"Thank you," she said whilst talking to the lady next to her.

I wanted to see her face when she tried the dessert. I didn't really know how much additional schnapps the chef had added but, judging by the strong smell, it couldn't have been too little. I stood at my service station and watched Mrs. von Schleicher. She finished her conversation, picked up the spoon, took an impressive portion of ice cream and whipped cream and eagerly shoved it into her mouth. Her eyes suddenly opened wide and her face lit up instantly. She searched the room and when she caught sight of me, she nodded her head ever so slightly and smiled. She was happy.

I took the orders for coffee and tea and served them a few minutes later. "Thank you, my dear," Mrs. von Schleicher whispered discreetly as I served her tea.

"You are most welcome," I whispered back.

They talked and laughed until early in the morning. By that time I was the last waiter still in the hotel; all others had gone home. Before Hendrick had left, he had helped me to prepare the bill and then said goodbye to Mrs. Suter. When he asked if everything was to her liking, she told him that she was *very satisfied* with the food and service. *Thank god,* I thought. I was not expecting any praise; as matter of fact, I was just proud that she had nothing to complain about.

"The service was excellent," Mrs. von Schleicher added to everybody's surprise. I looked at her, a little embarrassed. Shortly after one in the morning, Mrs. Suter finally asked for the bill. After everything was settled, they all said goodbye and left. I didn't get any tip because in Mrs. Suter's eyes I had not deserved it yet. In her mind, I got tipped in the form of her comment to Hendrick that she was "satisfied." And indeed, she had not criticized anything, which for me was already more than enough. When Mrs. Von Schleicher left, she had looked right into my eyes, squeezing my hand hard, and with a warm smile had repeated her praise, "Excellent evening, Andre."

When all guests had gone, I went back to the VIP room, stood at the door and looked at the empty table. It was very quiet and at this late hour I was the only one around. On the table there were still empty and half-empty wineglasses and red wine stains splattered all over the once white tablecloth. I looked at the table and thought, *This evening was not so bad after all.*

As I was clearing the table, I reflected on my interactions with Mrs. von Schleicher, who had surprised me more than anyone else. I somehow had managed to overcome my notorious lack of self-confidence and the strong feeling of not being good enough to handle such an important event. Not only had I overcome this negative feeling but I had also handled this demanding guest well. I had prepared myself mentally for disaster but, contrary to my expectation, it had turned out well. Contrary to my very worst expectations, I had made someone like Mrs. von Schleicher happy. Her words— "Excellent evening, Andre,"— still echoed in my ears and I was very proud, even though most of this success was achieved by keeping her wineglass full to the rim at all times. This had been the first time that I had identified a customer's need and acted on it. Later in my career, I would not only identify such opportunities and act on it, but I would do so to my advantage.

The next day I felt so motivated that I secretly hoped to be assigned to the VIP room again but of course it was not to be. Instead I was, for the first time in a long time, assigned to Johnny's station. To assist Johnny usually meant that I was running the station for him. Johnny was a strong waiter, probably the best one we had, but he was also notoriously lazy. He could run the largest and busiest station packed with guests and he would still joke with the girls in the kitchen. Whenever Mr. Hanter assigned a trainee to him, it would be left up to the trainee to do all the work. Johnny would greet the guests, entertain them with jokes whilst the trainee was running back and forth to the kitchen, serving, clearing and so on. If there were more complicated tasks such as opening a bottle of champagne or wine and the trainee asked for help, Johnny would simply laugh, "No, you do it; this is your chance to learn." Then, after all was finished, Johnny would present the bill to the guest, the guest would pay and he would keep the entire tip.

I had endured this many times and had grown used to it by now. It was pretty rough to work with Johnny but I did learn things from him and I always had fun. However, after having successfully run Mrs. Suter's function, I thought of myself as being too senior to assist someone like Johnny but for the time being, I kept quiet.

When I arrived in our station that day, nothing was prepared, as usual. The tables were empty, the side station and mise en place were not done. In short, nothing was ready. *Typical Johnny*, I thought, and went to the kitchen to get it all organized. When I returned, I found Johnny and Barrollo standing near our side station glancing through a magazine.

"Here, take a look, this is where we will be working soon." He held an expensive-looking, high-gloss brochure of a cruise ship in front of my face. "We will be traveling around the world, meet gorgeous girls and earn tons of money," he said.

I looked at them and realized that they were serious; they really wanted to apply for a job on a cruise liner. They agreed to write their applications together that afternoon. I knew nothing about cruise liners. I knew they were very large and glamorous ocean vessels with swimming pools, restaurants, etc. But I had never actually seen a brochure of one before. I flipped through the magazine and could not believe the prices they charged for such cruises; they were just astronomical. The countries these ships visited were absolutely amazing; it was virtually the entire world! South America, USA, Antarctica, Caribbean and all the other places which I only knew of from TV. There were pictures of beautiful beaches, tropical forests and crew members in white uniforms. I looked admiringly at Johnny and Barrollo thinking, *If only I could be as confident as they are.* I assumed that in order to be accepted on a cruise liner you had to be good in your job. I knew that for me the magazine would be as close as I would ever get to such a cruise liner. The likelihood of me working on that cruise liner was the same as wanting to become an astronaut; it was simply impossible.

The names of the two ships were MS *Deutschland* and MS *Europa;* the *Europa* was brand new and had just been launched the same year. The *Europa* was also much larger, weighing over 35,000 tons. In the brochure, the ships were prominently featured in different, exotic-looking locations. Not in my dreams would I have ever dared to send an application to one of these companies because I was convinced that I just was not good enough.

Little did I know that neither Johnny nor Barrollo would ever work onboard; in fact, they would never even write their applications. Instead, it would be me ending up onboard the MS *Europa*, but that was much later. For the moment I just admired these two guys who unknowingly had sparked a deep desire in me to discover the world. This secret desire was still more a dream than anything else but it would not go away in the years to come; quite on the contrary, it would grow stronger.

By February that year, I was well into my second year and only six months away from becoming the long awaited "third-year trainee." To be a third-year trainee carried a special meaning and status in the hotel. Third-year trainees were considered to be on the same level as a full waiter. Third-year trainees carried the same responsibilities as regular waiters. There was, however, one less attractive aspect of being a third-year trainee and that was the six-month tour of duty in the kitchen. So it was that one fine sunny Saturday morning, Ralf and I where summoned to the personnel office. "Don't be late," were the stern words from the ever-so-friendly personnel secretary.

Ralf and I wondered why we had been asked to see the personnel director. Had we done something wrong again? We were fully aware of our special status with the personnel director and because of this we had behaved exemplary over the past months. We arrived at the personnel office ten minutes early and nervously knocked at the door.

"Enter," the voice of Mr. Junger barked from behind the door. This was the same gentleman who, two years earlier, had issued two final warnings to us, nearly ending my apprenticeship before it had started.

"Sit down," Mr. Junger said and came straight to the point. "Both of you will be transferred to the kitchen as of March 1st to undergo your mandatory six-month kitchen training," he said, as usual neither displaying interest in the subject at hand nor the subjects sitting in front of him.

We took a deep breath. I don't know how Ralf felt at that very moment, but for me it was as if I had just woken up in hell. We were speechless.

Mr. Junger, unperturbed by our obvious shock, continued. "Pick up your chef's uniforms on Saturday and get in touch with Chef Karl regarding your work schedule." After that, he read out a whole list of things for us to do. "Do you have any questions?" Mr. Junger asked after he had finished his lecture.

"No," Ralf said and I just shook my head. I couldn't talk. I always knew I had to do the dreaded kitchen duty at one point but I never expected it to happen so soon and definitely not with so little warning. Two weeks was all I had left before going to hell! I had always hoped that I might be exempted from the tour of duty in the kitchen, especially since Ralf had never done it even though he had been at the hotel over three years already. We knew that there had been cases in other hotels where the management had conveniently left out this part of the mandatory kitchen duty, very much to the delight of the respective trainees.

Not so for us. We just had been told that we had to complete the full six months in the kitchen.

"That will be all," Junger said, and with that, we were dismissed.

I was unable to speak until we were outside Junger's office.

"Oh, God, they are really sending us to the kitchen," I said to Ralf, terrified.

"We are dead meat," Ralf answered laughing. I did not find this funny at all. "Looks like payback time for the chefs," Ralf continued. "I don't even dare to remember all the things I said to them because I was so convinced they would never send me there, and definitely not having nearly completed my third year." Well, at least he was still laughing, whilst I felt sick.

What we didn't know, of course, was that Karl knew all about our impending arrival and from that day onwards, he tried his best to put the fear of God into us. It started the same evening the moment he saw me.

"You will cry like a little boy when I have finished with you," and "I can't wait to have *YOU* in my kitchen!" he kept on saying, always pointing his short fat finger at me. Then, ten days before we had to start, he began counting down the days by writing them in large red numbers on the whiteboard in the kitchen. In addition, he encouraged his cooks to call out the remaining days we had left whenever they saw us.

"Hey guys, EIGHT!!" they would shout, then the next day, "He guys, SEVEN!" and so on. One day I was standing at the pass waiting for dishes when Karl suddenly grabbed the microphone of the announcer.

"Attention, attention, this is an important announcement. Only SIX days left until the arrival of our two waiters for kitchen combat exercise. I repeat, only SIX days left!" When he finished, all chefs were shouting and laughing.

"Hey waiter," Karl shouted one day. "Do you know that whatever doesn't kill you in the kitchen just makes you stronger? I promise you, when you leave my kitchen you will be very strong!" And then he laughed like a pirate. Although I didn't show it at the time, the teasing took its toll on me. I couldn't sleep anymore and turned quieter day by day.

Chapter 3: *"Welcome to My Kitchen!"*

When the big day finally came, I resigned myself to the fact that I was about to die. That morning, Ralf and I met in my room. We were both dressed in chef's whites and looked at each other full of doubt and apprehension.

"I wish it would be evening already," Ralf smiled sadly and I realized that he really meant it. As for me, I could not really concentrate; my thoughts were at home with my parents, my sister and brother. This was a little weird.

"Yeah, let's go," I answered and together we walked over to the hotel like two prisoners on the way to their execution.

On the way, we ran into Johnny who, with a huge grin on his face, said, "Ah, joining the enemy! Good luck with Karl. Get ready for a beating," he laughed.

I felt sicker by the minute. How I wished I could be him right now, looking forward to another day of routine in the restaurant. Over the past two years I had gone through more emotional experiences than ever before in my life. I had realized that whenever I managed to fall into some sort of routine, they gave me new responsibilities, pulling me out of my comfort zone. Every time this happened, I went through major stress. I did not handle changes very well; they came down hard on me even though I did not show it. Now, with the prospect of getting shouted at by Karl for mistakes on a daily basis, I felt nauseated. I had no illusions of what was about to happen because I knew nothing about the kitchen, or cooking for that matter, nor had I ever had any interest in it. Before I knew it, my notorious lack of self-confidence showed its ugly head. Why do they want me to do this? I asked myself. Why do I have to go to the kitchen now after nearly two years and why now that I have become a reasonably good waiter? Was this what working life was all about, constant change? This was not what I had signed up for.

By the time we reached the kitchen, I was a nervous wreck and the day hadn't even started yet. Then there was the dreaded Karl.

"Good morning, gentlemen!" he shouted as soon as he saw us. "Finally this hotel found some proper clothes for you to wear."

We just stood there, looked at him full of suspicion and kept quiet. Without wasting more time, he started to brief us on his expected code of conduct, which was very similar to Mr. Hanter's except that Mr. Hanter never had to brief us on his code; it was handed down word by mouth from trainee to trainee. I wondered how they had known that in the first place but I guessed it had to do with the natural respect we had for Mr. Hanter.

"Okay, Schwarz, you will be at the salad station for the next four weeks with Thomas Henkelman. Black, you join the gardemanger Matthias for four weeks. After that, we swap." Then Karl called the respective chefs and asked them to take us with them.

We were just about to walk off when he stopped us. "Um, there is one more thing, gentlemen," he said. "I forgot—*WELCOME TO MY KITCHEN!*"

I was ready for the worst but to my surprise, things turned out quite differently. As for the "beating" from Karl, our fears were totally unfounded, quite to the contrary. Of course they teased us a lot and we had to suffer the occasional practical joke here and there, but overall Karl and his chefs treated us in a very professional manner. Karl was tough but he definitely had an honest desire to teach us as much as he could during our short six-month tour of duty in his kitchen. He introduced us to the different sections in between meal periods and once lunch or dinner business started, we returned to our assigned stations. For me, this was the salad kitchen.

The salad kitchen, although simple and straightforward, was one of the busiest stations in the kitchen. Almost every dish of the regional cuisine at the Black Forest is accompanied by a salad and, with about sixty different dishes on the menu, there were about twelve different types of salads that had to be prepared at any given time. This meant that on an average day in summer, the salad station had to produce up to four hundred salads daily.

The salad kitchen was located just opposite of the announcer's station. It consisted of several refrigerators, sinks and the counter from where the waiters picked up the ready-made salads. The first thing I learned was to prepare the daily mise en place. Mise en place was required in the kitchen just the same as in restaurants; it was the pre-service preparation of all items required to prepare the different salads. In order to determine the quantity of mise en place required, we had to get information on the volume of business expected for the day. This included reservations in the restaurants, ballroom and, during the summer season, in the garden. We received this information from Karl, who in turn got it from Mr. Hanter.

So, for the first weeks, I prepared the condiment mise en place by cutting eggs, tomatoes, cucumbers and, to my horror, onions. I have hated onions ever since my earliest childhood. I don't know how and why this happened but I neither liked the taste of onions nor the terrifying look of this unpleasant vegetable. My mother had always shown great creativity in trying to make me eat onions. As for onions in sauces, for example, she would cook them to a point where they resembled some sort of cabbage or overcooked leeks and tried to sell them to me as such. I fell for this one only once because as soon as I bit onion—cooked or, worse, raw—I would feel as if my body went into shock. Yes, I despised onions then and I still despise them today.

Once I had finished the condiment mise en place, I helped Thomas with various other tasks, mostly the cleaning of lettuce and vegetables such as cauliflower, carrots and others. I was not yet allowed to prepare the salad dressing, which was the real secret of any good salad. It was now early March and the weather was still too chilly to open the garden restaurant. Business in most restaurants was slow. Just like Mr. Hanter, Karl too used these slow periods for cleaning jobs and training.

One day he called Ralf and me to the kitchen and asked us to follow him. He led us downstairs to the basement and stopped in front of the trout basin. The basin was large, about three meters long and two meters wide and it was full of trout. There must have been at least one hundred and fifty fish in that basin. He unlocked the heavy iron grid that covered the basin and opened it up.

"Gentlemen, today I will show you how to catch our famous Black Forest trout." After he had secured the grid, he took a wooden stick and shoved it into the side of his apron like a sword. *This can't be that difficult,* I thought as I saw the large sort of ladle standing next to the basin. The ladle consisted of a long handle with a kind of sieve at one end. Karl saw me looking at it.

"We never use that one," he said. "Too complicated. Now get up here and watch."

He explained that normally we would take out the dead fish first but since the entire batch had only been delivered in the morning, they were all pretty much alive. In order for us to be able to observe what was happening, we had to step onto a small ledge. Karl had his right hand already in the water, holding it completely still. I wasn't quite sure what to make of this. Was he trying to catch fish with his bare hands?

Through an opening on the side of the tank, water was pumped under strong pressure into the tank to simulate river conditions, enriching the water with oxygen at the same time. The trout normally "stood" in this artificial current, holding their position with constant short bursts with their tail fin. Karl's hand was wide open like the claw of a bear on a riverbank poised to catch a fish. After a while, he slowly moved his open hand towards one rather large trout that hung suspended in the artificial current. Ever so slowly, his large fingers encircled the fish without actually touching it, then all of a sudden his hand closed and the fish was caught in the grip of Karl's huge hand. His grip was so strong and tight that the fish couldn't move at all.

Ralf and I looked at each other, thoroughly impressed. Karl stepped from the ledge and held the trout up in the air.

"Can you see how my fingers dig deep into the stomach of the fish?" he said whilst showing us the underside of the trout. We could clearly see his fingertips embedded deep in the victim's underbelly. "This is why it doesn't move."

We stared at the fish that hardly moved except for its small mouth, which opened and closed frantically due to the lack of oxygen.

"Now we are going to kill it by giving it *one* strong blow to the neck but mind you, you have to hit the neck and never the head." With that, he took out the wooden stick and pointed out the exact spot. "This is the point you have to hit."

He lifted the stick and gave it one fast and strong blow. The trout died instantly. He placed the dead fish in a plastic bucket. To me it all looked simple enough.

"I will show you once more how it's done and then you two give it a try. We need eight trout." Within minutes, the second trout was dead.

"Who wants to go first?" Karl asked.

"I'll give it a try," Ralf said. *Oh good*, I thought; I much preferred to watch.

Standing up on the ledge, Ralf put his hand into the water and pulled it out in an instant. "Wow, it's cold," he said and looked at Karl.

"Get a fish, you sissy," Karl said mockingly.

Ralf put his hand back into the cold water. Like an open claw, his hand moved slowly towards a trout. So far he seemed to be doing well. Ralf's hand now reached the tail fin of his victim and all was going as instructed. Suddenly, the trout was gone. Ralf's eyes opened wide in surprise when he pulled out his empty hand. "I didn't even touch it," he said apologetically.

"Yes, you did. Otherwise, you would have caught it," Karl lectured him. "Try again."

Ralf started all over again with the same result. "My hands are freezing. Andre, it's your turn," Ralf said, capitulating.

I reasoned that from what I had seen, a quick and tight grip is the most important thing if I wanted to catch one of these fish, so I prepared myself mentally to squeeze the thing to death if I had to. I carefully put my hand into the water—Ralf was right; it was freezing cold—and, with a sudden splash, I pulled my hand out again. Not because of the cold, but it felt as if I had put my hand into a living thing; all those slippery moving creatures touching my skin had made me retract my hand instinctively. I put it back into the water filled with these slimy creatures but I held my hand as still as Karl had done and selected a victim.

I chose the closest one and moved my open claw towards the fish. My hands were larger than Ralf's so it was easier for me to encircle the fish with my fingers. When I reached the center of the fish I closed my hand and tightened my grip immediately and snap, I had the fish. I pulled it out and held it in the air when suddenly I felt the twitching muscles of the creature, which made me loosen my grip instantly, with the fish slipping out of my hand and diving back into the water.

To hold this fish was a strange experience, not because it was slippery and slimy but more because the feeling of the twitching muscles told me that the fish was fighting for its life. Karl praised and lectured me.

"Well done, but you have to push your fingers into the belly; otherwise, you will not be able to control it."

As I was still trying to get over my first near-kill, I asked Ralf to try again. This time Ralf grabbed the fish quickly and tightened his hand;

the fish didn't move an inch. "Now take the stick and hit it on the neck but try to hit the neck with the very end of the stick."

I moved closer to see how Ralf was doing. He lifted the stick and with a short strong blow, hit the trout. It all happened very quickly; Ralf missed the neck and hit the snout instead. The immense pressure of his blow onto the snout blew the eyeballs of the creature right out of their sockets, splattering all them all over us. It all happened very fast; I just felt something moist hitting my face and when I looked down on my jacket, I saw bloodstains splattered all over it. I noticed something gliding down the front of my jacket on a trail of blood. To my horror, I recognized one of the eyeballs.

Ralf had dropped the trout, which was now flapping wildly around on the floor in the dirt with empty eye sockets. It was utterly disgusting. Karl bent down, picked it up and killed it with one quick blow to the neck. He then cleaned it in the nearby sink and threw it into the bucket.

"This is what happens when you don't hit the neck at precisely the right spot. I need five more trout for lunch. I give you another twenty minutes," he said and left for the kitchen. It eventually took us more than thirty minutes to catch and kill five additional trout. We actually killed an additional eight but because they were in such bad shape when they finally died, we had to dispose of them secretly.

One trout had ended up on the floor and Ralf decided the fastest way to kill it would be to kick it against the wall. He kicked the trout, but instead of smashing into the wall, it shot into the air and got stuck in one of the safety grids of a compressor fan on one of the refrigerators. The fish got jammed tightly in the grid and was shredded to pieces until only the tail was dangling loosely from the grid. Bits and pieces of flesh were splattered all around the fan. It was disgusting.

The other trout was a very big one and even with several blows, we still did not manage to kill it. After three more heavy blows to the head, we decided that it would be easiest if I held the trout while Ralf delivered the deadly blow. I held the fish; Ralf grabbed the stick with both hands and hit the neck of the doomed creature with all his strength. He missed the trout and hit my thumb instead. A sudden nerve-racking pain shot through the thumb of my left hand, forcing me to scream. Whilst Ralf was chasing after the wildly flapping fish with a shovel, I was holding my thumb in terrible pain. Finally, the fish, or rather what was left of it, had stopped moving. Ralf had killed it or more appropriately, he had completely destroyed it with his shovel. It was totally unrecognizable as a trout and all that was left of it was a bloody fleshy pulp of fish. Ralf quickly and discreetly disposed of the bloody remains. My thumb was now red and had swollen to an impressive size. The pain had driven tears into my eyes. When Ralf came back, he looked at it and had a hard time controlling his hysterical laughter.

"Well, don't worry, you will live," he laughed.

"That's not funny," I protested in pain. "You have to kill the rest of these damned trout by yourself," I answered.

Twenty minutes later, it was done; we had a total of eight dead trout in our plastic bucket. Back in the kitchen, Karl briefly inspected our catch and then took us to the cold kitchen.

"Black, put the trout in the sink over there and wash them under running water." Then he took out a cutting board and a long and very sharp knife. "Schwarz, get me a trout."

I took one of the dead fish and handed it to Karl.

"Now, look," he said, holding the trout with its belly up in his left hand, with the head of the fish pointing away from him. "You insert the tip of the knife here." He poked the knife into the anus of the fish. "Then you slice it carefully open all the way to the head." The knife cut through the underbelly as if it were butter.

"When you cut, try to use only the tip of the knife and do not push it in too deep. Otherwise, you damage the gallbladder and the fish is spoiled." He pointed at a small green and long sausage-shaped sack. It was disgusting.

The fish was now cut open and I could see the intestines. I was surprised how little blood there was. I always imagined that if you poke a knife into any living thing, it would just burst with blood like a volcano.

"The intestines have to be removed. They are only connected to the body near the tail and here near the head."

With a short but strong pull, Karl separated first the intestines close to the tail and then, very carefully so as not to damage the gallbladder, pulled them out completely until they were only connected via a thin, vein-like string near the head.

"Now, you cut the vein." As he did so, the intestines fell into the sink. He opened up the empty belly of the trout and showed it to me.

105

"Here you go, completely empty. All we have to do now is to remove the intestine tract, which is this brown line running along the spine. Here, look," he said, poking his finger into the intestine and with his fingernail, scratched along the spine until nothing of the brown line remained.

"Now you wash the inside under running water once more and the fish is ready to be cooked." He handed me the trout.

I gave it back to Ralf, who was still cleaning the other fish. I showed him the empty trout and asked him to clean the inside as instructed.

"Schwarz, your turn," Karl ordered. I grabbed a trout and, with Karl standing next to me, did systematically exactly what Karl had done. It went perfectly.

"Well done, now do one more," he said. Again, it went well.

"Black, you are next. Schwarz, you show him how to do it and then you guys finish the rest." He asked us to call him when all was done.

I explained to Ralf step by step how to clean a trout and, just as Karl had told me, I said, "Ralf, your turn." We laughed. Ralf learned quickly and soon there was only one dead fish left.

"Let me do the last one," I said overconfidently after Ralf had finished cleaning out four fish. Everything went well until the moment when I had to remove the intestines. I poked my finger a little too hard and ruptured the gallbladder. A disgusting-looking green liquid substance gushed all over the fish. Ralf asked me what was wrong. I explained to him that the gallbladder had burst.

"No problem," Ralf said. "Let me clean it up under running water."

Since he had cleaned all the fish literally inside out, I left it up to him. When he finished, he opened up the belly and showed it to me.

"You see this here? I cannot remove the light green stains from the gallbladder liquid," he said.

I remembered how adamant Karl was about the gallbladder and wondered if we should dispose of the spoilt fish. Having observed the fish closely, we agreed that it was not too bad and nobody would realize it anyway. A few minutes later everything was cleaned up and we called the chef. Karl looked pleased when he came and saw that we had cleaned up after finishing the job without him having to tell us. He grabbed the bucket and took out each fish. The fifth trout he inspected a little longer and separated it from the others. The last one seemed okay.

"Gentlemen, well done. Now, follow me," he said, taking one of the fish.

We followed Karl to the hot kitchen. He grabbed a large frying pan and smashed it with a loud bang on the stove. He then battered the trout, added salt, pepper and lemon and placed the fish into the pan. We watched carefully because we were certain that he expected us to do the same. Karl was quiet and we wondered why he was not explaining anything. He turned the fish frequently as it sizzled away in the frying pan. Once it was finished, he carefully de-boned the fish, neatly separating the fillets. With a satisfied smile, he offered each of us one half to taste.

"Gentlemen, now try this fine Black Forest trout," he said with a strange grin.

Having grown up with only little fish in my daily diet, trout was not one of my favorite foods. However, this one, prepared personally by the feared executive chef Karl, I could hardly refuse. Ralf looked at me and whispered, "Enjoy your trout."

I took the fork and lifted one filet into my mouth. The moment it touched my palate, a sharp, acidic and bitter sensation attacked my taste buds. It was so disgusting that I spat the piece of fish back onto my plate.

The same happened to Ralf. "Yack! Ahhh…" I heard him swear.

The acidic taste in my mouth made me want to throw up. We both ran to the nearest waste bin and kept on spitting out every last piece of this foul-tasting meat. It seemed to burn itself into every corner of my mouth, forcing me to cough violently. Karl stood there with a serious face.

"Do you know what was wrong with this trout?" he asked.

Suddenly it hit me. "The gallbladder," I said.

"Yes, the gallbladder," Karl answered. "I told you, a spilled gallbladder will completely spoil the fish." He told us clearly it was better to dispose of a spoiled fish than trying to hide such a severe mistake. "Mistakes happen and there is nothing wrong with it as long as you admit to it," he lectured, then with a murky grin he added, "Do not forget you will never outsmart *me* in *my* kitchen."

The bitter foul aftertaste lingered in my mouth for hours and even the next day, I thought I could still taste it. We realized that Karl was not so bad after all and in the seven days we had been in the kitchen, we had learned a lot from him.

By mid-March, I was a seasoned salad chef and, with the exception of dressings, I was basically running the station by myself. Whenever there were quiet days, Karl would call Ralf and me for training which was conducted either by him or by one of the other chefs. The training covered all aspects of the kitchen operation. We learnt all about the gardemanger, saucier, entremetier, pastry and so on. The training was interesting and because most of the time Ralf and I were assigned together, we also made most of our mistakes together.

Just as we had secretly disposed of the shredded trout, we messed up an entire pot of mayonnaise that had separated and was beyond rescue. Considering the location of the pastry and the volume of traffic in front of it, it was a miracle that nobody saw the two of us carrying the huge pot full of spoiled mayonnaise to the basement, pouring it into the waste container. But we did it unseen. Our first ten liters of vinaigrette too disappeared down a drain after we realized that besides oil and vinegar, we should have added water, but by then it had been too late. Gone was the vinaigrette.

We loved the pastry and its products. We loved strawberry cake and the pastry had lots of it. I would sneak into the walk-in-fridge, with Ralf guarding the entrance and me on the inside gulping down sometimes up to three pieces of cake at once. Then it was my turn to guard and Ralf would eat. This we did many times and every time we got cheekier. But our luck was about to run out.

Although Karl never found out about the wasted dressings, mayonnaise and others, he did find out about the cakes. We had become so confident, and careless, I might say, that it was only a question of time until somebody *would* find out. That somebody was no other than Karl himself. Not only had he found out that we were decimating his cakes but he also had detected our preference for strawberry cakes. One day he asked the pastry chef to prepare five strawberry cakes, one of which contained twice the normal amount of strawberries. The extra large cake was left right in front of all the others. Karl assumed, correctly, that we would automatically attack the closest cake in reach which was, of course, the double-layer strawberry cake. And so it was. We came, saw and gulped down large slices of the voluptuous-looking strawberry cake.

Ever since I can remember, my mother has urged me to chew my food rather than just gulping it down. I gulped down the double-layer strawberry cake. By the time I realized that the entire base of the cake was drenched in Tabasco sauce, it was too late. Karl and his chefs must have emptied at least three bottles onto the base of the cake and I felt as if my mouth was on fire. Ralf was spitting and coughing. Unlike me, he had taken only a small piece whilst I had opted for one large piece and stuffed the rest in my mouth. It felt as if the concentrated spices of the sauce were burning its way from my mouth into my skull. At the same moment, Karl came in with half of his crew, roaring with laughter. Once the laughter had subsided, he made it clear to us that this was a last warning; the next time he would take things further. Another lesson learned. After that incident, we calmed down considerably, which is not to say we didn't have fun, but we took things far more seriously.

It was now early July and the summer season was in full swing. We served up to four hundred guests daily, the bulk of them during lunch and afternoon. I had moved on from the salad station to the cold section and from there to the hot kitchen—the real battlefield in any kitchen. With the arrival of the summer season, Karl had assigned Ralf and me to the busiest stations, which was the salad kitchen for me, and the cold kitchen for Ralf. Throughout July and August I made salads, salads and more salads until I had salads coming out of my ears. It came to a point where I thought I smelled vinegar everywhere. My hands always smelled of vinaigrette, even after taking a shower. I had turned into the salad man.

Besides making salads, the other big event in my life in August was that I finally passed the examination for my driver's license. I was happy and proud. Having failed the test twice, I had had little hope that the last and final test would go much better but, surprisingly, I passed. Finally, I would be able to drive my beloved Opel Manta.

At the time the Opel Manta was the closest that people of my income level would ever come to a sports car. I loved that car; the Manta was a two-door sports car lying fairly low on the road. Unfortunately it looked much faster than it actually was, especially the model I owned, but I still loved it.

Despite the fact that the Opel Manta had the notorious reputation of being a car driven mainly by lower-class hooligans, I liked it. Unfortunately, this unpleasant reputation made it an unpopular car with girls, which included my later girlfriend Tatiana, who would only go for rides with me after dark. She considered it to be bad for her reputation to be seen in a Manta. Although my love for the car was strong, my love for Tatiana was stronger. She never pushed me to sell it but, with clever female tactics, she made me see the light and finally I got rid of it.

As September drew to a close, our tour of duty in the kitchen neared the end. Overall it had been not so bad after all; Karl had been tough on us but we had gained a healthy understanding of the basics of a busy kitchen operation. Early October, we returned to the restaurant and it was as if we had never left. In the first few days, we had to endure the teasing of our fellow waiters. Johnny told us that he could smell the nauseating odor of the kitchen still clinging on to us like glue. Yack. He made a point of reminding us loudly in front of the chefs that we had to take additional showers to get rid of the smell. Johnny and the others also made a point of avoiding sitting next to us in the staff canteen. It was only after a few days during lunch in the staff canteen that Johnny officially declared us as "clean." Everybody laughed. Johnny told everyone that the kitchen stench had finally gone; our colleagues cheered, welcoming us back to the service brigade. It was all a little weird.

Towards the end of October it began to get colder and Mr. Hanter announced the closure of the garden restaurant. Once the garden was cleared, we began preparations for the annual inventory-taking and subsequent closure of the hotel.

Early December, I returned to hotel school for the final semester and preparations for our final examination. This semester was longer and far more demanding than the previous ones and it had a heavy curriculum. Almost daily, I sat in my room studying the different subjects until late at night.

Whilst I was busy studying, my colleagues in the hotel were busy preparing for Christmas and New Year's Eve. The hotel got inundated with so many bookings that Mr. Hanter decided to call me back to work on these evenings. I was the only one in my class who had been recalled for work; all the others went home for Christmas and New Year. The only consolation was that Mr. Hanter now looked at me as one of the senior guys and that made me feel proud.

Christmas and New Year went fairly smoothly and were uneventful, and since I only came to help on the busy days, Mr. Hanter had not assigned me my own station; instead, I assisted Peter in the Woodpecker. Our section was fully booked on both evenings but Peter and I worked well together and everything went very smoothly. New Year's Eve came and went and once again we toasted with Mr. Messer, who by now at least knew my name. We celebrated until the early morning hours. I returned to hotel school the next day still suffering the aftermath of a massive hangover.

The weather in Munster was terrible; it was cold and the sky was permanently grey. For some reason, snow never lasted long in this city but instead turned to a cold wet mess shortly after settling on the ground. There seemed to be a permanent icy breeze and the sky was mostly overcast and grey. For us, this was just as well since our teachers drove us hard, preparing us for our final examinations, and there was no time for leaving the school.

The exams were scheduled for August and I was determined to pass, if possible, with reasonably good marks. We had to complete a written exam and practical tests. The practical examination consisted of fine-dining service, bar and beverages and food preparation. Only on the day itself would I be told in which category I would be examined. I was not worried about the practical examination because I was confident that my level of operational expertise exceeded that required for the test. My real worry was the written exam. Throughout my school days, I had never done well in written examinations and that was the reason why this one gave me a tremendous headache. The reason for my failures in school was my complete lack of preparation for tests, which again, was due to my lack of interest in the subjects taught.

Even though I had studied like never before since coming to hotel school, the thought of this examination made me nervous. Again and again, I went over the main subjects, business economics, finance and all the food- and beverage-related subjects but I was still nervous. Had I really studied all there is to know or had I missed something? I had nightmares of me sitting in the examination room, looking at the questionnaires and not being able to answer the questions.

Then one day, there was an unexpected shimmer of hope—one of my schoolmates produced a full set of examination papers from the previous year. This was a gift from heaven and we all were tremendously excited. We made copies for everyone in our class and studied them. Although the papers were from the previous year, they at least gave us an idea of what we had to expect. We knew that the questions would not be exactly the same but at least it would give us an indication as to the number of questions, which subjects would be covered and so on. Finding these papers, even though they didn't help us at all in the end, at least gave me the mental boost I had so badly needed. In March, when the weather finally began to improve, it was time for us to return to our hotels. We would be back in August for our final examinations.

Two days before the imminent departure from hotel school, our feared and respected teacher Mr. Kapferer invited us for a farewell dinner outside the school. He took us to an up-market restaurant where we had a great evening with excellent food and some of the finest wines from Baden. Throughout the evening, Mr. Kapferer entertained us with tales and stories from his many years in the industry. I remember that some of his stories, whilst entertaining, sounded a bit fictitious to me, but I know now that, just as Kapferer was telling his stories that night, so am I writing a book about hotel experiences now. I fully understand that to non-hoteliers, some of these tales may sound difficult to believe, but it does not change the fact that all these tales are true and just as they had happened then, they are still happening now.

Kapferer had seen a lot during his days in large exclusive city hotels and listening to him made us realize that we were dealing with a pro. Kapferer had worked in many five-star hotels where he met most of the eccentric characters he was telling us about that night. He told us that the more expensive and exclusive a hotel, the more eccentric the guests it attracts. This is not to say that all guests in five-star hotels are eccentric, but these hotels do attract some of the weirdest characters.

The more expensive and luxurious the hotels, the higher the level of service they provide. These high levels of service include employees and management ignoring weird and eccentric guests. It takes skill and years of experience to communicate with such guests, pretending that they are actually normal. It almost seemed as if the wealthier the guests were, the weirder they became. I did not know it at the time but I would meet some extreme examples over the coming years.

Hotels cater to anybody and everybody who can afford it, twenty-four hours a day, three hundred sixty-five days a year. People fall in love in hotels and break up in hotels. People get married in hotels and hotels are the reasons for people getting divorces. Hotels are like theaters with dramas being performed every day, with guests being the actors and the employees the audience. In my three years at the Black Forest Grand Hotel, I thought I had seen it all; little did I know that I had only scratched the surface of this wild and wonderful adventure called the hospitality industry. Kapferer's farewell dinner whetted my appetite for more without my knowing it.

When I returned to Talasee after nearly six months at hotel school, I was pleasantly surprised to see a brand-new batch of trainees. This was not the only surprise; during my long absence, Johnny and Barrollo had the left the hotel to pursue other opportunities outside of our industry. Their departure elevated Ralf and me to the two highest ranks in the trainee hierarchy. Ralf and I were now the leaders of the pack and it felt great. I enjoyed the way the new trainees looked up to me in the same admiring manner as I had looked up to Johnny and Barrollo when I had first joined. Of course, seniority had its price and that was more responsibility. Mr. Hanter made sure that we did not become complacent in our new role.

I had to look after Hendrick's station when he was off, which in itself was an incredible compliment for me considering the caliber of Hendrick's guests. One of the new trainees was assigned to me, which was a very new experience for me. Up to that point, it was always me who had received training but now this had changed. I suddenly found myself in a position of having to train someone else.

This "someone else" was called Michael. I was supposed to teach Michael all there is to know about our profession. That was easier said than done. During the first few days, I was frustrated with Michael.

He didn't understand what I was talking about and generally seemed to be completely lost. It seemed that I had to say everything twice and sometimes even three times. I had never had to teach anyone before and didn't quite now where to start. I had not forgotten my first day with Kiki, remembering how badly she had treated me at that time. I wanted to make sure I did not do the same with Michael. Therefore, I bit my tongue and explained to him every task step by step, down to the smallest detail. But this was easier said than done.

For example, I would ask Michael to prepare the mise en place for our service station and he would ask me shyly what mise en place meant. I would then explain the term mise en place and what tasks it consisted of. When I finished, I could see in his eyes that he hadn't understood a thing. I asked him to prepare dessert plates, dinner plates and so on, but instead of doing it, he would look at me lost and I realized that he had no idea how to differentiate between all these different plates or where to find them. As I began explaining to him all about plates, I realized that there was no way for him to remember all those details. Even while I was talking, I caught myself using lots of abbreviations and other technical verbiage which must have sounded like Chinese to him. I was frustrated and I knew I had to take a different approach to training. Unfortunately, the training method I came up with was not much better than the first one.

My expectation was simply too high and I was moving too fast. I realized that I had to start from the very beginning and then go step by step. I let him clean ménages, polish cutlery, plates and other equipment. In doing so, he would learn names, sizes and the purpose of different plates, cutlery and all other operational equipment. In the coming weeks, I learnt that there was more to being a senior trainee than being admired for seniority and experience. Whilst Michael learned the basics of our trade, I had to learn how to share my knowledge effectively with him.

Another group of trainees joined the hotel in early April. Michael was lucky since he was automatically elevated to a more senior rank, even though the difference between him and the new trainees was only a few months. I felt a little jealous that Michael had moved up so fast because it had taken me over two years before moving up. The day the new trainees joined, I opened the garden restaurant for the first time. I was looking forward to working in the garden since temperatures at this time of the year were still quite chilly and I expected some idle days ahead. With Michael by my side, I prepared my service station. Michael practiced what I had taught him and I practiced coaching.

The weather was excellent with clear blue skies but still had rather chilly temperatures. It was a perfect day for a lazy waiter; most guests only peeked briefly outside to test the temperatures but went back inside almost immediately. By mid-afternoon, to my surprise, Mr. Hanter decided to send Michael home because we had no guests. This was another sobering experience; it was no longer I who was sent home but the junior trainee. This was the prize one had to pay for power.

Later that afternoon, some brave guests decided to take coffee on the terrace—a welcome change to my afternoon, which up to that point had been quite boring. I took the order and went to the kitchen to pick up my beverages. At that moment at the coffee station, the female trainees were going through their shift change. I disliked going to the kitchen during these shift changes because I could expect to be teased by all these girls chatting and giggling. They really resembled a flock of nervous chickens, which is quite a chauvinistic statement to make, but there is no other way of describing what was going on at the coffee station at that very moment.

I had to shout to get the girls' attention and even then there was no sense of urgency for any of them to get me my beverages. Seeing that I was not happy, one of the girls, Miriam, apologized and explained that they had a new colleague who had just joined their team. That wasn't really my problem; I just wanted my coffee. Miriam called the new girl to introduce me to her. I was getting impatient now, just as my guests would if they did not get their coffee very soon. The new girl came over and from the moment I looked at her, the coffee was all but forgotten. I just stood there and did not know what to say. I think I stared at her.

She was the most beautiful girl I had ever seen in my entire life. Her eyes radiated something that was difficult to describe; she looked like one of those supermodels on the cover page of glossy high-end fashion magazines. I felt as if my heart had stopped beating and a big lump had moved into my throat. The girl's name was Tatiana and when she cheerfully introduced herself, I was barely able to say my name. All I mustered was inaudible gibberish of some sort, after which I picked up my tray and left. I was dumbstruck by that girl's beauty.

As I served coffees to my guests, I recalled my encounter with Tatiana. What kind of experience had that been? I had behaved like an idiot; to be shy is one thing but to answer a greeting with a mumble is rather silly. I shook my head; this was a major blow to my already weakened self-confidence. She was truly a stunning girl and I had made a real fool of myself. I stayed away from the kitchen for the rest of the afternoon, which was not too difficult since I did not have any guests.

Rafaele arrived in the late afternoon and with his usual cheerful manner, he asked me if I had seen the new girl in the coffee kitchen. I told him I had but kept the rest to myself. In his typical Italian manner, he described her simply as *gorgeous*. I could just imagine how *he* had welcomed her. With his outgoing cheerful Italian personality, he had probably swept her off her feet by kissing her hand whilst making all sorts of flattering remarks. I was sure that with him, it was *she* who was embarrassed. I had to stay away from the kitchen as much as possible in order to avoid running into Tatiana.

The days that followed were not easy for me; every time I went into the kitchen, I would see Miriam and Tatiana chatting and giggling away and I tried to be as invisible as possible. Of course, I always thought they were talking about me, which, of course, they weren't, but all this made me feel even more embarrassed. The little self-confidence that I had left was slowly crumbling to pieces.

Tatiana seemed to hold a mysterious attraction for me and it was all very confusing. On one hand, I couldn't wait to see her when I picked up coffee and on the other hand, I was scared of all the giggling girls together. I was on an emotional roller-coaster ride. I was convinced she thought of me as a complete looser and—let's face it—who wouldn't have, the way I behaved? This had never happened to me and I had no clear idea how I should handle this situation. Of course, all this was just the beginning of a big crush, a crush on Tatiana.

Tatiana at the time was only eighteen years old and had just graduated from high school. She was an amazingly cheerful and outgoing character by nature. Her entire personality was such that almost everyone liked her instantly, with the exception of those girls who perceived her as a threat. It didn't take long for her to cause incredible pangs of jealousy amongst those girls who had boyfriends in the hotel, especially in the kitchen. She was always the center of attention and with her somewhat flamboyant way of entertaining the crowds, she was a little star.

Tatiana was very pretty. With her almond-shaped eye's she was indeed the most attractive girl I had ever seen. Her self-confidence and maturity impressed me immensely, probably because I lacked all of that. Her arrival at the hotel made an impact and everybody talked about her. Her eyes became the subject of much speculation, resulting in the rumor that she was of Asian descent. Her family name, Sputzwick, was reminiscent of the Russian-made satellite Sputnik and literally begged for some sarcasm on our part. Clever as we thought we were, we did not consider the possibility of her being used to this and her response was always instantaneous, sarcastic and left us looking silly in front of a bunch of giggling girls. Jokes about her name subsided soon thereafter.

Tatiana was always jovial, worked hard and slowly earned everyone's respect. From me, she earned not only respect but also wholehearted admiration. Deep inside me I knew that a girl of her caliber would never be attracted to an average person like me. This privilege was reserved for the Johnnys and Rafaeles of this world. They were not only self-confident and outgoing but they also looked the part. It wasn't that I thought I was bad-looking but I didn't think I was good-looking either. I was quite contented, happy and proud just knowing someone like Tatiana, even though I knew that she would forever be unreachable for me.

That summer was busier than others I had experienced in my three years at the hotel. Maybe it was because I was given more responsibility now that I had entered the final year of my apprenticeship. The months of May, June and July passed quickly and the dreaded day of the final examination was approaching. I was getting nervous. Mr. Hanter and the others did their best to make things worse by telling me horrible stories of *things* that happened to other trainees during their examinations. *Things* that made them fail.

To my surprise, Tatiana made an effort to encourage me whenever she saw them stirring me up. This was a nice gesture but it also gave me the sad reputation of being under her personal protection. The guys, of course, took the opportunity to tease me to death about it. I hated all this attention.

As if the mental stress of being teased about the examinations was not enough, my mother topped it all off by telling me that I had received a letter from the conscription office of the Federal Defense Department. I was invited to undergo the first round of medical examinations to determine whether I was fit for the eighteen months of mandatory service in the German armed forces. As requested in the letter, I informed the hotel.

Mr. Hanter suggested I take the opportunity to discuss my future career with the hotel. I met with him and we agreed that after successful completion of my final examination, I would stay on as demi chef de rang until I had to join the military. The date for the medical was still three months away so I decided that for the moment, I had other things to worry about.

August 15 was the day of my practical examination and only one week prior, we had completed our written tests which, to my surprise, I had passed with flying colors. The teasing, which I had to endure in the days leading up to the tests, had made me study even harder and because of it, my colleagues had, unknowingly, helped me to pass.

The practical examination was a different issue altogether. As examination venue, the school had chosen a four-star hotel in Freiburg, which was well known for its extensive banquet facilities. Having been unable to sleep the night before, I arrived in Freiburg far too early and went for a walk through the quiet and deserted city. At seven, I entered the hotel and followed the signs to the examination briefing room.

I watched the hotel staff set up a small buffet with coffee and croissants. I helped myself to coffee, sat on a nearby chair, and waited. Slowly the others began to arrive one by one. Being so early, I had plenty of time to prepare myself mentally for the task ahead. By eight, all had arrived and although the room was crowded with students, there was an eerie silence. Everyone, including myself, was obviously quite nervous. Then a team of examiners and observers entered the room and briefed us on the day's agenda.

I had hoped that I would be assigned to one of the restaurants to serve a five- or six-course gourmet meal, which was my strength. The same applied to most of the others. Our examiners must have known that this would have been far too easy so they came up with something far more challenging—a gourmet banquet.

I had done large functions before but mostly for groups of tourists rather than gourmets. The examination task consisted of preparing and serving a gourmet lunch for two hundred guests. The required setup included an aperitif bar for pre-lunch drinks in a separate function room. We were given two function rooms, appropriate event orders, a kitchen and a storeroom full of equipment. Everything had to be set up from scratch including the tables, the cocktail bar, tabletops, glasses, service station and so on. Each student was responsible for one part of the function. Some had to set up tables according to the floor plan issued by the hotel, and others had to prepare mise en place and other equipment needed for the service.

I awaited eagerly for my orders and when they came, I was in shock. To my absolute horror, I was asked to set up and run the aperitif bar! The aperitif bar!

I had been preparing for everything but not for the bar. I had prepared myself for gueridon service down to the last detail, I had studied wines and I even was ready to prepare a flambé and other dishes at the table; I was prepared for everything but the bar. If I had one weak point, it was the bar. My entire experience and knowledge in mixology was based on working with our bartender Hizli for two weeks at the hotel bar. In those two weeks, I had only learned some of the basic pre-dinner drinks like campari orange, martinis and similar aperitifs, but even then, Hizli had never actually allowed me to make them myself. We just studied the recipes and, on occasions when the bar was quiet and Hizli was in the right mood, he had allowed me to prepare a more complicated aperitif such as a Manhattan, White Russian and one or two others. This had never bothered me since I never saw myself as a future barman, a fact that I now regretted. Now I was standing in an empty room and was expected to set up a bar.

Sweat pearls were forming on my forehead because I had no idea where to start. I looked around the deserted function room; there was no bar and not even tables. Where could I find tables? I asked one of the hotel employees and she pointed me in the right direction.

Having found the equipment store, I manhandled two long rectangular tables into the function room. The examiner frequently stuck his head into the room to see how I was doing. I set up the tables and carefully boxed them in with a white tablecloth, just as I had learned at the hotel. I took my own sweet time and when the bar was finished I realized that I needed glasses. Once again, the examiner checked in on me but now he seemed to grow impatient. I still had no glasses, or anything else for that matter. My bar was completely empty.

Once again, it was a friendly hotel employee who told me where I could find martini glasses, highball glasses, tumblers and all the other glassware I needed for my bar. I found the glasses but, to make matters worse, they were full of water stains and I had to polish them all. This cost valuable time which I could have spent preparing the bar mise en place. When the examiner checked on me for the third time, he reminded me that I had only one hour left. One hour!

The examiner urged me to hurry it was, of course, in the examiner's interest to have the bar ready before our guests arrived and so he told me where to get lemons, olives and all other condiments for my mise en place. I got the lemons, olives and cherries and slowly it started to look like a bar. I checked the function sheet. I had to offer martinis, Camparis, gin and tonics, Bucks Fizz, Dubonet, Bloody Marys and Manhattans.

Manhattan! What the hell was a Manhattan again? I had done it before but I could not remember the recipe. There was no way for me to get the recipe from someone and I could not really ask the examiner, either, so I decided simply to forget about the Manhattan. I requisitioned the alcoholic beverages and set them up on my aperitif bar. I double-checked the bottles: sparkling wine, vodka, gin, martini, campari, Dubonet—it was all there. The mise en place was ready, too: cherries, olives, lemons, Worcestershire sauce, Tabasco—it seemed complete.

I looked at my watch—still twenty minutes to go, so far so good. Another examiner passed by my bar, scrutinizing the set up and frowned. He asked me if the setup were complete; I answered yes but wasn't really sure. Something was missing, he said. *Shit,* I thought, and ran through my checklist again. What was missing? I didn't know.

The examiner saw my face and knew that I was lost. The thought that things were not going well crossed my mind again. He asked me to get salt, pepper, and swizzle sticks. I tried to remember all the things he had told me and hurried to the service bar. The hotel bartender sensed what was happening and asked me for my function sheet. He looked at it, told me to get back to the function room and he would bring everything I needed. I would be eternally grateful to the man.

Back at the bar I counted my glasses. I had about eighty glasses of each type, *which should be enough,* I thought. The bartender came and discreetly handed over the rest of my mise en place. Now it looked more like a bar. I still had ten minutes until the first guest would arrive. The hotel bartender looked at me, smiled and assured me that I would be okay, saying that my mise en place was complete. I felt a little better.

The examiner came back and asked me if I was ready. Once again, I answered yes, this time more confidently, upon which he asked me where I was hiding my ice cubes. I looked at my bar. *Shit.* I had no ice cubes.

I rushed back to the service bar to get the ice. When I returned to my bar, I was shocked to see about ten guests waiting for aperitifs. I rushed behind the counter and with a forced smile, asked them politely for their orders. They all seemed to be talking at once and I didn't know what drink to prepare first. I had to get organized. I apologized, took a pen and paper and asked again but this time noting down every drink. I had just finished writing it all down when more guests arrived. Naturally, everyone went straight for my bar counter.

My heart was beating fast now. I made the martinis first, forgetting the olives. Next came the gin and tonics, which I served without the lemons. I managed to miss at least one ingredient in each aperitif. Some guests smiled, some rolled their eyes, trying to educate me along the way. The crowd in front of my bar got bigger and so did the sweat pearls on my forehead.

I dashed from left to right, pouring vodka here and tomato juice there. The room began to fill with the chatter and laughter of over one hundred people. I was far too busy to wonder why on earth they would leave me serving close to two hundred guests by myself; to this day, I haven't figured that one out. Then the first guests returned, complaining about too much gin here, too little tonic there, and all the time—more guests, more orders. After a while, I started to get the hang of it; my movements were smoother and I even started to take orders whilst mixing drinks.

Then it happened. "One Manhattan, please."

My heart stopped. I took a deep breath and clumsily explained that I had run out of Manhattans.

The guests raised their eyebrows in disbelief. "Never mind. One martini, instead."

Now I was getting really busy; I mixed and poured. The complaints became fewer; instead, I got requests for more refills. Bucks Fizz for the ladies, gin and tonics and Bloody Marys for the gentlemen. Half an hour later, the room was full and my bottles were nearly empty. I had begun to run out of lemons, ice, and glasses when, to my relief, the examiner entered the room, finally asking everyone to make their way to the dining room. Within minutes, the room was empty and I was alone.

This battle was over but the war had only just begun and I wondered if I had won or lost the one just now. Whilst I had been busy running my crowded aperitif bar, my fellow students had finished setting up the banquet hall for the gourmet lunch.

I rushed from the bar to the banquet hall where one of the examiners led me to my station. The room looked truly amazing; there were several long rows of tables, covered with snow-white and heavily starched tablecloths with red and yellow flower bouquets sitting on razor-sharp centerfolds. Between spotless polished silverware stood show plates with the hotel's crest in gold. The waiters stood erect in a straight line all facing the guests as they entered. There was one gap in the perfectly straight line and that space was reserved for me.

I rushed over and, still breathing heavily after the exhausting battle at the bar, I squeezed into the line of waiters. I glanced around the room, trying to find the wine and service stations. Since I had not been part of the setup team, I had not attended the pre-service briefing and therefore had no idea about the logistics. There was one wine station with wine waiter near the kitchen entrance. In each corner of the room, one service station had been set up. From what I could see, they were complete with all mise en place that I would need during the service. So far so good. I felt much more comfortable in this environment than at the bar. After all the stress I had experienced over the past hour, I had a sudden rush of confidence.

I looked around the banquet hall observing the faces of my colleagues; they all seemed a little nervous and intimidated by the approaching guests. This was not surprising because whilst I was fighting the cocktail battle, they had been idle in the banquet hall with plenty of time to ponder all the things that could go wrong. So by the time I assisted the guests at my table, I was perfectly calm and composed. From then on, it all went absolutely picture perfect. I took the orders with ease and I even had time to talk with my guests, many of whom recognized me from the aperitif bar.

Seeing some of my colleagues struggling nervously made me feel even better and soon I was on a roll. I opened the wines and answered probing questions from my guests with ease. The service went as smooth as butter and I got less and less attention from the examiners. Before I knew, it was all over. Despite my initial struggle with the aperitif bar, I had passed my practical examination with flying colors.

My three years of apprenticeship had come to an end but the learning had only started. Ten days after my final exams, I signed my first real contract with my first real salary. Because I was waiting to be drafted for my military service in the German Armed Forces, the hotel offered me an open-ended contract with the guarantee to re-employ me after I completed my eighteen months of military service.

With my new contract came a new rank and that was demi chef de rang. I was proud and everyone congratulated me for passing my final exams and for my promotion. As a demi chef de rang, I normally had to report to a chef de rang. Demi chef de rangs normally assisted chef de rangs in running their stations. Despite my title, I was always fully in charge of stations and more often than not, I was running one of the restaurants, supported by only one trainee. I didn't mind all that as long as I had fun. Gone were the days when I would nervously check the duty roster in the morning to see who I had to assist; now I checked to see which trainee would assist me. Gone were the days when I asked all the questions; now it was me who had to answer all the questions from my trainees.

I made a point, however, not to let my trainees do all the work; I never had the intention to be another "Peter" or another "Johnny." I shared the workload but I also shared the tip fairly, something that had never happened to me with my "bosses." I treated both trainees and guests with respect and in doing so they respected me as a "boss."

I got on well with everyone and even Karl began to treat me more and more like a human being rather than a monkey. I became more and more confident, a fact that didn't go unnoticed by Tatiana. We had been close friends for some time already but at one point, Tatiana had made her move. Her move came in form of a dinner and a goodnight kiss, with her only leaving my room the next morning. Before I knew it, we were a couple.

Then finally in early October, I had to report to the army hospital in Freiburg to complete medical examinations for my upcoming military service. I went and, although undesired and unexpected, I passed my medical with flying colors. I was accepted.

After the medical, I had to attend a personal interview with a recruitment officer. He asked me all sorts of questions including my political ambitions. I guess the fact that I didn't fully understand the meaning of "political ambition" was enough for the officer to raise my security clearance by one level. He then went on to describe the different services such as Army, Air Force and the Navy. It all sounded quite interesting. To my surprise, he asked if I had any preference concerning my posting; I didn't even know that I had a choice.

It was common practice for the German armed forces to base conscripts near their hometowns, presumably to save expenses of transporting entire armies of men every weekend from one end of the country to the other. I did not have to think twice and immediately answered, "I want to join the Navy." The recruitment officer made a note on a form in front of him and then asked me what branch of the Navy I had in mind. What I had in mind was quite simple and straightforward: I wanted to be a steward on a battleship. I dreamt of wearing a beautiful white uniform, serving the commander in the officers' mess whilst traveling around the world on a powerful battleship. The recruitment officer burst out laughing, telling me that the German Navy no longer had battleships and that the last one was sunk by the British in World War II. What a disappointment.

The recruitment officer then explained that the Navy had only very few steward positions available. I think I must have looked extremely disappointed at that moment since he asked me if I would be interested to serve as a cook on a destroyer. My answer came instantly—"Yes!" At this point I didn't care what they asked me to do as long as I could be based on a ship. He explained that I had the right background for a ship's cook, telling me that for this position I would have to complete a three-month basic training and then spend another three months attending the Navy's kitchen school. After six months, I would be assigned to a ship.

I could hardly contain my excitement; I could already see myself in a brilliant white officer's uniform under palm trees somewhere in the Caribbean. I suddenly got a craving for adventure. The interview was finished and the recruitment officer said quietly, "Welcome to the Navy."

Back in Talasee, my colleagues were quite excited when they heard that I would be joining the Navy. I especially liked the way the trainees looked at me, full of admiration. I had to think of the time when Johnny and Barollo studied the cruise ship brochures; then, I had looked at them in the same way, and now, here I was joining a destroyer. Maybe not as glamorous as a cruise ship but a ship nonetheless.

Chef Karl was of course overjoyed when he heard that I would be serving as a cook, telling me how lucky I was and I should be grateful that the Navy had offered me a way out from the miserable existence of being a waiter. My only concern was Tatiana; we had grown quite fond of each other and the thought of leaving her behind made me feel sad. We promised each other that whatever happened, we would stay together. My love for her went so far that I promised to write her one letter every day. I kept that promise and wrote to her every single one of my five hundred and sixty days.

For now, I still had several months before departing for Hamburg and I was dreaming of my white officer's uniform and all the exotic places I would see. I wondered what it would be like sailing on a destroyer through a storm and I wondered if I would be seasick. I was sure that I would find out soon enough.

Slowly, the excitement about my Navy career began to subside and other day-to-day occurrences took over. One of them was that Hendrick had decided to work on my wine knowledge. Throughout my apprenticeship, the wine training was focused on wines from our region, Baden. My knowledge of German wines was pretty good; I knew the German wine-label legislation inside out and I had adopted a taste for the Gutedel grape. We did have a reasonably good selection of fine French wines and even a couple of champagnes but they were expensive and, especially the French red wines, too heavy for the local taste. We also had a few new world wines from South Africa and Argentina but we did not think much of the New World as wine region and considered them cheap and of doubtful quality. They simply could not be compared to our wines from Baden.

The expensive French wines were reserved for out-of-town guests who had the money to spend. Several red wines had to be decanted into a crystal carafe. We did not sell many of these wines and therefore whenever we had such an order, Hendrick would be called to open the wine and decant it properly. Since we couldn't just open the most expensive wines for training purposes, Hendrick took an empty Bordeaux bottle, filled it with water and sealed it tight with a used cork.

We conducted the training in the Mountaindew, which was usually closed in the afternoon. Hendrick handed me the bottle and asked me to pretend it was a Chateau Pichon Longueville 1964, ordered by table five. Hendrick went and sat down at table five. I placed the bottle in a red wine basket, prepared my opener on a small silver plate, with one napkin and a candle. Satisfied that all was there, I walked briskly to table five. I placed everything on the gueridon, picked up the bottle and presented it to Hendrick.

Before he even looked at the label, he blasted me for shaking the bottle too much. He explained that such old wines have to be carried very carefully as they contain sediments which normally settle on the bottom of the bottle. If the sediments are stirred up, it can take up to thirty minutes for them to settle again. He confirmed the name and vintage of the wine, I thanked him and returned to my gueridon, where I carefully placed the bottle in the wine basket.

Once I had successfully removed the cork, I placed the candle next to the crystal carafe. I informed my guest that I was just about to decant the wine for him. Hendrick smiled gaily asking me to go ahead. I lit the candle.

With my right hand I carefully lifted the wine basket with the imaginary Pichon Longueville and with my left hand I grabbed the crystal carafe. I positioned the neck of the bottle just above the candle's flame and began to pour the wine slowly into the wine carafe. The candle illuminated the neck of the bottle perfectly, allowing me to see the typical brown streaks of sediments appearing from the bottom of the bottle. I tried to arrest the flow of the sediments in the neck of the bottle.

In order not to stir up the sediments, it was of utmost importance that the wine was flowing freely without creating air bubbles. When the bottle was empty I placed it carefully back into the wine basket and onto the gueridon. I suggested that my guest let the wine sit and breathe in the carafe for a moment in order to allow the bouquet of the wine to develop fully. Hendrick agreed and asked me at the same time *how* I would eventually serve him the wine since there were no Bordeaux glasses or any other glasses, for that matter.

Shit, I thought; I had completely forgotten to prepare wine glasses. I apologized to Hendrick and quickly polished two tall Bordeaux glasses and placed them in front of him. He asked me to serve the wine now and so I did. I knew from experience what would come next: first, critique on the decanting and then the question and answer session. The critique went fine with Hendrick only commenting on the way I had carried the bottle. The question and answer session was different. What are the grape varieties used by Pichon Longueville? I remembered the Cabernet Sauvignon and Merlot grapes but forgot the Cabernet Franc. In which part of Bordeaux is the vineyard located? I knew the answer—it was Pauillac, because I liked the sound of the name.

Then Hendrick wanted to know which other famous appellation bordered Pauillac. That, I did not know. It was St. Julien, Hendrick lectured. He asked me to describe the taste and made corrections along the way. He taught me how to stand properly at the table and where I had to put my left hand when I poured the wine. He taught me what to say and what not to say. I told Hendrick that his what-not-to-say was exactly what Johnny and Peter always *did* say. His answer was short and to the point, telling me what he thought of the two. We left it at that.

Once in a while, Mr. Hanter appeared out of nowhere, watched for a while and then disappeared again. We did these wine-decanting training sessions several times until I was reasonably confident in decanting an expensive bottle of red wine. I was grateful to Hendrick because I learned a lot from him. From wine, we moved on to champagne and then he began a series of training teaching me the skill of cooking at the guests' table. I prepared salads and flambé at the table as well as practiced the carving of Chateaubriands and other delicacies.

It was about at that time that another new trainee joined the hotel; her name was Anke Schworz. Anke and Tatiana, they became best friends the moment they met. They were like inseparable single-cell twins who, for some reason, looked different. It was a match made in heaven. Over time I would grow very fond of Anke who is still a close friend today. Anke, extremely attractive and sexy was like a bolt of lighting in disguise. Anke and Tatiana worked hard and played hard and they did almost everything together.

At the end of October, we went through the now familiar exercise of shutting down and closing the hotel. We had our traditional leaving party, said our goodbyes and left the next day. For me, it would become one of the most memorable holidays for various reasons. I spent most of the time with Tatiana, whom I was totally in love with by now. However, in order for me and Tatiana to become a couple, we had to overcome some serious hurdles since we both were engaged in relationships.

I had to say goodbye to my girlfriend Romy, a move which made me very unpopular with my mother. Tatiana had to say goodbye to her boyfriend, which made me very unpopular with him. Whilst my mother was very angry, not so much about the fact that I had left Romy but the way I had done it, she still mostly understood what was happening. Tatiana's boyfriend, on the other hand, did not understand what was happening and when he finally did, he focused his anger on me.

The problem here was that her boyfriend was thirty-three years old, physically very fit and he drove a seven-series BMW. He was a grown man whilst I was still trying to become one. That fact was confirmed on the day he was waiting in front of the staff house when Tatiana and I returned from a late-night snack. It all happened very fast.

He approached out of the dark, grabbed Tatiana and asked her to get into his car. I knew, by looking at him, that any offensive behavior from my side would spell certain death or at least severe pain for me. Despite this knowledge, I asked him to leave Tatiana alone and that was exactly what he had been waiting for. He looked at me, smiling, and before I knew it, his head shot forward, crushing brutally into my nose. The blow made me bend down in pain, and suddenly his right knee shot up, knocking me off my feet. I hadn't even had a chance to hit him back.

By the time I managed to get up, they had gone. I literally crawled to my room to lick my wounds. I didn't see Tatiana until the next day when she told me that she had broken up with him for good. I was overjoyed; there was nothing in our way that could stop us now. It took some time for my parents to forgive me the "cowardly" way in which I had finished with Romy, but eventually they forgave me and things returned to normal.

Tatiana's first task was to elevate me to an acceptable level in terms of personal presentation, including clothes, eau de colognes, shoes and everything else relating to my overall look. Of course my mother loved the fact that finally I got rid of my leather jackets, sleeveless jeans jacket, as well as the cowboy boots. Needless to say, I did not change overnight and there were some heated arguments between Tatiana and me, which she usually won.

So instead of jeans and leather jacket, I wore white linen pants with a pastel-colored linen jacket and I changed my beloved cowboy boots to flat white slippers made in Italy. My aftershave changed from Pitralon, a very famous and very cheap East German aftershave, to something called Aigner Pour Homme. The Aigner aftershave in particular left a long-lasting impression on me. I had never bought an aftershave and therefore had no benchmark in terms of pricing. The Pitralon aftershave cost me next to nothing; the Aigner aftershave that day cost me the equivalent of three days of tip. I initially felt dressed like a clown, but with Tatiana by my side I began to enjoy this new look. All that was left of my former self now was my car. Tatiana knew that it was too early to make me change my car, too, but the time would come. Before the end of November, Tatiana had transformed me into a new Andre.

Soon Tatiana and I began discussing my upcoming service in the Navy and our plans for the future. I had never planned that far in advance and was not really that interested, either. As far as I was concerned, I wanted to join the Navy and, after having done my time, come back to Black Forest Grand Hotel. Tatiana, unfortunately, did not agree with my plans. She told me quite clearly that after four years of working in the same hotel, it was important for me to move on to the next level. The "next level" for her meant not in the Black Forest Grand Hotel and not in Talasee. She had set her sights on bigger and better hotels for me. This was not quite what I had in mind; I liked the hotel and I liked the town; I felt comfortable here. We had endless discussions on the subject and finally we agreed to put it all on hold until later.

Other than that, we enjoyed a great holiday and before we knew, it was over. We returned to Talasee and went through the familiar routine of cleaning and preparing the hotel for the coming winter season. There were many new faces, including another new batch of trainees. I had risen to one of the most senior guys by now and because of this, I found myself doing more delegating and supervising rather than actual physical work. I was in a very good mood and smiled happily even when I went to the kitchen.

This was, of course, because of Tatiana. It did not take long for news of our liaison to spread and soon it was common knowledge. I don't know whether or not this was the reason why Mr. Hanter assigned Tatiana to assist me during Christmas Eve and New Year's Eve, but his choice could not have been better because we worked perfectly together. As matter of fact, we worked so well together that he frequently assigned us to the largest and busiest stations. Things were going well.

In March, I finally received my marching orders from the Defense Department. The simple computer-generated letter ordered me to report to the Kue.Dst.Schule in Glueckstadt on October 1. I had no clue where Glueckstadt was, but the fact that I didn't know it was a good sign because it had to be far away. I took out my world atlas and searched for Glueckstadt. I eventually found it about fifty kilometers north of Hamburg. This was near the North Sea coast and, hallelujah, very, very far away from the Black Forest. It was actually close to the border of Denmark.

Now I had to figure out the meaning of Kue.Dst.Schule, which was not that difficult, as it could only mean "Kitchen Service School." I worked it out as "Kue." for kitchen, "Dst." meant service and "Schule" was "school." Easy!

With the date for my departure set, the personnel manager now began talking about my return to the hotel after the Navy. By law, the hotel had to re-employ me after my military service if I chose to come back. In a meeting with the hotel manager, Mr. Holzl, and the personnel manager, Mr. Junger, I was asked if I was interested in coming back after completing my eighteen months' service. I confirmed my interest in coming back on the basis that I could always withdraw my intention to return at a later stage. I never told Tatiana about this, simply because I knew she would not have approved of it. I agreed with the management that I would leave the hotel in mid-September so that I still had two weeks to sort out my personal things at home.

In the remaining five months, I was running my own station almost daily and in the evenings I covered for station waiters who were taking their off-day. Whenever I was assigned to Hendrick, he asked me do the wines, champagnes and other service jobs that had to be done at the table. I enjoyed those remaining months when, for the first time since I had started my career, I was treated as a fully blown supervisor.

This showed in many different ways. I ate with the senior managers and I hardly did any mise en place jobs anymore. On the contrary, I checked what the trainees were doing and corrected or coached them if necessary. I watched the chefs playing pranks on the newcomers and provided mental support when things were taken a bit too far. I closed an eye when trainees or waiters took revenge on customers—only if I felt the customer deserved it. I now was truly in charge.

Tatiana and I had become an established couple and by the time we arranged my leaving party, we had become the most popular couple in the hotel. We were liked by all, probably because we were considered a perfect match. My leaving party was held in our favorite hangout, the Pferdestall disco.

The next morning I crammed my meager belongings into my car and after having a last coffee with Mr. Hanter, I said goodbye to everyone. As I drove past the main entrance of the Black Forest Grand

Hotel for the last time, I said a last goodbye to the hotel where I had spent the past four years of my life.

Chapter 4: *The Navy*

On the grey and chilly November morning I left for my service in the Navy, the main railway station in Freiburg was reminiscent of a train station during the war in some black and white movie. The platform was crowded with young men, some in uniform and some in plain clothes. Several officers with clipboards were answering questions from men in plain clothes, sending them to one of the different groups that had gathered in various areas.

I approached one of the officers and dutifully reported to him with my name. I considered for a moment saluting him but decided against it, purely because none of the others did. He searched all of his twenty-something pages without luck; my name was not on the list. A shimmer of hope, *maybe I could go home again.* He asked me if I was drafted to the Army or Air Force. I proudly told him that I was joining the Navy. On hearing this, he just laughed, telling me that there is no Navy here and I had to find my own way to Glueckstadt or wherever I was going. He ordered me to *make a move* and continued with the next one.

I had only one choice: find my own train, which I eventually did, arriving in Glueckstadt after a grueling twelve-hour train ride. I had never traveled that far away from my hometown and the experience of the journey itself, including a nerve-racking change of trains in Hamburg, had left me physically and mentally exhausted by the time I arrived at the barracks.

The Navy compound itself consisted of about twenty buildings, which included accommodations, crew mess, sports hall, weapons and ammunition storage buildings and training grounds. I don't remember exactly how I got to my room that night but I do remember that I was the last one to arrive because out of eight bunks, seven were already occupied. I crashed dead tired into the last bunk and fell asleep almost instantly.

I had barely slept an hour when suddenly the lights came on and all hell broke loose. There were loud metallic banging noises accompanied by ear-piercing whistling sounds. I shot up and nearly fell out of my bunk. *What was happening?* With half-open eyes, I saw an officer standing in the middle of the room dressed in full combat gear, with his foot resting on a steel helmet which he had been kicking noisily through the room only minute earlier. Had the Russians attacked?

He began shouting like a madman. "Get out of your bunks, you lazy bastards! Uniform check at 0530 hours! Schnell, schnell, schnell!"

I still had no clue what was going on. *Who was this man and why was he screaming at us?* I looked around the room and could see that my fellow roommates were just as surprised as I was. I looked at my watch, it was only four forty-five and I had hardly slept. *Was this a mad house?*

"Are you people deaf? Can't you hear what I am saying? Get the fuck out of your bunks and move your asses out of here!" the man barked, stomping his left foot on the steel helmet.

Slowly everyone got out of bed and after we had briefly introduced ourselves, we angrily discussed the unpleasant way we had been woken up. As it turned out, this was only a first taste of what was to come. Over time, we would get used to these "alarms" but for the first couple of nights, it was pure hell.

Later that day, we all had to assemble in the exercise hall. The exercise hall was the size of an aircraft hangar and simply huge. I was surprised at how many of us there were—a thousand men at least. There was a small stage with a podium at one end of the hall with a large German flag. Several officers walked stiffly up to the stage and one of the petty officers shouted an order for us to stand to attention. The officers on stage looked serious; none of them smiled.

After the rude awakening, I began to wonder if something might have happened with the Russians. The petty officer barked his order and over a thousand men in the hall fell silent in an instant. On stage, one of the angry-looking officers stepped forward. The man introduced himself as the commander and officially welcomed us to the German Navy and the Kuestendienst Schule in Glueckstadt.

What was that? I immediately looked up in surprise. *Did he say "Kuestendienst Schule?"* It couldn't be—that meant *coastal defense!*

I thought I must have misheard because this had nothing to do with the Navy kitchen school I was supposed to attend. *Damn, had I ended up in the wrong unit?* This was a disaster; I was supposed to be in kitchen school and instead I ended up in a coastal defense school. There was no doubt in my mind that that my posting in Glueckstadt was a mistake which I had to clarify before it was too late. I decided there and then that I had to see my platoon leader in this regard as fast as possible.

To say that this was a monumental mistake is an absolute understatement. I don't remember at all what the commander told us in his speech; I had only one thing on my mind and that was to sort out this mess with my wrong posting. When I went to the platoon leader's office, I was received with an icy stare from an officer in some sort of senior officer's uniform. The platoon leader listened patiently until I had finished my query. He just sat there looking at me with a strange glimmer in his eyes. Then all of a sudden, he took a deep breath and screamed from the top of his voice, ordering me to get the hell out of his office and asking me never ever to come back again.

Having never been screamed at in such a vicious manner, I was slightly startled. The platoon leader looked angry—very, very angry—angrier than any human being I had ever seen before and in the hotel, I had met many. In order not to aggravate the situation further, I turned on my heels and left his office.

I was totally devastated when I found out that my posting was no mistake. Coastal defense units were part of the Navy but based exclusively ashore and never on ships. My dream of traveling around the world had burst into pieces. There would be no leisurely strolls along the beaches of the Caribbean and no stories to tell after months and months at sea. My dreams of traveling the world with days out in the open sea were shattered. Instead, we traveled out to remote exercise grounds for days filled with grueling field exercises.

The coming three months were packed with all sorts of exercises—weapons training, formal training and field exercises. Although I was deeply disappointed by what the Navy had done to me, I did enjoy the immense physical challenges they put us through almost daily. More so because compared to some of my comrades, it turned out that I was quite fit. Seeing some of my comrades collapsing after thirty of forty kilometers of marching, with feet covered in blisters and tears in their eyes whilst I was still fine, made me feel great. As a waiter, I was used to that.

As for Tatiana, I kept my promise of writing her one letter a day and not only that, I made it a point of never writing less than three pages. I wrote, drew little pictures and sent her cool photographs of me in uniform, posing with my rifle. I also called Tatiana frequently. The barracks had three public telephone boxes, which were nearly always occupied, and, depending on time of day, I had to wait up to an hour to make a telephone call. I queued about three times a week to call Tatiana and my parents.

After the three months' basic training, I was physically as fit as ever and I felt great. The basic training did not kill me and time passed relatively fast. I finished basic training with high marks and at the end of three months I had risen to the rank of corporal, sporting two bright yellow bars on my shoulders indicating my new rank. The two bars did not make any difference in terms of authority but it did protect us from the teasing and pranks which full-time soldiers and petty officers played almost daily on us draftees.

A few weeks later, we were transferred to our permanent units. As coastal defense troops, our posting would be at naval air bases, Navy ports or any other shore- based Navy facility. Then the day came when the platoon leader announced that all transfers were posted on the notice board. We all stormed out of our rooms to the board, which was already surrounded by countless men all trying to find their names on the endless lists. I managed to elbow my way through the crowd and scanned the different postings. Most of our platoon went further north to the dreaded air reconnaissance base in Nordholz and to the Navy bases in Wilhelmshaven and Kiel.

My name was nowhere to be seen. I scanned the list again and finally found it on the very bottom, separated from all the others. It read: Andre Schwarz—Fue.Ak.BW—Hamburg.

What the hell was that? And why was it only me and none of the others?

I approached our group leader and asked him if he knew what the abbreviation stood for. He leaned forward and squinted his eyes. Suddenly, he laughed.

"You lucky little bastard," he said. "That's a nice and cushy job you got yourself. You are going to the Fuehrungsakademie der Bundeswehr"—the Officers Academy of the German Armed Forces. He then told me that the academy had a mixed contingent of seventy men from Air Force, Army and Navy. When I asked him what I would have to do there, he just laughed, saying that I probably would have to carry the briefcase of an admiral or something like that. He had a good laugh and left.

Officers Academy? I had high marks but I doubted that they would send me there to become an officer. For that I would have to sign up for a few years and as far as I knew, I hadn't done that—or had I? Now, I was worried; I had signed many documents over the past three months and most of the time I had not actually read them. Had I, by mistake, signed something saying that I wanted to become an officer?

None of the petty officers or platoon leaders was able to shed light on the nature of my upcoming transfer, but they all agreed that it would be a "cushy" job. There was only one way to find out and so I left Glueckstadt one week later to report for duty at my new unit at the officers academy in Hamburg.

My arrival in Hamburg was marked by a delay of over five hours due to technical problems with the train. When I finally reported to the academy's commanding officer, I was welcomed with a massive dressing down for my delay in front of the assembled platoon. It was not a good start and by the time he finished, he had nearly convinced me that I *was* the biggest loser in the German armed forces since I was not even able to make a simple train journey of sixty kilometers in time.

As he shouted at me in front of two hundred men, I just stood there in my green combat gear, holding my large green sea sack. He finally called a corporal of the Air Force to take me to the barracks reserved for the ratings. Up to that point, I still didn't have a clue as to my exact assignment; the only thing I knew for sure was that the commanding officer thought I was a complete loser. On the way to the barracks, the corporal asked me not to take the commanding officer too seriously and that he normally was "quite okay;" he just liked to "show off" sometimes.

At least this friendly corporal was able to shed some light on the nature of my assignment. I was surprised when he stated that I must have hotel background. *How had he guessed that?* I wondered. I found out later that I had in fact been chosen *because* of my food and beverage background in hotels. The officers academy in Hamburg had officer cadets not only from the German armed forces but from armed forces all over Europe and other countries and as such, they hosted many official events.

The academy compound occupied a large part of Hamburg's expensive suburb of Blankenese and was surrounded by lush parks with scenic greenery. The compound consisted of the university itself, the accommodation buildings, an officers club, one large banquet hall and one restaurant. There was also a large park with walkways and a large pond, home to a flock of ducks. And there were officers—lots of them.

To the utter delight of the friendly corporal, I dutifully saluted every officer we met until he asked me to stop it, explaining that we ratings were exempted from saluting. The reason for this wonderful exemption was that the officer-rating ratio was one thousand to one. The other pleasant surprise was that I had to share my room with only one other person, Senior Corporal Pauselius, who happened to be from coastal defense, too. It turned out that Pauselius and I were both assigned to manage the officers club of the academy!

The officers club very much resembled a private club for the rich and famous. There was a large bar stocked with every alcoholic beverage I had ever heard of, various comfortable lounge chairs, sofas and coffee tables. Next to the bar stood a temperature-controlled wine cabinet with various fine wines from Germany and France.

The bar was not our only responsibility; we also doubled as waiters for large receptions, dinners and balls, of which we had many. The academy hosted some serious receptions which were frequently attended by the defense minister, and once, even the foreign minister was present.

These events were quite impressive, even though I have to say that the wives of most officers were not the same caliber of guests I had met in Talasee. Most of these ladies were obviously not used to such high-profile events and looked rather uncomfortable in their tight-fitting ball gowns. This was probably the reason why many of them took the occasion to get viciously drunk on expensive champagne courtesy of the government.

The same wasn't true for the officers in their formal dress uniforms who looked truly impressive. I liked these receptions because this was the only time when we had a chance to wear our formal white Navy dress uniforms. Other than our Navy uniforms, there was very little in our daily routine reminiscent of the military. We worked as bartenders most of the time and occasionally, if the weather was good, we ventured out to the shooting range for some target practice with our rifles, presumably to remind us that we were still members of the German armed forces. Overall, life at the academy was easy and I truly enjoyed my time there. I kept on writing letters to Tatiana daily and she answered nearly every one of them.

Despite our "cushy" job, Pauselius and I were not happy. We had been in the Navy now for over one year and had not even so much as *seen* a ship. We wanted to be onboard a battleship and not in a bar serving wine and beer. This was not what we had volunteered for and we felt it was time for us to do something about it.

We filed an official complaint with our commanding officer. It did not take long for us to be summoned to the commanding officer's office. Needless to say, he was not impressed by our complaint but because we had done so in writing, he was obliged to take action. After a speech that bordered on a dressing down, we half expected to be court marshaled for our audacity but contrary to our wildest expectation, he got us an assignment for four days on the frigate *Hamburg* as "observers." We were in heaven!

Two weeks later, we boarded the mighty-looking frigate in Wilhelmshaven. For me, having never been to a seaport before, the sight of the harbor alone was fascinating. I remember that I stood there for several minutes just taking in the view; I was fascinated by what I saw. There were ships of all different shapes and sizes from all over the world. It was stunning. Up to that point the largest ships I had ever seen were the sightseeing boats on Lake Talasee, but compared to the size of our mighty frigate, they seemed minuscule.

What happened next was nothing more than embarrassing. We learned pretty soon that the North Sea in winter was the wrong place to be and definitely not on a fragile vessel like a frigate. Our mission took us from Wilhelmshaven to the island of Heliogoland and back. This is normally a short trip but in the winter storms of the North Sea, it was hell on earth. The waves seemed twice as large as the ship and we were scared to death. It didn't take us long to get as sick as puppies, tied to our bunks for two full days.

The crew of the *Hamburg* spared no efforts to make sure we "land rats" would remember this trip for the rest of our lives. As we found out later, they all knew about our letter of complaint, which presumably had a lot to do with the captain of the frigate sailing straight through the storm instead of going around it. When we eventually returned to Wilhelmshaven, happy to be still alive, it took us a day to get used to walking on steady ground again. On our return to the academy, we were greeted by our commanding officer with a knowing grin. We never complained again.

As my time in the Navy grew to a close, it was time to start thinking of the future. The easiest choice would have been to return to my beloved Black Forest Grand Hotel. Tatiana advised against it, saying that I should work for a five-star hotel or Michelin-star restaurant. I wrote several applications to some of the finest hotels and restaurants in Baden. I did it more for Tatiana than anything else since I had not much hope of being accepted by any of them.

I was wrong. To my surprise, several hotels invited me for interviews, including the prestigious Columbus Hotel in Freiburg. It came as an even bigger surprise when the Columbus Hotel offered me the position of demi chef de rang in its Michelin-star restaurant, The Stube. I accepted.

With my future secured, I enjoyed my remaining time in Hamburg. Three months before the end of my service, I got promoted to senior corporal, adding another two stripes to my shoulders. We began to count down the days to our departure by loudly announcing them every morning to all present in the officers' crew mess. Then, on the last day, we had the mother of all parties which left me with a massive hangover. At long last, the time had come to say goodbye to Hamburg and the Navy.

Little did I know as I boarded the overnight train from Hamburg to Freiburg that this was not only the beginning of a new chapter in my life, it was also the start of a wild and exciting ride through the world of five-star hotels which would eventually lead me from one end of the planet to the other, meeting wild and wonderful people on the way.

Chapter 5: *The Columbus Hotel*

The picturesque city of Freiburg is situated in the southernmost part of Germany close to the Swiss-German border. Wedged between Switzerland and France, the area is often referred to as the three-county-corner, a fact that is very much evident in the local cuisine. It is therefore not surprising that the region boasts the largest number of restaurants rated highly by both Michelin and Gault Millau. One of them was The Stube of the Columbus Hotel, my new employer.

The Columbus Hotel was, and still is today, the leading hotel in the city. With one hundred and twenty rooms, three restaurants and several function rooms, the hotel offered the latest in services and technology and has maintained that status today. The Stube was the hotel's signature restaurant, carrying one Michelin star and already aiming for its second one.

Michelin stars are awarded by the French restaurant guide *Michelin* and are probably the most recognized and influential gastronomic ratings in Europe. The guide awards one to three stars to a small number of restaurants of outstanding quality every year. Michelin stars are taken very seriously in the restaurant business, where the addition or loss of a star can mean a difference in turnover of millions of euros. Some three-Michelin-star restaurants are able to charge hundreds of euros for a meal on the strength of their reputation. I was joining this restaurant as demi chef de rang.

It took me while to get used to the black and white outfit again after nearly two years of wearing mostly green and navy blue. After serving in the Navy, I also had to get used to making my own decisions again since this was done for me by my petty officers for the past two years. How exciting it was to be able to choose once again what color underpants to wear or what time to go to bed at night.

My waiter's outfit at The Stube was very simple and very French, consisting of black pants, white shirt, black vest, black bow tie and a long white apron. The apron was very long, making it difficult for me to walk fast but then again, I was not supposed to do that anyway. I had a naturally faster walking pace than others did, which was made difficult by the tight apron, and so I wondered if it was meant to slow us down on purpose. This outfit was new for me; I looked like three-quarters waiter and one-quarter chef. I did not speak French, but maybe that's how the French came up with the name *chef* de rang?

The day I started, the hotel was reasonably quiet and the personnel director had plenty of time to show me around. He took me from top to bottom and finally delivered me to my new home, The Stube. The restaurant was covered in fine pinewood paneling and even the furniture was made of pinewood, upholstered with elegant pastel-colored fabrics. The table top setup was classic and simple—white tablecloth, highly polished silver tableware, wine glasses by Riedel and brilliant white napkins of simple fold sat on a beautiful silver show-plate. And next to each table stood a silver wine cooler, each with its own silver stand. It was time to meet my new colleagues.

The team of The Stube restaurant was pleasant, very experienced and highly professional, and I realized right from the start that I had a lot to learn if I wanted to reach their level of expertise. There was Thomas, for example, a young chef de rang acting as sommelier. With his skinny stature and round glasses, Thomas looked more like a computer nerd than a fine-dining waiter, but when it came to wines, he was unbeatable. He had a true passion for wines and he talked about nothing else. He could tell the grape, origin and the vintage of a wine simply by its taste. Thomas also oversaw the extensive wine cellar of the hotel, for which only he and the owner carried the key.

Located deep underground, the wine cellar, reminiscent of a dungeon, was truly magnificent. There were numerous alcoves full of dusty bottles of red wine. Wooden crates of the finest French Bordeaux and Burgundy were pilled up along the walls. In the middle of the cellar stood a high table with eight stools that was used for wine-tasting events.

We also had a female chef de rang and she was very pretty. Her name was Marion. Marion was a beauty beyond belief and I truly admired her. She was tall, slim and had beautiful long blond hair. She was a very professional chef de rang and was frequently assigned to the most demanding guests. She was also the girlfriend of the executive chef.

The oldest amongst us was Joerg. Joerg knew all there was to know about French food and wines and whenever he got the chance, he would drive over to France for a fine French dinner with wines and cognac. He had a high-strung temper that erupted on more than one occasion with his colleagues and, to my surprise, guests, too. On the other hand, he was *the* man when it came to preparing food or carvings at the guests' table. He cooked, carved and entertained guests like no other I had seen before and he always did it up to the required standards.

Leading this team was our restaurant manager, Slabov, and his assistant, Paul. We sometimes wondered how Slabov ever got the job because it was his assistant, "Tall Paul," who did all the work. Everyone called him Tall Paul for obvious reasons; with his one meter ninety, he was a giant. Paul prepared the duty roster, checked the menus and assigned the stations. His boss Slabov was from Yugoslavia and he was the type of manager who took the credit when things went well and quick to assign blame when things went wrong. I would find that out for myself very soon. Overall, it was a great team and working with them was fun and educational at the same time.

In the kitchen ruled Alfred Kraus, the chef de cuisine who had made The Stube the culinary icon of the hotel. It was he who earned The Stube the Michelin star and it was he who kept up the culinary quality and consistency with a relentless drive for attention to detail. He would not allow a single dish to leave the kitchen unless he had seen it personally. To watch him in the kitchen was like watching an artist; when he was cooking, he was completely immersed in the task at hand, totally focused and oblivious to the world around him. Quite different from the last chef I had worked with, Chef Karl. Although there was a big difference between Chef Kraus and Chef Karl, one thing they had in common was their distaste for waiters, unless, of course, they were female and blond. Despite this universal hatred of chefs for waiters, I have to say that Kraus was overall a very reasonable man and if he felt someone had an honest desire to learn, he would teach. He taught *me* a lot. His continuous spot checks on our menu knowledge alone taught me more than I had learned in six months working in the kitchen in Talasee. When I waited at the pass in the kitchen he would ask me questions about the dish I was waiting for, how it was made, what the main ingredients were and sometimes he would even ask about the history of certain dishes. For any waiter not to know the method of preparation, ingredients, variations or origin of any of his dishes was unacceptable to him.

The other reason, of course, was the fact that the wine and menu knowledge of the service staff was one point which the testers of restaurant guides always focused on. I got along well with Kraus despite his inborn distaste for waiters, which sometimes took over, resulting in me being disgruntled. Soon, I found a clever way of soft but firm retaliation and that was Marion.

Marion and I got on very well, so well, in fact, that we became close friends. So whenever Kraus had a serious go at me, I would drop some subtle hints with Marion, who would handle Kraus for me. It always worked. I should mention here that Chef Kraus did his spot checks on menu knowledge with everyone, including our restaurant manager Slabov, who, for this very reason, hardly ever ventured into the kitchen.

The most important character I have not mentioned yet was Mr. Kutsch, the owner of the hotel. Mr. Kutsch was hotelier by heart and a businessman by profession. He made a point of greeting every table personally during lunch and dinner. He did this in the most peculiar way. Mr. Kutsch wore suits wherever he went on his tour of the hotel, except in the restaurants. Before greeting his guests, he would take off his suit jacket and put on an apron. I have never figured out why he did this and neither could anyone tell me. He was not a chef, nor had he ever worked in the kitchen, but day in, day out, he would put on that apron and do his tour through the restaurants.

He also knew the menu inside out with zero tolerance for errors on our part. How he remembered even the smallest detail, such as the different side dishes and sauces for every dish on the menu, is an absolute mystery to me. Before he went into the restaurant, he would glance over the orders of the different tables, memorizing them in detail.

He had a keen eye for the smallest detail of a guest's table, such as bread crumbs, for example. This was one of the reasons why we crumbed the table several times during a meal and not only after dessert. He hated empty glasses, ashtrays, and, to him, unworthy beverages such as Coca Cola. He kept us on our toes.

Mr. Kutsch also had a very hot temper at times. His temper would only surface when things didn't go as he expected. He normally would be able to control this temper until he reached the kitchen but then he would explode. These explosions, when they occurred, were devastating. Other than that, he was a true professional. We respected him a lot and he was well respected in Freiburg.

The caliber of guests at the Columbus Hotel and The Stube in particular was very different from the ones I was used to from Talasee. In Talasee, our main clientele was tourists; not many people traveled to Talasee on business. In the Columbus Hotel, we hardly had any tourists; our key clientele consisted of local businessmen.

The guests of The Stube were mainly prominent members of the local high society, such as university professors, local politicians, and owners of various large companies. The guest profile of The Stube could roughly be divided into two types: the ones who knew their stuff about food and wines and the ones who pretended they knew. Those guests who knew their stuff were almost always quite pleasant to deal with and I am happy to say this was the majority. Guests who didn't know their stuff but pretended they knew it all were simply a pain in the butt.

Then there were the restaurant testers from reputable restaurant guides who definitely knew their stuff, and the testers from less reputable magazines who, most of the time, had little or no clue about food or wines but hoped to intimidate with their "powerful pens" in return for a free meal. Testers from publications such as the *Michelin* restaurant guide never identified themselves; it was part of our job to identify *them*. If we did not manage to identify them we would only find out once we got the official report.

Funny enough, this was one area where Slabov had a special instinct; he could literally sense them long before we realized they were there. Testers from less reputable publications, and there were surprisingly many, did everything possible to attract presumably desperately needed attention and many even told us why they were there. The moment a tester informed us of his intentions, the respect was gone and, sometimes but not always, *we* tested the tester instead.

My responsibilities during the first few weeks were not much different than those during my first weeks in Talasee; I had to do mise en place. Mise en place here and mise en place in Talasee were not quite the same. I folded napkins for all stations, prepared ice buckets and stands and prepared lunch and dinner menus. I polished cutlery and glasses and had to set up side stations.

To my relief, I did not have to prepare mustard pots, clean bottles of ketchup, oil and vinegar and so on. When I made the mistake of asking why we didn't have any such condiments, I was told, in no unclear manner, that the cooking was done by the chef in the kitchen and not the guest in the restaurant. Thomas added laughingly that there was one set of silver salt and pepper shakers on standby should a guest feel that the chef had no taste. He finished by advising me to make sure that *if* one of my guests requested salt and pepper, the chef should never find out. If that happened—he shook his head slightly—then I was dead meat.

If I hadn't any mise en place to do, then I watched Thomas, to whom I was assigned for the first few weeks. I observed that the service here *was* different.

Everything in the restaurant happened at a much slower pace and it was also much more solemn. I observed that my colleagues spoke very discreetly with guests but not with each other. There was no need for us to talk; each waiter was expected to know the status of each table in his respective station at all times. If a chef de rang, for example, wanted his demi chef de rang to get the next course for a specific table, he would simply indicate with two fingers the table number and the demi chef was expected to know what dish came next and call it up. If the chef wanted the demi chef to clear a table, he would simply give him a nod and indicate the table number with his fingers.

I was quite impressed when I witnessed all this for the first time but as with everything, after a while it too became second nature. Even when we served dishes, we were expected to know exactly who had ordered what dish. To achieve this, we used codes which were written behind each dish on the order pad, such as "L1" meaning first guest to the left. The most creative codes were the ones from Joerg, who used little drawings such as small breasts, big breasts, long legs, short legs, thick glasses or a large mustache instead of letters and numbers. We always collected his orders only to have a good laugh.

All this, of course, reduced the noise level in the restaurant considerably which, combined with the low and soothing background music, gave the restaurant a very solemn and exclusive atmosphere. Part of this atmosphere was created by the fact that the restaurant was clean and tidy even when fully booked. During the service, we kept the restaurant as clean as humanly possible. The service stations had to be empty and tidy at all times. The dining tables had to be kept clear of empty glasses and plates or other unnecessary items at all times. It came in handy that it had become second nature for me never to leave the restaurants empty-handed.

To "hang around" idle in the restaurant during quiet times was another unforgiving thing to do. We never just stood at the service station observing guests if it was quiet; this was a deadly sin in The Stube. Instead, we continuously roamed the restaurant, watching out for more brioches, wine refills or simply ashtrays to change. Everything was done as discreetly as possible, offering as little interruption as possible to the guests' dining experience.

One crucial part of the successful dining experience was the timing of service; unnecessary delays were simply not acceptable. From the moment the guest sat down we had to adhere to a predetermined time schedule for serving the bread, the menu, wine list and the dishes. The service had to flow smoothly and this is where the timing of food preparation in the kitchen played a crucial role.

The accurate call-timing of dishes was a special skill which required an intimate knowledge of the food preparation methods of the different dishes. If one dish was called too early and the guest had not finished the previous dish, the chef de rang was in trouble, the dish went into the garbage bin and the chef had to start from scratch. If, on the other hand, the dish was called too late, the guest would have had to wait unnecessarily and this was unacceptable in The Stube.

For the first two weeks I just watched and learned. I quickly identified two areas where I had to improve—wines and service timing. Whilst the timing of dishes was something I could improve simply by studying the menus and the preparation of its dishes on a daily basis, to improve my knowledge of wines took a little more than that. I thought that the best way to study was to get a book about wines; the question was: What book to buy? There was only one person who could help and that was Thomas. I wasn't sure if I should ask him; maybe he thought as demi chef de rang I should know all about wines.

After some days of contemplation, I decided to ask him anyway. Thomas's reaction was very helpful, of course; wines were his passion and he recommended I get the *Hugh Johnson Wine Atlas*. He explained that Hugh Johnson was one of the leading wine experts who rates wines from all over the world on an annual basis, publishing them in his wine buyers' guide. I bought the wine atlas the same day.

The book, divided into continents, talked about all the major vineyards of the world with emphasis on France. Having grown up in the wine making region of Baden, I wanted to see what he had to say about wines from our region. As expected, he rated the white wines highly for their unique flavor, much due to the predominant volcanic soil of the region. When I reached the section on red wines, I was shocked. Mr. Johnson had dedicated less than half a page to our red wines, saying that Germany produces a number of good red wines but they were not comparable to the heavier and tastier reds from France and the New World. *How could he say that?* I now had doubts about Hugh Johnson and his knowledge of wines.

Later that day, Thomas confirmed these views, saying to my surprise that German red wines were good but could not really compare with the French in particular. He explained in detail the why and how and promised he would let me try a really good one as soon as the opportunity arose. A few days later he called me to the service bar. On the bar counter I noticed an empty bottle and a half-empty crystal decanter.

"This is a 1978 Chateau Pichon Lalande from Pauillac in Bordeaux," he said with a big smile. He had decanted the wine earlier and the guest had only finished half of it. He poured a glass and offered it to me. "This is one of the top wines of the 1978 vintage and one of my favorites," he said.

"What, you want me to try these here and now?" I asked, slightly flustered since it was only lunchtime.

"This is a tasting, not a drinking session. Now, go on and try," he said. "But let it linger first before you swallow it."

I took the glass and sniffed the wine's bouquet. It smelled of oak. I took a sip without swallowing.

It was amazing; the wine was so smooth it felt as if it was hovering just above my tongue. I had never tasted a wine like this. There was an explosion of flavors and none of the acidity, which is typical in German red wines. It tasted wonderful. I swallowed.

"Wow, tastes really great," I said.

Thomas smiled. "Well, I hope so; this one is not cheap," he laughed and went on to explain that 1978 was not one of the best vintages for the vineyards in that area because of the poor weather in July. The harvest had been very small but produced an excellent quality.

I took another sip and he asked me to describe what I tasted. At first, I was hesitant since I didn't want to look stupid but he encouraged me to continue. How do you describe the taste of a wine? There was a light hint of herbs of some sort, I said. Thomas smiled. "Roasted herbs?" he asked and I agreed; roasted was a good word since it did not smell like freshly cut herbs. I came up with a couple of other comparisons that Thomas translated as chocolate and cedar wood.

Over the coming weeks, Thomas had me taste several other costly wines, amongst them a 1976 Chateaux Palmer and a 1970 Chateau Haut Brion Pessac from Graves. I would have never been able to afford such expensive wines and it was amazing to me how often guests left without finishing these treasures. Occasionally Thomas let me do the decanting of such wines but only on tables where he felt that no damage would be done if things went wrong.

I must have made good progress since Slabov and Tall Paul had begun to let me run entire stations during lunchtime. Although I was terribly nervous in the beginning, I started to get the hang of it and I always made a point of keeping my tables in spotless condition.

One day, we had just finished our lunch at table one when Mr. Kutsch appeared, dressed in his apron, holding a magazine in his hands.

"Good morning, gentlemen. How are you all?" he greeted in the friendliest of manners—a little too friendly for our taste.

"Good morning, Herr Kutsch," we murmured.

"I have here the *Regio* magazine from this week. In here is a report on a visit to The Stube," he said.

He opened and began reading the article. The report was overall good, commending the service as knowledgeable, the food superb and the wine recommendation by the waiter as excellent. There was only one point the tester commented on negatively and that was a slight delay in serving the main course.

To me the report sounded very good but when I looked at the faces of my colleagues, I could see that something was wrong.

"Gentlemen, I don't need to tell you that this should not happen in my restaurant." It was clear by the way he had pronounced 'my restaurant" that he was not pleased with what the tester had written, and although his voice was still relatively calm, I could sense that this was about to change. As my colleagues told me later, they knew exactly what was coming next.

"Who was in charge of table four on the fifth of this month?" he asked sternly. Slabov immediately shot up and got the roster. *What an ass kisser,* I thought.

Nobody talked; we all held our breath. Slabov returned.

"Table five on the fifth...that was Thomas' station," Slabov announced immediately. We sighed in relief; Thomas was off that day.

"I want to see him in my office first thing tomorrow," Mr. Kutsch said and with that, he left.

We looked at each other, happy not to be in Thomas' shoes.

"That was close. Poor Thomas, I don't want to be him tomorrow," Joerg whispered. We laughed.

I didn't feel like laughing; I liked Thomas and felt sorry for him. We speculated whether Slabov had not detected that tester or he had purposely not told Thomas. This was quite possible because Slabov and Thomas were not the best of friends.

"What will happen to him?" I asked innocently.

Tall Paul looked at me. "He will get a good dressing down and that's it. And don't worry, sooner or later it will be your turn," he said sarcastically. The others laughed in agreement.

The next day when I saw Thomas, he didn't look happy after meeting with Mr. Kutsch, not surprising since we had heard Kutsch screaming in his office all the way from the kitchen.

Over the coming weeks, I concentrated on studying my wine atlas. I was surprised to learn that Bordeaux is the largest wine region in the world, producing more fine wines than any other country worldwide. I learned all about the French classification system, which was better than the complicated German system. I was not surprised that the New World wine countries had no system. Australia and the USA were learning how to make good wines but for the time being they were considered mass-produced products.

One day at lunchtime, I was assigned to Joerg's station for dinner. Slabov approached me saying that a Mr. Eggers from the *Freiburg Gazette* had a booking for six at table ten. He also told me that Mr. Eggers was a food writer for that newspaper.

"We have a food tester for dinner?" I stuttered nervously, remembering what had happened a few days earlier with Thomas and the *Regio* magazine.

"Yes, Mr. Eggers has a booking for six on table ten. Joerg knows what he is like; he will look after him," Slabov said and left.

"I will let him know," I said.

Later when Joerg arrived, I briefed him immediately on the booking for Eggers from the *Gazette*. He simply smiled.

"Don't worry about him," he said. "This guy is easy, as long as we treat him as if he was a real tester."

"What if something goes wrong or the food is late?" I asked nervously.

"If anything goes wrong, he won't even realize it; that's the way he is. He talks a lot but has no clue about food or wines. Chef knows him and as long as the portions are larger and the dinner is free, he will always write good about anything. Eggers is a typical small-town writer who just needs some attention." Joerg laughed.

"So if that's the case, why do we need to take care of him?" I wanted to know.

"Well, that's his trick. The first time he goes somewhere he writes bad; the next time he comes back, he lets you know and then of course he gets the VIP treatment. Eggers will not be the last of his kind you meet, young demi chef," Joerg said mockingly. Joerg was right; throughout my career, I would meet many Eggers, people in desperate need of attention which they would not get anywhere else.

Mr. Eggers made quite an entrance when he finally arrived at seven-thirty. When he saw Joerg, he introduced him to his guests like a long-lost friend. Although I was standing right next to Joerg, Eggers hardly paid any attention to me. His body language struck me immediately as insecure with a strong craving for attention. He was a small man, measuring little more than one meter and fifty. I was always quite tall and from experience, I knew that some smaller people had a problem with that. So I decided to keep away from him as much as I could.

"Mr. Eggers, let me introduce you to our new demi chef de rang, Andre," Joerg suddenly said. I had no choice but to walk over and greet Mr. Eggers.

Standing in front of him, I had to look down and he had to look up at me. "Nice to meet you, Mr. Eggers ," I said, looking down on him and shaking his hand. He shook my hand briefly and then stepped back.

"I am Mr. Eggers and I write for the *Freiburg Gazette.* You know our paper, of course." That was a statement more than a question.

"Yes, of course, I know the *Gazette,*" I lied. I had never heard of it before.

"The *Gazette* is the leading newspaper in the region with a circulation of over fifty thousand copies daily," he said.

"That's very impressive, Mr. Eggers," I said, forcing a friendly smile.

"My food corner is one of the most popular sections in the *Gazette* and my readers are mostly gourmets. Your boss, Mr. Kutsch, knows that very well," he said with a strange smile. I was not quite sure if this man was trying to scare me or if this was the way he always talked. Thankfully, Joerg stepped in just in time.

"Don't worry, Mr. Eggers, I have already briefed Andre on how important you are for us, haven't I, Andre?" He winked at me. This conversation was nothing less than a farce.

"Yes, Mr. Eggers, we are happy to have you with us tonight." I couldn't think of anything else to say.

"Good. If you two do a good job tonight, I will certainly mention you in my review." Eggers said the last sentence so loudly that every one of his guests must have heard it. He had done this most probably on purpose. I had only known him for less than five minutes and all respect for the man was gone.

Eggers and his guests sat down and Joerg made some recommendations whilst I opened the napkins for Mr. Eggers and his guests.

"May I recommend a wine for you or would you like to choose one yourself, Mr. Eggers?" Joerg asked.

"I want you to recommend a wine for me, Joerg, but make sure it's a good one. You know I will have to write about it in my review." I had to control myself not to roll my eyes; this man was quite something.

I could not believe what came next—Joerg recommended a vin de pays from Bordeaux. I shuddered. *Not even a man like Eggers could possibly go for that,* I thought. The wine did not even have a vintage! Before Joerg had the chance to finish his description of the wine, Eggers had accepted it. It was amazing. Joerg gave me another wink when he left the table and I had to smile.

Whilst Joerg got the wine, I prepared bread and butter. Eggers didn't even look at the label when Joerg presented the wine and just when I thought that things couldn't get any sillier, Eggers asked for the wine to be decanted.

"Of course, Mr. Eggers, and may I suggest letting the wine breathe for a while before I serve?"

"Of course, Joerg. You know that any good Bordeaux has to breathe; that is very important."

I wanted to shake my head. I was just about to pass the menus when Eggers waved me towards him.

"I want Chef Kraus to prepare some of his special dishes for us," he said.

Before I could answer, Joerg stepped in.

"The chef will be delighted, Mr. Eggers," he said and pulled me away. We went to the kitchen, where Chef Kraus was already waiting.

"What does he want?" he asked Joerg.

"One of your *special* menus," Joerg answered.

"Excellent. You know what to do," he said and went back into the kitchen.

Joerg smiled and we went back to the restaurant. On the way we met Mr. Kutsch, who wanted to know how the restaurant was doing. Joerg briefed him on the business and then told him that Eggers was here.

"Not him again," Kutsch said, rolling his eyes. "Let's get this over with quickly. Give me five minutes; you know what to do."

I didn't quite understand what that meant but Joerg pulled me along and we went back to the restaurant. Eggers dominated the conversation at the table and it was clear from the faces of his guests that they enjoyed it as little as we did. When Kutsch came to the table Eggers shot up and introduced him to his guests and, judging by the loud tone of his voice, to the rest of the restaurant. It was simply embarrassing.

Eggers talked with one hand resting on the shoulder of Mr. Kutsch, who seemed to have difficulty maintaining his smile. Suddenly Joerg approached Mr. Kutsch, whispering something in his ear. Now I understood that's what Kutsch meant when he said to Joerg, "you know what to do."

"Mr. Eggers, I am afraid I have to attend to some urgent business. It is good to see you and I hope you have a pleasant evening." And with that, he left. Even Mr. Kutsch could not handle this annoying man and that meant something.

Joerg proceeded to explain the menu, which the chef would prepare for them. The menu Joerg explained sounded vaguely familiar but I couldn't quite figure out from where until it suddenly struck me that this was the menu we had served for lunch! Were they planning to serve a leftover menu from lunch? As I found out, that was the plan indeed.

Throughout the dinner, Mr. Eggers hardly paid any attention to the service and much less to the food. He was busy entertaining his guests with seemingly endless stories. I don't know exactly what he talked about but the fact that his stories weren't that entertaining was plainly visible on his guests' faces. The women had forced smiles on their faces whilst the men didn't smile at all. It was simply ridiculous. This Mr. Eggers obviously loved the tone of his own voice rambling on and on.

When we finally cleared dessert, Eggers complimented the chef on his excellent choice of dishes. He went into a frustratingly long review of the lunch menu, describing individual dishes with silly words like "fireworks of colors" or "revolution of flavors." Joerg and I were forced to stand at his table for over twenty minutes listening to his silly review. It must have been plainly visible that I was utterly bored by this since one of the women knowingly winked at me. I had to smile. It was clear that no one took him too seriously.

It was a mystery to me how people like Eggers were considered qualified to conduct restaurant reviews without any knowledge of the subject whatsoever. I can only guess that the people who chose them to do so were even less qualified.

Eggers finally asked for the bill and with it, relieved us from our misery. When Joerg informed him that the dinner was on the house, he faked mock surprise and thanked us profusely. Mr. Eggers and his guests left shortly before midnight, needless to say, without leaving any tip.

The printed review, published several days later, was nothing less than embarrassing. It clearly showed that Eggers had not taken any notes during the meal, describing dishes which we hadn't even served, and the vine de pays had become a 1976 Chateau Mouton Rothschild. We both had achieved our objective—for him a complimentary dinner and for us a good restaurant review. As usual for our boss Mr. Kutsch, he flatly refused to read this report.

I continued to polish my wine knowledge and as the days went by I became more and more proficient in wine-related matters. I frequently joined Thomas on his excursions to the Alsace where we had superb meals accompanied by excellent French wines. We sometimes spent the weekends there staying in one of the many vineyards. Despite my growing love for French red wines, I couldn't quite acquire a taste for their whites. One day Thomas took me to the Schwarzer Adler, a vineyard and restaurant in Oberbergen in the Kaiserstuhl area. Here, the Keller family ran a Michelin-star-rated restaurant whilst producing some of Germany's top white wines. I fell in love with their excellent Weissburgunder wines. We toured the cellars of the estate and tried many of their top vintages.

But the learning didn't stop with wines. On the food side I had made it a habit of meeting with Chef Kraus before every meal period to go through the menu of the day with him. I always carried a small notepad where I made notes of the methods of preparation of the dishes, ingredients and other details that Kraus explained to me. Over time I was able to predict styles of preparation simply by Kraus's menu descriptions, which pleased him immensely.

The knowledge I accumulated about food and wines also made me more confident in front of customers. More often than not, I would push my guests to order certain dishes or wines because I liked them personally and more often than not, they would follow my recommendations and liked them, too.

One day Mr. Kutsch summoned me to his office. I got the news from Slabov but he refused to tell me why I had to see the boss. I was petrified, half expecting a dressing down for a messed-up restaurant review. I checked with Joerg and Thomas but neither of them was aware of any recent publications about our restaurant. So I went.

Mr. Kutsch's office was surprisingly small considering his position. He asked me to take a seat in front of his relatively simple desk. The office itself was quite plain without anything on the walls. The only noteworthy feature was a large cabinet that was filled with cookbooks and gourmet magazines, presumably with articles about the hotel and The Stube. Mr. Kutsch was shifting through some papers on his desk, glancing through his half-glasses, which sat on the very edge of his nose. I nervously shifted in my seat waiting for him to say something. Then he looked up.

"Andre, how long have you been here now?" he asked. The way he had asked the question made me feel as if I had done something wrong. As matter of fact, it seemed to me as if he was going to talk with me about my performance.

"Ahm, a little over eight months," I replied.

"Eight months, eh?" he mumbled and leaned back in his chair.

"Yes, Mr. Kutsch."

"Slabov and Paul tell me you have made good progress over the past months, is that true?" This came as an unexpected surprise.

"Ahm, oh, I think so," I answered suspiciously.

"You think so, eh?"

"Ahm, yes, Mr. Kutsch."

"Well, I think so, too, and I also think it's time to promote you to chef de rang," he said and smiled.

I was taken aback. I had prepared for a dressing down and instead I got a promotion? I didn't know what to say.

"Really?" I replied shyly.

"Yes, really, Andre. As of the first, you are promoted to chef de rang. Congratulations." With that, he stood up and shook my hand. I was speechless.

"The personnel department will sort out your salary increase and your new contract," he said.

"Thank you, Mr. Kutsch."

"Don't thank me; you are doing a good job and we appreciate that." And with that, I was dismissed.

Back in the restaurant everyone knew already and congratulated me on my promotion. I was overjoyed. Finally I was a full-blown chef de rang in one of Germany's Michelin-star restaurants. I was proud.

After work I called my parents and then Tatiana to give them the good news. Of course they were as happy as I was. Later that evening we went out to celebrate. Thomas and Joerg had organized a bottle of Dom Perignon—at the time, the most expensive champagne I had ever tasted. The celebration lasted until the early morning hours, resulting in a massive hangover the next day.

A few days later Tatiana came to visit me from Talasee and we went for dinner in a small but reputable Italian restaurant near Freiburg's Cathedral. I was still in the clouds about my promotion, telling Tatiana all about my new responsibilities. Tatiana smiled and listened patiently.

During dinner she suddenly asked me what I would do next. I was taken aback; I had only just been promoted and she asked me what I would do next? Our conversation turned into a small argument with me insisting that she was too pushy. To make her point, Tatiana asked me how long it would take for my next promotion. I had no idea, of course;

maybe headwaiter or assistant restaurant manager in a few years time. It didn't really matter to me since I had only just been promoted.

Tatiana argued that my next promotion in The Stube was probably years away because in such a small hotel people didn't move very often. I was getting annoyed; I just had been promoted and didn't intend to contemplate my next move. I thought she would be proud; instead, she wanted to push me further. Ambition had not yet seeped into my blood and therefore I was angry with her.

We finished dinner and went for a walk though the city. It was a mild and pleasant night. In order to lay the subject of my future to a rest, I promised her to think about my next career move carefully. I also told her of my upcoming leave and we agreed to travel to Hamburg, where I wanted to show her the academy from where I had written her so many letters. We went back to my place where Tatiana stopped me talking about wines by kissing me suddenly and passionately. My anger was gone.

Tatiana left early the next morning, driving back to Talasee. The whole day I kept on thinking of what Tatiana had said. Maybe she was right, maybe I *should* be thinking of my next move. It was pretty clear to me that Slabov, Tall Paul and all the others were career waiters and quite happy with their positions and what they had achieved. Paul had been Slabov's assistant for over four years and Thomas and Joerg also had been chef de rang for several years already. Would I really be wasting my time waiting for the next opportunity for another promotion?

Tatiana and I traveled to Hamburg in November. The city was cold and overcast. We visited the academy, where I was allowed to show Tatiana the compound. Whilst I was proud showing her around the famous officers academy, Tatiana was quite visibly bored to bits. In view of this, I cut the tour short and after saying farewell to my former commander, we went to see the Hamburg harbor. I had been to the harbor before but somehow this time was different. The vast number of ships from all over the world left me with an itchy feeling, a feeling to discover the world.

We took a harbor cruise where a man explained the origins of the different ships. I was excited like a little boy with a brand-new toy seeing all these ships. I explained to Tatiana the different types— container ships, RORO, freighters and even some Navy vessels. That

Tatiana had no interest in ships and much less the different types was plainly visible on her facial expressions. I tried to make it sound more interesting by telling her that there were freighters from Africa, South America and ships from as far away as Hong Kong. I looked at the ships, wondering what stories they could tell. Tatiana had enough of my childlike excitement, saying that at the end of the day, ships were ships—some bigger, some smaller. And she reminded me that ships couldn't talk.

One of the ships we saw was a beautiful white cruise liner, the *Maxim Gorky*. It was huge but I didn't dare to voice my excitement to Tatiana. I looked at the ship and remembered Johnny and Barrollo when they talked about working on one of these. Tatiana must have read my mind. What came next was a dialogue sparked by her impatience with my lack of ambition and my pride, which I felt had been unjustly hurt.

"Why don't you apply on one of those?" she said, pointing at the cruise ship.

I laughed sarcastically. "They would never take me," I said.

"Why not?" Tatiana asked.

"Well, you probably need a lot of experience and..."

"And what?" she wanted to know.

"Tatiana, look, I don't know, but I don't think they would take me."

"You are a chef de rang in one of Germany's leading restaurants. What else could they possibly ask for?" she argued.

"I am sure you have to speak English, for example, and I don't."

"You know the basics."

"I don't think the basics are enough," I said.

"There are German cruise liners."

"Tatiana, come on, they wouldn't take me."

"That's what you said about the Columbus Hotel."

"I was lucky."

"No, you were not lucky. You had the right background and they invited you for an interview and accepted you."

"Yes, but this is different."

"How is it different?"

"Well, it is different."

"Andre, it is not different at all and if you don't try, you will never know."

"What is the point in trying if I know the outcome already?"

"Oh, you know the outcome?" she asked mockingly.

"Yes, I know the outcome."

"And what is the outcome?" she wanted to know.

"They will never take me."

"Oh, I see. Well, this is fine, then. At least we know now that they won't take you." And with that, she changed the subject.

I hadn't expected her to give up that easily but at least the subject was off the table. Unfortunately it wasn't off my mind. For the rest of the day I kept on wondering if Tatiana might have been right. *Maybe I should try and apply; the worst thing that could happen was that they reject me,* I thought. After torturing myself for the rest of the day, I overcame my pride and in the evening over dinner, I brought the subject up again.

"Do you think I should try and apply?" I felt so silly.

"Yes, I think so," she said without looking at me. I couldn't see her face but she obviously enjoyed this.

"From where do I get the addresses of the shipping companies?"

"We can visit to a travel agent tomorrow and get some brochures. I am sure they have the addresses in there," she said, pretending to be busy with something else. She knew already that she had won and I knew that I had behaved like an idiot.

The next day we went to several travel agents collecting several cruise line brochures. We spent another two days in Hamburg and then took the overnight train back to Freiburg. I selected two cruise lines, Hapag Lloyd and Deilmann, prepared my applications and mailed them to their respective personnel managers. After that, the only thing I could do was to wait and see. The next day I was back in the Columbus Hotel.

Having been promoted to chef de rang, I was now entitled to a demi chef or trainee to assist me. The entitlement came in form of Viola. Viola was from an influential Freiburg family. She had just completed hotel school and, despite her small size, she was devastatingly pretty and very sexy. We got on well from the start. I liked Viola because she worked hard, had an excellent sense of humor and she was very smart. It didn't take us long to become a good team—in more than one way, as it turned out. Our teamwork was first put to a test on a quiet Saturday. That day we had only one table occupied and we knew the four gentlemen well; they were businessmen from a nearby office. They had ordered four business-lunch menus and we had just served the main course when Slabov seated a single gentleman on table five. Slabov told me the guest's name was Kaiser and asked me to look after him. As if I wouldn't.

We went through the usual routine of me approaching the guest with the menus whilst Viola prepared bread and butter. I introduced myself and offered some recommendations but the gentlemen declined, saying that he wanted to look through the menu first. I left him with the wine list and went to check on my other table. The four gentlemen had nearly finished their main course and the second bottle of wine. Obviously they did not have to get back to work since they ordered a third bottle of wine. I got the wine and offered the host a taste but he politely declined, not because he trusted me but more likely because their glasses were empty. I opened the bottle, refilled all glasses and cleared the main-course plates. In the meantime, Viola had served bread and butter and I returned to my single guest to see if I could help. I walked up to his table, smiling.

"Hello, Mr. Kaiser, have you found something or would you like me to make a recommendation?" I asked. He looked up at me, smiling.

"Well, it's not easy; this is a fantastic menu," he said flatteringly.

"How about our set business-lunch menu?" I asked.

Mr. Kaiser frowned. "Hmm, no thanks. I want to be a bit more adventurous. Maybe the scallops?"

"Good choice," I said. "The grilled scallops are excellent. They were flown in from Hamburg this morning," I said.

"Hmm, okay. I try the scallops. What about the main course? I fancy something with beef."

"Oh, then I suggest the Tournedos Rossini with fresh goose liver, an excellent dish." I said that only because I really liked that dish.

Mr. Kaiser scratched his chin and flipped one page. "What about the Alsace beef stew?" he asked.

"Mr. Kaiser, if you like beef, I really recommend the tournedos with fresh goose liver. You will not be disappointed," I said. Alsace beef stew was packed with onions and I couldn't stand that dish.

"Oh well, you have convinced me. I take the tournedos then."

There you go, I thought. "You will not be disappointed," I said, happy that he had accepted my choice.

"Would you like a glass of wine with your lunch?" I asked.

"What do you recommend?"

"We have a 1982 Chablis Grand Cru by the glass. Excellent wine goes very well with your scallops."

"Nineteen eighty-two, I see. Which one?" he wanted to know.

"This one is from Drouhin," I answered.

"Drouhin, I see, not bad. And you really recommend the 1982 vintage?"

I was a little thrown off by his question. As far as I knew, there was nothing wrong with this vintage but the way he had asked, I wasn't so sure anymore.

"Do you have any good Muscadet?"

"We have a nice Muscadet de Sevre-et-Maine but I would still recommend the Chablis. It's a notch up from the Muscadet."

"Fine, you have convinced me. How about a nice red for my beef?" he asked.

"For your tournedos, I highly recommend our 1978 Gevrey-Chambertin from Faiveley, much better suited than Bordeaux for lunch,"

"Good choice, I have been to the Faiveley estate and love their wines. Gevrey-Chambertin, it is," he said with a big smile. *He has been to Faiveley—interesting.*

On the way to the kitchen, Slabov stopped me. "Table five, what did he order?" he wanted to know.

I looked at Slabov, puzzled; the way he asked the question had taken me by surprise. I handed him the order pad. He read and frowned.

"Could be a tester," he mumbled. "Keep an eye on him." He handed back the notepad.

I turned to look at table five.

"Don't look at him," Slabov urged.

I spun around. "Really, do you think so?" I said.

"I'm not sure, but let's keep an eye on him," he said, slightly annoyed, and walked off. *What's wrong with him?* I thought as Slabov left.

I was getting a bit nervous. Mr. Kaiser, a tester? He had asked quite a lot of questions but this happened a lot in The Stube. We had many single diners who were true connoisseurs enjoying fine foods and wines. I couldn't really see anything different with this guest but still mentioned Slabov's concerns to Chef Kraus.

"Really?" Kraus said as I handed him the order. Kraus knew that whatever his misgivings for Slabov were, he did have a sense for testers so better to be safe than sorry. He studied the dishes and asked me if Kaiser had ordered any wines. I told him about the Chablis and the Gevrey-Chambertin.

"Interesting," Kraus said. "Okay, go and serve him the wine. I get going on the scallops." He announced the order to his crew and was immediately rewarded with acknowledgments from his chefs. "I will finish this one myself," he added.

"Okay, Chef," I said and went to the service bar. To my delight, Michelle, one of the new girls, manned the bar. I had only seen her a few times and had not had the chance of talking with her. I had wanted to because she was simply gorgeous. Michelle was tall, slim and had a somewhat cheeky personality. She was also quite sexy with her neatly trimmed blonde hair and golden brown suntan. Michelle was also Viola's best friend.

"Hi there," she said as I approached the counter. "You must be Andre," she said before I could reply.

"Ah, yes that's me. How do you know?" I was surprised that she actually knew my name.

"Viola had given me a hint," she answered with a devastatingly cute smile.

"Oh, I see."

"What can I do for you?"

"Oh, ahm, one glass of Chablis Premier Cru."

"One glass of Chablis Premier Cru, no problem."

She turned around to take the bottle out of the refrigerator. Michelle wore the classic black skirt and white blouse of a female bartender. As she bent down to reach into the refrigerator, I couldn't help but notice her nicely shaped behind and the transparent white blouse clearly exposing the black bra she wore underneath. She remained in this position much longer than it was necessary and I wondered if that was meant for me. *Not bad,* I thought.

"Here you go," she said and placed the bottle and one white wine glass on the counter. I took the glass, as it was my habit, and held it into the light to check for water stains. It was spotless.

"Oh, you don't trust me?" she said mockingly.

"Oh, it's not that; it's just a habit. The glass is perfect," I said, slightly embarrassed.

"Hey, don't worry, I am just joking," she laughed. I packed the bottle and glass on a silver tray.

"It was nice to meet you, Michelle," I said.

"Same here, Andre. See you later" she smiled as I left. She was nice indeed.

"Nineteen eighty-two Chablis Premier Cru," I announced, presenting Mr. Kaiser the bottle.

He studied the label for nearly a minute and then nodded approvingly. "Very good, thank you."

I poured a little for him to taste. He held the glass in the light.

"When was this bottle opened?" he suddenly asked. *Shit,* I didn't know.

"Oh, this bottle? Ah, today, Mr. Kaiser," I lied.

"Today, eh?"

"Yes, today."

Kaiser held the glass to his nose, testing the bouquet, and then took a sip. Could he tell if the bottle had been open longer? I hoped not. He put the glass back on the table.

"That's fine. Go ahead, please," he said politely. I filled the glass slowly.

"Thank you," he said.

"You are welcome," I answered. At that moment I saw the small notepad and pen next to Kaiser's bread and butter plate. I was startled—a notepad! *This must be a tester.*

"It's a rather quiet lunch today," he said casually. My eyes flipped from the notepad to Mr. Kaiser.

"Quiet, yes. Saturdays are normally not so busy," I stammered.

"How about dinner?" he wanted to know.

"For dinner we are nearly full. Saturdays are normally busy for dinner," I said, forcing a smile. I had to tell Kraus that this was definitely a tester. "Let me see how the chef is doing with your scallops," I said. He nodded and I headed to the kitchen.

I found Viola on the service bar chatting with Michelle. "Viola" I said, "you need to keep an eye on table five. He might be a tester."

"Will do, Andre," the two girls giggled as I left for the kitchen. *They are both quite cute,* I thought, which nearly caused me to bang my head against the kitchen doors.

In the kitchen, I told Kraus about the notepad and my conversation with Kaiser. He confirmed that Kaiser had all the signs of a tester.

162

"Come back in five minutes and the scallops will be ready."

"Yes, chef."

I went back to the restaurant. Viola had started to clear the main-course plates from the only other occupied table in our station. I joined her at the table.

"Gentlemen, did you enjoy your lunch?" I asked.

"Very good. Tell the chef it was excellent," the host answered.

"Thank you. I will let him know. Would you like to take your dessert now or later?" I asked.

"We take dessert and coffee now because we have plans for the afternoon," the host answered. *I am sure, probably playing golf or something like that,* I thought. We cleared the table and whilst Viola got the dessert cutlery, I went to the kitchen to order the desserts and get the coffee.

At the pass in the kitchen, Chef Kraus was in the process of finishing my scallops. He carefully poured the sauce over a spoon in a zigzag pattern over the grilled scallops. He topped it off with some dill.

"Off you go," he said.

I placed a silver cloche on the plate and dashed off.

"Grilled scallops with a light champagne sabayon," I said as I lifted the silver cloche off the plate. I felt as if Kaiser watched my every move and I am sure he was.

"Nice presentation."

"Thank you, Mr. Kaiser, and enjoy your meal."

"Thank you."

He still was looking at the plate, turning it slightly with his hand. *He is studying the presentation,* I thought. *This must be a tester.*

In the meantime, Viola had served coffee and desserts for our four businessmen.

"They are asking for the bill."

"I will prepare the bill. You keep an eye on table five."

"Is he a tester?" she asked curiously.

"I think so. Let's make sure he is happy."

"Don't worry, I look after him," she giggled.

I went to get the bill. I was just checking the bill at the cash till when suddenly Michelle appeared next to me. She leaned casually against the cash till and crossed her arm and with a smile, she said, "So, how long have you been here, Andre?"

"Me? Oh, I have been here about eight months," I said, a little embarrassed. This was the first time that I stood next to her and I realized that she was taller than I had thought. When she smiled, her whole face lit up.

"Not bad," she said. "You like it here?"

"Yes, I do. How about you?" I asked.

"Too early to tell. I like the hotel and the team," she winked at me, which threw me completely off my tracks.

"Oh, I see."

"Hey, boss, what are you doing? Your guests are waiting for the bill," Viola shouted as she burst through the restaurant doors. I spun around.

"I have it here. Sorry," I answered and dashed off. The girls were giggling.

My four guests paid their bill and left. Mr. Kaiser had nearly finished his scallops when I approached his table.

"How are the scallops?" I asked. Kaiser looked up.

"Not bad," he mused. "Not bad at all."

Kaiser had eaten faster than I thought and it was time for me to get to the kitchen and fire the main course.

"Tournedos can!" Chef Kraus shouted whilst I prepared my silver tray. While I waited, Kraus asked me hundreds of questions.

"Did he leave anything on the plate? Did he ask for salt and pepper? Did he comment on the sauce?" and so on.

Five minutes later, I served Mr. Kaiser his tournedos and the Gevrey-Chambertin. Viola was still at his table when I approached. They both were laughing.

"You have quite an assistant here," he said mockingly.

"Yes, she is quite something," I said, slightly disturbed by the casual atmosphere between them as I served him the tournedos.

"Enjoy you meal," Viola said as she left the table, still giggling. I wondered what all that had been about.

He studied the main course just as he had done with the scallops, turning the plate from left to right, seemingly evaluating the dish in front of him.

Everything went well, with Viola entertaining him between the main course and dessert. She served him coffee and I served him the bill. Kaiser was pleased.

"That was an excellent lunch. Please tell the chef that everything was perfect and I hope you look after your demi chef de rang because she has a lot of potential." *Yep, I definitely know that, Mr. Kaiser,* I said to myself.

Viola and I saw him to the main entrance and once he had left I shook Viola's hand.

"I have no idea what you two were giggling about but I think overall it went very well. Thanks."

She looked up at me in surprise. "Well, well, a compliment. That's nice, thank you, boss." She grabbed my arm and dragged me through the empty restaurant. "I think we are a good team," she said and giggled.

"Yes, we are," I answered and laughed.

Deep down, I was still thinking about Kaiser and anxious to read his report but that would not happen so soon.

Throughout the meal, Slabov had kept away from the table and from Viola and me. This was typical for the coward. Only when Kaiser had left did Slabov crawl out from hiding, asking all sorts of questions. I patiently recounted Kaiser's lunch and his comments on the food, wine and service. Slabov seemed happy. I had no doubt that if the report turned out bad, he would deny having anything to do with it and if it was good, he would try to take all the credit. I didn't really care; I had done the best I could without his help.

That evening the girls invited Thomas and me out and, since we had no other important engagements, we accepted. We met in a nearby cocktail bar where I ordered a Captain Fantastic. I don't remember the ingredients of that cocktail at all but I do remember the name and above all, I do remember what happened after we left the bar.

After about six Captain Fantastics each, Thomas and I were ready to take off into space but gravity was pulling us down; in other words, we were drunk. Seeing us in this sorry state, Michelle must have felt sorry for us since she offered to take us to her place, which happened to be not far from the cocktail bar.

We left the bar and whilst Thomas and I fought an ongoing battle with gravity, the two girls giggled all the way to Michelle's apartment. I can't recall how I got to Michelle's apartment nor do I remember what we did there, but I do remember that I woke in the early hours of the next morning with Viola to my left and Michelle to my right. That was quite a surprise. I tried to see if Thomas was somewhere but he was gone.

What the hell had happened? Did I do it with two girls? This was incredible—I wake up with two girls in bed and I don't remember a bloody thing! It was still early in the morning and if I left now, I would still get a few hours of uninterrupted sleep. I got out of bed but not before taking a good look at the two stark-naked sleeping beauties. *What a beautiful sight,* I thought, and was quite understandably extremely excited. Something like this would never happen in my hometown; I began to enjoy living in a big city like Freiburg.

When I got up at ten I was still excited. Later that day, when I met the girls, they behaved as if nothing had happened; there was no sign of regret or embarrassment. They joked and giggled as usual. The only one who smiled sarcastically every time he saw me was Thomas. He never told me the full story of what happened that night but it couldn't have been much since I simply hadn't been in a state to do anything. I believe they had left me there because I was simply unable to move. I don't think, however, that Thomas ever realized that after he had left, the two girls had taken their clothes off and shared a bed with me. What a beautiful night—if only I had been sober.

I *would* eventually get lucky with both Michelle *and* Viola but not at the same time. It was about that time when something must have happened to me; either the damn puberty was finally finished or I looked more mature. I don't know what it was but it seemed that women had become more attracted to me. Working in a hotel, the opportunities and choices are endless; there are female room attendants, waitresses, female bartenders, secretaries, sales girls and then there are, of course, female diners. Although I went out with several female employees of the hotel, I was still not attractive enough for our female guests—unless they were married and desperate.

Besides female colleagues and guests, my main focus was still my job. To train and coach Viola was a good experience since she kept on asking question after question, many of which I couldn't answer. That was good for me because I learned, too. The Hugh Johnson wine atlas saved me more than once from embarrassment. As time went by, Slabov's confidence in me grew steadily and eventually I had to cover Joerg's station during his holiday.

Just as Hendrick looked after special guests in the Black Forest Grand Hotel, Joerg looked after The Stube's most demanding guests but "demanding" in Talasee and "demanding" in The Stube are not the same. As already mentioned before, our guests in The Stube were connoisseurs and as such it was important for the wait staff to be knowledgeable about food and wines in particular. It was a given that the waiter had to have a thorough knowledge of the method of preparation of each dish on the a la carte menu. The knowledge of the authenticity and origin of the ingredients the chef used was another basic requirement for each waiter. It was inexcusable if a waiter had to ask a guest to "wait a moment" because he was not able to answer a question.

The same, if not higher, standard applied to the wines. Due to the close proximity to France, many of our guests were absolute wine connoisseurs and they knew a thing or two about wines. Let's take the service of old red wines, for example; whilst I had opened and decanted many wines during my training, I had never served wines which were made long before I was actually born. In the Stube we served them on a daily basis. I had also never served wines costing as much as my monthly salary. To serve and decant such wines can be nerve-racking. Many things can go wrong: the cork breaks, the bottle slips, sediments are stirred up or sediments enter the decanter during the decanting process. Looking at the caliber of guests I had in my station day in and day out, it seemed to me that Slabov considered me as having mastered most of these tasks.

I also spent a considerable amount of time in the kitchen, where I watched the chef do his magic. The way he transformed simple food items such as sweet bread into culinary masterpieces was truly astonishing. He patiently explained the intricacies of his very own style in making terrines as well as giving me some insight into the preparation of his famous sauces. I did my best to pay the same amount of attention to detail in serving the dish as Kraus had given to the preparation of it.

I became fanatical with details. I insisted on having the tables in stations neat and tidy at all times. I did not like empty glasses, soiled plates or bread crumbs on the table. Aesthetics were important to me when serving dishes. Just as the chef had been pedantic with details during the preparation, so was I pedantic with the service of his masterpieces. If I served dishes from the gueridon onto plates, I made sure that none of the food items mixed with each other. I avoided having food items of the same color next to each other or vegetables mixing with the sauce of the meat. I always reconstructed the meat and garnish just as the chef had placed it on the platter. I always tried to make the plate and the dish look like the piece of art Chef Kraus had it intended to be. When serving the dish I flatly refused to do so from the left but always from the right. Unfortunately, due to the structure of The Stube, the table layout of the restaurant made it sometimes difficult to do so but I did it anyway, which many times left me in awkward poses trying to reach around a guest's right side.

The glasses of my guests were never empty and when they were, then it was because guests had finished their wines and I cleared the glasses immediately. Under no circumstances would I allow Slabov or even worse, Mr. Kutsch, to tell me to refill or to clear. In general I tried to avoid drawing attention to my station at all costs when Mr. Kutsch was around.

The reason for this was simple. If Mr. Kutsch observed anything he considered wrong then his temper would take control and not allow him to reason with anyone. He would immediately explode and once that happened, there was nothing anyone could do other than take it like a man and try to explain or apologize later. Mr. Kutsch did not like it when guests tried taking dishes apart, for example, ordering the trout with the potatoes from the chicken and the vegetables from another dish. As far as he was concerned, it was the responsibility of the chef de rang in charge of the station to educate the guest of the fact that the combination of main dish and side dishes cannot be changed, as it would upset Chef Kraus' intended balance of flavors.

Mr. Kutsch also had the habit of assisting us chef de rangs in serving the food if he saw us working on a gueridon alone. He would stop at the table, pick up a set of service cutlery and serve the side dishes, or if a piece of Chateaubriand had to be cut, he would take the knife and cut the meat.

My first encounter on a table with him was the—for me, unforgettable—Barberie-duck incident. It happened one day during dinner that one of my guests on table seven had ordered the chef's recommendation, which was Barberie duck with pommes gratin and red French cabbage. Unfortunately for me, the guest had asked for the very worst of possible side dish—spaghetti. I can honestly say that I tried my best to persuade the guest to try chef's pommes gratin but the guest insisted on having spaghetti.

I was standing at the gueridon and had just placed the Barberie duck on the dinner plate when Mr. Kutsch appeared next to me. He greeted the guests politely and picked up the service cutlery.

"What do we have here?" he whispered to me as he picked up some of the red cabbage.

"The Barberie duck," I answered.

"The Barberie duck, I see," he said with a totally artificial smile.

I could not see his face since I was still busy completing the garnish, but I could tell from the tone of his voice that he was not impressed to see a bowl of spaghetti on the gueridon.

"What are the side dishes for Barberie duck?" he asked with grinding teeth. I knew why he asked that question and wanted to explain to him that the guest had insisted to change to spaghetti.

"Mr. Kutsch, the guest wanted spaghetti instead of…" Mr. Kutsch had finished the cabbage and cut me off before I could finish the sentence.

"What are the side dishes for Barberie duck?" he asked again, this time more impatiently.

"Pommes Gratin, Mr. Kutsch," I mumbled.

"I see. And where are the pommes gratin?" he wanted to know.

"The guest wanted…" Again, he cut me off.

"See me in the back," he said. He looked at the guests, wished them an enjoyable meal and left. I served the duck with spaghetti.

"Enjoy your meal," I said nervously and removed the gueridon.

I went to the back where Mr. Kutsch was pacing up and down in front of the service bar. He looked at me as I entered through the restaurant doors. He stopped right in front of me and with his eyes half closed.

"Andre, tell me what are the side dishes for Barberie duck?" he asked me with a very low voice. He was tapping his right foot impatiently on the floor.

"Cabbage and pommes gratin, Mr. Kutsch."

"Pommes gratin, I see. If that is the case, why on earth did you serve a French Barberie duck with spaghetti?" The word spaghetti sounded as if he wanted to spit on the floor.

"Mr. Kutsch, the guest insisted to change from pommes gratin to spaghetti."

"The guest insisted, did you say the guest insisted?" he growled.

"I tried to persuade him…"

"If a guest asks for a hamburger, would you serve him a hamburger?" he growled, but this time much louder. His face was distorted with anger and I could see that he was slowly getting into a rage.

"No, Mr. Kutsch…"

"Are we running a fine-dining restaurant or a bloody Italian fast-food joint?" he shouted.

I looked to the floor.

"If a guest in the future asks for French fries, are we just going to say yes and serve French fries? Look at me when I am talking to you!" He wasn't talking now; he was screaming. From the corner of my eye, I could see my fellow colleagues trying to squeeze past Mr. Kutsch, who was blocking the way, and trying to get out of the firing line as quickly as possible.

"I have never seen Barberie duck served with spaghetti. Why don't you go out there and offer them a bottle of ketchup, eh?"

I observed two large veins popping up on his forehead, which was not a good sign. Mr. Kutsch's face was red as his voice got steadily louder. He now pointed his finger at me.

"If you serve spaghetti with a Barberie duck ever again in my restaurant I am going to throw you into banqueting and you can spend the rest of your days as a bloody banquet waiter, do you understand?" he screamed.

"Yes, Mr. Kutsch" I stammered. At this moment, Slabov appeared.

"I am sorry, Mr. Kutsch, Mrs. Sheridon would like to see you on table eight," he whispered. Kutsch looked at Slabov angrily.

"Slabov, haven't you eyes in your head? Don't you know what is going on in your restaurant?"

Slabov just stood there with a beaten look on his face.

"Spaghetti in The Stube, this is simply unbelievable," Kutsch growled and walked off. I just stood there in shock.

Slabov walked past me shaking his head. I felt like a schoolboy who had been severely beaten up. This was bad, very bad. For the rest of the evening I couldn't stop thinking about the spaghetti incident. Mr. Kutsch was very upset with me, that was obvious, but would he really transfer me to banqueting? This was bad indeed. Why had I accepted those bloody orders of spaghetti? I knew I shouldn't have. Mr. Kutsch hadn't even allowed me to explain or at least to apologize. I had to apologize to him before I left for the day. Otherwise I wouldn't be able to sleep and the feeling of guilt would eventually eat me up.

Thomas and Joerg didn't really help when they teased me. "Barberie duck with spaghetti, that's a first," they laughed. *Shit,* I had to apologize to Mr. Kutsch. The only ones who seemed to feel at least a bit sorry were the girls.

"Don't worry, that's Mr. Kutsch for you. That's the way he is. He will calm down." It didn't make me feel better because I knew I should have never accepted the order of spaghetti in the first place. I had to find Mr. Kutsch and apologize.

Much later when most guests had left, I asked at the reception for Mr. Kutsch. The girls told me that he was in the ballroom. I thanked them and went up the large carpeted staircase leading to the ballroom. On top of the stairs, I saw Kutsch walking towards me.

"Mr. Kutsch, can I talk with you for a moment?" I asked shyly.

"Yes, Andre, what is it?" he asked. His face had lost the angry look completely and it seemed that he had calmed down considerably since I saw him last.

"I wanted to apologize for the spaghetti but the guest had insisted and so I…"

He looked at me with a big smile. "Yes, and?" he asked.

"The guest had insisted on changing from pommes gratin to spaghetti and even though I tried to change his mind he kept on insisting on having spaghetti," I said, out of breath.

He suddenly laughed. "Why do you apologize, did I say anything?" He tapped me on the shoulder, smiled and left. I stood there on the large carpeted staircase completely speechless. What was that?

"Yup, that's Mr. Kutsch for you," Thomas laughed as I told him later that night about the strange reply from Kutsch when I tried to explain what had happened. "Just make sure it never happens again." After that incident, I never allowed guests to change side dishes.

As the year drew to a close, we began preparing for New Year's Eve. Christmas had been very busy with all restaurants fully booked. The service was easy and smooth since we only served one set menu. New Year's Eve was a far more elegant affair compared to the noisy parties we had in Talasee. The champagne we sold on New Year's Eve was truly amazing. I had never before seen so many bottles of Dom Perignon, Louis Roederer Cristal and La Grande Dame being sold in one evening. Money for our guests truly didn't matter.

At midnight, we toasted in the kitchen with regular Moet Chandon Brut Imperial, of which we had plenty. I drank plenty, too, which was evident the next day when I suffered a massive hangover. After work, we all ended up in Michelle's apartment where we continued celebrating until it was time to get back to work. Besides plenty of wine, there was plenty of hugging and kissing, but despite my secret hope of ending up with Viola and Michelle in bed, it was not to be.

Other than the headache, the new year started pretty much the same way the old year had ended—with plenty of work. I fell back into my old routine, until one day I got a call from my mother telling me that I had received a letter from Hapag Lloyd inviting me to Bremen for interviews. I could not believe it; they actually wanted me to attend interviews for the position of restaurant steward for the cruise liner MS *Europa*.

That day I was not able to concentrate on anything other than the letter and the interview. I was supposed to travel to Bremen the following week, which was a bit tight, but I was determined to make it happen. For the next few days, I was a mental wreck; on one hand, I was eager to work on a cruise liner traveling the world and on the other hand, I really enjoyed working in one of Germany's leading restaurants. I was content here and the prospect of leaving after only one year did not appeal to me at all. I had made new friends and over the past twelve months, we had grown quite close. I liked my small but comfortable apartment and I loved the growing attention I got from my female colleagues. Then of course there were Viola and Michelle—God knows what I might miss if I left now. No, I was not keen on leaving all this behind.

There was only one person who could help and that was Tatiana. She was excited and suggested I go to the interview and if they really accepted me there, I still had enough time to decide what to do. She had a point; I hadn't been accepted yet and there was no point in getting too excited; all I had was an invitation to an interview. I decided that she was right; I would go for the interview and if they really wanted me I could always reject the offer if I wanted to. I called a Mr. Bone of the personnel department at Hapag Lloyd and confirmed the appointment for eleven o'clock in the morning the following Tuesday.

Although I tried hard to concentrate on my job, I was constantly thinking about the upcoming interview. Would they accept me or would I be rejected? One problem was my English skills. If I had to do an English test then that would be it and one week was not enough time for me to brush up on the little English I had learned in school. Worst of all, I could not tell any of my friends that I had been invited by Hapag Lloyd for interviews. If Mr. Kutsch found out that I was looking for a job he would certainly have strangled me. In view of this, I kept quiet.

One Saturday Mr. Kutsch appeared at our lunch table with a serious face. He was wearing his reading glasses and held a magazine in his hands.

"Good afternoon, ladies and gentlemen, how is lunch?" he said.

Slabov jumped up immediately. "Good afternoon, Herr Kutsch, lunch is excellent," he said before any of us could answer. Lunch was not bad but it certainly wasn't excellent.

"I have here the *Gourmet* magazine for this week. They have an article about The Stube." He was waving the magazine for all of us to see. "Who was in charge of table five on January the tenth?" he wanted to know.

"I will check," Slabov said and disappeared. The moment he had mentioned the table number, I knew that had been mine. There was no doubt that this was *the* Mr. Kaiser who had sat in my station a couple of weeks earlier. *God help me,* I thought.

"I believe that was me, Mr. Kusch," I stammered before Slabov returned.

"I see," Kutsch said, looking at me from under his reading glasses.

Slabov returned. "It was Andre, Mr. Kutsch." He pointed his fat finger at me. I looked at the little weasel. Kutsch ignored him and began to read.

"The *Gourmet* magazine tester was thoroughly impressed by the food served, complementing the texture of the scallops of the starter and the tournedos, which he describes as the best he had tasted so far. " Mr. Kutsch looked at me and smiled. Then he frowned.

"What puzzled me was his description of the service," he said. *Oh shit,* I thought, *here it comes.* I prepared myself for a dressing down. Mr. Kutsch took the magazine and read.

"The professionalism of the service staff was evident in the recommendation of a superb 1982 Chablis Grand Cru from Drouhin and the 1978 Gevrey-Chambertin from Faiveley, matching the tournedos perfectly. Despite intense questioning of the waiter as to the compatibility of his recommendations, the waiter remained unperturbed, insisting that I should accept his suggestions. What followed was a match made in heaven—the Chablis perfectly toned down the rich sauce of the scallops, adding the finishing touch to an absolutely superb dish. My initial doubts about the Gevrey-Chambertin quickly evaporated when I tasted the chef's unique touch of adding a dash of what must have been reduced balsamic vinegar to his flavorful sauce, to which the red burgundy paid ample homage." Mr. Kutsch paused and looked at us for a moment and then continued to read.

"I must, however, complement the unique style of service which was both professional and well-timed and at the same time refreshingly entertaining. The entire meal experience from start to end deserves *Gourmet* magazine's highest score of ten points."

Kutsch closed the magazine and took off his glasses. He stuffed them in his shirt pocket and handed the magazine to Joerg, who was sitting closest to him.

"Gentlemen, this is what I would like to see," he said and then looked at me. "Well done, Andre," he said and left.

"You lucky bastard," Thomas said patting me on the shoulder.

"Yeah, you lucky bastard," Joerg laughed.

"What do you mean lucky?" I asked mockingly. "Is it my fault that I am good?"

Thomas patted me again on the shoulder. "Don't forget who taught you," he joked.

Everyone was happy that the report was good; we all knew what would have happened if it had been a bad one. I kept the magazine and took it back to my apartment where I read it over and over again. I was very proud. I was now more than ever determined to become as affluent in wines as possible. I had read the Hugh Johnson wine atlas so many times by now that I was able to recite certain paragraphs from memory. I had lost the taste for German red wines and had completely converted to red Bordeaux. When I went strolling though the city on my day off, I would more often than not stop in wine shops and see what wines and vintages they had on offer. There was of course no way that I could afford any of the really good wines with my meager salary but at least I could look at and touch the bottles. At work, Thomas called me whenever he had some really good leftover wines and so I tried many of the world's finest wines. This included names like the famous Chateau d'Yquem, which I found to be too sweet, the stunning 1969 Chateau Petrus from Pommerol, the equally stunning taste of which I still remember today. I tasted the finest vintage champagnes of Dom Perignon, Louis Roederer Cristal and many others and I am sad to say that many of them I have never tasted since. Before long, Thomas and I began to engage in discussions arguing the quality of different growers and their vintages.

Slabov had for some time observed my fondness of wines and to my surprise, made me take over as sommelier whenever Thomas was off. Although Slabov never said anything, I took it as a compliment nevertheless.

One day, I was in the middle of serving a table when I was called to the telephone. This was strange; the only people who normally called me were my parents or Tatiana and they never would bother me in the middle of lunch service. Viola took over and I went to the phone.

"Yes, hello?" I said.

"Is this Andre Schwarz?" a male voice asked; the voice sounded vaguely familiar but I did not remember where I had heard it before.

"Yes, it is and who is this, please?" I wanted to know.

"Hello, Mr. Schwarz, this is Bone from Hapag Lloyd, do you remember?" he asked. *Of course, I bloody remember.* My heart was beating faster now; it was Mr. Bone from the personnel department of the cruise line company. I began to sweat.

"Oh, yes, Mr. Bone. Um, good to hear from you," I stammered.

"Andre, are you still interested to join the MS *Europa* as a steward?" he asked.

My answer came the very moment he stopped talking. "Yes, yes, of course, I am."

"That's good, because something has come up and we need a replacement restaurant steward. Are you interested in that?" he asked.

"Yes, yes, I am," I answered again. Looking back now, I know that I was not actually in control of what I answered. The moment it had sunk in that *they* had called *me* and not vice versa, my brain had switched to autopilot, answering every question automatically with yes. The thought of working on a cruise liner had completely wiped out the Columbus Hotel, The Stube, fine wines, logic and anything else that only seconds ago had been important to me.

"Good, I would like to offer you the position of restaurant steward onboard our cruise liner MS *Europa*. If you are interested in this offer I will give you a rundown on how we will proceed from here."

"I am very interested," the autopilot answered on my behalf. It was as if reality had blurred away and I was floating in some sort of void. Bone continued talking.

"We need you very fast; you have to fly in three weeks' time. Is that possible for you?" Bone asked.

"Yes it is," I said.

"What notice do you have to give?"

"One month."

"Are you sure you can leave within three weeks?" Bone asked.

"Yes, that will be no problem, Mr. Bone," my autopilot answered.

"That's good. Okay, you will have to fly from Frankfurt to Anchorage in Alaska where the *Europa* will be three weeks from now. We have not much time; you need to apply for a U.S. visa and you have to come up to Bremen again to do complete health check and apply for your seaman's certification. When can you come up here to do all that?" he wanted to know.

"Next week."

"Next week, that's good. Let's see, how about Tuesday morning at ten?"

"That's fine Mr. Bone."

"Good, you will receive the documents in a couple of days. Please sign them all and bring them with you when you come to Bremen."

"Yes, Mr. Bone."

"Good, it was nice talking with you and I see you next Tuesday," he said and the line went dead.

I put the handset back into the cradle and stared at the telephone. The call had lasted less than ten minutes and had been completely surreal. My whole world had been turned upside down. Before the telephone call I was a happy, contented chef de rang in one of Germany's finest restaurants, and after I finished this call I had confirmed that I would be flying to a place I had never heard of in Alaska!

Alaska. This was really surreal. I had never left Germany except for one short excursion to Holland and now I was supposed to fly to one of the most remote regions on earth? It was like in a bad dream. I had confirmed I would fly in three weeks! My notice period was four weeks; how could I possibly explain that to Mr. Kutsch? Shit, shit, shit, he would kill me. I had to talk with someone; I was in desperate need for advice. *Shit, have I made a mistake?* I wondered. I forced myself to slow down and think rationally.

I went to the kitchen without looking at any of my tables. In the kitchen I went to the dishwasher and looked at crates full of chinaware as they were pushed out of the machine. I just stared at the steaming hot chinaware; the steward stared at me slightly puzzled.

"Are you okay?" he asked.

I looked at him. "Oh, me, yes, I am fine," I said and went back to the restaurant.

"Hey, where were you?" Viola asked, looking very busy.

"Sorry, I was just on the phone," I said.

"That's nice, but Mr. Schmidt over there on table four is not very happy. He had ordered the Chateau Pontet-Canet but Michelle says that we are out. Can you please talk with him?" she pleaded.

"Yes, no problem, I talk with him," I said. In my mind, I was replaying the phone conversation with Mr. Bone.

Suddenly I found myself standing in front of Mr. Schmidt.

"Are you telling me that you do not have the Chateau Pontet-Canet which is listed here on your wine list?" he shouted, holding the wine list up in the air.

I looked at the wine list and the finger of his right hand, which pointed at the Pauillac section of the Bordeaux page.

"Here you see?" he said.

I looked at his finger tapping onto the Chateau Pontet-Canet. The loud tone of his voice finally pulled me out of my stupor. I knew that the Pontet-Canet was out of stock but because of my telephone call, Viola had presented the wine list and I had not told her what was available and what was not. That was bad but it had been my mistake. I took the wine list from Mr. Schmidt.

"I am very sorry, Mr. Schmidt, this is our mistake but the Pontet-Canet is not available."

"What do you mean, is not available? I thought that this is a Michelin-star restaurant. How can you run out of wines?"

"The Pontet-Canet is a very popular wine and as you probably know, the estate has only released a limited number of the 1978 vintage because they had a substantial problem with a phytoplasma disease," I said.

This was an excuse that Thomas had taught me for just such complaints, or emergencies, as he had called them. The phytoplasma is a type of disease similar to flavescence doree; it is always present and depending on severity, can result in dramatically reduced yields during the harvest. Such details were not normally known to normal guests unless they were winemakers themselves. By showing off with such specialized names, the guest normally would realize that my wine knowledge was far superior to his and in order not to lose face, he had to accept my explanation. Even if the guest *was* a winemaker telling me that what I was saying was basically crap, I would simply hide behind the fact that I was just a waiter and that the information was given to me by our wine supplier. In this case, the guest would give me a lecture about the disease, after which I would promise to have a serious talk with the wine supplier. It was a win-lose situation for me.

Mr. Schmidt now realized that indeed my wine knowledge was far superior to his and backed off. "Oh, a phytoplasma disease, I see. Well, that's different then. What do you recommend me instead?" he asked.

I recommended him the 1978 Chateaux Lafite Rothschild, which, despite its close proximity to Chateau Pontet-Canet, had not been affected so much by the disease and was therefore available. Mr. Schmidt accepted my story without further questions or comments.

"You are quite a good liar," Viola said as we met in the kitchen.

"I am liar? Why?" I asked, mocking surprise.

"What is this bullshit about disease of the vine and so on? Michelle ran out of the wine and that's the true story."

"Oh, I see. You want me to tell the guest the truth and make us look like incompetent fools who can't even order wine? Viola, we can't do that. We have to preserve the credibility of our restaurant."

"You talk about credibility? What if Mr. Schmidt was a tester?" Viola challenged me with her hands at her hips.

"Mr. Schmidt is anything *but* a tester, don't worry."

"I said, *what if* he was a tester, what would you do then?"

"Well, I guess then I would be screwed."

"Exactly, so don't lie in the future and besides, it doesn't suit you," Viola said and walked off.

Still, per Thomas, the phytoplasma excuse had never failed so far and I was not going to give it up just because my sexy demi chef was throwing a tantrum.

Suddenly I remembered Bone, the telephone call and that he wanted me to fly to Alaska the following week. "Holy shit!" I said to myself.

Over the next couple of days, I began to warm up to the idea of becoming a steward on a cruise liner. In a bookshop nearby the hotel, I looked up Anchorage and was shocked to see just how far away this place was. I began daydreaming of a brilliant white ship, waiters and barmen in white uniforms and beautiful girls in bikinis sunbathing on deck whilst the ship slowly cruised from island to island in the Caribbean. The more I thought about it the more appealing the idea became and suddenly I said to myself, *Take it easy, you don't have a contract yet.* So I decided to concentrate on my current job until I sign a contract with Hapag Lloyd.

To concentrate on my current job was easier said than done. I simply couldn't concentrate; I thought about the ship all the time. I went to a nearby travel agent and took all brochures of the MS *Europa* I could lay my hands on. In one of the brochures, they had a graphic cut of the whole ship, which I studied for hours. The ship was impossibly big; there were restaurants, several pools inside and outside, bars, kitchens, a fitness center, a library, a ballroom and more. I could not stop thinking of the *Europa*.

The first person I told was Tatiana. She was very excited but somehow I could tell that she was not her usual self and I asked her if something was wrong. Tatiana told me that she had found a job in London and she would move there within the next four weeks. I was quiet. With Tatiana moving to England and me off to Alaska, the chances of survival for our relationship were literally nil and we both knew it. Nevertheless, we agreed that we had survived my time in the Navy and once again I promised to write her at least one letter per day. I had read in the brochure that even when the ship was at sea, there was a possibility to make telephone calls via the ship's satellite phone, which was expensive, but at least there was a possibility to keep in touch. We agreed that this would be the last time that we lived apart and once my time on the *Europa* was over, we would finally live together.

Next, I called my parents. My mother said she was happy but I don't think she meant it, which is understandable considering her son was off to one of the most remote places on earth. My father, on the other hand, fully supported my decision and I could tell that he was pleased about it. My contract arrived two days later and just as I said yes without thinking during the telephone conversation with Bone, I signed the contract before I actually read the document. There was only one more thing left to do: I had to resign from the Columbus Hotel and that meant facing Mr. Kutsch. I was not looking forward to that meeting.

I got an appointment the same day at five o'clock in the afternoon. I was as nervous as I had never been before.

I was not so much afraid of Mr. Kutsch screaming at me; I felt bad because Mr. Kutsch had been very supportive of me. Ever since that *Gourmet* magazine report, he had treated me like a true professional. It was he who had sent me, together with Thomas, on a sommelier course in France and it was he who had promoted me. I dreaded this meeting because I liked the Mr. Kutsch, the Columbus Hotel and The Stube. I wasn't really so sure anymore if leaving was the right thing to do.

Mr. Kutsch's reaction was the complete opposite from what I had expected. Not only was he supportive of my decision to join the MS *Europa*, he also had no problem with my request of being released after three weeks instead of the mandatory four weeks. The meeting went well; he shook my hand and wished me good luck. I was relieved because the meeting had gone better than I could have ever wished for. However, my happiness was not to last. I should have known.

At nine-thirty the same evening, Mr. Kutsch called me once more to his office and this time things proceeded quite differently. He first began to explain, in a very low voice, how hard he had worked to open The Stube and make it to what it was today. He then told me how many chef de rangs had become successful restaurant managers after working there at The Stube. His voice slowly grew louder, saying how I would waste all I had learned at The Stube by working on a cruise ship. His tone grew more aggressive, telling me that the coming weeks and months were going to be very busy and it was not a nice move of me leaving after two and a half weeks instead of the mandatory four. He now had worked himself into a state where he screamed at me. He screamed at me loud and long and eventually he asked me to leave his office.

I felt very, very bad. Outside Mr. Kutch's office, the secretaries looked at me with encouraging smiles and I realized that they must have heard everything since the doors of Mr. Kutch's office were not exactly soundproof. I forced a smile and walked out. Now I was definitely in his bad books and what was worse, I still needed a reference from him. I had no illusions of how that reference would look like.

Word of my resignation spread fast and took almost everyone by surprise, including myself. Somehow, everything happened too fast for my liking. I managed to get two days off from Slabov and traveled to Bremen to meet with Mr. Bone. I completed tons of paperwork. The medical test alone took nearly one full day and included several vaccinations for yellow fever, malaria and other tropical diseases.

In the end, I walked away with a certification from the World Health Organization, which allowed me to travel to exotic places like South America and Asia. It all sounded so surreal to me. I took an endless number of passport pictures and filled in lots of different forms. In my final meeting, Mr. Bone handed over a one-way ticket on KLM from Frankfurt to Anchorage. Bone wished me good luck as I left the Hapag Lloyd headquarters to go to the main railway station of Bremen to catch my train to Freiburg.

I watched the north German countryside rushing by, thinking of the incredible adventure I was about to embark upon. I studied the air ticket over and over again—Frankfurt to Anchorage. I had never been to any of these places—not even Frankfurt, as a matter of fact—in my twenty-three years of age. I had also never sat in an aero plane before and now I was about to fly to one of the most remote places on earth. I would have to fly from Stuttgart to Frankfurt, from Frankfurt to Amsterdam and then on towards Anchorage. I took a deep breath, wondering if I would ever arrive in Alaska. Suddenly I was gripped by panic. How could I possibly find my way around the airports? Frankfurt would be fine since everything was written in German but I also had to change in Amsterdam and that was a different story altogether; it was unlikely that the signs in Amsterdam would written in German and that was bad. I knew that many Dutch people spoke German but this did very little to make me feel better.

What had I done? It was one thing to dream of white cruise ships, beaches and palm trees, and quite another to actually get there without speaking the language. I had to stop beating myself up. I stuffed the tickets in my bag and tried to sleep but I was far too wound up and simply couldn't relax. By the time I arrived in Freiburg early in the morning I was mentally and physically exhausted and ready to beg Mr. Kutsch to give me back my old job. I went to my apartment, threw the bag in one corner, showered and went to work.

At breakfast I was reminded that it was a big day for the hotel. I had completely forgotten that we had the annual press ball the same night. I was assigned to assist in serving the gala dinner in the ballroom. *Why today?* I wondered. I had just traveled for over twelve hours by train from one end of Germany to the other and then we had a ball. *Shit.*

When Viola saw me at lunchtime she immediately commented on my tired looks, asking whether I had been out partying all night. I had not enough strength left to find her comments even remotely funny. After lunch I went back to my apartment, crashed into bed and fell asleep instantly.

The three-hour afternoon nap was exactly what I needed and when I got up at five, I felt already much better and rejuvenated. When I arrived in the hotel that evening, I went straight to the banquet headwaiter instead of reporting to Slabov in The Stube. He briefed me on the service sequence for the evening and showed me to my table in the ballroom.

The ballroom looked truly amazing. There were twenty-five round tables of ten. Each table was dressed in white tablecloths with large white flower bouquets and Christoffle silver cutlery. At one end of the ballroom was a stage with a backdrop and silver glittery letters reading "Fifth Annual Press Ball." It looked very much like a stage set up on a gala TV show. After the service briefing I went to change into my white gala dinner jacket with black bow tie.

"Wow, Andre, you look gorgeous," Viola exclaimed when she saw me after I had changed. So did she. I looked at her and gasped; she looked stunning. I hardly recognized her in her long black dress. Her hair was made up and I had to force myself not to stare at her cleavage. The dress was very tight-fitting, exposing her nicely shaped body perfectly. She looked elegant and very sexy.

"You look amazing," I said, for lack of better words.

"Really? Do you think so?" she giggled sheepishly.

"Oh, yes, definitely."

She turned on her heels. "I am glad you like it," she teased, wiggling around. "By the way, I am assigned to work with you, so what do you want me to do for you?" she asked teasingly.

182

"Oh, ahm, you can get the bread and butter?" I said, not getting her drift.

"Yes, sir, anything you wish," she laughed and walked off. *Anything I wish.* I stared at her as she left; the tight black dress pronounced every part of her beautifully shaped figure perfectly.

The annual press ball was one of the most prestigious and glamorous events in Freiburg and was attended by journalists, editors and publishers from large media conglomerates from all over Germany, France and Switzerland. Viola and I stood at our table watching as the invited guests slowly filed into the ballroom, searching for their tables. The ladies were dressed in long elegant and expensive-looking evening gowns and the men were uniformly dressed in black tuxedos, some better-fitting than others were.

I had never seen so much elegance before. Slowly our table filled up with beautiful-looking people. When the last of my guests sat down, I began to pour the wine. My guests were chatting away, hardly paying any attention to me as I served the ladies first and the gentlemen last. I did it by the book, the wine bottle tightly wrapped into a napkin with my left hand on my back. I had just finished with the white wine when it happened - I felt a hand on my backside! The hand was not just touching my bum; it literally grabbed my left cheek. I spun around and looked straight into the face of one of my lady guests. She was middle-aged, very attractive and very blond and wore a strikingly red dress. I had no idea what had happened and, thinking I had come too close to her by mistake, I apologized.

"Don't worry, sweetheart." The lady winked at me and said, "Can I have some more wine, please?" Then she smiled.

I looked at her glass and to my utter surprise, it was empty. At first, I thought I had forgotten her but I quickly realized that she was a fast drinker. I knew I had to take care of her and immediately poured her another glass. As I poured, I felt her hand grabbing my bum again and, once again thinking it was my mistake, I apologized profusely. She looked at me and winked again, patting my bum. I didn't know what to say so I smiled and left the table.

"Wow, she really wants you," Viola laughed as I came back to our service station.

"What do mean?" I asked innocently.

"That's so funny—she touches your bum and you apologize. You are soo sweet," she laughed, grabbing my bum in the same manner.

I spun around, hoping nobody had seen that. "What are you doing? For God's sake, we are in the middle of a function," I exclaimed.

"Yeah, and everybody is watching the waiters? Look around, nobody cares, they are all having fun," Viola laughed.

"Come on, we have work to do," I said.

Viola smiled at me, leaned over and whispered in my ear. "Hey, Michelle is coming over to my place for drinks later, want to join, sailor?" She laughed again.

I was stunned and again didn't know what to say. "Ahm, okay, yes, maybe, why not?"

"Great," she said. "Let's get this over and done with. I'll go to the kitchen and queue for the starters. See you later, sailor," she said and walked off, and, knowing that I would stare after her, she provocatively wiggled her bum. *What the hell was going on here tonight?*

The emcee got onto the stage, welcomed all invited guests, and kicked off the evening's program. There were speeches and awards whilst we served dish after dish of the seven-course menu.

I kept refilling the wine glasses for my guests and despite my best efforts to stay as far away as possible from the lady in red, her hand kept on touching my bum. For some silly reason I kept on apologizing even though I knew that it was not actually my fault. She called me and again I saw that her glass was empty.

"You are a sweetheart," she said. "What is your name?" she asked as I poured her more wine. Suddenly I felt her hand again, this time on my upper thigh, moving up to my bum and then slowly down again. She was stroking my bum!

"So what is you name?" she asked again.

"My name is Andre," I stammered.

She didn't seem to care about her husband or whoever that person next to her was. Her hand kept on stroking my backside. I blushed, looked around embarrassed but nobody paid any attention to us. Her hand kept on stroking me and I was getting hot. The ballroom was filled with background music, the chatting of people engaged in conversations, laughter, and—at one table—even singing. People took pictures, walked between tables and others danced on the large dance floor in front of the stage. No, nobody was paying any attention to us at all.

"Are you nervous, Andre?" she asked me. I wanted to scream, *You are stroking my bum in the middle of the ballroom. Yes, I am bloody nervous!*

"No, not really," I said. I could see, and feel, that my lady in red was getting drunk now. The other guests at the table were engaged in conversations and none of them witnessed my plight. Eventually it was Viola who saved me from further embarrassment when she called me to assist her with the main course. I excused myself and went to help Viola.

"You guys are really hitting it off," Viola joked but for me it was serious; we hadn't even served the main course and the lady in red was already half drunk and God knows what she was capable off when she was *really* drunk. I have to admit, though, that in some way, it was actually exciting and she *was* very attractive, even though she was much older than I was, but the fact remained that I was the waiter and she was a guest.

"Viola, come on, let's serve these main courses, please."

After we had served the main course, I quickly refilled the lady's wine glass. Since she was busy eating, I approached her stealthily, filled her glass up to the rim and left immediately. It happened so quickly that there was no time for her to put down the cutlery and touch my bum.

Viola was in stitches. "You are soo funny, Andre," she giggled.

"You see, that's what you call a 'hit and run mission.' I learnt that in the Navy," I said sarcastically.

Whilst my guests were eating, I looked around the ballroom. All tables had their main courses and most waiters just hovered around their tables pouring wine or standing idle waiting for their guests to finish. I saw Mr. Kutsch, dressed in a tuxedo and a white apron, going from table to table greeting every guest personally. One table was occupied by the annoying Mr. Eggers who, judging by the facial expressions of his guests, bored them to bits with his endless stories. There were also well-known journalists and news presenters from television stations.

Mr. Kutsch had now reached the table next to mine; I hadn't spoken to him since he gave me that dressing down in his office for resigning. He wished everyone at that table a good evening and came over to mine, greeting everyone with a big smile. When he saw the lady in red, he walked over to her and gave her a big hug. *Shit,* I thought, *he knows her.*

He was holding both her hands and looked at her admiringly up and down. I was sure he was complementing her on her looks. They talked for a while and suddenly both looked over to me and I saw her giggling. *Shit,* I thought, *what is she saying to him?* I hadn't touched her; she had started it. Thank God, Viola had seen everything; she would be my witness to prove that I hadn't started touching the lady in red.

Mr. Kutsch chatted with her a bit longer and finally kissed her on both cheeks and left. He gave me a brief look and what I thought to be a smile but I wasn't sure. Well, at least he didn't shout or scream at me and it seemed that the lady in red had kept the bum business to herself. I took a deep breath. This evening turned out to be more stressful than a busy day in The Stube.

It took my guests another fifteen minutes to finish their main course, not so much because they were slow eaters but because they talked a lot. Finally Viola and I began clearing the plates. Once the plates were gone, Viola crumbed the table and I set up the cutlery for cheese. I offered red wine to every guest and all, without exception and including my lady in red, took the Australian Pinot Noire. Mr. Kutsch had rejected the idea of serving this particular wine with the cheese course but since the wine was sponsored and the organizer had insisted on that, he had not had much choice. The moment we brought the bottles into the ballroom, Mr. Kutsch left, I guess out of protest.

"So, Mr. Kutsch told me you are going to become a sailor," the lady in red whispered to me as I poured her the Australian wine. Her tongue seemed to roll as she spoke. I looked at her in surprise. *Kutsch had told her? Why would he do that?* I was sure he was still very upset.

"Ahm, yes, madam, I will be working on the cruise liner MS *Europa*," I said, not without pride. *Kutsch had actually told her.* I couldn't believe it.

"Mr. Kutsch also tells me that he is not happy to see you leave, but I told him that if I could get a chance to work on a 'love boat,' then I would not hesitate to go," she said, giggling, and slapped my bum but hard this time.

I apologized again. *Bloody Hell!*

"That's quite okay, just don't do it again," she said and squeezed my bum. I didn't know what to do anymore; the continuous touching, slapping and now squeezing was getting me excited and annoyed at the same time and on top of all this, it was done by a lady who hugged Mr. Kutsch. How would I get out of this situation unharmed?

Once again, Viola saved me as she arrived with the cheese. "Are you still coming to our party or are you taking *her* out?" Viola asked, motioning to the lady in red.

"Are you joking?" I whispered. "Do you know that she had just hugged Mr. Kutsch a few minutes ago?"

"Oh, she knows him?"

"Yes, she knows him. He even told her that I am leaving to work on a ship," I said as we finished serving the cheese.

"I see," Viola said.

"Anyway, as soon as we have served the dessert and coffee, I am out of here. That was the deal with the banquet boys anyway."

"So are you coming to our party or not?" Viola wanted to know. Of course I was going; there was nothing in the world that could have stopped me accepting *that* invitation. I had already visions of me lying in between Viola and Michelle.

"Yeah, okay, I will be there," I said casually.

After we had served dessert and coffee, I went one last time to refill the wine and to my relief, the lady in red had disappeared; presumably she had gone to the bathroom. I filled her glass to the rim one last time and then Viola and I reported to the banquet manager that all was completed, he thanked us and he released us for the night.

I went back to my apartment where I took a long hot shower. In the shower, I began thinking of the ship again and remembered what the lady in red had said tonight. She had a point; to work on the *Europa* was a great opportunity and let's face it, how many young people of my age were able to go and see Alaska?

All of a sudden, I felt my initial apprehension about my upcoming journey changing into excitement. I got dressed in jeans and T-shirt and went downstairs to get a taxi. As it was already after midnight, it took me while to find one. I sat in the back of the car watching the deserted streets of Freiburg at night as the driver sped through the city. I thought of the lady in red and what would have happened if I had stayed longer. Would she have asked me to meet up later, somewhere outside of the hotel? Maybe she would have done so and maybe I even would have said yes if it had not been for Viola. My thoughts drifted to Viola; the anticipation of another evening with Michelle and her made me shiver with excitement.

Then I suddenly thought of Tatiana and I felt bad. I wondered why I felt bad since I hadn't done anything wrong - *yet*. I still loved her more than I loved any other girl in the world. It wasn't as if I was going to start a relationship with someone else; I was just going to a party and that's all. Was it my fault if girls started touching *me* like it happened tonight in the ballroom? *I* hadn't started that. There was the evening with Michelle and Viola where we all woke up in one bed, but nothing had really happened except a bit of hugging and kissing. None of this changed the fact that I loved Tatiana.

I tried to think of something else but it was difficult; Viola and Michelle kept on elbowing their way into my mind. The taxi came to a screeching halt in front of Viola's apartment building. I took a deep breath and wished myself good luck as I stood in front of the apartment door and knocked.

Viola opened the door and she looked sexy. She wore a tight-fitting T-shirt and the hottest hot pants I had ever seen. Her apartment was surprisingly noisy. *Did I hear voices?* My dreams of another night with two girls were shattered almost immediately; her place was packed with people! *Shit.*

"Hi there, better late then never!" she said and gave me hug.

"Hi there, what is happening in there? Do you have party?"

"Oh, well, Michelle decided to invite a couple of her friends," Viola said, rolling her eyes.

"She invited a couple of friends? Look at this place; it's like being in a discotheque," I said.

"Stop complaining. Come in and have a drink." She pulled me by my arm and closed the door. The apartment was packed with people and a thick cloud of cigarette smoke hung low beneath the ceiling. When Michelle saw me, she came over, giving me a big hug and then introduced me to her friends. I wasn't really interested in meeting any of them. I got a glass of wine and took a seat in one of the sofa chairs. I sipped a bit from my wine and studied Michelle's friends.

The guys looked like typical university students, which was not surprising since Freiburg was home to a well-known university. They were dressed in loosely fitting pants and jumpers that looked as if they had been made by their grandmothers. I didn't like the way they talked, maybe because I didn't understand half of what they were saying, and what's worse, almost all of them spoke pure High German.

The girls were of a similar type, wearing clothes which didn't really do them any justice. Not that I knew much about fashion or had some sort of superior taste, but my five years in deluxe hotels had left me with a little bit of an eye for style. Some of Michelle's friends didn't even wear makeup except one, which made her stand out like a sore thumb. This was definitely *not* my kind of crowd.

I decided to finish my wine and then get out as quickly as possible. I looked around Viola's apartment, which the students had turned into a real mess. *Thank God, it wasn't me who had to clean all this up the next day.*

"Hi there," a female voice suddenly said. In front of me stood the sore thumb with the makeup.

"Oh, hi there," I said.

"I am Erika," the sore thumb said and shook my hand. Without asking, she sat down next to me.

"I am Andre. Nice to meet you."

"Are you a friend of Michelle?" she wanted to know.

"Actually, I am working with both of them," I said. "How about you, what do you do?" I asked.

"I study medicine here at the university," she said.

"Oh, you study medicine. Do you want to become a doctor?" I felt this was a stupid question, but what else could I have asked a medicine student?

"In a way, yes. I want to specialize in heart surgery," she said.

I wanted to ask why she was slightly better dressed than the others and why she was using makeup but decided against it.

"What do *you* do, Andre?" she wanted to know.

"I am a chef de rang at The Stube in the Columbus Hotel," I answered proudly.

"Oh, really? I know the Columbus Hotel well. My parents dine there quite often," she said, exited.

"Oh, I see, that's interesting. Maybe I know them," I said, wondering if I had met her parents.

"Yeah, maybe. Oh, I love hotels. They are fascinating and there is so much elegance and glamour," she said.

"Yes, it is quite an exciting business and I love it."

"Yeah. So, what is a chef de rang? Some sort of junior manager?" she asked excitedly.

"Oh, ah not really, chef de rang is French and basically it is a waiter or rather a station waiter," I said to make it sound more impressive.

"You are a waiter?" she said; her voice had suddenly changed.

"Yes, I am a waiter in The Stube. That's the restaurant with the Michelin star."

"So, you do this temporarily as a part-time job?" she asked in the same voice.

"No, this is my full time job. I want to work in hotels, you know, work my way up to restaurant manager and then we'll see."

"Restaurant manager, I see," she said, very obviously not impressed, and sipped her drink. She was quiet and looked around the apartment as if she was searching for something. Suddenly she got up and shook my hand.

"Andre, it was nice to meet you," she said and walked away.

It was clear that the medicine student wasn't impressed with the chef de rang alias waiter. *Well that's too bad,* I thought, and got up, too. I decided that I had enough of this party and since it was quite clear that I would not sleep with Viola or Michelle and definitely not with both of them, there was no point in me staying any longer. I thanked Michelle and Viola and prepared to leave. I was just about to open the door when Viola grabbed my jacket from the back.

"Andre, follow me just for a moment. I need to show you something," she said. I followed her. She led me to her room, shoved me inside and locked the door.

"What are you doing?" I said. Viola just smiled, put her arms around me and kissed me. I left her place early the next morning.

Working the next day was a little awkward for me but Viola behaved as if nothing had happened. The next day was also the day Tatiana left for London and because she had been busy with packing her things and I had been busy with Bremen, we had not managed to meet before her departure. We talked on the phone for a long time and we both felt very emotional, a little more so for me because I also felt very bad about what had happened the night before. As I said goodbye to Tatiana, I wasn't really sure when I would see her again but I promised her that I would love her for the rest of my life. Tatiana promised me the same and suddenly I missed her a lot.

For the rest of that day my conscience gave me a very hard time about the night before. I defended myself with the fact that I had not initiated what eventually happened. On the contrary, I was already on the way out when Viola pulled me back. My conscience then argued why I had not simply left when Viola asked me to stay. My defense was clear: How could I just leave when Viola had a firm grip on my jacket, begging me to stay? And besides, what if it had been some sort of emergency? I could not have forgiven myself if something serious had happened to her after I simply ignored her cry for help. I finally came to the conclusion that what happened was not my fault but rather a combination of Viola striking with lightning speed and me being exhausted from the overnight train ride, the late night in the hotel and then the exhausting party. It made me feel a bit better but some guilty feelings kept lingering in my mind for the next couple of days.

My last weeks at the Columbus Hotel passed quickly and were filled with unexpected surprises. The first surprise came in form of my reference from Mr. Kutsch. I remember how I slowly removed the sheet of paper from its envelope and read. After my last experience with Mr. Kutsch, I hardly expected a positive reference. As I read the lines, I searched for the hidden codes.

Because the law protected employees and did not allow employers to give negative references, all references were generally positive. However, references always contained hidden codes that gave hints about the true performance of an employee. For example: "The employee reported for duty almost always on time" meant the employee was always late. Another example: "Completing projects within a given time frame has improved over the past year" meant that the employee never completed projects on time. I finished reading and then read the letter again and only then did I realize that Mr. Kutsch had given me a true and honest reference.

To Whom It May Concern:

The service activities in our gourmet restaurant The Stube make the highest demands on the professional and personal knowledge and personal attitude of our employees. Mr. Schwarz met these demands in every respect and always completed the work assigned to him to our utmost satisfaction.

He is a pleasant and refined person and was always friendly, attentive, polite and helpful towards our demanding clients. He is a hard-working, trustworthy and absolutely reliable employee who can be further highly recommended to any fellow employer.

His attitude towards superiors was irreproachable. Thanks to his cooperative, kind and helpful personality, he was also very much appreciated by his fellow employees.

Mr. Schwarz is leaving us in May of his own free will in order to improve his knowledge and capabilities onboard ship. We are sorry to lose him and we would like to emphasize that our establishment remains open to him at all times.

Our best wishes accompany him for his future.

I stuffed the letter back into its envelope and felt highly emotional. This was typical for Mr. Kutsch; on one hand he screamed and yelled and on the other hand, he was still a professional hotelier through and through. And, at least as far as I was concerned, he also had a good heart.

Thomas and Joerg organized my farewell dinner. To my surprise, it was attended by the whole team of The Stube. The menu consisted of goose liver, truffles, sweetbread and other delicacies and my favorite wines, Chablis and Chateaux Pichon-Longueville. My leaving gift was the latest Hugh Johnson pocket wine book and a bottle of Dom Perignon with a label that had been signed by all. We laughed, had fun and celebrated until the early morning hours. We ended up once again at Viola's place but I didn't want to leave Freiburg with a bad conscience. I found Viola terribly exciting but I still loved Tatiana. We said goodbye long after all the others had left.

Before I stepped into the taxi I looked up at Viola's balcony. She stood there with tears in her eyes; I waved at her and smiled. I got into the cab and closed the door. I would never see her again.

Chapter 6: *Cruiseliner, MS Europa*

The days leading up to my departure were filled with shopping for clothes and packing my two suitcases. I also had received my first-ever passport with my first-ever visa for my first-ever entry into the United States. I had less than one week left before my parents brought me to Stuttgart airport for my first-ever flight in an airplane.

I was booked on a Lufthansa flight from Stuttgart to Frankfurt and from there by KLM to Amsterdam where I would board my KLM flight to Anchorage. The thought of this journey made my stomach turn. I had never been to a city or an airport as large as Frankfurt before and I had no idea how I would find my way around there. I remembered the first time at Hamburg's main railway station with its gigantic hall, its multitude of different signs and its labyrinth of platforms where it took me some considerable time and effort to find my train to Freiburg. I knew that international airports were even larger than that. I admit I was scared.

Three days before my departure all my suitcases were packed. I still had difficulty comprehending that I would be flying all the way to Alaska. I studied the route the MS *Europa* would take over and over again. When I looked at the world atlas, I simply could not believe that I would see all these exotic and faraway places. Once I had reached Anchorage, if I ever reached that place, MS *Europa* would sail south along the west coast of Alaska, Canada and the United States. We then would cross the Panama Canal into the Caribbean and then cross the Atlantic back to Europe.

After a number of farewell dinners with family and friends, I spent my last day checking and double-checking my luggage. Finally, the last night before I would depart for my biggest adventure so far, I had dinner with my parents and went to bed early.

But I was unable to sleep. I had never been on an aircraft before and the prospect of taking off and landing several times was very unsettling and gave me a sleepless night. When I finally got up at five o'clock the next morning to take a shower I had not slept all night. My mother made breakfast but I was too nervous to eat. My father loaded my suitcases in the car and soon we were on our way to Stuttgart. My parents tried to make small talk in the car but I just couldn't engage in any conversation; I was simply too nervous.

We arrived at the airport and after my father had parked the car, we went to one of the many Lufthansa check-in counters. The check-in went relatively smoothly and since I was not able to talk, my father, having flown before, had to do the check-in for me and requested a window seat. The friendly lady behind the Lufthansa counter entered everything into a computer and then handed me my first-ever boarding card.

We still had over an hour before I had to depart and my parents took me for a coffee. I was in a sorry state—my face was black and I was terribly nervous. I was under immense stress that forced me to run to the bathroom every five minutes. My parents tried their best to cheer me up. The fact that my father was constantly joking, finding it funny to take pictures of me, didn't help to make me feel better. Finally, it was time to say goodbye to my parents.

At the passport control point, I said an emotional goodbye. My mother cried and gave me a big hug, asking me to take care of myself. I promised to do just that but wasn't really sure how. My feelings were completely sedated by my nervousness. I took out my brand-new passport, said my final goodbyes and stepped up to the counter.

When I had passed passport control I turned around once more and saw my parents still standing outside waving at me. I waved back, forced a smile and walked towards the departure gates. My gate was listed as C5 on my boarding card. I glanced at the multitude of signs and eventually found gate C5 after having walked from one end of the airport to the other. There was already a long line of people queuing in front of the gate. I was one of the last passengers to arrive.

When I finally reached the gate, a young lady took my boarding card and, to my horror, tore part of it off. She handed the other half back to me and with a smile wished me a good flight. Since I was afraid to board the wrong plane, I asked the lady if this was indeed the plane to Frankfurt. The lady looked at me slightly puzzled and then confirmed with a friendly smile that this was indeed the aircraft to Frankfurt. I was relieved and boarded the plane.

The aircraft was a Boeing 737 and the largest I had ever seen in my life. I was amazed when I saw the rows upon rows of seats to the left and right of the center aisle. A friendly flight attendant showed me to my window seat and helped me to store my bag in the overhead luggage compartment. The seat was smaller than expected and I had to fiddle for a while with the seatbelt until I managed to close it properly. I glanced out of the small window and saw part of the wing and underneath, workers were loading containers full of luggage into the plane. *Incredible that planes are able to fly with so much luggage and people onboard,* I thought.

A short while later the flight attendants closed the doors. Next to me sat a man in a business suit reading a newspaper; the seat in the middle had remained empty. Suddenly I heard a low whistling noise that became slowly louder, which I guessed must have been the pilot winding up the jet engines. They sounded very powerful, thank God.

Then the plane was pushed back and we taxied to the runway. There was a multitude of electronic noises and announcements. Then the pilot spoke, telling us that the flight time to Frankfurt was just under an hour. *That is fast,* I thought. After several minutes of taxiing, the pilot's voice came on again, asking the flight attendants to take a seat for immediate take off.

I could see that the plane turned onto the incredibly long runway and then it stopped. For a moment, I thought something was wrong. *Why would we stop now?* Then all of a sudden the engines began to wind up and the pilot released the brakes. It was incredible; the power of the jet engines accelerating the plane pressed me deep into my seat. I glanced out of the window and saw hangars and buildings rushing by at an incredible speed and then suddenly the front of the plane lifted and we began to ascend into the air.

I moved closer to the window and was instantly yanked back into my seat. The ground was disappearing at an incredible speed. To my surprise, the man in the business suit was still reading his newspaper. The plane shuddered several times, which made my heart jump. *What is wrong?* I looked at the man in the business suit and he still read his bloody paper. *What is wrong with him, couldn't he feel these bumps?* I didn't move. After a while, the plane began leveling out and I heard a loud pinging sound. *Is that an emergency bell?* The man next to me finally put his paper down and opened his seat belt. Several people suddenly got up and walked towards the front of the plane, disappearing behind a small door. *The toilets, thank God.*

The atmosphere seemed a bit more relaxed and I dared another glance out of the window. We were incredibly high. The aircraft shuddered several times but nobody seemed to be bothered by that and so I relaxed a bit, too. I still didn't dare to open my seatbelt, though. Then the pilot came on again telling us that we had now reached our cruising altitude of several thousand meters. He also said that the weather was perfect, which made me wonder why the plane still shuddered occasionally.

The man in the business suit returned to his seat, looked at me briefly with a smile and then picked up his paper again. I thought, *That is one cool customer*. He must have done this a thousand times. I stared out of the window, fascinated by the endless sky, the clouds and the fact that I was actually flying. Suddenly a young flight attendant asked me to fold down the small table in front of me and after I had somewhat awkwardly managed to do just that, she handed me a small tray with a sandwich and orange juice. The man in the business suit declined the tray and continued reading his newspaper. *What a strange guy.*

I suddenly realized that I had not eaten since five o'clock in the morning and gulped down the sandwich and the artificial-tasting orange juice. When the pilot spoke again, he told us that he would start the descent into Frankfurt in a few minutes and he hoped we had enjoyed the flight. I couldn't believe it; we had only just taken off and now we were already in Frankfurt? It was amazing.

Suddenly the plane began to descend and my stomach seemed to rise to my head. I grabbed the armrests thinking something was wrong, but since the man in the business suit simply kept on reading his paper, I gathered that everything must have been fine. The plane shuddered several times as we descended and a multitude of noises made me dig my fingers deeper into the armrests. When the pilot finally extracted the landing gear, I thought we had lost an engine. To my horror, even the man in the business suit put down his papers. I glanced outside and saw down below buildings, houses and a river rushing by. Then suddenly the buildings disappeared, we glided for a few minutes over some forested areas and then everything went flat green and the plane touched down. "Welcome to Frankfurt am Main Airport," a lady's voice announced. I had arrived in Frankfurt—alive.

The plane taxied to its gate and we disembarked. Frankfurt airport was a hundred times larger than Stuttgart. I didn't know where to go next and simply followed my fellow passengers. The main building of Frankfurt airport was huge and a beehive of activity. I wondered what to do next. There were hundreds of check-in counters. I took out my travel itinerary and approached one of the counters. The elderly and not very friendly Lufthansa lady behind the counter looked up and asked me what I wanted. I asked her for the number of the gate for the KLM flight to Anchorage in Alaska. It was obvious from the frustrated way she pronounced each word that I had interrupted her doing something important. She explained, or rather barked at me, that I had had to take the train to terminal B. I then made the mistake of asking her where I could find the train.

"That's why we have signs, young man," she barked and pointed at a yellow sign that said *Train to Terminal B*.

I was completely oblivious to the way she talked with me; I was just happy to have found my way. "Thank you," I said and followed the sign.

It was incredible; the airport was so large that I had to take a train to get from one terminal to the other. Terminal B was of the same gigantic size as Terminal A where I had arrived, except that there was none of the familiar yellow Lufthansa logos anywhere. I approached one counter and asked where I could find the KLM check-in desks, which turned out to be just around the corner.

I found the KLM check-in area and joined another long queue of passengers. The check-in again went smoothly except that there were no window seats left. I accepted the aisle seat offered by the lady dressed in bright blue and got two boarding cards. The lady informed me that I had to change aircraft in Amsterdam's Schiphol Airport. This worried me immensely because I didn't speak any English or Dutch. I would just have to see and hope for the best.

Once again, I found myself again wandering through endless corridors, passing numerous gates. I found the gate eventually and went through the same boarding procedure as in Stuttgart, except that this time I boarded a bright blue painted KLM aircraft, a DC9. The flight to Holland lasted just under an hour and once again, I gulped down a quick sandwich and a glass of water.

Schiphol Airport was just as huge and confusing as Frankfurt. I asked for directions; to my delight, most people I approached spoke German so I found my gate in good time. I even had some time left which I used to buy a postcard that I sent to my parents.

My dear loved ones,

I have just arrived from Frankfurt, where I had to wait for two hours here in Amsterdam. After a Boeing 737 and a DC9 I will now continue on a KLM Boeing 747 (flight to Tokyo). I still have one hour left and so far, everything is going well. I will be in touch with you again.

Andre

I posted the card wondering if it would ever reach my parents.

The departure gate for my flight was very large and to my surprise, there were a lot of Chinese-looking passengers. Since my flight was going to Tokyo via Anchorage, I found out that what I assumed to be Chinese were actually Japanese people, a small detail that, at the time, meant nothing to me. Fact is that there were lots of them, which indicated that the plane I was boarding this time was larger than the two planes I had flown so far.

The aircraft *was* larger, much larger; in fact, it was the largest plane in existence at the time—the Boeing 747 jumbo jet. I had seen this aircraft on TV before but never in my life had I imaged I would actually fly in one. Now I was about to board one to Alaska. It was incredible.

When I stepped into that aircraft, I was blown away by its sheer size. I even passed a staircase leading up to the upper part of the aircraft. The main cabin was three times as wide as the one of the Boeing 737. A Dutch flight attendant showed me to my seat.

Next to me sat a Chinese- or rather Japanese-looking man. He looked at me and I greeted him in German. Judging by his facial expression, he had not understood a word. I sat down and, with the trained hands of a seasoned air traveler, fastened my seat belts. The boarding took some time since the flight was packed, mainly with Japanese by the looks of it.

The immense size of the aircraft made a real impression on me. The cabin was so long that from my seat I couldn't even see the other end. The flight preparation was similar to the other two I had witnessed in the last twenty-four hours, except that here everything happened in much larger dimensions. When we taxied to the runway, everything vibrated. Every time we rolled over a bump the overhead luggage compartments in the center of the ceiling shook precariously. I wondered if that was normal. Then we rolled onto the runway.

The pilot stopped the plane for a few seconds and then suddenly the four powerful jet engines began to accelerate the large aircraft forward. The aircraft picked up speed but nothing happened; we kept on rolling faster and faster down the runway. It seemed to me like an eternity for the plane to reach its take-off speed and when it eventually lifted up, I was sure we were very close to the end of the runway. I was glued to my seat and my fingers dug deep into the fabric of the armrests and the pilot took us into a steep climb. My heart was beating fast; I expected the worst.

After about ten minutes, the aircraft began leveling out. It took another few minutes for my tensed up body to relax and finally I dared to move again. This gigantic beast was actually flying; the take-off had been an incredible experience. Finally, I was on my way to Alaska.

To my surprise the Japanese man next to me had gone to sleep. I assumed that he was either another seasoned traveler or he was simply very tired. It reminded me that I myself had not slept for the past twenty-four hours but I did not feel tired at all. An hour into the flight the girls in blue began serving meals. This time it was not just a sandwich with some artificial juice or water but a proper meal consisting of starter, main course and dessert. Unfortunately, the flight attendant didn't speak German and therefore I answered all her questions with *yes*. What I ended up with was a Japanese meal.

The starter consisted of some cold unidentifiable something and cold glass noodles as main course. Having never had an Asian meal in my life, the taste was simply horrific. The noodles were all gooey and the brown sauce, which turned out to be soy sauce, was salty as hell. I also tried the strange-looking green paste with a Chinese spoon that hardly fit into my mouth. This was a mistake and drove tears to my eyes, as it turned out to be wasabi that tasted like heavily concentrated horseradish.

Worst of all, I had to eat with chopsticks. I tried hard to figure out how to eat with these two little wooden sticks but I was not doing well. The Japanese man, seeing me struggling, taught me that first of all I had to break them in two. The Japanese man also realized pretty quickly that I did not speak his language and tried his best to show me what to do and how to eat. I eventually gave up; this food was not what I was used to. The only good news was that they actually served wines. The flight attendant approached me holding a white wine in one hand and the red wine in the other. I asked her if I could see the label, which she clearly didn't understand, so I shifted in my seat to look at the label. To my disappointment both wines were simple French vin de pays but, since it seemed to be the only choice they had, I opted for the red wine.

The wine tasted as expected, too young and full of acidity, not the best choice for my half-empty stomach. At least it took away the terrible salty taste of the soy sauce and eased the burning sensation of the wasabi. The Japanese man had finished his meal and gone back to sleep almost immediately. I don't know how he did that.

Three hours and three glasses of wine into the flight, I began to relax. The flight attendants had closed the window shutters and turned down the lights. There was a movie playing but it was only in English and Japanese and I didn't understand a word. The wine helped me to relax and I tried to sleep. I lay there for a while with my eyes open but eventually I fell into some sort of semi sleep.

The noise level was simply too much. When I woke up the cabin was still dark and everybody else was still asleep, including the Japanese man next to me. I just sat there and read the same magazine over and over again; it was incredibly boring. The flight was relatively quiet and only once in a while did the aircraft shudder a little. The longer the flight lasted, the more uncomfortable the seat became. Finally, I settled into a state of restless sleep, shifting in my seat for hours.

Suddenly, the flight attendants switched on the lights and opened the window shutters. It was very bright outside. Passengers started to wake up around me; some got up and others continued sleeping, including the Japanese man next to me. I looked at my watch and wondered why they would wake us up now since it was only four o'clock in the morning. Why was it bright outside in the middle of the night?

It finally dawned on me that it must be the time difference between Germany and wherever I was right now. The pilot made an announcement telling us that our present position was somewhere over Canada and we had another three hours' flight time left until we reached Anchorage. I had no idea what time of day it was but I felt suddenly very tired. The flight attendants began serving breakfast with warm bread rolls and hot coffee. This was much more to my liking. The Japanese man had declined breakfast and continued sleeping.

Finally, there was the familiar sensation of my body floating in the air as the aircraft began its final descent. The final approach was long and I couldn't see a thing because of my aisle seat. Suddenly the whole aircraft shuddered as the wheels hit the runway and everything shuddered. We rumbled along for a few minutes as the aircraft slowed down and eventually parked at its parking bay. After over thirteen hours of flight, we had finally arrived in Anchorage, Alaska.

After Frankfurt and Amsterdam, I expected my first American airport to be larger than anything I had seen before, but the Anchorage airport was surprisingly small, nothing compared to Amsterdam and Frankfurt. As matter of fact, the airport was even smaller than Stuttgart. All signboards were written in English and I had no clue where to go.

I followed the crowd until we reached immigration and joined the queue. When it was my turn to step onto the small booth, I was greeted by a uniformed Inuit-looking border guard. I greeted him with a friendly "guten tag" but I could see by his puzzled expression that he did not speak German. He just nodded and took my passport. After checking with his computer, he made a few notes and finally stamped my passport with a force that made me wonder if his intention was to destroy it. He handed me my passport and waved me through. I thanked him in German and passed through a metal detector that, quite surprisingly, didn't go off.

Just behind the metal detector lay the baggage hall. The baggage hall was again surprisingly small with only five or six luggage belts. Coming from Europe I had imagined that everything in the United States was much larger and more impressive but this was not the case here at all. The building was small with a very low ceiling and I had no difficulties finding my luggage since mine was the only flight to arrive that morning. Or was it evening? I had no clue.

I loaded my suitcases onto a trolley. Finding the exit was easy since there were only two—one with a red sign and one with a green sign. That was easy enough. I walked through the green channel, only to be stopped by a pair of uniformed Inuits. One of the two talked to me in English. I didn't understand what he was saying. He realized that my English was not that good so he pointed to my small carry-on bag and motioned for me to put it on a table. I did as requested. He spoke again and this time I guessed he asked me to open my bag, which I did. He looked inside and asked me something in English.

"Tut mir leid aber ich verstehe kein Englisch," I said in my best German.

He just looked at me, surprised. He tried his luck once more but I still didn't understand a word. He rolled his eyes and motioned for me to move on. I thanked him in the only language I knew—German—and moved on as requested.

I pushed my trolley towards a large automatic glass door that led into the arrival hall. As I walked towards the door I wondered what to do next; I had no clue where to find the ship and how to get there. Once I stepped though that door I would be truly on my own. I reached the door and it opened automatically. I walked through it into the arrival hall.

The first thing I saw were dozens of people dressed in heavy winter clothes, many of them wearing fur hats. I immediately realized why—it was terribly cold. Many of these people were holding signs with hotel names. I walked past all of them until I reached the end of the exit channel. There was a life-sized grizzly bear in front of what seemed to be a souvenir shop. I walked towards the grizzly bear. It was a scary-looking beast and I sincerely hoped I would never meet a live one. *Fat chance,* I thought, *unless they can swim.*

I looked around the arrival hall, wondering what to do next. I needed a taxi. I was just searching for a taxi stand when my eyes caught a glimpse of the familiar logo of Hapag Lloyd on a large board in the middle of the arrival hall. I let out a sign of relief when I saw the board with the logo surrounded by people with luggage trolleys. I approached the crowd and was happy to hear that they all chatted away in German. A man in a white sailor uniform holding a clipboard approached me.

"Are you joining the MS *Europa*?" he asked in German.

"Yes, I am," I answered.

He lifted up his clipboard. "Name?" he asked.

"Andre Schwarz," I answered.

He looked at his clipboard with a long name list, his pen tapping on each of the names on the list and he mumbled, "Schwarz, Schwarz, Schwarz...ah, here it is. Andre Schwarz, restaurant steward. You are a new hire, correct?"

"That's correct," I answered.

"How many pieces of luggage?" he asked in an official-sounding tone.

"Two."

He took two luggage tags and wrote my name onto them with a thick felt pen. "Here, attach these to your suitcases."

"Yes, thank you," I said and dutifully attached the luggage tags to my suitcases.

"Okay, we are still waiting for a few others. Wait over there with the others," he said, pointing at the crowd of people next to the board.

"Yes, thank you," I answered.

I approached the crowd of people and parked my trolley next to some others. Suddenly I realized that many of the passengers on my flight were actually crew members of the *Europa*. Many of them seemed to know each other, judging by the intimate way they hugged each other and most of them were guys with only a few girls.

None of them paid any attention to me, which was fine with me since I wasn't in a mood to engage in lengthy conversations after the twenty-four-hour adventure I had just gone through. There were several others like me who were simply ignored, which led me to believe that they too were "new hires."

When the last man had finally arrived nearly half an hour later, the sailor shouted for us to follow him. We all followed the sailor to the other end of the hall where we eventually stepped out of the building. It was much larger than I had thought. When I stepped out of the airport, I was hit with a gust of freezing cold air. It was really cold. Heaps of snow lined the streets and most cars were covered in crusty white patches, which I presumed to be salt. The sailor asked us to wait for the bus.

I looked in awe at the large American taxis that lined up in front of the airport building, just like I had seen them in the movies. I looked around and the view was breathtaking. In the distance just beyond a large car park, large mountain ranges with high snowcapped peaks ran along the entire horizon. I couldn't see any buildings in the distance, only snow-covered forests and mountains. It looked exactly as I had imagined Alaska to be like.

The bus arrived five minutes later. The bus was big in every aspect, very big. It had sixteen wheels, two in the front and four in the back; a gigantic luggage compartment underneath the passenger cabin; and on its side were the words—written in italic letters—*Alaskan Greyhound*. I was impressed.

We helped the sailor and the driver to stow away our luggage and then boarded the bus. I managed to sit just behind the driver; from there I had a good view ahead. I was excited and looked forward to seeing more of Anchorage and Alaska but to my surprise, after a drive of only ten minutes, we arrived at the Anchorage International Airport Hotel instead of the ship. I was even more disappointed when I realized that we hadn't even left the airport complex yet.

The hotel looked much more like an oversized log cabin than an "international" hotel. In front of the main entrance stood two large Alaskan trappers carved out of two very large wooden logs. The whole building had a very crude look.

We got out of the bus and assembled in front of the massive main entrance. Some of the guys went straight into the hotel without waiting for further instructions and it looked to me as if they had been to this hotel many times before. I looked at my watch; it was five o'clock in the morning for me but I had no clue what the actual local time was. I asked the guy standing next to me but he was just as lost as I was. The sailor asked the remaining few of us to proceed to the hotel bar and said he would join us later with the keys to our rooms. There was no doubt; we had to stay for the night. *Where is the ship?* I wondered.

We did as we were told and went to the bar. The interior of the hotel was very log-cabin-like too. Everything was made of thick wooden logs and looked pretty crude. The floor was covered with a thick crude carpet and the walls were adorned with the stuffed heads of grizzly bears and large antlers. It all looked remotely like some farmers' houses in the Black Forest but larger and cruder.

We reached the bar where we rejoined our colleagues. To my surprise, they toasted with cans of beer—at five in the morning. I wondered again what time it was. I moved to the massive wooden bar counter where a young blonde lady spoke to me in English. I guessed she asked me for my order so I asked for "one kaffee," which, to my surprise, she understood.

Still, nobody paid any attention to me so I just stood there and waited for my coffee. The lady returned at the same time that the sailor entered the bar with our keys. He called name after name and distributed the keys. When he called my name I collected my key, which had a large crude wooden tag with the number 235 burned into it. The sailor told us that wake-up calls had been ordered for five-thirty and the bus would leave for the port at seven. I was relieved; at least I could get some sleep in a proper bed before joining the ship. So far so good.

Back at the bar counter I got my coffee, which was only lukewarm and tasted terribly burned. *So much for the famous American coffee,* I thought. I finished only half of the terrible-tasting coffee and then went to my room. I suddenly felt very tired and couldn't wait to crash into my bed.

My room was on the second floor which I reached via a large wooden staircase. When I stepped into the room, I found two beds, one of which was already occupied by a roommate. He was curled up and fast asleep. There was a large window with its curtains drawn. I walked over to the window and peeked outside. To my surprise it was daylight.

Our room was located directly above the main entrance and I could see our bus still parked right in front of it. I closed the curtains, wondering what time it was. I quietly got undressed in semi-darkness, brushed my teeth in the small bathroom and then fell into bed. I couldn't sleep right away and lay awake for a while trying to comprehend that I was in a hotel in Anchorage, Alaska. Then I fell asleep.

When I woke up several hours later, I didn't know where I was. I sat up rubbing my eyes. *What time is it?* I began to remember the flight and my arrival in Anchorage. My roommate was still fast asleep and for a moment, I wondered if it was the Japanese man who had been sitting next to me in the plane. I smiled. *Not possible.*

I looked around the sparsely furnished hotel room. Then I saw a TV with a digital clock. Thank God, at last. I couldn't read the time and decided to get up to take a closer look. Suddenly I froze. The time read eleven o'clock.

"Shit," I exhaled. It was already eleven - we had overslept! I panicked, worrying that we had missed the bus. I dashed to the window and opened the curtains. It was bright daylight—and the bus was gone.

"Shit, shit, shit!" I shouted and rushed to my roommate. I shook him. "Hey, wake up! We are late. We have overslept!"

"What?" the guy mumbled, still asleep.

"Come on, wake up. It's already eleven and we have missed our bus!" I shouted.

The guy sat up and looked at me groggily. "What's the matter?" he said, still half asleep.

"The bus is gone. We should have gotten up at five-thirty," I said, pointing at the digital clock on the TV.

Suddenly, he shot up. "We have overslept?" he asked and ran to the window.

"What do we do now?" I said with a desperate voice.

The guy looked at the TV and began to laugh. "Jesus, you really scared me," he said, laughing.

I was lost. *Why is he laughing?*

"Relax, it's only eleven P.M.," he said. The P.M. didn't mean anything to me; all I knew was that it was eleven.

"Eleven P.M. What does that mean?"

"It's eleven in the evening, not morning. We still have over six hours until we have to leave."

"Oh?" Then I realized that the Americans read the clock in A.M. and P.M. instead of the twenty-four-hour time system I was used to.

"Oh," I said, feeling pretty stupid. "I see." I started laughing.

"By the way, I am Franz," the guy said and shook my hand.

"My name is Andre and I am really sorry," I stammered.

"That's all right, but you gave me real fright." Franz laughed and we began talking.

I found out that he too was a "new hire" and this was his first cruise. We talked until after midnight and then went back to sleep. Franz struck me as a nice guy and I liked him immediately, especially when I realized that he was from Bavaria. We both didn't realize it at the time but this was the beginning of a lifelong friendship lasting until today.

The next morning we received our wake-up call and Franz was the first one up. I had a shower and once we were ready, we went downstairs for breakfast. Breakfast was served in the same place we had met the evening before—the bar. When we entered, nearly all tables were already occupied so we sat on the bar counter. Franz spoke a little English, which made the ordering of breakfast much easier. The quality of the coffee hadn't improved much but at least it was hot. Like everything else so far, the breakfast was very crude and very American, consisting of a lump of burger meat, eggs and white bread. It all tasted terrible.

Half an hour later, the sailor informed us that the bus was ready. We went back to our room, packed our bags ands went downstairs to board the bus. I was very excited; at long last, I would see the ship, which would be my home for the coming months. I couldn't wait. At seven sharp, we left.

I managed to get the same seat behind the driver with an excellent view ahead. The countryside looked wild and seemed endless. The mountain range I had noticed the day before stretched as far as the eye could see. There were snow-covered pine trees to the left and right of the highway and we passed several gigantic American trucks with huge trailers. After about half an hour, we left the forested area and to our right, the sea came into view. It was an amazing sight.

I noticed bluish white lumps floating in the water, realizing at once that the lumps were sheets of ice. It was a stunning sight. Franz had taken his camera and was shooting one picture after another. Soon thereafter, we entered a more populated area with harbor installations. I saw several large tankers at anchor in the bay but there was no sign of the *Europa*. We drove through the city and the road was suddenly lined with several large buildings. The buildings gave way to large storage halls and stacks of containers. Our bus took a sharp turn and, after passing two large storage halls, we reached the container pier with several large cranes. The bus drove along the pier, passing several of these large ships. Then the driver stopped the bus in front of what looked like a white wall with a gangway leading up to an open door. He opened the doors of the bus and one by one we stepped outside.

The first thing I saw was the large gangway with a banner on its side reading *MS Europa—Hapag Lloyd*.

I stood in front of the MS *Europa*. The ship was larger than any building I had ever seen before in my life. It was gigantic.

"Wow, it's huge!" Franz said next to me.

"You can say that again."

"Come on, guys, hurry up, we don't have much time," the sailor shouted.

Most of the guys had already walked up the gangway, leaving only us, the "new hires," standing at the pier, marveling at the thirty-nine-thousand-ton cruise liner in front of us. Chased by the sailor, we picked up our bags and proceeded to the gangway.

We entered the ship via one of the passenger decks. I didn't know where to look first. When we entered the deck, I thought we were in the lobby of a five-star hotel. There was an elegant, modern-looking reception counter and the walls were adorned with expensive-looking paintings.

"Turn right to the purser's office," the sailor shouted to all the new hires.

The purser's office was crowded with people. There was a counter with several uniformed pursers attending to the newcomers. Franz and I reached the counter and the pursers asked us for our names.

"Schwarz," I answered.

"Schwarz, Schwarz, Schwarz..." He couldn't find my name, flipped a few pages and finally found me.

"There we are—Andre Schwarz, correct?"

"Yes."

"You are assigned to the main dining room and your cabin number is...455 on deck two," he said, and suddenly laughed. "Oh, you share your cabin with Wolfgang Wolany. Have fun," he said mockingly. Some of the other pursers giggled. I had no clue what that had been all about.

He retrieved a key from a box and handed it over to me. "Sign here," he said.

I signed for the key.

"Off you go, Andre," the purser said and laughed.

I thanked him and stepped out of the purser's office. I waited for Franz. When we all had our keys we were instructed to move to our cabins, unpack our things and then report to our assigned areas at ten sharp. This took me a bit by surprise since I had thought that I would only start work the following day.

We were taken to our cabins by a friendly purser. The size of the ship was amazing; we took an elevator to the lower decks and then traversed a maze of corridors and staircases to the crew quarters. We reached cabin 455 and the purser announced my name. I unlocked the door to the cabin whilst the rest of the guys continued.

I stepped into the cabin that would be my home for the coming six months. The cabin was larger than I had expected; as matter of fact, it looked quite comfortable. It was a so-called in-board cabin, which had no windows. I guessed the size of the cabin at about forty square meters with a table and an L-shaped bench. Opposite the table, there was a small mini-bar and a wardrobe. Above the mini-bar on the wall hung a calendar with the picture of a rather muscular man posing in swimming trunks. This struck me as a bit strange.

On top of the mini-bar were a number of photo frames with pictures of what I assumed to be my roommate. I guessed the pictures were taken in various countries the ship had visited; one was taken on a beach with palm trees and another in front of an icy glacier. There was something strange about the way the guys in the photo posed but I couldn't quite figure out what it was. I continued my tour of the cabin.

Looking around I found my cabin mate to be quite organized and tidy, which was a good sign. There were no clothes or other things lying around; everything was nice and orderly.

The beds were set into the wall and, just like shelves, arranged one above the other. Each bed had a small curtain which could be drawn to allow for a little privacy. The lower bed, obviously occupied, was neatly made up whilst the upper one was left bare with a set of neatly folded bed sheets and a pillow. Next to it, someone had left three white uniform jackets with my name embroidered on it. I opened one up and was surprised by how much starch they had used, it was as stiff as a board. I hoped it would fit.

Near the entrance door, there was also a small bathroom with a shower cubicle, wall mirror and a sink. A short while later my luggage was delivered. I began to unpack and, since the wardrobe space was quite limited, I had to leave one suitcase packed. I would try to figure out where to stow my remaining things later.

I showered, shaved and got dressed. My uniform consisted of black pants, white shirt, a simple black tie and the white heavily starched jacket which made crackling noises whenever I moved. I looked in the mirror and, satisfied that all was in order, I checked my watch. The time was five to ten.

Assuming that it would take me some time to find my way to the restaurant, I left ten minutes early. When I stepped out into the corridor, I found it deserted. I decided to turn left and walked down the long corridor, passing several heavy watertight doors, and finally reached an elevator landing with a metal staircase leading up. Next to the elevator doors were a sign indicating that I was on "Lower Deck 2." I decided to take the staircase.

I passed another sign indicating "Lower Deck 1" and finally reached a bright elevator landing with several large windows on the main deck. Here I found a waiter, dressed just like me, waiting for an elevator.

"Hi, can you tell me how I get to the restaurant?" I asked him. The waiter looked at me and, without so much as a smile, he pointed to a large, heavy-looking iron door. "Through there," he grumbled.

"Thanks," I said.

The door was very heavy and I literally had to force it open. When I stepped through it I found myself in a small room with two more doors. The one to the left led onto the "Main Deck," according to a small sign, and the one on the right to the "Restaurant." Both doors were again watertight doors and it took the strength of a body-builder to open them. Finally, I stepped into the main restaurant.

I knew from the brochures that the main restaurant had over four hundred and fifty seats. Since the ship carried over seven hundred passengers, all meals were served in two sessions, or seatings, as we called it. There were large round tables of ten, smaller tables of fours and twos. In the center of the restaurant, there was a large buffet counter with several green decorative plants. Huge glass windows ran along both sides of the restaurant with an excellent view onto the harbor on the left and the ocean to the right. At the other end of the restaurant, I saw a gathering of waiters and waitresses. I walked towards them. At the same time a gentlemen in a white officer's uniform joined the crowd. I reached the gathering just in time to hear his opening remarks of what turned out to be a briefing.

"Ladies and gentlemen," he began. "First of all, welcome to all our new colleagues, of whom we have quite a number here today, and welcome back to those of you who have just returned from you vacation."

The officer turned out to be the restaurant manager and it seemed that he didn't like to give speeches, as he continuously glanced around nervously.

"On this cruise we have six hundred and eighty passengers. The first seating will be quiet and the second seating is full. I will now hand out the station plans and then you can get your stations ready." He mentioned the names of a number of VIP guests and their backgrounds and after that, he handed out the station plans.

"Schwarz," he called out.

"Here," I said and stepped forward.

"Station two," he said simply as he handed me the sheet of paper. Then he moved on to the next one.

I looked at the sheet, which was basically a table plan of my station. Next to each table there was a name and the number of guests on that table. So far, so good. The question was: Which was station two?

One by one the older stewards left the gathering and went to their stations. I began to wonder if they actually expected me to start working right away without some sort of induction. As it turned out, they did expect me to do exactly that. I and some of the other new hires asked the restaurant manager where we could find our stations. The question obviously annoyed him and very gaily he pointed us in the right directions.

It was at this point that I realized the restaurant manager was a bit weird. My station was right where the briefing had taken place. I went to the service station, where I found one steward busy preparing his mise en place.

"Hi, I am Andre," I said to him.

"Hi," he grumbled without looking at me. He didn't bother to introduce himself and I wondered what was wrong with him. He obviously had no clue of my background and that I had worked in a Michelin-star restaurant, which, from what I had seen so far, was eons above this place even though this was a cruise liner.

So far the reception onboard had been anything but pleasant. It seemed to me that nobody took care of us newcomers nor did anyone bother to explain anything. This would have never happened at the Columbus Hotel.

The nameless steward had already prepared tea cups, saucers and several sets of service cutlery. As I was under the impression that we would be sharing the service station, I decided to ask him if there was anything else that needed to be done. He stared at me, slightly annoyed.

"Look, this is my side of the service station and this here is your side," he said, and with his finger drew a line through the middle of the service station. "You better get your mise en place ready because the doors open in half an hour." He walked off. *So much for teamwork,* I thought, realizing that I was on my own.

Finding out which were my tables was easy enough; they were all tables that had not been set up yet. If I only had half an hour left, I had to get going fast. First, I needed plates, napkins and cutlery. I studied "my half" of the service station. There was a stack of menus and some unfolded napkins. The service station itself consisted of four cupboards and four drawers. Two drawers and two cupboards were mine.

Now it dawned on me that we only shared the station but didn't actually work together. I opened the drawers and cupboards and found that all were fully stocked with cutlery and plates. My station consisted of one round table of eight, two tables of four and three tables of two, totaling twenty-two guests if the station was full. *Not too bad, I can handle that easily,* I thought.

I took a quick look at my neighbor's tabletops, which were laid out fairly simply and straightforward. It took me less than fifteen minutes to set up the individual covers consisting of main-course fork and knife, starter fork and knife, dessert cutlery and one show plate. When I began placing the menus on the show plates, I suddenly realized that I had no clue what the menu consisted of. There was no time to study it now, either.

I prepared the rest of my mise en place, which, once again, I simply copied from my neighbor. *So far, so good,* I thought. *What next?* It all looked ready to me. Five more minutes until the doors opened.

My nameless neighbor returned from a cigarette break together with several other stewards. They were laughing, joking, and ignored me completely. *Not the friendliest and most accommodating team,* I thought.

I studied the seating plan that I had received from the restaurant manager. In the first seating, I had only ten guests—eight on the round table and two guests on a small table. I was very nervous and my station mate's unhelpful attitude didn't really make things better. I walked the station to get a feel for my territory.

A girl in black pants, white shirt and blue vest came charging towards me. She carried a tray with wineglasses.

"Hi there, you must be one of the new guys. I am Angelika, your wine stewardess," she said with a big smile. It was in fact the first smile from anyone since I had boarded this vessel.

"Hi, Angelika. I am Andre. Nice to meet you," I said. She squeezed past me and began to place the wineglasses on my tables.

"Oh, shit," I said, realizing that there were no glasses on my tables. "I completely forgot the glasses," I said.

Angelika looked at me and, still smiling, she said, "Hey, that's not your fault. Beverages are my responsibility and you just look after the food." Her tray was nearly empty.

I didn't quite get that. I had studied wines for the past year and I had tasted some of the world's best wines, which Angelika probably had never even seen before, and here they would not allow me to use these hard-earned skills?

"Are you saying that I don't serve any beverages?" I asked, puzzled.

She looked at me, shaking her head. "This is so typical for this place. Nobody has briefed you on how things work here, am I right?"

She was, of course, right and this was the reason why I looked like a complete idiot in front of her. The more I thought about my experience so far, the more unorganized this place struck me. This was definitely not up to the standard I was used to. I had only boarded the ship at nine o'clock in the morning, had barely unpacked my bags and was now expected to run a station. What kind of quality did they expect me to deliver if I didn't even get the most basic information? I didn't even know the name of our restaurant manager or the chef, for God's sake. I wondered briefly how Franz coped with this chaos.

In the meantime Angelika had finished setting up her glasses. "Okay, listen, Andre, I don't have time now, I need to set up my other two stations, but since the first seating is quiet, I will try to brief you a bit more later, okay?" she said and dashed off before I could answer her.

In the meantime, all stewards had returned to their stations, waiting for their guests to arrive. Many blue-vested wine stewardesses were buzzing around their tables checking glasses one more time before the guests arrived. By now I had figured out by myself that one wine stewardess looked after the beverage service for three stations. I checked my tables once more and then returned to my service station. My grumpy and nameless colleague stood leaning at our service station reading the menu. *Shit, that's what I should have done rather than daydreaming.*

213

Then, at eleven-thirty sharp, the doors opened. Guests began streaming into the restaurant. Since my station was close to the entrance, I was able to take a good look at what I would be faced with for the next six months. I noticed that my nameless colleague had gone. I glanced around but could not see him anywhere; he had disappeared.

What I didn't really realize at the time was that we only had one and a half hours to finish the meal service for the first seating. In order to do this, every waiter had to stick to a very tight timetable and the clock started ticking the moment the doors opened. That was the reason why my nameless colleague had disappeared.

My first task would have been to immediately dash to the kitchen, pick up, serve warm bread rolls and butter to each table. By the time my guests had been seated, bread and butter should already be on the table. The next step would have been for me to introduce myself to my guests in the friendliest possible manner in order to create the best possible first impression (this was vital for the tip, but more about that subject later), followed by taking their order. The key objective was to take the orders from every one of my ten guests within the first fifteen minutes of arrival in order to get to the kitchen as fast as possible, securing the best place possible in the queue for the main courses.

However, I didn't know all that at the time. Instead, I took my own sweet time, very much like I would have done in The Stube. Service timing had always been an important factor whether it was at the Black Forest Grand Hotel or at the Columbus Hotel, but never in my wildest dreams had I expected anything like what eventually happened on my first day onboard the *Europa.*

I watched patiently as my guests arrived and chose their seats. I noticed that most of *my* guests were in their sixties, quite a difference from what I had expected. Judging by the way they dressed and the expensive-looking jewelry they wore, they were not the poorest people, either. They looked distinguished enough to deserve the best possible service from me.

Whilst my guests were busy agreeing as to who would sit where, I watched my fellow colleagues. My nameless neighbor had just finished putting bread and butter on each table and he was in the process of introducing himself to his guests. He did so with a sugar-sweet voice which surprised me considering the unpleasant way he had spoken with me. What an actor. When all my guests had settled, I decided to do the same, went from table to table, and introduced myself. I used pretty much the same lines as my neighbor had.

"Good afternoon, ladies and gentlemen…ahm…my name is Andre and I will be your…ahm…table steward for the next three weeks." *Damn, that sounded really stupid,* I thought.

One by one, my guests introduced themselves and I tried my best to remember their names. After the introductions were done, I went back to the service station and picked up my order pad. I found my nameless neighbor preparing fish and other cutlery on a tray and to my surprise, he had already finished taking his orders. The guy was fast, I had to hand him that. He picked up the tray and stopped briefly, looking at my station.

"Have you taken your orders yet?" he suddenly asked. I looked at him, annoyed at his challenging tone.

"I am just about to. Why?"

He didn't answer but continued. "Man, you haven't even served bread and butter yet. You better get your ass moving or you are never going to make it in time," he growled and walked off.

His comments, as annoying as they were, made me nervous. What the hell was wrong with this guy? I picked up my order pad and went to the large round table. In the meantime, Angelika had taken the beverage orders at a speed that was truly impressive. My order-taking went as expected—a complete disaster. I didn't know the menu or the dishes and wasn't able to answer any of my guests' questions. As much as I hated it, I had to tell my guests that this was my first day and I didn't know the menu yet and this was not a good start. I found out from my guests that soups and cold starters were ready-made at the buffet and I had to pick them up from there instead of the kitchen. *Guests telling me how to do my job; this was really a disaster.*

When I had finished taking all orders, I went back to my service station. I had to prepare some fish knives since some of my guests had ordered the fish of the day, fresh from the Anchorage fish market - so the menu had said. To my horror, there was not a single fish knife in my drawer. *Shit, shit, shit.* There was no way that I could serve fish without a fish knife. I had to borrow them from my neighbor. I checked his cutlery drawer and found what I was looking for.

Once the fish knives were done it was time for me to get the bread. In order to save time I decided to get the starters and soups first. I took a large tray and headed for the buffet. I picked up the ready-made plates of food, poured two soups and placed them all on my tray. This was as far away from Michelin-star service as I would ever get. It was terrible.

Whilst I served the starters, my guests started asking for bread and butter. *Shit*. I promised I would be back in a minute and dashed off to the kitchen. Suddenly I froze - the kitchen! Where the hell was the kitchen? I couldn't believe it; nobody had bothered to tell me how to get to the bloody kitchen. *Shit*. I looked around the restaurant, searching for the kitchen doors. There were none. There were only the two main entrance doors and the two fire exits at the back of the restaurant and none of them led to the kitchen. Other than that, there were no other doors. *Where on earth is the kitchen?*

I approached one of the wine stewardesses, a pretty blonde with a tray full of bottles and glasses.

"Sorry to bother you, but can you tell me how I get to the kitchen?" I asked.

She looked at me and laughed. "The kitchen is one deck down. Take the escalator over there," she said pointing at the buffet counter.

"Thanks," I said and rushed towards the buffet, where I found an escalator going down. The escalator was the fastest I had ever stepped on; it took me down to the kitchen deck at an incredible speed. I jumped off the fast-moving escalator and found myself in a beehive of activity. There were waiters and chefs everywhere. The kitchen had an incredibly low ceiling and overall was very compact. I didn't know which way to go and where to find the bread. There was a long queue of waiters in front of the main pass. There was no way that I could just drop my orders so I decided to get the bread and butter first, but from where?

I asked one of the waiters in the queue. He pointed towards the other end of the kitchen, shouting, "Over there, cutie pie. You better hurry, darling, you are late," he giggled and the other guys in the queue burst out laughing. This was a disaster.

I rushed to the other side of the kitchen and found the bread station. It was empty; there was not a single piece of bread left. The station looked as if it had been hit by a grenade; all that was left were crumbs but no bread. I asked one of the pastry chefs behind the counter for more bread. The pastry chef, a rather small man with a very distinct curled moustache, yanked around and looked at me angrily. His reply was short and to the point.

"Fuck off, you puff."

My eyes went wide and I looked as if someone had slapped me in the face. I just stood there and didn't know what to do next when suddenly another waiter appeared next to me. He smiled and with a sugar-sweet voice, said, "Don't worry, daaarling, Jumbo is just in a bad mood today." He giggled. Then, to Jumbo, he said, "Juuumbo, coomme onnn, can we have some more bread, pleeease."

Jumbo turned around, grabbed a bag of rolls and threw it towards the waiter. To my surprise he caught it with his right hand and handed it over to me.

"Here you go, honey," he said and winked at me. *He looks like a gay,* I thought.

"Ahm…thank you," I said and took the bread. I began to feel that I was running late. I quickly placed the rolls in six different baskets and placed all on a tray. It took me a few minutes to find the escalator which would bring me back to the restaurant. When I stepped onto the escalator, its speed took me by surprise and I nearly toppled over. Having safely reached my station, I served the bread and butter but most of my guests had already finished their first course and rewarded me with some unpleasant sarcastic remarks.

"Is that the dessert?"

Now I really got nervous. Instead of immediately rushing back to the kitchen, my fine-dining habit took over and I checked to see if my guests still had wine. I searched the table for soiled plates or ashtrays, remembering, *Never leave the restaurant empty- handed.*

When I saw that my neighbor was already serving his main courses, I panicked *Shit.* I went back to the kitchen were I joined the very end of a very long queue in front of the pass. I took a deep breath; at least having to wait would give me some time to collect my thoughts. I looked down the long queue of stewards in front of me; most of them were my fellow newcomers, including Franz, who was three stewards in front of me. Once in a while I heard one of them shouting, "Three grills in the queue," and "Five grills in the queue," wondering what that meant. Each of these shouted orders was repeated by one of the chefs in the kitchen.

I studied my order, which consisted of eight different main courses, and I wondered how I would get them all at once up to the restaurant.

Then I saw how my fellow stewards tackled this problem; they simply piled everything on one tray. I watched one of the stewards at the pass loading five plates with cloches on his tray. He covered them with a cloth and then he piled the next five plates onto the first layer and again covered them with a cloth. I shook my head when I realized he was about to add another two plates on top of the two layers. *Impossible, how can they carry this?* I thought.

The steward picked up the overloaded tray, heaved it onto his shoulder, adjusted his grip slightly and then walked away. The steward in front of me, a fellow newcomer, turned to face me.

"Did you see that?" he asked.

I looked at him and shook my head. "How the hell is he going to get up that escalator?" I mumbled.

"Imagine doing that during heavy sea," the steward said.

He had a point; at that moment we were still safely tied to the pier but what would happen once we were at sea?

"By the way, I am Tony and I am new here," the steward said.

"Oh, hi, I am Andre and I am also new," I answered.

"You know, I can see already that we are going to have a lot of fun here," Tony said. *You can say that again,* I thought.

Suddenly, Angelika appeared next to me. "Hey, your guests are getting impatient. Have you called out your grills yet?" she asked.

I had no idea what she was talking about. "Grills? No I haven't called them out."

"Let me have a look at your order," she said and took my order pad. "You have two steaks and two soles, you need to call them out so they are ready when you reach the front of the queue," she said.

"I see," I answered.

"Go on, call them out. 'Two grills and two soles in the line,'" she urged me.

I nodded and said, "Two grills and two soles in the line."

Angelika stared at me and then laughed. "Do you think any chef heard that? You will have to shout a little louder than that," she said with a cute Bavarian accent.

I took a deep breath and shouted again but this time much louder. "Two grills and two soles in the line."

The reply came in an instant.

"Hey, we are not deaf here. Two grills and two soles, you bloody moron," the chef's angry voice screamed back. Angelika giggled.

"At least he has heard you. Hurry up, I wait upstairs," she said and left.

Tony looked at me, checked his own order for grills and shouted, "Three soles and one grill in the line." The chef replied in the same unfriendly manner.

"I tell you, we will *most definitely* have lots of fun here," Tony said, half-joking and half-serious.

When I eventually reached the front of the queue I was the only steward left in the kitchen. All others had already left to serve their main courses. The pass was quite different from what I was used to. The counter was very high, with glass separating the kitchen from the front of the pass. I wondered if this was done to protect the stewards from the chefs. There was a small slot through which the chefs passed the ready-made dishes. The kitchen too looked quite different from the ones I was used to; everything was stainless steel—the walls, the ceiling, pillars—and there was a huge flat-top grill packed with at least twenty soles and another one next to it packed with several steaks sizzling away. All grills, shelves and work tops had small railings running along the edges, presumably to stop pots and pans from falling to the floor during heavy seas. This kitchen was made for a very busy operation and mass production.

I bent down to the slot and shouted my order into the kitchen but there was no reply. Suddenly someone grabbed my shoulder and pulled me violently backwards.

"He, you idiot, in this kitchen only one person shouts and that is me, you brainless moron." The voice belonged to a huge chef who grabbed my order pad and studied it for a moment.

"Look at this order. Where do they find you morons, in McDonald's?" he growled. Then he pushed me away from the pass and bent down to the slot, shouting my main course into the kitchen. The replies came instantly. The chef finished with "That's the last one!" and pushed the order pad into my breast pocket.

"You stewards are just fucking morons," he growled again and walked away. The chefs in the kitchen roared with laughter. "Bloody morons!" echoed through the kitchen. One by one my dishes started coming. I stacked them onto my tray just as I had seen earlier and ended up with three layers of plates and still one spare. When my tray was ready, I awkwardly heaved the tray onto my left shoulder. I had carried full trays before but this was simply too much. I tried to balance it on my left hand, supported by my shoulder, but it was loaded far too

219

high and I simply couldn't do it. The tray was terribly heavy and I could only balance it with two hands. There was no way that I could carry the spare plate; I had only one choice, and that was to pick it up later. I carefully walked towards the escalator with my three-layer tray shaking precariously with every step. I stopped in front of the escalator and, hesitating for a moment, stepped on it. I was literally catapulted up towards the restaurant. I nearly lost my balance but caught myself before disaster struck.

I reached the top, jumped off the escalator and stammered to my station where Angelika was already waiting. When my guests saw me, they began applauding. Many guests in the restaurant turned towards them to see what was happening; it was embarrassing. I carefully manhandled the tray onto my service station and Angelika immediate began removing the cloches. She expertly looked at my order and dashed off to the round table. I remembered the missing dish and went back to the kitchen. The big chef was standing at the pass with the missing plate in his hands.

"Hey, you moron, what is this?" he screamed, pushing the plate into my hands. "Don't fall asleep here. Get up there and serve your guests and don't you dare come back here claiming the food is cold—now run!" He barked the last world like a drill instructor in the army. I took the plate and literally ran towards the escalator.

Back in the restaurant Angelika had served most of the dishes. I served the last plate, for which I was rewarded with a sarcastic comment from the lady on my round table.

"Oh, you haven't forgotten about me after all."

I went from table to table and apologized to all for the delay. None of my guests was listening; they were all too busy gulping down the food for which they had to wait such a long time. It looked to me as if they were all starving to death.

Then the restaurant manager appeared next to me. He didn't say anything but simply watched my guests and then looked at me in the weirdest of manners. Without saying anything, he walked off. *That's it*, I thought, *I am history*. I was sure that I would get fired before the day was over.

"Hey, don't worry, this is normal on the first day," Angelika said as she saw me standing there looking shattered.

"Is it?" I mumbled. "I don't think the manager is very impressed."

"Don't worry about him, that's the way he always looks," she laughed. "Now get ready for the dessert and coffee. We are running a little late." *A little late* was an understatement considering that most of my fellow colleagues had already begun serving dessert and coffee. It was a disaster.

By the time I had cleared the main-course plates and served coffee and dessert, most other guests had left. Then only my guests were still sitting and chatting away. Angelika pushed me to get my cutlery and crockery down to stewarding in order to have it ready for the next seating. This was a disaster; I had to use all equipment from the first seating for the next one. I hadn't thought of this. This was simply too much. My coordination was totally out of the window and so was my self confidence; I relied now entirely on Angelika's guidance.

One by one the other stewards finished their preparations for the next seating and then left for a cigarette outside on the sun deck. I rushed to the kitchen to pick up my plates and cutlery and when I came back to the restaurant, I had only ten minutes left to get ready for the second seating.

The restaurant manager realized that I was running so hopelessly late that I would never finish in time by myself. Then he did something which would haunt me for a long time to come—he scrambled all other stewards to help me to get ready. They did so only under violent protests and outbursts, voicing out their anger about me being late. *So much for teamwork,* I thought. It was a true disaster. I would realize very soon that teamwork simply did not exist and everyone onboard worked for themselves, *their* guests and *their* tip.

I had just polished the last set of teaspoons when the doors opened and the guests of the second seating entered. I was mentally and physically devastated and had not much hope for the second seating to go any better than the first one. To my surprise, this was not the case; as it turned out, quite the opposite was true. These guests were far more friendly and relaxed than the crowd from the first seating. They were polite and even asked me lots of questions about myself, where I came from and how I got to work on the ship. This was much more the type of guests I was used to and they gave my shattered self-confidence a much needed boost.

Things went much more smoothly and, desperate to prevent another "three-layer tray-juggling exercise," I even managed to sell

221

only steaks and soles except for one chicken dish. With Angelika's advice still fresh in my mind I coordinated things a little better and dropped some of the attention to detail—habits I was used to from The Stube— which at least earned me the *third last* place in the much dreaded main-course queue. Whilst I was waiting in that queue I realized that I had to get away from The Stube's style of service in this new environment and adopt the more appropriate Talasee-garden-restaurant-style of working. I would eventually find my own style, with the speed and coordination I had learned in the busy garden restaurant in Talasee and the attention to detail of Michelin service from The Stube in Freiburg.

The fat chef was not much friendlier this time around, still calling me a *bloody moron*, but the fact that I was not the last one in the queue made it a little easier to ignore his childish comments. My tray ended up with only two layers of plates, which made it much easier to jump on and off the high-speed escalator. Once again, I reached my service station safely and although I was one of the last to serve the main courses, my guests remained friendly and polite. There were no sarcastic comments or other humiliating remarks but compliments for the food and, above all, my service.

By the time I had cleared the main course and served dessert and coffee the restaurant was nearly empty. I had plenty of time to clean up my station and prepare everything for dinner service. After all was done I went to the kitchen to familiarize myself with the different sections. I had to know the quickest ways to and from the pass, cold kitchen, pastry and stewarding.

The kitchen was amazingly compact; the stewarding area lay between the two escalators, which were systematically arranged to make it easy for stewards to drop off soiled plates at the dishwasher when coming from the restaurant. Moving clockwise, one would first pass by the cold kitchen for starters, then the pastry and finally the hot kitchen that was located close to the escalator leading up into the restaurant. Opposite the hot kitchen was the rear of the dishwasher where we would pick up clean plates and other equipment just before stepping onto the escalator to the restaurant. I made mental notes of the different sections which allowed me to plan for the coming dinner business. I then went back to the restaurant which by now was deserted; they all had gone on their afternoon break.

Nobody had bothered to tell me when I had to be back for dinner nor had anyone taken the time to explain what went wrong with my first seating. I realized that I was on my own and I had to find out for myself how things were done here. *I can do this,* I thought as I walked down the center aisle of the restaurant towards the door leading to the main deck.

I opened the heavy steel door which was marked with a sign—*Crew Only*. When I stepped through the door I found myself on an open deck at the back of the ship. The weather was perfect with a cloudless sky and fresh, crisp air. I took a deep breath and for the first time since I had arrived onboard, I allowed myself to relax a little. I took in the surroundings that were truly stunning. In the distance, a large mountain range stretched along the horizon as far as the eye could see. To the right side of the ship were the pier and the port installations. To the left there was the ocean reflecting the blue sky on its calm surface.

I bent over the side and was amazed to see how high above the waterline I was; the pier was at least three stories down from where I stood. I observed several trucks unloading hundreds of cardboard boxes, presumably supplies that sailors loaded onto wooden pallets. I bent a little further and saw people mingling around the gangway leading onto the main deck of the ship.

"Hey, don't fall over the side," a girlish sounding voice suddenly said. I turned and looked into the smiling face of a fellow steward.

"Oh, hi there," I answered back.

"You must be new here," the guy giggled. "My name is Manfred," he said in a most gay-sounding voice.

"I am Andre," I said. To say that I felt a little uncomfortable is an understatement. The way Manfred spoke and the way he wiggled around made me very nervous but at least he was friendly after my stressful lunch.

"So when did you get here?" Manfred asked.

"This morning."

"Oh, my God, and they let you work the very first day?" he asked, his face turning mock serious. "That's typical of them and let me guess, nobody told you how things work around here," Manfred giggled and joked.

"Yeah, that was a bit of a surprise," I mumbled, unsure whether he was serious or making fun of me.

"Don't worry, darling, we will take care of you," he giggled.

223

Darling, I thought, worried, *why did he call me darling?* I felt highly uncomfortable now. *Was he gay?*

"I saw you at station two with Peter. He is a nasty piece of work, that one," he said. My neighbor's name was Peter; at least I knew my station mate's name now.

"Yeah, he is not the friendliest of people."

"My station is right next to yours. If you need my help, just ask me, okay?" he sang.

"Oh, thank you, I will. " This conversation was getting too strange for me and I decided to try to get away from him.

"What time does dinner business start?" I wanted to know.

"You should be in the restaurant by five-thirty to get your station ready for the first seating. Doors open at six-thirty, okay?"

This was the first useful piece of information anyone had given to me since my arrival. I knew all I needed to know and decided it was time to leave Manfred. I suddenly felt tired and hungry, realizing that I had not eaten since breakfast. I didn't even know where we were supposed to take our meals. *Never mind,* I thought, *food will have to wait 'til dinner.*

I looked at my watch; it was three-thirty and I still had nearly two hours 'til dinner started. But for now I had to get away from here.

"I am a bit tired actually and I still have to unpack properly. It was nice meeting you and I'll see you tonight," I said.

Manfred shook my hand, holding it much longer then I felt comfortable with. "You take care, honey, and I will see you tonight," he sang. *Honey!*

He lit a cigarette. I forced a smile and left. It took me a while to find my cabin, more so because I wandered around the wrong deck at first. I finally reached cabin 455 after traversing a seemingly endless maze of corridors.

When I reached my cabin I wondered if I would finally meet my fellow roommate, but he was out and instead I found our cabin a terrible mess. The doors of a very untidy wardrobe stood wide open, a white steward's jacket and a pair of black pants were casually thrown onto the dining table. I picked up a bow tie and an undershirt from the floor and placed it on the table. *Who was this guy?* I wondered.

This was not a good start; I was by nature a very organized and tidy person and what I had seen of my roommate was troubling me deeply.

The bathroom was not much better—there were plenty of water stains everywhere and it seemed the sink hadn't been cleaned for some time. It was evident from the facial hair in the sink that my roommate shaved wet. It was disgusting but I was too tired to do anything about it.

For a moment I contemplated taking a rest but I was far to excited to sleep and so began organizing my belongings. Whilst I was folding shirts and trousers I recounted the past hours since my arrival. The first seating had been a nightmare and I did not look forward to seeing those guests again but I knew I had no choice. I remembered the angry remarks from my fellow colleagues, which said a lot about the kind of teamwork I could expect. This was worlds apart from what I was used to in Freiburg.

The more I thought about the first seating the more my self-confidence suffered. I literally had to tell myself, *Stop thinking about it and get on with the business.* If I could make it in one of Germany's top restaurants then this should be a piece of cake for me. What I had seen today could simply not compare with the professional service I was used to. Considering that I was thrown into the cold water without any prior briefing or explanation of how things worked around here and not even knowing where the bloody kitchen was, I fared actually quite well. At least none of my guests had walked out. *Mind you,* I thought, remembering the way they had gulped down their food, *it seems they had been far too hungry for that.* I promised myself that I would never again end up in a situation where I would need the help of those arrogant stewards.

Slowly I began feeling a bit more comfortable with our living quarters, at least with my part; everything was in its place and I had even managed to stow away the contents of my second suitcase. Having finished unpacking and cleaning there was just enough time left for a quick shower and to get ready for the dinner. I shaved, got dressed and, after a last look in the mirror, I left for part two of my first day. My roommate was still nowhere to be seen.

I locked the door and left. When I reached the restaurant I did not dare to look at any of my colleagues. Not so much because I was embarrassed about what happened at lunchtime but because the lack of teamwork had made me really angry. In any case, each of them was busy preparing his station, paying no attention to me anyway.

My fellow station mate by the name of Peter was already there and had nearly finished his setup. Without saying a word to Peter, I started with my own setup. It was an interesting experience, working so closely together without helping each other or even communicating with each other. As with everything, I would get used to it.

However, as I later would find out, the reason for Peter's silence and apprehension towards me was far more complex. Peter was straight. So was I, but *he* didn't know that yet.

The crew complement of MS *Europa* consisted of around 300, out of which about 250 were male and 50 female. Out of the 250 male crew members, over half were gay and that's a lot. In the main restaurant alone, over three-quarter of the whole team was gay and that included the restaurant manager. That's where things got complicated.

As I also would only find out after my first cruise, we stewards made incredible amounts of tip. The tip very much depended on the type of guests we had but generally, it was very good, seldom less US$4,000 for a three-week cruise. Not bad for a 23-year- old waiter.

Most of our guests were very regular passengers and in many cases they spent more time onboard our ship than ashore. They would complete a one-month cruise, go back home for a week or two and then return to the ship for the next cruise. Our restaurant manager knew them all. He also knew who the "tax" and "over-tax" payers were. The word "tax" was our slang for tip. The guidelines for passengers in terms of how much to tip were listed in the ship's cruise brochure and were calculated as follows: 16 German marks (US$6.50) per guest per day. If a guest was known to pay "tax" than this meant the value of the tip was in line with the recommendation in the ship's brochure. If a guest was known to be an "over-tax" payer then every waiter wanted to have this guest in his station. We also had "under-tax"-paying guests who, needless to say, were not very popular with us stewards.

The decision as to which guest sat in whose station was of course the responsibility of the restaurant manager. The distribution of the different types of guests was never fair. Depending on a steward's relationship with the restaurant manager, the quality of guests would vary up or down. More often than not the highest tax-paying guests would end up in stations run by gay stewards. Only on few occasions would the restaurant manager voluntarily place such guests in our stations. Therefore, my straight colleagues had come up with a simple and ingenious solution—they pampered their guests like no other, treating them like kings and queens. They went all out in their service, which resulted in guests asking to be served by certain stewards again on their next cruise. In this case, the restaurant manager had no choice other than to follow the guest's request.

Besides the paying guests, we also had artists, lecturers and celebrities who worked part-time onboard and had the privilege to dine in the restaurant. They never tipped and therefore no steward wanted them in his station.

Just try to imagine having to run a station full of artists and entertainers for a cruise of one month. The financial loss would be severe. Artists and entertainers were the ultimate weapon for the restaurant manager to use against those of us who were not in the good books with him. Artists and entertainers never sat in stations run by gay stewards. The gap of understanding between straight stewards and gay stewards was substantial and although it never turned physically violent, there were frequent violent verbal encounters.

The restaurant itself, with its over 400 seats, stretched over the entire width of the ship and was clearly divided in the middle. The stations ran by gay stewards were located on the starboard side and the stations of straight stewards were on the port side of the ship. In the center of the restaurant lay the buffet counter, the escalators and a number of stations which were ran by us, the newcomers and some straight stewards, but most of the time the center stations were a sort of no-man's land. I was assigned to a center station because I was a newcomer and nobody knew yet if I was gay or not. Peter my station partner was straight, very straight, but what I didn't know was that Peter had been assigned to our station as a penalty because he had gotten himself into some kind of trouble with one of the gay stewards.

To be assigned with newcomers such as me was dreaded by all for many reasons. Firstly nobody knew if the newcomer was gay or not and secondly, newcomers almost always ended up in the kind of trouble I had experienced at lunchtime. Whilst the gays in the restaurant worked together to a certain extent, the straight stewards were divided into two groups—the old-timers and the newcomers. The old-timers had absolutely no patience for the newcomers and of course the gays. The gays amongst the newcomers would sooner or later be absorbed into the restaurant's gay community whilst the rest of the newcomers would gather into individual groups. I would end up in one of the newcomer groups with Franz.

The sexual preference of a steward came into play in almost every aspect of the day-to-day operation, as in side jobs, for example. Side jobs were tasks which were not directly job-related, such as the cleaning of windows, buffet counters and others. Every steward was fully responsible for the cleanliness and maintenance of the surrounding area of his station. This included the walls, floor and ceiling. In addition, there were bi-weekly side jobs, which changed on every cruise. These were bigger and more complex tasks such as the cleaning of the escalators, cleaning of the plants in the restaurant, polishing of copperware and more.

There were difficult and not-so-difficult jobs. It was normal that the not-so-difficult bi-weekly jobs were assigned to gay stewards and the more difficult jobs to straight stewards. Some of the more difficult side jobs were frequently used by the restaurant manager as *unofficial* punishment for various offenses or, as it would happen to me, for being a little too vocal about our fellow gay colleagues. Whenever such jobs were completed, the restaurant manager inspected the quality of our work and hardly ever accepted the results at first inspection.

Overall, the prevailing atmosphere in the restaurant was not too conducive to and did not encourage teamwork; quite the opposite, every steward looked after *himself, his* station and *his* guest. Many newcomers never got used to this hostile environment and resigned before even completing the first six months onboard. I survived my first six months but not without difficulties.

For the moment, however, I was completely oblivious to all these details and it was in this strange environment that I tried to figure out why Peter ignored me. That afternoon I finished the mise en place in my station except for coffee cups and teaspoons. I remembered that there were enough for lunch and now some cups and spoons seemed to have gone missing. I went down to stewarding and ask one of the Chinese dishwashers if he had some tea cups and spoons. His answer— "Fuck-off"—was very much in line with the prevailing atmosphere onboard and therefore did not surprise me. I went back to the restaurant wondering what could have happened to my cups and spoons. I had only one unpleasant choice left and that was to ask my grumpy neighbor if I could borrow some of his equipment and this was not something I was looking forward to. Back in the restaurant, the chefs were busy setting up the buffet counter. It was a stunning setup with an incredible choice of delicacies from all over the world. The key feature was a tower of live lobsters. I was thoroughly impressed; never before had I seen such a large amount of lobsters.

To the left and right of the lobsters were silver platters with tiger prawns and gigantic Alaskan king crabs. Goose liver, all sorts of gourmet terrines, salmon, trout and various other delicacies were prepared on mirrors and silver platters. An incredible amount of work had gone into the garnish of the platters and the decoration of the buffet. Butter sculptures, ice carvings, fruit carvings and all sorts of sugar sculptures filled the few gaps that were left without food. There was even a small pedestal made of ice on top of which the chef had placed a 1000-gram metal tin of Beluga caviar. I had served caviar before but mostly out of 25- or 50-gram tins; never had I seen caviar tins of this size. Looking up and down the buffet there was food everywhere; the entire buffet gave the impression of lavish decadence.

"Get out of my way."

Someone rudely pushed me aside; it was the big chef whom I had encountered already at lunchtime. As it turned out this was the executive sous chef, Obermeyer. Obermeyer had been onboard for over four years and, as number two, he ran the kitchen. He was a typical chef and in many ways reminded me of Chef Karl in Talasee. He was rough, rude and had no manners but he was a good chef and a hard worker. He looked a little funny with his rather small head and small eyes in proportion to his immense big body, which must have easily topped 100 kilos. If he wasn't shouting at us stewards, he barked and screamed at his chefs. We respected him a lot.

I jumped aside as he passed me with a large platter of cooked ham. "Sorry," I mumbled, but he was already gone.

I decided to get out of the way and returned to my station, where I found Angelika preparing her beverages. Angelika hailed from Bavaria close to the town where I was born. Except for her small size of little more than one sixty, she was a good-looking girl with jet black hair and dark eyes. She had an outstanding personality, always jovial, friendly and polite. I liked her.

"Hi, Angelika."

"Oh, hi there," she said. "Have you recovered from lunch?" she smiled.

"Yeah, sort of."

"Is your station ready?" she asked.

"Yeah, I think so. I am just missing some cups and tea spoons."

"I am not surprised. Cups and spoons are sort of rare here onboard. I suggest you guard them at all times," she said.

I didn't understand. "I have to guard them?"

"Yes, some of the stewards even take them to their cabins after work."

"Really?"

"You see, every station has a set number of mise en place just enough for one seating and sometime passengers take them to their cabins or out on deck and then, well, you never see them again." This was a first and clearly another reason why every steward worked for himself. "Sometimes if stewards don't have enough equipment they steal it from other stations early in the morning or in the afternoon when nobody is around. We can't lock the stations so stuff disappears, but mostly tea cups and spoons because we don't have enough of them."

I just stood there and looked at Angelika in disbelief.

"Don't worry, you will get used to it. Everyone does," she laughed and walked off to the service bar.

"You think so?" I mumbled.

This was all very different from what I was used to back in Freiburg where we set the restaurant up together, we served together, we had lunch together and we went out together; in short, we were like a family. Even the one or two gay waiters that we had there were part of our team; there was no difference. We had always helped each other. Since I had left Germany for Alaska I had never felt so on my own and alone. The reception in Anchorage and on the ship had been less than pleasant and not been at all what I had expected. Although the company had arranged the hotel, meals and pickup, I would have expected some sort of welcome and at least a verbal rundown on the program we would have to expect. Instead, people got upset and impatient when I asked questions and nobody was willing to help. Everybody was extremely hostile towards us newcomers and even the restaurant manager hardly spoke with us. *Hostile* was the right word because so far everyone, except maybe Angelika and Manfred, had been very unhelpful.

Since my arrival on the ship, I had not eaten because I had no clue where the crew mess was, I had no idea where to bring my laundry and if any passenger asked me for direction, I would be lost. Nobody had bothered to explain anything.

At six-fifteen the stewards, including myself, settled at their stations awaiting the opening of the doors. I stood not far from my "partner," who watched Manfred entertaining some of his gay colleagues at his nearby station. They laughed and giggled like girls and even I could see now that they were queens. Suddenly Manfred looked at me and came over.

"Oh, hi there, hoooney, so here you are. Good luck with your first dinner," he giggled and then looked at Peter. "You be nice to him. It's his first day, the poor little thing, okay?" He danced back to his service station. *Honey!*

Peter looked angry and shouted after him. "Piss off, you faggot, or I stuff something up your backside."

Manfred turned around. "Oh, reaaally, darling, come on, give it to me, I can't wait," he sang and wiggled his backside provocatively at Peter.

I had to smile; at least Manfred did not take shit from this guy. Peter looked at me, noticing my smile. He grabbed his tray and I wondered where he was going.

"Get out of my way, you faggot," he said as he passed.

What an idiot, I thought, without replying to his silly comment. Less than a minute later the doors opened and our guests came rushing in, looking as if they had not eaten for several days. I stood there observing guests as they entered; I was oblivious to the fact that all the stewards had gone to the kitchen shortly before the doors opened to pick up bread and butter. I should have done the same.

Most passengers were dressed much more elegantly than they had for lunch; as matter of fact some guests even wore ball gowns, which struck me as a bit weird but I had other problems on my mind such as getting the service timing right this time. However, in order to achieve this, I should have rushed to the kitchen to pick up bread and butter *before* the doors had opened.

The first guests to arrive were my table of eight, the troublemakers who had given me so much grieve at lunchtime. I followed a very big lady to her seat, greeted her in the friendliest of manners and assisted her with her chair. Instead of saying "thank you," she continued from where she had stopped at lunchtime.

"I hope we don't have to wait again for our food for such a long time. Please make sure you hurry up tonight!" she grumbled.

"Of course…" I still didn't know her name. Her foul mood was obviously contagious.

"I agree with Mrs. Hart. I hope you serve us a bit faster than at lunch," one of the other guests said.

"Yes, I will," I answered, still standing at the table instead of getting bread and butter. I had already, unknowingly, wasted valuable time and only when I saw Peter at our service station with a tray of bread and butter did it dawn on me that I should have done the same.

Shit, I thought. I picked up my tray and was just about to dash off when Angelika appeared out of seemingly nowhere; she carried a tray with the bread and butter.

"This is for you, go and serve it and then take your orders," she said as she put the tray onto the service station. I felt like a silly little trainee.

"Oh, ahm, thanks" I stammered. She smiled.

"You have to get it just before the doors open in the future," she said. I never forgot that lesson.

Angelika had taken all her beverage orders for dinner and had them all set up before guests had arrived. This had left her time to get my bread. She would help and guide me a lot over the coming days until I got into the swing of things. I managed to take my orders without problems and, having served the starters in good time and without too many nasty comments from my rather demanding guests, I was rewarded with a place in the middle of the main-course queue in the kitchen. I shouted out my grills as loudly as I could, which was relayed immediately to the kitchen by Chef Obermeyer who stood at the pass like a wolf guarding his den.

As I waited to reach the front of the queue, I had plenty of time to observe the kitchen operation. Despite the fact that the attention to detail and finesse was nowhere comparable with The Stube, I had to admit that the chefs did an incredible job, considering the sheer quantity of different dishes they had to prepare in such a short time. They worked extremely efficiently and to my amazement, when I reached the pass, my dishes came one by one just as I had ordered them.

Throughout this time more and more stewards joined the queue screaming the number of grills at Obermeyer. He repeated all these orders to the kitchen. He was doing this whilst checking my dishes, cleaning up the plates and handing them into my care. How he kept an overview of what was going on in the kitchen *and* the queue amidst all this screaming and shouting was beyond me but he had earned my respect.

I had to be very fast in checking the dishes and placing them onto my tray and as soon as I had them Obermeyer immediately screamed, "Schwarz, you are done, what are you waiting for? Get the fuck out of here," and before I could answer the next steward had already started receiving his dishes. I still had not managed to "sell" the chef's recommendation but at least I ended up with only two layers of main-course platters on my tray, which made life a little easier on the high-speed escalators.

When I reached my service station Angelika had already cleared the starter plates and all I had to do was serve my main courses. To my surprise I finished this before Peter; that gave me a much needed burst of confidence. Angelika worked the tables like a little whirlwind—she dashed through our station refilling glasses here and there and when that was done she helped Peter clear his tables. She did so without saying a word to him because she didn't like him.

I walked through my station and suddenly I found myself in an idle state, waiting for my guests to finish their meals in order to take the dessert and coffee orders. Coffee! I suddenly remembered that I had not enough cups and spoons. When I mentioned this to Angelika she said she knew and asked me not to worry. I was worried.

We cleared the main-course plates and I took the dessert and coffee orders. Once this was done I took my order and a tray full of soiled plates and cutlery and went to the kitchen. I prepared the coffee and picked up the desserts from a much-stressed pastry chef. Having been told "to get the fuck out of here" for the second time in one evening, I returned to my station in the restaurant. I found Angelika with a full set of coffee cups and spoons.

"Where did you find them?" I asked her. She looked at me and gave me a mischievous smile.

"Don't ask, just keep an eye on your stuff in the future," she answered and picked up some dessert plates. When all was done I was just about to relax a little but Angelika reminded me that I had to get ready for the second seating and sent me to the kitchen to pick up my plates and cutlery from stewarding. I did as I was told and returned with a tray full of clean cutlery and other equipment.

My guests were happily chatting away and sipping coffee when I was already polishing forks, knives and spoons for my second seating. I looked at my watch; it was only ten to eight. *Good!* I still had more than half an hour to get my station ready for the second seating. This time I would not need the help of my so called "colleagues."

As I stood there at my service station polishing my cutlery I observed my guests, especially the ones at my large table. Although I didn't know it yet, they were the stereotypical MS *Europa* passengers—retired upper-middle class, reasonably well off, doing two to three cruises per year, average age sixty and up. Seventy percent of the total passengers were made up of this type. The next ten percent were the "artists," which included all singers, dancers, news presenters, bands and other types of entertainers who worked mainly in the evenings; average age of this group was forty and up. The remaining twenty percent of our passengers was a mixed bag of the very rich and those who had saved all their lives for a cruise; average age of this group was seventy and up for the very rich and fifty five and up for the rest.

Amongst the very rich we had some of our most eccentric and to put it a bit more bluntly—weirdest—guests. To have a mix of the different types at one large table was a recipe for disaster because they would never get along with each other. One has to remember that for three weeks or more these people take three meals per day together—breakfast, lunch and dinner—and there were bound to be disagreements and frictions. And there were—lots of them.

On my first evening, however, I was oblivious to all this; I was just happy to have successfully completed my first seating in time. Suddenly I felt as if the restaurant was moving. What was going on? I looked up and got the impression that the restaurant stood at an angle. I had to hold onto my service station to steady myself and when I looked out of the window near Manfred's station I realized that we had moved away from the pier. I had focused so much on the service and the timing that I had completely missed our departure from Anchorage.

The ship was in the process of making a turn, which was the reason for the restaurant standing at an angle. I could feel my system trying to adjust to the slow up-and-down heaving movement, which it was not used to. This was made even more difficult by the fact that the restaurant was so large that there were only very few visual reference points for the eye to confirm to my brain that it was the ship that was moving and not I.

My guests eventually left at ten past eight, by which time I had already completed my mise en place for the second seating. I was a bit disappointed that none of my guests from the round table had said anything about the service. I had expected to get at least a "thank you" from them instead of them just walking off. The timing had been good and we even had finished long before some of my colleagues.

I finished everything at twenty past eight, of course not without substantial help from Angelika. I saw that my station partner Peter was still struggling with his cutlery and I considered for a minute helping him but then I remembered how he had dealt with me at lunch and decided not to. If this is the way it worked around here that was fine with me, I could handle that.

I walked down the starboard aisle towards the back of the restaurant and stepped out onto the main deck. The first thing I noticed were the loud noises of plant exhausts which hadn't been there in the afternoon. The exhausts were located one deck below the main deck and the other loud noise was caused by the ship's propellers thrashing and churning up the sea at the back of the ship. A chilly wind blew across the deck and despite the deck's relatively protected location at the very back of the ship, there was no place to escape from the icy gusts.

As I approached the railing I noticed the stunning view of the open ocean before me. I could see the snow-covered peaks of the mountain range stretching along the entire horizon. I leaned over the side to look forward and saw that we were approaching the entrance of the protected bay of Anchorage. Beyond the harbor entrance was the open sea. It was a fantastic sight. The ship was moving surprisingly fast and I could see the white-crested waves ahead as the *Europa* sliced through the icy sea. I took a deep breath, inhaling the crisp fresh air; it was wonderful.

I felt excited to be onboard and suddenly all the stress from the past hours seemed blown away by the icy wind. There was some excited shouting and pointing towards the horizon. In the distance I saw something floating in the water, realizing instantly that these were icebergs! I looked at several large, deep blue chunks of ice floating freely in the sea; now I really had the feeling of being in Alaska. This would be the sight for the next two days at sea before we reached the famous Glacier Bay.

The second seating was much more relaxed than the first one and my guests were far more accommodating and friendly. I got my bread and butter before the doors opened and with Angelika's help I served my main courses in good time. I even had some time to chat a little with my guests. The conversations with my guests were still very much restricted to some polite chitchat and my main focus was still the timing and accuracy of the service.

When taking orders I gladly accepted any changes to the menu as requested because I didn't know better. Over the coming weeks I would learn how important it was to manipulate the orders in a way which suited me, the steward, best. I learned, for example, that in terms of dining habits and relationships between guests at my tables, there was a certain pattern to every cruise. In terms of dining habits it is important to remember that the prices of these cruises were always all-inclusive, which meant that my guests could order *what* they wanted and *as much* as they wanted.

The menu for lunch and dinner consisted of thirty-five to forty a la carte dishes plus one chef's recommendation set menu. During the first couple of days of every cruise this resulted in serious feeding frenzies. More than once guests ordered two or three main courses at the same time. Sad to say that this was not unusual and there was not much any of us stewards could do about it. Needless to say, this was hard work and plenty of trays with three layers of dishes to carry.

The only way for us to get these incredible appetites under control and to prevent us stewards from breaking our back was to play along and recommend as many dishes as possible. The objective was that each guest would leave breakfast, lunch and dinner with his or her stomach full. Especially for dinner, it was important to have them leaving the restaurant as fully stuffed as humanly possible. Not even the biggest eater could continue eating like this for more than three days and that was exactly what happened. After the third day many guests had overeaten so badly that they began cutting down their meals to little more than two dishes, with some of them even skipping one meal, mostly lunch. To me it was amazing how well this system worked.

The harmony and relationships between guests, especially at the larger tables, went along a similarly predictable pattern. The seating arrangements in the restaurant were such that each steward had the same guests for the duration of a cruise, which on average lasted between two to four weeks each. Throughout this time the same guests took their breakfast, lunch and dinner together, day after day, week after week. Most cruises started off in perfect harmony because the different individuals had never met before and didn't know each other. As the days went by the different personalities and characters started to emerge and with it the likes and dislikes of the individuals on the table began to surface. One week into a cruise these differences between characters and personalities began to clash and more often than not they resulted in open conflict. Such conflicts came in various shapes and sizes, ranging from simple gossiping behind each other's back to sarcastic arguments at the dining table. Under such circumstances I, the steward, had to be seen as being absolutely neutral in order not to endanger the expected tip at the end of a cruise. This was not always easy but over time I would find my own way to deal with these types of challenges.

The guests of my second seating, however, were pleasant and did not give me any trouble, at least not that first evening. I served dessert long before Peter and by the time I finished with coffee and tea, he *still* had not served his desserts. Half an hour later my guests left and Angelika helped me to prepare my station for breakfast.

I set up my tables except coffee cups and teaspoons. She advised me to hide them or take them to my cabin, otherwise they would be gone in the morning. Since I didn't fancy taking equipment to my cabin, I waited until Peter had gone to the kitchen and then stuffed them into our cupboard, hidden under some napkins. At ten-thirty most guests had left and only five or six stewards were still busy finishing their setup for breakfast. Angelika asked me to join them outside on deck.

The main deck was brightly lit but beyond the deck railing everything was pitch black. Temperatures had dropped considerably and it was freezing cold but despite this, the deck was crowded with stewards and stewardesses talking and smoking. I went to the railing and looked out into the dark nothingness of the night. Down below I could see, reflected by the spotlights from the upper deck, the frothy white sea rushing by churned up by the ship's powerful propellers.

Franz appeared behind me. "Hi, Andre," he said cheerfully, with a wine stewardess standing smiling next to him.

"Oh, hi, Franz how did it go tonight?" I asked.

237

"Good, very good, I have some really nice passengers in my station," he replied. Then he introduced me to the girl next to him; her name was Birgit.

"Nice to meet you, Birgit," I said just as Angelika joined.

"Hi there, guys. Hi, Birgit," she said with her usual big smile. I introduced her to Franz.

"So how was *your* first day, Franz?" Angelika asked, giggling.

Franz and I looked at each other.

"Mine was okay, a bit chaotic but with Brigit's help it went fine," Franz answered, laughing.

"Yeah, same for me. Without Angelika's help I would have died in there." I motioned towards the bulkhead door leading to the restaurant.

Angelika smiled. "Don't worry, the guys in there are not the most accommodating ones when it comes to newcomers but once you get to know them they are okay."

Not the most accommodating, she had said. *That is quite an understatement,* I thought.

"Angelika is right; as long as you do your job, you will be fine," Birgit added.

"You see, they are all here for the money and nothing else. Everything here onboard is about money, you will see," Angelika explained.

"What about the money?" Franz wanted to know. Angelika laughed.

"It's all about the tip; they are all desperate to get a good tip after each cruise."

"That is the reason why all stewards work for themselves and *their* guests and don't expect for a minute that they will help you because they don't get tip from *your* guests," Birgit added.

"What about the restaurant manager? I don't even know his name yet—does he get tip?" I asked.

"Oh, Bohne, no, he doesn't get tip" Birgit answered. *His name was Bohne,* I thought.

"He gets something else if he is lucky," Angelika giggled.

"Yeah, from Manfred, most probably," Birgit laughed.

Manfred was the steward I had met in the afternoon, the one who had called me *honey* and *darling* all the time; at least now I knew he *was* gay.

"By the way, where do we take our meals?" I asked.

"We have a crew mess on lower deck 1. We show you when we leave," Angelika said.

"Great, because I haven't eaten since breakfast."

"You haven't eaten? Jesus, you must be hungry," Angelika said.

"Don't worry, I'm okay," I lied. I was starving. The girls told me that the crew mess was closed now. I could get something to eat in the crew bar if I wanted but I was far too tired to go and look for the crew bar so late. Food would have to wait 'til the next morning.

We continued talking and the girls explained what would happen over the next few days. I found out that there would be a welcome gala dinner the next day, something that apparently happened every new cruise. I was amazed how little we were prepared for our job and wondered how we would have known about all this if Angelika and Birgit hadn't been kind enough to tell us. They told us that there was a parade at the end of the dinner where all stewards lined up in the kitchen carrying an ice cream cake with sparklers. The lights in the restaurant would be switched off and we would march into the restaurant in one long line. This was truly amazing, we had a major event coming up and nobody had actually told us newcomers about it. It became clear to me that there was a lot we had to find out for ourselves if we wanted to survive the coming weeks.

The girls then talked about the gala dinner, which happened when half of the cruise was completed and the final farewell dinner at the end of a cruise. The farewell dinner, according to the the girls, was the time when we would receive our tip. I didn't really care much about the tip; I was more interested in the actual cruise and seeing the world and from what I gathered Franz thought the same.

The girls talked a lot and obviously enjoyed enlightening us newcomers. Unfortunately at that moment I began to get really cold out there on deck but couldn't admit to that, of course. When Angelika finally said it was getting cold and, more importantly, late, I was glad. We left at eleven-thirty and retired to our cabins. I finally met my cabin mate.

"Oh, hi there!" a girlish sounding voice greeted me as I entered our cabin. In front of me stood a half-naked man offering to shake hands. I shook his hand somewhat hesitantly.

"I am Wolfgang and you must be Andre," he said.

"Yes, I am, nice to meet you."

Wolfgang was only about one meter fifty and he had to look up to me as I stood in front of him. He had dark curly hair and was slightly overweight but otherwise struck me as a friendly person. I hadn't noticed him in the restaurant at all.

"So this is your first day, eh?" he asked.

"Ahm, yes, my first day. And how long have you been, ahm, on this ship?"

"Me? Oh, I am part of the furniture. This is my fifth year. The plan was to stay not more than one year..." Suddenly he swung his arms in the air. "And here I am, alive and kicking after five years," he giggled.

"I see, so you like it here," I said shyly.

"Yeah, I like it. In the beginning I wanted to see the world and now I stay for the money," he laughed. *The money*, there it was again.

"I want to see the world," I said.

"Sure, and you should, but wait for the first farewell dinner when you get your tip, then you will know what I mean."

"Yeah, let's see," I muttered.

"So, how was your first day?"

"Oh well, it was okay. Maybe a bit chaotic but I am getting used to it."

"My station is near the dessert buffet next to the crew entrance if you ever need help or if you have questions. Some of the guys can be quite aggravating at times, especially with newcomers," he said.

"Thanks for telling me. I have realized that when I met my station partner Peter. He is quite and asshole." I got angry thinking of the way he had treated me on my first day.

"Oh, you are sharing the station with Peter? Well, he is one of the less friendly ones but don't worry..." He waved his hand like an angry woman. "Dogs that bark don't bite. He is one of Hartmut's guys. Hartmut is one of the oldest and longest serving stewards and he and his friends think they own the ship."

"I see," I mumbled.

"Anyway, overall it is fun working here, you will see."

"How about the restaurant manager Bohne? He seems very quiet. What is he like?" I wanted to know.

"Oh, Bohne, well, she...sorry, *he* is a little eccentric, that's all," he giggled. "Overall he is okay. Just be nice to him."

"Oh, okay. In that case I will be nice to him," I said.

Wolfgang walked over to the two bunks. "Now, this one up here is your bunk. I have the bottom one if you don't mind," he said pointing at the bunk below.

"No, that's fine with me."

"I see you have already unpacked. I left half of the cupboard over there for you and these two drawers are for you too." He opened two drawers just beneath the bottom bunk. I hadn't noticed them and was happy to have a little more space for my things.

"Are you an early riser?" he asked.

"I am."

"That's good. Breakfast service starts at 0700 hours. I normally get up at six-thirty so you may want to get up at six then you have half an hour in the bathroom."

This arrangement suited me perfectly. "That's fine, I get up at six."

"Great, then that is settled. As for the cleaning of the cabin, I am a bit lazy and have arranged for one of the cabin stewards to clean the place twice a week. I pay him one hundred marks per month; we can share that if you want."

"One hundred marks." I exhaled "That's a lot!" The price was exorbitantly high.

"Don't worry, this is nothing, you will see. I pay for the first month and when you get your first tip we can talk again," he chuckled.

There was no way I would pay such an amount for a little cleaning; I would rather do it myself.

"Okay, let's see," I said unconvinced.

"Has anyone told you how the laundry works?" he asked.

Of course not, I thought, *nobody had told me anything so far.* "Actually, no."

"The laundry is run by Chinese, crafty little buggers, and real businessmen, too, those Chinese chaps." He laughed. "You have three sets of jackets and one jacket lasts you only one day so you have to send your stuff to the laundry every second day. They will tell you that it takes seven days to get it back, which of course is too long. For a little extra payment of twenty marks per bag of laundry you get it back within a day."

I looked at him in disbelief; twenty marks per bag—that was ridiculous! In my contract it said nothing about me having to pay cash to get my laundry in time.

"Why do we have to pay extra for that?" I protested.

"You don't need to but they have the upper hand and it is common practice. If you don't pay you don't get your laundry in time; it's as easy as that," he explained.

"I can't believe it."

"That's the way it is but to be honest, twenty marks is next to nothing, considering our tip," he smiled. Are they all crazy here? You couldn't possibly make so much tip that you had to pay for everything extra.

"Anyway, it is getting late; I will tell you more tomorrow. Now we need to get some sleep otherwise you will be dead tomorrow. We have the welcome dinner and that's usually quite late."

Wolfgang took off his undershirt and went to the bathroom. When he finished I had a shower and brushed my teeth. By the time I climbed into my bunk Wolfgang had already closed his curtain and switched off the light in his bunk.

"Goodnight, Wolfgang," I whispered.

"Have sweet dreams," Wolfgang mumbled and giggled.

I closed my curtain and switched off the small lamp just above my head. Trying to sleep that first night was close to impossible; I still suffered a little from jet lag and the sensation of my bunk moving with the rhythm of the rolling sea outside was something new to me. As I lay there my mind was replaying the happenings of the past two days. I thought of the flight, the first night in the hotel in Anchorage, the shock of waking up in the middle of the night seeing bright daylight and the first day serving four meal periods without the slightest introduction. Never before had I been hit with so many new impressions in such a short time. *Incredible*, I thought, *here I am now lying in a bunk onboard the cruise liner MS Europa, cruising down the Alaskan coast. Incredible.*

The movement of the ship pressed me into my bunk one minute and the next it seemed to lift me out of it; it was an interesting sensation. The noise level also took some getting used to; there was the humming of the air-conditioner and the unidentifiable noises of various other machines somewhere in the ship.

The most surprising sensation however was the crackling and popping noises of the built-in furniture in our cabin. These noises were identical to those on old wooden sailing ships in movies except that this was no sailing ship. The crackling noises came from cupboard doors, wall panels, the built-in corner bench and other parts which were kept in constant motion by the ship's up and down movements. It was like in a movie.

I couldn't sleep, not so much because of the unfamiliar noises or the vibration from the ship's engines but because I was all hyped up from the experiences over the past forty-eight hours. My mind wandered to my parents who hadn't heard from me since I had left. *I have to try to call them or get in touch with them in the next port*, I thought. Then my cabin mate Wolfgang began to snore. Great, at least he could sleep. At least he struck me as a nice guy even though he acted a bit strange at times. I would get on with him. I liked Franz and my wine stewardess Angelika; she really had helped me a lot and saved me from certain disaster; I felt I owed her. I lay there for another hour or so and slowly I drifted off to a restless sleep. I woke several times, always afraid of being late for my first breakfast service. Then I fell asleep again.

Eventually my small alarm clock rang at six o'clock. I groggily sat up in my bunk and immediately hit my head on the ceiling, which was right above my head. *Shit*, I had forgotten that I was sleeping in this tiny bunk. I opened the curtain and when I wanted to get up, I slipped and fell from my bunk, landing awkwardly in front of Wolfgang's bunk below. He didn't move and kept on snoring. *Thank god*, I thought, *at least he hadn't seen that embarrassing exercise*. I felt my way in the dark to the bathroom and took a shower. After twenty minutes I was fully dressed and ready to go. Wolfgang still hadn't moved and I wondered if I should wake him up; it was six twenty-five. I was just about to call his name when his alarm clock rang. He immediately opened the curtain and with amazing agility sat up in his bunk.

"Good morning there," I said.

"Good morning," he mumbled, rubbing his eyes.

"Oh, you are all dressed already," he said.

"I am leaving now. I see you in the restaurant," I said.

"Yeah, you go on. I see you later," he said, resting his head sleepily on his hands, sitting on the edge of his bunk.

When I reached the main deck I looked around and found myself surrounded by nothing but ocean. The sun had just crept above the horizon, bathing everything in a glowing orange light. Instead of going to the restaurant I stepped out onto the open deck where I was greeted by an icy gust. I walked to the very end of the deck and glanced out at sea. The view was amazing; there was only water as far as the eye could see. No land, no ship, no nothing. We were all alone in the wide open ocean. It was beautiful. The ship left a long frothy wake seemingly all the way to the horizon.

I took a deep breath and stretched; the view by far exceeded my wildest expectations. I checked my watch; it was six-forty—time to get to my station. The restaurant was still empty and I saw only a few stewards with plates and other equipment setting up their stations; as usual, none of them paid any attention to me. Since I had set up my tables the evening before I only had to add cups and spoons and to my delight, I found them all where I had left them the evening before— hidden underneath the napkins in my service station.

After a few minutes all was done. Was there anything missing? The only way for me to find out was to approach one of the stewards and ask. I looked around and noticed Manfred standing at a side table folding napkins.

"Good morning, Manfred," I said.

As I approached him he swung around, looking at me through small puffy eyes. He looked as if he had partied all night. He had taken off his white jacket, exposing a substantial belly. Manfred was in his late twenties, of medium height, slightly overweight and sporting an unkempt moustache. There was something about his eyes which looked strange but I couldn't quite figure out what it was.

"Oh, hi there, honey, how you are today?" he sang with a big grin. There, he had said it again—*Honey!*

"I am good, thanks, and you?"

"Daaarling, I am sooo tired and would love to go back to bed," he said and winked at me.

"Ahm, Manfred, I was wondering, what do you normally set up for breakfast...I mean, on the tables?"

Manfred stared right into my eyes while I was talking, which made me feel very uncomfortable, forcing me frequently to look away. When I had finished my question he smiled and winked at me again.

"What do we set up on the tables for breakfast? Come on, follow me and I show you honey."

I wish he would stop calling me honey, I thought, embarrassed. He led me to one of his tables. The table had been set up and only the napkins were missing.

"There you go, you need one silver stand with different jams and honey, *honey*, and I normally use two stands with jam for the large tables and one stand for the smaller ones. Then you also need some of these little beauties here, silver butter bowls, I really love them, and don't forget the crushed ice at the bottom," he giggled. He picked up one of the silver bowls, lifted the cover and showed me the crushed ice.

"You should have it all in your service station. Any other questions?" he asked as he put the butter bowl back onto the table.

"How about milk and cream, where do I get that?" I wanted to know.

"In the kitchen, there is a large pot next to the coffee station. The creamers will be prepared by one of the girls."

"That's great, Manfred, thanks a lot," I said.

"Any time, honey, any time," he giggled as I walked off. Manfred was a nice guy but his habit of calling me *honey* all the time was annoying.

I found the stands for the jam and the butter bowls in my station cabinet. After having picked up and prepared jam, butter and crushed ice in the kitchen, my tables were set.

"Good morning, Andre, do you want to join me for breakfast?" Franz said, suddenly standing next to me. Breakfast—the word alone made me hungry already.

"Hi, Franz, good morning," I said, looking at my watch. "Do we have time?"

"It is only six forty-five. Let's grab a coffee and a croissant in the crew mess." Having not eaten for nearly twenty-four hours, I gladly accepted his offer. "Yeah, let's go," I said, hungry as a wolf.

The crew mess, located one deck below the restaurant, was surprisingly luxurious, bright and with an amazing selection of food. On the walls hung pictures of the different generations of MS *Europas*, starting with the first MS *Europa* in 1891 to the present one, which was the fifth luxury liner flying the orange and blue flag of Hapag Lloyd. Large windows on both sides of the restaurant offered an excellent view to the outside world. Considering that this crew mess had to serve a crew of over three hundred, I noticed that it was surprisingly small with not more than eighty or ninety seats.

The key feature, however, was the buffet with its extensive food selection. I was impressed because up to that point my staff canteen experience was limited to Talasee, Freiburg and the less than commendable food served by the German Navy. The open kitchen was part of the main kitchen, which also served the restaurant. This was evident by the fact that even here the omnipresent king of the kitchen, Obermeyer, stood behind the pass yelling at us stewards if he felt that we took more than we should. I must have been the only one intimidated by his nasty comments; most of the others simply ignored him.

Nevertheless, he and his chefs had done a great job in preparing our breakfast. There were different types of bread, rolls, toast, cereals and a hot station with fresh eggs, bacon, steaks and other delicious hot dishes. Next to the hot station I found a big basin of crushed ice with yogurts, fresh fruits, berries and freshly squeezed juices.

In addition there was the Chinese-food section. I took a closer look at the strange-looking dumplings and meatballs in small bamboo baskets. The baskets sat on a steamer next to which were several bottles with darkish looking sauces. I had no clue what they were since everything was written in Chinese. That was enough for me, and having never seen or tasted Chinese food before made me wonder how anyone could possibly eat this stuff in the morning.

Franz and I sat at a table near the window; each table had a pile of the *MS Europa News* which was the only available "newspaper" onboard. *MS Europa News* were simple A4-sized sheets of news telegrams which the radio room received every night. They were then copied onto the news letterhead and distributed throughout the ship. The news was very brief and never consisted of more than four or five lines and there were no pictures. Nevertheless it was an amazing technology to receive the latest news in the middle of the ocean thousands of sea miles away from shore.

Despite the large selection of food all I ended up with were two croissants and coffee. I was too nervous and intimidated by my new surroundings and there were still too many new impressions, which did not allow me to relax and indulge in a big breakfast. I sipped a little from my steaming hot coffee and gulped down one of my croissants, hardly chewing it.

"You look hungry," Franz said casually.

"I haven't eaten since yesterday morning," I said, already chewing on my other croissant.

"I couldn't sleep last night, the noises and the movement of the boat kept me awake for half of the night," Franz said, sipping his coffee.

"Yeah, same for me. It's quite strange to move back and forth, left and right and up and down when you lie in bed and want to sleep," I laughed.

"I guess we will get used to it," Franz said.

"I am sure that after two weeks of working five seatings every day and no day off we can sleep anywhere, even in the engine room." We laughed and although we didn't know it yet, that was exactly what would happen.

Five minutes later we were back in the restaurant ready to serve our first breakfast onboard. The doors opened sharp at 0700 hours and the first early birds headed to their tables.

For breakfast there was no fixed sating and although passengers had the choice of sitting at any table anywhere in the restaurant, most went back to their usual seat and steward. During the first few days of a cruise there were always some adventurous guests who wanted to try other tables, mostly those near the windows and the ones nearest to the breakfast buffet. Most stewards did not like having to serve somebody else's guests. The reason for this was of course the tip. If my guests sat in Peter's station, they would block the seats of his guests. Peter's guests would be disgruntled by having to sit at another table and this could quite possibly have a negative impact on his tip. For a steward to lose his guests meant he had not briefed them properly and the others expected that the mistake would be corrected the very same day. I didn't know all this then and what happened next that first morning was to be expected - I "lost" a couple.

Standing at my service station I observed the flood of hungry-looking people, greeting them with a friendly smile and a polite "Good morning" as they passed. Some answered politely back and some were in such a hurry to get to the buffet that they simply ignored me.

I could tell by the way the guests were dressed who the regulars were and who were the first-timers onboard. The regulars dressed in track suits and looked amazingly sloppy, not always a pretty sight considering the average age of our guests. Something else caught my eye that looked somewhat strange: Most ladies had put on an amazing amount of gold and diamond jewelry, diamond necklaces, bracelets, rings and watches that clashed with the sloppy tracksuit. Some of the elderly ladies wearing track suits and gala dinner jewelry had even put on high-heeled shoes that made them look truly comical.

As time went by I would learn that for many of our female guests, a three-week cruise was an important opportunity to parade the latest and most expensive jewelry and dressing gowns in front of other wealthy guests. Seven days into a cruise this would many times result in fierce competitions between guests, in particular at the larger tables. The first timers on the other hand were dressed in casual smart attire with jacket and some of them were even wearing a tie. The tie usually disappeared after the first couple of days. First-timers in most cases were friendly people and easy to deal with.

As I stood there observing the different characters entering the restaurant I realized that I still had to learn the names of my guests and breakfast would be a good opportunity.

"Hey you," someone poked a finger into my shoulder blades. I turned and looked at a blond and rather skinny steward. He looked angry. "Is this you station here?" he asked with a heavy Austrian accent.

I followed his skinny pointing finger, saw my empty tables and then confirmed that this was indeed my station.

"Good, follow me. I need to show you something," he said and walked off.

Who was this guy and what was wrong with him? I wondered. He hadn't even introduced himself. I followed him reluctantly and about halfway down the starboard aisle he stopped at his service station. He pointed at a table near the window.

"Are they yours?" he hissed. I looked at the table and recognized a couple from my first seating, not my most favorite crowd but yes, they were mine.

I looked at him. "Yes, they are from my station, why?" I said innocently. If he wanted to know their name, bad luck for him because I didn't know.

"What do you mean, WHY? *Your* guests are sitting in *my* station, that's fucking why! Get them out of here," he growled and stepped back to make way for me to approach the table. I didn't understand and I didn't move either.

"I thought there was free seating for breakfast," I stuttered.

"Free seating, there is no fucking free seating in my station and now pick up your guests and piss off my station," he hissed. Wolfgang had told me there was free seating for breakfast and from what I had witnessed for the past hour that was the case, so why was this guy so upset?

"Look, I can't ask them to leave when they have been seated already."

The skinny blond steward grabbed my arm. "If you don't go over to that table and offer to take them to your station, you will be in the shit, sissy. That, I promise you."

Where was the restaurant manager or his assistant? Was there nobody who kept an eye on these guys or, rather, us? How could this guy ask me to take my guests back to my station when there was free seating for breakfast? The whole thing did not make sense.

"What is the problem here?" someone said. A tall elderly-looking steward with thinning straw-blond hair stood next to the skinny one. I had not seen him before but he appeared in control and projected an air of authority.

"Hartmut, look at this," the skinny guy said. "This pussy's guests are sitting in my station and he is doing nothing," he complained. Hartmut looked at the table with the couple and then at me.

"You are new here," he said calmly.

"Ahm, yes, my name is Andre and this is my second day," I said.

"Okay, Andre, look, there are certain rules here which apply to everybody and one of them is that we make sure our guests never block another steward's paying guests' tables, do you understand that?"

I could not believe what I was hearing; they really wanted me to tell these people to get up and come with me.

"But these guests are also paying," I defended my couple.

"Yes, they pay *you* and not *him*," Hartmut said, putting his hand on the shoulder of the skinny guy.

"Exactly!" the skinny one said.

"Now, because you are new, we will make an exception. You can leave them there under two conditions," Hartmut said. I didn't say anything and just nodded.

"First, *you* have to serve them and second, you make absolutely sure that this won't happen again. How you do that is your problem. Do you understand?" Hartmut's face had moved so close that I could smell his nicotine breath; he had a threatening smile on his face. The skinny blonde guy looked angry at Hartmut; he was not happy with me getting away so easily.

This was really something; they expected me to treat my guests like sheep. How could I tell my guests what to do and what not to do? I had no right to do that. What was wrong with these people?

"Do you understand?" Hartmut asked again.

"Yeah, sure, no problem," I mumbled and went over to the table with my two troublesome guests.

"Good morning," I said uncomfortably, the couple stopped staring out of the window and looked up at me.

"Do you know how long we have been sitting here waiting for someone to take our order?" the lady hissed at me whilst her husband just shook his head. *Here we go again, this is not a good start for my first day at sea.*

"My apologies for that but this is not actually my station and I just saw you sitting here…" The lady cut me off.

"We are not interested in your excuses, we want two freshly brewed coffee with milk and cream and we want them fast," she growled.

"Try to make it faster than our lunch yesterday," her husband said sarcastically.

There was no point in trying to explain the situation so I left to get the coffee. Five minutes later I served the coffee and despite them giving me the cold shoulder I wished them a nice day and retuned to my own station but not without being threatened again by the skinny guy. I was not happy; to get shit from guests is already bad but getting threatened by colleagues for something so minor was simply ridiculous. What was wrong with them?

Back at my station I found two guests from my second seating sitting at one of the small tables. *Damn, how long have they been sitting there?* I hoped not long.

"Good morning," I said as sweetly and humbly as I could.

"Good morning, Andre," the lady said with a friendly smile. Her husband looked briefly up from the *MS Europa News* and with a smile nodded at me. That was a good sign.

"What can I get you? Coffee or tea?" I asked.

"Tea for my husband and I'll take coffee, please."

"Would you like to order something from the breakfast menu?

"No, thank you Andre, we will get everything else from the breakfast buffet."

"Well, it's a great selection. Let me get your coffee and tea," I said and left.

On the way to the kitchen I had to think over and over again about the incident with Hartmut. Where had the restaurant manager Bohne been? I wondered if I should talk with him but then decided against it; it wouldn't be a good way to start my career onboard. In the kitchen I ran into the skinny blond steward who made some nasty comments when he saw me but with his heavy Austrian accent I couldn't understand and couldn't be bothered anyway.

When I poured the coffee for Mrs. Steiner—I got her name from my table plan— she had just returned from the buffet with an amazing amount of food. Mr. and Mrs. Steiner were not fat and not slim but looked fit and in good shape. The friendly couple was in their fifties and therefore amongst the younger ones on this cruise. To my delight they were not dressed in the sloppy tracksuit but in simple casual clothes. Mrs. Steiner must have been a beauty in her youth and with her long blonde hair and sharp features, still looked rather attractive for her age. Mr. Steiner looked like a chief executive on holiday and I guessed that he was some sort of senior manager in a large company.

"I can't wait to see Glacier Bay tomorrow morning," Mrs. Steiner said as I poured her coffee. "Have you been there?"

"No, I haven't. This is my first cruise," I said, slightly embarrassed.

"Oh, you must bring your camera tomorrow morning. Glacier Bay is stunning and if we are lucky we will even see a piece breaking off one of the glaciers," she said excitedly. *Glaciers?* I didn't know that we were heading towards glaciers.

"Have you been there before?" I asked Mrs. Steiner.

"Only once two years ago, but we had bad luck; we spent the entire morning in the bay but nothing happened. But I am sure it will be different tomorrow," she said and sipped her coffee. I suddenly realized that I didn't actually know where exactly we were heading to and made a mental note to check. I had of course checked the route briefly in the brochure back at home but all I remembered is that we would sail down the west coast of the states, not in what ports we would stop or any other details of the program.

"Just make sure you have your camera with you," she said again.

"I will make sure I bring it, Mrs. Steiner, thank you. But for now, enjoy your breakfast."

The friendly couple thanked me and just as I left their table another couple arrived. Slowly my guests began to appear one by one which made the service easy for me. Guests from the first and second seating mixed at the large table and I was amazed how different they were in character and mentality even when seated together; it was as if the second seating were guests of more class than the ones in the first seating.

Breakfast service overall was a leisurely exercise even though I ended up with my full complement of guests amounting to nearly thirty breakfasts served. Bohne showed up twice and on both occasions he just stood there at my service station watching me. This made me highly uncomfortable and had without doubt something to do with the fact that I had messed up the lunch service on my first day. I was determined to prove to him that I knew my job and dashed from table to table, clearing cups and plates, refilling coffee and having quick chats with my guests.

Bohne just stood there—he didn't smile, he didn't frown, he just stood there. I remember vividly thinking, *This guy is a bit weird,* especially because every time I tried to make eye contact with him he would look away. When I said "Good morning" to him he just grunted something unintelligible. *He was strange.*

When I had just cleared some plates and cutlery, he suddenly turned, bumped into me, and without apologizing he walked off. I was nervous and wondered if he was evaluating me. *Most probably,* I thought, *I am the new guy.* Breakfast finished at nine-thirty and my last guests left just after ten. My timing was good, all my crockery and cutlery was down with stewarding and I had already exchanged the linen on my tables with new ones. All I had to do now was to pick up my equipment, polish plates and cutlery and set up the tables. The rest would just be a repetition of the previous day.

I was determined to make the first seating work today and I ran through the service sequence over and over again. *Before the doors open set up bread and butter then take the orders, change the cutlery for starters and immediately go down to the kitchen to pick up soup. On the way back pick up starters at the buffet counter, serve starters and soups, then back to the kitchen and jump into the main-course queue and call out grills.* It wasn't really that complicated; speed was everything, speed and the coordination of the different steps of picking up and serving.

I looked at my watch; I had to get into the main-course queue before 1945 hours. That meant I had only fifteen minutes for the first five steps of the service sequence. I wanted to make sure that I had not forgotten anything and began to write the service sequence on a piece of paper. I started on top of the list with "bread and butter" then I drew an arrow down and wrote "taking order" and so on. Eventually I had noted down all steps and reviewed my masterpiece. By preparing this simple piece of paper I had unconsciously prepared a map of the service sequence in my mind and over the coming weeks I would focus entirely on reducing the time it took for each step to as little as possible.

For example, the escalator—initially I had always stepped onto the escalator carefully and then walked down rather slowly. With a bit more speed I could gain valuable minutes, both up and down. After a few weeks' practice and watching my colleagues I would literally jump onto the escalator, hold the moving handrail with my right hand, balance the tray on my left hand and then I would jump, literally flying over five to six steps in one go. In the end, when I had gained sufficient practice, I managed to take a leap from the top of the escalator halfway down, take another leap from there all the way to the bottom. All this was of course helped by the fact that I was tall and quite fit. Both Bohne and Obermeyer learned to hate me for this and more than once I ended up in trouble because one of them was waiting for me at the bottom of the escalator.

Another example where I could save valuable time was to limit the number of trips to the kitchen to the absolute minimum. The minimum was three trips per seating— one for starters, one for main courses and one for desserts; any additional trip would cost valuable time and endanger the timely completion of the service. In order to achieve this I had to be able to carry at least sixteen main courses all at once from the kitchen to the restaurant.

In order to achieve this I had watched my colleagues closely. They had developed methods and ways to load trays with up to four layers of platters and to carry them supported on the left shoulder. In addition they carried another three plates in the right hand. Such loads only became necessary if I had not managed to sell effectively the same dishes that would drastically limit the number of platters I had to carry. As with the escalator, I became quite sufficient in carrying such enormous loads.

Then there was the mise en place. If I had sufficient mise en place to set up the entire station twice, it would allow me to eliminate the need for having to polish cutlery and crockery between seatings. I know that several stewards, mainly Hartmut's guys, had double mise en place in their stations but nobody would, of course, dare to question them from where they got all this equipment. This was also the reason why I had found my station nearly empty when I started; they had literally plundered it. It was still too early for me to think of having double mise en place and I would eventually get it but I still had a long way to go.

At ten-thirty I was ready for lunch and to my surprise I had beaten Peter, who was still setting up his tables. I had a relatively relaxed lunch with Franz, Angelika and Birgit in the crew mess. This was the first meal I could enjoy in some sort of peace. Angelika told us all about Glacier Bay and how scary it was seeing pieces of the glacier breaking off and gliding into the sea. I couldn't wait to see it.

Chapter 7

After lunch we went back to the restaurant and by the time the doors opened for the first lunch seating, my bread and butter had been on the tables already for half an hour. The first seating was pretty rough with my guests ordering nearly half of the dishes on the menu. It was only because of Angelika's help that I made it in time without needing help from any of my colleagues. The attitude of my guests hadn't improved much; quite on the contrary, the couple that had breakfast in the skinny steward's station was trying to wind up the others because of it. I had identified them as Mr. and Mrs. Schulze, and that they were first-timers was plainly visible according to Angelika. Throughout the service I had the feeling that Mr. and Mrs. Schulze were trying to turn the other six couples on the table against me. I mentioned my concerns to Angelika who told me not to worry, saying that she had seen it all before. They just had a desperate need for attention. In time I would learn how to deal with this type of customers but in those early days I struggled to cope with it. Angelika urged me to simply ignore them because she reckoned that soon they would turn against each other and that they then would try to side with me.

I did my best to follow her advice and focused on the service rather than on Mr. and Mrs. Schulze. We finished lunch in good time with Bohne frequently "observing" me during the service. Strangely enough he "bumped" into me twice during his observations and I began to wonder whether he had a problem with the ship's movements.

What I didn't know at the time was that he was gay and had an eye on me. I only found that out much later when the penny began to drop as to how things worked on the *Europa*. If I had known I would have stayed away from him as much as possible. But, naïve as I was, I assumed he was still not sure about my capability as a restaurant steward and deemed it necessary to observe the way I was running my station. I was still afraid that he might transfer me out of the restaurant to another less demanding job. So I did my best to look as good as I could in front of him.

The second seating went smoothly; Mr. and Mrs. Schulze were as friendly as ever and I began to memorize the names of my remaining twelve guests. There was a table of six consisting of two couples and two elderly ladies. They hardly paid any attention to me during the service because they were engaged in lively conversations. The only ones frequently chatting with me were the two elderly ladies, Mrs. Straub and Mrs. Kern. Then there was a table of two couples who had been onboard several times before. Angelika had told me that they were "over-tax"-payers and if I took care of them there would be a handsome tip at the end of the cruise.

At that moment I didn't care much about the tip; for me all guests were the same as long as they treated me with a little respect. Overall the guests of my second seating were pleasant, much like the ones I was used to from the Columbus Hotel. Everything went smoothly that second lunch; by two-thirty my station was empty and by three I had finished the preparation for the welcome gala dinner in the evening.

For this gala dinner we used white, heavily starched tablecloths and napkins, three-stick silver candelabras and tall Riedel wine glasses. Once again it was purely by accident and a passing remark from Angelika that I found out I had to get a short white dinner jacket from the laundry. The lack of communication was truly amazing.

I got my dinner jacket the same afternoon from the laundry, which I only found after an adventurous journey through the endless corridors of lower deck 2. When I returned to my cabin I found that we had a visitor, Manfred. Wolfgang and he were sitting at our small table, looking at a photo album, giggling and laughing.

The two stewards looked at me as I entered the cabin with the dinner jacket over my arm.

"Oh, hi there, sailor," Manfred chirped.

"Hi guys, what are you two up to?" I asked shyly.

"Oh, nothing, really just hanging out, *honey*," Manfred giggled. He had called me honey again which made me feel very uncomfortable.

"Leave him alone. Can't you see that he is shy?" Wolfgang said mockingly.

I was not shy; I was embarrassed. I walked over to my wardrobe and hung the dinner jacket on a coat hanger.

"So tell us, how was your second day onboard?" Manfred asked.

"Better than yesterday. I think I am getting the hang of it."

"You will be okay, don't worry," Wolfgang said, as if he was talking to a small child.

"Well, I better leave you two alone then. I am sure you want to get some rest before the gala dinner tonight," Manfred said and got up.

"Hey, don't worry about me, you don't need to leave," I was not used to this kind of talk.

"I have to, I had a late night last night and I am in desperate need of some sleep." He winked at Wolfgang.

"Oh, I see."

"Now then, you two honeys have a good rest and I see you tonight fresh and beautiful," he giggled and left.

"See you tonight."

"What a queen," Wolfgang said after Manfred had left. "Don't worry, Andre, he is harmless."

"Don't worry, that's fine," I lied. It was not fine; *The way he talked was bloody weird,* I thought.

"So do you know what's happening tonight?" Wolfgang asked.

"Not really," I said, thinking, *How could I know?*

Wolfgang went on to explain that there was only one set menu and that the service sequence and the timing was important, especially for the first seating because of the parade. The parade was performed by us stewards whereby we all gathered in the kitchen with one ice cream cake—or ice bomb, as we called it–each. Each ice bomb had ten sparklers, which would be lit just before stepping onto the escalator. In the restaurant all curtains would be closed and the lights switched off and when Bohne gave the sign we all would walk in one long line into the restaurant with the ice bomb on our left hand. There were three gala dinners per cruise—at the beginning, the middle and at the end. I wondered how they expected me to know all this without any kind of orientation from my restaurant manager. We talked about the service sequence in more detail and Wolfgang answered all my questions patiently.

"Thanks a lot for this, Wolfgang," I said, truly grateful. "Is there anything else I should know?" I asked, to be on the safe side.

Wolfgang giggled. "Oh, there is a lot more. I don't even know where to start. We all have to do afternoon coffee and tea on deck once a week and then there is the midnight buffet which we also do once a week."

I looked at him, trying to figure out if he was joking or not but he wasn't.

"How do I know if and when I have to do this?" I asked.

"Bohne will put up a roster, probably tomorrow after breakfast. He normally waits 'til after the welcome dinner."

"I see. And is there anything else?" *Better to ask now than to find out later,* I thought.

"Oh, there is more. We have also a number of side duties like cleaning the escalators, polishing copper and air-condition grills and other ghastly jobs which Bohne will assign to us. He does a roster for these too and normally puts it up when we are halfway into the cruise."

"We have to do cleaning jobs? I thought we have housekeeping to do that?"

"We have housekeeping but they only do the day-to-day cleaning. The deep cleaning we have to do ourselves," Wolfgang said, wiggling in his chair.

"I see."

"You want more?"

"Is there more?"

"Of course, don't forget we are on a ship after all so we have to do lifeboat drills by law in every port. Mind you, not everyone, but we do it in groups."

I listened up. *Life boat drills—at least that sounded like fun,* I thought.

"Let me guess—Bohne is doing a roster for that too?" I guessed.

Wolfgang laughed. "Yes, there is a roster but it's not done by Bohne; it's done by the first officer, Lange, a really nice guy," he added.

"I see. And that's it then?"

"No."

"No?"

"No."

"So what else do I need to know?"

"We have to do fire drills, a lot of fire drills." Wolfgang exhaled, waving his hands in obvious disgust.

"How does that work?" I asked.

"Fire drills normally happen between breakfast and lunch and you will have the same station all the time. Look over there," he said, pointing at a small plaque on our door. "On that plaque you see our lifeboat station and the fire station."

I looked at the plaque, which indicated the location of our assigned lifeboat and the location of our fire station.

"I guess there is more," I said, expecting him to come up with something else.

"No, that's all, but the fire drills they take quite seriously when it comes to timing and so on. You see, if there is a fire somewhere out at sea they can't simply call the fire brigade so that's why we have to do it," he explained.

"Makes sense," I agreed.

"Yeah, and the first officer can get really pissed off if someone doesn't show up in time or stays away completely which happens sometimes, especially if there was a party the evening before," he giggled.

"So what happens if you are late or don't show up?"

"Then your ass is grass," Wolfgang chuckled, pronouncing the word ass as "aaaass."

"No, be serious, what happens?" I wanted to know.

"You get a warning and if you have three such warnings you have to see the captain and that's bad news because he can send you home."

"Oh, really?"

"Yes, really."

I knew that would never happen to me because I would take this seriously and besides, it sounded far too exciting to me to miss; it had an air of adventure to it.

"If there are no other questions I will take a nap, Your Honor," Wolfgang joked.

"No other questions," I replied.

Wolfgang got up and, without being shy, began to undress. I took the opportunity to go to the washroom. When I came back he had disappeared, with the curtains of his bunk closed. I climbed in my bunk and before I knew it I was fast asleep.

When I returned to the restaurant three hours later it had been transformed into something like a large fine dining room. The tables were all laid up with shiny silver cutlery, highly polished candelabras and beautiful flower bouquets. The buffet counter in the center of the restaurant was covered in live lobster, illuminated ice carvings and the chefs were setting up caviar stations. It looked truly splendid and so did I. I wore my short white dinner jacket with bow tie and for the occasion I had used my most expensive Boss after shave.

On my station I found a stack of gala menus fresh off the ship's press, which I began to fold immediately to make sure that my station was ready in time.

"You look absolutely splendid, honey," Manfred suddenly chirped next to me. "Let me take a look at you."

"Hi, Manfred," I said, slightly embarrassed. Of course at the same moment Peter appeared at our station. He was dressed in the same outfit but somehow looked uncomfortable in it.

"Can I get to my station, please, ladies?" he said and pushed his way in between Manfred and me. *Ladies!* I really didn't like this guy.

"Hey, don't be so rude, you whore," Manfred said and walked away wiggling his backside. *They are all nuts here,* I thought.

"Hi, Andre, nice outfit," Angelika said as I was in the middle of setting up bread and butter on my tables.

"Thanks, same for you," I lied. Angelika was still wearing her usual blue vest and black skirt.

"Yeah, right," she answered and we both laughed.

Just before the doors opened Bohne came to check if everyone was ready. When he had finished his round through the restaurant he stopped right next to me and just stood there looking at my tables; he didn't say a word, the weirdo. He just stood there staring at my station. I followed his glance but I could not find anything missing or wrong. When he eventually turned around to walk away I quickly stepped back to make sure he didn't bump into me again and he didn't. That man *was* weird; so far he had not spoken one single word to me.

He opened the doors as usual at seven sharp and our guests, all dressed in their most expensive and glamorous-looking evening gowns, hurried to their tables. Dinner service was easy and smooth since we only served one set menu. Once every guest was seated Bohne ordered us to the kitchen to pick up the starters; this was the first time I saw him actually working. There was a long line of stewards waiting for their starters in front of the cold kitchen. I joined the queue and patiently waited with my tray until it was my turn to pick up the starters for my guests.

As usual Obermeyer stood there like King Kong yelling at us "morons" to move faster. The more senior stewards were not afraid of him and yelled back at him to keep his "trap shut," which caused laughter and some rude remarks from the rest of us. I realized that I had never met the actual chef before and wondered where he was; it seemed that Obermeyer was running the kitchen all by himself.

I reached the front of the queue, picked up my plates and carefully placed them onto my tray. Obermeyer watched with eagle eyes and suddenly he began to scream.

"Be careful, for God's sake, this is food and not your bloody girlfriend. Or should I say boyfriend? With you morons, one never knows."

In the kitchen the chefs were laughing and yelling. I was still too new to answer back but one day I would have to say something otherwise this would never stop, especially the reference to boyfriends and other remarks insinuating I was gay, which really began to annoy me.

When I served the starters my guests hardly paid any attention to me, which was a first. As usual Mr. and Mrs. Schulze dominated the conversation whilst the others had to listen. Judging by the looks on their faces they had the same problem I had with Obermeyer; they too would soon have to say something Mr. and Mrs. Schulze would never stop.

After we had cleared the starters we served the soup and finally the main course. The service went smoothly and the timing was perfect; I did not give the Schulzes any opportunity to give me grief. On the other hand, Mrs. Schulze was far too busy telling her fellow travelers where she got her dress, emphasizing several times how expensive it was. *It doesn't look expensive,* I thought. The lack of interest in her dress was plainly visible on the faces of the others around the table but so far they were still too polite to ask her to shut up.

Twenty minutes later I cleared the main-course plates and cleaned the tables, set up the dessert cutlery and, having learned to coordinate as many tasks as possible, I took the order for tea and coffee before going down to the kitchen to prepare for the long awaited parade. In the pastry Jumbo had already prepared over twenty round platters with the ice bombs, each topped with ten sparklers. We all took one platter as we passed the pastry and then lined up in front of the escalator.

The escalator had been stopped to allow the parade of stewards to enter the restaurant in a properly spaced fashion. For this we stewards had to wait in the right order that allowed us, once we were in the restaurant, to walk around the buffet counter and then leave the parade to go to each of our tables. This had to happen in sequence, starting with the first steward in line then the next one and so on.

Bohne walked down the line of waiting stewards and checked if we stood in the right sequence and, of course we were not. He moved us around until he was satisfied that the sequence was in order. He grabbed my arm and moved me from the middle of the queue to the front where I ended up just behind Peter. Bohne, as usual, did all this without saying a word. Manfred stood slightly ahead of me and as he saw me coming he greeted me with a girlish voice.

"Oh, hi there, honey."

I could have died. I was embarrassed in front of my fellow stewards and forced a smile. At the same time Peter looked at me with disgust in his face and I could see that he thought that I was one of them. When the last steward had taken his place in the queue Bohne signaled to Obermeyer, who was waiting in front of the queue, to light his mini-torch.

In the meantime, in the restaurant, the assistant restaurant manager had switched of all lights and it was now pitch black. Then Obermeyer received the signal from Bohne to light our sparklers, which he did while making his usual rude remarks as we passed by–"Come on, honeys, let's get this gay parade on the roll."

"Oh, yeah, give it to me, daaarling," Manfred chirped excitedly. "Light my fire, dear Obermeyer."

The whole kitchen roared with laughter. One by one we passed by Obermeyer who lit our sparklers with his handheld mini-torch. When ten waiters had crowded the escalator, Bohne stepped aside, shouted "Go" and we began marching up the escalator into the restaurant.

In the kitchen the queue began moving and when I reached Obermeyer he torched my sparklers which lit up instantly, exploding into a mini volcano, sparkles flying to the left and right. I entered the restaurant walking just behind Peter.

It must have been an interesting sight as our long column of stewards, each with his mini-volcano, entered the pitch-black restaurant. Suddenly the restaurant exploded in applause with guests yelling, "Aaahh" and "Oooh," accompanied by a multitude of camera flashes. We solemnly moved around the buffet in a column of sparkling fire and when the round was completed the stewards ahead of me began to sheer out of the parade, walking towards their tables. When it was my turn I simply followed Peter to our service station where we were greeted with more "Aaahh"s and "Oooh"s from our guests.

As Wolfgang had told me in the afternoon, I went from table to table presenting the ice bomb to my guests. A moment later the lights came back on, instantly bathing the restaurant in glaring bright light. I was called by my guests from one table to the next where they took pictures with me and the ice bomb, all except the Schulzes, who didn't appreciate the fact that I was suddenly the center of attention.

When the photo sessions finally finished my sparklers had all but disappeared. I returned to my service station and began cutting and portioning pieces of the ice bomb onto dessert plates. With Angelika's help I served desserts. I went to the kitchen to get the coffees which I had taken orders for earlier. This had been a wise decision which earned me a place in the very front of the coffee queue. I served my coffees in good time.

I didn't waste time and immediately began preparing my station for the second seating. I got my customary visit from Bohne, giving his usual weird performance of watching me silently. Unfortunately I didn't pay attention and therefore didn't see when he turned to leave, allowing him to "accidentally" bump into me with his hand brushing against my back side. *Shit,* I thought, *and he got away with it.* He really began to annoy me.

When my guests eventually began to leave, I felt that they had changed for the better and to my surprise, they all thanked me one by one for a wonderful dinner, all except Mr. and Mrs. Schulze, who left without saying a word.

My guests of the second seating looked truly stunning with ladies in beautiful evening gowns and the gentlemen in elegant tuxedos. I realized again that there was a distinct difference between the guests of the first and second seating, with the latter being far more sophisticated. The gala dinner went smoothly and once again our parade ended in applause and lots of photos. When all guests had left I began preparing mise en place and setting up my tables for breakfast.

We had been at sea now for two full days and I had seen nothing but ocean, and whilst we had been serving our welcome dinner that night, MS *Europa* continued cruising due south through the Gulf of Alaska which would bring us into Glacier Bay early the following morning.

That night, however, I had no idea where we were or where we were going. All I knew was that I had to get used to the gentle and ever-present sensation of constant movement. I wasn't seasick but I didn't feel perfect either; it was some weird feeling in between. Normally during the service I was too busy to feel anything but once I began to relax, the movement of the ship seemed to become stronger and I began to feel a little nauseated, just enough to remind me that I was on a ship. Things were slightly better when we gathered outside on deck which presumably was because of the ample supply of fresh air.

As I was polishing my cutlery for breakfast the next morning I tried to ignore the gentle up and down movements of the 39,000-ton ship. I tried to think of something else to divert my attention. That "something else" was Tatiana, who I realized hadn't heard from me since I had left. *Damn, how could that have happened?* I promised myself to write to her immediately that same night. Half an hour later I finished and after I had hidden my coffee cups and spoons under the napkins in my cupboard I joined the others out on deck.

Outside on the main deck was party time. It was extremely chilly, as to be expected in Alaska, with freezing gusts blowing across the deck. Beyond the brightly illuminated main deck was nothing except pitch-black darkness.

To my delight I found that some chefs had set up a makeshift bar from which they sold Gluehwine by the cup for a couple of German marks. Next to the steaming hot pot of Gluehwine stood a small HiFi system playing the latest in rock and pop. The HiFi system was working at full blast to exceed the background noises from various unseen machinery and the thrashing of the ship's propellers at its stern. The deck was crowded with stewards, chefs and other ship personnel. I found Angelika and Franz standing with some other colleagues near the starboard railing.

"Over here," Angelika called out when she saw me, waving her hands. I joined the group and Angelika immediately asked me if I wanted a cup of Gluehwine. *What a question,* I thought, *I could down an entire bucket by myself in this freezing cold.*

"Yes, please," I said. Angelika dashed off to get me a cup.

"How are you guys?" I asked no one in particular and because I didn't know what else to say. Besides Franz there was Birgit and two other colleagues, both of whom I hadn't met yet. The two introduced themselves as Michael and Iris. I could see by their red faces that the Gluehwine had started to lighten the mood and atmosphere already. This was the case not only in our group but there was laughter and chatter coming from all across the main deck.

"Where is your cup?" Franz shouted as he looked at me with glassy eyes.

"Angelika is getting me one," I said just as she returned holding a cup with steaming hot Gluehwine.

"Let's drink to your first cruise onboard the *Europa*," she laughed. They all raised their cups shouting "Cheers."

"Cheers," I joined in and took a sip. The Gluehwine was excellent and I could feel the warmth spreading throughout my system as the hot liquid found its way to my stomach. It felt wonderful out there in the middle of the freezing cold Alaskan sea.

"So how are you guys settling in?" Michael asked, looking at me and then at Franz.

"It has been quite a ride," Franz smiled.

"Getting there," I answered.

Michael nodded his head, laughing. "Trust me, I know how you feel. Working on this steamer takes getting used to but don't worry, we all had to go through this in the beginning."

"Did you enjoy your orientation?" Iris asked jokingly.

What orientation? Nobody has oriented me on anything, I thought.

"Can be improved," Franz answered.

"Yeah, I know but that's Bohne for you. He doesn't give a shit about newcomers and neither does anyone else. You either make it or you don't," Michael said, and from the tone of his voice I could tell that he didn't like Bohne. "He only looks after his fellow sissies," he said, talking like a girl. We all laughed.

"I think his problem is that he doesn't know how to handle straight guys," Angelika said, taking a sip from her Gluehwine.

Michael and Iris nodded. "That's a bloody understatement," Michael said.

Suddenly Manfred appeared out of the dark and elbowed his way into the center of our small group. "Hello, darlings, are we having fun?" he chirped, wiggling his lower body like a woman. *He is definitely, undoubtedly gay,* I thought.

"Hi, Manfred," Angelika imitated his voice and we all laughed.

Manfred took her in her arms. "Oh, my darling Angelika, why are you not my wine bitch on this trip? I miss you sooo much." He squeezed Angelika and she grimaced at us.

"I can't breathe, Manfred." Angelika pretended to be struggling in his grip.

"I am sorry, darling. Oh, I wish you could be a man, darling. I would show you a good time or two."

We roared with laughter; the tone of his voice and his body language was simply too much. Then Manfred moved on to the other girls and hugged and kissed them one by one. He suddenly stood in front of me and I instinctively stepped back because I was afraid that he would do the same to me. Everybody laughed.

"And how are our two newcomers doing?" he sang, winking at me.

I didn't know what to say to that and so all I could do was try to smile and say something clever—which I did. "Good thanks," I mumbled.

"Darlings, tomorrow we will be in Glacier Bay. I have booked a boat and I can't wait to see these gigantic wet ice cubes popping into the sea." We laughed at the way he described the gigantic glacier.

"Be careful that none of these *ice cubes* squashes you when they *pop* into the sea, Manfred," Michael joked.

"You are soooo funny, Michael, but enough now, my darlings. I need to move on; we have a little party tonight - in my cabin. If any of you want to join you are most welcome." He looked at the three girls and with a sad face, he continued, "Sorry, ladies, men only."

"That's quite okay, Manfred, you go ahead and party," Birgit said.

"We will, darling, believe me, we will. And as for you two," he said looking at Franz and me, "you can knock on my door anytime, lower deck two, cabin 550, write it down so you don't forget. Bye bye for now." He danced away.

Jesus Christ, he is so gay, I shook my head as I looked after him.

"Quite a handful, that one," Angelika laughed.

"He is quite okay and doesn't give a shit what people think about him. He is harmless but it is the quiet ones you have to look out for," Michael said.

"Yeah, like Bohne. *She* is the worst of the lot," Iris chuckled.

We talked for another hour and Angelika made sure we always had plenty of Gluehwine to keep us warm. By midnight it was getting freezing cold despite each of us having had nearly five cups of Gluehwine each. I wasn't sure anymore whether the ship was moving or I, probably both. It was time to go to bed. We emptied our last cup and then made our way back to our cabins.

When I reached my cabin the lights were on and parts of Wolfgang's steward's uniform were spread everywhere. It looked as if Wolfgang had exploded. The cabin was a mess but thanks to the Gluehwine I couldn't really be bothered. I took off my clothes and even though I was very lightheaded, I did so in an orderly fashion by neatly stowing away my uniform. After a quick shower I climbed into my bunk and fell asleep instantly.

The next morning was as to be expected—I had a headache. I got up and saw that Wolfgang had added his private clothes to the already substantial mess in our cabin. I took a long hot shower which at least took some of my headache away. I got dressed as quietly as I could so as not to wake my cabin mate. Wolfgang was still snoring when I left our cabin.

The restaurant was still deserted so early in the morning and there were only two or three other people. After I had finished everything I went outside onto the main deck. The air was chilly and fresh with hardly any wind. The view took my breath away; we were cruising in-between two mountain ranges with peaks higher than I had ever seen before. The top of the mountain ranges were covered in snow whilst the lower parts were bare rock. I could even see whirling gusts of snow blowing high up on the mountaintops and by the looks of it the wind speeds must have been incredibly high up there. The sky was deep blue and cloudless whilst the color of the sea around us was deep green. There were countless pieces of ice floating by, some flat and covered with snow and others rocky like miniature icebergs; it was a fantastic sight. Surrounded by this wild and majestic beauty I felt small and at the same time I was grateful for being here. It was truly beautiful.

"Wow," I mumbled, causing small puffs of white transparent clouds appearing from my mouth as I spoke to myself. I leaned over the side of the railing to get a better view of what lay ahead; we seemed to be traveling down a fjord several kilometers wide. I couldn't see the end of the fjord and had no idea how much further it went. *I have to get my camera,* I suddenly remembered and went back to my cabin to get my camera.

To my surprise Wolfgang was still asleep. I looked at my watch; it was nearly six-thirty.

"Hey, Wolfgang, time to get up. Come on, there is a fantastic view up there," I said.

Wolfgang remained quiet.

"Wolfgang, get up," I repeated.

Then I could hear some shuffling and he lifted the curtain of his bunk. With his eyes still closed he blinked at me, blinded by the light. I took my small Olympus camera out of my wardrobe.

"It's nearly six-thirty; you have to get up."

"Mmmh, what?" he whispered, still half asleep.

"Come on, get up. I am going back up there. Come on, it's time." I left the lights on as I rushed out of the cabin.

In an instant I was back on the main deck taking countless pictures of the wild and icy landscape around me.

Breakfast that day was quiet with most of our guests spending the time on deck admiring the wild beauty all around us—except for Mr. and Mrs. Schulze.

I approached the table were I found Mrs. Schulze alone; her husband had gone to the breakfast buffet.

"Good morning, Mrs. Schulze," I said with a sugar-sweet voice. She answered with an unidentifiable growling which, if it had been in the middle of the night, would have scared the shit out of me.

"Would you like coffee or tea this morning?"

"Andre, we have been here now two days and you should know that we never take tea in the morning. " She hadn't even bothered to look at me when she spoke.

I knew that they always had coffee in the morning but I had to say something and at that moment asking for coffee was the only intelligent thing that came to my mind. Obviously it hadn't been that intelligent.

"Of course, Mrs. Schulze, can I bring you anything else?"

"If you give me some time to study the menu, then yes."

"I am sorry, Mrs. Schulze, I will get your coffee first." I went to the kitchen cursing this unhappy lady from the very bottom of my heart.

When I returned minutes later Mr. Schulze had joined his wife at the table.

"Good morning, Mr. Schulze."

"There you are. I thought already you had forgotten about us," he grumbled, completely ignoring what I had said to him. I poured two coffees and placed the thermos on the table.

"I hope the coffee tastes better than what you served us yesterday," Mr. Schulze grumbled.

"The coffee on this ship is awful," his wife complained.

"I am sorry, Mrs. Schulze."

"Is that all you can say—*I am sorry?* How about serving us some decent coffee for a change?" Now she *did* look at me but with an angry face.

"Get me some scrambled eggs with ham and mushrooms but make sure they are not as runny as yesterday. Otherwise I am quite happy to go down to the kitchen and show your chef how to make scrambled eggs."

Mrs. Schulze snorted sarcastically.

"The eggs not too runny, yes, Mr. Schulze, I will tell the chef. Will there be anything else?"

"No, there will be nothing else. Just make sure you get my eggs right."

"Yes, Mr. Schulze."

These two had a serious problem and all I could do is let them grumble and smile. I ordered the eggs and told the breakfast chef to make sure that the eggs were not too runny. He was the only chef on duty, he literally had many eggs to fry, and so his answer to my simple request was short and to the point—"Fuck off."

Ten minutes later I served Mr. Schulze his eggs. "Enjoy your breakfast," I said and smiled, but there was no reply.

From my service station I watched as he began poking his fork into the scrambled eggs. He took the first forkful of eggs and suddenly his face changed into a disgusted grimace. It was obvious the eggs were too runny.

"Andre," he shouted.

"Yes, Mr. Schulze," I said and rushed to him.

"I thought I had told you to make sure the eggs are not runny?"

"Yes, Mr. Schulze."

"So what is this then?" He lifted some egg and I saw that it was soft but couldn't really call them runny.

"I am sorry, Mr. Schulze, would you like me to change them?"

"All I am asking for is eggs which are not runny. Why is this so difficult for you to understand?"

"I am sorry, Mr. Schulze."

"This is not acceptable."

"Yes, Mr. Schulze."

"Take this plate away from me before I get sick." At that moment I was close to giving him the same answer I got from the egg chef but that would have been unwise.

"Yes, Mr. Schulze, I will change them for you."

"Forget it, your chef has no clue how to make scrambled eggs."

"I am sorry, Mr. Schulze."

"Do you know how much we pay for this cruise? You don't earn that much in two years and we can't even get some decent scrambled eggs." He began to raise his voice.

"Take it easy, Paul, we will complain to the manager," his wife tried to calm him.

"You bet we will complain; this is simply not acceptable."

"I am sorry, Mr. Schulze." I didn't know what else to say.

"Take those eggs away, I can't see them anymore."

I wasn't sure if he meant me or the eggs, but I took the plate and left. From my station I observed the two and the more I watched them the more I was convinced that they had a problem with each other rather than with me—or the eggs, for that matter. I don't think they were a happy couple; otherwise why would they behave like this? Unfortunately this wouldn't be the last time that I had to deal with this type of customers but as time went on I learned how to deal with them in a much more direct manner, which normally would bring them down to earth quite quickly.

The more I thought about the incident the angrier I became. Now I noticed that Mr. Schulze was grimacing as if he had swallowed something utterly disgusting. Then he lifted his coffee cup and held it just under his nose. I wasn't quite sure what he was doing but it looked as if he was sniffing the coffee, then he grimaced in utter disgust and put the cup back on the table. Obviously he wasn't impressed. His wife gesticulated wildly with her hands, presumably agreeing with her husband concerning the taste of the coffee.

At this point I had enough and I quickly turned my back to them before they could call me over to complain about the coffee. I had had enough for the day and I couldn't have managed another round of abuse from this miserable couple. I took an empty tray and left the restaurant in the hope that by the time I came back they would be gone. When I came back I saw they hadn't gone.

The Schulzes left me alone for the rest of their breakfast and then left without saying a word. I was worried what would happen to me if he really complained to the hotel manager. This was only my third day and I quite possibly had a major complaint on my hands. *Shit.*

The complaint never came and *if* Mr. Schulze *had* complained it would have had no consequences for me. What I didn't know at the time was that Mr. and Mrs. Schulze had similar problems everywhere on the ship. They complained about the service in the ballroom, the quality of food at the midnight buffet and the lack of attention to detail from their cabin steward. They had so many complaints that the hotel manager himself had stopped listening to them and all he could do was answer with "Yes, Mr. Schulze," and "I am sorry, Mr. Schulze."

I had only two other guests that morning and they had been in such a hurry to get out on deck that we had hardly talked. When I cleared their table after they were gone, I saw they had left behind a small two-page brochure entitled "Landing Information." This brochure was printed onboard and contained all necessary information relating to our next port of call or, as in the case of Glacier Bay, all information relating to an upcoming attraction.

I read the brochure, which was short but informative. From here I learned that Glacier Bay was a national park and contained almost sixteen different glaciers out of which twelve calve, meaning they shed broken pieces of ice to produce icebergs, or as Manfred had put it, "ice cubes popping into the sea." There were several glaciers descending from high snowcapped mountains into the bay to create one of the world's most spectacular displays of ice and iceberg formations.

One of the most famous of these calving glaciers was the Muir Glacier at the end of the icy strait which was also our final destination. MS *Europa* continued cruising up the icy strait of Glacier Bay towards the Muir Glacier where we were scheduled to arrive at eleven that morning. The ship would drop anchor near the glacier itself and would remain there for most of the day. If we were lucky we would see the glacier calve, which, according to Angelika, was one of the most spectacular events I could witness in my live. We would raise anchor at five in the evening and would then make our way towards the small port Skagway, Alaska, where we were scheduled to arrive in the early hours of the next morning.

At ten-thirty that morning I went outside to the main deck to take some more pictures of the stunning landscape. The first person I bumped into was Wolfgang, my cabin mate. I realized that this was the first time I saw him outside of our cabin and in daylight. Wolfgang stood leaning against a white painted metal staircase smoking a cigarette.

"Wolfgang, this is the first time I see you up here," I said.

"I am always here. How are things with you?"

"Good, breakfast was very quiet."

"It's always like that in places like Glacier Bay, or when we arrive in large ports. Most passengers prefer having morning coffee and pastries on deck, watching the scenery at the same time." Wolfgang finished his cigarette and flipped it casually overboard.

"The scenery is really stunning," I said.

Wolfgang glanced at my camera and then there was a sigh. "You know, I have been here so many times now it has become something I've gotten used to, and I just realized I have never actually taken any pictures. I think I should start doing that."

"You should. Just look at these incredible mountains and the floating icebergs. It's really amazing," I said enthusiastically. I noticed that the ice on the straits had become denser and the captain had reduced speed. This could only mean that we were close to the Muir Glacier now and that we would stop soon.

I went over to the railing and looked forward and I saw the glacier in the distance. The glacier was still quite far away; I could see that eventually we would not be able to go further but it was an amazing view looking at this gigantic wall of deep blue ice.

The floating ice around us had now become so dense that the bow of the ship had to smash its way through the ice, constantly pushing large ice sheets to the side. It was as if we were in Antarctica. I could have stood there and watched for hours.

"Just wait until you have been here several times. Then you will remember this conversation and you too will be bored going down this icy strait."

"I don't think so. Something like this can never get boring," I said enthusiastically.

Wolfgang smiled at me. "We will see."

I saw that the decks along the entire ship's length were lined with passengers taking photos and watching the scenery. They all wore thick winter coats, scarves and fur hats, which reminded me that I was actually freezing cold, but the view was simply too fantastic for me to leave. The ship seemed to be slowing down further and I guessed that we would soon stop completely. Several stewards had gathered next to me, some had cameras, others just smoked a cigarette. Suddenly they started pointing at something out on the ice.

"Look over there! A seal!" someone shouted. I searched the ice but couldn't see anything.

"Can you see a seal?" I asked Wolfgang.

"Yeah, over there, see? The little black dot on the ice."

I squinted my eyes and then I saw a small black something lying on the ice. I couldn't really make out any black dot but took a picture anyway and so did many of my colleagues. I never saw the seal, not even in the pictures.

"So how are your guests on this cruise?" Wolfgang wanted to know.

"They are okay."

"Do you think you have any over-tax payers?"

"I don't know."

"I think I have two or three. Can't wait to find out," Wolfgang said as he lit another cigarette.

"I have one very troublesome couple, though, complaining all day long."

"There are always some. I had one guy at my round table who thought he could treat me like his personal slave but he stopped that quite quickly," he laughed.

"How did you do that?"

"Easy, just keep on embarrassing him in front of the others, make him look stupid."

"I see." I didn't ask further because I didn't want him to think I couldn't handle my troublemakers.

The ship had come to a halt and the captain had dropped the anchor; we had arrived at Muir Glacier. I couldn't see the glacier because of the ship's position. It was time to get back to the restaurant.

Lunch was not much different from breakfast, with less than half of my guests showing up. The first seating consisted only of Mr. and Mrs. Schulze, Mrs. Kern and Mrs. Straub. The service of only four guests was easy but the atmosphere at the table seemed tense. My two elderly ladies chatted happily with each other whilst the Schulzes tried hard to find things to complain about. They were constantly nagging about the food, the service and me. It was clear that the two ladies did not like the way the Schulzes were behaving at the lunch table and when Mr. Schulze gave me a hard time because he felt the food still took too long, Mrs. Kern asked him to stop it immediately. From that point on the two ladies stopped communicating with the Schulzes completely.

At one point during the lunch service there was a sudden announcement from the captain.

"Ladies and gentlemen, this is your captain speaking. We have word that within the next few minutes the Muir Glacier will be calving. We have been observing a large piece of ice which we believe will sheer off at any moment."

There was a sudden commotion in the restaurant and all passengers suddenly got up and ran to the starboard windows and so did several stewards. I quickly took my camera from my service station and rushed to the starboard side windows. I squeezed in between Manfred and two of his guests and glanced across the icy landscape outside. I saw the gigantic wall of ice in the distance—it looked majestic. I could clearly see the deep valley which the glacier had carved onto the mountain range. The top of the glacier was rugged and dark with sediments whilst it was deep blue in the middle. The sea around us was full of floating icebergs. The captain's voice came on again.

"Look at the left side of the glacier where YES, there it goes!"

Suddenly the entire left side of the glacier sheered off, gliding majestically into the sea. It all seemed to happen in slow motion but that, the captain explained, was due to the distance and the immense size of the piece that had broken off. The captain drew our attention to the mini-tsunami caused by the calving that was now traveling towards the ship. It was almost like a Mexican wave running through the floating ice towards the ship. It didn't look particularly big but once it hit the ship I realized quite quickly just how big the piece of glacier must have been since the wave rocked the ship left and right. The entire event had captivated me so much that I had not taken a single picture even though I was holding my camera firmly in my hands. The excitement slowly subsided and our guests returned to their tables. To my surprise the Schulzes hadn't moved an inch from their table and instead were rolling their eyes as Mrs. Kern and Mrs. Straub recounted the calving at their table. They were a strange couple indeed.

As soon as the desserts were served Mr. and Mrs. Schulze got up and left without taking coffee.

"Those two should be thrown overboard," Mrs. Kern commented as I offered her more coffee. I smiled.

"If we are lucky the sharks will get them," Mrs. Straub added, laughing.

I wasn't sure what to say. I knew that I had to stay neutral when guests talked about other guests but deep down I fully agreed with them.

"I will try to get your dishes faster in the future," I said, lamely.

"No, you don't need to. There is nothing wrong with the speed of your service, Andre. The Schulzes just need something to complain about. You are not doing anything wrong."

"Yes, but…" Before I could finish, Mrs. Kern chipped in.

"There is nothing wrong with the way you serve, it is perfectly fine, this is not your problem. It is Mr. Schulze and he can't handle his retirement," she said. The ladies laughed and chuckled.

Mrs. Straub nodded. "That's right. You see, Mr. Schulze has just retired from an important managerial position where he was in charge of a large international company. Imagine one day you are fully in charge and the next day you are just a passenger of a cruise liner surrounded by fellow retirees."

"But it is still no reason to behave like this." Mrs. Kern shook her head.

"Mind you, his wife is not much better and she has problems dealing with his retirement too. She was of course the First Lady in the company as long as her husband was still on top. Now she is just like us." Mrs. Kern and Mrs. Straub giggled, holding each other's hand.

"That's right, but don't worry, Andre, we will keep them in line in the future." The two ladies kept on giggling.

I had to laugh. I really liked the two elderly ladies; they were kind with a good heart. I would do anything for them as long as they were my guests. The two ladies left in time for me to get ready for the next seating which was just as empty. Finally at two-thirty I finished lunch and my dinner setup was completed.

When I stepped out onto the main deck there was commotion at the stern with many of my fellow stewards and stewardesses leaning over the side of the railings. I saw Franz and walked towards him.

"What is happening?" I asked.

"Here, take a look. They are trying to fish one of the icebergs out of the water," he answered and moved a little so I could squeeze in. I looked and saw one of our lifeboats with several sailors dressed in thick orange-colored jackets and life vests. They were in the process of trying to wrap a large net, suspended from one of the ship's lifting cranes, around one of the smaller floating icebergs. The entire process was accompanied by shouting and yelling from some of the stewards on deck.

After some considerable manhandling of the net by the men in the boat, the boat moved away and the sailors signaled to the crane operator the *all clear* for lift. The rope of the net strained and loud crackling noises echoed across the ice as the net began to take the weight of the ice. We could hear the whining of the crane's motor as the heavy piece of ice slowly lifted out of the water. The stewards on deck cheered and yelled as the iceberg was finally suspended high in the air. Then sailors appeared on the main deck and began chasing us out of the path of the crane. I realized that they were planning to set the iceberg down on our main deck. The crane swung around and slowly set the piece of ice carefully onto the deck.

Franz and I approached the iceberg once the sailors had removed the net. It was much larger than it had looked floating in the water. The ice had a deep blue color and looked like a gigantic crystal. I carefully touched the ice like a child touching a new toy; it was incredibly cold and as hard as stone.

"What are they going to do with this?" I asked Franz.

"No idea," he answered.

Angelika joined us and having heard my question, she answered. "The chefs will use it to make ice carvings and the bartenders will shave part of it off to be used in cocktails. The ice is actually made of freshwater mixed with seawater and it is said that it gives a special taste to cocktails. Think about it—this ice may have frozen thousands of years ago and you have a chance to taste it in one of our cocktails," she giggled with her Bavarian accent.

276

"Great, maybe with a dash of dinosaur pee," Franz said and we laughed.

She took some pictures of Franz and me posing in front of our "catch." We waited for another half-hour hoping to witness another piece of ice sheering off the glacier but nothing happened. Angelika, having been to Glacier Bay several times, lectured us on what we saw. For example, she told us that the air here was so clean and unpolluted that it was difficult to judge distances correctly and that's why the glacier itself was apparently much farther away than it seemed. She also told us that the glacier was pushing constantly towards the sea and she asked us to listen to the crackling noises. I stood at the railing and listened carefully and indeed there were loud crackling and popping noises echoing and bouncing off the steep rock faces of the surrounding mountains. *Nature is really amazing,* I said to myself.

We stayed outside for a while and when it became too cold we retreated to the more comfortable and warm atmosphere inside the ship. We had coffee in the crew mess and then went back to our cabins for a rest. Back in my cabin I suddenly remembered that I had not written a single line to my parents or Tatiana. I decided to do just that. I got changed and took out pen and paper and began to write my first letter. By the time I had to get ready for dinner I had written six pages to my parents and started three to Tatiana. I would finish her letter in the evening.

In the evening, I just had finished my shower when I heard a deep rumbling noise and vibration under my feet which meant the ship had started its engines and we were leaving Glacier Bay. I could feel the ship turning and slowly it began picking up speed. It was only now that I realized the ship had been unnaturally quiet since we had arrived here in the bay. MS *Europa* was now on the way to the small port of Skagway, Alaska, a town which was a leftover from the gold-rush days. Wolfgang only came back as I was just about to leave. After a quick chat I left for the restaurant.

Once my station was ready I had dinner with Franz and Angelika in the crew mess. Dinner went smoothly with the Schulzes being unnaturally quiet, presumably kept in check by Mrs. Straub and Mrs. Kern. After dinner we gathered for a while outside and then went back to our cabins early. I finished my letter to Tatiana, which amounted to seven pages outlining all my recent experiences from the long flight to

Anchorage to the happenings at Glacier Bay. At midnight I went to bed and fell asleep immediately.

When I got up the next morning the ship was dead quiet—no rumbling of the engines and none of the usual vibrations, only the humming of the air-conditioner. I had a shower and got dressed. Wolfgang was snoring away as happily as ever.

Instead of going straight to the restaurant I went outside onto the main deck and saw that we were already at the pier; we had arrived in Skagway in the early hours of the morning. We were still surrounded by mountains with snow-capped peaks, the sky was blue without clouds and the air was chilly and fresh. A little further in the distance I saw several large industrial raw-oil storage facilities with a large tanker at a pier. Other than that there were only sea, mountains and some floating sheets of ice.

Most of my guests showed up for breakfast early because they had booked tours and excursions. As I was clearing my station Wolfgang approached me, asking if I wanted to join him in going to town quickly after breakfast. I asked him about posting my letters and he told me that there was a post office in town which he would show me. I was happy to join him because my English was far from sufficient to ask for stamps and much less for getting my letters successfully posted.

It was a strange feeling after three days on the ship to have once again firm ground under my feet. I instinctively missed the constant vibration and movement of the ship. The town was not far from the pier and it took us less than fifteen minutes to reach its center. The town itself looked like something out of a Western movie; most buildings, including the church, were made of wood and most of them had small verandas with wooden roofs in front of them.

Wolfgang took me to the post office which looked not much different from the ones in a Hollywood Western movie. At the counter Wolfgang did all the talking, asking to have two letters posted to Germany. The lady behind the counter handed him a set of stamps which I moistened on a small sponge pad and stuck them onto my letters. The lady took the letters and stuck them into a bag. Wolfgang paid in cash and then we left. I wondered if the letters would ever arrive in my small hometown so far from this place. We had just enough time left to look around a bit and then headed back to the ship. It was only when we walked back towards the *Europa* that I realized this was the first time since boarding that I saw the ship in full size. It was bigger than I had thought and it seemed to grow bigger the closer we got to it.

"She is a beauty," I said to Wolfgang.

"Yeah, she is, isn't she? And soo big," he giggled. I briefly wondered what that was all about but didn't think much of it.

At the gangway we presented our crew ID cards and after checking them thoroughly the sailor allowed us back onboard. We walked up the gangway and entered the familiar surroundings of the ship. We got changed and before I knew it I was back at my service station waiting for my guests. If I had hoped for a moment that most of my guests would spend the day in Skagway, I had been dead wrong. They all came for lunch.

Because we were in a harbor we had only one free seating, meaning our guests could sit in any station they wanted. It was amazing; every single one of my guests showed up for lunch. My station was packed with some of my guests sitting on neighboring tables. During the service I found out that the Schulzes hadn't even left the ship, claiming that there was "nothing to see anyway" and that they had no plans for leaving the ship in the afternoon either. To make their point they stayed last, which left me with only two hours to venture back into Skagway with Wolfgang.

Skagway consisted of one main street which stretched for about one mile. The main street was dotted with Alaskan souvenir shops, supermarkets and a couple of Western-style saloons. We bought a couple of postcards and other souvenirs. The town had something idyllic about it with the low buildings and the surrounding snow-capped mountains. The locals were friendly but in an artificial American sort of way. When we reached the end of the main street we turned around and walked back towards the port. The massive superstructure of MS *Europa* was much larger than any of Skagway's buildings and we could clearly see it in the distance.

We returned to the ship and after a quick shower we were back in our stations. Dinner went smoothly and because we were scheduled to depart at eight o'clock, most guests of the first seating finished their dinner early to watch our departure outside on deck. Unfortunately this was also the reason why my guests of the second seating were late and because the evening program in the ballroom was not attractive, they sat even longer.

We were now on our way to the capital of Alaska, the port city of Juneau where we were scheduled to arrive the next morning. The sea was reasonably calm and I could hardly feel that we were on a ship. By eleven my guests had left. I was just about to go back to my cabin when Wolfgang approached me, asking if I wanted to join him for a drink in the crew bar. Since most of the others had left, including Franz and Angelika, I said yes.

The crew bar located on lower deck 1 was more than just a bar; it was the place where we licked our wounds after frustrating days with guests like the Schulzes. Licking our wounds normally was done with plenty of Beck's beer. The bar was known as the Piesel and it was always packed. There was a small bar counter, several standing tables with barstools and two sofa corners.

When I entered the bar I found it packed with stewards, stewardesses and chefs. There was chatter, laughter and plenty of loud music. We fought our way through the crowd and the dense layer of smoke that hung in the room. We settled at one of the standing tables near the bar. Wolfgang bought me a large beer. I saw Hartmut and his gang near the bar and I noticed that some of his friends were eyeing us curiously.

Wolfgang raised his glass. "Cheers," he said cheerfully.

"Cheers," I said and took a sip of the cold refreshing beer. I kept on glancing over to Hartmut and his friends, wondering why the kept on watching Wolfgang and me.

"What's wrong?" Wolfgang asked.

"Nothing, it's just Hartmut and his friends—they keep on staring at us," I said.

"Don't worry about them, that's just the way they are. They are not only the longest-serving stewards here on this ship but they have already been the longest-serving stewards on the old *Europa*," Wolfgang explained.

Suddenly Manfred appeared with two of his male buddies. "Hi, you two, what are you doing here all by yourself? Having a romantic evening? That is sooo sweet." He was waving his hands and wiggling his behind as he spoke. His two friends were giggling like girls. It was embarrassing.

"We are just having a drink," I said to Manfred defensively. I wanted him to leave; I didn't really fancy being seen having drinks with him.

"Of course, honey, of course," he giggled, rolling his eyes, and then continued whispering in my ear. "Don't worry, I won't tell a soul," he giggled again.

"Manfred, for God's sake, this is not what you think..." But Manfred kept on patting me on my shoulders like a little child. It was humiliating and all the while Hartmut and his friends were watching us.

"Okaaay, honey, I am leaving. I am not bliiind and I can see that you don't want to be disturbed." He grabbed his two buddies and danced away in the rhythm of the music.

Hartmut and his gang had been watching and were roaring with laughter, imitating Manfred. Throughout the encounter Wolfgang had remained completely quiet.

"He is quite something," I said to Wolfgang, shaking my head in the hope that everyone in the bar could see it.

"Yeah, you can say that again," Wolfgang whispered, taking a sip of his beer.

"Hey, Wolfgang, you know, I think there are a lot of them here on board."

Wolfgang looked at me slightly confused. "What do you mean? What do you think we have a lot of?"

I looked around to make sure nobody could hear me. "Gays, there are a lot of gays here on the ship, don't you think so?" I asked him innocently.

Wolfgang stared at me without moving his eyes for several seconds and then began to smile. He looked to the left and then to the right and then he leaned forward in a conspiratory manner. "You are right, there are a lot of them here on this ship," he whispered to me with a big smile.

I took a gulp of beer. *I knew it, I just knew it and I wouldn't be surprised if half of the restaurant crew was gay!*

Wolfgang leaned forward again. "Listen, Andre, there is something else you should know," he whispered.

"Yes?"

"I am one of them. I am gay, too, just so you know," he said and leaned back.

It took me a moment to process his words—I was dumbstruck. The moment he had said *I am gay too,* I froze. I didn't know what to say, much less what to do. The only thing that I could do in that situation was...to drink my beer.

I picked up my glass and emptied it in one go. Wolfgang looked at me. I couldn't look at him. Nobody had ever told me *I am gay* straight to my face. What was I supposed to say? Something like, *Oh, okay, that's nice?* I couldn't and so I did what I thought was the only sensible thing to do—I got up and left. I didn't say "Goodnight" or "I have to go," I just got up and left. I was too shocked to say anything.

On the way back to my cabin the full meaning of Wolfgang being gay began to sink in. Everybody knew he was gay and I had been going out with him and much worse, I shared a cabin with him! Now I understood why Peter and Hartmut had been calling me female names all the time; they thought I was one of them—they actually thought I was gay too.

I reached my cabin and all I wanted was to go to bed as quickly as possible before Wolfgang returned. That night it took me a long time to fall asleep and, unknown to me at the time, it was the beginning of a serious paranoia of people suspecting me to be gay. This paranoia would last for many years to come, which resulted in my becoming very apprehensive and aggressive toward gays. Over time Wolfgang and I would get along but whenever he teased me in the cabin I would take it so seriously that I ended up sleeping with a razor blade under my pillow. I threatened Wolfgang, saying that I would use it if he dared come too close to my bunk. From that day on we never went out together and I tried my best to stay away from him as far as possible.

When I entered the restaurant early the next morning we were already tied to the pier in Juneau. The weather was abysmal; it rained the whole day and the sky was laden with low-hanging dark rain clouds. It was the perfect weather for Mr. and Mrs. Schulze, which gave the miserable couple plenty of reasons to complain about the weather all day long. It sounded almost as if it was my fault. Mrs. Straub and Mrs. Kern communicated in no uncertain terms to the unhappy couple that in fact it wasn't.

That day I had my first afternoon tea shift on the lido deck which was the highest open deck of the ship. Since nobody had ever bothered to show me around, it took me a while to find the lido deck and it was only thanks to a fellow steward that I eventually got there. The lido deck was the uppermost deck of the ship and featured an all-weather swimming pool. The swimming pool with its retractable glass roof was truly amazing. That day there was a light drizzle and the glass roof was closed. I could imagine that during sunny days this would be the perfect location for sunbathing.

The service was a straightforward and boring affair; all I had to do was stand behind a buffet, smile and offer a selection of cakes to guests. Because of the weather not many passengers had left the ship and therefore the pool was crowded with people. What made this shift interesting, however, was the fact that I had never actually been on the lido deck before and I had a chance to meet many guests I would otherwise never see. The amount of cakes I served was incredible but what was even more stunning was how many cakes I served to the same guests who kept on coming back for more. One gentleman alone came back six times for the same strawberry cake which must have added a considerable amount of fat to his already substantial belly. One lady approached me and asked for a piece of my popular strawberry cake and when I went to place it on her plate, I saw to my surprise that the plate was already full of other cakes, pastries and even two scoops of ice cream. There was clearly no space left for my strawberry cake. Seeing my hesitation and the puzzled look on my face, she smiled sheepishly and asked me to place it on top of the cheesecake which, according to her, was fine. It has to be remembered that all these guests had just finished lunch; where exactly they put all that food was beyond me.

This was a far cry from the service I was used to in the Columbus Hotel. The fact that the afternoon buffet was free put some considerable stress on some of our guests who began stockpiling cakes, pastries and ice cream on their tables out of fear it would be gone by the time they returned. This, of course, never happened, even though I have to say that the chefs were hard-pressed to keep a steady supply based on the vast number of people that day.

The wastage was a different matter altogether. We cleared plenty of plates with half-eaten cakes, molten ice cream and other items that hadn't even been touched yet. It all went into the bins. What happened there on the lido deck that afternoon struck me more like a feeding frenzy rather than an afternoon tea buffet. The shift lasted only forty-five minutes but combined with the awkward timing, it was still enough to spoil the afternoon. There was not enough time left to take a nap and it was still too early to go back to the restaurant. All I could do was to lie on my bed and, hoping that my gay cabin mate

Wolfgang would not return, write letters to my parents and Tatiana. Of course there was plenty to write about, like my troublesome guests and the feeding frenzy on the lido deck. The only thing I didn't mention in my letters was the fact that I was living with a colleague who was gay.

I had also realized that whenever Bohne stopped at my station he was not actually observing my performance as a steward but…my butt. Whenever I saw him approaching I made sure that I had something to do which kept me away from my station or I took soiled dishes to the kitchen. I learned how to evade him successfully whenever I could and soon he stopped standing at my station trying to "accidentally" bump into me and my butt.

Unfortunately all this went unnoticed by Hartmut and his friends who kept on treating me like a gay. They kept on calling me "Andrea" until one fine day I finally lost it. Franz had to grab me at the last moment when I was just about to lose my temper trying to physically attack Hartmut, who had called me Andrea once again in front of several stewards. If my attack had been successful it would have most certainly spelled the end of my career as a steward.

Bohne witnessed all this but did not interfere. The reason for this lack of interest I would find out much later. The only good thing was that they began to leave me alone, not because they believed now that I was straight but because they were worried that I would lose my temper again. The weeks that followed were intensely stressful for me whenever I saw Hartmut. Even though he toned down considerably after my near-attack, he never quite stopped teasing me.

When the doors opened as usual at six-thirty sharp that night I was ready for my first seating. My guests rushed to their tables looking as hungry as ever, not surprising since they had not eaten since afternoon tea. Two hours without food was quite a challenge for my guests.

The main topic on most tables was the bad weather and how little everyone had seen of Alaska's capital. In order to bring Alaska closer to our guests the chef had created a special menu consisting mostly of fresh fish and fresh Alaskan king crab which he had bought in Juneau. I started to take the orders. Angelika had told me that whenever the chef bought fresh fish, most of my guests would go for the fish.

I started with the Schulzes who, of course, had nothing good to say about the quality of Alaskan fresh fish. According to them the Alaskan sea was polluted with oil ever since the oil spill in Valdez some years back. The Schulzes ordered two steaks. Mr. and Mrs. Steiner were not sure and even though I tried hard to convince them that the fish was okay, they too ordered two steaks.

With these steak orders I was ripe for a heavy-duty beating from the chef. At least Mrs. Straub and Mrs. Kern trusted me and ordered the fish. The two elderly ladies would be the only ones ordering fish and all the others ordered steaks and tenderloins. News about the oil spill seemed to have spread to other tables and I ended up with only two fish, seven steaks and eight tenderloins. That would not go down well with Obermeyer—I was dead meat. Angelika had finished her wines and joined me at the service station.

"Okay, I do the fish cutlery, you go down to the main-course line. How many fish do you have?" she wanted to know.

"Ahm, two."

"What?" Her eyes went wide.

"Two fish, one for Mrs. Straub and one for Mrs. Kern," I said, slightly embarrassed.

"You have only two fish?"

"Yes."

"Did you tell them that it's fresh?"

"Yes, I did, but according to the Schulzes there was an oil spill and the fish is not clean.

Angelika laughed. "Come on, that's ridiculous."

"I know, but that's what they said."

"Jesus, Obermeyer will kill you, he will rip you apart. I really feel sorry for you. Good luck, you better get down to the kitchen," she said and I dashed off.

In the kitchen the main-course queue was still relatively short. I took a deep breath and called out my grills. "Two fish and ten grills in the line," I yelled.

I saw Obermeyer at the front of the queue staring at me; he looked really, really angry. He walked up to me and stopped right in front of me.

"What did you just say?" he said in a threateningly quiet voice.

I stepped back a little and moved my tray like a shield in front of my lower body. "Ahm, two fish and ten grills," I whispered. My colleagues burst out laughing.

"Are you aware that we have FRESH Alaskan king crab onboard?"

"Yes, Chef, but…"

"If you are aware we have these delicacies, why the fuck did you not tell your guests about it?"

"Chef, I did, but…"

"Oh, you did."

"Yes, Chef, I did, but they preferred…"

"They preferred, what, the steaks?"

"Yes, Chef."

"So, what did you do, simply take the order?"

"Well, I didn't want to but…yes, eventually I did."

Obermeyer leaned forward and suddenly screamed from the very bottom of his heart.

"You morons are all fucking useless, the whole bunch of you— fucking pussies. Are you people too incompetent to sell fresh fish or do you simply not have enough fucking brainpower to say "fresh fish," you goddamn idiots?" He stormed back to the pass.

As it turned out eighty percent of all guests had decided to order steaks and tenderloins. The chef had only added the ever-popular steaks and tenderloins as an alternative because he had expected most guests to order the fish and had been worried that he didn't have enough of the "normally" popular fish. Obermeyer screamed and shouted at each of us as we picked up our red meats. I wondered if this had happened because my guests, the Schulzes, were spreading the rumor about the oil spill in Valdez. I was happy to be out of the kitchen and serving my main courses but just when I thought that things couldn't get any worse, the Schulzes claimed that their steaks were not as they had ordered and both demanded to have them changed. Now I was really dead meat.

When I went back to the kitchen the queue had gone and I went straight to Obermeyer, who stood at the pass counting the number of main courses they had served.

"Excuse me, Chef," I said, standing next to him with Schulzes steaks in my hands. He didn't move and didn't even look at me. I just stood there waiting.

"Ahm, excuse me, Chef," I said again, mentally preparing for the worst.

Obermeyer very slowly put down his pen, rolled his eyes and then looked at me. His eyes wandered to the two plates in my hand and then back to me. "Yes, what can I do for you?" he asked with a sugar-sweet voice.

I saw several chefs gathering behind the pass with angry faces. They all began staring at me.

"Ahm, my guests wanted to have their steaks medium and these are well done."

Obermeyer stood up and crossed his arms. "Sorry, I didn't hear that, say that again," he whispered.

I was puzzled. How could he not have heard me standing so close to him?

"I said, my guests wanted to have their steaks medium and these two steaks are well done," I said and swallowed nervously.

"I see. And why did you not tell me that before?" he asked with the same soft voice.

"I did."

"You did?"

"Yes, Chef, I did."

"But we didn't fire any well-done steaks," he said and turned to the assembled chefs behind the pass. "Or did we?" he yelled.

"No well-done steaks, Chef," one of the chefs behind the pass answered.

"There you have it; we didn't make any well-done steaks."

"But, Chef, these steaks are well done."

Obermeyer leaned forward. "So you are saying that I am lying?" he whispered into my face, his breath a mixture of garlic and cigarettes.

"No, Chef, of course not…"

"So why the fuck you are saying that we have made the wrong steaks?" he screamed.

"I am not saying you made the wrong steaks…"

"So it was your fault?"

I knew that there was no way out of this and if I wanted to get some medium steaks quick, I had to claim it was my mistake.

"Maybe it was my mistake," I mumbled.

"Of course it was your mistake, you fucking moron." He turned to the chefs behind the pass. "Two medium steaks for this idiot here," he yelled. One of the chefs swore and threw two steaks on the grill.

Then Obermeyer looked at me and barked. "Listen to me, you moron, when your medium steaks are ready you take them and get the fuck out of my kitchen and don't you dare to come back here, do you understand?"

"Yes, Chef," I mumbled.

"What was that?"

"Yes, Chef," I said a little louder.

"Idiot," he said and walked off.

This would not be the last time I had such encounters with Obermeyer but over time I would learn how to retaliate. I ignored the nasty comments from the chefs behind the pass when I finally got my steaks. I took the two plates and rushed back to my station where Angelika was already waiting.

"You better hurry before Mr. Schulze asks for Bohne. He is pretty pissed."

Shit, I thought, *that is not good.*

"Two steaks medium," I said as friendly as I could when I served the steaks. Most of the other guests at the table had finished their meals and everyone was staring at the angry couple.

"It's about time; we have been waiting for over fifteen minutes," Mr. Schulze complained. *Yeah, I know, and after six cakes and all that ice cream at the afternoon tea buffet you must be pretty hungry,* I thought.

"My apologies for the delay, Mr. Schulze, but the chef made them fresh for you."

"I hope they are medium this time," he said in a challenging tone. *I hope so too,* I thought. There was no way on earth that I could go down to the kitchen a second time.

The steaks were fine this time and the two gulped down their meals so fast that by the time I had cleared the other dishes, they had finished theirs too.

I could feel that the atmosphere at my round table was deteriorating by the minute because of this unpleasant couple and although my two elderly ladies Mrs. Straub and Mrs. Kern tried their best to losen the atmosphere, the Schulzes always came up with new ways to spoil everyone's mood. It was only a matter of time until this situation turned into open conflict between them. What was worse was that the table of Mr. and Mrs. Schulze always kept me so busy that I never spent much time with my other guests. The good news was that the others fully understood the situation and always made encouraging comments whenever I had such unpleasant encounters with the Schulzes.

I served desserts and coffee and once again I finished preparations for the second seating in good time, leaving me over twenty minutes' break which I spent outside on the main deck. As usual most of the stewards and stewardesses had gathered there having casual chats and smoking cigarettes. I began to enjoy the time out on deck because they were a refreshing break from the hectic dinner business in the restaurant. I joined my usual group of friends and we talked about the coming days at sea and gossiped about our guests.

Franz had been lucky on this cruise; all his guests without exception were very pleasant. If only I could say the same. It seemed that everyone else had been lucky with their guests and I was a little jealous. I stood near the railing and looked at the brightly illuminated port of Juneau. The air was fresh and crisp and although I only wore my steward's outfit, I wasn't feeling cold.

I had been onboard for nearly six full days which now seemed to me like an eternity. I took a deep breath of the fresh cool air. Despite my troublesome guests I was happy and proud to be here. *Hey, you are in Alaska,* I said to myself. I felt good.

"What are you thinking about?" That was Angelika standing next to me.

"It's a shame that I haven't had a chance to venture into Juneau," I lied.

Angelika laughed. "Hey, don't worry, it wasn't too pleasant out there in this weather."

"Yeah, but who knows? Maybe I will never come back here."

"Oh, you will, don't worry. We'll come to Alaska again and anyway, the best places are still to come," she said.

"Yes, of course, I am just thinking…" I mumbled.

"Just wait until we reach San Francisco. I can tell you that's an interesting city."

"San Francisco?"

"Yeah, great place. It's even worth it to sell your afternoon tea there if you are on duty."

I didn't understand. "Selling my afternoon tea shift? What do you mean by that?" *How could I "sell" my shift,* I wondered?

"Well, that's one of these weird practices—some of the stewards buy your shift if you don't want to do it in a port like San Francisco, meaning you pay them and they do it for you."

"Pay them? You mean I pay them and they actually work for me?"

"Exactly."

"Why not swap shifts?" I asked.

Angelika laughed. "Swap shifts? Nobody will swap shifts with you, Andre, not unless you pay them."

This is typical, I thought, *there is no teamwork here; it's all about the money.* "So how much do I have to pay?" I wanted to know.

"That depends on the harbor. Places like San Francisco, New York, Los Angeles and so on are expensive and you pay anything between one hundred and two hundred marks."

"One hundred to two hundred marks!!" I exclaimed. "That's crazy!"

"Hey, I don't make the prices," Angelika laughed, "but trust me—considering the tip you will get, it's nothing."

"That's extortion."

"Yeah, everybody talks like that in the beginning but then you will do it, too," she said. "Just wait, when we are at sea, prices range from fifty to one hundred marks."

"Why would I want to have someone do my shifts at sea?"

"Maybe because you want to sleep?" she mused.

"I will never do that," I said.

"What, you never want to sleep?" she giggled.

"No, I mean I never will sell my shifts."

"You won't?"

"No, I won't," I insisted. I had no intention of paying people to do my shifts; I was sure that by the time we reached these ports I would find someone to swap with rather than having to pay.

"Okay, then don't," Angelika said, knowing very well that after I had received my first tip three to four weeks into the cruise, a few hundred marks would be nothing if it meant being able to go out and see a once-in-a-lifetime city or getting a few more hours of sleep. In the end Angelika was right; eventually I would sell my shifts just like all the others, but I didn't know it yet.

The thought of having to sell shifts in order to get some sleep or get to shore kept my mind occupied for the rest of the evening. We talked for a while on deck before we returned to our stations in the restaurant waiting for our guests of the second seating.

As mentioned already, the atmosphere amongst my guests of the second seating was completely different and much friendlier than that of the first one. They were always engaged in conversations and discussions and paid little or no attention to me at all. This was good and bad—good because I was much more relaxed and focused, and bad because I had time to concentrate on other things, such as the ship's movements, for example.

We left Juneau late that night and I had not seen anything of the city or its surroundings. Our next port of call was another small town called Sitka which we would reach after two days at sea and remain there for only half a day. As we left Juneau heading out to sea later that evening, the movements of the ship got stronger and so did my feeling of seasickness. As long as I had to move around I felt fine but as soon as I stood idle at my service station I began to feel dizzy and nauseated. It was bad.

The glimmering lights outside told me that we were still close to shore and we had not yet reached the open sea. We were still within the confines of the protective wave breakers of Juneau port. At about nine-thirty we passed the port entrance and from then on things got really bad—at least for me.

I had just served coffee and desserts when the first breaker hit the ship head on. There was a sudden *wham!* Everything shuddered and I instinctively grabbed hold of my service station. I felt the restaurant tilting slightly forward and split seconds later there was the second loud *wham!* I stood frozen at my service station, half expecting alarm bells to ring at any moment but all remained quiet; not only that, it seemed that nobody except I paid any attention to the weather or the ship's strange movements. Fear had temporarily replaced my seasickness and I began to realize that nobody really cared about what was going on. I felt sick again.

I moved around as much as possible but eventually I had to fold my napkins and that I couldn't do whilst walking. As we headed out to sea it became more and more uncomfortable for me. The skyline outside had shrunken to tiny pulsating lights reminiscent of hundreds of fireflies. The ship fell into an up-and-down rhythm interrupted frequently by violent *whams!*

When I finally finished folding my napkins, my station was ready for breakfast. I headed straight for my cabin with only one thought on my mind and that was to lie down and sleep. I was relieved to find that Wolfgang was out so I had a quick shower and went straight to bed.

Chapter 8

I woke up very early the next morning after a good night's sleep. The first thing I noticed was the movements of the ship seemed as if it had settled into a steady rhythm. I showered, got dressed and went up to the main deck where I was greeted by a glorious sunrise at sea. There was not a soul on deck when I stepped out of the heavy watertight door and walked to the back of the ship. If there hadn't been the ever-present humming of exhaust fans and other machinery, I would have only heard the howling of the gusty winds.

It was still dawn but the bright orange glow just above the horizon began to grow brighter. There were some scattered clouds bathed in an eerie orange-gold color. It was a stunning sight. The ship left a white frothy trail which seemed to stretch all the way to the horizon. I looked around and saw nothing but water. The endless ocean with its long-drawn swells was a sight that made me forget any worries or anxieties I had. The experience gave me a feeling of wanting to discover the world that lay beyond that glowing horizon.

Leaning over the railing, I stared at the white foamy water rushing by down below. The speed at which we were cruising was amazing considering the size of the ship. I looked at my watch and to my surprise it was only just six o'clock; I had plenty of time until I had to face the Schulzes again.

I took my breakfast in the crew mess and then finished my station for breakfast. To my surprise Bohne was already up doing his usual weird walk around and I wondered why so early. He stopped at my station and looked at me; no correction—he stared at me, right into my eyes. He just stood there watching me.

"Good morning, Mr. Bohne," I said.

"Morning," he whispered so quietly that I could hardly hear him. Somehow he gave me the strange impression that he would launch himself at me at any moment and therefore I stood there in front of him all tensed up.

He stared at me and I didn't know whether I should laugh or cry. *What is wrong with this man?* I asked myself.

292

He suddenly stopped staring at me and his eyes wandered to my neat pile of folded napkins. Then he pointed at the pile and said, "That napkin is dirty. You cannot use that"

The comment was unexpected and left me perplexed. I checked the napkin and noticed a stain. I took the napkin and threw it into the linen bin under the drawers of my service station.

"We can't use dirty napkins," Bohne said with an excited high-pitched voice and then he walked off. There was no doubt in my mind that that man had a serious problem.

Mrs. Straub and Mrs. Kern were my first guests to arrive and, as usual, in a good mood.

"Good morning, ladies," I greeted them cheerfully.

"Good morning, Andre. Are we the first ones?" Mrs. Straub asked.

"Yes, you are."

"Good. Let's hurry before our troublesome couple arrives," Mrs. Kern smiled.

I brought them to their seats and took the order. "Can I get you two coffees as usual?" I asked

"Yes, my dear, two coffees as usual," Mrs. Straub answered. The two elderly ladies went to the breakfast buffet and I picked up their coffees. When I returned to the table they had already accumulated an amazing amount of pastries, rolls and various cold cuts.

"I can see you are hungry this morning," I said.

"You have no idea, especially after what happened last night," Mrs. Straub answered, giggling.

I didn't know what she was talking about so I asked, "What happened last night?"

"Oh, you are not going to believe this," Mrs. Kern answered. She grabbed my arm and pulled me down. She looked around as if to make sure nobody was listening and then she continued. "Last night, we had just arrived in the Europa Salon when the Schulzes joined our table."

"Yes, and they seemed to be in a very bad mood," Mrs. Straub added.

"What's new?" I said casually.

"Correct, but it seemed that they had a fight before joining us. Anyway, we all sat down and ordered our drinks. When Mr. Schulze asked for a whiskey, Mrs. Schulze whispered something like, 'You had enough' or something to that extent."

"Yes, and he didn't like it," Mrs. Straub giggled.

"That's right, because suddenly he stood up and yelled at her."

"He yelled? I asked.

"Yes, he yelled so loud that everyone around us looked at our table; it was quite embarrassing."

"In the middle of the Europa Salon?"

"Yes, in the middle of the Europa Salon," Mrs. Straub giggled.

"What did he say?"

"Well, he told her sternly that he can order whatever he likes and that his drinks are none of her business."

"Wow," I said. I didn't feel very comfortable listening to this but there was no way that I could just walk away now.

"That's not all, because now the headwaiter arrived, asking him to keep his voice down because the show would start at any moment."

"Ha! And Mr. Schulze didn't like that, either," Mrs. Straub giggled again. "So he starts screaming at the poor headwaiter."

"Jesus, really? What did he say?"

"He told the headwaiter that he was a paying customer and he could order whatever he wanted and talk as loud as he wished."

"By this time all the attention was on our table; everyone watched what was going on. But the headwaiter kept calm and asked him again to lower his voice."

"And did he?" I asked.

"God, no, quite the opposite. Now he was screaming and yelling, asking to see the hotel manager," Mrs. Kern said mischievously.

"What did the headwaiter do?"

"Well, he told Mr. Schulze that he was intoxicated and it would be better for him to take a rest," Mrs. Straub said.

I couldn't believe what I was hearing and I was sure that after such an embarrassing incident, the Schulzes wouldn't bother me for some time.

"Yes, and then he really lost it because now he started screaming from the top of his voice. Several of the men in the salon came up to our table and asked the headwaiter if he needed help but he declined politely and asked them to take a seat."

"When Mr. Schulze noticed the men he began to shout, 'What is your problem? Do you want to fight?' He asked them over and over again. Then several waiters arrived and together with the headwaiter they ushered Mr. Schulze out of the salon whilst he was screaming and shouting. It was just hilarious."

"Where did they take him?"

"We don't know but he never came back. Good God, it was just so terribly embarrassing," Mrs. Kern answered.

"Mrs. Schulze was just standing there crying her eyes out and at that moment I felt sorry for her and asked her to take a seat."

"I see," I nodded.

"Yes, but instead of sitting down, she called us 'stupid old women' and stormed out of the salon with everybody watching her."

"The whole episode was just too embarrassing," Mrs. Straub added.

Mrs. Kern finally let go of my arm and I stood up. "Well, I don't think we will see them this morning," I laughed.

The two ladies chuckled. "Yes, I guess they'll have room service for a few days," Mrs. Straub said and then they laughed.

"Well, you better have some breakfast before your coffee gets cold," I said.

At the same moment more guests arrived. I saw several of them passing by the two ladies, whispering and laughing with them. I was sure they were talking about the incident with the Schulzes the night before.

I was back at my service station, watching Mrs. Kern and Mrs. Straub having their breakfast. Throughout my conversation with them I felt the ship heaving up and down but to my delight it did not seem to affect me as much as on the day before. I hoped it would last.

Bohne kept on coming to my station doing his weird watching thing and I wasn't sure whether he was watching my guests or my butt. I assumed it was the latter and so I disappeared every time I saw him coming. Eventually he ended up at Manfred's station and I could see them watching me, whispering and giggling. I really didn't want to know what they were talking about.

The party in the Europa Salon must have been a good since only one other couple showed up for breakfast. Not everyone was as lucky as I had been; several stewards had their stations packed. I went leisurely to the kitchen and watched the "egg chef" on duty as he frantically prepared the many egg orders from my colleagues. He was swearing and complaining. The egg chef was quite obviously gay and the girlish way in which he shouted at my colleagues was extremely entertaining. We had plenty of laughs with him. Then Obermeyer arrived and the atmosphere in the kitchen changed. Obermeyer looked as if he had had a long and intoxicating night, which probably was the case. He was not in a good mood. He picked up a gigantic mug of black coffee and disappeared into the chef's office. Some of the senior stewards took the opportunity to stick their heads into his office, sarcastically wishing him a "good morning." His thundering reply in form of screams and shouts echoed through the kitchen. I decided it was time to leave the kitchen now that Obermeyer was back.

At the service station I found Peter busy polishing his cutlery, a task which I had already completed earlier. As usual he decided to ignore me completely. This was something I was used to by now.

It seemed as if I had mastered the coordination of the different service jobs better than he and frequently finished my first seating long before he did. I was sure that this was due to the fact that I knew if I ever needed the help of the others again, I was finished.

I was so focused and obsessed with timing that I moved further and further up in the daily main-course queue in the kitchen. The escalators no longer presented a problem for me and my overloaded trays; quite the opposite, as the days went on, I climbed them faster and faster and before long I would even use the escalator's momentum to literally catapult me up and into the restaurant. I began to enjoy my job.

The only problem I had not quite mastered yet was dealing with the different kinds of people I had to interact with daily—the senior stewards, the chefs, the gays and some of my guests. My gay colleagues in particular presented a massive problem. I simply didn't know how to interact with them. I wasn't able to joke with them about the fact that they were gay and so I simply ignored them, which was not a good way to deal with the problem. Throughout my time on the ship I never got any better at this and therefore my relationship with them would always remain strained. It seemed as if they were trying to figure out forever and a day whether I was one of them or not.

Case in point was Bohne, who, over time, would try pretty much every trick under the sun to make me lose my temper and sometimes it worked. It was not much different with the senior stewards for whom any newcomer was automatically gay until proven otherwise. The only way to prove them wrong was of course to go out with one of the girls onboard. Considering that there were not that many of them, this was a rather difficult task but a task which I would eventually master, too.

Chefs were another story altogether. They were rougher and more uncut than the ones I had met at the Black Forest Grand Hotel and in the Columbus. They had to handle much larger volumes and deal with incredible time constraints during lunch and dinner business. Considering the speed by which the main courses came out of the kitchen, I have to say they did an incredible job. The much higher speed of service also meant that they were much more stressed than chefs in land-based operations, which made them naturally much more tense, resulting in frequent agitated shouting and screaming. The atmosphere in the kitchen during these times took some getting used to but over time I began to grow into it and learnt to love it.

Obermeyer in particular seemed to have a never-ending repertoire of swear words that he used extensively and although most of his yelling during busy times was good natured, it did instill a healthy sense of urgency into all of us. In many ways he reminded me of a drummer on one of those old fashioned Roman rowing boats where slaves provided propulsion with long oars in the rhythm of the drummer. All in all I have to say he was just as strict with his chefs as he was with us. Because of this, we respected him.

Then there were of course my guests, who sometimes were the most difficult characters to handle, especially if they were gay, too. Most of our guests were rich, spoiled, extraordinarily demanding and generally behaved as if they owned the ship. There were of course exceptions, but because we were always so busy with the spoiled ones, the exceptions mostly went unnoticed.

The overall atmosphere onboard was like no other I had ever experienced before; it was almost as if people changed their personalities as soon as they got onboard. Here they could show off their hidden and maybe real personalities. Nobody seemed to care about the whims and fancies of each other—the weirder the better. Elderly ladies dressed as if they were twenty and well-known TV stars dropped any inhibitions they may have had ashore, especially if they were gay. It was as if they were trying to compete with each other as to who could dress, behave or act the weirdest. And in midst of all this there was us—the stewards who had to act as if all this was nothing out of the ordinary. It was a strange and utterly unreal atmosphere reminiscent of movies like *The Rocky Horror Picture Show*.

I still had the urge to offer Peter my help as I saw him struggling with his mise en place, but I knew that all I could expect were sarcastic comments.

One day, I was just about to add some finishing touches to my setup when Wolfgang approached me. "Hey, Andre, we have a lifeboat drill at eleven," he said.

"A lifeboat drill?" This was news to me.

"We always take it in turns at sea and today is our turn," he said.

I had no idea what he was talking about. "What do I have to do?"

"Just meet me at ten to eleven in our cabin and we'll go up there together," he said.

"Up there where?"

"Up there to the lifeboats, Andre," he laughed.

"Okay, I see. Well, then, I'll see you at eleven." I looked at my watch; it was ten-thirty.

At ten to eleven I went to my cabin, where I found Wolfgang in the process of donning a bright orange life vest.

"Are we sinking?" I asked sarcastically.

"That's funny, go and get your life vest and put it on."

I looked around, wondering where I could find a vest.

"Oh, sorry, the vest is here in the bench."

He lifted the bench behind the table and pulled out another orange vest. I had no clue how to put it on so he helped me.

"Every cabin is assigned to one boat. Ours is C5. Wait for the announcement and then follow me."

"How do you know it is us today?" I wanted to know.

Wolfgang laughed. "I hope one day they come up with some sort of orientation for you new guys. There is a roster at the notice board in the purser's office. You should always check it once in a while because they sometimes change the dates without telling anyone," he said.

Why I was not surprised? Communication on this ship was virtually non-existent.

At eleven sharp, a klaxon sounded and the speakers crackled. "All hands man the lifeboats. I repeat, all hands man the lifeboats."

"That's it, follow me," Wolfgang said and dashed out of the cabin. I followed. Outside of our cabin several stewards wearing the same orange vests were rushing down the corridor and we followed. Other off-duty stewards pressed themselves against the walls to make space for us, at the same time shouting and yelling for us to move faster. We ran down the corridor and entered one of the emergency exits where we dashed up the stairs, back into long corridors and up the stairs again. After a while I had no clue anymore where we were; I just followed Wolfgang.

We finally entered one of the guest elevator landings and through a watertight door onto the sundeck where I found myself underneath one of the surprisingly large lifeboats. I followed Wolfgang along the deck, passing one lifeboat after another. Finally he stopped underneath the second to last boat which was marked with a large yellow sign reading "C5." We fell into line with several other stewards and waited; everyone was breathing heavily from the long run.

I had never been to this deck before and I was amazed by the incredible view in front of me. There were hardly any clouds and the sky was bright blue. There was only deep blue ocean as far as the eye could see, with long, rolling white-crested waves. There was a chilly gust of fresh crisp air which made me seek cover behind the steward next to me. Once gain I was impressed by the speed at which we cruised through the towering waves. I felt a light vibration and the frequent shuddering, whopping noise as we hit waves head on. Standing there high up on deck wearing my life vest gave me a feeling of adventure and I liked it. *This is actually quite cool,* I thought.

Then one of the officers dressed in white approached our group and conducted a roll call. One by one he called our names and when he shouted "Andre Schwarz," I answered with a loud "Here." He made a note on his clipboard and then continued. When he finished the roll call he tucked the clipboard under his arm and checked our life vests one by one to see if we had put them on properly. When he came to me he grabbed the front of my vest with both hands and shook me violently from left to right, then he nodded and moved on to the next steward. After all vests had been checked he reported his findings to another officer dressed in white. Overall there were six boat crews assembled at eleven-thirty. After a short speech by the first officer, he pronounced the exercise a success and the drill was over.

"That's it, that wasn't too bad," Wolfgang laughed.

The way back to our cabin was a maze of corridors and staircases and I knew I would never find our boat unless I memorized the way. I knew I had to walk this way a few times in the afternoons if I ever wanted to have a chance of finding this boat by myself.

"Hey, Wolfgang, thank you for taking me with you." I was truly grateful.

"Don't worry, I know how it is to be new here. We are not the best in welcoming new crew members," he answered.

"Tell me about it. If it hadn't been for you, I would still be in the restaurant folding napkins," I said and Wolfgang laughed.

"When you are back in the restaurant, go to the purser's office and study the emergency drill plan. We still have to do our fire drill and one lifeboat drill."

"We have to do another lifeboat drill?"

"Yes, but for the next one we will be in port and we take the boats down and row them around a little. It's quite an experience if you have never done it before."

"I guess so," I mumbled, unsure what to expect.

After some small talk we went back to the restaurant for lunch service. As expected, the Schulzes didn't show up for lunch, which was just as well. The atmosphere in my station was relaxed since there was no busy afternoon schedule for my guests. After nearly one week of eating, my guests began to slow down in terms of the amount of food they ordered. Most other stewards had overfed their guests on purpose right at the beginning and so they had already slowed down earlier. I had not learned to do this yet but I knew on my next cruise I would use the same tactics. By now most guests only ordered starter and main course and then took dessert at the afternoon tea buffet on deck. This saved nearly fifteen minutes of lunch service. I finished lunch with half an hour to spare.

During lunch I had an interesting conversation with Mr. and Mrs. Knaub, who sat at a small table for two. Because I was always so busy with my large table, I had never had the chance to talk much with them. The couple was in their early fifties and therefore of a slightly younger generation than the others. The conversation began with Mrs. Knaub asking me how long I had been onboard.

"I joined in Anchorage," I answered.

"Oh, is this your first cruise?" she asked.

"Yes, it is."

She laughed. "Well, we are onboard at least three times a year," she answered.

"Three times a year?" I was impressed.

"Yes, we have done two world cruises, one cruise around South America and several cruises in the Mediterranean and Norway."

"Wow, that's a lot." I was surprised that no one had ever told me about them. At least Bohne should have known that they were regulars.

"This is our first Alaskan cruise; we always wanted to do this," her husband explained.

Mrs. Knaub laughed. "Yes, we know this ship inside out."

"I would think so," I said.

"So, how about you, Andre, where are you from?" she wanted to know.

"I am from the Black Forest in Southern Germany."

"Oh, that's a beautiful area. We know it well; we have a house in Hinterzarten, do you know it?"

"Of course I know Hinterzarten. My hometown is only ten kilometers from there," I said.

"I see, but where are you originally from?" she asked.

I had to laugh; I was used to this question because I was tall and dark and didn't really look much like a German.

"Born and bred in Germany by German parents both" I answered.

Mr. and Mrs. Knaub looked surprised. "You don't look German," Mr. Knaub said.

"Yes, I know, it's the story of my life," I joked.

"Well, I think you are a very good-looking young man," Mrs. Knaub said and I blushed.

"Hey, hey, hey, leave that young man alone," her husband said jovially.

"So what do you do when you are not on this ship?" I asked.

"Oh, we are retired. Our sons have taken over the business." Mr. Knaub went on to explain that he had run a very lucrative private bank in Hamburg. His customers included some of Hamburg's most well-known names, which I have heard many times before but of course I knew them only by name.

"We have our own yacht but we prefer the *Europa* with its excellent food and service," Mrs. Knaub said laughing.

"It's of course smaller than the *Europa*," Mr. Knaub chipped in. "But we have done cruises to the States before."

"All the way to the United States?" I asked. *This cannot be a small yacht,* I thought.

"Of course we don't have couples like those troublemakers you have at the round table over there." Mr. Knaub motioned to my large table.

"Well, Mr. and Mrs. Schulze, they are not too bad," I said, slightly embarrassed. I had to be careful not to talk behind other guests' backs.

Mr. Knaub laughed. "Don't worry, we know exactly what you are going through. We had this type of guest at our table once. All you can do is let them be, even though we have to say that this one is quite something. Have you heard what happened last night in the Europa Salon?"

"Yeah, I heard about that. Must have been quite embarrassing," I said quietly.

"Embarrassing is not the word; it was a show all by itself. The way this Mr. Schulze behaved was just ridiculous, I tell you. The way he screamed and shouted at his wife was just bad. I will mention this to Mr. Huber when I am back in Hamburg," he said. When I heard the name Huber, I listened up. The CEO of Hapag Lloyd, the owning company of the *Europa,* was Huber—could it be the same? "I don't think he will be happy when he hears what guests he has on his ship."

It was the CEO, I thought, they *actually knew the CEO.* I didn't know what to say. I definitely had paid much too little attention to these guests. I began to wonder whether this couple was the reason for Bohne's frequent visits to my station rather than my bum. I was sure he knew and he hadn't told me - *that bastard.*

"Darling, I don't think there is anything he can do, he doesn't choose his guests," Knaub's wife said, smiling. She put her hand on her husband's arm.

I smiled. We talked for a little longer and I decided that I liked that couple and I would definitely pay them more attention in the future. When I told Angelika about this conversation later, she was surprised, saying that she had never seen them before. At least we knew now who they were and we were prepared. I also knew now that I had to be careful with Bohne; if he didn't tell me about these guests, God knows what other important guests I had sitting in my station. Like many other things, I would have to find that out for myself.

In the afternoon I started to write some letters, much to the delight of Wolfgang, who told me that he had given up on that a long time ago. Since Anchorage I had written about twelve letters to my parents and

Tatiana, which I planned to send off in Sitka as soon as I knew how. Instead of finishing the letters, I fell asleep with my face resting on the writing paper.

The same day after dinner I was invited to my first party in Birgit's cabin. When I arrived at Brigit's cabin after getting lost several times in a maze of corridors, the party was already in full swing. There were several off-duty stewards, stewardesses and chefs. I was surprised at the large number of people crammed into the tiny cabin. They had set up a small bar on the cabinet near the bunks, and on the table in the center of the cabin, I found baskets of bread and platters of cold cuts and smoked salmon. Loud music and the chatter of people provided the background noise for the party.

"Hey, Andre over here," Franz called out as he saw me. I made my way through the crowd over to Franz. He passed me a bottle of Beck's beer and we toasted to having survived the first week onboard.

Then Obermeyer burst into the room. "What the hell is going on here?" he barked.

For a split second I felt as if I had been caught doing something illegal with all this food around, but when he shouted, "Where is my beer?" I knew that all was in order. Contrary to my expectation, Obermeyer turned out to be quite a jovial character with a stinging sense of humor when off duty. This was also the first time that I saw some of the girls off duty, realizing that they looked much better without their uniforms.

We talked and drank plenty of Beck's beer until far too late. At one point I ended up next to Obermeyer who was just recounting stories of previous cruises. Most of his stories evolved around embarrassing incidents in the kitchen, the cause of which almost always being we, the incompetent stewards. His focus was of course the latest incident, with him preparing tons of freshly caught fish which, in the end, he had to throw away because we stewards were too stupid to sell and instead inundated him and his chefs with orders for steaks and tenderloins. He closed by saying that the only way to deal with us retards was to do exactly the opposite of what was planned because that's the way our retarded brains seemed to work.

Listening to him and his reasoning, influenced by lots of Beck's, I began to wonder if maybe he was right. I didn't tell him that, of course. We all had a good laugh when someone pointed out that despite

Obermeyer's tirade, the girls still favored the retards and we all, except Obermeyer, toasted to that with more Beck's.

I left the party at three-thirty after countless bottles of Beck's and for some reason it took me a while to find my cabin. For a change, Wolfgang was already fast asleep when I returned. I did my best to be as quiet as possible when I climbed into my bunk but judging by the grunting noises from Wolfgang I wasn't too successful. When I finally settled in my bunk, everything seemed to be moving and I wondered if it was me or the ship that moved and shifted constantly but most likely it was me. Then I fell asleep.

As expected, the next morning was a very unpleasant one. I awoke with a massive headache. I had a very long shower which eased the pain I was in at least a little. Getting dressed happened in slow motion and was pure torture. Every time I bent down I was reminded that I had too many Beck's the evening before. Beer had never been my beverage of choice; I was much more into fine wines. I promised myself never to do that again.

Instead of going straight to the restaurant, I went outside on deck and savored the fresh and crisp morning air. The cool breeze on deck was heaven for my pulsating headache. I glanced across the empty ocean which was of a dark grey color because the sun had not risen yet. Long-drawn swells heaved the ship up and down and back and forth as the massive hull of the *Europa* pushed at over thirty knots through the sea. At least the ship's movements did not make me feel nauseated anymore, a sure sign that I was beginning to grow my sea legs. I glanced around and inhaled the fresh air. I took several deep breaths and the view of the endless ocean elated me despite the dilapidated state I was in.

Breakfast went smoothly and again there was no sign of my special guests, the Schulzes. Mr. and Mrs. Knaub updated me on the movements of the troubled couple, saying that they had seen them together the evening before in the Europa Salon sitting by themselves at a small separate table. It seemed the Schulzes were not yet ready to face their fellow passengers after the by-now famous incident. I wasn't in a state to engage in friendly chats with my guest and so I spent most of my time at my service station folding lots of napkins and polishing even more cutlery. My headache eased off a bit as the morning went on and I couldn't wait to finish breakfast and head back to my cabin for a nap.

At lunchtime, after having slept for about two hours, I felt already much better. The one person who seemed to have noticed the change in me compared to the morning was of course none other than Manfred.

"You look much better, darling," he chirped as he stopped at my station.

I wasn't prepared for that. "Sorry?" I mumbled.

"Had a rough night last night?" Manfred asked with his girlish voice.

"Oh, ahm, not really," I lied.

"Come on, I am not blind. You looked pretty bad this morning."

I was shocked—had it been that obvious? I hoped my guests hadn't noticed.

"You should invite me to your party the next time. That would be fun."

"I didn't have a party, Manfred."

"Don't worry, honey, I won't tell anyone. This is between us, our own little secret," he giggled.

"There is no secret. I just had some drinks with some of the others."

"Is it now? I wonder why Wolfgang was so quiet this morning," he said and winked at me.

"Manfred, for God's sake, I didn't even see him last night. I don't know where he was or what he did."

"Oh, I see. Was it that dark?" he giggled again.

"I just told you that I don't know what Wolfgang did."

"So why do you get so excited then, honey?"

"I am not excited."

"Doesn't look like it to me." The way he had pronounced the last word made it sound as if he was singing.

"Look, Manfred, I don't have time for this. I have to get ready."

"Okay, okay, if you don't want to tell me, I will find out anyway, honey," he chirped and walked off to his station.

I was angry—why in God's name did he think I was gay? If he continued talking to me like that, I would never be respected by the others. There was only one way out of this—I had tell him straight to his face that I was straight.

After I finished my mise en place, I walked straight and very determined to Manfred's station. "Manfred, I have to talk to you," I said in a challenging tone.

He spun around, waving his hands like a girl. "Oh, Andre, it's you. You have startled me, you know?"

"Yeah, right. Anyway, I really have to talk with you."

"What can I do for you, honey?" he chirped and crossed his arms.

"Now look, I just want to tell you that I am not gay. I am straight and I have a girlfriend back home." I looked at him in anticipation of what he had to say to that.

"Oh, you have a girlfriend, that's great. Is she nice, honey?"

"Yes, she is, and I would appreciate it if you don't call me honey and darling all the time, because I really I don't like it."

"Oh, I see, I am sorry, honey."

"You said it again."

He looked in mock surprise. "I said what again?" he asked.

"You called me honey again."

"Oh, did I, darling?" he laughed.

"I told you not to call me that."

"Call you what?" he giggled.

"I told you not to call me honey or darling. It's stupid and I am not gay, so stop it, okay?" I was really unhappy now.

"Look, darling…"

"Stop it!" I protested.

"Look, no offense, but I call everyone honey or darling, not only you. It's just what I do."

"But I don't like it!" I insisted.

Manfred was enjoying this and I didn't get it.

"That's your problem, but I don't like to be called honey or darling because it is stupid."

"Hey, relax, darling…"

"Manfred, I am serious, stop it or…" I couldn't believe it; he went too far now.

"Or what, honey?"

"MANFRED!" I yelled.

"Okay, okay, there is no need to get excited, hon…Oops, I nearly said it again," he laughed and put his hands in front of his mouth.

"For God's sake, why do you do that?"

He bent forward and said with a serious tone. "Come on, Andre, I am only joking, don't take it too seriously."

"Yeah, whatever, but I still don't like it." I was pissed off with him.

"Look, I will be a nice gir...ahm, boy, and call you by your name, okay, hon... Damn, there it was again. Okay, it might take me a while but I will try, okay?"

"Yeah, whatever, I have to go." I just couldn't be bothered and walked off.

Back at my service station I found Angelika talking with Peter.

"Hi, Andre."

"Hi, Angelika," I said. When Peter saw me he walked off without saying a word. I looked at Angelika.

"You know what I think? I think this one is also gay. That's why he behaves like an idiot."

Angelika laughed. "Hey, what's wrong with you? Had a bad morning?"

"Not really, but Manfred is pissing me off calling me honey and darling all the time."

"But he calls everyone girlish names. He is a queen, didn't you know that?" she smiled.

"I don't care if he calls others stupid names. I don't like it and if he says it again I don't know what I am going to do to him."

"Don't say that too loud," Angelika answered.

"Why? Do you think I am afraid of him?"

"Of course not, nobody is afraid of Manfred. He is just making fun of you." She patted my shoulder reassuringly.

"That's not funny," I said.

"Look, just play along and you will see he will stop it soon."

"What, you want me to pretend I am gay?"

"No, that's not what I meant. I meant just play along. If he calls you honey, call him darling."

"I can't do that."

"Why not?"

"Because I am not gay."

"You don't have to be gay to joke around a bit."

"Look, I can't, it's not me. Everyone here already thinks that I am one of them."

"And who is that?" Angelika asked.

"Everyone—Hartmut, this guy over there..." I pointed at Peter. "Everyone."

"You care about what they think? Come on, everyone knows that they are just a bunch of hooligans. Who cares what they think?"

"Angelika, if they continue calling me girl's names, I will lose it one day."

"I wouldn't do that if I were you."

"Yeah, and why not? Do you think I am afraid of them?" I was really angry now.

"I don't think you are afraid of them, but if you lose your temper and do something stupid, then you are on you way home in the next port."

I was quiet; I knew she was right and there was not much I could say to that. She looked at me and then smiled.

"I can tell you that there are a couple of girls that like you and they know you are not gay, believe me, but don't tell them I told you, okay?" she whispered. That was unexpected and I didn't know what to say. "Anyway, let's forget about that. We have to get ready for lunch." She picked up her tray.

Her words echoed in my head—*There are a couple of girls that like you and they know you are not gay*—and I wondered if it was true or if she just wanted to make me feel better.

"So who said that?" I wanted to know.

"Who said what?" she mocked.

"Which girls are you talking about?" I felt silly asking.

"Hey, I can't tell you that. I promised them."

"That means you are lying."

"I am not lying."

"I think you *are* lying," I insisted. I wasn't really interested in knowing if it was true or not but it was a good way out of this silly conversation. But then again, what if it *was* true? It would still be nice to know.

"I am not lying and I won't tell you. Sooner or later you will find out anyway," she said and walked off. She left me standing there wondering if what she had said was true.

I had only six guests for the first seating; the Schulzes were still nowhere to be seen. Not that I missed them, but I began to wonder where they were. Mrs. Kern and Mrs. Straub were in their usual jovial mood, speculating as to the whereabouts of my troublesome couple. Mrs. Straub thought that they may have jumped overboard whilst Mrs. Kern was sure they had gone on an involuntary diet. Mrs. Steiner agreed with Mrs. Kern, saying that both of them could use a few days without stuffing themselves. Everyone laughed. I wondered what it would be like when the couple eventually returned to the table. Would they still make such comments? I would find out the next day.

That day I came third in the main-course queue, which was a first for me. When I reached the pass Obermeyer greeted me in his usual brisk manner.

"Who do we have here, another steak and tenderloin clown? What do you want?" he barked at me.

I just smiled and announced my order. "Two chicken, three fish and one steak, Chef."

"Oh, only one steak? What is wrong with you today? Looks like you had one Beck's too many last night or what?"

Although he barked as usual, there was something different in his tone; it sounded more like the barking of a fellow drinking partner. It seemed to me that it had been good for me to attend the party the previous night; it meant we shared common friends.

"Two chicken, three fish and one steak for Mr. Beck's here," Obermeyer shouted into the kitchen and that was it—no further sarcastic remarks.

"So how are you feeling today, having a hangover?" he asked.

"Not really, Chef, I am okay."

"Good, at least you are not one of those hussies like them back there," he shouted out loud. He looked at Manfred and some of his gay friends at the back of the queue.

"Just wait 'til I am down there, darling," Manfred giggled and the rest of the queue burst out laughing. "Oh, hoooney, I am sooo afraid, what are you going to do to me—give it to me?"

Obermeyer had to laugh. He walked threateningly toward Manfred. "The day will come when I will really give it to you with my frying pan, you old woman," he barked. Everyone roared with laughter at the verbal engagement.

"You mean the big, big frying pan with the long handle?" Manfred shouted back, wiggling his lower body.

"Yeah, that one. I am going to shove it up your backside 'til it comes out of your big mouth," Obermeyer yelled.

At the same time the first of my main courses were finished. Obermeyer walked back to the pass and added the final touches to my dishes. When he had finished I covered the plates with cloches and placed them onto my tray.

"I tell you, that guy is so confused it's not funny anymore," Obermeyer whispered to me.

"Yeah, he really doesn't know whether he is male or female," I answered.

To my surprise Obermeyer burst out laughing. "Of course not. He is an old bloody woman with a moustache," he answered whilst whipping the rim of a plate with the steak. "That's the last one, off you go."

I was surprised; this was the first time he had not ordered me out of his "bloody kitchen."

"NEXT!" he screamed as I lifted the tray onto my shoulders.

As I walked away I heard him shouting at the next steward in line. "What the fuck do *you* want?" he barked.

I had to smile because he had addressed him in a much ruder fashion than me. *Thank god I went to that party last night,* I thought again as I climbed up the escalator. It seemed I had an ally after all.

Angelika was already standing by to help me serve. I carefully placed the tray onto the service station. She immediately started to remove the cloches of the plates on top. "You do the Knaubs, I'll start with the others."

I checked my order pad and took one chicken and one fish for Mr. and Mrs. Knaub.

"That was quick," Mrs. Knaub said when I served her the fish.

"I was lucky today," I answered.

"This has nothing to do with luck," she said. "We have watched the way you work—very efficient."

I didn't know what to say; the compliment had taken me by surprise. "Thank you, Mrs. Knaub. Enjoy your lunch."

I went back to the service station and picked up the last remaining two plates for Mrs. Kern and Mrs. Straub. The plates were piping hot and I dashed to the two elderly ladies to get rid of them as quickly as possible.

"Mm, I love fish," Mrs. Kern said.

"Yes, it looks good today," I answered, trying not to show that I had burned my fingers. "Enjoy your lunch."

Back at the service station, I found Bohne staring at the Knaubs.

"Good afternoon, Mr. Bohne," I said, as friendly as I could. He mumbled something unintelligible. Whilst he stood there staring at my guests I cleaned up the cloches in my station.

"How are the Knaubs?" he suddenly asked. Since I had only heard him talking once, I didn't immediately understand his question.

"Excuse me?"

He looked at me, annoyed. "The Knaubs, how are the Knaubs?" he asked again, with his voice one octave higher.

"Oh, they are fine. I think they really enjoy the cruise."

"Are you sure?" he whispered so quietly, I hardly understood what he was saying.

I looked at Mr. and Mrs. Knaub and they looked very content as they ate their lunch.

"They are very important." Again, I hardly heard him talking.

"Excuse me?"

Bohne stepped back and looked at me, annoyed. "I said, they are important. The Knaubs are very important, do you understand?" He looked very nervous.

"Yes, I understand, and I *will* look after them."

What was wrong with this man? I thought, as he stood there eyeing me nervously. Couldn't he see that I was on top of things? I had looked after them for the past six days and he hadn't bothered once to tell me who they were and that they knew the CEO of the company.

He just stood there watching the couple as they enjoyed their food. I didn't know what to do or what to say. What did he expect me to do, pat him on the shoulder and say, "Don't worry, it will all be fine?" *He is a real weirdo.*

"They are important," he suddenly said again to no one in particular and walked off. *This guy definitely has a screw loose,* I said to myself as I watched him walk off. Even the way he walked was strange, as if he had something between his legs.

"What did he want?" Angelika startled me; she had appeared out of nowhere.

"I have no idea. He kept on telling me the Knaubs are important."

"I see. That means they are really important. He does not pay that much attention to guests unless they are someone special."

"Well, they seem to know Huber, the CEO."

"Huber? Really? I see, that explains it."

"Yes, they know Huber and as far as I can see, they are perfectly happy. By the way, this is not the first time I've had important guests," I said, smiling mischievously.

"That's not what I meant," Angelika protested.

"I see. So what did you mean then?"

"You are just being silly."

"I know." I had to laugh. "You know, Obermeyer was different today."

"Really? How different?"

"I don't know, but he didn't shout at me in his usual way in the kitchen."

"Look, Obermeyer is not that bad. He is quite a funny guy when he is off duty."

"Yes, I think so, judging by last night," I said.

"I think he likes you because you are not so pretentious like Hartmut and his gang and of course you are not one of them," she said, motioning over to Manfred.

"Of course I am not. How often do I have to tell you people?"

Angelika laughed.

"So how about you? Who is your boyfriend here?" I asked.

Angelika blushed. "I don't have a boyfriend onboard," she said.

"So you left him ashore?"

"That's none of your business," she said.

"Of course not, but how about Franz?"

She suddenly looked away. "Franz? Why him? He is new."

"I've noticed the way you look at him."

I meant it; I noticed the way she had stared at him several times and especially at the party the previous night. I thought they would make a good couple, not only because they were of a similar character but also because they seemed to be on the same wavelength. I had also noticed that whenever she was close to him, she would touch his arm when she laughed. There was no doubt in my mind that she liked him.

"You are so silly."

"Am I?"

"Yes, you are and now I have to go because I am busy. Your guests have finished, by the way." She turned and walked off. *She definitely likes him,* I thought, smiling.

When I cleared the main-course plates my two elderly ladies couldn't stop praising the food they just had. I thanked them and made a mental note of telling Obermeyer. The Knaubs were just as happy, which was good. I considered telling Bohne but decided against it; I didn't want to initiate any conversations with that man unless it was absolutely necessary.

I served desserts and coffee and prepared my station for the second seating. Bohne passed by a couple of times but he remained quiet, which was good. I hoped that he could see that his "important" guests, the Knaubs, were happy with me and my service.

I finished long before my station mate Peter, which must have been very frustrating for him. With over half an hour left before the second seating, I joined the others out on deck. It was only out there that I realized the sea had gotten a bit rough. The entire stern of the ship heaved up and down considerably and for a moment I tried to figure out if I felt nauseated or not. I didn't. A chilly but refreshing breeze whisked over the deck.

"Hi, Andre," Franz said as he saw me. "How are things with you?"

"I am fine, how about you?"

"Good, thanks. Do you know where Angelika is?" he asked.

I had to smile. "I think she will be here soon. Why do you want to know?"

"Tony and I are thinking of having a little get-together in our cabin after Sitka, and we need her to arrange for some drinks," he said with a smile. *Yeah, right,* I thought.

"Hi, guys," a voice said from behind. I turned and saw Angelika standing next to me.

"Jesus, don't give me a heart attack."

"Hey, it's freezing out here," Angelika said. It was very chilly but I couldn't really admit that.

"Don't be such a wimp," I joked.

"Yeah, you can talk."

We planned the party for the first night after Sitka. Angelika agreed to organize the drinks whilst Tony and I volunteered to organize the food. I had no idea how I would accomplish that but Angelika kindly offered to help.

After I had finished my second seating I went back to my cabin to get some well-deserved sleep. Wolfgang was out and that was good. I finished one letter to Tatiana, describing the happenings from the last few days without mentioning the fact that some girls seemed to have a crush on me. I still didn't know whether that was actually true or Angelika had just said it to make me feel better. I liked to think it was true and wondered who these girls were. Since I had just written a letter to Tatiana, I told myself to stop thinking about this. Then I fell asleep.

When I woke up nearly three hours later something seemed wrong, my bunk was moving! *What was happening?* I wondered drowsily. I tried to sit up and nearly fell out of my bunk when the whole cabin suddenly shuddered and vibrated violently. There were strange screeching noises like on an old sailing ship. *There must be a storm up there.* I carefully climbed down from my bunk and awkwardly stumbled to the bathroom. I could feel that the ship was going through some rough seas.

Taking a shower under these conditions was an interesting experience, especially seeing the shower curtain and the water in the shower basin moving back and forth to the rhythm of the ship. I finished my shower and got dressed—another interesting exercise. Suddenly the door flung open and Wolfgang stormed in. "Hey, how are you doing?" he gasped. "Shit I am late."

"What's up with the weather?" I asked.

"Nothing, a bit bumpy, that's all. What time is it?"

I looked at my watch. "Ten past six."

"Damn, I am late," he said again. "I haven't prepared a thing for dinner. I wanted to finish early and now I am late." He didn't seem to care about the shuddering and shifting of the ship.

"Is this normal?" I asked.

"Is what normal?" he gasped again as he undressed. I really got the impression that he couldn't care less about the rough sea.

"This weather."

"The weather? Come on, this is nothing. Just wait 'til we go through a storm."

"So this is not a storm?"

Wolfgang looked at me and then he started laughing. "Come on, the sea is a bit rough and that's it. You don't need to worry, this happens all the time."

He turned and rushed to the bathroom. There was no point in talking to him; he was too preoccupied with getting ready for dinner. I decided to leave him alone and headed for the restaurant.

When I reached the main deck I was surprised at how dark it was. The sky was overcast with dark grey clouds hanging low above the waves. The massive hull of the ship was thrust up and down by seemingly gigantic waves. Canvas sheets strapped over winches and other machinery flattered noisily around in the gale. Instinctively I grabbed one of the hand rails running along the ship's walls. Sea spray filled the air, soaking everything in the open in cold seawater. I quickly turned on my heels and went back inside.

In the restaurant I realized quickly that I was the only one seriously concerned about the weather and the safety of the ship. I studied my colleagues and judging by their faces and their general demeanor, the weather seemed to be the least of their concerns. That evening was not an easy one for me and although the service itself went fairly smoothly, the violent movements of the ship and the stormy sea outside made it difficult for me to concentrate. Angelika must have sensed my anxiety because she frequently tried to make jokes about the ship's movements. I did not feel like laughing. After I had served the guests of my second seating, I went back to my cabin, showered and disappeared in my bunk. I drew the curtains and, to my surprise, despite the continuous heaving of the ship, I fell asleep instantly.

The next morning all signs of bad weather had disappeared and the sea around us had quieted down considerably. The waves rolled in long lazy swells and seagulls trailed the ship, chirping noisily, hoping to catch some food leftovers. *Stupid birds,* I thought. The sky was bright blue with only a few scattered clouds. We were on our way to the port of Sitka where we would remain for one short day before continuing on south.

I stood on deck as I had done pretty much every morning for the past six days and savored the peace and quiet of the early morning hour. As I stood there gazing at the horizon, I realized that my morning walk on deck had become something like a habit. To stand there all alone surrounded by nothing but ocean and the superstructure of the ship gave me the energy I needed to master the daily challenges with my difficult guests and colleagues. The past eight days had not been easy and it was only now that I had a feeling of having found my place in this daily rat race. The hectic timing of serving up to six meal periods a day had quickly become a habit and I began more and more to concentrate on my guests and colleagues rather than on the service itself.

I had found my daily routine. I woke up at six sharp every morning and always left our cabin long before Wolfgang opened his eyes. The long and seemingly endless corridors of lower deck 1 and 2 had also become more familiar and I hardly got lost anymore. The kitchen and its chefs had also become more familiar and I felt that I had gained a certain amount of respect amongst the chefs. I had found my group of friends and, lucky for me, Obermeyer was part of that group. No doubt I owed much of my standing in this group to Angelika, who simply didn't like pretentious and arrogant people, something which I liked to think I was not. To this day I have no desire to pretend to be bigger or better than others and to this day I am immensely proud of where I come from—a small, decent and down-to-earth town in the beautiful Black Forest.

That morning on deck, I felt at home for the first time on this big luxurious ship. For the first time I felt excited and looked forward to discovering new places and meeting new people. All my worries and anxieties had disappeared, just like the bad weather the night before. I suddenly felt ready to face the troublesome Schulzes and Hartmuts of this world.

We arrived in Sitka at eight, by which time most of my guests had finished their breakfast in order to witness our arrival in port. To everybody's surprise, the Schulzes had made an appearance at the breakfast table. Not surprisingly, they had been very quiet and although far from friendly, they had not complained about the food or the service. The atmosphere at the table had been tense and it seemed as if my two elderly ladies, Mrs. Straub and Mrs. Kern, were keeping them in check.

Breakfast finished at nine and I quickly cleaned up my station. Angelika and Franz had asked me to join them for a quick trip into town before lunch, which I had gladly accepted. I liked the two a lot and because I thought they would make a nice couple and hoped that they would somehow get together. At nine-thirty I waited at the gangway for my two friends.

The city of Sitka is located west of Baranof Island in the Alexander Archipelago which is part of the Alaska Panhandle in the U.S. state of Alaska. Sitka is the fourth largest city in Alaska with a population of just over 8,900 souls. The fourth largest city of Alaska struck me as rather small as we walked down its main street with its variety of souvenir shops, drug stores and saloons. Some of the buildings looked a little out of place and Angelika told me that they were Russian. As I later found out, the town of Sitka used to be part of Russia and was sold in 1867, together with the rest of Alaska, to the United States. Sitka also was the site of the ceremony in which the Russian flag was lowered and the flag of the United States raised after the purchase.

Even though the town itself was small and could be explored within a matter of hours, I found its history immensely interesting. We visited the Saint Michael Russian Orthodox Cathedral, which was an interesting wooden building where we took plenty of pictures. After buying some postcards and a small number of souvenirs, we made our way back to the *Europa*.

We returned to the ship at eleven-thirty, which left me just enough time for a quick shower and at eleven forty-five I was back at my station. Because many of our guests had booked sightseeing tours, we had one open seating instead of two. To my dismay most guests of my first and second seating came for lunch and because I had only twenty-one seats, two couples sat at Peter's tables. He was furious and because he flatly refused to serve them, I had to do them as well.

With Angelika's help I served twenty-five guests in a record time of less than an hour. At twelve forty-five it was over and by one o'clock all my tables, including the two from Peter, were set up and ready for dinner. My station mate was seriously cheesed off but I couldn't be bothered.

In the afternoon we ventured once more into town and I finally posted my letters to Tatiana, all thirteen of them, and several letters and postcards to my parents. After the post office, there was not much else to do so we bought more souvenirs and then went back to the *Europa*.

That evening I watched our departure from the main deck because we left at eight and that was exactly between the two seatings. I was surprised at how many well-wishers had shown up for our departure; the pier was packed with people, all waving their arms at us. The decks of our ship were just as crowded with passengers waving back at the crowd ashore. Two pier workers manhandled one of the *Europa*'s heavy stern ropes from a massive bollard on which the ship had been tied to the pier. It landed splashing in the dirty harbor water, from where it was slowly pulled in by one of the ship's winches. After a short while, pulled by two harbor tugs, the ship slowly edged away from the pier. I glanced at the upper decks of our ship, where hundreds of passengers waved frantically with scarves and handkerchiefs. When we reached the harbor entrance the tugs said goodbye with three blares of their ships' horns. Then I felt a light vibration resonating through the ship as the captain increased the revolution of our two gigantic propellers, slowly accelerating the ship towards the open sea. The skyline of Sitka began to fade away until its lights eventually were merely tiny dots on the horizon.

By the time we started serving our second seating it was already dark outside and the lights of Sitka had disappeared in the distance. During dinner Angelika brought a large platter of smoked salmon to our service station and asked me to hide it in the lower cabinets of my service station. I was stunned. *What if someone had seen this?* Angelika just laughed, telling me not to worry because everyone was stealing food like this for parties. To my surprise, even though my miserable station mate Peter saw what we were up to, he kept quiet.

The platter of smoked salmon was followed by cheese, steak tatare and a selection of breads and rolls. After dinner we smuggled our bounty of delicatessen out of the restaurant to Franz's cabin. We had to shuttle several times back and forth to the restaurant until we eventually had assembled an impressive little buffet two decks below the restaurant. The party started at eleven-thirty and was attended by our usual crowd, including my newfound friend Obermeyer.

I washed down plenty of steak tatare with the usual large amounts of Beck's beer. At one point I ended up talking once again with Obermeyer. It was actually him who did all the talking and I listened as well as I could, considering that more Beck's kept coming. Obermeyer told me the story of his life and until today I am not sure that he actually knew it was me he was talking to since he spiced up his story with plenty of personal tragedies, mostly involving girls.

We partied once again far too long and when I eventually returned to my cabin, all I had left were a couple of hours sleep. I got up the next morning feeling just as bad as I had felt after my first party a few days earlier. I had been onboard now for a little less than ten days and because of our intense working schedule, it felt as if it had been months.

I survived the next day, albeit with a splitting headache. Since we were at sea, the day after the party I went to bed in the afternoon to catch up on badly needed sleep. The day after such parties was normally accompanied by sarcastic comments from Manfred which I had learned to ignore.

The day passed and before I knew it we had reached the Alaskan port of Ketchikan, the "Salmon Capital" of Alaska. The one day we spent in Ketchikan followed pretty much the same routine as the others before—after breakfast we ventured out into town and bought plenty of delicious smoked Alaskan salmon. After lunch in the afternoon we ventured out again, bought postcards, souvenirs and took lots of photographs. We then tried local beer in one of Alaska's most famous bars, the Red Dog Saloon, taking plenty more photographs. In the evening we returned to the ship just in time to serve dinner for our starved guests.

Ketchikan was followed by two days at sea, the first of which was marked by another lifeboat drill and another party with all sorts of marinated and smoked salmon and plenty of Beck's beer. Looking at the incredible amounts of Beck's we consumed made me wonder where they stored all this beer. I would find out weeks later when I was taken on a tour of our storerooms onboard.

On the second day at sea, I was in the middle of serving lunch when the captain announced that we had entered Canadian waters. I looked outside but couldn't see any difference; there was still plenty of water, except it was now Canadian and not American water. Nevertheless, we had reached Canada.

Our first port of call in Canada was Victoria, a city that, if it had not been for the large American cars, struck me more as European than anything else. Victoria is the capital city of British Columbia, the westernmost province of Canada. Located on the southern tip of Vancouver Island, Victoria is also a major tourist destination and popular port for cruise ships. Most of the buildings were made of bricks and stone rather than the Alaskan wooden structures. The city of Victoria with its nicely arranged walkways and plenty of greenery was in stark contrast to the plain and simple towns of Alaska. The shops and stores along the main street of Victoria looked like something out of a storybook.

We walked through the clean and neat city, visited the famous Empress Hotel and the Thunderbird Park where we took lots of photographs and bought postcards. I liked this city and hoped that I would have the chance to come back one day when I had a little more time.

At Thunderbird Park we relaxed in a café before heading back to the ship. I watched Franz and Angelika and more than ever I had the impression that the two of them had a crush on each other. Whenever we went out, we did so always in the same group—Franz, Angelika and I—and throughout this time the two of them got closer until eventually, the day after Victoria, they started holding hands. It was now official; Angelika and Franz were a pair.

The day at sea was also the last for this cruise because the next day we would arrive in Vancouver, where most of our guests would disembark, traveling back to Germany. First, however, we had the customary gala farewell dinner. This was the time of reckoning for us stewards because this was the day when we would get our well-deserved tip. For me of course the focus was still on the successful completion of that final dinner rather than the impending tip.

The restaurant that evening looked as good as ever with lots of silver cutlery, candelabras, flower bouquets and a lavish buffet with plenty of caviar and other gourmet dishes. Obermeyer and his team had done a truly fantastic job and I was sure our guests would be impressed. Once again I wore my short white dinner jacket with bow tie looking "absolutely gorgeous," according to Manfred.

I had learned to ignore him. Our guests too had put on their most expensive evening wear, complemented by even more expensive jewelry. Everyone arrived in time and I went through the usual ritual of taking orders and making small talk. I noticed that the atmosphere at my troubled table had improved immensely, with everyone being in a jovial mood and that included the Schulzes. This was due to the fact that for them the cruise was over and everyone would fly home the next day.

This was part of a pattern that would repeat itself on every single cruise. One has to remember that each cruise lasts two to three weeks and throughout this time, these guests had breakfast, lunch and dinner together and in addition, they would meet at afternoon tea, at the pool and so on. For the first few days this was fine but then they would begin to notice each other's peculiarities. One guest snorted when laughing, another slurped and others wore the same clothes day in and day out—there was something annoying for everyone.

Halfway through the cruise these peculiarities would result in conflict, with me, the steward, caught in between. This was the time when I, the steward, had to be seen as completely neutral since otherwise this could have serious repercussions when it came to the tip. This was not always easy since they all had only one person to talk to and that was me. Then, as the cruise neared the end, tempers settled and eventually they all became friends again.

And so it happened that on that last day of our Alaskan cruise, they all laughed and chatted happily with each other and for once, hardly anyone paid attention to me. After having served a sumptuous seven-course menu, we ended the meal with our famous ice parade which left the entire restaurant cheering and applauding. Mr. and Mrs. Knaub called me to their table and complemented me on the menu and, of course, the excellent service.

"Thank you," I said shyly.

"We really enjoyed having you as our steward," Mrs. Knaub said as she passed me an envelope. I said "Thank you, Mrs. Knaub" and stuffed it into the inner pocket of my jacket. One by one my guests called me to their tables and handed me envelopes with money—all except the Schulzes. Mr. and Mrs. Schulze left without even saying goodnight and that was quite fine with me; I much preferred not having them around.

The turnover for the next seating was so tight that I hadn't even had time to open my envelopes. The second seating went pretty much like the first one, ending with emotional goodbyes from my guests and several envelopes with tip. Having received several of these envelopes, I couldn't wait to open them.

When my guests had finally left, I cleaned up my station and rushed to my cabin. I was relieved to find the cabin empty. Wolfgang was still out and that was good; at least I had some privacy when I counted my well-deserved tip. I took the envelopes out of my inner pocket, placed them all on the table and sat down.

The first envelope I picked up was from Mrs. Straub and Mrs. Kern. They had written my name and "Danke" in neat Old-German script. I had grown quite fond of the two ladies. I opened the envelope with my pen.

What I saw next took my breath away. I had expected the tip to be something in the range of fifty to one hundred marks but the two banknotes I held in my hands left me completely speechless. What I held there in my hands were two brand new, five-hundred mark notes. I stared at the two banknotes, not knowing whether to laugh or cry; it was simply unreal. *Could it be a mistake?* I wondered. One-thousand-marks tip! I had only seen five-hundred-mark banknotes few times and here I got two of them—as tip! My monthly salary was only one thousand eight hundred marks and here two elderly ladies had given me one thousand as tip; this was simply unreal. I carefully stuffed the banknotes back into the envelope.

I picked up the next envelope which was from Mr. and Mrs. Knaub, the couple who knew the CEO of Hapag Lloyd, Mr. Huber. I opened it. I retrieved another five-hundred-mark banknote. This was simply unbelievable—one-thousand-five-hundred-marks tip! *Who were these people?* I asked myself. I knew they were wealthy but this by far exceeded my wildest expectations, if I ever had any. I had only opened two envelopes and already I had received tip equivalent to one month salary.

When I had opened all envelopes, I had counted a total of three thousand and four hundred marks. I counted the banknotes again and again but the amount remained unchanged—three thousand and four hundred marks. "WOW!" I shouted out loud. I walked up and down the cabin, thinking of all those banknotes—three thousand and four hundred marks. "Wow!" I shouted again. Suddenly all the problems and challenges I had experienced since boarding the *Europa* in Anchorage had disappeared. I am working on a cruise liner, I will see the world and the way it looks, I even will make a bit of money on the way. I felt like celebrating. I called Franz in his cabin but he wasn't there so I went to the crew bar.

The Piesel was so packed with chefs, stewards and stewardesses that I had a hard time negotiating my way through the mass of people. I had never seen the bar so full and the noise level was amazing. The speakers of the HiFi system must have been at its highest but the chatter and laughter of the people were still much louder. I found Franz and the gang near the bar.

"Hey, Andre, it's about time you came, we have been waiting for you," Franz shouted. I just smiled. "Here is your beer and cheers to our first cruise."

"Cheers," I replied and took a sip. "The place is packed today," I shouted at Franz.

"Yeah, apparently it's always like this after the farewell dinner."

"I see." My answer drowned in the background noise.

"Hey, Andre, tell me, how was your tip?" Franz suddenly shouted in my ear.

I didn't answer but looked at him with a very big grin. "How was yours?" I shouted back at him.

He nodded knowingly. "Bloody amazing, biggest tip I ever got in my life," Franz shouted from the top of his voice.

"Yeah, it's the same for me, just unbelievable," I said and raised my glass again for a toast. "To the next six months!"

Franz smiled and raised his glass. "To the next six months of tip!" We laughed.

Once again we drank until the early morning hours and the only reason for leaving was the barman who insisted in closing the bar. We took several bottles of Beck's and went onto the main deck where we sat for another hour. By the time I got back to my cabin it was time to get ready for breakfast. Wolfgang was still not there and our cabin looked exactly as I had left it after dinner. I took out the envelopes which I had buried deep underneath layers of socks and underpants and found that all the money was still there. I shook my head and put the envelope back into the drawer.

"Amazing," I mumbled to myself. "Absolutely amazing."

The next day we arrived in Vancouver, British Columbia. We were scheduled to stay in Vancouver for two days. On the day of arrival most of our passengers disembarked and were shuttled to the airport from where they returned to Germany. The next batch of guests would arrive on the second day of our stay, and then at eight in the evening we would depart for the next cruise, which would take us down the west coast of the United States and all the way to Acapulco in Mexico.

At breakfast I had an opportunity to thank my guests for their generous tips, followed by some very emotional goodbyes. The only ones who had not even shown up for breakfast were the Schulzes. I guess this was because they were afraid of Mrs. Straub and Mrs. Kern, who had promised me they would publicly expose them for the fact that they had not tipped me. Of course the Schulzes never showed up but at least we had a good last laugh.

After all guests had left we had a major cleaning exercise where I was assigned my first side jobs. I know now that those side jobs were pretty easy ones compared to what would come later. I had to clean the handrails of the elevators leading from the restaurant to the kitchen. When that job was completed there was not much more to do and I had the evening off—what a treat. We went for dinner at a revolving restaurant located on top of one of Vancouver's tallest buildings.

The next morning I had to start at nine and it felt like three days' holiday. We did more cleaning in the morning and after that I had my first real lifeboat exercise. Since I had not paid any attention to the exercise schedule, I wasn't actually aware of it until Wolfgang came to my station asking me what I was still doing there. We rushed to our cabin, picked up our life vests and went to our lifeboat station.

Initially we went through the same routine as we did a week earlier but this time we actually had to launch the boat. When the boat was at the same level with the deck, we boarded and the sailors slowly let it down inch by inch. It was quite an experience to sit in that boat, dangling ten meters above the water. Thankfully, the sailors knew what they were doing and so we reached the surface of the sea unscathed. They released the ropes and we floated away from the ship.

Our lifeboat was one of the open boats capable of carrying over one hundred and twenty people. Despite the impressive size, the lifeboat seemed tiny next to the gigantic hull of the *Europa*. Our task was to take to the oars and row the lifeboat away from the ship. Sounds easy enough but the oars were just as big as the boat itself and I was struggling to get to grips with these long and heavy wooden things. There was much screaming and shouting from the officer calling us all sorts of names. Our laughing and joking of course did not help; quite the opposite, the officer kept on reminding us that in a real emergency situation, lives would depend on our rowing skills and from what he could see, we would have drowned already.

We tried our best but all in all it was more fun than anything else for us. The officer kept on shouting, saying that we should row according to his count but somehow we couldn't manage to coordinate our rowing to anything resembling some sort of rhythm. The boat turned around on its own axis and before we knew it we bumped into the hull of the *Europa*.

The officer was not happy and was screaming and shouting at us; he stepped over to the worst offenders and showed them what to do. We tried again and at long last we began to move away from the ship, albeit in a zigzag pattern. Our performance must have looked quite funny, almost comical, from above the ship, much to the dismay of the officer who knew that the captain was watching the exercise.

When we had managed to get far enough away from the ship, the officer announced the exercise was completed. He started the lifeboats' engines and we made our way back to the *Europa*. He repeatedly told us that in a real emergency, we most probably would have gone down with the ship and therefore we would have to repeat this drill again in a few weeks.

Despite the bad outcome of this drill, I had enjoyed it and looked forward to the next one. Reason for this was of course the fact that I had not done so badly and got away without being shouted at. Other colleagues had fared less well, which was plainly visible on their faces. We managed to row back to the *Europa* in a more or less straight line.

Somehow, I had expected to get back onboard via the gangway but instead, we stopped beneath an open watertight door about three meters above the water line. Suspended from the door was a rope ladder that dangled idly in the wind. I guessed correctly—we had to climb it in order to get back onboard.

One by one, we awkwardly climbed the dangling ladder until finally, assisted by several sailors at the door, we were back onboard. We were welcomed by several other officers who made sarcastic remarks about our performance. This was too much for one of my fellow stewards, who felt it was necessary for him to remind them that we were stewards after all and not sailors. We all made the mistake of bursting into roaring laughter. The first officer instantly rewarded my fellow steward with a severe dressing down that brought us back to reality and the laughing stopped.

At the same time that we stewards were learning how to row a lifeboat away from a sinking ship, our new passengers began arriving at the pier. They came straight from Vancouver International Airport where buses had picked them up. At the pier, the gorgeous pursers from our guest relations department welcomed them. They boarded the *Europa* via a large white gangway with a two large banners reading "MS Europa Hapag Lloyd." By three-thirty, the boarding was completed and most guests had settled in their cabins.

Bohne had scheduled a meeting at four o'clock to brief us on the upcoming cruise, expected VIPs and the table arrangements. At four sharp, we all had assembled in the restaurant waiting for Bohne to enlighten us. He finally appeared at five past four, flanked by his two assistants Yankowich and Koenig. Seeing the two assistants there surprised me since they normally kept a very low profile and never interfered in the operation at all; as matter of fact, we were not really sure what exactly they did onboard, if anything.

Yankowich was Yugoslavian and looked more like a ship's officer in his white uniform and short-cropped hair than an assistant restaurant manager. The girls onboard considered him good-looking. He was fully aware of this and used it to his fullest advantage. His colleague Koenig must have been about fifty years old, was of medium build and was one of those people who was easily overlooked because he blended in with the masses. They were a strange pair and from what I had seen since my arrival, I wondered what exactly they were doing onboard except sitting in the purser's office trying to look busy.

Bohne stopped in front of Manfred's service station and without saying a word, he just stood there. I guess he expected everyone to stop chatting automatically, which of course did not happen. He just stood there and looked at us with an unhappy face. He struck me as very immature with his eyes darting nervously back and forth.

"Be quiet!" he suddenly shouted with his high-pitched voice. Some of the guys had to laugh just hearing his voice and I thought for a moment that I had detected a slight grin on the faces of his assistants but I could have been wrong. When it had turned reasonably quiet, Bohne opened the briefing.

"The next cruise is ten days and ends in Acapulco."

On hearing Acapulco, someone in the back whistled, earning him an angry glance from Bohne.

"The passenger count is eight hundred and forty-six. In the first seating we have three hundred and eighty-one guests and in the second seating, four hundred and sixty-five."

There was murmuring and mumbling amongst the assembled stewards.

"Quiet, you keep quiet now!" Bohne yelled, with his head twitching nervously to the left and right. The way he acted was weird and I still did not know what to make of that man.

"The first seating will be busy, very busy, no time for cigarettes on deck, ha!" he giggled like a child. "We have fourteen artists onboard, seven band members, two television presenters, two magicians and three pianists. The presenters will sit in station four with Manfred, the magicians and pianists are with Karl Banhauser in station eleven and the band will sit in station three with Andre Schwarz." Bohne looked up from his notepad and grinned.

I had heard that having artists is considered a punishment amongst stewards because they never tipped. To have a table of seven with band members was a loss of tip that could literally run into the thousands - but that meant nothing to me. I was onboard because I wanted to see the world and not to make money. Of course, the tip was a nice side effect but it would never be so important to me that I would get upset because I had a table full of musicians.

Station three was not the station I had for the past two weeks and I also didn't know where station three was. *Will I have to share with Peter again?* I wondered. Bohne seemed sadistically satisfied with the unhappy faces of my fellow colleagues who had just been awarded with artists. He continued.

"There are a number of important guests like Mr. Feiler..." He read out a list of several names of guests, their positions and the reasons why they were very important. These guests were over-tax tippers and literally worth their weight in gold. Not surprising, all but one over-tax couple were assigned to gay stewards. Again, Bohne glanced around the assembled stewards in the hope of detecting some disappointed faces.

"Now the station plans...hee hee," he chuckled like a child who was just about to get a big bar of chocolate as a present. "Manfred - station one, Oliver and Paul - station two, Wolfgang and Andre - station three..."

Shit! That was the starboard side. Not only had Bohne assigned me to the starboard side in midst of all the gays but on top of that, he made me share the station with my cabin mate Wolfgang, who everyone knew was gay, too. In addition, to top it all off, station three was right next to Manfred's station. I was convinced that Bohne had done this on purpose. I was angry.

When he had finished reading out the list, he looked up and observed us one by one. As he glanced along the line of stewards, our eyes met and I could see his face glowing with sarcastic delight as he saw my angry expression. At that moment, it became clear to me that we would never be friends. Unfortunately he was still my boss so there was not that much I could do except bite my tongue and keep quiet.

After announcing the table plan, he gave us all a rundown on the entertainment program for this cruise as well as the forecasted weather.

Lastly, he announced the days and dates for the welcome, gala and farewell dinner on this cruise. Normally this would have been the end of the briefing but what followed next was an episode I will never forget.

Bohne glanced at us and asked, "Are there any more questions?" His eyes moved from person to person in the front row but no one had a question. He was just about to dismiss us when one steward in the back raised his hand. This was Karl Banhauser, one of the stewards who, just like me, had a couple of artists assigned to him. Karl had been onboard for over seven years, four on this ship and three on the old *Europa*.

"Mr. Bohne, I have a question," he said.

Bohne's head jerked back; he had not expected anyone to ask questions. "Yes, Karl?"

"Why have you assigned me artists again? I had five on the last cruise." Karl's voice was calm but carried a very challenging undertone.

"Because that's the way we have made the plan." Bohne's face had turned completely red. He turned to leave but Karl hadn't finished yet.

"Why me? I have had five artists on the last cruise. It has always been common practice not to have artists on two consecutive cruises—why now?"

All heads turned to Bohne, who looked very nervous and agitated now. His two assistants just stood there probably wishing to be somewhere else.

"I don't owe you any explanation. I can assign you any guest or artist I want and that's it," Bohne said and turned to leave.

"No, you cannot, Bohne!" Karl yelled.

Bohne stopped dead in his tracks and turned round. "Excuse me?" he shouted.

"I said, you cannot do what you want!" Karl yelled back.

Bohne's eyes went wide. "You cannot talk to me like that." His voice resembled more that of a hysteric woman rather than a man.

"I can talk to you in whatever way I bloody well want and you have still not answered my question. Why do you give me artists again after I had five on the last cruise? Answer me that!"

"You are out of line; you have no right to treat me like that!" Bohne cried and stomped his foot several times on the floor. He looked like an angry upset housewife. It was pretty clear to me that there was something seriously wrong with him.

"Mr. Bohne, I am warning you—either you change that table plan or I am seeing you in the hotel manager's office," Karl shouted at Bohne.

I would have expected Bohne to order Karl to his office or something like that but instead he shouted back in his high-pitched voice. "Leave me alone, YOU BITCH!"

There was instant silence!

All heads turned to Bohne and everyone fell silent. The silence lasted for another few seconds and then we all burst into roaring laughter. Bohne stomped his foot on the floor once more and then he walked off. His two assistants remained behind, asking us to get back to our stations. Some of the senior stewards told them to piss off and soon after they disappeared, too.

I could not believe what I had just witnessed; Bohne had completely lost his temper and called Karl a bitch in front of over thirty witnesses. Bohne had no choice, he had to change the table plan. Most of the guys went over to Karl and congratulated him on his performance.

I decided to check out my new station and see if the mise en place was complete. Of course it wasn't—all the teaspoons and most of the teacups had gone. *Damn, I should have thought of that and taken the teaspoons and cups from my old station,* I thought angrily, but now it was too late.

"Hi there," Wolfgang said and placed a cardboard box on top of our service station.

"Hi Wolfgang."

"So now we have the pleasure of living and working together. I hope you don't get sick and tired of me," he giggled.

"Don't worry," I mumbled, still upset about the loss of my cups and spoons.

"What's wrong with you?"

"I am a bit upset because just realized that I left my cups and spoons in my old station because I didn't know that we would have to change."

"You are in luck, young man," Wolfgang said, patting his cardboard box.

I didn't understand what he meant. "What is it?"

"This, my friend, is our stock of coffee cups, saucers and spoons. I never travel without them," he giggled.

"You are lucky. I have to go and start from scratch begging for spoons and cups."

"Of course not, young man, in here is enough for the two of us," he winked at me. I was surprised, not at him winking at me but at the fact that he was willing to share his equipment with me.

"Are you sure?"

"Of course I am sure. We work as a team correct?"

"Yeah, of course," I mumbled. After the past three weeks with Peter, this was quite a difference.

"And hey, who knows, we may spend the next six months on this station together so at least we should hit it off together, correct? I am sure you don't want another Peter in your station, or am I wrong?"

Wolfgang was well-informed even though I had never shared any of my frustrations with him. I wondered how he knew that the stations would change on this trip.

We unpacked the cups, saucers and plates and placed them neatly in our cabinets. Working with Wolfgang was completely different; for example, when he was in the process of placing ashtrays on his tables and saw that I hadn't done that yet, he simply continued placing them on my tables, too. It did not take me long to do the same and soon we worked as an excellent team.

"Do you know who is doing our wines?" I asked him.

"Doris," he answered.

"You mean Doris, as in—Hartmut's girlfriend?"

"Yes, that's her," he giggled. "Beautiful, blonde Doris."

Doris was without doubt the prettiest girl onboard. She was blonde, had deep blue almond-shaped eyes and turned out to be a very nice person, which made it all the more difficult for me to understand why she would go out with a guy like Hartmut.

"What do we have heeeere?" I shuddered; Manfred's voice had startled me.

"Hi Manfred."

"You two again. I see you are sharing a station together—how nice," he giggled. Wolfgang just smiled and I rolled my eyes. Wolfgang winked at me.

"Yes, Manfred, we are sharing a station and you better be nice to your guest. Otherwise, we steal your tip," he joked.

"Ah, my guests will never leave me. You will never be able to match Manfred's special service, my dear," he wiggled his body like a woman.

"Manfred, can't you see that we are busy?" I said.

"Hey, darling, you still have plenty of time, what's the hurry?"

"Don't call me, darling," I insisted.

"Ooops, sorry, I forgot hon…ah, there it is again, hee hee hee." He acted like a child.

"Yeah, righ."

"Look, my dear, you are now on the starboard side and I can call you whatever I like, sweetheart."

I was just about to ask him to shut up when Wolfgang interrupted. "Manfred, leave him alone. We are really busy here."

"Okay, okay, take it easy. Anyway, honeys, I am over there if you need me. Bye, bye." He waved his hand, wiggled his bum and walked off.

I grabbed a stack of plates and began setting up our tables. "You know, I wish he would stop that," I said to Wolfgang.

"Stop what?"

"Stop calling me darling and honey all the time."

"Don't worry, he does that with everybody but you are the only one asking him to stop and that's why he likes to tease you."

"But it really bothers me, Wolfgang, and if he doesn't stop I will give him a piece of my mind."

Wolfgang laughed. "That will make things only worse."

"I don't care."

"Look, Manfred is a nice guy and he knows that you are straight and that's why he likes to tease you. Just don't think about it."

"Yeah, whatever."

Whilst I was setting up plates for our stations, Wolfgang was placing napkins on each plate and before I knew it, our tables were ready. I then began folding napkins for the second seating, for both of us, whilst Wolfgang polished our cutlery. This was a completely different way of working—as a team—and I liked it.

"Andre, look, if I may make a suggestion, don't be so vocal about gays. Bohne doesn't like that," Wolfgang said in a serious tone. "You should count yourself lucky to be on this side of the ship and you have only seven artists. It could be worse," he said and winked at me again.

I didn't feel comfortable with him doing that but I kept quiet. "I am not complaining, I am just not used to people like Manfred."

"No worries, you will get used to it. Everyone does," he laughed.

At the same moment, Doris joined us at the station. "Hi, guys."

"Hi there, sweetie," Wolfgang chirped.

Doris looked at me. "You must be Andre," she said and offered to shake my hand. "I am Doris."

"I am Andre." I shook her hand.

I have never been very comfortable with good-looking girls but Doris seemed like a nice person, quite different from what I had expected, especially in view of the fact that she was going out with Hartmut. Why she did that was a mystery to me.

At five-thirty I went to the crew mess for dinner where I met up with Franz, Angelika and the rest of our gang. Franz told me that he had been moved to my old station and Angelika was now his wine stewardess. He also thanked me for the excellent mise en place I had left for him, which I didn't think was funny. We finished our dinner and after a short break outside on deck we waited in our stations for the doors to open.

As usual Bohne came into the restaurant to see if everyone was ready. He walked down the aisle looking left and right and then turned and came back. Several stewards made faces as he passed by them. Judging by the way he kept on looking back over his shoulder, he must have known that this was happening. I tried to keep a straight face as he passed, which was not easy. He stopped briefly, looking at Wolfgang and then me, and walked off. I wanted to shake my head but decided against it.

Then the doors opened and our guests came streaming in, looking for their tables. I greeted every guest politely and pointed them in the right direction when they asked for help. I noticed that the average age of our guests was slightly lower than on the previous cruise. Suddenly I noticed a very jovial bunch of younger people, quite different from the rest, entering the restaurant. One of them walked up to me, pointing at my round table.

"Hi there, is this table number eight?"

"Yes, it is," I answered.

The man turned to his friends. "Hey, guys, here it is."

It was my band. There were seven of them in total, four guys and three girls. When they had all sat down, I went to the table.

"Hi there, I am Andre and I will be your steward for this cruise."

One of the guys got up and shook my hand. "Hi, Andre, I am Anton Seller and this is my wife Karin," he said politely.

I shook Karin's hand. I froze when I heard the name Anton Seller and wondered briefly if he was THE Anton Seller of the Anton Seller Orchestra which was famous in Germany. I didn't dare to ask.

Anton introduced me to the rest of the band, including a lady by the name of Michelle. She was obviously Asian, very slim with long straight black hair and had a beautiful exotic and delicate face. With broken German, she introduced herself. Her incredible exotic looks caught me a bit off balance and my reply sounded just as broken as hers.

"Ni...nice to meet...you," I stammered. There were plenty of grins around that table.

Anton finished the introduction. "There you have it, Andre, the Anton Seller Orchestra."

So it was them, I thought. Amazing. I couldn't wait to tell my parents and Tatiana. The Anton Seller Orchestra had been hired for three months to perform in the Europa Saloon after dinner. They had numerous concerts in Europe, Asia and the Middle East but their home turf was still Germany, where they were famous. I knew the Anton Seller Orchestra well from television shows even though admittedly their music was not really my style. But they were a very entertaining bunch and my first "famous" guests. I could see that there was no trouble on the horizon for the next few weeks.

My other guests in the first seating consisted of only one more table and that was one very friendly couple by the name of Melle. Mr. and Mrs. Melle were in their early fifties and had done several cruises before and they knew many of my colleagues. Even Doris knew them and had them as guests on a previous cruise before. She also told me that in terms of tip they were over-tax payers but not by much. She mentioned that I should still look after them. My answer to her was of course I would look after all my guests, including those like the Anton Seller guys who would most probably pay no tip at all. She laughed. *I am not here for the money,* I told myself again.

Overall, I was happy with my first seating; they all struck me as nice people. In the second seating, I had twelve guests—four couples at my round table and two couples at my smaller tables. They all were polite but a little more reserved than my previous guests.

Bohne had taken it easy on me with the number of guests; some other stewards had eighteen guests in the first seating and nearly twenty in the second seating. They worked like slaves, especially in the first seating. I found out that there were a number of stewards who were only onboard for the money and nothing else; they *wanted* to run full stations on as many cruises as possible only because of the tip. These were also the guys who "bought" afternoon tea shifts, midnight buffet shifts and any other jobs which could make them some additional money. I never saw them ashore because they hardly left the ship when we were in port. For the moment, I was happy with my first seating of nine and the second seating of twelve.

Interestingly the four couples at my round table were all friends and had booked this trip together, but even though they were friends, the atmosphere at the table was always very subdued and sort of stiff. They always talked with each other but I hardly heard them chatting or laughing louder than the average conversation. In more than one way, they were a little strange, which was quite okay with me since they left me alone. They were not demanding but they did pay attention to detail and brought shortcomings to my attention. Then there were two tables of two nice, typical German upper-middle-class couples, Mr. and Mrs. Farb and Mr. and Mrs. Zumstein.

We departed Vancouver at eight in the evening. A large crowd of people saw us off and there was even a band playing at the pier. As usual, our decks were crowded with passengers and crew all waving their goodbyes to Vancouver. I was of course excited because we were now on our way to the famous city of San Francisco with its even more famous Golden Gate Bridge.

I had seen and heard so much about San Francisco on television and in songs but I would have never dreamed that I would actually see this city for myself. I knew that according to American television series broadcasted in Germany, it seemed that most crimes were committed in San Francisco. I always remember Karl Malden and Michael Douglas in the police drama *The Streets of San Francisco* that was broadcasted for many years on Saturday nights. Then of course there were countless songs about San Francisco and because I did not speak English at the time, the words San Francisco were usually the only words I recognized. Here I was, in three days time I would be sailing underneath the famous Golden Gate Bridge into San Francisco. I was very excited. First, however we had three days at sea.

Early the next day we left Canada and entered the territorial waters of the United States. There was only one person aboard for whom this made a big difference and that was Obermeyer. The Americans had quite strict food safety laws and as soon as we entered American waters, we were required to adhere to these laws. We also had very strict food safety laws in Germany but some of the American requirements went a bit too far, which was clearly visible on Obermeyer's face. Everyone entering the kitchen was required to wear hair nets which looked very much like shower caps. This included us stewards. Of course none of us wore them but we carried them in our pockets just in case there was a surprise inspection. Our Chinese dishwashers all wore hairnets, which made them look a little like wannabe-ninjas but more like the turtle version. Obermeyer had to remove all non-plastic or non-stainless-steel containers and everyone, including our Chinese stewarding crew, had to wear plastic gloves. Just as we did with the hairnets, so carried the chefs the gloves in their pockets.

The same day, we had the welcome dinner with the gala buffet setup, caviar stations and our famous ice parade. As usual everyone applauded and cheered and we ended up posing for countless pictures. It was the same for the second seating where even my four stiff upper-middle-class couples asked to have a picture taken with me, not that they did much smiling but at least they were happy. The only challenge I had with them was that they did not leave after they had their dessert and coffee. Instead, they sat and talked and when they eventually left, I had just enough time to reset the table for the second seating. If that happened again the next day I would have to address it somehow.

We finished the welcome dinner for the guests of the second seating and again, everyone wanted to have their picture taken with the ice bomb and us stewards. I was surprised to see two very well-known TV news presenters onboard. I knew them well from the news on television; I had literally grown up with them. I found out later that we had an internal ship television channel which broadcasted daily news. The news presenters were from different German, and sometimes even Swiss and Austrian, TV stations and changed for every cruise.

What was even more amazing to me was that they both seemed to know Manfred very well. I saw them several times come all the way from the other end of the restaurant only to chat with him. Of course, what I did not know was that the two were gay as well and that Manfred had a reputation for organizing outstanding parties. Nevertheless, they were famous and I was proud to be in such high-profile company.

Wolfgang and I got on very well and contrary to my initial concerns, he treated me with respect and only occasionally did he drop some gay jokes that even made me laugh. He was an excellent station mate and we really worked as a team.

As for Doris, she helped too but as soon as she saw that we were fine, she would leave us and spent time at Hartmut's station. At first I thought she would just stand there chatting with him, until I realized that he actually made her polish his equipment! There was no doubt that she was one of the prettiest girls I had met or at least the prettiest *blonde* girl I had met. In any case, I had a girlfriend whom I loved very much so there was no point looking out for others—at least not intentionally.

I still was busy writing long letters to both my parents and Tatiana. Most of my letters were between four and six pages long and I never ran out of things to write. It was not that difficult because every single day I experienced a "first"; having never lived in larger cities in Germany and having never been exposed to traveling outside of Germany, everything was new for me. My letters resembled more diaries than letters, diaries of a boy from the countryside exposed to the big wide world. The only thing that was not new for me was the service of fine foods and fine wines. I missed the real service as we practiced in The Stube and I strongly believed that, coming from a Michelin-star restaurant, I stood far above the others, both in terms of knowledge and in terms of skill.

Chapter 9

I t was my twentieth day onboard and I had not had a day off since my arrival. I did not feel tired anymore; I felt as if my body had adopted a routine that did not require a day off but focused heavily on the afternoon breaks. If we were at sea in colder latitudes, I would spend my afternoons in my bunk catching up on sleep whilst in warmer regions, I would sleep on deck in the sun. This was quite an interesting experience; at home, if I was asked to work ten days without day off I would feel it after only eight days. Here I would work for six months without a day off and simply did it.

My sleeping rhythm had changed and instead of feeling the missing day off, I missed sleeping in the afternoon. The more time we accumulated without rest, the more important the afternoon nap became. When we were in ports, especially big ones like New York, San Francisco, or exotic places like the Caribbean or the South Pacific, we sacrificed the afternoon nap and instead went ashore for sightseeing trips or to beaches. If we were then assigned for afternoon tea shifts, the following day at sea many of us sold our shifts in order to catch up on missing sleep. There were plenty of examples where stewards fell asleep between seatings whilst sitting outside on deck. There have even been cases of stewards falling asleep standing at their service stations. Tiredness and the stress of serving two seatings also caused some memorable incidents, like Tony who began serving his main courses before his stewardess had placed the plates on the table and the food ended up on the tablecloth instead of the plate. My worst incident was serving the wrong food to the wrong guests which was bad but could be fixed quite easily.

One afternoon during those three days at sea, Wolfgang took the time to show me a bit more of the ship. After twenty days onboard I ventured for the first time into areas which were normally reserved for guests. He took me to the shop, the indoor pool, theater, disco, hairdresser and all other places where we were not normally allowed to go. Working on a cruise liner is quite different from working in a hotel ashore. In a hotel waiters constantly move around public areas such as lobby, reception, restaurants, bars, etc., whilst the back-of-house areas were limited to kitchen, stores and canteen. On the *Europa* I worked exclusively in the restaurant and occasionally outside on deck for afternoon tea or midnight buffet. All other areas were off limits to us.

Facilities for the crew were completely separate from those of the passengers. It was like two different worlds—we had our own indoor pool, crew bar, cabins, decks and we even had our own shop. There was no need for us to mingle in passenger areas. One steward was asked once by an elderly lady whether we stewards also lived onboard. He considered for a moment of telling her no and that he had to swim home every night but then decided against it and told her the truth that we all lived onboard.

There were even tours for passengers to the kitchens, stores and crew facilities because we had so many requests from passengers to see how and where we lived. The crew facilities onboard the *Europa* was definitely amongst the best. On many of our competitor ships, crew had to share cabins with six to eight colleagues whereas on the *Europa* only two shared one cabin. Each cabin was about the size of a shipping container and had its own bathroom, dining table, minibar and more than sufficient space to store personal items. We had no reason to complain.

Wolfgang finished the tour in the half-moon-shaped lido bar overlooking the bow of the ship. In the center of this bar stood a shiny white piano in midst of comfortable sofa seating. The entire bar was surrounded by large glass windows with a stunning view of where the ship was headed. I would have one of my most memorable experiences in this bar on my second turn one year later. We returned to our cabin in the late afternoon with another hour to spare for a nap.

On the evening before reaching San Francisco, we finished early because everyone wanted to get up early to watch our arrival. Wolfgang told me that the timing of our arrival was such that we would pass underneath the famous Golden Gate Bridge at sunrise, which was a spectacle I wouldn't want to miss.

The next morning I got up very early in anticipation of our arrival. Franz, Angelika and I met on the main deck and from there Angelika took us to the "signal deck," which was the highest open deck on the ship—thirteen floors above sea level. This deck got its name from the gigantic mast with all sorts of radars, antennae and other navigational and radio gadgets. This deck was off limits to passengers but accessible to crew. We would spend many hours on this deck roasting in the sun.

We took the elevator to the Columbus deck which lay one deck below the signal deck. From there we had to climb up a very narrow and steep set of stairs that finally led onto the highest point on the *Europa*. The first thing I saw was the gigantic dark orange signal mast with its rotating radars. The deck itself was much larger than I had expected and the view from up here took my breath away. It was fantastic.

We walked around the mast to the very front where we had an unobstructed view ahead. The deck was already crowded with several stewards and chefs, all equipped with cameras. I noticed that most of the older guys were missing; there was no Hartmut, no Manfred, Peter or any of the other "old-timers." Most of the people present were newcomers such as myself or photo buffs.

I remember very well Angelika's answer to my question of how many times she had seen the arrival in San Francisco when she said, "I can't remember how many times but I would not miss it for anything in the world." She had expressed it with an enthusiasm that had impressed me immensely because it seemed that even after three years working on the ship, she had not lost the excitement which was normally reserved for us newcomers.

Just beneath our deck was the Columbus deck, the highest outdoor deck for passengers, and it was crowded with people. Even the two decks below were crowded with passengers. Of course it helped that over the past couple of days the weather had turned much milder and even now, early in the morning, it was pleasantly warm with only a light breeze.

I looked down at the gigantic bow of the ship, which gave me the impression that the ship was literally gliding across the water. I noticed straight ahead the long dark grey shadow on the horizon, which Angelika explained was the California coast, and that we were heading straight for the San Francisco peninsula. I was surprised how far out we still were. I had expected to see the Golden Gate Bridge in the distance; instead, we could not even make out the shore properly. Still, I took my camera and shot a couple of pictures.

"Save your film until we come closer to the bridge," Angelika said.

"Don't worry, I have enough rolls with me." I was not lying; I had another three rolls with me just in case.

I looked again at the bow of the ship as it glided over the waves at a surprising speed. To stand up there made me feel great, as if standing on top of the world. *I am really lucky,* I thought, *to be able to stand up here on Germany's most famous cruise liner, searching the Californin coast in the distance for the first glimpse of the world-famous Golden Gate Bridge of San Francisco.*

I looked down at the dense crowd of passengers on the Columbus deck and recognized the slim figure and long black hair of Michelle, the Asian musician. I had never met an Asian girl before and I still remembered the moment Anton had introduced me to her. The way she looked at me with her exotic almond-shaped eyes had blown me away. Her entire demeanor was far more graceful than anything I had seen before and there was no doubt that I had a little crush on her. All of a sudden she turned around and looked up at us standing on the signal deck. Because there were only a few of us up there, she recognized me immediately and with a smile she waved at me. That was unexpected; I waved back at her and smiled, too.

"Hey, hey, hey who is that?" Angelika interrupted. "There is only one very good-looking young lady amongst the elderly crowd down there and she waves at you?"

Here we go, I thought; I had expected so much. "Her name is Michelle and she is one of my guests."

"Oh, I see. Can you see any of my guests waving at me like that?" Angelika asked cheekily.

"Yeah, right, maybe they don't like you because you serve them the wrong wines," I replied.

"Don't try to change the subject."

I wish some of my gay colleagues or some of the senior guys could have witnessed this little scene; *This would have been good for my reputation,* I thought.

"Angelika, she is one of the musicians in the Anton Seller Orchestra."

"She is still a woman."

"You sound jealous."

"Oh, please."

"Please, what?"

"I have a boyfriend."

"So? I think you are jealous."

"You are trying to change the subject."

"OVER THERE," someone cried, pointing at the horizon. "THE GOLDEN GATE!"

With squinted eyes, I tried to find the famous bridge and then suddenly I saw it. It was still quite small but clearly recognizable as the famous Golden Gate Bridge. To my surprise I only saw the bridge and no San Francisco; I had always been under the impression that the Golden Gate was right in the middle of the city but from what I could see now, I was wrong. The bridge was built to connect the two sides of the bay, which was the actual entrance to San Francisco Bay. There was a light fog just above the water's surface, which seemed to get denser in the distance. The closer we got to the coast, the denser the fog became and all we could see were the tops of the towers of the Golden Gate Bridge.

From the Columbus deck we could hear the lecturer's metallic voice talking about the bridge and its history.

"...bridge was the largest suspension bridge in the world when it was completed in 1937 and has become the internationally recognized symbol of San Francisco and the United States. It is currently the second-longest suspension bridge in the United States after the Verrazano-Narrows Bridge..." I listened as he went on talk about its size, length and other interesting details.

After a while the fog began to lift, the bridge became clearly visible and we could also clearly make out cars moving about. Just behind the bridge the skyline of San Francisco moved into view, brightly illuminated by the rising sun. To me this was a majestic spectacle and I took picture after picture with my small Olympus camera.

"Look over there," Angelika suddenly shouted, pointing at the bridge. "See that island over there?"

I squinted my eyes, searching for the island. Then I noticed an elongated building sitting on a sort of rocky island. "Yes, I can see it. What is it, a factory?"

"No, that's Alcatraz, the famous prison," she answered.

"Oh I see. Wow."

The captain reduced speed as we approached the Golden Gate Bridge and with the rising sun from behind, the entire structure was glowing bright orange. It was truly an impressive feat of engineering.

"This afternoon we'll take a taxi into the city and take a trip with one of the famous cable cars. I'll show you the Lombard Street with its beautiful flowers and then we'll have coffee at Fisherman's Wharf," Angelika said. The names didn't mean anything to me but it sounded interesting and I was looking forward to once again having some solid ground under my feet after three days at sea.

Franz had been standing quietly next to us taking picture after picture with his Canon camera.

"Hey, Franz, what do you think of all this?" I asked him.

"Great, this is just great. I can't wait to show these pictures to my friends at home," he mumbled.

Angelika grabbed his hand. "It's beautiful, isn't it?"

I smiled and at the same moment, Michelle looked up at us again and smiled. I blushed and smiled back, hoping that nobody had witnessed this little episode.

"Mm, somebody is blushing," Angelika giggled.

Shit, I thought, *she has seen it.*

"Come on, leave me alone," I answered mockingly.

After we had passed under the bridge, two harbor tugs joined us and escorted us all the way through San Francisco Bay towards the pier. The lecturer kept talking about the history of the city, its foundation in 1766 by the Spanish, the California Gold Rush in 1848 and the devastating earthquake in 1906.

"Hey, it's time to move, we have to get ready," she reminded us.

Breakfast started early with most guests arriving at the same time. They couldn't wait to go out and discover San Francisco—just like us.

Immediately after breakfast we changed, met at the gangway and took a taxi into the city. For the first time I saw all the things I only knew from television—the big American taxis, American police cars, American policemen and policewomen, American telephone boxes and more. Much to the delight of my friends, I photographed everything. This included an American newspaper-dispensing machine, which I had seen so many times in *The Streets of San Francisco*. We took a ride in one of the famous cable cars and visited one of San Francisco's many landmark buildings, the Transamerica Pyramid, which was not a pretty building but who cares—it was famous. Another taxi ride and two rolls of films later, we returned to the *Europa* to serve lunch.

Once again, I was amazed how many of my guests showed up for lunch. I thought that in a port like San Francisco my guests would have lunch in restaurants ashore but I was wrong, very wrong. My station was packed and so were the others. Obermeyer was pissed and for the first time since I joined the ship, he ran out of food. Obermeyer was furious and not even the fact that we shared the same friends could protect me from his wrath.

"You are all useless losers," he screamed.

"Five grills in the queue," another steward shouted at the end of the queue.

"No more grills - piss off," Obermeyer shouted at the poor guy.

"Come on, Chef, just five."

"Are you deaf? I have no more grills so piss off," Obermeyer screamed.

The steward shook his head, left the queue and went back to the restaurant. I was third in the queue and had been lucky to arrive early. Obermeyer slammed the platters onto the trays, swearing from the top of his voice.

"We are in San Francisco, did you idiots not tell your guests? There is plenty to see out there and instead you all come back and waste my time here. Losers, that's what you all are, goddamn losers."

When I finally got my dishes I took them and left the kitchen as fast as I could. Even as I stood on the fast-moving escalator I could still hear Obermeyer's angry voice echoing through the kitchen.

Several of my colleagues had to return to their guests and inform them that the food of their choice was not available. This caused numerous complaints, all of which were reported to Bohne. Well, that is, only the newcomers reported them to Bohne; the older stewards knew that they were on their own. If they had expected Bohne to support them by charging into the kitchen, pushing Obermeyer to prepare more grills, then of course they would have been dead wrong. Even if Bohne's life had depended on such action, he would have rather died. This is our weirdo restaurant manager; the older guys knew all this. There was no way on earth Bohne would risk a confrontation with Obermeyer, a confrontation which he would certainly lose. Whenever someone went to see Bohne with a complaint or any other problem, for that matter, Bohne's first reaction was a disgusted frown as if the steward approaching him carried a contagious disease. If he didn't

343

simply wave the steward off, he would add disgustedly, "They are your guests, you handle it. Don't bother me with these things, go, go, go." Bohne was weird and it was as simple as that.

Lucky for me I had made the kitchen in good time and got all my grills. All my grills on that day meant every single one of my eighteen guests had opted for this dish and I had therefore been a major contributor to the fact that Obermeyer eventually ran out. At least all my guests were happy, all except my four stiff couples who were not too pleased by the fact that I had added two chairs to their table so it now had to accommodate eleven guests instead of eight. They looked even stiffer than usual.

By one o'clock the last guest had gone. Wolfgang and I cleaned up our station, went back to our cabin, got changed into shorts and T-shirt and at one-fifteen sharp, we waited at the gangway for Angelika and Franz. We spent the afternoon at Fisherman's Wharf, strolling along the numerous souvenir shops and restaurants. I took more pictures of anything typically American, including cars, policemen, letter boxes and other day-to-day items which normally would go unnoticed.

We found an interesting-looking restaurant called Alioto's No. 8, where we made a reservation for dinner. For the rest of the afternoon we sat in a cozy little café overlooking the wharf and the harbor. The weather was perfect with a light breeze and clear blue sky. Hundreds of screaming seagulls provided the fitting background noise to the excellent view across the harbor.

Sitting there in the sun with my shorts and sunglasses, I felt relaxed for the first time since I had joined in Anchorage, probably because I had grown comfortable with my new friends and my new surroundings aboard. I was surprised by how close I had become with Franz and Angelika, both of whom I felt I had known far longer than only twenty-one days. I glanced at San Francisco Bay with the prison island of Alcatraz in its center and I had to smile; here I was, sipping a coffee in San Francisco. I began to enjoy this.

For dinner we again had one open seating. My four stiff couples entered the restaurant the moment Bohne had opened the doors and they immediately stormed to their table. Because we had only one seating, I had prepared eleven chairs at my round table, which was not well received by the stiffs. One of the gentlemen, Mr. Keller, was the spokesperson for the group and asked for the additional chairs to be removed because he felt the seating was too tight. This was a problem for me because if the turnout for dinner was anything like lunch then I would not have enough seats. After some discussions we agreed on removing one chair.

Another couple of my second seating, Mr. and Mrs. Zumstein, took the two remaining seats. They turned out to be a jovial pair that I hoped would lighten up the atmosphere at that table. The only guests who did not show up that night were my band; they had chosen to have dinner outside. Other than that, my station was packed with eighteen guests.

Without wasting time, I took my orders, served starters and dashed down to the kitchen where I was eighth in the main-course queue. Obermeyer, having hoped that the bulk of our guests would take dinner in one of San Francisco's many excellent restaurants, was again deeply disappointed by the fact that none of us stewards had managed to persuade our guests to take dinner outside. And as usual he expressed his disappointment in his unique way by screaming and shouting at us.

To his further dismay, most guests had chosen grilled meat dishes rather then the fresh fish and the famous Dungeness crabs which the chef himself had procured in the afternoon from the local fish market. In anticipation of a rush for fresh fish and crabs, Obermeyer had concentrated his mise en place accordingly with hundreds of fillets and crabs sizzling on the grill. One by one the meat orders came in and each of them was answered with nothing less than pure damnation from Obermeyer. It seemed to me that none of our guests wanted his fresh fish, much less the famous Dungeness crabs. More and more fish fillets had to be removed from the grill to make space for steaks and tenderloins. The chefs in the kitchen were just as annoyed and swore at every order relayed to them by Obermeyer. The atmosphere in the kitchen was like on a battlefield. None of us looked forward to reaching the front of the cue and repeating our meat orders to an angry Obermeyer.

"NEXT!" Obermeyer screamed as one steward left with his tray. Next in line was Peter, my former station mate.

"Three steaks, five tenderloins and four Dungeness crabs," he shouted in his usual arrogant manner.

"What was that?" Obermeyer leaned forward, mockingly putting one hand on his ear as if he had not heard him.

Peter rolled his eyes, annoyed, and repeated his order. "I said three steaks, five tenderloins and four Dungeness crabs."

"Wow, look at this guy, he has actually sold four crabs. Let's give him a promotion to personal lackey of Bohne," he cried. "New order for this joker - three steaks, five tenderloins and four Dungeness crabs," he screamed into the kitchen. The chefs behind the pass repeated the order. Obermeyer gave Peter a disgusted look, which Peter answered with a short "Piss off."

Obermeyer froze and then leaned forward in a mock surprise. "What was that, my friend?"

Peter stared at him defiantly.

"I ask again, what was that, my friend?"

"I am not your friend," Peter mumbled.

"Of course you are not my friend, because I don't have pussies like you as friends." Obermeyer was talking with a low and challenging voice.

"Yeah, yeah, just leave me alone," Peter said and took one step back.

"You better be careful when you come to my kitchen in the future, you loser." Peter remained quiet; this was not the time and place to challenge the Number Two in the kitchen. Obermeyer turned to the pass and slammed cloches angrily on Peter's platters. When the order was completed, Obermeyer told Peter to get the hell out his kitchen. Peter left like a beaten dog with his tail between his legs.

We all had watched the encounter quietly and only Manfred, last in the queue as usual, had made some obscene remarks. I was nervous and did not look forward to presenting Obermeyer with my order of six steaks, eight tenderloins and only four fish.

When my turn came, Obermeyer had quieted down enough to grace me only with some sarcastic remarks. I quietly and efficiently packed my tray and left, hearing Obermeyer shouting, "NEXT!"

I served my main courses and Doris did the side dishes.

"I see you survived Obermeyer," she whispered at the station.

"Yeah, just about. He is in a real foul mood tonight."

"Not surprisingly. I am sure he has his garbage bins full of fish and crabs tonight since none of you sold any of them," she said.

"Hey, it's not that I have not tried, but for some reason they all want meat."

"Don't worry, this is not the first time. Sometimes everyone orders fish and he has not enough and sometimes he has everything left over—like tonight," she grinned.

"That means he would be in a bad mood in any case."

"Exactly," she said and grabbed a plate of potatoes.

One hour later all my guests had left except the stiff ones; they sat and talked and talked. It was difficult for me to understand why they would not leave and discover San Francisco at night; we had another day at sea ahead of us and there would be plenty of time to sit on the ship and chat. Thirty minutes later only few guests were left in the restaurant, including my four couples—and they kept on talking.

Wolfgang and Doris had already gone and I was one of only four stewards left with guests. Instead of getting ready to leave, Mr. Keller in particular kept on ordering coffee. They always ordered one coffee at a time and whenever I got back, someone else would ask for one; it was almost as if they did it on purpose. Then just when I thought they had finished, Keller would ask for something silly like a glass of water. I could see in his face the he was well aware that I was itching to leave and it seemed to me as if he enjoyed giving me the runaround. The other thing that annoyed me was that he kept on calling me "waiter" rather than by my name and it seemed to me as if he got some strange satisfaction out of it. The thought of a "pervert" briefly crossed my mind. Other than that. they ignored me completely.

When they eventually left, everyone else had gone. As I was just about to leave, I heard someone entering the restaurant. I turned and there was—Manfred.

"Hiiiii, daaaarling, how are you, my dear? I forgot my keys in my service station," he giggled like a girl.

I just stood there frozen in place, staring at his incredible outfit. "What *are* you wearing?"

I could not believe my eyes. Manfred wore black shiny leather pants, a black sleeveless leather vest and a black leather cap. There were a number of steel chains around his waist, on his vest and on his hat. He looked like one of the singers of the Village People.

"Do you like it, honey?"

"Ahm, not really," I answered, then I suddenly noticed that he was also wearing make up! *How could he possibly dare walk through the guest areas dressed like this?* I wondered.

"You have no taste, my dear. Well, never mind, where I am going they will go crazy about me," he giggled, wiggling his whole body. "See ya, my dear!" He waved his hat and wiggled out of the restaurant.

I shook my head, cleaned up and rushed to my cabin to get changed. Franz and the others had already gone but he had left the address of the restaurant so I could follow later. I took a taxi from a taxi stand not far from the pier. Since my English was less than sufficient to communicate with the taxi driver, all I could do was show him the address Franz had left me and hope he would understand. He did.

To my surprise, the taxi driver talked a lot, obviously not realizing that I spoke no English. He talked all the way to the restaurant and until today I have no idea what exactly he was telling me during that trip. I managed a "thank you" and "goodbye," upon which he said a few more things which I didn't understand and simply answered with, "Yes, yes," and "thank you."

There was a much larger group than expected, which to my surprise included Doris and Petra, our two best-looking stewardesses, who normally only went out with the senior guys. I greeted them and took the only seat left next to Angelika. We sat outside on a beautiful wooden terrace overlooking San Francisco Bay and glimmering in the distance was the brightly illuminated Golden Gate Bridge.

The waitress passed me the menu which, of course, was in English. Angelika was kind enough to translate the dishes for me. They had a large selection of fresh seafood and a variety of U.S. beef. With Angelika's help I ordered, ironically, beef tenderloin, despite the recommendation from her and the waitress that I should try the famous Dungeness crab. I wondered briefly if the chef would give her a hard time for not selling his precious fresh fish and seafood.

"Did Mr. Keller finally let you go?" Doris laughed.

"Yeah, just about. He kept on ordering coffee and water and so on."

"Maybe he likes you?" Petra joked and winked at me.

I smiled. I could see that the wine had begun doing its part. "No, I don't think so. I think they are just a very frustrated, stiff and conservative bunch."

"But I do know that they are not happy with you because you added a few chairs for breakfast and lunch today," Doris said.

"Yeah ,but we always do that when we have one seating," I protested.

"Sure, but I know from Yankowich that they had specifically requested not to have any other guests at their table and I understand they were quite insistent on that."

"Don't you think someone should have told me that before the cruise?" I could not believe that they had this kind of information and did not tell me.

"Yankowich only told me tonight. I also didn't know," Doris said.

"That's typical Yankowich—he only gives this kind of information to his boyfriends," Tony shouted from the other end of the table.

"Oh, shit, talking about it," I had just remembered Manfred. "You'd never believe what Manfred was wearing tonight when I saw him before I left."

"Oh, let me guess, was he in his skimpy-looking black leather outfit?" Angelika asked.

"Yeah, and he doesn't hesitate walking around the restaurant in that outfit." I still couldn't believe that he actually would run around like that. What if guests saw him?

Everyone was laughing at my naivety and as they later explained, San Francisco was one of the top destinations for gays. Apparently, they all were out tonight partying.

Our dinner was served at around eleven and I have to say the tenderloin was amongst the best I ever had and together with the excellent California red wine, the whole experience came pretty close to being perfect. We finished a few more bottles of red wine before we finally asked for the bill. We went for a leisurely walk along the harbor front, enjoying the mild pleasant night.

At eleven o'clock the next morning, dockworkers untied the heavy ropes from the bollards and threw them into the dirty harbor water. Slowly the winches pulled the ropes aboard and the harbor tugs pulled the over-35,000-ton ship away from the pier with ease. The timing of our departure between breakfast and lunch was perfect for our passengers, who crowded the decks waiving goodbye to San Francisco. Once we had reached the center of the bay, the harbor tugs pulled away and we began moving forward under our own power.

I stood on the main deck as we passed underneath the Golden Gate Bridge and wondered, *Would I ever come back here again?* San Francisco had been a very pleasant experience, which was also the turning point in my life onboard; I had my group of friends and I was now part of the crew.

The one and a half days in San Francisco had been quite busy with work and sightseeing so naturally there had not been much time to

349

sleep. We would only spend one day at sea before arriving in the Port of Los Angeles where we would have the same gruesome schedule again. It was obvious that Bohne knew this because he had assigned me for afternoon tea duty on deck. But I was not the only one; strangely enough, most of the newcomers were assigned this duty and the usual senior guys offered to buy them. First, I didn't want to consider, but after breakfast I was so exhausted that I was longing for a few hours sleep in the afternoon. I sold my shift for an unbelievable one hundred and fifty marks.

When I got up the next day, we had already arrived in Los Angeles and the *Europa* was already secured safely to the pier with the gangway down. The Port of Los Angeles is located in San Pedro Bay and is about thirty kilometers away from the city of Los Angeles. The port complex was gigantic and had a sheer endless number of container ships from all over the world tied to its piers. As far as the eye could see there were ships, cranes and thousands of containers piled up in stacks. The part of the port where we had docked was part of the largest cruise ship center on the west coast of the United States.

The most interesting sight for me was five huge aircraft carriers in another part of the harbor, clearly visible in the distance. It was an impressive sight; even at a considerable distance, the carriers looked gigantic, and next to one of them, the *Europa* would have looked tiny. The weather had also changed—it was considerably warmer, which showed in the way we dressed. We went out in shorts and T-shirts and, as usual, our camera bags.

Los Angeles was only the second city I visited in America but I could see and feel that it was very different from San Francisco. First of all, the city didn't seem to have a center like other cities; instead, it seemed to consist of several different centers in different parts of the city. Because the city stretches over such a wide area, it took time to get from one district to another and therefore we had not much time for sipping coffees in cafés. We literally spent half of our time that afternoon in long taxi rides.

We visited the three main districts of Los Angeles: Santa Monica, and then Long Beach, where we went on a tour of the mighty cruise liner Queen Mary, and last but not least, the famous district of Beverly Hills. In Beverley Hills we took a walk in the wealthy area surrounding the famous Beverly Wilshire Hotel. The houses and villas were simply out of this world and so were the cars parked in front of them. There were Rolls Royces, Lamborghinis, Ferraris and all the other super expensive cars of this world. The cafes and restaurants were full with stylish-looking people, almost all of whom wore expensive-looking sunglasses. The girls in the cafes and on the street looked as if they were movie stars and all were dressed in short skirts and high heels. On more than one occasion I thought I recognized one or another Hollywood star but I was wrong.

That we were tourists was obvious based on our clothes and we were treated accordingly. When we entered expensive shops we were made to feel as uncomfortable as possible, presumably to have us out as quickly as possible. The people in San Francisco had definitely been far more accommodating than the beautiful and posh-looking crowd in Beverly Hills. It was clear that money ruled this place and that of course was something we did not have. Nevertheless, we managed to take a few pictures in front and inside the Beverly Wilshire hotel before security asked us to leave.

Overall we didn't feel welcome and so, after I had taken some more shots of Beverly Hills police cars and letter boxes, we flagged down a taxi and went back to the Port of Los Angeles. I liked this system of just stopping a taxi anywhere, something which would have been unthinkable back home in Germany.

We stayed overnight in Los Angeles but because of the time it took to get to any of the major districts, we decided to stay onboard and so did most of our guests. We had two seatings for dinner that night. In the first seating I only had one couple, Mr. and Mrs. Melle; the Anton Seller band had ventured into town for dinner.

With only two guests, I had of course a very leisurely first sating, even though I wouldn't have minded at all to see Michelle again. In the second seating all my guests graced me with their presence. My large round table that I now called the "Keller Gang" was as punctual as ever and, as usual, complete. Since they had boarded the ship, I had never seen them not being together, which was a bit strange for four couples. But then again, the couples themselves were strange so it all fit together. I politely greeted them as I always did and as always they all greeted me too, but in a very formal and reserved manner.

"Tonight I have a challenge for you," Mr. Keller said as I asked him for his order. *What challenge?* All eight of them were staring at me as if to see how I would react. I looked at Mr. Keller and it was strange; even though he was seated and I was standing, I had the feeling that he was looking down on me.

"What is the challenge, Mr. Keller?" I asked cheekily.

"Tonight I am going to order something which is not on your menu." He pronounced every word very precisely so as if to make sure I understood him properly.

"No problem, Mr. Keller. If the chef has the ingredients for your dish, I am sure he will be able to prepare it for you."

"I very much hope so, since you call yourself a six-star cruise liner," he answered.

I felt a little nervous now; this was the first time that someone asked for a dish that was not on the menu and our a la carte menu had over forty a la carte dishes.

"Good, I would like to have a T-bone steak."

That is not too bad, I know we have T-bone steaks, I thought.

"One T-bone steak, no problem, how would like to have that done?"

"Not so fast, young man," Mr. Keller interrupted. *Oops!* "Make sure the chef trims all the fat off the meat. I can't stand it when there are bits of fat left on the meat. Do you understand that?" The way he had asked me that last question definitely insinuated that he thought I hadn't understood.

"No problem Mr. Keller, I make sure the chef trims all the fat off the meat, every last bit of it. Clear."

"How would you like the meat done, Mr. Keller?"

"I have told you before—not so fast, I have not finished yet," he said with an impatient tone. "Tell the chef that for the preparation of the steak, he should not use a fork to turn the meat. I don't want him to poke a fork or a knife or anything else in that T-bone steak, do you understand that?" He looked deep into my eyes as if he was trying to figure out if I had really understood the meaning of his words.

"Understood, Mr. Keller, I will make sure the chef does not use a fork to turn the meat on the grill," I said politely. I looked around the table to see if this was some kind of joke but judging by the expressions I saw, they were quite serious. I just hoped that they would not all start ordering their individual dishes.

"Is there anything else, Mr. Keller?"

"Yes, tell the chef I would like my T-bone medium rare."

"Medium rare, no problem."

"I am very sensitive when it comes to steaks and I hate it when they are too dry. If your chef pokes his fork into that steak, I *will* be able to taste it and if it is dry, then you can tell your chef I *will* send it back without hesitation."

"I understand, Mr. Keller and I will tell the chef. What would you like to have with your T-bone steak?"

"I would like to have some steamed vegetables, but only carrots and broccoli without oil or butter, do you understand? No oil and no butter."

The way he kept on asking me if I had understood confirmed to me again that he did not credit me with much intelligence. It was not that he was rude but the way he talked to me showed quite clearly that he did not respect someone like me whose only job was to serve others. This must have been the reason for him calling me waiter all the time instead of Andre like all the other guests.

This type of guest was not new to me; I had encountered them before and I had learned that the best way to handle them was simply to ignore the way they acted. This is of course easier said than done because I also had my pride. There where occasions when the lessons I had learned from Raffaele at the Black Forest Grand Hotel in terms of revenge came in handy.

"I fully understand, Mr. Keller—one portion of steamed vegetables, only carrots and broccoli, without oil or butter. Would you like some potatoes with that?"

"Oh please, spare me with those superfluous carbohydrates," he said, disgusted.

"That's fine, no potatoes. Will there be anything else?"

"Tell the chef to make sure all is hot."

"I will make sure the food is hot, Mr. Keller. May I repeat the order? You ordered one T-bone steak, all the fat trimmed off, no fat at all to be left on the meat, no fork to be used for the preparation, the chef should not pierce the meat at all. And as side dishes, you ordered steamed carrots and broccoli without oil and butter. Your dish will be served hot." I looked at Keller and smiled politely, thinking, *You pompous old fart.*

"That will be all, thank you." I took the orders of the other guests.

Just as I turned to leave the table, he called me back. "Oh, and waiter!"

I stopped. "Yes, Mr. Keller?"

"Tell the chef that we want all main courses together."

"I will tell the chef."

I smiled once more and went back to my service station. I was boiling inside, angry about the humiliating way he was treating me. It had never been in my nature to show my feelings in front of guestss— angry or sad—even if they were openly rude to me because I respected people too much, but there have been occasions when I did resort to revenge on guests.

The main dining room of the *Europa* served over one thousand seven hundred guests per day from a very compact kitchen. The lunch and dinner menu was fully a la carte with an option of a chef's recommendation. The selection of dishes was designed in a way that catered to all tastes—vegetarian, dietary and even vegans were catered to. Serving such an extensive menu within a specified period of time from a very compact kitchen required detailed planning and a skilled and efficient kitchen brigade. The chefs knew the menu inside out even though it changed on a daily basis.

Part of this careful planning was the mise en place, which had to be carefully balanced so as not to run out of food but also not to end up with high wastage. The amount and type of mise en place depended of course on the selection of dishes on the respective menu. Because of all this, there was little or no room for the chef to accommodate out-of-menu dishes and on the occasions when he did, they had to wait until the bulk of the main courses had been served.

Generally we were discouraged to "sell" such dishes because of the aforementioned reasons. At the time I took Keller's order, and coming from a Michelin-star environment, I didn't know all this. I didn't know that the biggest incentive for stewards not to accommodate such dishes was their fear of the wrath of the chef. Because I didn't know that and I also didn't ask anyone, I was doomed.

Because of Keller's order, which had taken far too long, I was nearly last in the main-course queue. Seeing all those stewards chatting and joking in front of me was a bad sign. I called out my grills except for the T-bone steak. I had to find a way to get my order across to Obermeyer without making to much fuss. The only way to do that was to write the order down, leave the queue quickly and give it to him— that way they would have enough time to prepare my special order. I scribbled everything on a piece of paper and went to the front of the queue. I waited patiently next to Obermeyer until the time was right.

"Excuse me, Chef."

"What do you want?"

"I have one special order here. Can I just…"

He cut me off. "Special order? What special order?" he barked impatiently.

The first few stewards in the queue had stopped chatting and looked at me with knowing grins.

"One T-bone steak with…" Before I could finish the sentence he cut me off again.

"T-bone steak?" he growled. He turned around and put his hands on his hips.

"Ahm, yes, Chef, one T-bone steak, medium rare with…"

"Hey, hey, stop it right there. There is no T-bone steak on the menu today."

"I know, Chef, but the guest insists on having…"

"Having what?"

"The guest insists on having a T-bone steak," I mumbled. My eyes fell on one of the stewards behind Obermeyer who was waving his hand in front of his throat, which meant, "Shut up."

"Look, Chef, I know that there is no T-bone steak on the menu but my guest really would like to have one."

"I see, your guest would like to have one." He turned to the kitchen and shouted, "Gentlemen, we have to stop cooking for a moment and get a T-bone steak from the freezer for this clown here. Who wants to go all the way down to the freezer?"

All the chefs in the kitchen stopped what they were doing for a moment and began shouting, screaming, "Get the hell out of here and piss off," and other obscenities.

Obermeyer faced me again. "Sorry, as you can see, my guys have no time for clowns like you and now get back into the queue," he yelled.

Some of the stewards now began shouting for me to get back into the queue. I just stood there not knowing what to do. Obermeyer continued to bark orders into the kitchen. I was just about to slip back into the queue when he turned around abruptly.

"Give me that fucking order and get back into the fucking line." He ripped the paper out of my hands and read.

I wasn't sure whether to leave or to explain the order to him.

He looked up. "I said, get back into that bloody queue, are you deaf?"

I walked off and behind me I heard him screaming, "One T-bone, medium, no fat. Oh, and don't poke your forks or knives into the meat. One portion steamed carrots and broccoli—no oil, no butter." The response from the kitchen was as expected, all the chefs screaming "boo" and "bloody clown." It was a nightmare.

When I eventually loaded all my dishes onto my tray, I did so under a barrage of nasty shouting and screaming from the kitchen. Obermeyer's last words echoed loud and clear in my head: "Don't you ever give me such an order again." I would remember that for the rest of my time onboard; I had learnt my lesson, or rather—another lesson.

Keller gulped down his T-bone steak without a single comment and even when I asked him after the meal how it was, he just mumbled, "Okay." My timing was out of the window because of that T-bone steak and after several liters of coffee, I was the last to leave the restaurant. That evening I felt depressed, humiliated by both guests and chefs. This was not what I had expected after an interesting day in Los Angeles.

The next day when I got up, we were already at sea on our way to Mexico. I couldn't wait to see the famous Acapulco. I didn't quite know what to expect but I hoped for gorgeous beaches, girls in micro bikinis and lots of palm trees. The day at sea started slowly with most of my guests being late for breakfast or not showing up at all. We spent more time outside on deck chatting than serving our guests. It was a quiet morning. Lunch service was a little busier but because of the warm weather, most guests hardly ate and clearly couldn't wait to get out on deck and into the sun. It was the same for us. Immediately after lunch was finished and the station was made ready for dinner, we got changed and Angelika took Franz and me all the way up to the signal deck from where we had watched the arrival in San Francisco.

This was the first time we went sunbathing on deck since I had arrived onboard. This would be our afternoon routine for the months to come. Already in Anchorage, I had noticed that most of my colleagues had strong suntans and now I would find out why. That afternoon there was not a single cloud in the sky and if it had not have been for a refreshing breeze, it would have been too hot up there.

Whilst Franz and Angelika moved three deck chairs into position, I walked around the signal mast to the front of the deck and the view that opened up before me was fantastic. There was nothing but deep blue ocean all around us and the *Europa* seemed to literally float above the water. I stood there on the railing looking down at the white painted decks crowded with passengers baking in the sun. I watched the deck stewards dressed in white short-sleeved shirts and white shorts as they served cocktails and other drinks. Compared to those crowded passenger sundecks below us, the signal deck was truly an island of peace and quiet.

That afternoon made up for much of what had happened the evening before; standing up there thirteen floors above the sea with that warm breeze in my face gave me an exhilarating feeling. By the time I stretched out on the deck chair, Franz and Angelika had already fallen asleep. As I was lying there in the sun looking at the clear blue sky above, I could feel the ship's motion as it heaved up and down in the rhythm of the long-drawn swells. It could be felt much stronger up here than down below and soon I was fast asleep.

I woke up groggily an hour later feeling as if I had slept under a salamander. As usual I hadn't bothered putting on any sun protection, which had been a mistake. Because of the strong breeze, I hadn't actually felt the sun at all and only later after my shower when I attempted to dry myself with a towel did I realize that I had been very badly burned.

There were plenty of comments from my guests that night asking if I had been in the sun. More interestingly, Mrs. Farb, a polite elderly lady from my second seating, wanted to know where we stewards go for sunbathing since she never saw us on the passenger decks. I told her that there were three decks plus the bow section of the ship reserved for the use of the crew. When I told her that we also had one indoor swimming pool, a shop, a bar and other facilities for the crew, she could not believe it, asking where all this could possibly be located since she had done a tour and thought she had seen the whole ship. Her husband and I had a good laugh.

MS *Europa* entered Mexican territorial waters in the early hours of the morning and by the time I woke up, the crew was busy securing the ship to the pier of Puerto Vallarta in Mexico. Puerto Vallarta was little more than a small resort city which had become famous through a number of Hollywood movies that had been shot there in the sixties and seventies. It had only recently been discovered by the cruise line industry and was not yet fully developed for tourism. Angelika, who had been in Puerto Vallarta several times, had briefed us already that the only interesting thing to do here was to venture into the city, take a few photographs with a reptile called iguana on our shoulder and then head for the beach.

After the breakfast service we headed out to take the pictures with the famous iguana and then we headed for the city center. In the city of Puerto Vallarta, I came face to face for the first time in my life with the realities of a Third-World country. Many of the souvenir and other shops in the city were located in old buildings which were in a very bad shape. There was litter on the streets and worst of all there were children approaching us, begging for money. They ran after us and kept on pulling on my shorts and T-shirt. My first instinct was to take out my wallet and give them a couple of dollars, which would have been nothing for me but probably would have meant a lot to them. Angelika immediately stopped me, telling me not to do that.

It was difficult not to give anything, looking at these poor little things. The clothes they wore were very dirty and torn and none of them looked older than nine or ten years old. Having to beg at such a young age must be a terrible thing and *God knows*, I thought, *they may not even have parents.* I am not a sentimental or soft person but the way those children looked at me was something quite different. Looking at them and not giving anything made me feel like a criminal but Angelika insisted that we don't give because, she explained, then we would not be able to get rid of them and even more would come.

Although I understood her reasoning, it was difficult. It came as a shock to me to hear from her that in many cases this was even organized crime and that the children were dropped in these locations in the morning for begging from tourists and then collected in the late afternoon to hand in their proceeds from the day. This was my first real culture shock and it was not easy to return to a ship where guests threatened not to eat a T-bone steak if the chef had poked his knife into the meat. This was the world I was used to; the one I had seen outside that day was new for me.

Because this was new, I was not able to get the images of those begging children out of my head. Never mind whether they were organized beggars or not; at the end of the day they were children who should be playing with each other instead of having to beg for money from rich tourists. Not that I was rich, at least not in my world, but in theirs I was a millionaire. I kept on seeing their images, wondering where they slept and what they would eat and then I asked myself again if I could have made a difference by giving them at least some money. Children as I have seen them all my life have always been laughing, playing, smiling or doing other things which made me smile too. Never before had I seen kids that wore dirty and torn clothes and had nothing to eat. This was not the Mexico I had expected to see.

In the afternoon we went to one of few local five-star hotels and gate-crashed onto their beach. The white sandy beach was beautiful, quiet and clean. We put our towels down in the sand, took off our clothes and dashed off into the water. We played around and swam a little and then went back to our newest hobby—sleeping and bathing in the sun. At least I tried, but in the end I couldn't sleep.

The sunbathing felt more like sunburning even though I had put on a thick layer of sun lotion. My skin was painfully protesting the fact that only one day after having been badly burned, I had decided to go out into the sun again. It was stinging all over and finally I had to put on my T-shirt and baseball cap. When I could not stand it any longer, I excused myself and headed back to the ship.

After a long and not-so-hot shower, I covered myself in so much after-sun lotion that my white shirt had several dark oily stainss, but at least I smelled good. My face was as red as a lobster. Whenever we took pictures in those days, our heads were red most of the time and if a flash was used, it reflected in our faces drenched in after-sun lotion.

In the evening, we had an original Mexican mariachi band perform for our guests in the Europa Salon. I did not actually see them performing but I saw the band musicians in the restaurant dressed in their traditional, typical Mexican outfits. They wore large straw sombreros with chin strap and hat band, red ponchos, long baggy, straight-cut muslin pants, cotton shirts of the same material, red sash around the waist, and simple sandals.

My first seating was quiet with only Mr. and Mrs. Melle coming for dinner. The Anton Seller gang presumably was busy setting up for the evening entertainment. For the second seating I had anticipated everyone to be in a hurry to finish dinner and to get as quickly as possible to the Europa Salon to secure the best tables. This was the case with the Farbs and the Zumsteins but not so for my four couples under the leadership of Mr. Keller. Once again they ordered late, ate slow, asked for plenty of coffee and were the last ones to leave.

I had finished cleaning my station and had already set up all my tables for breakfast. There was nothing else to do but to wait for Keller and his friends to leave. It was eleven and I hovered around their table to see if there was anything to clear.

"Would you like some more coffee?" I asked in the hope they would get up and leave.

"No, thank you, we are fine," Keller answered on behalf of everyone.

Maybe they don't know that we have a special program, I thought, and decided to let them know. "I am not sure if you know but we have a traditional mariachi band performing in the Europa Salon tonight."

Keller looked up at me and again I had a distinct feeling that he was looking down at me. "Do you want us to leave?" he said in a very provocative tone.

The question took me by surprise. "No, of course not, not at all, Mr. Keller," I stammered.

"I see. Well, then, we will continue our conversation if you don't mind," he said. He was not rude or anything like that but the way he had said it was humiliating.

I walked away. They finally left at eleven-thirty and only one woman bothered to say goodnight.

The next day was another sunny day at sea. Our next port of call was the famous city of Acapulco. I had heard that name so many times in movies and documentaries and never in my wildest dreams would I have thought that I ever would get to see this exotic place. My expectation of Acapulco was very much what I had seen on televisionn—white sandy beaches, palm trees, beautiful exotic-looking girls in sexy bikinis and wealthy people mingling in stylish street cafes and restaurants. I could not wait.

Breakfast, as it was usual at sea, started late with most guests dressed for a day on deck in the sun. I was just serving breakfast to Mr. and Mrs. Melle when Michelle arrived. The way she was dressed took my breath away. She wore a thin transparent sort of gown and underneath, for all to see, she wore a very, very small bikini. She had her long straight black hair tied back in a ponytail that emphasized her exotic Asian facial features beautifully. She took a seat at the empty round table. After I finished serving Mr. and Mrs. Melle, I took a deep breath and went over to her table.

"Good morning, Andre, how are you?" she said in her broken German. I just loved that accent.

"Good morning, Ms. Yeoh," I answered. True to German custom, I could not bring myself to call her by her first name.

"Hey, call me Michelle," she said immediately.

"Okay, ahm, good morning, Michelle," I whispered. She smiled.

"What can I get you?" I asked, even though I knew that she always took black coffee with one sugar for breakfast. *Why didn't I offer her that? I am such an idiot,* I thought.

"Can I have a black coffee please?" she asked. Her smile revealed a perfect set of brilliant white teeth.

God, she is pretty. I had to concentrate hard not to look at her bikini top, which was exposed as she turned to talk with me.

"One…one black coffee, no problem," I said and dashed off to the kitchen. Less than two minutes later I returned with her coffee.

"So are you working all day or do you guys get a break in between?" she asked as I poured coffee.

"Oh, we do have breaks between breakfast and lunch and lunch and dinner," I said, and because she was not looking at me, I stole a quick glance of her breasts. They were beautiful.

"So what do you do in your breaks?

"Well, if we are at sea and the weather is nice we go sunbathing on deck and if the weather is bad we normally catch up on sleep." I wondered why she wanted to know that. *Maybe she wanted to meet up with me when I had my break.* I was getting excited.

"That's nice. At least you get to enjoy this cruise a little bit too. It must be a dream job working here onboard this beautiful ship, traveling all over the world," she said.

Wow, she is impressed by my job. I liked that and I had never thought of that. She wasn't wrong, of course—here I was traveling from one exotic place to another, meeting all sorts of people and I guess I wasn't looking too bad after all.

"Yeah, it's not too bad, I guess." I tried not to show that I was proud; she definitely seemed to like me.

"You know, my husband even suggested that this would be a job for me."

What was that? Did she say "my husband"? I could not believe my ears. I was shocked—she was actually married!

"Oh, did he?" I said dryly. I was very disappointed. One moment ago, I thought that this beautiful woman might be interested in me and the next moment, she tells me that there is a husband.

"Yes, but I wouldn't like to be away from him for such a long time. It wouldn't work," she added.

"That's understandable," I said without really meaning it.

"So your husband is part of the Anton Seller band?"

"Yes, Herman has been with Anton ever since they started. We met when I was still singing but I have given that up now—for him." *Oh great, she was actually in love with the guy.*

"That's great, sounds like real love," I said again without meaning any of it.

"Yeah, but now I will have my coffee and enjoy the rest of the day on deck."

"You should—the weather is great, lots of sunshine."

"I can't wait, Andre." The way she pronounced my name was simply out of this world.

After I finished breakfast I decided to give my sunburned skin a break and instead of joining the others on deck, I went back to my cabin to take a nap. I still had to finish some letters to Tatiana and my parents. I finished the letter to Tatiana without mentioning my short mental affair with Michelle. Of course I loved Tatiana and nothing had happened with Michelle but I felt a little bad anyway. So I wrote all about Puerto Vallarta and the poor children begging for money. I wrote about the afternoons we had spent on deck and that I had managed to get sunburned. In my mind, I could see Tatiana laughing when she read this because she knew very well how careless I sometimes was.

That afternoon, it was as if I wanted to prove a point—I went sunbathing again, albeit with a thick layer of sun protection spread all over my body. To lie up there on the signal deck was simply too big an attraction for me to miss. After a nice, hot and sunny afternoon on deck, we were sufficiently relaxed for another gala dinner.

That night the board photographer took plenty of pictures of us stewards performing our famous ice parade and of course of us posing with guests. Our lobster-red faces on those pictures were simply hilarious; it was as if we had covered them in some sort of reddish lotion.

The next day we arrived in the famous exotic and historic city of Acapulco. On arrival, a mariachi band playing at the pier and a large crowd of people greeted us. We all assembled on deck watching our arrival in the early hours of the morning. We would remain in Acapulco until the next morning and Angelika had already made a plan for our short stay. After breakfast, we planned to take a walk along the famous white sandy bay of Acapulco, dotted with shops, restaurants and bars. In the afternoon she wanted to take us to the Acapulco Princess Hotel with its lush green gardens and beautiful beaches. It all sounded fantastic.

To my utter surprise, most of my guests had booked full-day excursions with lunch and that included the four couples of the Keller gang. Eight large buses were parked in front of the ship, ready to take our guests on their tours. They all went on extensive tours, which included a trip to the famous La Quebrada cliff, watching the Mexican cliff divers performing their daring and impressive jumps.

As for us, we took a taxi to the Acapulco bay beachfront with its bars and restaurants. We flagged down one of the many old banged up Volkswagen Beetles, which looked as if they had just been rescued from a scrap yard. To call our taxi a taxi was a complete overstatement, and at first, I really thought it was a joke. Because of my halfhearted protests, I was rewarded with the front seat that hardly provided sufficient space for my legs. My grandfather used to own a Volkswagen Beetle about twenty years ago and even then it was already a novelty.

The traffic into the city was one massive traffic jam. In order to provide us with at least some relief from the stifling heat outside, the taxi driver had opened all windows, which did not make much difference and besides adding more hot air from the surrounding car engines, he also let in their exhaust fumes. Once we got out of the suburbs surrounding the port area the traffic improved a little but as soon as we hit the four-laned poorly maintained highway along the bay, it began to slow down again. Along the highway scraps of litter had accumulated in small heaps and it was clear to me that this road had not been cleaned for a very long time.

So far, I had not seen the Acapulco I knew from television—the white sandy beaches, exclusive cars and beautiful people. Angelika told us that the beach was somewhere to my right behind rows of high-rise buildings lining the highway. These high-rise buildings along the beachfront formed part of Acapulco's famous skyline. This skyline was on nearly every postcard of Acapulco and the buildings had looked quite good from afar but as we drove past them, I noticed that they also were very poorly maintained, with paint peeling off and litter scattered everywhere.

Every once and so often, our taxi driver pushed the brakes sharply in order to avoid one of the many potholes in the road. Our taxi driver had just lit his third cigarette when we arrived at our destination. Angelika paid the driver and then took the lead to show us the city. My first impression was disappointing—there was no beach. So far, I had not seen any exclusive cars and except for super-large American cars, most of the vehicles I saw were in a dilapidated state. The beautiful people must have been away because the people we saw on the street were average and some even looked a little scary. We walked for a while and then all of a sudden the view to the ocean and the whole bay opened up.

It was a fantastic sight—the deep blue ocean, the snow-white beach lined with high- and low-rise buildings in front of mountains of lush green vegetation. This was more like the Acapulco I had expected to see. I took my camera and began taking pictures. There were several large white luxury yachts and a number of medium-sized sailing yachts anchored in the bay. It was truly an amazing sight.

I also noticed how hot it had become since San Francisco and not only hot but also very humid. As we walked along the bay I was struck again by the large number of children running around the beach begging for money from tourists. What I noticed on the streets in terms of cleanliness left me disappointed. After we bought some postcards and some souvenirs, it was already time to return to the ship.

We flagged down a taxi, this time a large American car that was in the same dilapidated state as the Volkswagen Beetle earlier. For me this was the first time to sit in one of these large American "street cruisers," as we used to call them. Franz and Angelika once again let me sit in the front and this time there was plenty of space. The bonnet of that car was huge and must have been at least the size of a Volkswagen Beetle. The suspension was the softest I had ever experienced because every time the taxi driver stopped the car on a traffic light, it swerved back and forth like a ship.

We completed lunch service in exactly one hour and by one-thirty, we sat in another rusty taxi on our way to the Acapulco Princess Hotel. Angelika had told us that a visit to this hotel was an absolute must. First, we had to cross the bay, which alone took us nearly an hour, before ending up on a small two-lane road leading up the east mountain. The traffic was still horrendously slow, which trucks creeping up the steep and hilly road caused. The traffic on the other side of the road was just as bad but our taxi driver could not have cared less; he was busy overtaking these trucks, slipping in and out of our lane in a manner that made my hair stand up. The way he overtook them despite oncoming traffic was simply suicidal and many times, we slipped back into our lane only centimeters from oncoming cars or trucks.

The road became steeper as we continued up the mountain and the higher we climbed the better the view became. When I looked out of the car window, I could see the entire bay with its white beach, blue sea and deep green tropical forests. I had only one concern and that was how close we drove along the edge of the road beyond which there was a drop of several hundred meters. When we reached the top of the mountain, the driver suddenly drove onto the hard shoulder and stopped the car. He was trying to tell me something in English but as usual, I had no idea what he was saying.

"Let's get out of the car. I have to show you something," Angelika said from the back.

I forced open the massive rusty car door and stepped outside. It was hot and humid but luckily, on top of the mountain there was a refreshing breeze. We stood at the edge of a cliff which dropped several hundred meters to the sea below. The view from up there was fantastic. Just opposite from where I stood there were several expensive-looking villas and beyond them in the distance lay the open ocean. I took a few pictures. I noticed several other cars stopping and I could see that the passengers were quite obviously tourists like us.

Our driver pointed at the villas and kept on shouting the same word repeatedly but I did not understand what he was saying.

"What is he saying?" I asked Angelika.

"I think he is saying 'salon' or something like that," Franz laughed.

Angelika laughed. "Guys, let me get out of the car first," she said and joined us at the edge of the cliff. "Look over there, can you see the futuristic-looking villa over there?" She pointed at one of the buildings. "The white one with the round windows."

We saw the villa she was talking about. It was a strange building with round windows and from what I could see it had no corners; everything was round. I saw two expensive-looking cars parked outside but I could not make out the brand.

"So what is it?" I asked

"That is Sylvester Stallone's villa. He actually lives there," Angelika said.

"Oh, Rambo, the muscle man," I joked. "Are you sure he lives there?"

"Of course, why do you think they all stop here?" she said, pointing at the other tourists taking pictures of the villa.

I could not believe it. *Did they really stop here just for that? Oh, what the hell.* I took a few pictures for my collection. "Okay, done, let's go," I said.

"Wait, maybe we see him."

"Angelika, come on, do you think he will just step out of this place and wave at you?"

"Believe it or not but sometimes he does," she protested.

"Yeah, good luck," Franz said and took a few more shots.

Twenty minutes later, we arrived at the entrance gate of the Acapulco Princess Hotel. I had never been to a five-star resort hotel and was surprised to find an entrance gate but no hotel. We drove through the gate and entered what looked like a beautifully landscaped park. As it turned out, this was actually a golf course with stunning greens, artistically trimmed bushes and walkways with tall coconut palms as far as the eyes could see.

We drove five more minutes before I caught a glimpse of the incredible hotel. The hotel was built in the shape of an ancient Aztec pyramid with a spectacular fountain at the main entrance. We got out of the car, paid the driver and walked into the completely open lobby. Angelika led us through the lobby, passing the reception as if she were regular customer here. Every hotel employee greeted us politely, which made me feel out of place. For some reason I felt like an intruder, like someone who was not supposed to be here.

Angelika stopped. "Here we are, the Acapulco Princess Hotel," she said.

We stood at the entrance to the garden of the hotel. Like so many times already on this cruise, the view took my breath away. I looked at a lush tropical garden with several swimming pools, waterfalls and a huge artificial tropical river. The lush green garden stretched for several hundred meters and its size absolutely amazed me. I noticed in the distance a hanging bridge crossing the tropical river just like in one of the movies with *Indiana Jones*.

Beyond the garden lay a private lagoon with a snow-white beach. To me it looked just like paradise. Angelika led the way through this paradise whilst Franz and I shot picture after picture. Soon I had finished the first roll of film and changed it for a new one. We passed by pools with bars packed with gorgeous and wealthy-looking girls and bars hidden behind waterfalls. I felt completely out of place. We settled in one of the poolside bars where Angelika ordered three signature cocktails for us. As we sat there sipping our cocktails I could not get enough of the amazing sight. I wanted to take more pictures but I had only one roll left.

"This is amazing," I mumbled.

"It's great, isn't it?" Angelika said, sipping her cocktail.

"I will come back here on my holiday," Franz said.

"Yeah, as if you could afford it," I said.

"With the tip we are making? We can go anywhere we want." We all laughed. After we had finished our cocktail, we took a walk through the rest of the garden and eventually ended up in the deserted lagoon where Franz and I went for a swim. One hour later, it was time for us to return to the *Europa*. We took a hotel taxi. I was happy to see that we would not have to drive home in another rust bucket but instead a brand new Cadillac with dark tinted windows and air conditioning. The ride back to the ship in this car was so comfortable that I fell asleep almost immediately.

MS *Europa* left Acapulco early the next day and on the pier a large crowd of people waved us their goodbyes with scarves and handkerchiefs. I stood on the main deck and in my mind, I said goodbye to an Acapulco that had not really lived up to my expectations. The reality was that there was a huge gap between the very rich and the very poor in this city and I concluded that if you want to experience the Acapulco as seen on television, you need money and then lots of it. Ironically, places like San Francisco, Los Angeles and Acapulco, cities that I had really been looking forward to, had not been as I had imagined them to be, and instead Alaska, out of all places, with its wild stunning beauty, had left a lasting impression on me.

We now sailed along the west coast of Central America toward Panama. During the night, we entered the territorial waters of Nicaragua, where we briefly stopped over in Granada. In the late afternoon, we departed and after sailing overnight, we arrived early the following morning at Puntarenas in Costa Rica.

Since we had departed from San Francisco, the weather had been a blessing, with cloudless blue skies and steadily increasing temperatures and humidity. The days at sea and in ports always followed the same routine. At sea we served breakfast, lunch and dinner and in between, if we were not assigned for afternoon tea service or other duties, we went sunbathing on deck. When we were in ports, we went out to visit places of interest, went shopping or tried local specialties. In smaller ports like Granada and Puntarenas, we normally only managed to venture out to places close to the ship where we bought postcards or souvenirs to prove that we had actually been there.

Our entry into the Gulf of Panama marked my thirty-first day onboard. After thirty-one days of continuously working without a single day off, my body had settled and my requirement for rest had changed. A nap between breakfast service and lunch service would be like sleeping for half a day and a nap for a few hours in the afternoon would completely revitalize me for the next two days.

The actual meal service had turned into something like a competition as to who got the best place in the main-course queue or who could carry the largest number of food platters. I was good at both. Gone were the days when I was afraid and nervous, hoping that I would get my station ready in time.

In the afternoon, after crossing the Gulf of Panama, we reached the port of Panama City. This looked like a very busy port; the inner and outer harbor area was crowded with ships of all shapes and sizes waiting to be admitted to enter the first set of locks of the Panama Canal.

I had heard much about the Panama Canal but I did not really know much about it. I picked up a copy of the landing information and read all about the famous waterway. The Panama Canal is a truly impressive feat of engineering, connecting the Pacific and the Atlantic Ocean.

Construction began in 1880 under French leadership. However, plagued by problems including diseases like malaria and yellow fever, the attempt collapsed. The United States continued where the French had failed and completed the canal in 1914 but the project had come at a high cost. It is estimated that as many as 27,500 workers died during the construction of the canal.

I was surprised to learn that the canal consists of seventeen artificial lakes, several artificial channels, and two sets of locks. The locks had to "lift" ships from sea level up by twenty-six meters and before entering the Atlantic, they lifted them back down to sea level. In view of this, I was not surprised to see that the bay was crowded with ships. Even the piers of Panama City itself were busy with countless ships. We did not enter the port; instead, we dropped anchor offshore just outside the harbor.

On the evening prior to our arrival, I had served my second farewell dinner that had yielded only meager tips. The reasons for this were of course the Anton Seller band and the Keller gang of the second seating. I did not really mind—the Anton Seller band had been fun to be with throughout the cruise and in most ports they had never taken their meals in the restaurant, which of course had been good for me. We had become friends and that was more important. The Keller gang of course was a different story altogether. They had tipped but far below the expected tax. I also did not mind because I was happy to see them gone. They were just a bunch of strange people and in my mind I wished them good luck with whatever they were up to next.

Our schedule was quite tight because our existing guests had to depart the ship before lunchtime and the new passengers would arrive in the early afternoon. This was a tremendous task because all the transfers of people and luggage had to be done by boat since we were not on a pier. Our tenders had been busy the whole morning shuttling back and forth to shore. None of this really affected us restaurant stewards but for our colleagues, the cabin stewards, it was extremely busy getting the cabins ready in time for the new arrivals.

This meant for me that once I had finished cleaning up after breakfast service, I was free until dinner. Theoretically, we could have gone ashore but because the shuttle boats were busy with passengers, we stayed onboard. In any case, the recommendation from the company was not to venture into the city due the high rate of crimes. We could not go sunbathing either because there was absolutely no wind and it was simply too hot and humid outside. There was one positive aspect to Panama City and that was the fact that it was also a so-called "mail harbor."

There were only a limited number of ports or cities during our cruise where we could receive mail and this was always an exciting event. I had not heard from my parents or from Tatiana since I had left home. San Francisco and Los Angeles had also been mail harbors but it had been too early for me. I was full of hope to be one of the lucky ones this time.

Before my departure from Germany I was given a list of "mail harbors" in different countries which the *Europa* was scheduled to visit. Each of these mail harbors had a deadline by when mail had to be sent from Germany in order to arrive on time in the respective harbor. I had given copies of this list to my parents and Tatiana. I could not wait; according to Angelika the mail boat had delivered two large bags of mail in the morning. The mail was in the process of being sorted in the purser's office and they would distribute it before dinner service. I had written many postcards and posted many letters so far but I had no clue if they ever had arrived. Today was the day that I would find out.

In the early evening that day, we had our pre-cruise briefing again, which went pretty much along the same lines as the one in Vancouver. Bohne announced the station plan that had not changed much; I would remain in my station with Wolfgang and Doris. Bohne announced the side jobs and the seating plan. I had no artists this time and there were also no complaints from anyone concerning the seating plan. We all were desperate to see whether we had any mail.

Finally, Bohne made the announcement. Once again I had the impression that he was in one of his sadistic moods and that he had dragged the briefing on longer than usual because he seemed to enjoy seeing us look desperately at the two mail bags sitting next to him on the floor. One of the bags looked a little bulkier and I wondered if there were parcels inside.

"Are there any questions?" Bohne cried, knowing very well that we wanted our bloody mail.

"No questions, Your Honor. The mail, please. " That was Hartmut who sounded as if he was losing his patience.

Bohne rewarded him with an angry stare but I could see that Hartmut could not be bothered less. Yankowich, standing next to

Bohne, grabbed a pile of letters and handed them to Bohne. He shifted through the letters as if to choose who would be first and who would have to wait until last. Everyone was quiet, staring at Bohne in expectation of their name being called. This included me.

Bohne, of course, was enjoying the attention. Then he looked up and began. "Albert....Anton...." He called out the name and then handed the letters to Yankowich on his left or Koenig to his right. The respective people stepped forward and took their letters.

"Brinkman....Berger....Baumann...."

It was quite amazing to see how the faces of the men and women changed when their names got called. One moment they looked very serious and anxious and suddenly their faces would glow with happiness.

"Calder....Cromer....Pressman....Dieter...."

Some received a bundle of letters, others only one or two and some got nothing. Bohne distributed the letters in alphabetical order and therefore some of the stewards knew that they had no mail once their letter of the alphabet had passed. I could see on their facial expressions that they were deeply disappointed when they left.

"Ebert....Eckert...Junkers....Schwarz...."

A sudden jolt shot through my body when I heard my name; it sounded wonderful. I had mail!

Bohne handed a bundle of three letters to Yankowich who passed them on to me. I grabbed them full of excitement and joy. I looked at the envelopes, which were full of postage stamps. One letter was from Tatiana and two from my parents. I would have never thought that three simple letters could make me so incredibly happy.

Since I stood near my service station, I put the letters into the drawer because I did not want to read them just yet. I wanted to enjoy and savor the excitement for as long as I possibly could.

"Last but not least, we have three parcels," Bohne cried with his customary screechy voice. Koenig manhandled the bulky parcels out of the mailbag and Bohne read the names.

"Scherer....Manning....and Schwarz."

That was my name again. I looked around to see if it was a mistake. I could not believe it and because I did not believe it, I had to ask. "Mr. Bohne, was that Schwarz, as in my name?"

He looked at me with his usual mixed expression of discontent and disgust. "Schwarz, yes, I said clearly Schwarz, are you deaf? Get you parcel." The way he talked, it sounded to me as if he was jealous and from what I had seen so far, this was probably true.

I walked up to Koenig, who handed the parcel to me with a smile. The parcel was from my mother. It was incredible—my first mail harbor and I had received three letters and one parcel! I was ecstatic and in the best of moods; the world for me was in order. I had a great job, I traveled the world and now I had received more mail than anyone else. Life was good.

I was in the perfect mood to meet my new guests. They arrived in good time for the first seating and contrary to expectation, they did not overorder and overeat. Quite the opposite, it seemed to me as if they kept each other in check. My ten guests of the first seating were nondescript, polite, friendly and very reserved. At first I thought that after an hour together that might change, but from what I observed, I wondered how they would get on.

For these guests, the waiter, food and service were of no importance; they focused exclusively on themselves and nothing else. That was fine with me; all I had to do was to do my job. The second seating was not much different except for Mr. and Mrs. Knaus, who were not impressed with their quiet and "boring" neighbors. From what I could see, this cruise had the potential of being a pretty civilized one for me.

We should have entered the Panama Canal early the next morning but at nine-thirty, we were still at our anchorage. We finished breakfast service, cleaned up our stations and then went outside onto the main deck to watch our impeding departure. There was a party atmosphere on deck—someone had set up a small tape recorder playing Latin music and several stewards and stewardesses had taken off their uniform tops and relaxed in deck chairs. Franz, Angelika and I sipped from our freshly brewed coffee that tasted great despite the stifling heat and incredible high humidity.

We had seen one of our tender boats with the first officer aboard leaving the ship for the port but nobody knew why or what was the reason for our delay. The first officer returned twenty minutes later but still we did not move. *What was the problem?* I wondered. After some time another boat—this time from the canal administration—approached and once the boat had stopped at the gangway, a man disembarked and disappeared inside the ship.

I wondered if there were some serious problems but Angelika told us otherwise. According to her, the average waiting time for ships wanting to cross the Panama Canal was three days and sometimes even longer. Needless to say, we couldn't wait three days and therefore the captain had to find a way to speed up the process. After half an hour, the boat left with the man standing on the stern of the little craft waving us goodbye. He looked happy, which was a good sign.

When suddenly the anchor was pulled up and the harbor tugs approached us, I knew that everything was fine. Angelika explained that what had happened just now repeated itself every time here in Panama. In order to move up in the queue of ships waiting to enter the Panama Canal, the captain had to resort to paying an additional "incentive" to someone important in the canal administration. The incentive must have been up to the administration's expectation because less then five minutes after the gentleman from the harbor administration left, I felt a light vibration under my feet as the captain started the ship's engines and a short while later we were on our way.

Angelika, Franz and I watched the long line of waiting ships as we passed. I noticed the different types, freighters, tankers, gigantic container ships and even some ro-ro ships waiting to make their passage. The heat and humidity here was incredible; everything was moist or wet and even after only ten minutes outside my uniform felt damp. I had never before experienced such high humidity. Later, back at home, when I tried to explain to my parents what the weather was like, I always asked them to go to the bathroom, run the shower very hot for about twenty minutes without opening the bathroom door—and that's what the weather was like. There was hardly any wind because we literally crept at snail's pace towards the entrance of the Panama Canal.

As we drew closer to the entrance of the canal I observed for the first time the vegetation to the left and right, and soon I noticed that the banks were covered in dense, lush green jungle with palms, large ferns and other unidentifiable plants. To me the jungle looked exactly like I had seen in the Indiana Jones movies.

Close to shore, several local boats sped toward the canal. The boats were typical for this region with their long and narrow hull and the powerful single outboard engines made them fast little crafts. They also sat quite low in the water, which was perfect for entering the shallow side arms of the canal. As we neared the canal entrance, the shore began closing in around us and after a while, it looked as if our 39,000-ton ship was cruising up a river. Once we had entered the canal, a smaller tug joined us. This tug would stay with us for the rest of the seventy-seven-kilometer journey through the Panama Canal.

We entered the channel leading up to the first locks. The channel banks were all evenly slanted at the same angle and nicely overgrown with grass that looked like part of a golf course. A wall made of natural stone supported the green slope, which looked more like a park than a major shipping channel.

Further in the distance I noticed a high wire mesh fence with heavy barbed wire at its top. It looked as if the fence was built to stop the jungle from invading the canal area because beyond the fence there was nothing but thick and dense jungle. On the other side of the fence, the area was covered in what looked like the finest cut English lawn. The fence ran along the canal as far as my eyes could see and I wondered whether it had been built to keep out wild animals. *There is still a jungle out there,* I thought and smiled.

What I didn't know at the time was that the fence was built by the Americans and although we were in Panama, to my surprise, the Panama Canal itself was actually American territory. Our lecturer explained that the United States began works on the canal in 1904 after helping Panama to declare independence from Colombia in exchange for control of the Panama Canal Zone. At the time of our crossing, the United States and Panama had already agreed on the formal return of the canal to Panamanian control on December 31, 1999.

Soon we reached the first of three locks, the Miraflores locks that would lift the *Europa* up by over sixteen meters. The locks assembled a gigantic dock with four massive iron doors at both ends. The operation of the locks was controlled from a three-story building in the typical colonial style from the 1920s. Large signs on each side of the building read in large letters "Miraflores" and to me it very much resembled a railway station.

In the distance, I saw the fence with the thick green jungle seemingly pressing against it. I also noticed a strong military presence with soldiers patrolling along the canal and the lock installations. I also noticed several armed jeeps driving slowly along the fence and frequent sweeps by dark green helicopters overhead. I found out later that this was due to tension between the U.S. and Panama surrounding the ownership of the canal, which Panamanians felt belonged rightfully to them. Apparently, there had been violent student protest over the past weeks in connection with this issue.

There was no immediate danger to our lives and so we continued watching with interest as we steered toward the Miraflores lock. Its two huge open steel doors looked like a giant mouth that was just about to eat us alive. Our small but extremely powerful tug pushed us gently into the locks and once the tug had safely brought us to a halt, the massive steel doors began to close. Overall it was an exciting maneuver.

Finally, the doors completely closed. We waited but nothing happened. The main deck was now at the same level as the ground level of the locks. I noticed two locomotives that slowly moved into position and stopped to the left and right of the ship. I asked Angelika what they were doing and she explained that they would pull us out of the locks as soon as the lock had filled and the doors on the opposite side opened. She told us that we could not run our engines here since our massive screws would turn the locks into a gigantic blender. I had never even thought of the havoc the twin screws of a 39,000-ton ship could cause in a confined environment like the locks.

The whole system was quite simple but effective. I looked down and saw that they had run a steel cable from one locomotive to the one on the other side. Once the doors opened, the two locomotives would slowly pull us out of the locks.

It was now close to lunchtime and we had to return to the restaurant, which was just as well because after over two hours on deck I was wet all over. It was incredibly hot. The restaurant was refreshingly cool which was exactly what I needed.

Most of my guests looked hot and had red faces from the sun; they all would spend the day on deck watching our passage through the Panama Canal. It was an easy lunch; my guests arrived in time and none of them ordered much. They did not talk much, neither with me nor with each other. They also did not eat much, presumably because of the hot weather outside. For me to hope that this would be the same for the rest of this cruise was simply too much to hope for.

There was quite a difference between my current guests and the previous ones. On the last cruise, I was constantly entertained in the first seating by the Anton Seller guys and in the second seating, I was kept on my toes by the Keller gang. My new guests were completely different; I do not even know what they talked about, *if* they talked that was. Mr. and Mrs. Knaus of the second seating were the only ones to keep me somewhat entertained. They were a jovial couple in their late fifties and they had done several cruises on the *Europa* and other ships before. They were also the only ones who came in shorts and generally looked as if on holiday.

The rest of my guests, typical for Germans, had changed into something more formal, a little too much considering where we were. In any case, lunch was very quick because everyone wanted to get back on deck to watch our cruise through the Panama Canal. When I came out on deck after I had cleaned up my station, they had just opened the locks' steel doors and I immediately saw that the locomotives had disappeared and we were much higher now. When I looked over the side, I was amazed to see that we had really risen by several meters.

"That's incredible," I said to Franz, who was shooting away with his camera.

"That was fast, wasn't it?" he answered.

"Look over to the other side," Angelika suddenly said.

On the other side, going in the opposite direction, was a huge container ship that had just undergone the same procedure. Each lock had two identical dock-like basins, one in each direction. It was just like a two-lane road. I hadn't noticed the ship before and it was huge. I took my camera and began shooting away. In the meantime, the *Europa* was slowly pulled out of the locks by the tug.

Once we had cleared the locks, the little tug began pushing us farther into the canal and then a familiar vibration announced that the captain had started our engines again. We slowly cruised through a narrow channel into the canal. We had an absolutely stunning view—to the left and right of the ship there was dense lush green jungle and it looked as if the ship was in the middle of a tropical rainforest, which was truly weird. We were in the middle of the canal that was not more than a few hundred meters wide and we were cruising along the left side close to its banks. On both sides, there was jungle, which was an amazingly beautiful sight. We rushed to our cabins to get our swimming trunks and met upstairs on the signal deck. The view from up there was even more impressive than from the main deck. It was still terribly hot and humid and Angelika warned us to watch out for mosquitoes but because of the strong wind, she reckoned we would be quite safe.

We gathered alongside other stewards in front of the signal mast where we had the best view. In front of us, the canal stretched for several kilometers into the distance. I could clearly see how the canal had been carved through mountainous jungle; it was really an astonishing sight. An hour later, after cruising at seemingly a snail's pace, the canal began to widen and Angelika explained that we would now enter the Miraflores Lake.

We crossed the lake with our little tug still trailing us. Having learned the hard way that sun lotion was important in these climates, I covered myself from head to toe in that oily stuff. For the duration of the crossing, we all settled into our deck chairs. I had brought my walkman and as I was lying there in the sun listening to Duran Duran, Scorpions and Pink Floyd, staring at the cloudless blue sky, I felt like being in heaven. At one point I closed my eyes and dozed off. Franz woke me half an hour later; we had just reached the end of the lake. I opened my eyes under my sunglasses and looked drowsily at the smiling face of Franz.

"Hey, wake up, we are at the next lock," he urged. "You want to see that or not?"

Of course I wanted to see that; I could still sleep in the evening after dinner. I took off the headset of my walkman and got up. I had been sweating heavily in the sun so the light breeze that came as I stood was refreshing. I walked around the signal mast to the front of the deck.

The surrounding landscape had flattened out a little and it seemed that we had left the more mountainous region behind us. The passenger decks beneath us were crowded with hundreds of guests. Looking at our elderly passengers standing there in their bathing suits and bikinis, I wondered if we ever would get some younger guests, offering us something to look at. I shared my observation with Franz who started laughing. Angelika told us then that we normally had a younger crowd during school holidays when parents or grandparents sometimes took their daughters and nieces on cruises. I noted that she had only mentioned daughters and nieces without mentioning sons or nephews.

Great! The next holidays would be Christmas, which was still a few months away. Franz and I still had to wait a while before we could see some more attractive bathing suits and bikinis on deck.

We were already much closer than I had expected and the gigantic steel doors of the Pedro Miguel Locks were already wide-open, ready to swallow us. Once our tug had maneuvered us safely into the locks, the doors slowly closed and we underwent another nine-meter lift. Throughout this procedure, the onboard lecturer explained in detail what was happening. The actual raising of the ship went amazingly fast once the water started entering the locks under high pressure. The power must have been immense considering the enormous weight of our ship. Thirty minutes later, everything was completed and the doors slowly opened in front of us.

Once we were released from the locks, we entered another ten-kilometer stretch of the canal that was completely manmade. As we cruised down the canal, we passed a large memorial dedicated to all the poor souls who had died during the construction of the Panama Canal. Naturally, I took many pictures. Since we had entered the Panama Canal, we had also observed and photographed many exotic birds flying close to the water's surface and to my surprise, most of them were pelicans. Contrary to my expectation, they were not white but dirty grey.

We passed several ships of different sizes traveling in the opposite direction on their way to the Pacific Ocean. Every time we passed one of these ships everyone onboard would wave at them, but many times the sailors we saw on deck just raised lazily their hands and sometimes they just looked bored at us, probably thinking, *Silly tourists.* It was quite an experience.

After the artificial part of the canal, we entered another partially natural stretch of river. The Chagres River, or Rio Chagres, as it was called in Spanish, was a stretch of about ten kilometers that was followed by the large Gatun Lake. The Gatun Lake was a gigantic semi-artificial lake leading to the last set of docks, the Gatun Locks. When we entered the lake, we returned to our deck chairs and baked a little more in the sun. To my relief a cooling breeze had started to pick up just as we had entered the lake. By the time we reached the center of the lake, it was already time for us to get back to our cabins and get ready for dinner.

Back in my cabin, I found Wolfgang snoring in his bunk. He later told me that he had crossed the Panama Canal many times and he had seen it all before. I got undressed and took a long cold shower. After an entire day in the stifling tropical heat of the Panama Canal, a cold shower struck me as the best thing on earth.

When I had finished drying my hair and getting dressed, I still had some time and decided to read the letter from Tatiana again. She had given me an update on what had been happening in the Black Forest Grand Hotel and her upcoming exams. I suddenly realized how much time had gone by since we had last met. Tatiana also told me that she wanted to work in London and had already sent several applications to various hotels. She insisted that working in a London hotel was a must in order to improve her English and if she wanted to work even further abroad in the future.

When I read this, the fact that I did not speak English came back into my mind and I realized that I had to do something about it. I could not always rely on others to translate for me every time I wanted to order something when we were ashore or when I wanted to ask a question. Eventually I had to sit down and start learning English in earnest. After I had finished reading the letter, I stuffed it back into its envelope and stored it safely in my drawer. I heard Wolfgang yawning in his bunk and then he opened the curtains.

"Ah, what time is it?" he asked with a sleepy voice.

"It's nearly five-thirty, time to get up, you lazy bugger."

He sat up on his bunk, rubbing his eyes. "Wow, have you been in the sun?" he suddenly asked.

"Yes, why?"

"Jesus, you are dark," he laughed. He was right; my earlier sunburn had now turned into a dark suntan after nearly four days sunbathing every afternoon.

"Oh, well, it was quite hot up there today but very interesting."

"I forgot—the Panama Canal. Are we through yet?"

"We just entered Gatun Lake when I left the signal deck," I said.

"Oh, good, then we should be back at sea sometimes tonight. I hate these canal crossings—they are so slow and boring."

"I thought is was quite interesting."

"Yeah, I said that too in the beginning. Just wait until you have done it four or five times—then it becomes a chore."

He got up and walked to the bathroom. At that moment, I thought that even if I crossed that canal ten times I would still be up on deck taking pictures; it was just too interesting an adventure to miss. If the day ever came that I would be sleeping in my bunk whilst crossing the Panama Canal, then it was time for me to leave.

By the time we entered the Gatun Locks, the dinner service for the first seating was already in full swing. Whilst I was feeding my hungry guests, hundreds of tons of water slowly drained out of the locks and the ship slowly descended back to sea level. By the time I cleared my guests' empty dessert plates, we had long left the locks and were on our way to Limon bay, where countless ships lay offshore awaiting admission into the Panama Canal.

Our next cruise would take us first to the San Blas Islands, which was still part of Panama, then to Colombia in South America and from there we would go island-hopping in the Caribbean. When I saw the names of the Caribbean Islands, I had tears in my eyess—Bahamas, Barbados, Antilles and Jamaica. I would be visiting all famous islands that other people could only dream of; it was like in a wonderful dream.

The sparsely lit coast of Panama slowly disappeared in the darkness. By the time we got up the next morning, we would be far out somewhere in the Caribbean Sea, where we would spent the day before reaching San Blas Islands the next morning.

This next day also marked my thirty-fourth day onboard and I wondered where the time had gone. It was remarkable how quickly I had adapted to this very different working environment where we served two fully-booked seatings for lunch and dinner. Even when we were at sea, there were only few occasions when we went to sleep earlier than one or two in the morning, due to our intense and hectic working schedule which differed at sea and ashore. At sea, it would typically look like this:

06.00—06.30 Wake-up call, get up and take a shower. After shower, get dressed and up to the restaurant
06.30—07.00 Preparation of station and tables for breakfast
07.00—07.30 Breakfast in the crew mess.
07.30—09.30 Breakfast service for guests—open seating, no fixed tables .
09.30—10.00 Preparation of station and tables for lunch.

10.00—11.00	Break or fire/lifeboat drill or lifeboat exercise (at sea)
11.00—11.30	Lunch in the crew mess
11.30—13.00	Lunch service for guests of the first seating
13.00—14.30	Lunch service for guests of the second seating
14.30—17.00	Break or afternoon tea service/fire drill/lifeboat drill or lifeboat exercise (at sea)
17.00—17.30	Shower, shave, get dressed and back into the restaurant
17.30—18.00	Preparation of station and tables for dinner
18.00—18.30	Dinner in the crew mess
18.30—20.15	Dinner service for guests of the first seating
20.15—22.00	Dinner service for guests of the second seating
24.00—01.00	Midnight buffet on the sun deck and lido deck (twice a week)

Not included are the frequent parties we had at sea and they normally never ended before three or four in the morning. If we were not partying, then the evening was the only time left to do other essential jobs such as writing letters to our loved ones. Because of this tight schedule, we hardly ever got more than five hours sleep at most and therefore, the afternoon nap at sea became very important for us. After two months working like this, even I sold my afternoon tea shifts in order to get some additional sleep.

Days in ports were of course filled with sightseeing tours, shopping tours, eating out, and clubbing in the evenings after dinner service. Before reaching large and well-known cities, we would get as much rest as possible during the days before in order to be physically fit for the hectic schedule *ashore* and it looked something like this:

06.00—06.30	Wake-up call, get up and take a shower. After shower, get dressed and up to the restaurant
06.30—07.00	Preparation of station and tables for breakfast
07.00—07.30	Breakfast in the crew mess
07.30—09.30	Breakfast service for guests—open seating, no fixed tables
09.30—10.00	Preparation of station and tables for lunch
10.00—12.00	Break or sightseeing tour ashore/quick bite to eat ashore

12.00—13.30 Lunch service for all guests, open seating

13.30—18.00 Break or more sightseeing, shopping or other activities ashore

18.00—18.15 Very quick shower, shave, get dressed and back into the restaurant

18.15—18.30 Preparations of station and tables for dinner (at the same time, gulp down a few rolls to satisfy stomach)

18.30—21.00 Dinner service for all guests—open seating, no fixed tables

21.00—21.15 Preparation of station and tables for breakfast the next day

21.15—21.30 Get changed and leave the ship for an evening out

21.30—04.30 Eating, drinking and partying in restaurants and bars ashore

04.30—06.00 One glass of water, two Panadol and crash into the bunk

06.00—06.05 First wake-up call

06.10—06.12 Second wake-up call

06.12—06.30 Get up painfully slow and take a shower. After shower, get dressed and up to the restaurant.

06.40—07.30 Preparation of station and tables for breakfast

Most of our days in port were like this and if we stayed for two or more days, we normally were completely shattered for the coming days at sea. Those sea days were the most difficult ones and every single available minute would be used to catch up on sleep, resulting in a schedule like this:

06.00—06.30 Wake-up call, look at the clock, decide to skip breakfast and sleep a little longer

06.30—07.00 Second wake-up call, look at the clock and decide to nap for ten more minutes

07.10—07.20 Get up in a hurry and take a shower. After shower, get dressed and hurry up to the restaurant.

07.20—07.30 Quick final preparations of station and tables for breakfast

07.30—09.30 Breakfast service for guests, trying hard to stay awake. Open seating, no fixed tables

09.30—09.45 Quick preparations of station and tables for lunch, looking forward to going to bed

09.45—11.15 Hope there is no fire/lifeboat drill or lifeboat exercise (at sea), skip lunch and sleep instead

11.30—13.00 Lunch service for guests of the first seating, feeling tired

13.00—14.30 Lunch service for guests of the second seating, close to falling asleep

14.30—18.00 Hope there is no afternoon tea service or fire/lifeboat drill. If so, sell the afternoon tea service or get any drill over as quickly as possible and go to sleep

18.00—18.10 Wake-up call, take showers, shave, get dressed drowsily but quickly and, feeling slightly better, rush back into the restaurant

18.10—18.30 Skip dinner in the crew mess and prepare station and tables for dinner service

18.30—20.15 Dinner service for guests of the first seating, feeling just good enough to survive the first seating

20.15—22.00 Dinner service for guests of the second seating and already tired again

22.00—22.05 Check if assigned to midnight buffet on the sun deck and lido deck and if that's the case—sell!

22.06—06.00 Go to bed and get a good night's sleep

This may sound a little funny but after two or three days ashore we struggled through work just like this. For the moment, I enjoyed my job and I enjoyed going to bed in one country and waking up the next day in another. The excitement of seeing all these exotic and faraway places was something that would last for many years to come.

I also had begun to find my way around the ship without getting lost. Over time I discovered shortcuts which saved valuable time, especially if we were at sea and I was desperate to get into my bunk and sleep. I had also found my favorite spot on the signal deck for sunbathing and I had my regular seat in the crew mess. Everyday noises of all sorts of machineries had become so familiar that whenever the chief engineer switched any of them off, I would know instantly.

With my increase in knowledge of the ship corridors, staircases and elevators, of which we had many, my confidence level grew in proportion and before long I was confident enough to concentrate on things other than my work and that was—girls. As mentioned before, we did not have many girls onboard and those which we did have were therefore in high demand. Out of the limited number of girls the prettiest were of course spoken for, meaning they had boyfriends. The other girls had various affairs and some of them had rather questionable reputations. Over time I got to know them all.

In such an environment, major crew changes were more like meat markets where we stewards would stand on deck watching and observing the quality of our female newcomers. I was watching and observing too and I made my comments but deep down I knew that I would be faithful to Tatiana—at least for the moment.

All this was much easier for our gay colleagues, not only because the number of gay stewards by far outnumbered the straight ones, but also because many of our male guests were gay. AIDS was not so much an issue then and I was told that some of the parties they had onboard were quite wild. The relationship between straight stewards and our gay colleagues was generally good although clashes between the two were common. I have to be honest in saying that I was never quite comfortable dealing with my gay colleagues such as Manfred and Wolfgang, even though I knew that most of the time they were just joking and making fun of me, much due to my visible fear of them.

There was only one person I learned to dislike with a passion and that was Bohne. He was simply weird and as far as I could tell, not even my gay colleagues had quite figured him out. Most of the time when he talked with me I didn't quite understand what he was saying, and that was not because he spoke quietly or in a different language, he simply couldn't talk—he mumbled. During cruises, he never talked with guests nor did he try to communicate properly with any of us stewards. The only time he seemed to make an effort to speak in a way that everyone could understand him was at the customary pre-cruise briefings and even then, some of the things he said were disconnected. His eyes constantly darted nervously from left to right as if he was worried that at any moment someone would scream or throw something at him. He was simply weird and I never understood how he had survived all these years in his job.

The ship's crew of over three hundred and fifty was divided in two main sections: the ship's technical personnel consisting of captain, first and navigation officers, engine room crew, sailor, printers, etc.; and the hotel personnel consisting of hotel manager, cabin and restaurant stewards, bar tenders and so forth. We did not have many dealings with the ship's technical personnel and most of the time we only socialized with them in the crew bar.

There were also the Chinese who did all the cleaning jobs such as laundry, stewarding and public-area cleaning. Most of them were from Hong Kong, Malaysia and Singapore and had been working on ships for decades. They were also the unofficial traders of the ship. They changed currencies at better rates than the purser office, one could buy anything under the sun from them ranging from video cameras to tailor-made suits and jackets, and if they did not have the desired item onboard, they would magically produce them a few ports later. They never socialized much with us nor did they eat in the crew mess. Instead, they always prepared their own meals. I didn't really know what to make of them; they were just too different.

The only time when the Chinese gathered in force in the crew bar was after farewell dinners, for good reason of course, because that was the time when our pockets were full with envelopes of cash—a lot of cash. The Chinese of course knew that very well. That was the one and only time when they invited us stewards to play a Chinese game called *mahjong* with them. Mahjong is an ancient Chinese game, played with small tiles, each of a different value. A set of mahjong tiles has usually around 144 tiles split in three categories: suits, honor and flowers. The value of each tile is expressed with dots, bamboos, Chinese characters and flowers. I watched with interest some of these games between stewards and the Chinese and honestly, I had no idea how it worked. What I did know was that the stakes were incredibly high; I'll never forget the five-hundred- and one-thousand-mark banknotes on the table. The minimum entry for a game was five hundred marks.

It didn't take me long to figure out the nasty game the Chinese played. They would always let their victim win the first couple of rounds, earning him hundreds and sometimes thousands of marks. Most of the guys didn't know of course when to stop and once the Chinese had their victim at a point where he or she felt invincible, they began to take them out. I have seen many stewards lose their entire earnings from a three-week cruise in one of those nights. They would leave the bar angry and upset, with their tails between their legs. Occasionally the Chinese would pretend to be beaten, letting the victim walk away with impressive winnings only to ensure that we stewards kept on coming back. At the end of the day the stewards were the losers and the Chinese walked off with their pockets full of cash.

There was only one steward, Martin, an Austrian, who had been in the business for over twenty years; he had mastered the game and he was the only one amongst us who was strong enough to beat the Chinese at their own game. We knew they didn't like him challenging them but he was an exception to the rule; most of the time we stewards were the ones walking away with empty pockets. I watched the game many times and more than once the Chinese offered to teach me, but I simply didn't trust them and so I never tried.

Chapter 10

The two most senior officers onboard were, of course, the captain and the first officer. I hardly ever talked with them but I respected them a lot. I am not sure if that was because of their impressive uniform or the fact that I always felt that my life was in their hands, especially after my first visit to the bridge, which to me looked like an enlarged version of an aircraft cockpit, with its many radar screens and consoles full of gauges and switches.

Whenever I saw them in the restaurant they seem to radiate confidence and authority. The captain took lunch and dinner in the restaurant at the famous captain's table. This was the most prestigious and sought-after table on the entire ship. Only sixteen guests per cruise had the chance of getting a seat at the captain's table. These much-desired seats were assigned by Bohne and could not be requested. The captain's table was reserved exclusively for very regular guests, business partners of the company or other very important guests. We knew that whoever was chosen by Bohne to sit with the captain had to be special one way or another.

When the captain's table was occupied, heads turned and everyone wanted to see who the "chosen" ones were and everyone wondered who they were. First-timers had no chance whatsoever to join the captain's table and the same applied to us stewards; only the most senior stewards were assigned to serve the captain's table.

If the captain were not able to attend, which happened frequently, then the first officer would sit in for him. I found them both to be friendly and polite but other than that, we did not interact with them. They never got involved in the hotel operation except for the most serious disciplinary cases and we all knew that if we were ever asked to see the captain or the first officer, we had done something seriously wrong. Luckily, I never had to see the captain or the first officer.

The San Blas Islands were quite different from what I had expected. But then again, what had I expected? I had never even heard of them before. Being in the Caribbean, I was looking forward to my first white sandy beaches, palm trees and azure blue ocean. Instead, I found that San Blas consisted of hundreds of small, picture-perfect tropical islands with white sand and coconut trees and was covered entirely with dwellings.

The indigenous Indian tribe, the Cuna, inhabited the islands and this meant that we could not go to the beach. The Indian culture we found more than made up for it. Apparently, the Cuna had been resisting changes to their culture since the Spanish first arrived over five hundred years ago. The Cuna had managed to maintain their way of life and the San Blas province even had its own government. Interestingly, each little island was run by its own chief and before we could visit any of the surrounding islands, we had to get permission from its respective chief. Many of these islands had no electricity or water supply. Out of the many islands only a small number was accessible to tourists; the others were off limits.

MS *Europa* dropped anchor about one mile out at sea and guests were shuttled in our lifeboats to and from the islands. We took the shuttle in the afternoon to one of the islands where we went on a sightseeing tour on foot. The village on this island consisted of hundreds of huts made out of straw, some of which were built on stilts over the water. It very much reminded me of the Neolithic lake village at Lake Constance with similar huts on stilts in the water. As matter of fact, many details were exactly like I had seen them there, such as "ladders" which were made out of one piece of log and the dugout canoe which was made from a single tree.

For me it was the first time in my life to come face to face with an indigenous tribe. There was one unique detail—we hardly saw any men. Wherever we looked, we saw women of all ages in their colorful dresses. I couldn't take my eyes of them, not because they were particularly pretty but because they were the first "native" people I had ever seen and, especially if they greeted me with a smile, the experience was intense. The Cuna looked to me more like Maya or Aztecs than Indians. The dresses they wore where reminiscent of South American Indians with red as the dominating color. The clothes they wore, which included wrappings on both arms and legs, looked rather warm to me and I wondered if they were uncomfortable and hot wearing them in this weather. Obviously, they were not.

The Cuna women had one thing in common with me and that was they hardly spoke any English. I didn't need to speak English to understand that they didn't like to have their pictures taken—unless one paid. Franz tried to take some pictures without paying, with the result that the women got very angry and covered their faces. They would allow people to take some shots but only for a few dollars.

We strolled through the village photographed its straw huts and the very large "meeting house" where apparently all villagers gathered to hear the stories and advise of the elders. It was an amazingly large hut that again was made out of wooden poles and straw and covered with leaves of coconut trees.

We finished our tour of San Blas at five o'clock and took the short ride back to the ship in one of our lifeboats. San Blas had been an interesting experience and one I will never forget. From my conversations with the Knaubs that evening, I gathered that they had had the same experience as me. For me it had been so intense that when I lay in bed that night, I could not stop thinking of the Cuna and the fact that they had no electricity, light and water. I fell asleep trying to imagine what it must be like to sleep in a straw hut on the floor in this heat and without air conditioning.

We entered Colombian territorial waters sometimes in the afternoon the next day. When I got up, we were already cruising along the Colombian coast. The weather in the Caribbean was perfect, with a cloudless blue sky and calm seas. We were surrounded by deep blue ocean and only the light breeze caused by the ship's forward movement brought some relief from the burning sun on the signal deck. The deck was crowded with crew baking in the sun. I had managed to secure a deck chair, equipped with my walkman, and, covered in suntan lotion, I listened to Duran Duran.

We were scheduled to arrive in Cartagena, Colombia late in the evening. I have heard many horror stories from Angelika about stewards being mugged in Columbia, which hadn't been what I wanted to hear about the place. I didn't really know much about Colombia and the little I remembered from television usually involved drug lords and police raids. She assured Franz and me that despite this we still should go ashore in Cartagena, where she wanted to show us the downtown area with its old colonial buildings. Angelika emphasized that as long as we stayed together we would not be in any danger. Her comments did not really make me feel better about that place but at the same time, I said to myself, *If Cartagena was really that dangerous, why would we stop there in the first place?* I came to the conclusion that there was only one way to find out and that was to go ashore and experience it for myself.

When it was finally time to get back to work, I looked like a freshly baked loaf of brown bread. Dinner was uneventful and all my guests behaved in a civilized way. I had already adopted the "stuff-them-with-food" routine that would hopefully result in my guests longing for a diet after the first couple of days. I served double portions of every dish they ordered which, to my delight, worked extremely well and only half of them finished their desserts. Another two days and I would have them fed to a point where they would cut their food input voluntarily by half and my workload would reduce proportionally.

We watched the arrival in Cartagena from the main deck after dinner service. There was not really much to see because it was already dark. The pier was brightly lit, with several people greeting us on arrival. Beyond the port installations, I saw the pulsating lights of the city of Cartagena. I leaned over the side and watched as the sailors brought down the gangway and the first person to step ashore was the pilot who had guided us safely into port. The next person coming down the gangway was an officer dressed in white but I couldn't make out if it was the first officer or someone else. He greeted a group of uniformed people and after a short conversation, he led them up the gangway.

"Those are the Customs officers," Angelika explained. "They will be given a tour of the ship, check that the beverage stores are locked and then after a nice dinner, we will be cleared for landing," she laughed.

I laughed too but naïve as I was, I still couldn't quite believe that we would get the clearance based on a nice dinner rather than the fact that everything was okay. I liked to think that we got it for the latter.

"So what exciting sightseeing tour have you planned for us tomorrow?" Franz wanted to know.

"I will show you the Plaza del Bolivar and an old monastery in downtown Cartagena, which is the oldest and most interesting part of the city."

"Is it dangerous?" I asked, causing Franz and Angelika to roar with laughter. "That's not funny," I said a little offended.

"Come on, Andre, don't be a wimp," Angelika joked.

"I am not a wimp. I am just asking a question after all the horror stories you told me."

"Cartagena is not the safest place but then again, it's not that everyone who walks around the city gets mugged," she said.

"Except, of course, unsuspecting tourists such as us," Franz laughed.

"Yeah, funny."

None of us felt like going out that evening; there would still be time for that the next day. I went back to my cabin and wrote another letter to Tatiana. Writing those letters every night was for me like talking to her. Here I could say what I wanted and here I could express my deepest feelings, good or bad. That night, however, the fact that Tatiana had written only one letter to me bothered me immensely.

So far, I had written about twenty-eight letters since my arrival and I was in the process of writing the twenty-ninth. I was not too happy because I had received only one letter from her. I wondered why—I knew she was not the letter-writing type but then again, it was not that I would be back home in two weeks. Quite on the contrary, we would not see each other for at least six months. This was a long time for people to be apart and Tatiana was quite an attractive young woman. Should I be worried?

I tried to concentrate on the letter I was writing but my thoughts kept on slipping back to question why she had written only one letter in over a month. Even if she was not the type who wrote letters, didn't she have an urge to put her thoughts down on paper? Wasn't it like talking to me in person?

I put down the pen and told myself to stop it; Tatiana loved me and I knew it. I knew that she was proud to tell friends that her boyfriend was working on a cruise liner— who wouldn't be? That was a definite plus and besides, we were as good as married anyway. The more I thought about it the more I realized that for our friends, Tatiana and Andre were a given. For them we were already married and deep down I knew that eventually we would make it official. So why was I worried?

Maybe it was Tatiana's outgoing and bubbly personality. The more I thought about it the more I realized that it was actually not difficult to fall in love with Tatiana because of her fascinating, energetic and captivating personality. We had been together for four years and somehow it felt as if I had known her for an entire lifetime. It was almost as if she was part of me—Tatiana. The more I thought of her the more I began to miss her. Why had she only written one letter?

I took a new sheet of paper and began to put my feelings down on paper. The letter turned into a love letter of over six pages. When it was eventually completed I put my pen down and looked at the six sheets of paper in my hand. I read the letter from the beginning and—it was a disaster. It seemed as if I had written the same lame sentences over and over again. I sounded more like a little child who had its toy stolen. There was no way that I could send this letter to Tatiana. Even if she had decided to see someone else, the last thing that would make a difference was my letter.

I tore the letter apart and threw it into the bin because if Tatiana chose to be with someone else, there was nothing I could do about it anyway. I didn't sleep very much that night, constantly thinking of Tatiana and wondering why she was not writing to me. That night I was homesick for the first and last time in my life. That night it struck me just how far from home we were and I realized that whatever happened, I could not just leave, get into my car and drive home. I couldn't even just pop out and make a phone call to Tatiana or my parents; I realized that I was stuck on this ship for the next five months. It was a terrible feeling.

When I woke up the next morning, my homesickness had disappeared completely and after a long and hot shower, I felt fresh and ready to face the world. Breakfast went well and as if we had nothing else to do in Cartagena, the first officer hit us with an unannounced fire drill. *So much for discovering the city.* After the drill, there was just enough time to get ready for lunch. To my surprise, most of my guests had gone on sightseeing tours and I finished already at one o'clock. The only annoying thing was that Bohne had begun lingering around my station again. Wolfgang found that quite funny. I didn't.

In the afternoon Angelika, Franz and I went out. We didn't have any local currency and Angelika suggested we visit a local bank to change money because we would get a better exchange rate than in one of the many currency-exchange shops. Not even the Chinese could beat that rate, she said.

The weather was something I had to get used to. There was not a single cloud in the sky; it was incredibly hot with a humidity that made me wonder if we were in a sauna.

In front of the port entrance, we flagged down a similarly banged-up taxi as we had already experienced in Acapulco. We left the harbor complex and entered the suburbs of Cartagena. If the traffic and the poverty that we had encountered in Acapulco had left me with a slight culture shock, this place was far worse. The road on which we drove was covered in potholes and cracks and the tar on its surface had turned soft from the scorching sun. Both sides of the road were lined with litter of all sorts—plastic bags, bottles, papers and what was even worse, I saw people who seemed to live along the road in tents made out of plastic sheets and cardboard.

The cars, buses and trucks on the road were mostly American and just as dilapidated as our taxi. The buses and trucks were in a particular bad shape and it seemed as if they were held together only by wires and tape. I didn't see a single truck which had a profile on its tires and the buses were hopelessly overloaded with people even sitting on the roof. I felt completely overdressed in my brilliant white shorts, white polo shirt and white slippers. I looked at the taxi driver, whose unshaven face was covered in sweat with a cigar stump in one corner of his mouth. He didn't talk at all.

We reached the outskirts of Cartagena, where the traffic slowed down even more. The streets became busier with people and soon we reached downtown. The traffic had come close to a standstill and the people crossed the street wherever they found a gap in between the cars. The noises of loud car horns and shouting street merchants reverberated through the city. Most of the buildings I saw were built in the typical Spanish colonial style and very old. Unfortunately, they all were in advanced stages of deterioration with paint peeling off and in the immense humidity, mold was growing happily on the walls.

As we drove past these buildings I thought that properly renovated, they could look quite beautiful. The streets were buzzing with life— there were people, children and small animals wherever I looked. Huge advertisement boards fixed to building walls showed the same deterioration as the buildings themselves and some of them could hardly be read.

We reached a large square and the driver stopped in front of a bank. Happy to have survived the trip to downtown Cartagena, I jumped out of the car. I was happy to get out of that damn taxi and finally having solid ground under my feet again. I glanced at the bank, which looked to me as if Bolivar himself had used it already during his days.

"Hey, Andre, are you coming with us?" Angelika asked, standing on the first steps of a huge half-moon-shaped staircase leading up to the main entrance of the bank.

"No, thanks, I wait here." I had no intention of buying anything and having been stuck on the ship for several days and now for nearly forty five minutes in a hundred-year-old taxi, I was happy to just stay in front of the bank and relax a little. "Make it quick!" I called after them as they dashed up the staircase.

I walked up to the center of the staircase and sat down. From here, I had an excellent view across the square in front of the bank. It looked actually quite idyllic; the entire square was covered in cobblestone and there were several large trees with huge canopies. Underneath each tree stood several old fashioned cast-iron benches, some of which were occupied by people sleeping. Several stone-carved water troughs, complete with iron rings to fasten horses to, bore witness to a time long gone by.

It was quiet and pleasant where I sat. As I gazed into the distance I noticed an armored truck driving into the square. It was one of those large and heavily armored American trucks which were used to carry large amounts of cash. Now that looked interesting! The truck slowly drove towards the bank and stopped at the bottom of the staircase. For a few seconds nothing happened. Suddenly the doors opened and several guards dressed in bulletproof vests and armed with pump-action rifles jumped out of the truck and into defensive positions.

To me it looked just like in a movie; I had never seen an armored truck before and definitely not American. I also had never seen heavily armed security guards with such rifles and those cool-looking vests. Four guards surrounded the truck whilst two others quickly opened the door and retrieved a metal case of some sort. The two dashed up the staircase, looking suspiciously at me as they passed.

I got up, staring at the truck, thinking that it would make a cool picture. For a moment I wondered if I should ask one of the guards to take a picture of me and the vehicle but decided against it. While I walked down the stairs I took out my camera, trying to see which angle would give me the best shot. At the bottom of the staircase, I turned towards the truck and walked around it, past one of the guards who eyed me suspiciously. I decided that a shot from the front would look cool. I was just about to take the picture when all of a sudden one of the guards blocked my way.

Before I could say something, he rammed the nozzle of his rifle violently into my belly, shouting something in Spanish. I instantly gasped for air with my eyes wide open. I instinctively braced myself to be shot and froze. I stared into the guard's angry, unshaven and sweaty face. He kept on shouting in Spanish but I didn't understand. I was close to panicking and with an immense pain in my stomach, I stepped back. The guard waved for me to get away from the truck. I carefully turned and walked off, expecting any moment to be shot in the back. The shot never came.

I rounded the front of the truck and walked back up the stairs all the way to the main entrance. Down below I saw the guards laughing, shouting something at me in Spanish. I didn't understand what they were saying and I didn't care. Although they had probably been joking, I had the fright of my life and was just happy to be still alive. Franz and Angelika appeared a short while later, talking and laughing.

"Let's get out of here," I said as I saw them.

"Hey, what's wrong?" Angelika asked.

"Nothing. Let's go."

"Okay, okay, it's not far from here, we can walk." she said. I just wanted to get away from the armored truck and the trigger-happy guards.

We crossed the square and walked until we reached the entrance to a large complex consisting of more colonial buildings. It looked like the entrance to a palace but it was, as Angelika explained, a monastery—the Augustinian Fathers convent. We stepped through the entrance in an inner court with a cobblestone floor and several large and ancient-looking trees. The inner court was pleasantly cool and seemingly deserted. There were several cast-iron benches and a little further away a wooden structure of some sort.

After my unpleasant experience with the guards and my near-death experience, the peacefulness of this place came as a relief. Franz and Angelika asked me to take some pictures of them on a bench under one of the trees. Then Franz insisted on taking a picture of Angelika and me, for which I only managed a forced smile. We walked around the court and when we reached the wooden structure I immediately recognized it as a wooden gallows. The only thing missing was the rope on which the victim would hang.

"Jesus, look at this, you know what this is?" I said.

"Of course, that's where they hung people," Franz answered whilst taking a few shots.

"Hey, I have an idea," I said. "Why don't you climb up there pretending to hang and I take a picture?"

"Good idea," Franz laughed and climbed up the wooden ladder. On top of the platform, he stood right underneath the pole where the rope would normally be dangling. Franz stood on his toes with his head at an angle and his tongue hanging out. I took the shot.

"Hey, there is even a door on the floor," Franz shouted and with his tongue hanging out of his mouth, I could hardly understand him. It looked funny and scary at the same time.

"You guys are like little boys," Angelika complained. Franz climbed back down.

"Take one of me," I said excitedly and handed him my camera. I climbed up the ladder and stepped up on the wooden platform. I was surprised at how high I was; it had looked smaller from down below. I carefully stepped onto the door that made some crackling sounds but it held.

"Are you ready?" I shouted at Franz, who had the camera in position.

"Yes, go ahead, prisoner," he laughed.

I stood on my toes and jerked my head to the right. With my tongue hanging out of my mouth, I shouted, "Okay, go ahead."

I never finished the sentence because at the same time, something cracked underneath my feet and the doors swung open. I screamed. It all happened very fast—one moment I was standing on top of the wooden platform and the next moment I sat dazzled on the ground underneath with my head spinning. Franz and Angelika came running toward me and I still didn't know what had happened.

"What...what happened?" I stuttered.

When Franz and Angelika saw that I was okay, they started laughing.

"I am fine," I said, still a little groggy from the fall. I looked around and saw that my left knee was full of blood and suddenly I felt a stinging pain in my leg. I had been lucky that I fell clean through the door; only my left knee had struck the edge of the frame as I fell. Angelika took out some tissues and gently patted my knee. There was a deep cut bleeding heavily.

"Looks bad. You need to get back to the ship and see the doctor," she urged. I could see that for myself.

Franz helped me up and together we walked out of the convent. I continuously had to pat my knee to stop the blood running down my shin. I had enough of this city and was happy when we finally sat in the taxi on the way back to the ship.

Back onboard I went to the hospital immediately, where the doctor checked my wound. He cleaned it thoroughly and fixed it with six stitches. When all was finished, he bandaged my knee.

"That was a deep cut; I had to stitch it up. You better be careful in the future," the doctor said with a solemn voice.

"Yeah, will do," I mumbled.

"You come back in three weeks and I remove the twine. Until then, try not to get it wet and stay away from the beach," he said.

Stay away from the beach?? This was a disaster. We were just about to begin our island-hopping tour of the Caribbean and I was not allowed to go into the water. This was really a disaster.

When I told Franz and Angelika, they pretended to feel sorry for me but eventually they couldn't stop laughing. In a way, I was lucky because knowing me, if there had been a rope, I would have put it around my neck and then the incident would have surely ended differently.

We left Cartagena that evening shortly before the second seating started. I didn't feel like watching our departure from Cartagena, which had not really been a very pleasant experience for me. To complete the first seating with my hurting knee had been a painful exercise because my trouser legs kept on rubbing on the bandage whenever I walked up and down the escalator. I tried to walk more slowly than usual but it still hurt. My strange way of walking attracted Bohne's attention, causing him to hover around my station like a shark circling his prey. God knows what he thought had caused my strange way of walking.

The only relief was when I was standing still at my service station and that's the way I stood when the guests of the second seating entered the restaurant. I greeted them all in the politest of manners without moving an inch. I waited until everyone was seated and only then did I approach the tables slowly to take the orders. Mr. and Mrs. Knaus were the only ones asking me if anything was wrong.

"I had a little accident this afternoon," I simply answered.

"Oh, was it bad?" Mrs. Knaus asked with a concerned expression.

"No, not really, I am fine," I lied.

"What happened?" Mr. Knaus wanted to know.

"Nothing really, but more importantly, what would you like with your chicken?" I tried to change the subject.

At least the hunger got the better of Mr. Knaus and he ordered his side dish. "I'd like some potato puree and steamed vegetables."

"Potato puree and steamed vegetables, thank you." I slowly walked back to my side station and picked up fish knife and fork for Mrs. Knaus, who had ordered fillet of sole.

Seeing me crawling rather than walking, Mrs. Kraus asked again. "Is it bad?"

"No, not really, I am fine." Even a blind man could have seen that I was lying.

"Just be careful," she said with a motherly voice.

"I will, don't worry, Mrs. Knaus."

It was time for me to get down to the kitchen. I slowly crawled to the escalator and instead of running down as usual, I just stood on one step until I reached the kitchen. My knee felt wet and I was sure the blood was soaking through the bandage from the constant rubbing. I was happy when I could just stand there in the main-course queue without having to move. I called out my grills to Obermeyer who repeated my order in his usual angry manner. Because I moved much more slowly, I had only gotten a place at the end of the queue but I couldn't be bothered. At that moment I just wanted this evening to be over as soon as possible.

"Hi there, honey," Manfred chirped from behind.

"Hi, Manfred," I mumbled annoyed.

"What happened to you—can't walk?" he giggled.

"Yeah, but it's not what you think."

"Oh, is it now? What do I think, then?" He was one of the most annoying creatures I had ever met.

"I don't know what you think but whatever it is, you are wrong," I said, annoyed.

"Was it Wolfgang?" He suddenly stepped back as if he was afraid I would smack him.

"What?"

"Did Wolfgang do something nasty to you? Was he a bad boy?"

"Oh, shut up."

"Come on, you can tell me, darling."

"There is nothing to tell, Manfred. Leave me alone."

"Was it the first time?"

"I said, leave me alone."

"It was, wasn't it?"

"Oh, piss off."

"I remember my first time, it was soo good," he sang.

This was too much—my knee was hurting and the last thing I needed was this idiot making fun of me again. "I had an accident and that's all. Now shut up, you pussy," I shouted.

"An accident—is that what they call it now?" he continued, giggling like a little girl.

I just stood there in the queue and kept quiet. I really didn't need that at that very moment. My knee felt moist and I was sure now that blood was soaking through the bandage. Several stewards had witnessed our encounter with interest and I knew what they were thinking—*Is he gay?* At that moment, I hated Manfred.

The queue moved. I stepped forward, trying not to pay any attention to Manfred, who was just behind me, but Manfred just couldn't stop.

"Mum," he mumbled as I walked forward.

That was it for me. I turned around and shouted, "Shut the fuck up or get the fuck out of here!" I was boiling on the inside and I could feel my heart beating hard. My sudden outburst took Manfred by surprise and he immediately stepped back.

"Okay, okay, relax. I was only joking," he said with a somber voice.

My shouting had attracted the attention of most stewards in the queue as well as Obermeyer's. He suddenly appeared next to me.

"What the fuck is wrong with you two?" he screamed.

"Nothing, Chef, we are fine, don't worry," Manfred said, still a little surprised about my outburst.

I was angry and couldn't care less about the chef or anyone else, for that matter. I was fed up with this ongoing teasing, joking or not joking.

"If you two sissies want to have fun then do it somewhere else but not in my kitchen, is that clear?" Obermeyer shouted. Several stewards whistled and others imitated Manfred's voice, shouting "Ooohhh" and "Aaahhh."

"Tell *him* that, not me," I said, angrily pointing at Manfred.

Obermeyer was momentarily taken aback by my serious face and determined expression. "Manfred, that's enough, stop it," he said.

"Hey, honeys, take it easy," Manfred said soberly.

"Oh, shut up," Obermeyer said, turned on his heels and walked back to the front of the queue.

The rest of the guys teased and shouted for a while but Manfred had learned his lesson for the day and remained quiet. When I reached the front of the queue, I picked up my dishes and packed them onto my tray. The tray was heavy and its weight with the platters pressed heavily onto my injured knee. By the time I reached my station I had sweat pearls on my forehead. Having served my main courses, I stood by my side station patting my knee. The blood had seeped through the bandage into my trousers, creating a small shiny patch.

"Are you okay?" Wolfgang asked, seeing me nursing my knee.

"I am fine, don't worry, just a scratch."

Wolfgang had witnessed the episode with Manfred in the kitchen but had remained quiet.

"What's wrong with him?" Doris asked as she joined us at the station.

I didn't like all this attention, which sooner or later would attract the attention of Bohne. "Guys, really, I am okay. Let's get on with the service. We are nearly finished anyway."

"I suggest you finish dinner and then go back to your cabin," Doris said.

"Trust me, I will do that," I said and forced a smile.

When all my guests had finished their main course, I cleared the plates and served coffee and desserts. By the time I finished, the patch on my trouser leg had grown to the size of a plate. I was one of the last to leave the restaurant and went back to my cabin without the customary stop outside the main deck.

When I took off my pants the full extent of the mess became plainly visible. The bandage was completely soaked in blood and my whole shin was smeared with blood. I took off the rest of my uniform and went to the bathroom where I took off the bandage and cleaned the wound. When I had finished I put on two large plasters and crawled exhausted into my bunk. To lie there was a relief and slowly the throbbing began to subside. A short while later I fell asleep.

The next day, after a good night's sleep, I felt much better and the bleeding had stopped. We spent the day at sea before reaching Willemstad/Curacao in the Dutch Antilles the next morning. In Willemstad, we visited the town with its typical Dutch buildings and the small factory from which the famous Curacao liqueur originated.

Over the next eight days, we visited many famous islands in the Caribbean like Aruba, Dutch Antilles; Bridgetown, Barbados; Santo Domingo in the Dominican Republic, Kingstown, Jamaica and many more before we eventually reached Nassau in the Bahamas. We visited some of the most beautiful beaches but whilst Franz, Angelika and the others had fun on the beach and in the water, I sat in the sand reading books. Slowly my knee got better and two days before reaching Nassau, the doctor removed the stitches from my wound. I was over the moon when he told me that in Nassau I would be allowed into the water again. I couldn't wait.

We were scheduled to stay in Nassau for two and a half days for a major crew and passenger change. Nassau was also a mail harbor where I hoped to receive some letters from Tatiana and my parents. We reached Nassau in the early hours of the morning on my forty-sixth day onboard. We all had lined up on deck to watch our arrival. My wound had healed nicely and I couldn't wait to hit the beach. Angelika told us that she would take us to the famous half-moon beach, which was a semi-private lagoon and apparently one of the most beautiful beaches in the Caribbean.

Nassau was much more to my liking, as compared to the Central and South American ports we had visited recently. The port was clean and designed to accommodate tourists on a large scale. Tall coconut trees surrounded most of the colonial-looking buildings painted in white. There was a large banner suspended at the main terminal reading "Welcome to MS *Europa*." At the pier, a local band played some sort of reggae music, using the parts of oil barrels as drums. Everyone was dressed in white shorts and colorful tropical short-sleeved shirts.

In the harbor, I noticed several large white yachts and one of the brand new Windstar computerized cruise liners with automated sails. The weather was picture-perfect—no clouds, deep blue sky and the water in the harbor was literally crystal clear.

Our first day was marked by a hectic breakfast, with most guests and part of the crew leaving the ship to fly back home. There would be no lunch and only a small dinner since the new guests were only expected to arrive the next day. This was like a holiday for us.

After breakfast, a full deep cleaning of the restaurant was scheduled. Once Wolfgang and I had brought our station back into tiptop shape, we went on to do our side duties as assigned by Bohne. I was given the task of cleaning the buffet counter. I had to empty out all cabinets underneath the counter, clean and polish the mirrors running along the buffet and clean all its surfaces. Equipped with a bottle of glass polish and stacks of newspaper, I cleaned these mirrors until they looked like new. Shortly after lunchtime, we had completed our cleaning jobs and the restaurant looked spic and span. For dinner, only some of us had been assigned to open our stations and luckily, I was not one of them. I went back to my cabin and had a long shower. At two, I waited at the gangway for Franz and Angelika. I looked like a typical tourist with my white shorts, colorful tropical short-sleeved shirt and cool-looking sunglasses. We went into Nassau where we did a quick sightseeing tour of the town and after some shopping, we returned to the ship in the late afternoon.

In the evening, Angelika took us to the Nassau Hotel where we had dinner in a restaurant near the beach. Half of the diners in the restaurant were colleagues from our ship. After dinner, we went to a bar near the beach. This was the first time for me to watch a sunset on a Caribbean beach. The bar, set on a wooden platform on the beach, had a straw roof and several wooden fans on its ceiling. The sounds of the ocean beyond the bar and the flapping of waves hitting the white sandy beach lined with coconut trees couldn't have been more perfect. Caribbean tunes playing from invisible speakers added to the idyllic atmosphere. To me it was like paradise.

"This is what our job is all about," Angelika said, sitting on a barstool next to me. She wore a colorful tank top and a surprisingly short skirt.

"Let's drink to all our friends back in cold Germany," Franz said and raised his glass.

"Yeah, and may they have lots of snow," I joked.

"Cheers!"

"Tomorrow we leave the ship early to go to the half-moon beach, where we'll stay 'til about three in the afternoon because we have no breakfast and lunch service."

"Let's drink to the beach," I said and we all raised our glasses.

"Cheers!" We all downed our drinks in one go and ordered another round.

"Who do we have here?" a familiar voice chirped. It was Manfred, Wolfgang, Doris and a whole group of others from the *Europa*. I turned around and rolled my eyes; Manfred was exactly what I did *not* need right now.

"Hi, guys," I said.

"Do you mind if we join you?" Manfred said, playing with Angelika's ponytail. I did mind but couldn't say so, of course.

"Of course not, darling," Angelika mocked.

The black bartender immediately was taken aback; he obviously felt a little uncomfortable dealing with Manfred who kept winking at him.

"I wish he would go away," I whispered to Angelika.

"Come on, he is not that bad," she defended him, at that moment Doris joined us. "God, it is beautiful here. Look at the sun—how low it hangs over the horizon."

She was right; the sun had dropped just above the horizon and looked like a red fiery ball that reflected on the surface of the ocean, causing the foamy waves flapping onto the beach to glow deep orange.

"Very nice indeed," Franz said to Doris.

"I could stay here forever," she added.

"Yeah, me too," I agreed.

Without asking, Doris sat down on the empty chair beside me. She looked gorgeous in her extremely short hot pants and a white shirt with only two buttons closed. She was extremely sexy.

"So, Andre, how have you settled in so far?" she said just as I inhaled some of her expensive-smelling perfume. I was still surprised that she had chosen the chair next to me even though there were plenty of other unoccupied chairs. I briefly wondered where Hartmut was but I didn't ask.

"Not too bad. I am getting the hang of things."

"It can be a little rough for newcomers but once things have settled you will enjoy it," she said. Her immense beauty struck me again. With her large deep blue eyes, delicate facial features and her voluminous blond hair, she ranked amongst the prettiest of the girls we had aboard. Her figure was nearly perfect—maybe a little on the small side—but her well-shaped body more than made up for it.

"Oh, that's quite okay. I am finding my way around now," I said, a little insecure.

"So I heard you have a girlfriend back in Germany. What is she doing?"

This question had taken me completely off guard. Why did she ask about Tatiana?

"Ahm, yes," I mumbled.

"Yes, what?" she laughed.

"Yes, I have a girlfriend and she is working in a hotel."

"Don't you miss her?" she asked.

"Ahm, yes, I do…a little." *Shit, why did she want know all that? I wondered. Can't we talk about something else?*

"I am sure she misses you too," she said with a smile. I wasn't so sure if Tatiana missed me, judging by only two letters she had written to me so far.

"Hey, look, the sun is setting. Shall we move down to the beach?" she asked.

I hardly believed my ears; she wanted to go down to the beach with *me*. I was ecstatic but couldn't show it of course; I remained as cool as possible. "Yeah, okay, let's go," I said quickly before she changed her mind.

We took our drinks and walked towards a row of sunbeds. The sand was soft and still warm. We settled in two sunbeds and placed our drinks on a small wooden table between our chairs. The sun was now sitting right on the edge of the horizon and the sky was glowing deep orange.

"This is really something," I whispered. "It's beautiful.

"Yeah, it's nice, isn't it," Doris said.

For a while we just lay there in our sunbeds staring out at sea. The waves kept on rolling in and washing up the beach, accompanied by a light breeze in the same monotonous rhythm. It got darker as the sun began disappearing behind the distant horizon.

I couldn't quite believe that I was lying on one of Bahamas' most beautiful beaches next to one of the ship's most beautiful girls. We could hear the laughter and chatter of the others back on the veranda but here at the beach we were surrounded only by the soothing sounds of the ocean. Doris shifted in her sunbed and suddenly her arm lay next to mine and her hand touched my arm. She just left it there and I didn't move. I froze. I was sure she could feel that her hand touched my arm but she didn't move it away.

My heart began beating fast and my brain went into overdrive—what was I supposed to do now? This was definitely an invitation, or was it not? She took a deep breath, was that a sign? Shit, I didn't know what to do. She was quiet and didn't move an inch. I had to do something—should I just stroke her arm a little? I still could excuse myself and make it look like it was unintended. This was obviously an invitation; otherwise she would have moved her hand away already. What about Hartmut? Would she tell him? *Shit,* I thought, *this was very awkward.*

Doris didn't move and neither did I. It was now or never; I might just be seconds away from a wonderful night. I was just about to make my move when we were rudely interrupted by an annoying voice.

"Hey, you two lovebirds enjoying the sunset?" It was Manfred.

Doris sat up in her sunbed and in doing so, she removed her arm. *Shit, shit, shit,* I thought, *why had he come now, why?*

"Hi there, Manfred, come and join us. It is beautiful here," she said. *Oh, no, she asked him to stay.*

"I don't want to disturb your peace here," he said, wiggling his body in his usual girlish manner. *You do disturb us, go away—right now!* I thought angrily.

"You don't disturb us, correct, Andre?" Doris said.

Of course he does. Ask him to get the fuck out of here and leave us alone, I wanted to scream this sentence right into his face.

"No, of course not," I answered without any enthusiasm.

Manfred sat down next to Doris and with that, the moment was gone; the atmosphere was completely destroyed. I had never really liked Manfred very much but at that moment, I hated him like I had never hated anyone before. My only hope now was that he would get bored quickly and disappear.

Of course he didn't. He was there to stay *for-bloody-ever.*

"It is wonderful here, isn't it, darling," he chirped at Doris.

"Yeah, I could stay here forever," Doris chuckled. "We have been here so many times but I can never get enough of the sight of these sunsets," she added.

"Yeah, and do you remember the last time we came here and we had the beach party just over there?" he said, pointing at an empty stretch on the beach to the left.

"Oh, yes, I remember. Hartmut pushed me into the water and I was really upset with him."

This conversation was going in the completely wrong direction. Manfred was slowly but surely eroding what little was left of the atmosphere. I heard more voices coming towards us; it was the rest of the gang, all of them equipped with their drinks. They settled all around us in sunbeds and in the sand. That was it—the moment was gone, probably forever. *Shit.*

We sat there on the beach, talked and had plenty of drinks. Despite the missed opportunity, if there ever was one, I had a good time. We stayed 'til very late and by the time we left it was pitch black and the bar had closed.

The next morning I got up late—at eight. There was no breakfast duty and it felt unreal. After working forty-six days nonstop, I woke up early as if on autopilot. We all met in the crew mess for breakfast and then we went out to spend the day at the half-moon beach.

I was in the best of moods and couldn't wait to jump into the sea. Equipped with towels and plenty of sun lotion, we took a taxi from the harbor to the beach, where we arrived half an hour later. We joked and laughed and at one point, we even sang in the car; we were in the very best of moods. This was life as I had never experienced it before. The half-moon beach belonged to a hotel and was basically a lagoon in the shape of a banana. It was a truly lovely sight—a long white sandy beach with many coconut trees and plenty of good-looking people.

We chose a spot underneath a coconut tree and dropped our towels. To make a point after three weeks sitting on Caribbean beaches without being able to go into the water, I dumped all my stuff and ripped the clothes off my body. Then I ran through the hot white sun towards the incoming waves. I reached the water and dashed through it like a mad dog. "Yippee," I screamed. The water was pleasantly warm and I took large jumps, ready to dive into the next wave and...suddenly I screamed. I screamed out loud.

An excruciating stinging pain shot up my right leg, traveling at lightning speed through my spine, and I kept on screaming. My senses told me that some unseen creature had dug its fangs into my foot and instinctively I panicked. I had no clue what had just happened but the pain in my foot was tremendous. I came to a standstill and began hopping on my left foot back towards the beach where I fell into the sand holding my pulsating right foot. I looked at my toes and at first I could see nothing wrong. I sensed the pain in the big toe of my right foot but still I couldn't see that there was anything wrong. Franz, Angelika and some others came running toward me and kneeled down.

"What's wrong?" Angelika asked.

"I don't know. I think something bit me in the foot," I said with a pain-ridden face.

"Let me take a look—where is it?"

"I think it's the toe."

Angelika lifted my foot and took a close look at it. "Oh, shit," she suddenly said with a frown which made my heart jump.

"What is it?" I asked.

"Sea urchin," she answered. "I think you stepped on a sea urchin."

"A sea urchin - and?"

"Here, you see—some of the spikes are still in there," she pointed at my toe but I couldn't see a thing.

Franz bent down, looking at my toe. "Yep, I can see some spikes there. That was definitely a sea urchin."

"Can you pull them out?" I asked.

"I don't know, let me try."

"No, don't," Angelika urged. "There are different types of sea urchins; some of them are poisonous. You better get back to the ship and let the doctor take a look at this."

When I heard the word *poisonous,* I looked at her in horror—this simply couldn't be true. I checked if I felt dizzy or nauseated but I seemed to be fine so far. I felt the stinging pain now clearly pulsating in my right toe.

"Can you not pull them out?" I asked again.

"No, you have to go back to the ship. Even if it is not poisonous you still have to have it looked at."

"Come on, let's go. I come with you back to the ship," Franz said.

"No, don't worry, I can go by myself," I said. I didn't really want to crawl back to the ship and attract lots of attention again as I had in Cartagena.

I tried to get up but the moment I put weight onto my right foot a sharp stinging pain shot through my foot and I nearly collapsed.

"That's it—I bring you back to the ship," Franz said and helped me up. Together we hobbled to the taxi stand.

The doctor in the ship's hospital greeted me with a simple, "It's you again. What happened this time?"

He checked my foot and confirmed that I had stepped in a sea urchin but luckily not the poisonous one. I had nine spikes in my large toe and the bad news was that the top of the spikes began to dissolve the moment they entered the flesh and the doctor explained that he had to cut around them to clean the wound. He gave me four shots of anesthetics that left half of my foot without any feeling whatsoever. It was a messy affair with lots of blood on the operating table, but it looked worse than it was. In the end he wrapped half of my foot in a thick white bandage and asked me to keep the foot still until the next day. That was easier said than done since I had to work that night.

I was just about to leave the hospital when the doctor called me back.

"One last thing—you know that you cannot go in the water for at least three weeks," he said.

"Three weeks??" I cried in disbelief. We were just about to embark on another tour of the entire Caribbean and I was not allowed into the water—again! This trip was turning into a disaster.

"Yes, three weeks. You come back every week and we see how it is healing. If things go well then I might let you go back a few days earlier."

"That's nice of you, thank you very much," I said with a trace of sarcasm in my voice.

I went to my cabin and into my bunk until it was time to get ready for work. The doctor's words kept on echoing in my mind—*You cannot go into the water for at least three weeks.* We were scheduled to visit some of the world's most famous beaches and I was not allowed into the water—AGAIN.

I took a shower, which was not that easy with my right leg hanging out of the shower cabin. When I finished, the whole bathroom floor was wet and messy. I got dressed and then tried to put on my shoe, which was virtually impossible with the thick bandage around my foot. I took some of the bandage off and tried again but it was still too thick. I took off a little more but it still didn't work; my foot was simply too thick to fit into the shoe.

I had no choice. There was no way that I could call in sick; I had to get my bloody foot into that shoe. The only way to do that was to take the entire bandage off and stick one or two plasters on my toe. Finally, I forced my foot into the shoe. There was just a little stinging pain; otherwise, it was fine, but I literally hobbled to the restaurant rather than walked.

This was the first night of my fourth cruise with half of the crew being new. We had our pre-cruise briefing and to my delight, Franz and I would share a station with Angelika as our wine waitress. I doubted very much that this station arrangement had happened accidentally nor did I believe for one minute that Bohne had assigned us together because he thought we would work well together. Someone must have helped a little but I couldn't quite make out who.

There were plenty of new faces in the pre-cruise briefing and amongst them were several girls who were quite pretty. Not all of them were new; most had returned from a three-month holiday. Angelika introduced me to one of her very close friends, another wine stewardess by the name of Helga. Helga was a pretty girl with blue eyes, shoulder length brown hair and a very attractive figure. She had the cutest Bavarian accent when she spoke.

Bohne conducted his briefing in the usual weird manner, with his eyes darting nervously from left to right. To my surprise, the normally elusive executive chef Winterhalter and his number two Obermeyer attended the briefing. Bohne finished with his briefing and then gave the floor to Winterhalter.

"We have not finished yet!" Bohne cried as he detected some movement in the back of the assembled crowd. "Chef wants to say something."

Chef Winterhalter glanced at Bohne and shook his head slightly; it was obvious that they were not the best of friends. He looked at each of us and then started talking in his usual calm and collected manner.

"Ladies and gentlemen, you may or may not know that at the moment we are preparing for the Chaine des Rotisseurs certification. If we get this certification then we will have the first restaurant onboard a cruise liner to be appointed a member of the Chaine des Rotisseurs."

There was murmuring throughout the ranks with some stewards smiling and others shaking their heads. I smiled when I heard "Chaine des Rotisseurs" because I knew about the society from my days in Freiburg. To become a member wasn't really that difficult and what I didn't like was that membership was partly based on financial considerations rather than profesional merits. I thought the chef was just making a bit of a show and possibly trying to elevate himself a bit. Of course if we really were the first restaurant on a ship to become a member, then from the marketing angle it was a good move, one which would certainly soon be followed by others.

"As part of the preparation I have planned to improve and upgrade the quality of our menus over the coming weeks," Winterhalter continued. He paused and looked at our faces.

The way he spoke always annoyed me. I don't know why but it annoyed me. Not that I didn't like him; on the contrary, I liked Winterhalter as a person very much and of course he was the mastermind behind our menus and buffets and he probably was a good chef too, but I just didn't like the way he talked. It was purely a personal thing. He stopped looking around and reckoned that his words had impressed us enough for him to continue.

"Our current menus are good but we have to fine-tune them a little further. We do not want to turn this restaurant into a fine dining room but we have to make improvements in order to fulfill the expectations of the Chaine. Now, the first of these improvements will be the addition of a daily flambé to our dinner menu, prepared at the table."

The moment he finished his sentence there were instant protests from all the assembled stewards. There were shouts of "Oh, no!" and "Not possible!" and "Are they crazy?"

I couldn't believe what I had just heard; adding a flambé to our dinner menu would be quite a challenge considering our tight timetables for the two seatings. Obermeyer stepped in front of Winterhalter. "QUIET! Be quiet, for God's sake," he screamed. The protests subsided into a murmuring. Obermeyer stepped back and nodded to Winterhalter.

"Let me finish. First, there will be two types of flambé, one sweet and one savory. We will give you the entire mise en place you need to make it as quickly as possible. We know that time is of essence and therefore Obermeyer and I have come up with some ideas to speed it up. We know that you can't do a full flambé from scratch on the table; you don't have time for that. For all the sweet flambés, we are thinking of having a general base of caramelized butter ready in the kitchen which we give you in a bowl together with the already-prepared ingredients for the flambé. All you have to do is put the ingredients in the pan and flame it up. We are still working on the details.

As for the savory ones, we will have meat, sauces and everything else ready to the extent that all you basically need to do is heat up the meat and sauce, lace with alcohol, flame it up and the dish is ready,"

"Chef, we don't have enough burners and flambé pans," one of the stewards shouted from the back of the crowd.

"You don't need to worry about the equipment. Mr. Bohne has ordered more than enough additional burners and pans and I understand they should arrive any time," he said with a smile. There was excited whispering and murmuring amongst the other stewards.

"What do we do if five guests order flambé?" another steward asked.

Chef Winterhalter looked at him puzzled. "That's even better for you. There is only one daily flambé on the menu and if five guests order them, then it's easy. You just cook five...why do you ask?"

I had to agree with the chef—that *was* a stupid question. The more you had the better for you. It was annoying if you had twenty different main courses and only one flambé.

From what I could see, Winterhalter and Bohne, although not the best of friends normally, on this occasion they had actually worked together and removed any obstacles before talking to us. This was a first - at least since I was onboard. From what I could see there was no way to protest; the decision was made—we would start cooking flambé at the table. I wondered how that would end.

The questions finally subsided and the meeting ended. We were dismissed.

Bohne had assigned me to a center station where I felt much more comfortable than on the starboard side. The other advantage of this station was that it was a little further away from Manfred, who had really become annoying lately. Franz and I went and inspected our new station; its mise en place looked fine and complete.

"Fresh of the press, here are the new menus," Franz said and handed me a menu. I opened it and there it was—the infamous "Flambé of the Day."

"He really did it," I said. "He really added a flambé." I looked at the menu in disbelief.

"He could have at least waited until two or three days into the cruise, which would have at least given us time to get to know our guests first," he said.

"He could have chosen a quiet cruise and not a fully booked one."

"Yeah, the chef's revenge for all we did to them," Franz said and laughed.

"Well, let's see how many of my new guests will order flambé and hate me afterwards because it took a long time and so on."

"Looks like and interesting cruise. By the way, how is your toe?"

I had not thought of my injury at all with all the excitement of a new cruise, the newcomers and the flambé. "It's much better than I thought; I can't feel a thing and the shoes keep everything nice and tight. The only problem is that I am not allowed into the water for the next three weeks."

"Three weeks—are you sure?" Franz asked.

"Yes, three weeks."

Suddenly Franz began to laugh. He laughed and couldn't stop.

"What's so funny?" I wanted to know.

"Nothing, it's just…"

"What…?"

"First the gallows and then this. It's just too funny…" He kept on laughing.

"Yeah, thanks, Franz, but I don't think it's funny. We are six weeks in the Caribbean and I am not allowed to go to the beach. That's not funny."

"But you *can* go to the beach," he said.

"Yes, I know, but I can't go into the wa…"

Franz burst out laughing until he finally had tears in his eyes. "I am so sorry," he said. "I really didn't mean it, it's just…"

"Yeah, don't worry, as long as you are having fun—in the sun," I said with a smile.

"At least you have no pain, that is at least something."

I looked at him, trying to see if there was something sarcastic to his comment. "Yes, at least I have no pain," I said, carefully watching his face.

What I didn't know at that moment was that my foot was still well protected by the four injections of anesthetics which would sooner or later wear off. The anesthetics did wear off at the beginning of the second seating and it was only then that the full extent of the operation dawned on me. I had just left the pass and was standing on the escalator when all of a sudden an excruciating pain shot up my leg, through my spine and into my brain with the force of a bolt of lighting. This happened so fast and the pain was so severe that I nearly threw my tray away. The stinging pain had been so severe and so sudden that I had sweat pearls all over my forehead. As it turned out, it was the first of many such bolts hitting me in shorter and shorter intervals until eventually, it happened every time I stepped on my foot. By that time I had nearly finished and went straight back to my cabin.

Chapter 11

The passengers of my fourth cruise was an interesting mix of people ranging from the "once-in-a-lifetime-cruise" passengers who had saved all their lives for the trip and the very frequent return passengers who knew the ship, my colleagues and the captain better than I ever would. The good news was that they were not overly demanding and what was even better — none of them seemed to like flambé.

We left Nassau late that night and after one long and sunny day at sea we reached Miami on Florida's east coast. I remember Miami mainly because on the pier where we docked was also the famous liner SS *Norway,* one of the last large ocean liners at the time. It was a leftover from the glorious times of the transatlantic steam ships. The SS *Norway* was about double the size of the MS *Europa* but with certain elegance. I very much liked her elegance and aesthetic lines that to me, reflected the grandeur of the old steamship era. To me she was far more elegant than the famous QE2, which at one time had been her most severe competitor. Other than that, I don't remember much about Miami except the many surf and souvenir shops along the beach road.

From Miami we cruised south to the southernmost point of the United States, Key West in Florida. We did not have much time in Key West and so we just went to see the spot that is claimed as the southernmost point in the United States. We took the customary pictures, bought some postcards and went back to the ship.

We left Key West the same evening and cruised for a day and a half in a northwesterly direction toward New Orleans, where we arrived in the early morning. I didn't see anything in New Orleans either because the first officer had me assigned to a lifeboat drill in the morning and Bohne had me doing afternoon tea on deck in the afternoon. I wondered if the two had worked together on that. I saw the roofs of the city from the signal deck and took two or three lackluster pictures and that was it.

My toe had begun to recover and although the pain had gone, it was still bleeding heavily. At midnight, we left New Orleans and the United States to cross the Gulf of Mexico for one day toward Mexico. The weather was perfect and we spent every available minute on deck sunbathing. We reached the sunny port of Playa del Carmen in Mexico after one day at sea in the Gulf of Mexico. Playa del Carmen was a small town and still relatively quiet and idyllic.

From Playa del Carmen it was only a half-day cruise to the island of Cozumel and by lunchtime, we dropped anchor off the island's east coast. We spent the half-day in Cozumel on the signal deck doing what we did best up there—sunbathing. At five o'clock, we lifted anchor and steamed south toward San Andres in Colombia. It took us one and a half days to reach the collection of small islands off the coast of Colombia. We went ashore in the afternoon and were greeted by native islanders dressed in similar colorful dresses as we had seen already in San Blas. We took our pictures, bought some small souvenirs, and went back onboard in the late afternoon. In the evening we left San Andres to spend the next two days at sea, which were once again marked by lots of sunbathing.

So far I had been lucky with my guests—none of them had showed any interest whatsoever in Chef Winterhalter's flambé of the day. Franz had not been that lucky and had already served several of the time-consuming dishes prepared at the table. It showed quite clearly that our system of having two seatings was not very "flambé-friendly" and if it hadn't been for my constant help, especially in the first seating, Franz would have never finished in time.

Other stewards had not been as lucky and they really struggled to complete their service in time. Despite the many shortcuts the chef had provided, the service of only one flambé took over fifteen minutes. The preparation of the burner, pan and ingredients had to be done together and whilst the steward was doing this, he was not able to serve his regular main courses. Most stewards served their main course first and then the flambé, which left guests still eating their flambé when all the others had already completed their meals. This caused a number of complaints.

Some stewards tried to serve the flambé first, which ended in a disaster because by the time the steward reached the main-course queue he was at its very end. This caused considerable friction between the stewards and the chefs which on several occasions turned quite ugly. By the time guests got their main course, they were itchy and upset from the long waiting time. The guests with the flambé had long since finished and were upset because they had to wait for all the others.

415

During what would later become the infamous "flambé cruise," the kitchen was a war zone. Those stewards who had managed to convince their guests not to order the flambé had a good laugh witnessing the screaming and shouting in the kitchen between the seriously pissed-off flambé stewards and a very angry Obermeyer.

By the time we reached Bridgetown in Barbados the flambé experiment was declared a failure and taken off the menu for good. The last evening of the flambé cruise, we had our farewell dinner, which went smoothly for all of us because the chef had wisely opted for a menu without flambé. The tip that evening was amongst the best I had so far, yielding more than three thousand marks in total. Even Franz, who had to serve a damn flambé nearly every night, got away with mostly over-tax payers.

We would spend two days in Bridgetown deep cleaning the ship, exchanging passengers and visiting the beaches of Barbados. Because I was still not allowed to go into the water, I sat on my towel in the sun watching the others jealously.

In the afternoon of our first day in Barbados, we had our pre-cruise briefing and we all were surprised to see Winterhalter and Obermeyer attending again. This spelled bad news. As it turned out, Winterhalter was still determined to "upgrade" our service and presented us with his next vicious plan.

"We have decided to re-think the service of flambé at the table and postponed it until further notice," he began. This was greeted with cheers and clapping from us stewards. This came as no surprise since the continuation of this plan would have certainly ended in mutiny on our side.

"QUIET," Obermeyer barked at us.

Winterhalter glanced at each of us and then continued. "If you think that we will go back to the old style of plated service, you are wrong. We may have postponed the flambé but this doesn't mean that this will stop us from improving and enhancing the service we offer our guests," he announced.

We all eyed him suspiciously in expectation of what crazy plan he had cooked up now. He stood there and waited until we had quieted down.

"We will go for the Chaine des Rotisseurs membership no matter what," he said and again there were murmurs of obvious disagreement amongst our ranks. "We will start with the service of fish. Up to now we have filleted the fish in the kitchen. In the future, I want you to do that at the table."

I glanced at Bohne, who was standing behind Winterhalter and Obermeyer with a sarcastic grin. He definitely enjoyed this, the old sod. There was no murmuring or whispering at first but then the first objections were voiced out.

"This is no different from the flambé," one steward protested.

Winterhalter's face went dark. "Of course it is different. You have to serve the fish from a platter on the table anyway and it doesn't make a difference if you serve the entire fish or take off only the fillets," he argued.

"And how are we supposed to do that without side tables?" The steward had a point; we didn't have any side tables. Several stewards mumbled "Exactly" and "He is right" in agreement.

"You don't need a side table. Do you want me to show you how to do that with one hand?" Winterhalter challenged the steward. Now there was laughter echoing through the crowd.

"We can't fillet fish with one hand—that is not possible," the steward insisted.

I didn't really agree with him since I had done this many times in Talasee before. It wasn't easy and it only worked when the fillets came off the bones easily. Sure, it wasn't the most sophisticated way of filleting a fish but with a bit of focus it was actually possible.

"Do you want me to show how it's done, you sissy?" Winterhalter shouted at him.

"It will be messy and time consuming," the steward insisted.

"Then you have to move your lazy steward's ass and work a bit faster, you sissy." Everyone roared with laughter. The steward remained quiet.

"I have discussed this with Mr. Bohne and he agrees that we will give it a try." Nobody said anything, knowing that a false remark about Bohne would have had consequences. I looked at Bohne, whose eyes darted from steward to steward trying to detect a smile or other reaction. There was none. I was sure that Bohne had just said yes when Winterhalter presented him with his latest idea. I was sure he wouldn't have fought for us to make things easier. He was simply a hopeless cause.

"Are there any more questions, gentlemen?" Winterhalter asked.

"I have a question, my dear chef."

Everyone laughed at the sudden girlish-sounding voice; it was Manfred.

"What do you want to know, sissy?" Winterhalter asked with a smile.

"Mm, he calls me sissy, I think he likes me," Manfred said and wiggled his lower body.

"Don't get your hopes up, you…"

"I still think you like me, Chefy," Manfred chirped and everyone broke into laughter.

An angry looking Obermeyer stepped forward. "Manfred! Do you have a question or not? If not, shut the fuck up," he shouted.

"Okay, okay, don't get violent at me, Herr Obermeyer. You scare me," he said with a mock sour face.

We nearly cracked up listening to this comical exchange.

"Chef, do we have to fillet every single fish or do you allow us to ask the guest first if he wants us to do this to the poor fish?" The way Manfred had pronounced the "poor fish" caused more laughter.

Winterhalter rolled his eyes and answered. "Yes, you may ask your guest if he wants you to fillet the *poor fish*," he said, imitating Manfred.

"That's really nice of you, Chefy," he chirped. "No more questions, Your Honor."

"Okay, gentlemen, that's all I have to say," Winterhalter said and he and Obermeyer walked away.

Bohne stepped forward looking nervous. "You heard the chef, and now get back to work. The briefing is finished."

We all dispersed and Franz and I went back to our service station.

"Now that was an interesting briefing," I said to Franz.

"Filleting fish with one hand—now that will be even more interesting," he said.

"Yup, Winterhalter definitely makes sure we don't get bored around here." We laughed.

On the evening of the first day in Bridgetown, our old passengers had departed and the new ones had not yet arrived. We had a Caribbean costume party on deck for all the crew. For the party we decorated the main deck in colorful balloons and plenty of leaves from coconut trees. There were rows of foldable tables and benches and the chefs had set up an extensive buffet. Because we had no breakfast to serve the next morning, we didn't have to worry about the time we finished—and we didn't. The official Caribbean costume party ended at around one in the morning and we all split up in smaller groups and continued partying in our cabins.

That night was a milestone for my standing amongst my colleagues because for some reason I ended up in one of the party cabins with one of the ship's nurses. Her name was Angie and she had only joined the ship in Nassau. Angie was in her early twenties, blond and incredibly sexy. This was her first cruise and as it turned out, she was a party animal. Angie and I left the party cabin together sometime early in the morning and retired to another cabin which I believe was hers. I don't remember at all what happened that night or if anything happened at all, but the fact that we left together, arm in arm, was the talk of the ship the next day. It was a milestone for me because I had proven unknowingly once and for all that I was not gay.

The next day was for me marked by a terrible hangover and although Angie and I became good friends after that night, that was as far as it went. My love for Tatiana was too strong to pursue this escapade further. Unknown to me at the time was that my little escapade had sent out another message to the rest of the female crewmembers and that was I was available!

The next day I received two letters from my parents, one letter from Viola and three letters from Tatiana. My parents informed me that they would try to visit me in Bremerhaven in two weeks. I was very happy about that because they would be my first visitors. There were some interesting news from Tatiana—she had applied for a job in London and apparently, they had accepted her. She didn't tell me if she would actually go but I was sure I would find out. She had also repeatedly assured me that she loved me. That made me feel really good and—bad. As happy as I was hearing those loving words and receiving those letters from Tatiana, for some obvious reasons, I felt bad. I promised myself never to do that again, which was an honest and heartfelt promise at the time. Because I felt so bad, I decided not to go on deck after dinner but to write her a long letter that night.

The next day our new guests arrived. I celebrated my sixty-first day onboard and my sixty-first day working without a day off. My need to sleep had shrunk to the bare minimum and even on days like in

Barbados where we could sleep a little longer, I woke up early thanks to my perfectly tuned-in body clock. I spent the afternoon walking around Bridgetown by myself. I couldn't face another day on the beach watching the others play in the water whilst I had to bake in the sun, unable to go for a swim in the Caribbean.

We departed Bridgetown the same evening shortly before midnight. The timing was perfect for us and as usual, we gathered after dinner on the main deck, watching our departure. It was a beautiful tropical summer night with a cloudless night sky and hundreds of sparkling stars. Although it was quite warm, as soon as the captain turned the ship towards the open sea, a light refreshing breeze provided relief from the heat. With my jacket off and sleeves rolled up, I sipped on my Beck's beer and chatted happily with our newfound friend Helga. We got on very well, which was very much due to her excellent sense of humor. I liked Helga from the first moment we met. Helga and Angelika were best friends and I felt that we would get on really well.

I was excited about this next part of the cruise because it would take us all the way back to Europe, my first Atlantic crossing. There was already lots of talk about the upcoming days at sea. The crossing itself would take a little over five days and according to our colleagues, Atlantic crossings were never without incidents. They talked about passengers getting bored because day in day out they would see nothing but ocean around us and, especially for some newcomers, this could be a scary experience. They called it the "Atlantic Syndrome" which, to be honest, meant nothing to me. According to them, there had been cases where members of the crew disappeared, allegedly gone overboard. Then there was talk about the weather; because we would leave North America from Canada, we would be crossing a part of the North Atlantic, which at this time of the year saw heavy seas and sometimes storms.

All this talk didn't really bother me. At the end of the day we were on a cruise liner and with all our modern navigation equipment, I was sure that the captain would not purposely head into a storm with over seven hundred human beings onboard. No, I was not afraid. Maybe a little nervous, but definitely not afraid.

Once we had crossed the Atlantic we would visit Ponta Delgada on the Azores and then, via Spain and France, to Bremerhaven in Germany. I couldn't wait.

It was still too early to judge my guests on this cruise since I had only served them one dinner so far. Overall, they seemed fine but they were all individuals and hadn't known each other before coming onboard, which was fine in the early days of the cruise but could be a problem during the long and boring days at sea. According to Angelika, that was when they began to notice each other's whims and fancies. I didn't fully understand what she meant and decided that there was only one way to find out and that was to cross that bridge once we got to it.

As we passed the harbor entrance of Bridgetown, a light vibration announced the increase in speed and with it the wind picked up. Slowly the lights of Bridgetown faded into the darkness of the night until they were just some brightly shimmering dots in the distance. At one in the morning, only Helga and I were left on the main deck. We had settled in some of the sunbeds, she with a glass of wine and I with my sixth bottle of Beck's. We just sat there and talked. The main deck was still brightly lit but other than that, all was dark.

The ship was running now at full speed and we hardly noticed the loud howling of some invisible machinery and frequent gusts of wind whistling all around us. We talked and talked and completely lost track of time. At one point during our long conversation, I began to wonder if Helga would invite me back to her cabin once we decided to leave. We got up at around three in the morning and as we were on our way back to our cabins, I waited for her to say the magic words. The magic words never came. Instead, she gave me a hug and kiss, telling me how nice this evening had been. I assured her that I felt the same although, deep down, I was of course disappointed. I brought her to her cabin and with a last glimmer of hope, I said goodnight to her. I stood there saying goodnight for the fifth time, still hoping for the magic words but they never came.

The next morning we were far out at sea with no land in sight. It was a glorious day with lots of sun and not a single cloud. To my delight and my friends' disappointment, there would be no more beaches until we reached the Azores and by that time, I would be able again to join them. The day at sea was uneventful except for the fact that my guests ordered plenty of fish.

It was almost as if the two seatings had agreed that on this cruise they would indulge themselves in nothing but fresh fish. To make things worse, Winterhalter and Obermeyer had bought plenty of these slimy creatures of all shapes and sizes in Barbados. It was almost as if my guests together with the chefs had agreed to make my life as miserable as possible with all that fish. I took the orders in good faith and whenever I asked my guests if I should fillet the fish, they answered with yes. I then stood at the table and, in one hand holding the plate, with the other I attacked the fish, sometimes gently, sometimes virtually ripping the fillets of the bones. With the added pressure of having to work within a certain timeframe, the result of my filleting was not always pretty. I hated the chef for that.

The only good thing was that I was not alone in my plight. Whilst Franz was lucky with most his guests ordering meat, many of my colleagues went through the same trauma as I—having to fillet fish with one hand. This in turn caused me to join a group of unhappy stewards voicing our frustration with the fish filleting procedure in the kitchen whenever we got the chance to do so. The chef would have none of this and the torture continued. Some of my colleagues simply stopped asking their guests, which was something I couldn't do. As long as the official instruction was to fillet the fish at the table, I would continue to do so. The only time I took shortcuts was of course when more than five guests ordered the fish and it was impossible for me to do them all. Angelika was of course a great help and did what she could to assist.

The rest of the day at sea, we spent nurturing our suntans by exposing our skins as much as possible and as long as possible to the sun. By now I had an incredible suntan, which caused several of my guests to ask me where I was from. Whenever I told them that I hailed from the south of Germany, they would acknowledge that and then ask me, "But where are you from originally?'

I had heard this question many times because I never really looked typically German; I had the height but not the blond hair and no blue eyes. I would then insist that I really *was* born and bred in Southern Germany, which my guests would acknowledge but in many cases, they never truly believed that I was. It has to be said here again that the average age of our passengers was probably around sixty-five to seventy, which meant that they had lived through times when the stereotypical German was supposed to be tall, blond with deep blue eyes. I knew this, of course, and always made the additional joke, telling them that my ancestors actually descended from a Roman centurion by the name of Leffo who had been given a piece of conquered land on which he founded a small settlement that eventually became my hometown of Loeffingen in the Black Forest. This was the reason, I told them, that I sported slightly darker features. Judging by their reaction, some guests actually believed me.

Early the next morning we arrived in the Bermudas, where we would spend most of the day in Hamilton and depart at eight for Baltimore. There had been much talk about the Bermudas because of the famous Bermuda Triangle—a region of the Atlantic Ocean between Bermuda; Miami, Florida; and San Juan, Puerto Rico—where disappearances of ships and planes had defied explanation and continue to do so. Many of the senior stewards and of course the chefs had tried their best to put the fear of God into us while crossing this region. They told stories of lost crew members who apparently disappeared overnight and were never seen again.

I didn't believe any of these stories but then again, I had heard a lot about this area. It was one thing to watch a documentary about this mysterious region on television while sitting in a comfortable armchair. It was quite another to actually be there, standing on deck of an ocean liner plowing through the ocean with gusts of wind blowing in one's face. The evening before reaching Hamilton, I stood at the stern of the *Europa* watching our white frothy tail of churned up ocean fading into the night and I have to admit—at that moment I actually was a little nervous.

There was much talk about the Bermuda Triangle amongst our guests and many of them asked me if I had been through the area before, which of course I hadn't, and when they then asked me if I was afraid, I laughed and said no. My guests of that cruise were divided into believers and non-believers and this made for some interesting discussions at the table, with most of the non-believers frequently ridiculing the believers. We had a lecturer onboard who took a far more realistic view. He actually gave a lecture on the Bermuda Triangle the afternoon before we reached Hamilton. I was assigned to the afternoon tea and, standing behind the buffet on the lido deck under blue sky and sunshine, I listed to his theory on the Bermuda Triangle. Unfortunately, guests asking for more cakes and pastries frequently interrupted me but I still got most of his lecture. One guest had just asked him a question about missing ships in the Bermuda Triangle.

"There have been many theories about missing ships. A significant factor with regard to missing vessels in the Bermuda Triangle is a strong ocean current called the Gulf Stream. It is extremely swift and turbulent and can quickly erase evidence of a disaster. The weather also plays its role. Prior to the development of telegraph, radio and radar, sailors did not know a storm or hurricane was nearby until it appeared on the horizon," he said.

"But ships have also gone missing after the invention of modern navigation equipment," the guest insisted.

"That is correct, and there is an explanation for this too. Sudden local thunderstorms and water spouts can sometimes spell instant disaster for mariners and air crews. Finally, the topography of the ocean floor in this area varies from extensive shoals around the islands to some of the deepest marine trenches in the world. With the interaction of the strong currents over the many reefs, the topography of the ocean bottom is in a state of flux and the development of new navigational hazards can sometimes be swift," he explained.

The group of guests from which the question originated struck me as believers and they were obviously not happy with the lecturer's theories. I watched with interest as the group whispered and it was obvious that they were preparing another challenging question for the lecturer.

"Can I have a strawberry cake, please?" someone suddenly startled me. It was an elderly woman with a big smile and a plate already occupied by two other cakes. I picked up a piece of strawberry cake and placed it on the already crammed plate.

"Thank you so much, young man," she said and walked off. I had to smile.

I returned my attention to the group of believers who already had another question ready.

"What do you have to say about the fact that compasses often go crazy?" one of the believers asked.

"Well, gentlemen, they don't actually go crazy, but it has been inaccurately claimed that the Bermuda Triangle is one of the only two places on earth at which a magnetic compass points towards true north. Normally a compass will point toward magnetic north. The difference between the two is known as compass variation. The amount of variation changes by as much as 60 degrees at various locations around the world. If this compass variation or error is not compensated for, navigators can find themselves far off course and in deep trouble," the lecturer said.

It was obvious that the group of believers didn't fully believe him and was ready to challenge him further. I didn't witness the rest of the interesting lecture because my shift was finished and I still had a chance to catch some sleep in the sun. The lecture was interesting but it hadn't really made me feel much better about the fact that we would still be cruising around the Bermuda Triangle for a few more days. To me it seemed that there were still plenty of open questions about the happenings in this mysterious region. Despite all this, we traversed the Bermuda Triangle safely and reached Baltimore unscathed. What's more, the weather had been stunning with calm seas and a fresh cooling breeze and endless sunshine.

During our short time in Baltimore, I was selected once again to participate in a lifeboat drill in the morning and Bohne had kindly chosen me for afternoon tea service on deck. Sometimes I had the feeling that he really did this on purpose. After another day sailing through glorious weather, we reached New York the following morning. We all got up early to watch as we slowly cruised up the Hudson River toward New York. We were scheduled to stay for only one night before departing on our five-day Atlantic crossing.

When the Statue of Liberty came into view in the distance, it a felt all a little unreal. New York had always been a special place because for us it was the epiphany of a big city, if not *the* biggest city of all. Names like the Empire State Building, Manhattan and the Statue of Liberty were synonymous with America and the land of unlimited possibilities. How many times had I seen these icons of America on TV? How many times had I used these names, never thinking that I would actually see them? It was an exhilarating and at the same time emotional feeling.

I took tons of photos of the Statue of Liberty and if I didn't take photos, I just stood there marveling at the famous structure. We docked on one of the ocean piers where once the famous transatlantic ocean liners docked. From the moment of our arrival to the moment we departed, time was money—literally. Unfortunately for me, all my guests came for breakfast and because they had booked tours only for the afternoon, they took it very easy, much to my dismay. After breakfast, I had just enough time to leave the ship and walk around a little on the pier where I took plenty of pictures of one lonely parked NYPD police car.

After lunch Franz, Angelika, Helga and I immediately headed out to the city. First, we took one of the famous yellow cabs to the Rockefeller Center where we took plenty of pictures, and then we headed to the Empire State Building where we went all the way to the top. The view from up there was incredible. The weather was warm but up there a strong wind blew. We saw all of Manhattan, the Hudson River and the Statue of Liberty in the distance. There were hundreds of skyscrapers all around us, to me an absolutely incredible view.

After the Empire State Building, we had just enough time left to take a quick snack in one of America's finest and most famous fastfood restaurants—Kentucky Fried Chicken, another first for me. After having gulped down a portion of chicken nuggets with French fries, I stole the paper tray mat and took some pictures of us in the restaurant. We headed back to the ship in the late afternoon after three hours of very hectic sightseeing. We left New York at eight in the evening, cruising along the incredible skyline of Manhattan. Thousands of brightly lit skyscrapers dominated by the two towering buildings of the World Trade Center left me in awe, an experience I would never forget. I would come back to New York several times on later cruises but I never forgot that first time, even though we had spent less than four hours ashore.

We had started our Atlantic crossing and what came next were five long days at sea. That evening was the first time since joining the ship that we had a storm warning pinned to our notice board! At that stage, it was a warning only and no storm preparations had to be made but for me, it was enough to put the fear of God into me. I didn't know what to expect. Angelika told us that storm preparations included emptying our side stations, plate warmers and any other unsecured items. I got a little scared. The *Europa* had a gross tonnage of nearly 39,000 tons and it was difficult for me to imagine that anything could shake this giant to a point that plates would be thrown out of our warmers or cabinets. Nothing happened that night.

The second seating finished as it had started - relatively quiet. The ship didn't move any differently than usual and my worst fears thankfully never came true. Everything was as usual, including the fact that all my guests ordered fish. It was clear that the filleting of fish would continue for some time to come. On the other hand, after over a week of filleting *several fish a day* at the table, I really got the hang of it. My new strategy now was to recommend fish whenever I could in the hope that one day soon they would get tired of the slimy little creatures.

By the time I got up the next day we were already far out at sea, and the moment I got up, I felt the the ship rolling heavily. I stepped out on deck and glanced out at the open ocean and I could immediately see the difference. The sea had become rougher, the waves were higher and had white foamy crests on their peaks caused by strong windy gusts. There was no land in sight, only ocean as far as the eye could see. It was a truly majestic sight, completely different from the relatively calm seas of the Caribbean.

Since Anchorage, we had always cruised along the East and West Coast of Central and North America, where the weather conditions were calmer and more protected. Out in the open ocean and with the change in weather conditions, the movement of the ship had increased substantially. We were cruising through long oncoming swells separated by deep watery valleys. These long-drawn swells heaved our 39,000-ton ship up and down at steep angles as if it were a sheet of paper.

To walk around the restaurant in such conditions with a heavy and fully loaded tray took me a while to get used to. One moment I was walking upwards and the next moment, I was walking down and so it went day and night. It was only now that I really felt like I was on a ship. On the fourth day of our Atlantic crossing, the sea conditions grew worse with larger swells, and the ship's bow frequently hit one of the larger waves head-on so that the entire ship shuddered and trembled. In the beginning, my heart stopped every time we hit one of these waves, but because the sea condition hardly changed and the heaving and trembling was never-ending, soon I hardly noticed it. My system began to adapt to these conditions. After a while instinct took over and my body began to automatically adjust my balance depending on what angle the ship stood. This was an interesting experience, especially when I realized that I had started to sense in what direction the ship would be angling next and immediately shift my weight accordingly. I had found my sea legs.

The experience of not seeing any land for five full days was also something that I had to get used to. It was not that I was afraid of not seeing land, but it was strange to get up in the morning day after day and there was absolutely nothing but water and sky. I tried to imagine what it must have been like for someone like Christopher Columbus who spent months at sea without seeing land and not knowing where he was going. Being there in the middle of the Atlantic, I suddenly had a hell of a respect for the man.

On this long voyage across the Atlantic, my guests naturally spent much more time together and had much more time to observe and notice each other's little peculiarities. These peculiarities could be simple things like slurping when eating soup or any other habit that would normally go unnoticed. Five days at sea were anything but normal and although none of these peculiarities mattered much on the first and second day of the crossing, on the fourth day this began to change. As an outsider, I noticed the changes more than anyone else did. A guest who slurped his soup or coffee a little bit would hardly be noticed on the first day (or at least it would be openly pointed out to him out of politeness) but after hearing the slurping for four days, four or five times a day, any consideration disappeared and the first signs of aggression flared up. Suddenly guests would roll their eyes openly to convey their dissatisfaction with other guests' behavior and some even would get up, making sarcastic remarks.

All this was part of the Atlantic Syndrome, as we called it—a combination of frustration due to the absence of land on one hand and the seemingly increasing proximity to their fellow passengers on the other. On this cruise, it was particularly bad with *my* guests because they were all couples that had never met before and they were therefore instinctively suspicious of each other. They hardly talked at the table and the atmosphere was very stiff. I had thought that over time they would get to know each other and become one big happy family but in that, I was dead wrong.

At one point, they started to get me involved quite a bit when I was asked for my opinions on matters that really were none of my concern. As an example, at one point they all began criticizing each other's wardrobe and several of them asked me, when we were alone, what I thought of the design of this dress or the hairstyle of that guest. Naturally, my answer had to be something more or less meaningless like, "Oh, I am not very good with clothes…" Some of the problems they had with each other were simply ridiculous and it was not always easy to smile and nod, pretending to agree with them.

The focus was normally on suits, dresses and hairstyles. Unforgivable crimes included wearing the same dress twice to a gala evening, wearing the same jewelry twice for a gala evening, wrong dress with wrong-colored shoes or vice versa and many more. Then of course, there was the way couples addressed each other at the table. Some were perceived as overly romantic—kissing was a definite no-no—and then there were others who were perceived as too disrespectful. In short, anything that *could* be commented on *would* eventually be commented on and, depending on the length of the cruise, they dissected each other.

On day five, the relationships between my guests at the large round table was at its worst. The two couples at the small tables observed the happenings at the round table with interest and freely shared their opinions with me. "Freely" in this case meant that they shared their opinion so loudly that someone at the large table would hear it and this was when sometimes such disputes spilled over to other tables.

Overall, my transatlantic cruise was an incredible experience. Every day I watched in awe the endless ocean around us. I observed the long swells that struck me as capable of easily doubling or tripling in size, given the right weather conditions. I had a good deal of respect for the Atlantic.

On the morning of the sixth day, we reached Ponta Delgada on the Azores. When we first sighted the islands, I felt immensely relieved even though I had never doubted that we would find them eventually. It was good seeing land again after such a long time at sea. We only stayed in Ponta Delgada for one day and because my guests had no interest in going ashore, they stayed onboard or, more precisely, they stayed in the restaurant and so did I, albeit involuntarily.

After departing the Azores, we spent another day at sea before sighting the coast of Spain. We entered Spanish territorial waters around lunchtime and I could clearly see the Spain coast to port. Franz and I took plenty of pictures even though there was not too much to see once we got them developed except endless sea and a little of the coast in the distance.

The next morning we docked in La Coruna. After cruising in the sunny and tropical parts of the world, we now headed for the icy north.

429

Before that, we were scheduled to stop over in our home port of Bremerhaven. My parents were planning to visit me there but I wasn't sure since I had not received any more letters after the last one. We arrived in Bremerhaven four days later, after stopping over in the port of Le Havre in France.

I saw my parents almost immediately, standing at the pier and waving at me. For me this was an emotional moment after almost three months being away from home, the longest I had ever been away. Bremerhaven seemed to me almost like home. I couldn't wait to finish breakfast and rush out to see them. My mother was in tears when she saw me coming down the gangway and when she hugged and kissed me, we both felt very emotional. For a change, I also hugged my father, which was something I had only done once before and that was at my departure from Stuttgart three months earlier. It was a nice and very emotional reunion. I had organized passes for my parents to come aboard and I proudly showed them every part of *my* ship.

Bremerhaven was our temporary homeport for cruises to Northern and Eastern Europe. We would remain in Bremerhaven for three days for a major change of passengers. Part of our stopover here was the customary deep cleaning exercise of the restaurants, bars and all other hotel-related areas. My parents stayed in Bremerhaven for the three days and during this time, we went on shopping tours, sightseeing tours and every evening we had dinner together. It was a nice and much needed break.

We departed Bremerhaven on the morning of the third day. The day had been marked by the arrival of our new passengers and throughout the day, pursers were busy with check-ins. Luggage was piled high in front of the ship, ready to be moved to the cabins. The crew was busy storing supplies. For us the day was still relatively quiet; we inspected our new stations as assigned by Bohne. Mine had thankfully not changed; I still worked with Franz. Once the preparation was completed, we went out on deck to watch our departure.

I stood on the railing of the main deck and waved goodbye to my parents. I could see my mother wiping her eyes as the *Europa* slowly moved away from the pier. I took off my jacket and waved it at my parents and my father, typical for him, did the same. Finally, it was time for me to get back to work. I put on my jacket and waved goodbye to them for one last time. We passed the harbor entrance just as the first lunch seating started. I looked outside and in my mind said goodbye to Germany and my parents.

The coming cruise would be quite different from what we had experienced so far. We headed all the way to the most northern point of Europe into the icy regions of the northern Arctic Ocean. The first evening was uneventful and to my surprise, in my first seating, I had only two guests. I was not the only one with an empty station; Franz only had four guests in the first seating. Mr. and Mrs. Berger turned out to be a nice and friendly couple in their early sixties and not at all demanding. They watched their diet very carefully, a clear sign that they had been onboard before.

The second seating was not much different; eight guests occupied my round table and Franz had only six. The ship was not full at all. My round table seemed fine but it was still too early to tell. All in all this promised to be a quiet cruise, even for us waiters. Although this cruise would have a negative impact on our tip, we were happy to get a little break after the busy Alaska-Panama-Caribbean cruise which we had just completed.

On the morning of the second day, after having spent one day at sea, we reached the port of Kirkwall on the Orkney Islands. After breakfast service, we completed an open lunch seating, for which all my guests showed up at once, but even then the service was a piece of cake. Immediately after lunch, Franz, Angelika and I went ashore.

Why we stopped in Kirkwall is a mystery to me until today because there was absolutely nothing to see. It was simply a tiny fishing village with one or two shops and that was it. We walked through the entire city in less than an hour and finally, tired of the cold windy gusts blowing constantly through the city, we returned to the ship.

The gala welcome dinner on the same evening was served in an almost leisurely manner. I only had two guests, Mr. and Mrs. Berger, and they were eating nearly half an ice bomb by themselves. The second meal period finished at quarter past nine. That was a first for me, having us sitting in the crew bar at nine-thirty—another first. In view of the abysmal weather outside where the temperatures kept dropping by the hour, the crew bar manager had prepared a large pot of Gluehwine. When we left in the early hours of the next morning, we were anything but cold.

The next day we reached the capital of Iceland, Reykjavik, which really had not much more to offer than Kirkwall except it was larger and colder and sported street names that were impossible to pronounce. Considering that it was July, I wondered what this place would be like in winter; the temperatures must have been deadly. The one and only attraction in Reykjavik was the building that housed the government. We watched the change of guards, noticed many good-looking blond-haired girls and then returned to the ship.

We cruised further to the north and reached Isafjordur on the northern tip of Iceland the next day. After Isafjordur we spent two uneventful days at sea before we reached the first true highlight of this cruise, Trinityhaven on the island of Spitzbergen. We entered the Magdalenefjord just after breakfast. The landscape around us was untouched and wild and reminded me very much of Alaska. We dropped anchor in the fjord and remained there for the rest of the day. The main attractions of this desolate place were graves of sailors of whaling ships who had been buried there centuries ago. There was not much to see of the graves except eroded pieces of wood, presumably from coffins and scattered bones, but it was a remarkable sight nevertheless.

The next day we traveled further north until suddenly were surrounded by drift ice. It was an amazing sight; we had seen drift ice in Alaska but only small single pieces, whilst here we literally cruised through large sheets of ice. The ship was cruising at a very low speed, presumably so as not to have the hull damaged by one of the many icebergs floating past the ship. It was especially eerie in our cabin—throughout the night we could hear ice sheets scraping along the hull and every so often, there was a light shudder when we hit larger pieces.

The next day the temperatures had plummeted far below zero. There was an icy wind and the only reason we ventured outside was some quick photos. In the afternoon we turned south again towards another bay called Moellerhaven, which we reached in the late afternoon. We ventured ashore and had drinks in the "most northern bar in the world," which was not more than a foldable banquet table packed with drinks and Gluehwine, set up by our bar staff. Nevertheless, at that moment it *was* in effect the northernmost bar in the world.

We also visited the "Hapag Lloyd Hotel," which was not more than a small wooden hut painted in the Hapag Lloyd company color -

orange. The hut was so small that it could only accommodate four people at a time. Apparently the hut had been standing there for centuries and had been visited frequently by German war ships during the Second World War. They all had left wooden planks which bore the names of their ships like the *General von Steuben 1933* and the *Prinz Eugen.* These ships had been hiding there, waiting to attack convoys on their way from Murmansk in Russia to England.

The landscape in Spitsbergen was of a stunning beauty; the bay was surrounded by snow-capped mountains and icy blue glaciers. Although the landscape vaguely resembled that of Alaska, Spitsbergen struck me as more serene. The mountains were less rugged and there were far more ice sheets floating in the bay.

We returned to the ship in the late afternoon with a little too much Gluehwine in our stomachs. That evening, my eight guests of the second seating became, for a few minutes, the center of attention in the restaurant. To me it came as a complete surprise because they had been exemplary guests up to that point. I had just returned from the kitchen with my main courses when one of the gentlemen, a Mr. Laubenstein, got up and screamed from the top of his voice at one of the other guests, Mr. Hombach.

"This is outrageous behavior. You are out of line," Mr. Laubenstein shouted, staring angrily at Mr. Hombach.

Mr. Hombach had been fairly quiet throughout the cruise and I had no idea what could have possibly caused this outburst.

Mr. Laubenstein grabbed his wife. "Helen, we do not need such company. Let's go," he said. His wife got up quietly without saying a word.

I stood at my service station and nearly forgot to serve my main courses. The restaurant was quiet and every guest stared at Mr. and Mrs. Laubenstein as they got ready to leave.

"You are a perverted, low-class pig!" Mr. Laubenstein suddenly screamed at Mr. Hombach as he walked away from the table. There were several "ohs" and "ahs" emanating through the restaurant from shocked guests.

I still had no idea what could have possibly caused such a violent reaction. Mr. Laubenstein and his wife stormed out of the restaurant. His wife had not said a single word throughout the incident and neither had Mr. Hombach. That was a bit strange. With the couple gone, the other guests started talking again and I quickly served my main courses. At the table nobody spoke and I noticed that Mr. Hombach was as red as a lobster. The others just seemed happy to bury their heads in their plates in order to not have to look at the flabbergasted Mr. Hombach.

"What the hell was that?" Franz whispered.

"I have no idea but something is strange. The only one screaming was Mr. Laubenstein. All the others hadn't said a word."

"Just ask them," Franz said.

"Come on, Franz, why do you want to know? This happens on every cruise, God knows what's the problem. Maybe Laubenstein didn't like his tie or Hombach had bad breath—literally anything could set them off."

"Yeah, but I really want to know." Franz smiled; he was just a nosy little person.

Suddenly I saw Bohne coming with large steps towards me. "Andre, Mr. and Mrs. Laubenstein insist on leaving your table and changing the station. What have you done?" he asked like a stubborn little girl.

His attitude was annoying. Normally he didn't say a word and as soon as something went wrong, he suddenly remembered your name and automatically assumed it was the steward's fault. I guessed it would have been different if I had been in his "inner circle of friends."

"I didn't do anything. The Laubensteins had an argument with Hombach then they got up and left. This has nothing to do with me," I said angrily.

He was taken aback by my stern reply. "Okay, okay, so what happened?"

I couldn't believe it—I had just told him what happened and now he asked me again.

"As I said, the Laubensteins had an argument with Mr. Hombach then they got up and left."

"How about the food? Did they complain about the food?"

"No, the food was perfect. The argument was about something else."

"What else?" he wanted to know.

"I don't know," I said. I had to smile because this was getting silly.

"This is not funny, okay? Just so you know, Mr. and Mrs. Laubenstein do not want to sit in your station anymore. " He really acted like a girl now.

"But this has nothing to do with me. I told you that already!"

"You should know what is going at your tables," he said to me like a spoiled angry girl and walked off.

I looked at Franz, who had been standing behind Bohne making funny faces at me. "You know, I have no idea what is wrong today. First, my guests lose it and now Bohne. What the hell is going on here?"

"That's what I want to know too," Franz laughed. "So go and ask them, come on."

"I can't believe it, you are worse than a woman. We will find out, don't worry. Anyway, looks like I have only six guests now in the second seating."

"Yeah, that episode cost you at least five hundred marks," Franz laughed.

I did find out what happened from one of the ladies at the table. She was in her early seventies and traveled by herself. I couldn't believe my ears when she told me. Apparently, Mr. Hombach had had an eye on Mrs. Laubenstein since they met for the first time and ever since then he had been flirting with her openly.

"He was flirting with her? She must be at least seventy years old," Franz laughed.

"So what? Are they not allowed to flirt?"

"Well, yeah, but…"

"There is no but. Anyway, in the first couple of days, everyone thought that it was for fun and that he would stop—but he didn't. Apparently, he had asked her for a dance and she had accepted—while her husband went to the bathroom. What happened next is that he grabbed her behind and several people witnessed this but by the looks of it she didn't really mind.

The husband came back and found that Hombach had joined their table. Initially he was still smiling but then Hombach apparently completely ignored Laubenstein. At one point Laubenstein had enough and left with his wife. From what I was told, it looked as if there was quite an argument between Mr. Laubenstein and his wife because of this. Anyway, it seems that Hombach called Laubenstein's cabin three times last night trying to speak with Mrs. Laubenstein and that's when the husband lost it for the first time.

"You must be kidding," Franz said.

"Not at all, and listen to this—so today at lunch, Hombach started to abuse Laubenstein because he had not allowed his wife to speak with him last night, calling him a tyrant."

"What?"

"Yes, and not only that, apparently Hombach said to Laubenstein that he had heard of people like him who keep their wives locked up at all times—like a dog. An that's when Laubenstein lost it and left."

"This Hombach has a serious problem," Franz said.

"You can say that again. Just imagine me trying to call Angelika and you don't let me talk to her and then I abuse you because you don't let me flirt with your girlfriend."

"You wish, my friend," Franz laughed.

"Are you challenging me?"

"Try and you are dead."

"You see, you act just the same as Laubenstein, you are a tyrant." We had a good laugh.

I never saw the Laubensteins again, not in my station and not otherwise. I think they tried to stay away from me, thinking that by now I had sided with Hombach and the rest of the table, which of course was not the case at all; quite the opposite was true. For the next couple of days hardly anyone talked with Hombach and the other two husbands at the table kept a close eye on their wives.

We spent the next day at sea without any major incidents. That evening we had a party on deck - at several degrees minus. Since reaching the Arctic, it had never really gotten dark at night; instead, we found ourselves in an eerie twilight. It was a strange feeling sitting out on deck at one in the morning in daylight, downing steaming hot Gluehwine. It was fantastic. Early that next morning we reached Europe's northernmost town of Hammerfest, where I joined the "Polar Bear Club" - the most northern club in the world.

At midnight, I participated in a football game, Chefs vs. Stewards. Unfortunately, we stewards lost and I blame it mostly on our football outfit. It was not easy chasing a ball dressed in thick warm winter clothes.

After a short visit to the Norwegian port of Tromsoe, we spent another quiet day at sea and then visited three of Norway's most beautiful fjords, the Moldefjord, Romdalfjord and Eidfjord. The landscape was truly fantastic. It was like a different world. Entering these fjords was like entering a river which had cut through bare bedrock. To both sides of the ship mountains rose hundreds of meters almost horizontally into the sky. Sometimes the channels were so deep that there was not sufficient light to take pictures until the channel opened up into a clearing. I had never before seen such majestic beauty. When we left Norway and its fjords, I promised myself to come back here one day with a little more time.

The Arctic cruise neared its end and the highlight of our last day at sea before reaching Bremerhaven was the farewell dinner. The first seating went by quietly and I had lots of time to talk with my only two guests, Mr. and Mrs. Berger. My stories must have been good since it yielded five hundred marks—over-tax!

My guests of the second seating had somehow not recovered from the Laubenstein incident and, judging by the meager tip, they somehow blamed it on me. It was an awkward evening—they hardly talked, I hardly talked, and so the atmosphere was gone. Not even our famous ice parade could save the day. After dinner, we gathered in the crew bar for our own farewell party where I ended up with two girls sitting on my lap. I was happy that this cruise was over and although I had seen some stunning places, it hadn't really been a happy end.

The next day we docked at our pier in Bremerhaven. We spent two days in port before departing for our Summer-in-England-Ireland-and-Scotland cruise. Having been spoiled with many interesting and exciting places and countries for the past three months, this cruise was interesting in some ways but I yearned for places that were more exotic. I didn't know it at the time but this cruise was to become one I would never forget, albeit for different reasons.

The first leg of our cruise took us from Bremerhaven to Southampton, the Channel Island of Guernsey and then to Glengarriff in Ireland. The weather was pleasant and the three cities were interesting but nothing really special. When we left Guernsey the weather began to deteriorate and by the time we reached Glengarriff we had gone through some pretty rough sea. After a windy and rainy day in Ireland, we departed Glengarriff in the early morning, only to be greeted again by an incredibly rough sea. The horizon was overcast and it rained cats and dogs. Heavy winds howled over the deck and in the afternoon, the captain issued a heavy weather warning and ordered all lower open decks to be closed to passengers and crew. Bohne called us together and ordered us to "rig the restaurant for storm."

When I heard that, I was shocked—rig the restaurant for storm did not sound good. As we stood there listening to Bohne's instructions, the whole ship was already heaving precariously up and down, causing all sorts of clanging noises from the kitchen. I kept on looking outside and what I saw made me really nervous. The waves had grown so high that they were slapping against the windows of the restaurant and considering that we were at least three meters above sea level, this was scary. Bohne asked us to empty all plate warmers and clear our service stations of anything that could be damaged. To empty the plate warmers was a real concern to me; could it really get so bad that plates would be thrown out of their warmers?

The answer came from the ship itself, as it suddenly shuddered as if it was hit by a hammer. I held on to something so as not to fall. It was at this point that I started getting scared. The older guys of course had a good laugh but I really didn't feel like making jokes. We started clearing our stations and I emptied the plate warmer near our station. Walking around with stacks of plates in my hand had become difficult because of the ship's violent movements. The ship kept heaving up and down, shuddering every so often when waves hit us head on. As the day went on the weather got progressively worse and I began to wonder if they would suspend the service. Of course they didn't. Obermeyer had rigged the kitchen for storm too; it was interesting to see plate trolleys and other items tied to the wall to keep them from rolling uncontrolled through the kitchen. Despite all the preparation there were noises of pots and pans crashing to the floor—it was scary.

The restaurant opened for lunch and to my utter surprise, many of my guests actually came to eat. My guests hardly seemed to notice the weather and ordered from across the menu as if nothing had happened. Funny enough, I didn't feel seasick but had a strange nauseated feeling in my stomach. To serve lunch under these conditions was an absolute nightmare; I had real difficulties getting up and down the escalator with my fully laden tray. After a while, I got the hang of it and managed to finish lunch unperturbed, although there were several cases where trays landed on the escalators and they had to be stopped to be cleaned up.

Finally, lunch was over and we cleaned up the damage as much as we could. I spent the afternoon trying to get some rest, which was virtually impossible with all the movements and screeching sounds in my cabin. I had no windows in my cabin, which was probably a good thing because I couldn't see the storm outside, but everything that was not fixed kept on moving from the left to right. A small palm tree in our cabin kept on swaying from left to right in the rhythm of the ship's movements, my waiter's jacket on the wardrobe door swayed together with the plant and all was accompanied by screeching noises reminiscent of the noises on an old wooden sailing ship.

Having a shower in such rough weather was another interesting experience since the shower spray also moved with the rhythm of the boat and most of the time that meant a wet floor in the bathroom. Throughout the afternoon, the weather had gotten worse and the ship's movements had become far more violent. I managed to get dressed and when I came up to the restaurant at five-thirty, I found a letter to all guests posted on our notice board:

Dear Ladies and Gentlemen,

Due to the deteriorating weather conditions, it is absolutely impossible to enter the port of Dublin. The gale-force winds, the stormy sea, the narrow harbor structure, and consideration for the safety of passengers, the crew and the ship have forced me to cancel the visit to Dublin. I would like to ask for your understanding and wish you an enjoyable additional day at sea. Thank you.

Captain U.B.

I stared at the letter, in particular the wording he used to describe the weather. "Deteriorating weather conditions" worried me immensely. The weather was well and truly deteriorating and the ship was now listing at some very steep angles. I looked out of the window and what I saw was frightening. The size of the waves in comparison to our 39,000-ton ship was simply unbelievable. The sea was boiling with waves of at least fifteen to twenty meters in height. Dark grey clouds were hanging low above the stormy sea and I looked in awe at foamy walls of water rolling towards the ship.

The ship's heaving and rolling was immense. We continuously climbed mountainous waves and once we had reached the crest of these gigantic walls of water, we plunged forward, diving into the sea with the entire ship shaking and vibrating violently. I could not walk straight without holding onto something. In front of my service station, I found several menus and one broken ashtray on the floor. All decorations from tabletops and the buffet had been removed and some of the planters near the buffet had been secured with ropes. One by one, my fellow colleagues arrived from their afternoon break. Some joked and laughed and others pretended to find it funny whilst deep down they were a little scared. I was one of them. Seeing large waves crashing continuously against the restaurant windows at three stories above sea level was very discomforting.

When I had stepped onto the ship for the first time in Anchorage, it had struck me as unbelievably big and not in my wildest dreams had I ever thought that the sea would have the power to throw our massive ship around like a sheet of paper. Little did we know that this was only the start. Of course I assumed that in such weather not many guests would come for dinner and once again I was wrong—very wrong. They all came.

One by one, my guests stumbled to their tables and sat down. I was holding on to my service station whilst the entire restaurant heaved and shuddered. Taking the orders was not easy—I constantly had to hold onto something when the ship climbed up a wave and plunged down again. My guests had fun and they seemed completely at ease despite the commotion all around us.

Halfway through the first seating Franz told me that he heard the captain and first officer would not join dinner tonight. I was not surprised and happy to hear that the two most senior officers stayed where they were supposed to be—on the bridge steering the ship through this mess outside.

Throughout the first seating, the weather got worse, judging by the violent shudders that emanated through the restaurant. Down in the kitchen the preparation of dishes had become a real torture for the chefs. They had fixed railings to the stoves to prevent pots and pans sliding over the side and falling to the floor. Equipment such as deep fryers could not be used and pots had to be half-empty to ensure there was no spillage of boiling water or oil.

Obermeyer himself stood at the stove and not as usual at the pass. Despite all the rigging that had been done there, unsecured trolleys with stacks of plates were still rolling around and crashing into walls. It was quite a mess. After the first seating had finished, we managed to turn the restaurant around just in time for the second seating. Once again absolutely everybody showed up and then with an immensely big appetite. Just when I thought things had stabilized a little, we were hit by a big one. I had just cleared my dishes when I felt the ship climbing a wave at a very steep angle, to a point where I had to hold my tray to keep it from sliding over the side of the service station.

Then it happened. All of a sudden, the entire restaurant began to vibrate violently. Plates and cutlery on my tray began to shudder with an ever-increasing clattering noise until all of a sudden we heard a loud bang! It sounded almost like an explosion. The mayhem was followed by sounds of glass bursting and glass splinters raining to the ground. There were breaking noises everywhere, then the ship rocked and listed violently before shuddering again as if hit by a giant hammer. Everything shook and there were more clanging and banging noises everywhere, then after some "aftershocks," it slowly stabilized again.

Nobody knew what had just happened. In an instant, all chatter and conversations had died and the restaurant had turned completely quiet. I had grabbed my service station and had literally frozen when it happened, wondering if we were about to sink. The vibration had subsided but the shuddering continued. As I found out later, the ship had climbed up a giant wave and when it reached its crest, the ship dipped forward at such a steep angle that the ship's screws shot out of the water. The moment the twin screws had lost the water's resistance, they accelerated instantly and that was when the ship had begun shaking violently. The vibration caused the decorative mirrors on the buffet literally to explode with pieces of glass flying everywhere. It had been an incredible experience.

When things had settled a little, I took the order for desserts. Surprise, surprise—only two of my guests still had an appetite for something sweet. The others left fairly soon and the evening was over. The weather was still bad but as the evening went on, the heavy seas began to subside. The ship still rolled and heaved heavily but by no means as bad as the Big One, as we called it afterwards. The next day the weather was still bad but never again in my nearly three years onboard would we experience weather as bad as on that day and never again would we stumble into a Big One.

The rest of the cruise was uneventful. We reached Helensburgh in Scotland the following day and after three days of constant heaving and rolling, I had once again solid ground under my feet. After Helensburgh we sailed north to the Scottish port of Oban and then onward to the by-now-familiar Kirkwall on the Orkney Islands. From the Orkneys we visited Dundee and then after one more day at sea we docked once again in Bremerhaven. What came next was another three-week Artic cruise that followed nearly the same route as the first one. We sailed into some of Norway's finest fjords, played football in Hammerfest and after plenty of midnight Gluehwine parties, we finally reached Bremerhaven again.

The three days in Bremerhaven were filled with cleaning, cleaning and more cleaning. The stench of the horrible cleaning liquid was literally coming out of my ears, so much cleaning had I done. We had one entire day without passengers and during that time, we cleaned our stations from top to bottom. We all had tons of side duties assigned to us, which left us almost no time to explore the city of Bremerhaven.

On the third day our passengers arrived—almost six hundred of them! The ship was packed. As it turned out, it was the fact that we would visit Leningrad that had made this Baltic cruise so attractive. During my time in the Navy, they had taught us that the USSR would be our potential enemy and so we had learned a lot about their weapons and tactics. We had also learned that the USSR was not a place where people would travel on holiday; as matter of fact, it was a place from which people tried to run away. All this had made the prospect of visiting the Soviet Union even more interesting. The passenger profile was over sixty-five years old and it turned out that many of them had been there before—during the war.

My station was full for the first and the second seating, with an average age of sixty-five and above. This cruise had all the signs of a very busy one for us stewards. Our first port of call the evening after leaving Bremerhaven was Gdynia in Poland. I knew only a little about Gdynia and at first, the city name was completely unknown to me. Later I found out that its German name was Gotenhafen and it used to be part of East Prussia.

Gotenhafen had been a major German naval port during the war. This was also the port from which the famous cruise liner *Wilhelm Gustloff* had sailed in the winter of 1944-45, only to be sunk by a torpedo of a Soviet submarine. It was the worst loss of life in a single sinking in maritime history. Of course, by the time we strolled through the streets of Gdynia, all that was ancient history. This was the first time for me to travel to an Eastern European country and Gdynia was exactly as expected—run-down, dirty and badly maintained. Although there were countless old buildings with baroque-style columns and richly decorated facades, they all were all in a deplorable state and covered in dark gray dirt. It was plainly visible that once upon a time these buildings had been real palaces.

The same applied to other buildings in the city; if they were not old then they were of the ugly Soviet-style design looking just as old. The windows of shops were empty; except for dust and faded old posters there was not much to see. Halfway through the afternoon, Franz and I decided that we had seen enough and we returned to the ship. I still had two hours until dinner, which I used to catch some sleep.

The doors opened as usual and within minutes, my station was packed with lots of elderly guests chatting eagerly away and trying to decide what to eat. Once again we were wrong in thinking that because of the higher average age, our guests would eat less. They ordered far more than they could eat, which called for our old tactic of recommending as many dishes as possible in the first couple of days in the hope that they would be so stuffed that they would eventually order less. It worked only for some; others continued stuffing themselves to a point that they could hardly walk.

After Gdynia we reached Stockholm, where we would remain for one night. Stockholm was a beautiful city and already the arrival that led us through the famous archipelago was an incredible experience. The archipelago consisted of thousands of small islands and inlets, each of which was not more than a large rock with a few trees and sometimes a wooden hut. Each of these islands seemed to be different and together with the deep blue sea and the clear blue sky, they looked gorgeous. I took hundreds of photos. It was beautiful at the time but when we looked at the pictures later, it became a little bit boring— island after island, rock for rock, one looking like the other.

Stockholm was full of gorgeous blonde Swedish girls. In the evening Angelika took us to a nightclub that was packed with these Nordic beauties - it was heaven. The only downside was that the prices for drinks were so high that each of us could only afford two drinks. It was worth it—the view was out of this world.

After leaving Stockholm we spent a very busy days at sea. The weather was excellent but too chilly for sunbathing and so the restaurant was full for lunch and dinner. We were scheduled to arrive in Leningrad early the next morning and I was determined to get up so as not to miss the arrival in this extraordinary city.

I knew only little about Leningrad except the fact that it was in the Soviet Union. I had seen many faded black and white pictures that my father had taken during a trip in the early sixties organized by the local Chamber of Commerce. I had looked at these pictures hundreds of times and they had fascinated me ever since. Now, I was only one night away from Leningrad.

The next morning I was the first one on deck. We were still out at sea and so I set up my station first. By six, everything was ready and I went back outside. It was a chilly morning and the sky was overcast with low-hanging clouds and a light fog but at least it didn't rain. In the distance, the skyline of Leningrad came slowly into view and because of the weather, everything looked like in my father's pictures - black and white.

Then the pilot's boat arrived and I watched with interest as the pilot boarded our ship. I was so fascinated by the Russian boat that I noticed every little detail that was different—the small red Soviet flag and the Cyrillic letters at its stern that I presumed was the name of the little craft. We entered the harbor about twenty minutes later and I watched with interest all the Russian ships moored at the pier. Each of them had the famous red band with hammer and sickle at its funnel. The view of the many dilapidated and badly maintained buildings along the harbor front had been disappointing. Of course, the weather didn't help and so everything looked dark and grey. There was hardly any greenery and the few trees I saw looked naked without any foliage. Our brilliant white ship looked completely out of place.

We docked at a pier next to an old rusty ship with some curiously large satellite dishes mounted on its deck. By now, several other waiters had joined me and for them it was clear - this was a spy ship. Whether or not this was true I didn't know.

Angelika had given us an interesting briefing as to what to do in Leningrad. She had told us that we could roam around the city as freely as we wanted, which was different for our passengers. If our passengers wanted to go ashore in the Soviet Union, they had to book a tour and were not permitted to venture individually off the ship. Angelika had described it as: out of the ship, into the bus, driven to a sight, taking pictures, back into the bus and come back onto the ship.

For us it was different. Under international law, we were considered sailors; we had the right to move around freely. Russian sailors were granted the same rights in Western countries. In order to keep us together during our visits, the Russians usually organized great parties for us in the sailors' clubs. These clubs were normally within the harbor compound. The parties were great fun and always attended by plenty of gorgeous Russian girls. Officially, these girls were students trying to practice their foreign language skills. The girls might have been students but more likely from a KGB spy school rather than a normal university.

Breakfast that morning was served in one open seating, which had been a major foul up by Bohne because everyone came at the same time and we hardly had enough space to serve them all. My station was packed with guests I had never seen before and I would never see again. At eight o'clock sharp, they all left at the same time for their sightseeing tours. There were nearly twenty buses parked in front of the ship, all ready to take our passengers on their sightseeing tours.

By the time the buses left, the ship was nearly empty. We hurried to our cabins to get changed and at nine, Franz, Angelika and I met at the gangway. We had to walk all the way to the entrance gate of the harbor that looked more like a border post between East and West Germany than an entrance. The guards were anything but friendly and asked us why we would not attend the party. We politely declined, telling the guards that we wanted to see the winter palace of the tsar. The guards looked not very pleased and told us in broken and very heavily accented English that we had to exchange the mandatory twenty-five dollars, hoping that this would change our minds. Angelika had prepared us for that and we each exchanged twenty-five dollars in exchange for Russian rubles. The exchange rate was pure extortion but we knew better than to complain.

445

We pocketed the brand-new Soviet banknotes and finally we were permitted to leave the harbor. In front of the harbor building, we flagged down a Russian taxi. I don't remember what car that was but by the sounds of it, it had only a small two-cylinder engine. I didn't even know that such small engines existed.

I gazed out of the car window and looked at the majestic buildings and cathedrals as we drove through the city. The city was full of interesting details, including long, straight boulevards, vast spaces, gardens and parks, decorative wrought-iron fences, monuments and decorative sculptures. However, just as in Gdynia, the city was covered in a dark layer of charcoal dust and the buildings and structures were badly maintained. Then we saw the river. The Neva River with its many canals and granite embankments and bridges gave the city a unique and striking ambience. These channels led to St. Petersburg, being given the name "Venice of the North." I tried to imagine what this city would look like in fully restored condition and concluded that it would be a fantastic place.

The other detail I noticed were the many bridges. There seemed to be bridges everywhere, some decorated in medieval styles with lions, horses and griffins, and others in the typical Soviet style lacking any decor. As we had already seen in Poland, there were not many cars on the streets and those few cars we saw were either government vehicles or military trucks. Electric-powered buses with their typical long rods connecting them with a network of electric feeder wires roamed the streets. The buses, just like everything else, were in a deplorable state without any of the typical colors and advertisements as I was used to from back home. Talking about advertisements, there was nothing of that sort at all. The only posters we saw were those glorifying the army, the worker and the Party, and all of them had the red flag with hammer and sickle in it. In a way, they actually looked quite cool.

Despite our concerns that the fragile little car would never make it to the tsar's winter palace, we arrived there safely. I got out of the taxi and was immediately struck by the sheer size and elegance of this famous structure. The palace looked exactly as I remembered it from my father's photos; it was a truly magnificent complex. I wondered what genius mind could have possibly dreamed up such a monumental palace. The huge square in front of the palace was nearly deserted except for some lonely individuals selling postcards from under their coats.

I had taken the landing information for Leningrad and read with interest about the history of the palace and its monumental proportions. The green-and-white palace had 1,786 doors and 1,945 windows. Interestingly, the winter palace was not actually built by Peter the Great but Catherine the Great, who also was its first imperial occupant. I wondered if she had ever used all those doors and windows—probably not—and anyway, the palace was no longer a palace and nobody actually lived there anymore.

The palace had been converted and was now part of a complex of buildings known as the State Hermitage Museum, which held one of the world's greatest collections of art. We visited the museum and I realized that the art pieces on display were just as magnificent as the palace itself; there must have been millions worth of paintings and sculptures. As part of the museum, many of the Winter Palace's 1,057 halls and rooms were open to the public.

We visited also the Military Gallery, which accommodated 332 portraits of military leaders of the Russian army during Napoleon's invasion of Russia. Unfortunately, we only had time for about half of them. We left the museum through one of its gigantic doors and ended up on the square. The centre of the square is marked with the Alexander Column. This red granite column (the tallest of its kind in the world) is over fifty meters high and weighs some 500 tons. The eastern side of the square is occupied by the building of the former Guards Corps headquarters and the western side opens towards Admiralty Square. It was simply an impressive complex.

On the other side of the square, just behind the Winter Palace, was the incredible palace garden. The garden was more like a park and featured several large fountains, golden statues, walkways and exotic flowers. Strangely enough, this park was in an excellent condition compared to the rest of the city. We walked around the park all the way down to river Neva River and took lots of pictures along the way. Walking back from the river to the palace took us nearly forty minutes and by the time we ended up at the palace square, it was time for us to get back to the ship.

We flagged down a taxi and to our surprise, it was exactly the same car and driver as we had in the morning. Angelika explained that the taxi had not picked us up accidentally but he had been assigned to watch us and that he was not actually a taxi driver but a KGB agent. Franz and I laughed but she reminded us and insisted that that was what the Russians did—they kept an eye on foreigners who ventured into the city by themselves and had them followed around. We never found out if the taxi driver was in fact a spy but at one point when we visited Yalta, we were actually followed and eventually we concluded that the Russians did keep an eye on people like us. All this was just an incredible adventure for me. I couldn't wait to come home and tell my family and friends all about my travels.

When we arrived back at the ship, we had just enough time left to take a quick shower and get ready for dinner. We were scheduled to depart shortly before our first seating, which was great because this would allow me to watch our departure from Leningrad. The main deck was packed with stewards, stewardesses and chefs, and even Obermeyer made an appearance. The weather had gotten a little better but it was still dark and chilly and the heavily overcast sky had only opened up in some places, revealing patches of clear blue sky.

We all talked about our experiences ashore and from what I heard, we were not the only ones suspecting that we had been followed around. Obermeyer had been to the party organized by the Russians and vocally shared his experiences with a group of chefs and stewards. They came to all sorts of conclusions about the girls who had been present at that party and I began to wonder if they had not watched too many James Bond movies.

We finally cast off our mooring lines and the ship began to move away from the pier. There were only a few people at the pier waving us goodbye and it seemed to me that they were only there to make sure we had left no spies behind. Our friend the little pilot boat escorted us out of the harbor and soon Leningrad began to shrink away in the distance. I felt the familiar vibration under my feet as the captain slowly increased the speed of the ship. The sea reflected the grey overcast sky and the horizon looked as if a storm was racing towards us. I had seen enough and I was just about to go back inside when suddenly someone shouted.

"Hey, look over there, there is a periscope." It was one of the chefs pointing with his hand towards the sea. All heads turned.

"It's a Russian submarine," someone else cried.

I walked over to the railing and searched the sea for a periscope. I couldn't see a thing.

"Look, there it is again," someone shouted. By now, most people on deck had gathered on the starboard railing, trying to detect the periscope of a Russian submarine.

I looked at Franz who was standing next to me. "Can you see a periscope?"

"I can't see anything," he replied.

Neither could I, but I kept on searching and all of a sudden, I saw something moving through the sea. The "thing" seemed to be traveling at the same speed we were but I was not quite sure if that was a periscope or something else. Then again, I had never seen a periscope before and didn't really know what I was looking for. I imagined it should have looked like a pipe or something like that sticking out of the water.

"Is it that thing over there?" I said, pointing in the direction of the thing I imagined to see.

"Where is it? I can't see it," Franz said.

"Over there—can you see it?"

"No, I'm sorry, but I can't see anything."

By now I had lost the thing again and searched for it but without luck. "I think I lost it."

"Maybe it has dived," Franz said a little sarcastically.

"I don't know, maybe it was nothing."

"Why would a Russian submarine follow us? Don't you think they have better things to do?" Franz said mockingly.

"Well, maybe they are getting ready to attack," I joked.

"Yeah, remember your lifeboat station just in case," Franz said. We had a good laugh.

We never found out if there was a Russian submarine out there or not but several of the others swore they had seen that periscope. I had seen something too but whether or not that was a periscope I never found out. It was time to go back inside to feed our hungry passengers. As it turned out, they were very hungry indeed and ate as much as ever.

The next day we arrived in Helsinki for a one-day stopover. Franz, Angelika and I went ashore and did some sightseeing where we took some pictures of street names that were the longest and most unpronounceable I had ever seen. Not only were the street names unpronounceable but also the names of shops, dishes on menus and everything else, for that matter. Thankfully, most Finnish people spoke English.

After Helsinki, we spent one day at sea, which Franz and I spent packing our belongings and cleaning our cabin. My cabin mate Wolfgang, as usual, left the cleaning to me and hardly ever came home during those last few days before our holiday. He was simply too lazy and couldn't be bothered doing any type of cleaning. For Franz and me there was only one thing on our mind since we had started packing and cleaning—holiday! Even during our short stopover in Karlskrona we stayed onboard to finish cleaning our cabin.

At the arrival in this Swedish port city, something interesting happened. We were not able to enter the harbor because the ship was too big for the small port and so we dropped anchor and remained offshore. In the afternoon, we stood on deck and watched as a number of small fishing trawlers approached us. The trawlers stopped close to our stern and the fishermen began to talk with some of our sailors who were one deck below. After a while, our sailors dropped a rope to the trawler and the fishermen attached a large basket with freshly caught prawns, lobsters and other delicacies. The basket slowly ascended as our guys pulled it up. Then the basket disappeared somewhere inside the ship and a short while later it hung empty, or rather, nearly empty, on the rope.

What I saw next made me laugh. At the bottom of the basket there were several bottles of vodka, rum and whiskey. They had actually traded live seafood for bottles of alcohol. Alcohol was in short supply in Sweden and because of the immense taxes, it was also very expensive. To our delight, the seafood appeared again the same night, perfectly cooked in our crew canteen. It had been a gift from the technical crew to the rest of the crew. That did a lot for our teamwork with those chaps.

After dinner that night, Holiday Group Three—and that included Franz and me—organized a farewell party. I didn't get much sleep that night but I couldn't be bothered. It was the last night onboard and I had over forty-five days to get rid of a terrible hangover, if there was one.

There was one - a big one. It was a great party and even Franz drank himself silly. He normally controlled himself much better than I did, but on that night, he went all out. By the time I crawled out of bed the next day, I had a splitting headache and we had already docked at the pier. My cabin mate Wolfgang had disappeared. He left me a note apologizing for not being able to help with the final cleaning, saying that he had to catch the morning train to Frankfurt. He had left his keys and apologized for not being able to help me with the clearing of the cabin.

Despite my headache I had to smile. I had not expected him to help me anyway but at least the lazy bastard had left a note. I spent the morning clearing our cabin and once the crew purser had signed off, confirming that the cabin was clean and tidy, I brought my suitcases to the main deck. There was lots of activity in the corridors, with crewmembers of Holiday Group Three manhandling their luggage up on deck. There were people dragging suitcases, bags and boxes everywhere. There were many happy faces, smiles and whistles as we all got ready for our leave. Finally, I had completed everything and was ready to leave but not without saying goodbye to Franz and Angelika. After we had exchanged addresses and said our goodbyes, I took one last look at the ship where I had spent the last five months, said farewell, and took a taxi to the train station of Bremerhaven.

Twelve long hours later, the ICE came to a screeching halt at Freiburg Central Station. I stepped out of the train and saw my parents almost immediately. It was a very emotional reunion, especially with my mother after over five months away from home.

This was the longest I had ever been away from my parents. I spent the next one and a half months visiting friends, family and of course, I went to London to see Tatiana.

Strangely enough, for the first few days I was unable to sleep, mainly due to the extreme change of environment. On the ship, I was used to a hectic working environment with constant activities and being surrounded by many crew and guests. There were noises and movement day and night. Back at home, all that was suddenly gone. I missed the constant rolling and rocking of the ship. I also had to get used to the incredible quiet and peacefulness at night without the constant humming of the air-conditioning units and all the other noises which were normally present on the ship. It was for these reasons that I could not sleep—it was simply too quiet. It was only after a few days when I had sufficiently acclimatized that I enjoyed good night's sleep.

Over the coming weeks, I invited family and friends to my MS *Europa* slide shows of all the countries I had visited. I had an honest desire to share my experiences with them and after five months traveling, I was desperate to tell people about all the places I had seen. I was excited about my travels and wanted to tell them about Alaska, New York, Washington, the Panama Canal, the Caribbean and all the other exotic places I had seen. Of course, I was very young then and did not immediately realize that others might get jealous and feel that all I wanted was to show off. Unfortunately, that was how some of my friends perceived my slide-show evenings.

The first four weeks passed quickly and before I knew it, I had only two weeks holiday left. I flew for one week to London to visit Tatiana. It was my first time in London and I liked the city immediately. Tatiana worked at the Britannia Intercontinental Hotel and shared a flat with her best friend Anke in Golders Green. We spent a relaxing week of shopping, sightseeing, dinners and late nights out with Anke.

That holiday I fell in love with Tatiana all over again. My desire to be with her was as strong as ever before, and I think she felt the same. On the day I had to depart, I saw Tatiana, for the first time since I had known her, with tears in her eyes and suddenly I felt very bad. Of course, typical for Tatiana, she tried to hide it as best as she could but her emotions were stronger. Was it fair to leave her like this and disappear again for over five months? This question bothered me on the flight all the way back to Germany. Our farewell was very emotional but typical for Tatiana, once we had said goodbye, she walked off and did not turn around. Now *I* had tears in my eyes.

Back at home, my mother welcomed me with a letter from Hapag Lloyd; I had received my marching orders in form of a new contract. I was very excited about my next trip because the Brazil–Amazon–Caribbean cruise would take me all the way to South America. Suddenly I felt restless and I had itchy feet again. Of course, on one hand, I was sad to leave my family and friends behind but on the other hand, the thought of sailing all the way to South America was very exciting. I signed the contract and sent it back to Bremen and a few days later my air ticket with travel itinerary arrived. I was scheduled to fly out to Genoa in Italy, where I would rejoin the ship.

The remaining days went by quickly and once again, I found myself in the middle of an emotional farewell with my parents at the airport in Stuttgart. I kissed my mother goodbye and gave my father a hug and with tears in my eyes, I walked towards passport control. I turned around once more, smiled, waved at my parents one last time and then walked towards the departure gates.

The flight to Genoa lasted less than two hours and compared to the miserable autumn weather back in Germany, Italy was pleasantly sunny and warm. Already at the airport, I met many of my colleagues of Holiday Group Three. We boarded a bus which drove us to the ship. There were several new faces in the bus including a number of girls. They all sat very quietly staring out of the window, just as I had done in Anchorage seven months earlier. Then we entered the harbor and the MS *Europa* came into view. It was strangely comforting to see the ship again, almost like seeing an old friend after many years. I knew it there and then—this ship had somehow become my second home.

I completed all the usual arrival details in the purser's office. I asked the purser whom I would be sharing my cabin with. When he told me that it was with my good old friend Franz, I was of course extremely happy. We only found out later that Angelika had arranged this. Franz arrived on the same day but late in the evening. We unpacked and talked until late in the evening.

The next day we got a briefing from Bohne about the upcoming cruise. This included some new procedures in the restaurant. Although he had been on holiday too, he did not say anything like "Nice to be back" or "Nice to see you all again," he just warbled on as usual. That was Bohne. The rest of the day was spent with cleaning jobs in the restaurant and in the evening, Franz, Angelika and I went out for dinner. We talked about our holiday and the upcoming cruise to South America. It was good seeing the two again.

The next day we prepared our stations, mise en place and studied our guest lists. Bohne had assigned Franz and me in one station with Helga as our wine stewardess. Helga was also Bavarian, a good friend of Angelika's and had an excellent sense of humor and admittedly she was also cute. My station was full but not busy; I had eleven guests in the first seating and fourteen in the second.

The profile of our guests was slightly different on this cruise than it was on my last cruise to Leningrad. Of course, it had to be, since the Brazil–Amazon–Caribbean cruise and the ones that followed were amongst the more expensive cruises we offered. The guests of my first seating made a very sophisticated impression and they struck me as not very warm but very polite. I had one table of eight—Mr. and Mrs.

Schneider, Mr. and Mrs. Baumann, Mr. and Mrs. Kalf and Mr. and Mrs. Knitt. The four couples knew each other and that was good for me because I would not have to expect any fights or arguments there.

I had one more table of three—Mr. and Mrs. Pfeiffer and their daughter Michelle. The family was late, which completely messed up my timing but when I saw their daughter, who was an extremely gorgeous, young dark-haired girl wearing extremely short hot pants, the delay was forgiven. The arrival of Michelle had made many heads turn, not so much heads of guests but those of my colleagues from the stations on the port side. We had over five hundred passengers on this cruise and the only cute girl was sitting in my station. It was fantastic and by the looks of it, Michelle loved to wear as little as possible. This was bound to be an exciting cruise for me in more than one way.

Despite the late arrival of the Pfeiffers, I managed to finish the first seating in good time. My large table left without dessert and coffee, which was a bit strange. At first, I thought I had done something wrong but one of the women joked, telling me that I would finish every night early because they preferred to take coffee in the Europa Salon. The Pfeiffers were a little different. Not only did they take dessert and coffee but they also ate very slowly, but of course in view of having Michelle around a little longer, that was quite okay with me.

In the second seating I had fourteen guests, with one table of eight consisting of Mr. and Mrs. List, Mr. and Mrs. Knapp, Mr. and Mrs. Vogel and Mr. and Mrs. Kaufmann. The four couples didn't know each other but struck me all as reasonably friendly. Then there was one more table of four and again it was a family—Mr. and Mrs. Klar and their daughter Katie and son Peter. When they arrived, I could hardly believe my eyes. Katie was another gorgeous young woman, this time blonde and with a very attractive figure. Franz and I looked at each other with a big smile; this would really be a good cruise. After dinner, we went outside on the main deck where all members Holiday Group Three gathered for drinks, toasting to the upcoming five months together.

After leaving Genoa we had two days at sea, whereby on the second day we were scheduled to cross the straits of Gibraltar. The strait of Gibraltar is only thirty-three kilometers wide and connects the Mediterranean with the Atlantic Ocean. During the crossing, the decks of the ship were packed with passengers. To starboard, we could see the famous Rock of Gibraltar and to port was the coast of North Africa.

I took plenty of pictures but when I later developed them, there was not really much on it except ocean and coastline in the distance. *Well,* I thought, *at least I have been there.*

The next day we reached Casablanca in Morocco where we docked for one day. After another day at sea we arrived in Las Palmas on the Canary Islands. We went ashore in the afternoon and walked around the city center, which was crowded with German tourists.

After Las Palmas we cruised farther to the south towards Dakar in Senegal. Temperatures steadily increased the further south we traveled and more and more passengers spent their days outside on deck. Before reaching Dakar, we had two days at sea and luckily for me, my guests were dedicated sunbathers. During the day, my station was relatively empty with most of my guests outside on deck.

To Franz's and my delight, Michelle and her parents were amongst those passengers who interrupted their sunbathing for lunch in the restaurant. It was not that we were keen on seeing our passengers day and night but Michelle was a different story. She had the beautiful habit of wearing only little when she came for lunch. She would sit there in her bikini with nothing else but an extremely transparent scarf wrapped loosely around her shoulders. It was great, even though it was sometimes difficult to concentrate on my main task of serving food. More than once my eyes wandered to places other than the food platter in my hand. The places were, of course, none other than Michelle's bikini top.

Young Katie from the second seating was even better; she would sit there in her bikini top with a T-shirt wrapped around her waist. I am not sure if her parents approved of that but I had the impression that she was a bit of a rebel and the reason why I say this is because she had the habit of flirting openly with me.

After the second day at sea we arrived in Dakar in Senegal. We were scheduled to stay in Dakar for only one short day and because not many of our guests went ashore, we finished lunch late. Franz, Angelika and I went ashore in the afternoon. We didn't have much time but because we would spend the next five days crossing the Atlantic towards South America, we thought it to be a good idea to get once more some solid ground under our feet. At midnight that day we left Dakar and we all watched our departure from the signal deck with plenty of Beck's beer. Our Atlantic crossing was blessed with perfect weather, much of which we spent on deck sunbathing.

On the third day at sea, Katie invited me to a party. It was a hot day and most of my guests stayed on deck for lunch—except for Katie. She came as usual in her bikini top and a T-shirt wrapped around her waist. Franz winked at me with a smile on his face as she walked past; I jokingly wiped my forehead and followed her.

"Hello, Katie, how is the weather outside?" I asked.

"Oh, you wouldn't believe it, it is sooo hot. I wish I could take all this off," she said and winked at me. I hadn't expected that and, typical for silly me, I didn't know what to say.

"Ahm…well, maybe not a good idea here in the restaurant," I said shyly.

"Yeah, I guess so."

Helga approached the table and, standing just behind Katie, she winked at me, making funny faces.

"Hi, Katie, you want the usual Diet Coke?"

"Yes, please, Helga, thank you," Katie said and Helga left to get her Coke.

"Why don't you try the Europa salad today? It's light, refreshing and just right for this weather."

"Sounds good, I don't want to eat too much," she said.

I went to my other two guests and successfully sold another two Europa salads using the same line. I served the salads fifteen minutes later, first Mr. and Mrs. List and then Katie.

"Enjoy your salad," I said. I had to control myself to not look at her bikini top, which was quite a challenge.

"Thanks, Andre. By the way, what do you guys do in the evening after work? Do you have any place to go?" she asked.

"Oh, we have plenty of things to do. We have crew bar and sometimes we have parties on deck."

"Oh, really? You know, there are a couple of guys and girls of our age and we have a party tonight up on the FKK deck. Why don't you join us?"

The FKK deck was a small deck hidden away just behind the lido deck. It was completely separated from the rest of the ship and completely private and—it was off limits for crew members. I had heard from Angelika that younger passengers sometimes had parties there and I knew that some of my colleagues had even attended them but I didn't really fancy running such risks.

"Ahm, thanks, but we are not actually allowed in passenger areas after work."

"Come on, nobody will know and I am sure there is a way to get up there undetected."

"I don't know, if they catch me I will be in trouble," I said.

"If anyone comes up there, I will tell them that you were invited by us."

It was risky but she had a point. If a passenger invited me then - why not? I knew I shouldn't accept the invitation but in view of that bikini top and the way Katie smiled at me, there was no way on earth I could say no.

"Okay, let me think about it. What time does it start?"

"We will be up there by nine but you can join us any time after you finish your work. I will be there."

"Okay, I'll try," I said, a little nervous.

Katie finished her salad and left shortly thereafter for the sundeck. After that conversation I could think of nothing else than the invitation—and her bikini. I told Franz about it and he, of course, warned me of the consequences if I was caught. I knew about the consequences but thinking of Katie in her bloody bikini top made the decision very difficult for me.

The problem solved itself when another steward by the name of Peter approached me and asked if I also had been invited to the party on the FKK deck.

"Yes, I was. You too?"

"Yes, from Petra. She is the daughter of a single lady in my station. Look, why don't we go up there together at around ten. What do you think?"

"Okay, no problem. Where do we meet?"

"I'll meet you at the main deck at ten sharp, okay?"

"Good. See you there at ten."

At dinner that night, Katie had changed completely and behaved just as a good daughter should. I hardly dared to look at her when I served so as not to arouse any suspicion from her father or brother. She was very cool and other than the occasional "thank you," she treated me just like stewards should be treated by their guests. After the second seating, I rushed to get my station cleaned up and after a quick shower, I dashed up to the main deck. Peter was already waiting.

"Hi there," I said.

"Hi, Andre. Okay, let's go," he said and walked off.

I followed him. Peter had been onboard three years and knew the ship inside out. He led me though the corridors of the crew quarters and from there we climbed up the emergency staircases all the way to the lido deck. The staircase was deserted and we met not a single soul. We reached the top of the emergency staircase and there he stopped.

"We have to cross the lido pool and then through the door just next to the bar," he whispered. I felt as if we were about to break into a bank but I nodded and smiled. He carefully opened the door and scanned the surroundings.

"All clear," he whispered and stepped outside. I followed him. We walked fast and crossed the deserted pool deck. The deck was empty because all passengers were in the Europa Salon attending the ball. This was also the reason why the youngsters had organized their own party on the FKK deck.

We reached the door to the FKK deck, Peter opened it carefully, took a quick look and then whispered, "Good, let's go." We stepped onto the FKK deck.

The FKK deck was dark but there we could hear subdued music from a small Hi-Fi set. As my eyes adjusted to the darkness, I saw about twelve people, some sitting, some lying in deck chairs.

"Oh, hi guys, nice of you to come," someone said. It was Petra, the girl from Peter's station.

"Hi, Petra, good to see you. This is Andre." We shook hands.

Suddenly, someone grabbed my waist from behind. "Hi, Andre, nice to see you," she said and squeezed herself against me. This came quite unexpectedly and for a moment, I didn't know what to say.

"Oh, ah, hi, Katie, nice to see you," I stuttered.

"Come on, let's have a drink," she said and took my hand and led me to one of the empty deck chairs.

"Tonight, *I* serve *you*. What can I get you?" she asked.

"Oh, I see. Ahm, a beer will be fine."

"One beer for the gorgeous steward, right away," she said jokingly and walked off.

It was only now that I realized she only wore her bikini and a transparent top. The weather was excellent with temperatures in the mid-thirties and a clear sky with thousands of brightly shining stars.

From my deck chair, I looked straight at the huge funnel of the *Europa* with the brightly illuminated Hapag Lloyd logo. I decided there and then that this was a great place and a great party and that it had been worth the risk.

Katie came back with my beer and sat down next to me. "Cheers, Andre," she said and we drank. As the evening went on we settled comfortably into the deck chair and an hour later, we were lying side by side gazing at the stars. We talked and talked and slowly Katie came closer and closer until I could clearly feel every part of her body next to mine. We talked and forgot the time and only when Peter suddenly appeared next to us did we realize that most of the others had already gone.

"Hey, we are going to my cabin. Do you guys want to come?"

Before I could answer, Katie whispered, "No, we will stay here," which was quite fine with me.

After half an hour only Katie and I were left. We were completely alone. At one point Katie leaned over and kissed me. I didn't object. Her famous bikini top came off easily and so we had a wonderful night up on the FKK deck.

The night ended far too soon and by the time we left, the entire horizon was bathed in a deep orange glow. We kissed each other goodbye and I quickly dashed over the pool deck and via the emergency staircase back to my cabin. When I returned at five in the morning, Franz was still fast asleep. I quietly undressed and carefully slipped into my bunk.

An hour later, my alarm clock rang but I had just fallen into a deep sleep and couldn't hear a thing.

"Hey, time to get up, wake up," Franz said, standing fully dressed next to my bunk.

I drowsily opened my eyes. "What time is it?"

"It's six-thirty. Come on, get up. You were quite late last night, where have you been?" he asked.

"Just went for a drink."

"Yeah, yeah, you went to that party on the FKK deck, didn't you?"

"No, we just had a drink."

"Yeah, right. I have to go and you need to get up. Come on, let's go. I'll see you upstairs," he said and left.

I was dead tired and only with difficulty was I able to get up. I took a long hot shower that helped to make feel at least a little better. I got dressed and left for the restaurant. I arrived just in time to set up my station when the doors opened. For the first half an hour I had no guests, which gave me a little more time to wake up.

"Hi, Andre, how are you today?" a girlish voice asked from behind.

I turned around and looked at Manfred, who stood there with a dirty grin on his face. *Good God, not him again, and not now.*

"I am great, thanks."

"You don't look great, darling."

"I am okay."

"Did you have a party last night?"

"No, I didn't."

"Well, *we* had a party and only Wolfgang was missing. He wasn't with you, by any chance?"

I could not believe what I heard. "Manfred shut up. I have no idea where Wolfgang was and he was most definitely not with me. So leave me alone."

"Mm, it's a sensitive subject then, is it?"

"Manfred, yes, I partied but not with Wolfgang. And if you want to know, I was with a very pretty girl."

"Oh, I see, with a girl. And who was it?"

"That's none of your business."

"Oh, trust me, I will find out anyway. Have a gorgeous day, my dear."

"Yeah, go and serve your breakfasts," I said angrily.

Manfred laughed and walked off. Franz was laughing next to me.

"So who was the girl then? Was it Katie?"

"Franz, don't you start now, please."

"Don't worry. I don't care as long as you don't do anything stupid."

"I won't do anything stupid, don't worry."

Katie did not come for breakfast that morning and I assumed she was still fast sleep. I only saw her again for dinner when she came with her parents. I felt more than a little uncomfortable making small talk with her parents, knowing that the night before I had made love to their daughter—twice. Katie didn't say a word and although she smiled at me when I served her, she remained completely cool.

The two remaining days at sea passed quickly and throughout this time, I only saw Katie for dinner. I began to wonder if she regretted having been with me. That she had *not* regretted that evening I found out several days later when she handed me a letter, telling me how nice it was and that she missed me. That was enough for me and from then on, we met another three times before the cruise was over.

We arrived in Salvador the following morning and remained there until midnight. There was not much time for us to go ashore because of another lifeboat drill. All I saw of Salvador was the harbor but it gave me a good indication what to expect in Brazil. The next day we docked in Recife, the second largest city in northeastern Brazil. We only remained there for half a day and at two in the afternoon we departed for Belem. The two days at sea were quiet with most guests taking lunch on deck. This was great for us because we finished lunch early and sunbathed on the signal deck in the afternoon.

On the morning of the third day, we arrived in Belem, capital city of the Brazilian state of Para and most importantly, this was the entrance gate to the Amazon River. Franz, Angelika, Helga and I went to visit the Nazareth Basilica, an old Portuguese church. I only joined them under protest because I would have preferred to see the old Portuguese fortress Forte do Castelo but the others opted for the church.

We left Belem in the evening of the same day and finally entered the largest river in the world, the Amazon, for what would become one of the most impressive experiences by far. What I didn't know was that I would also have one of my most memorable experiences so far.

The Amazon River is extraordinary in all aspects and I was amazed to learn that it is the largest river in the world by volume. Its total river flow was greater than the next eight largest rivers combined. The entrance to the Amazon River is over 325 kilometers wide. The main river is on average about four kilometers wide and navigable for large cruise liners such as MS *Europa* to sail the 1,500 kilometers all the way to Manaus, which was our destination.

We entered the mouth of the river that night. The next morning when I glanced outside for the first time, the river was still so wide that I could not see its banks on either side. During the afternoon of the same day, the Amazon began to narrow and by late afternoon, we could clearly see the riverbanks.

The landscape along the river was simply breathtaking; there were lush green rainforests as far as the eye could see. As we cruised along the right banks of the Amazon, we passed tiny villages which reminded me very much of the Stone Age settlements in Unteruhldingen at Lake Constance. Even the long boats that lay on the riverbanks seemed to have been carved out of one single piece of log, just as they had them on display in Unteruhldingen. I saw children playing on the banks and some were even swimming in the river. Various domesticated animals like dogs, pigs and one or two very skinny cows gathered on the waterfront. The river itself was of a very brown color, which was mainly due to the large amount of sediments it carried. The weather had become very hot and humid and it was only thanks to an ever-present breeze that we could stay outside for any prolonged period of time when we were sunbathing.

Chapter 12

The next day at lunch, I experienced for the first time in my life real panic, an experience that I will never forget. We were just in the process of serving lunch when Katie's brother Peter engaged me in an unwanted conversation after I had once again made love to his sister the previous night. He had somehow become interested to know what it was like to work on a ship like the *Europa* and asked me all sorts of questions. I answered him patiently, wondering if he knew about Katie and me. Katie was sitting right next to him and I had to work hard not to look at her. Suddenly he caught me completely off guard when he said that I must meet plenty of pretty girls in this job. I guess it could have been a joke but I was not prepared for that, not when his sister— my lover - was sitting next to him. I didn't know what to say and stuttered some lie. Katie looked at me wide-eyed and probably wondered if she had just been one of the "many pretty girls."

I told him something about the average age of our passengers and that we hardly had any young people onboard and I definitely did not lie when I told him that this was my first cruise where we had some younger folks onboard. This was turning into a very uncomfortable conversation and I knew I had to get out of it as quickly as possible before he came up with even more embarrassing questions or statements. Franz saved me by telling me that my main courses were ready. I excused myself, went back to my service station and finished serving my main courses. *That was close,* I thought, and tried my best to avoid that table.

I was just standing next to Franz when the ship suddenly began to list slightly to the right; that was not really anything unusual, especially if the ship made turns. Franz was teasing me about Katie when somewhere in the restaurant a fully laden tray fell crashing to the floor. We looked up trying to see what happened when I realized that the ship continued listing to the right side but at a much steeper angle. I stopped what I was doing and looked around. I noticed that the rainforest, which I normally saw when I looked straight ahead, had disappeared, and all I saw was blue sky. Something was wrong.

The ship continued listing to the right and, it seemed, at an increasing speed. I looked out of the starboard window and to my horror saw only the brown water of the Amazon River. Something was horribly wrong.

The restaurant suddenly had turned dead quiet; nobody moved and nobody spoke. The sudden silence of four hundred passengers in the restaurant made things worse; it seemed that with their silence, they all had agreed in their minds that something bad was happening. Then another tray slipped from a nearby service station. The more the ship listed to the right the more things began falling noisily to the floor. At the same time there were loud clanging noises coming from the kitchen; it sounded almost as if all plates, pots and pans fell out of their shelves. In the very quiet restaurant, these noises sounded almost like explosions.

Franz and I now had to lean forward and hold onto the service station so as not to fall backwards. I remember that the moment I held on to that service station I could not think straight anymore; it seemed as if my brain had completely stalled. I expected that the ship would flip over at any moment with water bursting through the windows.

Suddenly the first passengers started to panic as a female voice screamed, "We are sinking!" I looked to the right and there was a woman standing up with panic in her eyes. One steward rushed over and tried to calm her down. At the same time on the other side of the restaurant another lady started to scream; she didn't say anything, she just screamed. Another one of my colleagues rushed over trying to calm *her* down. The listing continued further and all of a sudden, I froze. I was terribly scared and simply froze.

I stood there at my station and stared at the restaurant, which stood now at such a steep angle that empty chairs began slipping towards the window and it didn't look as if it would stop. Then in a fraction of a second a thought shot through my mind: *I can't get out of here, I am trapped!* I could not move and everybody in the restaurant seemed to be waiting for something to happen. *How do I get out if the water comes?* I was close to panicking.

Then within minutes, the ship began dropping on the port side, settling back to its normal level again. The restaurant was still dead quiet but as the restaurant returned to its normal level, people slowly began talking again. There were only whispers at first and then it seemed that everyone was talking at once. Relieved laughter and chatter suddenly replaced the silence. I still held on for a few more minutes as my brain began to power up again.

Franz came up to me. "What happened just now?" He looked a little shattered but otherwise seemed fine.

"I have no idea but I am glad it's over," I said.

A short while later the captain made an announcement explaining what had just happened. He started off by saying that everything was fine and there was no reason for concern. He explained that some of the buoys along the deep channel of the river, which were supposed to guide large ships, had come loose and the ship had begun drifting towards the riverbanks. The keel of the ship had already made ground contact and in order to avoid running aground, he had to make a sharp turn which was the reason for the steep angle at which the ship stood for a few minutes.

I understood quite clearly what had happened but what I could not understand was my reaction to it. The fact that I had worried how to get out of the restaurant when the exit to the main deck was only five steps from my station had shocked me. For the coming weeks, I pondered a lot about this incident because I wanted to find a way to make sure this never happened again. I concluded that the key is to realize at the earliest possible stage when the brain begins to shut down and do something about it, like talking or moving about. Fortunately, I never got the chance to try it out.

We had a short stopover the next day in Boca da Valeria, which was little more than a collection of little houses on stilts. In the town center there was a tiny market where locals sold handmade crafts and some offered to take pictures with us in their tribal costumes. The further we sailed into the Amazon the more the humidity increased until it eventually came to a point where all our clothes where soaked with moisture when we stayed outside on deck for more than five minutes.

The next day we arrived in Manaus, our final destination for this cruise. The city of Manaus was much larger than I had expected and, as I found out to my surprise, had a population of over two million. As soon as breakfast was finished, we went ashore following Angelika who had been to Manaus already twice. She took us to one of Manaus' main attractions that was well-known to all Germans, the Teatro Amazonas. The Teatro Amazonas was an opera house built in the late 1800s and was one of Manaus' most notable landmarks. It reflected the massive wealth that was made here during the turn of the century rubber boom. The German director Werner Herzog that made it famous all over Europe featured the theater in the movie *Fitzcarraldo*. From the outside the building looked not much different from other older theaters in Europe, except this one was in the middle of the Amazon River and, surrounded by small little huts, looked completely out of place.

The first thing I noticed when we went inside was a strong lingering moldy odor and when I saw the exuberant interior of the 1896 opera house, I was not surprised. The interior contained massive red velvet curtains, velvet seats, crystal chandeliers, wrought iron banisters and Italian frescoes. The velvet caused the moldy odor, which was not surprising because it was stifling hot inside and there was no air circulation whatsoever. Nevertheless, it was an impressive building and as usual, I took tons of pictures.

Manaus was the last port of call on the Brazil–Amazon–Caribbean cruise and in the evening of that day, we had our farewell dinner. This was also the time for me to say goodbye to Katie. We did so after dinner and for one last time we met in total secrecy at the FKK deck. It was very humid but thankfully, we were blessed with a refreshing breeze. From the FKK deck, we had an excellent view over the city of Manaus with its myriad of glimmering lights. Beyond the sea of lights was the pitch-black rainforest that surrounded Manaus. All this added tremendously to the romantic atmosphere. When I looked at Katie, I noticed real tears in her eyes. It was an extremely emotional evening and we made each other many promises. We promised each other to write as much as possible and we wanted to meet up when I was back in Germany. We left at one in the morning after we got dressed and she went back to her cabin. The next day she left with her parents and her brother. I never saw her again.

We departed Manaus with new passengers, commencing our three-week Christmas and New Year's Eve Caribbean cruise. The route took us up the Amazon River back to Belem and from Belem to Montego Bay in Jamaica. We celebrated Christmas in Montego Bay and for the first time in my life, I had sunshine and blue sky for Christmas. In the afternoon, we went swimming on a snow-white beach and in the evening, we sang Christmas carols standing in front of coconut trees. It was all a weird and strange Christmas for me.

From Jamaica we headed towards Santo Domingo in the Dominican Republic, then to San Juan in Puerto Rico and on New Year's Eve we reached the island of St. Thomas before we eventually docked in the port of Charlotte Amalie on the U.S. Virgin Islands. We celebrated New Year's Eve after dinner when we went out to the beach at Magens Bay equipped with plenty of food and drinks.

Our New Year's Eve party on the beach was a very memorable one because in the early hour of the following morning we had some gatecrashers in form of a group of pretty female American students. They had never met Germans before but by the time the party finished and we said goodbye, they knew us, literally, inside out.

Before our five-day Atlantic crossing we had one final stopover in the Caribbean in Pointe-a-Pitre on the island of Guadeloupe. One incident I remember vividly about Pointe-a-Pitre, besides beautiful beaches and topless French girls, was that I was nearly bitten by a poisonous snake. If it had not been for a very alert taxi driver, I would have surely seen the ship's doctor again.

We left the Caribbean and steered towards Funchal on Madeira, which we reached after five beautiful and sunny days at sea. The stopover in Funchal was only short and in the late afternoon, we departed for the Mediterranean. After visiting Casablanca once more, we crossed the straits of Gibraltar and reached Genoa the following day. We remained in Genoa for three days before departing for our fifty-four-day "Around South America" cruise.

The "Around South America" cruise was a very special one because from the customer service point of view, it became the biggest challenge in my career up to that point. The reason for this was one guest who had booked for the entire fifty-four days; his name was Karl von Kraufnitz. Mr. von Kraufnitz would test my patience as no one had ever done before. It was also during this cruise and because of von Kraufnitz that I made up my mind as to my future career.

The "Around South America" cruise route included some of the world's most famous port cities in South America:

Genoa	Italy
Tangier	Morocco
Arrecife	Lanzarote, Spain
Santa Cruz	Tenerife, Spain

Sao Vicente	Cape Verde
Recife	Brazil
Salvador	Brazil
Vitoria	Brazil
Rio de Janeiro	Brazil
Santos	Brazil
Paranagua	Brazil
Montevideo	Uruguay
Puerto Madryn	Argentina
Ushuaia	Argentina
Cape Horn	Argentina
Magellan Strait	Argentina
Puerto Montt	Chile
Valparaiso	Chile
Arica	Chile
Callao	Chile
Guayaquil	Ecuador

The cruise as such was a very memorable one in terms of the countries and cities we visited, but as far as work was concerned, Mr. von Kraufnitz made sure that for me, every day was like hell on earth. He complained at breakfast, lunch, during afternoon tea and dinner. He complained about the food, the service, the cleanliness of his cabin, the artwork on the ship, the quality of the carpets and more; in short, he was not a happy man.

Mr. Kraufnitz traveled with his wife, who was a very quiet and timid person. I always was under the impression that she suffered heavily under her husband's behavior because by nature she was not like him. I do not know what sadistic pleasure von Kraufnitz got out of embarrassing me on a daily basis in front of his fellow passengers but I am certain that it must have satisfied him somehow. Von Kraufnitz had a seemingly desperate need to be in total control of his table and all seven guests with it. He dominated every conversation and did not like others challenging him or his views.

I vividly remember the first time I met him. Mr. and Mrs. von Kraufnitz were assigned to my large table together with six other couples. On the first evening they arrived late, which I know now he had done on purpose to have the appropriate audience for his grand entrance. I stood at the table and was chatting away with the six couples already present. We talked about the South American cruise and I told them how much I looked forward to seeing the famous Cape Horn.

"Hey there, steward," someone suddenly called from behind.

When I turned, I stood face to face with Mr. and Mrs. von Kraufnitz. My first reaction when I looked at him was to smile because he wore a…monocle. I had never seen someone actually wearing one of these except in old movies. He wore dark brown shoes, beige pants, and a navy blue double-breasted jacket with gold buttons and instead of a tie, he had a scarf wrapped around his neck. He had silver grey hair and a small, quite familiar moustache and as if that was not enough, he carried a walking stick with a silver head of a German shepherd on one end and a silver cap on the other. He was the epiphany of a German aristocrat.

"Yes, you, where is my seat?" he barked.

"Can I have your name please?" I asked him and without saying a word, he handed me his voucher. "Ah, Mr. von Kraufnitz, this is your table."

I stepped aside to let him pass. I assumed that he would wait for his wife but to my and the other guests' surprise, he just walked past me and sat down without even trying to help his wife with the chair. I assisted Mrs. von Kraufnitz and she thanked me with a polite smile. It was now my turn to introduce myself.

"Mr. and Mrs. von Kraufnitz, my name is Andre…"

Before I had finished he began to talk. "*My* name is Karl von Kraufnitz and this is my wife, Hannelore von Kraufnitz. We have purchased a cruise on this ship only because our beloved *Queen Elizabeth II* is undergoing a complete overhaul in Hamburg for six months. "

He had simply cut me off as if I wasn't there and introduced himself to his fellow passengers. Then he looked up at me. "I do expect the same quality of service that I am used to onboard the *QE2*. Do you understand that?" he asked.

"Yes, Mr. von Kraufnitz," was all I could muster; I was too stunned at the way he talked to me. I did not know what to do next; I still had not finished my introduction and I thought that at least I should tell him my name.

"Mr. and Mrs. von Kraufnitz, my name…"

"Ja, ja, that's fine, bring us two glasses of your best champagne but nothing less than Moet," he said without even looking at me.

"Jawohl, Mr. von Kraufnitz," I said and walked off. Von Kraufnitz had taken me completely by surprise with his rude and humiliating behavior. I would have not expected this in my wildest dreams.

Back at the service station, I whispered to Franz. "I have a real troublemaker over there. I tell you, there will be problems."

"Who is it?" Franz asked.

"Over there, see the guy with that bloody monocle stuck in his eye? That's him."

Franz suddenly laughed. "You got to be joking. He looks like a retired Army General but from the First World War."

"Well, that's the way he behaves, anyway."

I asked Helga to get the two glasses of champagne. After she had served them, Von Kraufnitz called me back to the table.

"Yes, Mr. von Kraufnitz, can I help you?"

"I am not happy with the service of the champagne." *Shit,* I thought, *I hope the champagne is not flat.*

My concern was justified. Because premium beverages had to be paid for, we did not sell much champagne and if we did then it was by the bottle, not by the glass. Therefore it would not have surprised me if they had used a bottle that had been open for a few days.

"Is it not cold enough?"

"I don't know. I haven't tried it and I won't because I don't know what it is," he said in an arrogant tone.

"I am sorry?" I said, but I had no clue what he was talking about.

"You are sorry? You don't know how to serve two glasses of champagne and all you can do is to say sorry? Get me your manager," he barked. The other guests around the table were quiet and nobody spoke.

I could not believe it; he wanted to see Bohne. That had never happened before. I had to try to solve the problem by myself.

"Mr. von Kraufnitz, can I …"

"You are still here? I had asked you to get me your manager, or had I not?"

"Yes, but…"

"GET ME YOUR MANAGER," he shouted.

I went to get Bohne; I had no other choice. To go and have to ask Bohne to solve a problem for me was even more embarrassing. I went to Bohne's office. He sat behind his desk and looked at me, surprised, when I entered.

"What are you doing here? Have you finished with your first seating?" he said nervously.

"Ahm, there is a guest who wants to see you."

"A guest wants to see me? Why, what happened? What have you done?" he cried.

"Nothing, he is not happy with the champagne."

"Who is the guest?"

"Mr. von Kraufnitz. He has booked the full fifty-four days."

"Von Kraufnitz, I have never heard that name before," Bohne muttered. "Get back to your station, I will come later." I couldn't be bothered telling him it was urgent; he would just start shouting again.

I went back to the restaurant to tell von Kraufnitz that Bohne was on his way.

"Mr. von Kraufnitz, the manager is on his way to see you."

"You didn't tell him it is urgent? I have been sitting in front of this lukewarm champagne for ten minutes and all you do can do is to make empty promises."

"But Mr. von …"

"I would like to place my food order now." He had cut me off again.

I was taking their order when Bohne arrived.

"Good evening, Mr. von …"

"Are you the manager?"

"Yes, I am."

"I have ordered two glasses of Moet and this is what I get," he said and pointed at the two glasses in front of him. Bohne was taken aback; he had not expected such an aggressive reaction.

"Is the champagne not good?" Bohne asked with his eyes twitching nervously.

"I don't know. I haven't tried it and from what I can see, you are not much better than the steward or the girl who was serving us. Let me explain to you how champagne is served aboard the *QE II*. They present the bottle at the table, let the guest taste the champagne and then pour the glasses. Do you understand that?"

"Yes, of course, Mr. von Kraufnitz, let me get you two new glasses."

"Now I don't want your champagne anymore. Take it back and bring me the wine list."

Bohne took the two glasses and handed them to me. "Wine list." he whispered angrily and left.

I took the two glasses to my service station. Helga delivered the wine list and after he had chosen his wine, she took the order.

He had already messed up my timing and there was no way for me to catch up. I went back to the table and took the order for Mr. and Mrs. von Kraufnitz.

"I'll have the cream of mushroom soup and the sirloin steak, medium rare, with steamed broccoli, carrots and béarnaise sauce. Have you got that?" he asked.

"Yes, Mr. von Kraufnitz."

His wife ordered another cream of mushroom soup and the fillet of sole with steamed potatoes and a selection of steamed vegetables.

I repeated the order and left for the kitchen. When I arrived, I was hopelessly late and ended up at the very end of the main-course queue. Helga took the soups and served them to von Kraufnitz and his wife whilst I waited in the long line of stewards. I had only moved about three places further when Helga came back with the soups—the cups were still full.

"What's wrong with the soups?" I asked.

"Mr. von Kraufnitz sent them back because he said there was parsley on the soup and it didn't say that on the menu."

"But that's only garnish" I protested.

"I told him that too but he insists to get the soup as it is on the menu—without parsley."

"Okay, just get him a new one." This was going a bit too far.

Of course, Obermeyer was not pleased at all but because it was Helga, he ordered two new ones. After a few minutes, she left with two soups *without* parsley.

Fifteen minutes later it was my turn and when I had all my main courses, I went back to the restaurant. Franz was just finishing clearing his main courses and I had not even started serving yet.

"Hey, just so you know, von Kraufnitz said the soups were not hot."

"Yeah, I would have been surprised to hear that he liked them." In view of the complaint, I decided to serve him and his wife first.

"One sirloin steak and one Dover sole. Enjoy your meal."

I carefully placed the plates in front of them just as I had always done it with the right hand from the right side; I felt like I was back at the hotel-school examination. I continued serving the other guests when von Kraufnitz called me again to the table.

"Steward, on the menu it didn't say anything about mushrooms and now I have broccoli, carrots and there are some mushrooms."

"Ahm, the sirloin steak comes with sautéed mushrooms, Mr. von Kraufnitz."

"I only want what's on the menu. Take them back."

"Yes, Mr. von Kraufnitz."

I took the plate and went back to the kitchen. I didn't need Obermeyer to remove the mushrooms and so I picked them out with my bare hands on the escalator, dumped them in a bin and went back to the restaurant. On the escalator I re-arranged everything nicely on the plate with my hands and served the steak to von Kraufnitz.

"We have taken off the mushrooms, Mr. von Kraufnitz."

He looked at the plate and, without saying a word, began to eat. The peace lasted only for about two minutes before he called me back *again.*

"Steward, the steak is cold," he said and pushed the plate away. "I want a hot steak."

It does not say hot on the menu, you freak, I thought of saying but kept quiet and removed the plate. I went back to the kitchen already dreading Obermeyer's wrath. He stood in front of the pass talking with his Number Two. I approached him ever so carefully and explained what had happened.

"Of course, it's cold if you fuck around with it for half an hour before you serve it. One sirloin, medium well done," he screamed. *That was not too bad; at least he had not argued,* I thought.

Ten minutes later, I had a new, piping hot steak that I served to von Kraufnitz. He ate it without comments. The atmosphere at the table was a disaster; everybody watched von Kraufnitz eat and nobody spoke. When he finished I cleared the table, asking everyone if they had enjoyed their meal.

"If you could have served it correctly the first time, it would have tasted much better, but instead *you* embarrass *me* by keeping everyone waiting."

473

"I am sorry, Mr. von Kraufnitz," I mumbled and left the table.

"How is it going?" Franz asked

"Don't ask. The guy is an absolute nightmare and this is only the first day."

"Don't worry, maybe he is jetlagged and he will be fine tomorrow."

"Jetlagged from a flight of two hours? I don't think so," I answered.

"He will be fine tomorrow, you will see."

"Let's see."

I took the dessert orders and, needless to say, he again found something wrong with the dessert of his wife. She had ordered a peach melba and it did not say on the menu that there were chocolate shavings on top. I got her a new one. The coffee was not hot enough and I had to change that too. When he and his wife had finished, he got up and waited for everyone else to get up too, but except for his wife, nobody moved. He nodded and then left the table with his wife following him. As he passed by me, I wished them both a good night.

"You have a lot to learn, young man," he simply said and left. I just stood there and thought, *Go to hell, you freak.*

The moment the two left, everyone at the table started talking. They called me over and told me how bad they felt for me and that I should not pay attention to him and his unjustified complaints. It was nice of them and I appreciated their concern but it didn't really make me feel much better.

Von Kraufnitz wasn't fine, neither the next day nor the day after; the first night had just been a preview of things to come.

We departed Genoa and docked the next day in Tangier. After Tangier we cruised to Arrecife, Santa Cruz and arrived in Cape Verde on the tenth day for the last stopover before our Atlantic crossing to South America. Throughout this time von Kraufnitz hadn't missed one meal in the restaurant and hadn't left the ship once. Every day he found something else and continued complaining about every little detail. Obermeyer was furious with my constant questions about garnishes and requests to have this removed or that added. After ten days, I had von Kraufnitz barking at me in the restaurant, Obermeyer screaming at me in the kitchen and Bohne staring at me angrily every time he saw me and so it went day in, day out. By the time we left Cape Verde I was already stressed like never before in my entire short life. My mood began to dwindle and it was only because of the constant encouragement from my other guests that kept me from saying something stupid.

During the five days at sea that followed, things got worse. Some of the other guests had started to speak up, asking von Kraufnitz to tone down. Exactly the opposite happened and he humiliated me even more. The atmosphere at the table was at its worst when one of the other guests lost his temper and told von Kraufnitz to shut up. It must have worked because von Kraufnitz "punished" them with his absence for one entire day. It was like a day off duty for me and I managed to recover a little. It was only after we had reached Salvador that von Kraufnitz had booked excursions in nearly every port. I hardly saw him except on the days at sea.

We reached Rio de Janeiro where we stayed for two days. Von Kraufnitz and his wife were out for most of the time. We visited some interesting bars but in view of having to face von Kraufnitz the next day, I could not really enjoy what I saw up there on stage in one of those bars.

We left Rio and after visiting the Brazilian port cities of Santos and Paranagua, we spent another two days at sea. Although he still complained about this and that, von Kraufnitz had toned down a little. The only benefit for me was that Bohne had kept out of my way, trying to avoid my station and me at all costs. Von Kraufnitz never came when we had an open seating, very much to the displeasure of my colleagues who repeatedly urged me angrily to keep him in my station. Nothing was further from my mind than that.

On the morning of the third day, we were scheduled to arrive in Montevideo, the capital of Uruguay. I got up early in the morning to prepare my station and, to my surprise, I was not the first one up. The sun had only just started to rise above the horizon and the sea was flat and calm. It was a glorious morning. Several stewards had already finished their preparations when I arrived in the restaurant. I did not know much about Montevideo or Uruguay, for that matter. I was in the middle of setting up my coffee cups when the loudspeakers crackled to life and the voice of the captain came on. "Ladies and gentlemen, we are about to enter the harbor of Montevideo and in about fifteen minutes we will be passing the wreck of the German pocket battleship *Graf Spee.*"

Graf Spee? I had heard the name before but I knew nothing about this ship or how it had ended up here in the first place. I quickly finished my breakfast setup, grabbed my camera and went outside onto the main deck. The deck was crowded with crew members from all different departments: stewards, stewardesses, chefs, technical crew and even some officers. I joined Franz and the others. We looked at the sea where the sun had just crept above the horizon, bathing the entire sky in a glowing orange red. It was an incredible sight.

"Jesus, look at the upper decks," Franz said and when I turned around, I saw the decks were crowded with passengers. I could clearly hear the lecturer explaining the history of the pocket battleship *Graf Spee*. *What was a German battleship doing all the way here in South America?* I wondered. I was surprised to hear that its captain scuttled the ship after having been hunted by some English cruisers.

"Ladies and gentlemen, on the right side you can now see the wreck of the *Graf Spee*," the lecturer announced.

"There she is," someone cried and all heads turned.

I looked to the right and noticed a number of masts and what looked like a broken rusty tower sticking out of the sea and just behind it, the sun was rising majestically into the morning sky. *Amazing, this was once a German battleship,* I thought. I took some pictures. Then when we were at level with the wreck, all of a sudden the ship's horn blasted three loud whistles in honor of the German battleship. It was quite an emotional affair. After the experience I wanted to find out more about this ship and bought two books in the ship's boutique telling her interesting but sad story.

In Montevideo, some of our passengers left us and new ones joined. Unfortunately for me, von Kraufnitz and his wife where not amongst the departing guests. After Montevideo, we headed further South and by the time we docked in Puerto Madryn in Argentina, temperatures had dropped considerably. From Puerto Madryn we cruised down to the southernmost port of Argentina, Ushuaia. We attempted to cruise down to Cape Horn but the weather conditions were at its worst and with wave heights of over ten meters, the captain abandoned the idea. We managed to get a few shots and we returned towards the Strait of Magellan.

The Strait of Magellan is a sea route immediately south of mainland Chile and north of Isla Grande de Tierra del Fuego. The strait is the most important natural passage between the Pacific and Atlantic oceans but is considered too difficult a route to navigate because of the inhospitable climate and the narrowness of the passage. It is about four kilometers wide at its narrowest point. Until the Panama Canal was finished, this was the main route for steamships traveling from the Atlantic Ocean to the Pacific and was often considered the only safe route rather than having to round Cape Horn, the waters of which are notoriously turbulent, unpredictable and frequented by icebergs and sea ice. I read all this *after* the crossing of the Strait of Magellan, which was good, since otherwise I would not have enjoyed the crossing. The landscape in the strait was magnificent: high mountains and some pine forests and then, when I least expected it, a glacier.

After successfully crossing the Strait of Magellan, we dropped anchor offshore at Punto Arenas for one day and then continued on to Puerto Montt in Chile. Von Kraufnitz was always booked on excursions, which gave me a much needed break. After Puerto Montt we cruised along the Chilean coast to Valpariso and then via Arica to Callao in Chile. This was our last port before Guayaquill, where our "Around South America" cruise would finally end. I counted the days and then the hours and I could not wait to see von Kraufnitz finally leaving the ship for good.

We served our farewell dinner with the customary ice parade the evening before Guayaquill and I was determined not to take any crap from von Kraufnitz for missing parsley or some other silly complains. Strangely enough he kept quiet and what made matters worse, he paid over-tax. I contemplated for a moment refusing to accept the envelope but then decided against it since I would have only punished myself. I took the envelope without much fuss and mumbled a hardly audible "thanks."

Although the tip from this cruise was not bad, the fifty-four day experience with von Kraufnitz had been a stressful one for me. It had made me think a lot about my future and I had begun to ask myself if this is what I really wanted—serving people like von Kraufnitz for the rest of my life? There is no doubt that I had met many people who were truly wonderful but there had also been many who were like von Kraufnitz, unhappy people who let their frustrations out on people like me—stewards and waiters—knowing that because of the nature of our job, we were easy targets. I decided there and then that this was *not* what I wanted for my future. I did not have a clear idea at the time how to get out of this but a thought had been planted in my mind and over the coming twelve months, a clearer idea would begin to take shape. For the moment, however, I looked forward to the upcoming Caribbean cruises.

We left Guayaquill the next day with new passengers onboard, heading toward the Panama Canal. We crossed the Panama Canal three days later back into the Caribbean where we remained for a full two months. We cruised from island to island and in the process visited some of the Caribbean's most beautiful beaches in Jamaica, Barbados, Haiti, Puerto Rico, Antigua, Martinique, British Virgin Islands and many more. Having learned from experience, I had become very careful when stepping into the water to avoid sea creatures like sea urchins and stingrays. The weather was perfect with blue skies and lots of sun and soon all of us had an incredible suntan. After two months in the Caribbean we headed towards the Bahamas where we remained for two days in Hamilton, from where we eventually embarked on my third Atlantic crossing. After five days we reached Cape Verde and from there we headed northeast through the Strait of Gibraltar and arrived in Genoa two days later.

Mediterranean cruises were normally shorter in length and generally tailored to a more budget-conscious clientele. When we departed from Genoa two days later our passenger profile had changed completely. The crowd was younger and more active and above all—more attractive. The average age had gone down to about forty and there were much more attractive women in bikinis roaming the decks of our ship. Suddenly we had something to look at from the signal deck.

The type of entertainment had changed too, with live bands and artists much more suited to the younger crowd. One of the bands was assigned to my first seating, consisting of three male and three female musicians. They were relatively easygoing and although I could not expect much in terms of tip, the fun we had more than made up for it. Especially the fun *I* would have was worth more than any tip to date.

Mediterranean cruises were slightly cheaper and shorter in duration. The only downside to this was that the younger crowd had also a much bigger appetite, which meant more work for us stewards. Winterhalter was kind enough and had suspended his fish filleting exercise, which, of course, was a tremendous relief for us. Despite this, we still had to work hard.

The guests literally ordered up and down the menu and it was during these Mediterranean cruises that I carried the fullest trays ever.

It was seemingly impossible to streamline orders; my guests listened patiently to my suggestions but in the end, they just ordered whatever they wanted. Most stewards had the same problem and the only way for us to get this under control was to revert to our old tactic of "stuffing" them in the first couple of days. We took their orders and Chef Obermeyer made the portions larger, which, at least for some of the ladies, was finally too much. After a few days, more and more of my guests skipped meals or went for the diet set menu instead. After about three days, more and more of my guests requested smaller portions, which normally signaled the end of the eating frenzy.

The dress code in the restaurant had changed too; it was far more relaxed. Many of my guests interrupted their sunbathing on deck to take lunch in the restaurant and they did so dressed in their swimming gear and T-shirts. It was a great time, even though it was not always easy to concentrate on my main task of serving food, especially when women were sitting there in bikini tops again. As usual, many times my eyes wandered to places other than the food platter in my hand.

These were also the times when we stewards and stewardesses got invited to party with guests and vice versa. There was a party of some sort almost every night and whilst Franz and Angelika attended only some of them, I was on the prowl almost every night. I enjoyed myself tremendously and some of the parties we had were truly memorable. The order of the days in the Mediterranean was serving three meals per day and partying at night.

Our first port of call was Syracuse in Sicily and contrary to my expectations, the landscape was beautiful. We left Syracuse and spent one day at sea before reaching Heraklion on the island Crete in Greece. We went ashore in the afternoon and for the first time in my life I saw the famous blue-and-white-painted buildings Greece was so famous for. We took lost of pictures and bought little souvenirs.

We departed Heraklion late that evening and after dinner, we had a party on deck where the band from my first seating provided the entertainment. It was an excellent party and I spent most of the evening and the early morning hours with the band members, in particular with Katrin, the pianist. Katrin, with her twenty-one years of age, was two years younger than I was and had a very outgoing personality. She had short blonde hair, a petite face with deep blue eyes and a gorgeous body. We got on well from the first moment we talked.

The next day I woke with the customary headache and received the customary sarcastic comments from Manfred. I still had not learned to ignore him and I knew that he knew that too. Therefore, we had our usual silly argument. The band, including Katrin, did not show up that morning, presumably fast asleep in their beds, exactly where *I* wanted to be at that time. We spent the day at sea and instead of sunbathing in the afternoon, I went for a good four-hour nap, after which I felt much better.

Early the next day we arrived in Istanbul where we stayed for one night before cruising down the Bosporus into the Black Sea. Our departure from Istanbul was delayed by one day because we had "lost" one of our stewards. He had not returned from shore leave and because nobody knew where he had ventured to, the captain made the decision to delay our departure. He divided crew into search parties that had to visit hospitals, police stations and hotels. The police finally delivered him to the ship in the late afternoon. He looked pretty beaten up and refused to talk about what had happened to him. As we later found out, he had ventured to a dodgy district on the Asian side of Istanbul where the police picked him up. He had lost all his money, jewelry and other personal items, which he claimed had been taken by the police. We never found out if this was really what had happened.

We finally departed Istanbul in the early evening for Varna in Bulgaria. The stopover in Varna was a short one but we had time to go ashore and visit the Theotokos Cathedral where we took some pictures.

Our next destination was Yalta on the Crimean peninsula in the Soviet Union. I was looking forward to that port city only because it was in the Soviet Union. First, however, we had another day at sea. That day it had been five days since we had left Genoa and the mid-cruise gala dinner stood on. The dinner went well and our ice parade went exceptionally well.

This was the first time that I participated in the Europa Seaman's Choir in the Europa Salon. I did not do that voluntarily but was forced to do so by Franz and Angelika and not because I was a good singer. The seaman's choir consisted of crew members from all departments who performed traditional sailor songs on evenings after the welcome dinner, mid-cruise gala diner and the farewell dinner. The focus here was not so much quality but quantity—the more crew members the better.

480

An additional incentive was the champagne buffet before and after dinner. In order for me to get out on stage and sing in front of five hundred passengers, the champagne buffet before our performance was an absolute must. By the time we began to sing I had downed already five glasses of champagne and although I did not remember a word of the lines, I hummed as best as I could and tried hard to match at least the melodies of the songs. To my surprise, we got a standing ovation for our performance. Afterwards we had a party on deck that continued until the early hours of the morning. At about one in the morning, the band and other artists had finished their performances and joined our party, which at that time was still in full swing. The pool deck was crowded with members of the choir and there was loud chatter and laughter. It was pleasantly warm on deck and there was a light breeze.

The pool deck was located at the very stern of the ship and the white frothy trail left in the ship's wake was brightly illuminated by rows of spotlights. The night sky was covered in countless brightly shining stars and a beautiful full moon provided the backdrop to our party. I was just talking to one of the stewards, Tony when someone patted me on the shoulder—Katrin.

"*That* was an excellent performance," she said, looking at me with her deep blue eyes. She still wore the long white dress that she had worn during her performance; it was so tight that I could see every curve of her perfect body. For a moment, I did not know what to say and I just stood there with what must have been my eighth glass of champagne. Then the champagne took over.

"That was because of me, wasn't it, Tony?" We all laughed. "But first, can I get you something to drink? A glass of champagne, maybe?"

"Yes, please," she answered and I dashed off to get her champagne. I came back with a glass, I toasted to her and Tony—"Cheers to our seaman's choir"—and we all drank to the choir.

Then Katrin asked, "So how long have you two been singing?"

"Let me think, that must have been now…ahm…three hours," I laughed.

"For me it's already the second time but I haven't attended any practice sessions," Tony said.

"So you are the one with experience," Katrin said to me and giggled.

"Yeah, he is the one with experience. He knows five words of the song and I am still humming."

We all laughed. We chatted away and after a while, Tony excused himself, saying that he had an early morning and it was time for him to go to bed. Frankly speaking, I should have done the same but there was no way I would leave Katrin standing there just like this.

"Tony is right; it's late and you guys have to get up early," she said.

"No problem for me. I don't mind another glass of champagne," I said with a smile.

"Let me get this one for you."

Katrin went to the bar and got two more glasses of champagne. She came back minutes later with two full glasses. Suddenly Katrin leaned over to me and in a secretive tone whispered, "You know what, why don't we go up to the lido bar and have the champagne there? They have a wonderful white piano there."

I had had plenty of champagne that night but not enough not to know that I was not permitted into the lido bar after work.

"Ahm, that would be nice but I am not allowed up there."

"Hey, the bar is closed now and I know how to get in. I practice there in the afternoons and sometimes late at night. I always have to use the back entrance and that one is always open."

"I don't know—if someone sees me up there I am in trouble."

"Nobody will see you, they are all gone. Come on, trust me, it's safe."

I knew the bar was closed now but I didn't know it was accessible at night. Still, it was a risk.

"So what do you think?" she said, winking at me with her blue eyes.

On the other hand, I'll just go with her upstairs and if anyone asks, I can still say I'm just showing her the way and then I can still excuse myself, I thought, aided by the champagne.

"Okay, let's go, but I can't say long."

"Sure. I also must get some sleep," she giggled.

We took the emergency staircase to the lido deck and then walked all the way towards the bow of the ship. The lido bar was located at the very front of the ship, just above the bridge. Because of its location on top of the bridge, the lido bar commanded an excellent view forward through a large half-moon-shaped row of windows stretching across the entire length of the ship. There were rows of tables and comfortable armchairs along the window front and in the middle of the lounge stood, slightly elevated, a shiny white piano. All the lights had been switched off and the white piano reflected the full moon outside. It was a beautiful setting.

For me this was only the second time to be up there and I carefully negotiated my way towards the piano. All the champagne I had that night did not really help things much and suddenly Katrin took my hand.

"Come on, I show you where I work," she whispered and stepped onto the stage. She placed our glasses on top of the piano, pulled a little white stool from under the keyboard, and sat down. She moved to the very edge of the stool and pulled me down next to her, and then she opened the cover of the keyboard.

"This one is for you," she said and began to play ever so softly.

I had never sat in front of a piano and had never actually considered this an interesting instrument but then she started to play "Moonlight Serenade." First, I was worried that someone would hear us but her fingers whisked like a feather over the keys, playing as gently as I have never heard anyone play before. Her body began to move in the rhythm of the melody and I just sat there stunned. I glanced across the piano and beyond the bar's windows I saw the full moon reflecting on the calm surface of the ocean. It was like being in a dream.

All my worries about someone finding us up there had completely gone and the longer she played the more captivated I became by her sheer gentleness and passion. After a while her playing began to fade away until eventually she gently touched the last key with her eyes closed. The tones of her play ebbed away until eventually it was completely quiet. I just wanted to jump up and tell her how wonderful this had been when she turned around and kissed me. This was unexpected and I slowly put my arms around her. Her white silky dress literally floated off her body and we had a wonderful night in the lido bar. When we left the bar later that night we said goodnight and I felt as emotional as I had never felt before. I sneaked into my cabin and silently crawled into my bunk. I lay awake for some time with "Moonlight Serenade" echoing through my mind before I eventually fell asleep.

The next morning I was in the best of moods and despite the late night, I felt great. I could not wait to see Katrin again and when I did, all the memories from the previous night flared up again. Katrin and I met several more times in the lido bar at night and every night was more romantic and beautiful than the one before. We did this until we returned to Genoa two weeks later and once again we promised each other to write and stay in touch. But just as with Katie, I never would see Katrin again.

In the afternoon, we entered the harbor of Yalta. Yalta at that time was partly a commercial harbor and partly for the Soviet Navy's use. For this reason, the pursers had handed out printed warnings to all passengers that taking photos in the harbor area was *strictly* prohibited. Already as we entered the harbor, I could see several frigates, destroyers and some naval high-speed jetfoil crafts at the pier. The jetfoil boats in particular caught my attention; I had never known that these aerodynamic crafts with the plane-like wings underneath their keels were used in any navy. They had small gun turrets on their bows and torpedo barrels to the left and right. They struck me as very cool and aggressive-looking. *I had to get some shots of them,* I thought.

In the afternoon Franz, Angelika and I went ashore and as we had done already in Leningrad, we had to walk quite a distance to the harbor entrance. Just as in Leningrad, our passengers were not allowed to venture into Yalta individually but only as part of sightseeing tours arranged by Intourist, which was the Soviet tourism agency. On our way to the harbor entrance, we passed several of the jetfoil boats and I decided to take the risk of taking a quick picture. I took my camera and pointed it at the boat but before I could take the picture, Franz yelled at me to stop. I looked up and suddenly saw one of the guards from the entrance gate come running towards us. It was a frightful sight; he was dressed in a long green greatcoat and wore a Red Army fur hat with the hammer and sickle emblem on its front. He carried a rifle and was screaming and yelling in Russian. We were all scared to death.

The Russian soldier stopped right in front of me and, still screaming, he pointed with his rifle at my camera. I did not understand what he was saying but he kept on yelling, then he shouldered his rifle and took the camera out of my hands. He beckoned me to open the camera and then I understood — he wanted me to remove the film. He looked at me with a determined and fierce expression and without hesitation I opened my camera, took out the roll of film and handed it over to him in the hope that this would save my life. He grabbed the film and shoved it into his coat pocket. He ordered us to follow him, which, in view of his menacing-looking rifle, we did. We had to give our names and other personal information, including a photograph of each of us and once everything was completed, he sent us back to the ship. We were not allowed to leave the harbor premises. That was quite fine with us; we were happy that we had not ended up in a Russian military prison or worse—shot on the spot.

We stayed onboard for the rest of the day but managed to get out the next day, which was only possible because the guards had changed. We dutifully exchanged dollars for rubles and then walked along the picturesque sea promenade. We also visited the famous Livadia Palace, located in the nearby town of Livadia where the Allies held the famous Yalta conference during World War II.

There was also one supermarket in town, which normally would not be visited by tourists, but Angelika had told us so much about the famous Russian supermarkets with empty shelves that we simply had to take a look. It was truly an amazing sight; there were shelves, display cabinets and everything else you would find in any other supermarket in the world except there were no goods. Even more interestingly, there was plenty of sales staff with nothing to do. I would have loved to take some shots but after the experience in the harbor one day earlier, I did not dare to even look at my camera. Despite all this, Yalta was an idyllic and picturesque seaside town which would have been an attractive holiday destination if it had not been in Soviet Russia. We returned to the ship in the late afternoon and departed Yalta and the Soviet Union in the late evening of the same day. After Yalta, we headed back via the Bosporus into the Mediterranean, and after stopovers in the beautiful Greek port cities of Skopelos, Skiathos and Piraus, we ended our cruise in Genoa. Katrin left, together with most of our passengers, and when she had gone I felt bad, not because of the fact that she had left but because of the fact that I was still in love with Tatiana. I had fun with Katie and Katrin but I realized that my heart still belonged to her. That night I wrote her a long letter, partly because I had very guilty feelings.

The next cruise lasted nearly a month and we visited many of the most famous Mediterranean destinations like Greece, Sicily, Malta and many more. On this cruise I had two more troublesome guests, which strengthened my resolve not to stay onboard for very much longer. It was around that time that the company announced another world cruise commencing at the end of the year. I definitely wanted to be part of it but I reckoned that after doing a world cruise, there was not really much more to see and eventually I had to make a decision whether I wanted to do this for the rest of my life or start thinking of my future career. I decided to postpone my final decision until the time of the world cruise came.

The Mediterranean cruises ended one month later and we eventually departed Genoa, which had been our home port for a little over two months, for the last time and headed towards Bremerhaven in Germany. From there we embarked on another England and Scotland cruise and two more Arctic cruises, after which we returned to Bremerhaven where Holiday Group Three—that included me—would leave the ship for a nearly two-month leave.

During this holiday Franz and Angelika visited me in the Black Forest and I went to Munich to visit them. We had a great time exchanging stories of our adventures with friends and family. I also visited Tatiana in London and was surprised to see how fast she had risen to an assistant manager position. I admired how confident she interacted with the senior management in the hotel where she worked. It was during this holiday that we began talking about me possibly moving to England to work. I had not much confidence at the time, considering the fact that my English was nonexistent. Tatiana told me several times that it would be easy for me to find a job there and that she would help but I was still a little apprehensive. I did not even think I would ever be able to master this language to a degree that I could converse in English with the same ease as she did. Back in Germany, I spent the last few days with my parents.

I received my new contract, which would have me joining the *Europa* in Genoa. My parents drove me to Stuttgart airport from where I would take a Lufthansa flight to Genoa. When it was time to go to the boarding gate, I said goodbye to my parents, which for me, as usual, was an emotional affair. I arrived in Genoa two hours later and stepped aboard the *Europa* in the afternoon.

The impending world cruise would be the crown jewel in my two and a half years on the cruise ship *Europa*. We virtually covered every continent on the globe and traveled to places that I had never seen nor heard of before. During this cruise, I met many more interesting, entertaining and sometimes annoying and stressful guests and had many more exciting and exhilarating experiences. There were times when I wanted to stay onboard forever and sometimes I wanted to catch the next plane home, but overall it was an experience and an adventure I will never forget. To describe each and every experience on the world cruise would be a book in itself and maybe one day I will put it all down on paper, but for the moment I will only list down the names and places we visited on this longest of my cruises.

We departed Genoa on the evening of the following day for:

Genoa, Italy
Valetta, Malta
Ashdod, Israel
Haifa, Israel
Port Said, Egypt
(Crossing of the Suez Canal)
Sharm-el-Sheik, Sinai
Port Sudan, Sudan
(New Year's Eve at sea)
Aden, P.R. Yemen
Bombay, India
Marmagao, India
Madras, India
Port Blair, Andaman
Phuket, Thailand
Penang, Malaysia
Belawan, Sumatra
Sibolga, Sumatra
Nias, Indonesia
Jakarta, Indonesia
Singapore, Singapore
Pdang Bay, Bali
Fremantle, Western Australia
Adelaide, Southern Australia
Melbourne Victoria, Australia
Hobart Tasmania, Australia
Sydney, Australia
Bay of Islands, New Zealand

Auckland, New Zealand
Nuku'alofa, Tonga
Date Line at Sea
Apia, Western Samoa
Mopelia, French Polynesia
Bora Bora, French Polynesia
Papeete, Tahiti
Tahanea Atoll, Tuamotu Archipelago
Amanu Atoll, Tuamotu Archipelago
Pitcairn Island, Tuamotu Archipelago
Easter Islands, Chile
Callao, Peru
Guayaquil, Ecuador
Balboa, Panama
(Crossing of the Panama Canal)
San Blas, Panama
Cartagena, Columbia
Willemstad, Curacao
Kralendjik, Bonaire
La Guaira, Venezuela
St. George's, Grenada
Kingstown, St. Vincent
Fort-de-France, Martinique
Philipsburg, St. Maarten
St. John's, Antigua
Bridgetown, Barbados
(Crossing of the Atlantic)
Cape Verde
(Crossing of Gibraltar)
Genoa, Italy

We arrived back in Genoa nearly four months after we had left and once again, Holiday Group Three went on leave, albeit only for one month. My leave this time was only short and the four weeks passed quickly.

I had received my new contract only two weeks after going on leave and once again, my flight destination was Anchorage in Alaska. I was booked on a Delta Airlines flight. I would travel from Frankfurt to

Anchorage, from where we would embark on the three-and-a-half-month around-the-world cruise. My parents drove me to Stuttgart airport, from where I would take a Lufthansa flight to Frankfurt. When it was time to go to the boarding gate, I said goodbye to my parents, which for me, as usual, was an emotional affair. I arrived in Frankfurt two hours later only to find that my onward flight was delayed by two hours.

Because of this delay, we missed the connecting flight in Dallas/Fort Worth. For someone who did not speak any English, this was, as usual, a stressful affair. I finally got onto a flight to Seattle where I had to change again to catch a flight to Salt Lake City. We landed in Salt Lake City in midst of a terrible snowstorm, which at one point I thought I would not survive. From Salt Lake City I boarded the flight for my final leg to Anchorage, where I arrived after having traveled for altogether nearly thirty hours.

From Anchorage, we followed the same route down the east coast of the United States as we did on my very first cruise, which now lay nearly two years back. We crossed the Panama Canal and then did some island hopping in the Caribbean. From the Caribbean we visited Acapulco, Playa del Carmen and Cozumel in Mexico.

We reached the sunny island of Cozumel on a very special day because on that day I celebrated my twenty-fifth birthday. This day was special not only because it was my birthday but because it was on that day that, in the middle of a very wild birthday party, I made up my mind concerning my future.

I realized that night that in five years I would be thirty! I was twenty-five years old and all I had achieved so far was being a waiter on a ship. This thought had bothered me already for some time but on that birthday it really struck me. It was now or never; I had to make a decision—stay onboard or leave and focus on my career. I decided there and then to focus on my career and resigned the next day.

I had given three weeks' notice as per contract; that meant I would leave the ship in Bremerhaven. In the next port, I called Tatiana and my parents to give them the news. Tatiana was overjoyed and my mother was in tears; finally, their son would come home. Out of the three weeks I had left onboard, I would spend six days in the Caribbean, then we would travel up the east coast of the U.S. and then after my fifth and final Atlantic crossing, I would stay in Europe for good.

We left Cozumel at midnight and headed north towards Key West in Florida. One of the more interesting ports for me was Port Canaveral where we took a taxi to Spaceport USA, otherwise known as Cape Canaveral. We saw many of the famous Saturn and Apollo rockets, we inspected the Eagle moon lander and we even stepped into the cockpit of a space shuttle. I could have stayed there for several weeks just looking at these incredible machines.

After Port Canaveral, we visited Newport News in Virginia and then left for Baltimore. In Baltimore, we took a cab to Washington where we explored the city. We took plenty of pictures at the Capitol, the White House and the famous Arlington Cemetery. After a busy and hectic day in Washington, we flagged down a large yellow cab. I fell asleep almost immediately and only woke up when we entered the harbor area in Baltimore. We departed Baltimore around midnight for our passage through the Chesapeake and Delaware Canal towards New York. My last visit to New York was marked by endless sightseeing tours and one final dinner at Windows of the World with its incredible view over Manhattan.

We stayed in New York for two days and then departed for Halifax in Nova Scotia, Canada. The weather in Halifax was very bad with an overcast sky and it never stopped raining. We stayed onboard and watched with growing concern the deteriorating weather. In the evening of our departure, Bohne called us together informing us that the captain had raised a storm warning for our upcoming Atlantic crossing. *Great,* I thought, *what a way to spend my last few days onboard.*

We went through the usual routine of securing everything that was not permanently fixed, glued or otherwise bolted to the surface. Bohne had told us that the sea would be rougher this time because we would be crossing the Atlantic much further to the north. I was not really looking forward to this but if anything else, I would at least get some great last shots, especially in view of the fact that I was now the proud owner of a video camera that I had bought especially for the world cruise.

The first two of our six days at sea were rough but not as bad as expected. The third day was a little worse and in the afternoon of that day, it got bad with waves up to fifteen meters in height. On the fourth day, the weather was still bad and I decided to capture my last stormy crossing of the Atlantic on video. After breakfast, I sneaked down to the lowest open deck normally reserved for the massive winches for the thick ropes used to tie the ship to the pier. Because of the stormy sea, the deck had been completely closed off for safety reasons. It was strictly forbidden for anyone to venture out there but of course, with the prevailing waves, it was the most exciting place to be. This deck was located at the very stern of the ship and whenever the ship dove into the sea the stern came precariously close to the water's surface. It was an exciting place to be and I was sure to capture some incredible shots. I pressed myself against one of the gigantic winches and began to film. I got some great shots of the boiling and churning sea. Through my tiny viewfinder, I saw the world in black and white and everything looked far less exciting than it really was. I had to get closer to the action.

I switched the camera off and moved to one of the open windows; the view here was much better. The heaving of the ship, the stormy gusts and wet spray, however, made this an unpleasant experience. The size and height of the waves were truly frightening. From down here they looked far larger than from up on the main deck where we were still about three meters above sea level. By now, I was covered in wet spray and had a salty taste on my lips. The ice-cold stormy gusts that hit me constantly made me shiver.

I pointed the camera out of the back and captured the up-and-down movement of the ship perfectly; it looked fantastic. This would be a great movie and I could not wait to see it all in color on TV. I put the camera on pause and searched for a spot where I could capture this mayhem from a better angle. Several times, I had to grab onto something because the stern of the ship dove so deeply into the sea that the frothy water was only inches from flooding the deck.

We seemed to plow through a series of very high waves that came rolling head-on toward us. Every time the ship climbed a wave on one side, it would take a steep dive down the other side. This was a perfect opportunity to take a shot of the ship as it traversed the churning sea.

I positioned myself on the outermost winch and began to film. I got some excellent shots as the over-39,000-ton ship was pushed up and down by the sea as if it were a sheet of paper. Through my tiny viewfinder, I saw a miniature version of what was happening in reality. Everything was black and white and appeared very small and distant. It was almost as if I was watching it on TV. Because of this I did not see that the next series of waves were much larger than the previous ones. I just kept on filming until suddenly, in an instant, all hell broke loose.

I do not know exactly how it happened; the only thing I remember is that I was staring through my viewfinder when I suddenly had the sensation of being hit by a giant, freezing cold sledgehammer. The wave that hit the ship that moment was so powerful that I never knew how it happened. I only remember than one minute I was standing up leaning against the winch and the next minute I was lying facedown on the deck, soaked with water and shivering. The wave had hit me with the force of a steam train, covering me instantly with tons of freezing cold seawater. I thought my heart would stop at any moment. The wave had pushed me all the way to the center of the deck.

I held onto the handrail of a staircase and stood up. I was still trying to figure out what had just happened when I realized that my camera was gone. I looked around and found it in pieces near the starboard winch. The ship was still rolling violently when I picked up the pieces. I carefully climbed up the staircase to the main deck where those who witnessed what had happened to me greeted me with intense laughter. I shivered violently as I crossed the main deck with pieces of my destroyed camera in my hands. Back in my cabin, I immediately ripped off my soaked clothes and took a long hot shower. After the shower, I got dressed and inspected my camera that was scratched and soaked in seawater. I removed the videotape, which still seemed intact but I would only find out once I had access to a video recorder. I dried the camera as best as I could in the hope it would still work. Several pieces, such as the microphone and part of the handle, had come off but I reasoned that should not stop it from functioning. Several days later I saw the real extent of the damage; the camera, covered in crusts of salt, would never work again.

That day I had been lucky; the force of the incoming wave could have easily thrown me against one of the winches or worse, it could have flushed me overboard and because not many people had been on deck that day, nobody would have found out until much later. Nevertheless, the videotape was still intact and is now a lasting souvenir from that last violent Atlantic crossing.

After three more days at sea we docked in Southampton, England where Franz, Angelika and I ventured ashore together for our last sightseeing tour in a foreign port. From Southampton we crossed the

English Channel and finally arrived in Bremerhaven. As we entered the harbor I stood on deck and watched the tugs maneuvering us towards the pier. This was the last time I would be watching this maneuver and I felt sad. That moment I was wondering if leaving the *Europa* had been the right decision. The money was good; I had the unique chance of traveling around the world and I had many good friends on the ship.

On the other hand, I was now twenty-five and others of my age had already climbed to managerial positions whilst I was still a waiter. True, to work as a steward on such a beautiful, elegant and luxurious ship was a great experience but then again, there was another side to the story—having to deal with the likes of von Kraufnitz. I did not intend to be the servant for such people for the rest of my life and that moment I knew I had made the right decision in wanting to move on. I still loved hotels and never considered to work in any other industry but I wanted to do so in a position where I could choose the time when to socialize with customers and when not to. I took a deep breath and looked around the main deck where I had spent so many hours with my friends and whispered a silent goodbye.

I went back to my cabin and began to pack my bags. I completed my final clearance in the late afternoon and brought my luggage down to the pier. The *Europa* was scheduled to leave the same day and I had promised Franz and Angelika that I would watch their departure from the pier.

As I stood there in the late afternoon watching harbor workers cast off the ropes, I had tears in my eyes. This was the first time that I watched the *Europa*'s departure from the pier instead from its main deck. I saw Franz, Angelika, Helga, Doris and all the others standing at the main deck with a large bed sheet in their hands, waving it frantically. I waved back at them and said goodbye . I watched until the ship had disappeared in the distance, then I took my two suitcases and walked to the taxi stand. The taxi took me to the railways station in Bremerhaven where I boarded the overnight rain to Freiburg. Ten hours later, after an emotional reunion with my parents, we drove the last fifty kilometers home by car. Two and a half years working onboard Germany's most luxurious cruise liner had finally come to an end.

I had planned to spend three weeks with my parents before flying off to London. For the next two weeks, I was busy writing applications to five-star hotels in London and surprisingly I secured several appointments for interviews. The applications had been written by Tatiana and I had just copied them, not knowing what I was actually writing. Tatiana had also lined up an interview for me with the assistant food and beverage manager at the Britannia Intercontinental Hotel for a position in banqueting. She had urged me to accept that position which he would surely offer me because with him being her friend I would be able to move faster. I was not too comfortable taking a job because of her connections but then again, I always knew that Tatiana knew what she was doing.

After I had packed my bags, my parents brought me once again to Stuttgart airport from where I had left so many times to join the ship. We said goodbye and I departed Stuttgart two hours later to begin a new chapter in my hotel life.

Chapter 13: *London*

My Lufthansa flight touched down in London Heathrow after a short flight of only one hour and fifteen minutes. My impression of London that day was not at all what I had expected. Instead of rain, fog and overcast sky I found excellent weather with sunshine and a clear blue sky. As we taxied to the terminal, I looked out of the small window of the even smaller Boeing 737 and I immediately had a very good first impression of England.

I couldn't wait to see Tatiana again and I was of course excited that finally, after having been together for over five years, we would, for the first time, actually live together. I had not told her but I was a little nervous about that, after having two years of absolute freedom traveling the world. I was also a little nervous about my job, which I did not actually have yet.

Just before I left Germany, Tatiana had assured me she had taken care of everything and I would have an interview with the assistant food and beverage manager of the Intercontinental Britannia the same afternoon. I was nervous simply because I did not speak any English. But then again, that was not entirely true; I knew the very basics, enough for ordering a cup of coffee or asking for directions. Still, I wondered how I could possibly survive an interview in English. Tatiana had told me that I had nothing to worry about; the interview was just a formality and the job was as good as secured because the assistant food and beverage manager was a good friend of hers. I did not feel too comfortable about this but I trusted her.

We disembarked the plane and I had to elbow my way through the incredibly busy Heathrow Airport. Heathrow was one of these airports that had been constantly enlarged over time, adding a building here and another one there. Over the past two years I had learned that in order to get out of airports, one simply had to follow the sign "Exit" or "Immigration." This is what I did and eventually I ended up at the passport control counter.

The officer behind the counter asked me something like, "How long are you planning to stay in England?" which of course I did not understand. I just smiled, shaking my head in the hope that he would stamp my passport. The good man quickly realized that my English was nonexistent and waved me through. In the baggage hall, I picked up my luggage and proceeded through the green channel where British Customs officers eyed me suspiciously. They did not stop me, presumably due to my innocent looks, and seconds later, I stepped into the crowded arrival hall.

There were hundreds of people waiting for arriving friends and loved ones. Pushing my luggage trolley, I slowly walked along the waiting crowd of people trying to find Tatiana but she was nowhere. For a split second, I was worried she was not here but then all of a sudden I saw her standing at the other end of the crowd. I walked towards her and when she saw me, her face lit up. She immediately darted towards me and we fell into each other's arms. I had not hugged Tatiana for over seven months and although I knew her better than I knew anyone else, it felt a little strange holding her after such a long time.

After we had finished our little welcome, she led me through the crowded terminal to her car. We left the airport some fifteen minutes later and it was only now, as we drove along on the highway from Heathrow to London, that I realized a new chapter in my life had just begun. I looked at the English countryside rushing by and I did not talk much in the car, thinking of the days on the ship when I would go to bed in one country and wake up in another. I realized that gone were the glorious days of lying in my deck chair baking in the sun, the sightseeing trips in exotic new countries and above all, the generous tips. I suddenly wondered if I had made the right decision after all but then I asked myself again, *Do I want to stay a waiter all my life?* and the answer was, *No, I don't.*

We entered the suburb of Ealing some forty-five minutes later and eventually turned onto Valetta Road. I observed my surroundings and saw rows upon rows of identical houses made of red brick. The road and some of the houses were not very well maintained and I noticed litter along the walkways that lined the road.

Despite my secret hope that we were on the wrong street, we were not. Tatiana stopped in front of a red brick house with a completely overgrown garden surrounded by a broken fence. I still hoped that we were on the wrong street, maybe visiting someone, but when Tatiana switched off the engines saying, "Home Sweet Home," I knew that this was it. This was where she expected me to live with her.

I got out of the car and stretched. I looked at the red brick stone house which looked utterly deplorable. The grass in the tiny garden in front of the house had not been cut for ages and the walkway had cracked tiles everywhere. It was an utterly deplorable sight. Tatiana noticed my face and asked me if anything was wrong which I immediately denied.

We unloaded my suitcase and walked across the dilapidated walkway to the entrance door. Tatiana entered first and I followed. We entered a small hallway with a narrow wooden staircase leading up to the first floor. Although everything was clean and tidy, it could not hide the fact that the house was old and pretty run-down. This was the place where I would live from now on. It was an anticlimax.

The house had three bedrooms, which she shared with two other girls. Tatiana's room was on the first floor and at one point it must have been the master bedroom. The girls had left it to her in expectation of my arrival. I was in a somber mood and still had not said much. All this was very different from the luxury liner where I had spent the past two years.

"You are very quiet," Tatiana said.

"I am okay, I just have to get used to my new surroundings," I lied, but Tatiana knew me better than that.

"So what do you think?" she probed.

"It's nice. It's different, but nice." I must have sounded very unconvincing.

"You know, accommodation here in London is very expensive and everybody has to share flats or houses," she said.

"I believe you, but this house is quite...ahm...sort of old," I mumbled.

"Look, you have just arrived and you have to go for your interview with Serge. Let's get changed and we'll talk later," she said, a little annoyed.

This was definitely not a good start. I had a shower, got changed and we left for the hotel.

The Britannia Intercontinental Hotel was located in the very heart of London at Grosvenor Square near Hyde Park. The hotel was a typical seventeenth-century building with many little arches, balconies,

Roman columns and tall windows which were all painted in white. Four large white columns supported the roof of the main entrance, above which six flags hung lifelessly from their flagpoles made of brass. Tatiana had been working in this hotel for a little over a year and in this time had earned two promotions to her current position of housekeeping supervisor. She was tough, demanding and respected by her peers.

Tatiana had parked the car on a meter and we went to the staff entrance located at the back of the hotel. She whisked me through the maze of corridors and finally we were in the food and beverage office on the fourth floor. Tatiana asked me to take a seat and disappeared. The walls were full of framed culinary awards; I could not really read what it said on them but judging by the chef's hats, they must have been for the kitchen.

There was a steady traffic of restaurant managers, chefs and other food and beverage staff coming in and out of the office. Then Tatiana came back and asked me to follow her. We stepped into one of four office doors with a brass plate reading "Assistant Food and Beverage Manager." In the center of the windowless office stood a large mahogany desk behind which a small middle-aged man was busy writing something. Tatiana and I stood there waiting for the small man to notice us. He must have heard us coming in but still he just kept on writing. *How long is he going to let us wait?* I wondered. After another couple of minutes, he suddenly looked up, pretending to be surprised.

"Oh, my apologies, but I had to finish this urgently," he said with a heavy French accent. He got up and we shook hands; he was even smaller than I had expected. "So, you are the famous Andre."

I didn't understand what he had said except for my name which he had pronounced the French way.

"I have heard much about you from Tatiana and it is a pleasure meeting you finally," he said and motioned for us to take a seat.

I had no clue what he had said except that he had mentioned Tatiana's name. I knew I had to say something so I just said, "Yes, thank you," which was the best I could muster.

"So when did you arrive?" he asked.

I did not understand but I immediately guessed he wanted to know how I was. "I am good, thank you," I answered.

Tatiana's head jerked around and she whispered in German, "He wants to know when you arrived."

Shit, I thought, *what do I say now?* "Sorry," I said.

In the meantime, Tatiana told him that I had arrived today. I felt like a complete idiot.

"Do you understand English?" he asked me, talking very slowly.

Tatiana and Serge looked at me expectantly to see if I had understood. I had understood only one word and that was "English" and from the way he had pronounced the sentence, I guessed he wanted to know if I spoke English. The answer was easy.

"A little," I said. Tatiana smiled immediately and Serge looked satisfied.

"Okay, based on what Tatiana had told me, we will assign you to the banquet department and based on your previous experience, we will give you the position of banquet captain. We will send the contract via Tatiana tomorrow for you to sign and if everything is fine you can start on Monday."

Serge looked at me as if he was expecting me to say something. He had talked a lot and he had talked fast; I had not understood a word of what he said. I looked at him and then at Tatiana, she smiled and nodded to me and then I looked again at Serge who still sat there looking at me expectantly.

"Yes," I simply mumbled.

"Good, welcome to the Britannia Intercontinental Hotel," he said and smiled. Then we shook hands and Tatiana ushered me out of the office.

Back in the car, I replayed the interview with Serge in my mind. I had not understood half of the things this Serge person had said and I did not know what kind of person he was but something inside me told me that I did not like him.

"Darling, you have the job, congratulations!" Tatiana said, which took me a little by surprise.

"Thanks," I answered. For me the entire "interview" had been a farce; I had no clue what the little Frenchman had said to me and I had hardly spoken. It had been a real farce and I felt silly.

"You don't look happy—what's wrong?" she wanted to know.

"I didn't say or do much in this interview," I said.

"So what? You got the job AND he made you a banquet captain."

"What is a banquet captain?" I asked.

"Well, captain is something like a chef de rang. It's just the English name for it," she answered.

"I see, and how will I communicate with my staff if I don't speak English?" I asked. The interview had made it plainly clear to me that I had some tough times ahead of me.

"You will learn it fast, don't worry, and by the way, there are more Germans and Austrians in the hotel than Brits."

"That is not the point. There are still the customers."

"You have to go to English classes, of course. I have already an application form for the St. Andrews School of English. You can go there on Monday. It's a good school, we all went there."

"But I am working on Monday."

"Don't worry, I have checked with human resources. You induction lasts three days and each day from nine to five. After that, you are on late shift in banqueting. So from Monday to Wednesday you will go to school *after* work and after Wednesday you go *before* work, which works perfectly. I have spoken with the school already," she said.

"Oh, I see. Looks like long days ahead for me."

"Nothing you are not used to from the ship, correct?"

"That was different."

Tatiana had everything arranged for me: my accommodation, my job, my English school—in short, everything. Instead of appreciating all she had done for me, I felt as if I had no control over my life. I felt a little lost.

On Monday morning at eight o'clock sharp, I was at the hotel. It took me a while to find my way to the human resources office. I do not remember how I did that but somehow, I did. I joined a group of about fifteen newcomers for a three-day introduction to Intercontinental hotels that included a hotel tour on the last day.

It was only as we walked through the hotel, always following the human resources director, that I realized just how five-star this hotel really was. There were marble, brass and crystal chandeliers everywhere. For the first time of my life, I came face to face with a real five-star hotel. Even the customers seemed to look different—the gentlemen were very distinguished and the ladies carried an air of elegance and exclusivity. It was an exhilarating atmosphere.

Finally, we got to the banqueting area, which was where I would be working. The function rooms looked more like private palaces with thick velvet curtains and expensive tapestry and silk carpets. It was an intimidating sight of wealth and decadence.

After each day of induction, I went straight to the St. Andrews School of English. We were a mixed bunch of students from all over Europe. We all had one thing in common: We could not speak English but we were willing to learn. It was a painful experience since the teacher, a woman of about sixty years, did not speak any of our languages and we did not speak hers—English. We had started by looking at pictures of simple objects like a house, a flower, a dog and so on. The teacher would point at the picture and then we all had to repeat, "The house, the flower, the dog..." In the evening I would sit in my room looking at photocopies of these pictures, practicing "The house, the flower, the dog..."

I was determined to learn this language and in order for me to learn it fast, I came up with an additional and very simple method: I bought a novel by Dale Brown, *Wings of Fire.* My plan was to read the novel and every time I encountered a word which I did not know, I would look it up in my dictionary and write it down on a notepad. It took me about three days just to finish one page since I did not know a single word but for some reason it worked. Slowly, over time, words repeated themselves and I began to remember them.

After my induction, I was released to the banqueting department. Jonas the banqueting manager greeted me. Jonas had been in this position for over twenty years and it seemed to me that he had never done anything else. He was a small, medium built man of about fifty years of age and he greeted me in the politest of manners. He was dressed in a typical English suit with grey pinstripes. He spoke Queen's English and his whole demeanor reminded me of that of a butler.

First, he took me on a tour of the department. Jonas realized quickly that my English was nonexistent but from the way he treated me, it was clear that I had not been the first such candidate he had dealt with. He spoke slowly and after each sentence he asked me if I had understood, which, in the absence of anything else to say, I always answered politely with "yes."

The banqueting department consisted of one medium-sized ballroom on the ground floor and three function rooms on the third floor. The Britannia Ballroom on the ground floor was large by my standards, capable of seating up to one hundred and fifty people comfortably. The Britannia room was very British in its design with heavy velvet curtains, a thick dark blue and yellow carpet and very tall windows facing the street. Three oversized crystal chandeliers hung from the stucco ceiling. There was a small pantry and a small storeroom at the end of the ballroom.

We then moved on to the third floor where he showed me the three smaller function rooms, each of which was designed in a different color theme but with the same heavy velvet curtains and thick carpets. Our banquet team consisted of only five: Jonas, Damien, two waiters and I. For larger functions, we enlisted the help of part-time workers who were drawn from the hotel's restaurants and bars and sometimes part-time staff from outside. I guessed he explained all this to me as we viewed the rooms but at the time, I did not understand a word. I would find all this out as time went by.

In the Grosvenor Room, one of the smaller function rooms on the third floor, he introduced me to Damien, another banquet captain. We were of the same rank except that he was Irish and spoke English fluently and I hardly spoke any. Damien and I would become very good friends. Looking back, I must say that Damien had a lot of patience with me, never hesitating to take time explaining to me with his hands and feet what he was trying to say. Jonas left me with him.

Damien showed me everything in detail—the pantry, storerooms and the different banquet setups. The banquet department of the hotel had a good mix of lunch and dinner functions. Because the hotel was surrounded by embassies, most notably the American embassy just opposite the hotel, much of our lunch business originated from the various embassies' trade sections. The format of these lunches always consisted of a pre-lunch aperitif bar and a three-to-four course set menu depending on the budget of the organizer. Throughout the week we had lunch and dinner functions of various sizes and only on the weekends did business slow down.

For the first couple of days Damien and I worked the same shifts until he deemed me ready to run smaller functions by myself. It had not taken me long to grasp the intricacies of the relatively simple banquet service. After less than two weeks, I was running my own functions, from setup to service to settling the final bill.

The English language, however, still proved to be challenge for me, especially when it came to taking orders. Many times I had to ask guests to repeat themselves and even then, I did not clearly understand what they wanted. On occasion, this lack of understanding caused puzzled faces when I served drinks which were not what guests had actually wanted, but because they where busy with other things, most of the time they just accepted them.

I learned quickly that the prevailing aperitif for the English was the gin and tonic, or G&T, in short. For every lunch function, we set up a small aperitif bar and in the beginning, when guests simply ordered "one G&T," I just stood there with a puzzled look on my face. Seeing my obvious perplexity they would then say slowly, "Gin and tonic, please," pronouncing the word *please* in an irritated manner. It was not always easy standing there behind my aperitif bar, listening to humiliating and sarcastic comments from irritated guests but I patiently ignored them. Over time my understanding improved and with it, the speed and accuracy of my drinks improved as long as my guests did not speak too fast.

I was used from the ship to working independently without much supervision; I soon had taken complete ownership of "my" banquet department. One of my first tasks was the cleaning and tidying up of the pantry and storeroom, just as I had done on the ship with my service station. By doing this, I knew exactly where everything was in the shortest possible time. My beverage stock was always on par and I never faced shortages during functions. Much to the surprise of Jonas and Damien, I never left the hotel without having prepared the setup for the next day.

Located just behind the Britannia Ballroom was the hotel bar that only opened in the evening. There was a connecting door from the ballroom to the bar and during the day, we used the bar's dishwasher to clean our glasses after lunch functions. One day we had just cleaned up the ballroom and I was busy behind the hotel bar polishing wine glasses, which we had used during lunch. The two cast-iron gates of the bar leading into the hotel lobby were closed but the busy lobby was clearly visible. Watching the comings and goings of guests in the lobby provided me with at least some entertainment whilst polishing hundreds of wine glasses. Whenever the small dishwasher had finished one cleaning cycle I took out the rack with clean but wet glasses, shoved in a new one, and then continued polishing. I was just in the process of removing another rack when the doors to the bar flung open and a woman stormed into the bar. I stood up and looked at her.

"Hey you," she said in a very rude manner. Although my English was not that good at the time, I understood that she was talking to me.

"Yes?" I answered.

"I have been waiting out there with my guests now for over ten minutes for someone to take my orders but no waiter is around. I have important guests and they cannot wait."

"Yes?" I said, although I hadn't the faintest clue what she was rumbling on about. I looked around hoping for Damien to show up.

"Hey you, I am talking with you," she barked. "I need two English teas and two freshly brewed coffees on that table." She turned and pointed at a table in the lobby with three distinguished-looking gentlemen. "Hurry up, I am waiting," she said and dashed off.

I just stood there with a wine glass in one hand and a drying cloth in the other and no idea what this woman had just said. I had a faint suspicion that she had been placing an order with me but I was not sure. I had to wait for Damien. I glanced at the table in the lobby where she had sat down again. Judging by the pin on her suit jacket, she worked for the hotel but again, I was not sure. I continued polishing my glasses.

After five minutes she came storming back into the bar looking even angrier than before.

"Where is my order?" she barked.

"Yes?"

"Yes"? What do you mean, 'yes'? Do you understand what I am saying?"

"Yes?" I was getting nervous now and did not know what to say to this agitated and hysterical woman.

"Coffee and tea, do you understand? I want two coffees and two teas!" She stood with her hands on her hips waiting for a response.

I gathered that she wanted two coffees and two teas. "Two coffees and two teas," I repeated.

"Yes, and now hurry up and get them," she growled and disappeared through the cast-iron gate.

I walked over to the coffee machine that was switched off. There was no point in switching it on because I knew it would take too long for it to warm up. Since there was no way for me to explain this to her, I had only one choice: I had to use some of the leftover coffee from my lunch function. I did not intend to get into trouble and therefore I went to the ballroom and prepared a tray with four cups and four saucers.

From my pantry, I got two English breakfast tea bags, which I placed in the two cups. There was still coffee in the silver coffee urns and from what I could see it was still reasonably hot. I poured two cups and went back to the bar.

I searched the fridges for milk and luckily found a small creamer which I placed on my tray. I took the tray and went to the lobby. The woman was busy talking when I approached the table so I stood there and waited. Suddenly she stopped in mid-sentence and stared at me with an angry look.

"Coffee for Mr. Peros and Mr. Kant and tea for Mr. Smith and myself, thank you."

I had heard her talking but I couldn't remember who got what and so just placed a cup in front of each of them. Whilst I was doing this, the woman suddenly stopped talking again and looked at me, puzzled.

"The coffee is for Mr. Peros, not me." She took her cup and exchanged it with one of the gentlemen. "I am so sorry, he is new," she apologized to the guest with a forced smile.

I could see that she was very angry with me. I stood there not knowing what to do. She looked up at me again.

"You can go now." This, I had understood.

"Yes," I said and walked off. Back in the bar, I found Damien behind the bar counter.

"Where have you been?" he wanted to know.

"Two coffees and two teas," I said in broken English and pointed at the table in the lobby with the angry lady.

"Oh that's Linda, our director of sales and marketing," he laughed.

"What?" I had not understood what he had said.

"Is she okay? She can be quite a bitch, that one," he laughed but of course I hadn't understood a word.

"A bitch—you know what that means?" He made a grimace, waving his hand in front of his face, indicating that she was crazy. I laughed.

As it turned out, she later went to the food and beverage director and complained heavily about the two lukewarm coffees and the disgusting teas. The food and beverage director took the complaint but nobody ever came back to me about the incident.

Over the coming weeks, my English began to improve. Every day I went to the St. Andrews School of English for my four hours of classes, after which I started my hotel duty at one o'clock. I never finished work before one or two in the morning except on those days when we had no functions. My salary compared to that from the ship was minute but I made up for it with plenty of overtime.

One day I had just finished preparing the Grosvenor Room for lunch and I was in the process of cleaning up the pantry when I heard a sudden noise that sounded as if a bag of potatoes had been dropped from a great height onto the function room floor. I immediately rushed into the room to see what had happened. What I saw made my heart jump. One of the curtain rails with the heavy velvet curtains had ripped out of the ceiling and dropped to the floor—this was a disaster. My function was supposed to start in fifteen minutes and now this had happened. I panicked, trying to figure out what to do. I went back to the pantry and picked up the phone. I dialed the number of the engineering department and tried to explain what had happened.

"Hello?" someone answered the phone in engineering.

"Hello, hello," I stammered, trying to find the right words.

"Come quickly," I said.

"Who are you?" the voice on the other end asked.

"I am Andre in banqueting. Come quickly."

"What is the problem, mate?" the voice asked. *There* was a useful word—problem.

"Problem, yes, problem, come quickly," I uttered.

"Listen, mate, calm down and tell me where you are and what the problem is."

I gathered that he wanted to know what had happened and I tried to remember the word for curtain and suddenly, I got it.

"The carpet, the carpet is fallen down, come quickly." I was panicking now because at any moment my guests would appear.

"What?"

"The carpet, the carpet—it's fallen down," I said again. *Why didn't this guy understand?* I wondered.

"Look, calm down and tell me where you are right now."

"Grosvenor Room, the carpet is fallen down in Grosvenor Room," I said.

"Stay there, we are coming," the voice said and the line went dead.

A few minutes later two engineering staff members equipped with tools and a ladder showed up. They looked at the fallen curtain and began laughing.

"Hey mate, this is a curtain, not a carpet," one of the two said as he walked through the room.

I checked my watch, only five minutes to go. "Oh the curtain," I said.

"Yes, the curtain, and we cannot repair this now. We have to take it away," he said and the two engineers began removing the curtain from the floor.

"Today they will have a lunch with a view," one of them said, still laughing.

I was horrified when I saw them dragging the massive curtain out of the room, disappearing into the service corridor. They couldn't just leave the window like that, what were they doing? Under the circumstances, it was the only sensible thing to do and so I served my lunch with one curtain missing. The lesson I learned was of course the difference between a curtain and a carpet, something I would never forget.

Five months into my career as banquet captain, I grew tired of the boring banquet service and I told Tatiana this on every occasion, which ultimately was the cause for many arguments between us. Somehow, word of my dissatisfaction with my current job got to Serge, who quickly promoted me to banquet headwaiter. This was a nice gesture but I had long since harbored ill feelings towards this little Frenchman, who I felt was taking advantage of me by letting me work so much overtime that my salary at the end of each month was higher than Tatiana's. Tatiana kept on telling me how good the hotel was and how I should appreciate the promotion but I felt that I had gotten it because of the both of them and not because of my professional performance. I began to hate the sight of the slimy little Frenchman who I felt let us do all the work and he himself just sat in his office all day long. Tatiana would have none of it, constantly telling me he was a good guy.

Besides my animosity towards the Frenchman, I had also grown tired of guests. After two years on the ship dealing with the most demanding and obnoxious of characters, I felt it was time for me to do some job other than the constant "What can I do for you?" and "What may I bring you?" I had grown tired of being other people's servant, getting abused and still having to smile as if nothing had happened. The famous phrase "the customer is king" had been recited at the Britannia so many times that I was literally sick of it because I felt it was nothing more than an invitation for guests to abuse me. I wanted to get away from these obnoxious guests, be it in hotels, restaurant or on a ship. I did not want to end up as the eternal waiter. All I wanted was to resign.

I wrote the letter, much to the dismay of Tatiana, but I could not be bothered. The day I handed in my resignation was a good day and I felt great. I went to the office of Serge and told him that I was leaving. Just to see the way he was sitting behind his desk feeling important made me angry and I knew that whatever he would say I couldn't have cared less about. True to his character, he gave me a long speech, telling me what he had done for me and what he could do for me in the future. I was not interested in anything he said and just listened to him sitting there rumbling on. When he finally finished, he asked me again if I really wanted to leave, which I answered with a loud, "Yes, I am sure," and with a big smile on my face, I got up and left.

For the coming months, I took a break and did what I had always wanted to do—discover England. In the first few weeks of freedom, I went to all the important sights in London. I visited Madame Tussauds, the British Museum, the Museum for Natural History and I strolled up and down Piccadilly Circus. I did a tour of the HMS *Belfast* and the old war rooms; in short, I truly discovered the city of London. After London, I went to see a different castle every day—first, Windsor Castle then Leeds Castle and so on. In the third month of doing nothing, I felt ready to start looking for a job again. I still wanted to work in hotels of course but as far away from guests as possible and there was only one way to do that: working in the back of house. The "back of house" in a hotel included all those areas which normally remain invisible to guests, like accounting, human resources, engineering, housekeeping and other administrative areas. My long-term goal was to become a food and beverage manager of a five-star hotel and in order for me to achieve that, I knew I had to experience the back-of-house operation of a hotel. My reasoning for becoming a food and beverage manager at the time was simple: I would still be working in the field I knew best, food and beverage, and it would be left to my discretion as to when I wanted to see guests and when not. Only two weeks into my search for a job—by that time I had dropped my CV in most five-star hotels in London—I got a call from the Belgrano Sheldon Hotel. The lady from their personnel department didn't tell me on the phone what exactly what they were looking for but instead invited me for an interview. My English had made major leaps in the meantime and I had already completed the third novel by Dale Brown. I was able to speak more or less fluently and had even discovered the British sense of humor.

One of my Christmas presents from Tatiana was a videotape of Billy Connolly live at the Royal Albert Hall. Billy Connolly was Scottish and one of Britain's foremost comedians at the time. I had to watch the tape about seven times before I started to understand what he was going on about but once I did, I could not stop laughing.

The Belgrano Sheldon Hotel was located in Belgrano on Chesham Place, which was only a five-minute walk from the famous Harrods department store.

I liked the hotel, with its dark wood paneling and shiny white marble floor, from the moment I set my foot into it. The hotel was surprisingly small and compact. I was met by a friendly young lady by the name of Lucy who invited me to the lobby lounge for a coffee. She carried a small folder with my CV and after we had been served the coffee, she asked me to give her a summary of what I had done before. When I had finished she sat up and smiled.

"Thank you, Andre, that was interesting. Now, let's see what we can do for you," she said and opened the folder.

"You have a very strong food and beverage background, but I understand you want to try other areas, correct?"

"Yes, that's correct."

"Good. Now, we have the position of assistant food and beverage controller coming up, which I thought might suit you, not right now, mind you, but in about two months' time…"

I was very disappointed; this was exactly the kind of position I was looking for but two months was too long and I could not afford to be without a job much longer.

"We currently have an opening for a chef de rang in our fine dining restaurant. What do you think about starting as chef de rang in our grillroom? Once the current assistant food and beverage controller leaves, we will offer you a transfer to cost control. Would that be acceptable to you?" she said with another big smile.

I had no desire to go back to fine dining restaurants. I was not sure about this, even though it sounded like a reasonable alternative. *What if they do not transfer me?* I wondered.

"If you would like to think it over, that's fine with me. You don't need to tell me right here and now," she said, seeing my hesitation.

"I am very happy about your offer. It's just that I had planned not to go back to restaurants."

"I understand that but I can assure you it would only be for two months," she said.

"What if the assistant controller is not leaving?"

"Well, this is actually confidential but since you don't know him, I can tell you. He is on notice already and his last day will be the thirtieth of June."

"Oh, I see," I said. That was good news.

Lucy nodded and smiled.

"Can I think about it and let you know tomorrow?" I asked.

"Of course you can, Andre, no problem at all."

When I stepped out of the hotel onto the road, I took a deep breath. As I walked through Belgrano towards the Knightsbridge Underground station, I thought about the offer and decided that it was not a bad offer. The entire interview experience had been a very pleasant one and seemed to me much more professional than what I had experienced at the Britannia Intercontinental Hotel.

By the time I came home, I had made up my mind to accept the job. I called Lucy the same afternoon and signed my employment contract the next day. Four days later, just I completed my three-day induction, I was dressed once again in a chef de rang uniform consisting of black pants, white shirt, black vest, bow tie and a long white apron. Back to the good old days of "What can I get you?" and "Was everything to your liking?" and so forth.

I stood at the entrance of the fine dining room of the Sheldon Belgrano Hotel and waited patiently for the restaurant manager. I looked into one of two big Art Nouveau mirrors near the entrance, rolled my eyes and thought, *Here we go again, another two months and then it would be goodbye to fine dining service, goodbye to wearing funny uniforms and goodbye to serving spoiled customers.*

The restaurant manager, Terry O'Connor, who, needless to say, was Irish, greeted me. As matter of fact, he was the epiphany of an Irish man, with his red hair, white face covered in red freckles and a very heavy Irish accent. Terry was a very reserved character and never talked much. It seemed to me as if he tried hard to play the stiff English gentleman, with his face always pointing a little to the ceiling when he walked.

The restaurant was quite small and with only a little over forty seats, it was the smallest I had ever worked in. The design of the restaurant was distinctively Belle Époque and Art Nouveau with its typical floral and other plant-inspired motives. The main entrance of the restaurant featured two large wrought iron gates displaying flowing floral art typical for the Art Nouveau style. The restaurant was very elegant with tables covered in white linen and silver flatware and beautiful high-stemmed wine glasses.

The chef, as in any reputable London restaurant, was French and his name was Jean Pierre. Jean Pierre was the first real skinny chef I had ever met, which did not stop him from preparing excellent dishes. Jean Pierre had joined the Belgrano only six months earlier from the Le Gavroche Restaurant, where he had worked with the famous Albert Roux. He had not yet been awarded a Michelin star, but that was the plan for the future because the hotel had planned a multi-million-dollar renovation of the entire property that included the re-branding of our fine dining room. We *were* in the Gault Millau restaurant guide, where we scored fourteen points. Our fourteen points was not a bad result considering that the chef had only been there for less than six months.

The style of service practiced in this restaurant was a strange mix of old and new and some homemade additions. For example, Terry insisted on decanting every red wine, whatever the vintage, but no one used a candle when doing so. It was painful for me to watch them decant very good vintage Bordeaux without checking for sediments in the bottle. It was even more painful when I realized that they did not actually understand the full purpose of decanting old wines; all they knew was that "the wine has to breathe." Another example was cutting beef at the table; it irritated me immensely to see my demi chef de rangs or commis de rangs pocking their forks into the meat as deeply as they possibly could when cutting beef. It was very frustrating for me having to explain such simple basics, especially when I received silly responses like, "But won't the beef move on the cutting board?"

There were many more examples where attention to detail was completely lacking. Because of this, I lost professional respect for Terry pretty soon and, although I really liked him as a person, I realized that behind his gentlemanly façade there was not much else. As I found out later, Terry had actually grown up in this restaurant and worked his way up from bus boy to restaurant manager. He had never experienced any operation other than this fine dining room.

The restaurant was not very busy and the management perceived this outlet to be purely in a supporting role to the rest of the hotel. This was the outlet where breakfast was served and that was its main purpose. Lunch and dinner was quiet most days and the few customers we had were elderly regulars—they were retired, wealthy and, above all, very, very English. This was part of the problem of this restaurant; there was no energy, no buzz, just wealthy retirees and an Irish restaurant manager trying to run a Le Gavroche-style restaurant.

There was no way I would lower my standards and so I did my own style of service, that of Michelin restaurants. Jean Pierre shared my criticism of the restaurant operation with a passion. In his opinion, the running of fine dining restaurants should be left to the French and the running of pubs to the Irish. More than once he would get angry, telling me, "An sis is se reason why you 'ave waitars poking forks into se finest beef and young American red wines are being decanted. It is really awful. Se should go 'ome and run their poebs." Even though it was true and he had a point, I had to laugh every time at his accent. Jean Pierre and I became friends mainly because when it came to restaurant operation, we shared the same standards.

We worked in two shifts: early and late shift. There was no split shift, which was at least one advantage. I preferred the early shift, which included breakfast and lunch service and ended at around four o'clock when all preparation for dinner was completed. This was my favorite shift. Late shift started at three until closing, which normally was around eleven-thirty. I hated late shifts simply because there was nothing to do. We never had more than ten covers, which made late shifts a painful and boring exercise.

About seven weeks after I had started, rumors of the impending departure of our assistant food and beverage controller began circulating. I was getting excited and one day I was promptly summoned to the financial controller's office. The financial controller, by the name of Chris McCarthy, was another Irishman but of a very different caliber. He quizzed me for about an hour on all aspects of food and beverage cost control. We had learned cost control in hotel school but that had been a long time ago. Whatever I said in that interview could not have been too bad because at the end I got the job, and finally, after nearly eight years of working in restaurants, I said goodbye to the black pants, white shirt, black vest and bowtie.

I said goodbye to Terry and his team and promised to be on his back if his beverage cost was out of line. He tried half-heartedly to persuade me to stay, telling me that I could move on to become his assistant in no time if I would stay, but that was pretty much the last thing I wanted for myself. He could not really understand why I wanted to move from the hotel's fine dining restaurant to food and beverage control in the basement but that was to be expected. I do not think that when it came to his career he ever thought further than the next day.

Then on a Monday morning three weeks after my interview with Chris, I reported for duty to the food and beverage controller's office— in the basement. Rob van Krachten was from Belgium and had been in the job for nearly two years. He was an accountant by profession and had never actually worked in a kitchen or restaurant before. Rob was one year younger than I and he knew his numbers inside out. He was very polite and proved to be fanatically pedantic when it came to figures and reports. On my first day, he asked me to give him a summary of what I had done before. He listened attentively and when I had finished he gave me an overview of my new job.

"We are responsible for the controlling and receiving of food and beverage items, as well as storing and inventorying them. This includes wines, spirits, liqueurs, meats, fish and anything else that the chef or the food and beverage manager order. We monitor food and beverage costs, report potential shortfalls and suggest corrective action to maximize profitability."

"I see, okay," I lied, having completely lost track of what he had just said.

"At the end of every day we issue a daily flash food and beverage cost report which is then distributed to the chef, the food and beverage manager and the general manager."

"I see, okay."

"The daily flash food and beverage cost report is a summary of direct purchases, store issues and complimentary issues—do you follow me so far?" he asked.

I did not follow him at all, mainly because he had used so many new words like direct purchases, store issues and others that I was completely lost.

"Yes, I do," I lied.

"Good. Now, for the first two weeks I want you to complete the daily receiving sheet." He went on to explain that the daily receiving sheet was a summary of all items received. Each delivery was accompanied by a delivery note or invoice. "Do you have any questions?" he asked and smiled.

I had many questions and considered asking him to repeat what he had just said but at the end, I decided not to.

"No questions," I lied again.

"Good. I want you to finish the receiving lists by lunchtime," he said.

Rob had the unique habit of assigning deadlines and timeframes to everything he asked me to do. This put a little bit of pressure on me but at the same time, it was an excellent measurement tool for my effectiveness.

He showed me my desk, which was located just behind his. Our office was strategically perfect—to our left was the delivery entrance, to our right was the chef's office and next to the chef's office was the entrance to the main kitchen. The office itself was located in the basement and because of this, there were of course no windows. In front of our office was a long corridor which led to the storerooms, the housekeeping office and the room service office. Our dress code was smart casual but tie was a must. I had never worn anything other than my waiter's outfits and had only a limited inventory of smart casual clothes. I still had a long way to go before I settled into a respectable smart casual outfit.

Our office was quite small and there was just enough space for our two desks, one filing cabinet and one small table with a computer. The computer was used to record the inventory, issues and deliveries of our stores. This inventory had to be updated at the end of each day by taking off all items, which had been issued, and adding all items, which had been delivered. If we did everything right then the total inventory in the computer would balance with the actual inventory in the stores. It did not always.

Rob gave me a pile of receiving sheets and some deliver notes of items which had been delivered already. I began to write.

Rob checked on me an hour later. "You are a bit slow there. Don't worry about your handwriting, the important thing is to get it all recorded," he said. *Shit,* I thought, *that was clear. I have to do all this a bit faster.*

I finally entered the last invoice at three-thirty. Now I had to add everything up, subtract or add the corrections and then Rob asked me to check, check and double-check. In the end, he checked everything again and finally he allowed me to sign off on it. I had completed my first task with a three-and-a-half-hour delay. Rob then took me on a tour of the storerooms. By the time we finished our day had officially ended but we still had to update the inventory on the computer. Rob sat me down next to him and showed me how to enter new additions to inventory and how to take out the store issues of the day. He told me that we would do this together for the first few weeks and then he would leave it up to me. I liked his systematic approach, which was exactly what I needed with my limited knowledge of the job.

At six-thirty, we had completed the update and finally finished for the day. We had a quick bite to eat in the staff canteen and at seven I left. I had completed my first day as assistant food and beverage controller. I had found the job by myself without connections and it felt incredibly good.

At home things got a little better with Tatiana. She was happy that I had a job and I was happy to have a job I actually enjoyed. A few days later Tatiana announced that she had applied for a job on the cruise liner *Queen Elizabeth II* and that she had been short-listed and put on a waiting list. I was happy for her even though I was so preoccupied with my new job that it did not really fully register.

Over the coming weeks, my speed of completing tasks assigned by Rob picked up and at the end of my third week I did the receiving sheets. After some training by Rob, I had taken over the receiving and checking of deliveries. I was very thorough and issued more correction notices than Rob had ever done before. By doing this, however I had made myself very unpopular with several suppliers and in particular the fish supplier. Fish deliveries had caught my attention simply because the weight listed on the delivery notes were hardly ever correct. Day in, day out, the fish man delivered his fish and day in, day out, I corrected his quantity and weight until one fine day he decided to pay me back.

The fish man had learned to hate me from the very bottom of his heart. The fish man always came around ten in the morning but on one particular day he was half an hour late. "FISH!" he shouted as usual when he passed our office.

"Oh, your friend is here," Rob laughed.

"Yeah, let's see if he is trying to short-change us again today," I said.

"Well, there is only one way to find out. Off you go," Rob laughed.

"FISH!" the fish man screamed again.

"I am coming," I shouted back when I stepped into the corridor.

"Hurry up, I have parked on a double yellow line. I don't want to get a ticket because of you," he barked.

I was used to his rude manner by now and had learned to ignore him. He had dumped two large Styrofoam containers with salmon, halibut and sole on the floor next to our weighing scale. The fish man did not like my method of weighing every fish individually; he much preferred the old method of putting the entire container with fish and crushed ice on the scale and then subtract the estimated weight of the box and ice. This is how it was done before.

I felt that this method was far too inaccurate and at one point, I had started to weigh them individually. Weighing each fish was a dirty and slimy affair because I had to remove each fish by hand and place it on the scale. The fish man had expected that I would grow tired of sliding my hands into the crushed ice and into the gills of the fish in order to retrieve them for weighing. I did not, and the more he complained, the more determined I was to continue. The result had been a revelation because more often than not, the weight and quantity were different and I had to issue correction notices in favor of the hotel. The fish man hated me for that.

That morning we had a particularly large delivery of fish because we expected a busy weekend.

"Let's get on with it, you kraut."

I was used to that too and just smiled and suppressed my urge to say, *Fuck off, you slimy limey.* Without hesitation, I slid my hand into the gills of the first salmon and placed it on the scale. I recorded the weight and went on to the next one. The fish man stood there grumbling on about me. When I came to the last fish of the second container—a salmon—I could hardly lift it up. It was so heavy that I had to use both my hands but still it was impossibly heavy. *What is wrong with this fish?* I thought. The salmon literally crashed with a loud metallic clanging noise onto the electronic scale, which immediately jumped to 29.9 kilograms. This was completely impossible; something was wrong. I glanced at the fish man who was in tears, laughing.

"That's *real* Scottish salmon, laddie!" he cried, mimicking a Scottish accent.

I squatted down and took a closer look at the salmon and then I saw it—the underbelly of the fish had been crudely stitched together to stop whatever was inside from falling out. I picked up a knife and cut the twine where the belly of the salmon had been stitched together. The moment I cut the first twine several pieces of old rusty metal began dropping onto the scale; screws, steel plates, pieces of metal chains and other scrap metal had been stuffed into the salmon, apparently to teach me a lesson. In the meantime, several chefs had gathered, watching me remove the scrap metal from the fish. Everybody found it quite funny and the fish man was laughing with tears in his eyes.

I did not find it funny simply because it was so crude and unsophisticated but then again, so was the fish man's mind. I took the fish and threw it back into the Styrofoam box.

"Minus one fish which is not up to the hotel's quality standard," I said and prepared a correction note. The fish man stopped laughing.

"Hey, there nothing wrong with that fish!" the fish man protested suddenly.

"Nothing wrong? It was full of filthy dirty scrap metal in case you haven't noticed."

"There is nothing wrong with that. You wash the fish and it's gone," he yelled. Seeing him plead with me to accept the fish made me feel great. I was determined to send the filthy salmon back; I had enough witnesses to prove what had happened. I finished my correction note, ripped it off the pad, handed it to the fish man, and walked out of the kitchen.

The fish man was screaming and shouting, "You will regret this, mate," but I could not be bothered. I was sure that I had made the fish man my mortal enemy and expected more annoying encounters but instead he simply stopped talking with me. He would pass by our office, shout "Fish!" dump the Styrofoam container on the floor and with crossed arms, he would stand there and wait until I had checked the quantity and weight of his delivery. Once I finished I would hand him his copy of the delivery note and without saying a word, he would walk off. Suddenly the fish deliveries turned into very peaceful and quiet affairs.

Then on the thirtieth, we prepared for my first month's end. During lunch that day Rob told me all sorts of what he called "horror stories"—all the bad things that could happen during a month's end. The way he talked made me nervous. However, as he went on, I began to realize that his horror stories were only horror to the ears of an accountant. Horror in his view was, for example, not being able to balance the inventory on the computer with the actual inventory in the storeroom. Horror in his eyes was if he had to search for shortages or overages in the balance sheet.

"Sometimes," he said "you are looking for small amounts like four pence or twelve pence which would take you hours and hours to find."

"But in the end you find it, correct?" I wanted to know.

"Yeah, we always find it but it's hard work and it stresses me out because I have always this vision that one day I can't find it." He looked at me with a horrified expression in his face.

This is overdoing it a bit, I thought, *there is nothing horrifying or stressful in looking for a mathematical error.* I pretended to be sympathetic to his plight but it was difficult.

"Has it ever happened that you couldn't find a shortage or overage?" I wanted to know.

"Only once."

"So what happened? How did you balance the numbers in the end?" I asked.

"I went to see Chris the next day."

"I see. And?"

"It was amazing." Suddenly Rob's face lit up like a Christmas tree. "You should have seen him—he asked me to give him the balance sheet, I gave it to him and he placed it in front of his desk. For a few minutes, he just sat there and looked at the sheet; he did not move. Then he picked up the calculator, made a few calculations and suddenly he said, 'Here is your mistake.' It was amazing. Chris is incredible when it comes to numbers."

"How did he do that?"

"Until today he has not told me; he calls it the 'controller's eye' or something like that. He promised me that if it happened again he would

518

teach me. Sometimes I wonder if I should just put in a mistake on purpose just to find out how he does it."

Rob talked about Chris and his skills with the calculator as if he were a superstar or a famous singer. The more I thought about it the more I had to laugh. *How exciting can it possibly be to look for a mistake on a financial balance sheet and when you eventually find the mistake, you are treated like a hero*? I hoped that I would not end up like that one day. I promised myself that if the day ever came that I started talking like Rob, it was time for me to get back to the front of the house.

The month's end turned to be a lot of work but I could not associate any part of it with the word "horror." Two and a half months into the job, I was taking care of all deliveries, the completion of the receiving sheet, issuing of store orders and the daily update of the inventory. I loved the sensation of beginning to understand the essence of cost control. Over the coming three weekends I cleaned all storerooms and in the end we had super clean and tidy stores. It also gave me one great advantage—I knew exactly where everything was.

One day Chris the controller called me to his office, which was the first time since my interview with him. I was nervous.

"Hi Andre, take a seat," he said as I entered his office.

"Hello, Mr. Mc….." I said, a little shy.

"Call me Chris, please," he said.

I hated this habit of the Brits calling each other by first names. He was the financial controller, the most senior manager after the general manager—how could I possibly call him by his first name? I really did not like this habit.

"Ahm…yes," I did not intend to call him by his first name.

"André, you have been with us for a little over three months and I hear a lot of very positive things about you."

I was relieved; he had not called me to give me shit. I had half expected that maybe the fish man or his company had complained about me and my correction notes but it seemed that was not the case.

"Thank you, Mr. Mc…."

"Chris, call me Chris, please," he asked me again.

"Yes, Chris." I had said his name in such a low volume that it was hardly audible. Chris had to laugh. "Anyway, first of all, I am happy to tell you that you have passed your probation. Here is your letter of confirmation." He handed me the letter and shook my hand.

"Rob tells me that you have a lot of potential and therefore we have decided to send you to a workshop which is organized by the London Association of Chartered Accountants. The workshop is tailored for food and beverage cost controllers of international hotels. You will spend three weeks at their compound in Surrey in September."

I sat with my mouth open. I had passed my probation and now they are sending me to this workshop. I was very happy.

"Mr. Mc...sorry, Chris, this is very nice of you, thank you very much," I stammered. I wondered if the workshop would be for free or did they expect me to pay for it. I suppressed the urge to ask.

"Don't thank me, thank Rob for the recommendation and yourself for your hard work," he said and smiled.

This was the first time since I had left school that I had to study and then—in English. On our last day when we received our certificates, I was proud and happy. It was about at that time that Tatiana got her fateful call from the *QE2* telling her that they had a post as a purser and asking her to join within the next three weeks. It was a surprise. Although Tatiana was over the moon when she heard from Cunard Lines, for our relationship it spelled another long period of separation. Tatiana had asked them to give her twenty-four hours to think it over. She had done it for me and that night she told me that if I said no then she would not accept the offer and she would not go. I am sure she knew that I would never say no to her taking such an excellent opportunity to see the world, especially not after I had done the same.

The surprise was not that they had accepted her but the fact that she had to start within three weeks' time. We have had our difficulties lately but this came a bit as a shock. Tatiana's departure meant for me that I had to look for a new flat because with my current salary, I would not be able to afford the master bedroom in our existing house. My first thoughts were, *How do I survive in London without Tatiana? How do I find a new flat?* I had grown very lazy since we had been living together; she did everything and I did nothing. Tatiana had opened my bank account and Tatiana paid the monthly bills; in short, she did all the daily chores of an independent adult. I had never really lived by myself, except of course in Talasee and on the ship, but in Talasee everything was done by my mother and on the ship everything was done for us by the company. Not that I was not capable of doing them but I simply had never done them before. So of course we discussed the offer and opportunity and she even asked, out of courtesy, if I wanted her to stay but I could have never asked her to let such an opportunity slip through her fingers.

For the coming weeks until the day of her departure, we were busy finding a new flat for me and assuring each other of our eternal love. The closer the day of separation came, the more certain we were that whatever happened, we would never separate. No, there was no way I would hold her back. She called them the next day and accepted the position and three weeks later we kissed, hugged, and said goodbye at Heathrow Airport. The next time I would see her would be in six months' time.

Once Tatiana had left, I had to move out of the house on Valetta Road. I found a nice apartment again in Ealing. The apartment was located on the first floor in a house that belonged to a friendly Russian woman. When she introduced me to my flatmate, my heart nearly missed a beat. I shook the hand of the sexiest Norwegian woman I had ever laid my eyes on. She was gorgeous. To forestall any wrong ideas, she had a boyfriend— he was very tall, very strong from going to the fitness center every day, and he was very black. He did not live with us, he only came occasionally to visit but when he did, things could get quite noisy in her room.

As the months went by I began to settle into a very monotonous accounting routine of coming to work in the morning, receiving and checking goods, issuing stores, completing food costs reports and so on. It was the same every single day. The excitement of the first few months had gone and by now, I knew my job inside out. I was just about to voice my boredom to Rob when he announced one fine day that he intended to resign. I was stunned; this had come completely unexpectedly. He planned to return to Belgium where he wanted to get married. He also told me that he had recommended me as his successor to Chris. All of a sudden, the old excitement was back—I had a feeling that things began moving in the right direction.

Rob left the hotel six months after I had joined the cost control department. On the day of Rob's departure I was once again invited to the controller's office and once again, I was given a letter—my promotion to food and beverage controller.

Chapter 14

The day after Rob's departure, I started my life as food and beverage controller, which was not much different from before except that now I had to do everything by myself because Chris could not find an assistant for me. In order for me to finish all tasks in time, I had to start a little earlier and finish a little later. I did not really mind since Tatiana was not here anyway and I knew that this would only last until I had my assistant.

Two months later, I was still alone. Unfortunately for me, I had settled in a daily routine with the result that I managed to do everything by myself. The only time when Chris sent me help was for the end-of-month stocktaking. Then one day Chris called me to his office to tell me that they had found and assistant. By that time, I had been soldiering on alone for over four months. My assistant's name was Jerry and he was from Nigeria. When Chris first briefed me, he urged me to be patient with Jerry, saying that he came from a different culture and I had to train him up slowly. I was patient by nature and I was confident that Jerry and I would work well together. Jerry started the next day.

I had planned to start him off in the same systematic manner as Rob had used with me. After the introduction and a casual chat, I gave him a rundown on cost control and then went on to explain how the receiving sheet worked. I told him everything there was to know and ended with the instruction to complete the receiving sheet by noon. Jerry confirmed his understanding and began.

After one hour, I checked on him and that things were not going too well for Jerry was clear to me when I saw that he had not even completed copying the first delivery note. To my surprise, he had entered the *items* in the column meant for the *item code* and he had written the *cost* in the column for the *item description*. That was bad. I knew I had to start from scratch.

I tore up the first sheet and did the first one by myself. I gave it to him as a sample and asked him to continue. He continued and for a moment, it looked as if he had understood. I let him continue. By lunchtime, he had entered three delivery notes.

"When will we have lunch?" he suddenly asked. I was just in the process of preparing several purchase requests and turned to face him.

"Have you finished the receiving sheet?" I asked, surprised.

"Not yet, but I am hungry," he answered. I had not expected that.

"Have you not had breakfast?" I wanted to know.

"I did, but that was early this morning."

"I see. Okay, I suggest you go for a quick lunch and continue afterwards."

"Thanks. I will see you later," he said and disappeared.

I got up and looked at his receiving sheet. It was a mess. He had again used the wrong columns and half of the descriptions I could not read. *If he does not hurry up, he will never get this done in one day,* I thought.

I waited and waited but Jerry did not come back. I went looking for him and found him in the staff canteen. When he saw me, he gave me a big smile and asked me to join him.

"Jerry, I haven't finished my orders and you have to finish your receiving sheets."

"But I haven't finished my lunch yet," he said, looking at me with big eyes.

"You haven't? But you have been gone for nearly an hour."

"I cannot eat that fast; it's not healthy," he said. This was getting a little too much.

"Okay, finish your lunch and I'll see you in the office." I left.

Jerry came back to the office thirty minutes later. He sat down and continued to write. By five o'clock, he had still not finished and when I saw his receiving sheet, I knew I had to do it myself if I wanted to get it finished the same day. I decided to send him home for the day and complete the sheet myself.

This was the first time for me to work with someone from a completely different culture and I told myself that I had to be more patient. Unfortunately, things did not go much better the next day and the day after. I went to see Chris and told him the problems I faced. Chris asked me to be more patient. I wondered how much more patient I could possibly be with him but I promised to try again.

It was not easy. I liked Jerry as a person; he had a pleasant and humble personality but he just could not get any work done. After a while, it took me so much time looking after him that I could not get my work done in time. Two weeks later, I was back in Chris' office.

"Chris, it just doesn't work. I have tried to let him do the receiving but he is so slow that the delivery guys started shouting at him, which made him upset, upon which he refused to continue. He cannot do the receiving and he cannot finish the receiving sheets in time. I just think he is in the wrong job."

"Look, Andre, I understand, but we have to make this work. You know he went through a very bad time over at Heathrow."

"I know that, but if he worked over there as he does here, I am not surprised," I said.

"Why don't you let him do the stores? At least there he cannot do anything wrong," Chris pleaded. "Come on, what do you think?"

"Okay, okay, I'll let him do the stores but if he can't do that either, you have to put him somewhere else," I insisted.

I really did not like the idea of him running around in my well-organized storerooms. It had taken me a long time to get the par stocks in place and clean up the bin cards. The last thing I needed was for someone to come and mess everything up again. I was determined to have him transferred if he messed up my stores.

Chris looked at me and smiled. "Okay. I promise if he doesn't work out, we'll see what to do with him."

Jerry did mess up my stores and I was angry. As much as I tried to understand him and the world he came from, I could not work with him. After only one week, he had issued stores without recording half of the items he had given out. When we did the stocktaking, we missed items in one section and were over in another. It was bad. My bin cards were a mess with items crossed out, others added—everything was out of whack. In the end, I left him with cleaning jobs only and I did all the receiving, issuing, recording and so on. I did the daily flash food and beverage cost report, the end-of-month by myself and I was upset. It simply did not work out.

Rescue came in form of a Sheldon Grand account audit conducted by our Sheldon Grand head office in the States. For several days, the auditor interviewed me about my daily administrative tasks, reports I generated and all other tasks. He reviewed my files, my inventory lists and any other records I kept. When he finally finished he thanked me for my help and that was it—or so I thought.

The audit was conducted in all hotels and the outcome of it was a surprise for all of us. The day the report arrived Chris called Jerry and me to his office. He informed us that there would be a meeting with the general manager the same afternoon to inform us of some upcoming changes. Chris looked serious and I wondered what this was all about. I had been with the hotel now for over one year and in cost control for over eight months and I had never seen him this serious before.

Our general manager at the time was a very competent and impressive lady, Mrs. Michelle Burnes, and until today she remains one of the best GMs I've had the pleasure to work with in my career. We met in one of our small boardrooms on the third floor. There were seven of us: Chris the controller, his assistant controller Singh, our chief accountant Jim Spencer, my assistant Jerry and I. There was also the auditor and one more gentleman whom I had never met before. We all sat around the oval-shaped boardroom table. Chris did some chitchat with the unknown man but otherwise it was quiet. Our GM, Mrs. Burnes, entered the room a few minutes later.

"Good afternoon, gentlemen," she said with a strong and commanding voice. Mrs. Burnes was in her fifties but she struck me as a very attractive woman. She was tall, slim and had medium-length blond hair. Mrs. Burnes was divorced and there were rumors that she was once married to the CEO of British Airways.

"I am not sure if you all have met Clark here before. Clark is the purchasing manager of the Sheldon Park Tower Hotel." Clark looked around and nodded to everyone.

"Clark, you know Chris, Singh and Jim. Over here, we have Jerry and Andre. Andre is our food and beverage controller." Clark looked at Jerry and me and smiled.

"Nice to meet you," I said.

"And over here we have Mr. Carlson, who conducted the accounts audit." Carlson smiled at us.

"Now, you are all wondering why we are here. Well, as you know, Mr. Carlson here has conducted a thorough audit of our finance division. The audit went well and I fully support Mr. Carlson's findings and recommendations. So without further ado I give the floor to Mr. Carlson."

"First of all, I would like to thank you, Mrs. Burnes, for your kind hospitality during my audit. I also would like to thank Chris and his team here for your support and the assistance you have given me during this audit. Audits are always a pain and everyone is happy when it's over." Everyone laughed at this comment, probably because it was true. He had been a pain.

"Let me say on the outset that you all are doing a magnificent job and what's more important, you do it by the book."

I was relieved; at least this was a good start and it seemed there were no major problems. I relaxed a little.

"However…"—*Oops, here it comes,* I thought—"there was one area which caught my attention and that is the way you do purchasing." He paused and looked at Mrs. Burnes. She smiled and nodded knowingly.

"You don't have a purchasing manager and a large part of all purchases is done by Andre, your food and beverage controller, because he is looking after the stores. The department heads themselves purchase all other items needed. All food and beverage items are also purchased by Andre."

I suddenly had a bad feeling about this; my name had come up several times and I was not sure if I had done something wrong here.

"We currently have no process of frequently checking the competitiveness of prices at which we buy all these items. This means that if suppliers increase costs we simply accept them and take it as a given. From what I can see, this has been going on for years."

That definitely did not sound good, I thought, and shifted uncomfortably in my seat.

"On the other hand, you have a food and beverage controller and an assistant food and beverage controller in charge of controlling a rather small inventory."

Oh shit, I thought, *this was definitely not good.*

"Let me tell you that there is nothing wrong with this setup, but some simple calculations will show you that with this setup, the financial priorities are wrong and the efforts are not focused where they should be."

I swallowed, thinking, *I have definitely done something wrong here.*

"From what I have seen, the chef controls his costs pretty well. Andre, with the help of his assistant, is producing a number of reports which confirm that this is the case. A lot of his time is spent on month's end and counting the small amounts of beverages and stationary items in the stores during the month's end. He again produces a report to confirm that all is well controlled."

Mrs. Burnes looked at me and she was smiling. Unsure what to make of it, I forced myself to smile back at her.

"Andre, you don't need to look so worried. There is nothing wrong with cost control," she said.

Mr. Carlson looked at her and then at me. "Oh, there is nothing wrong with cost control. As matter of fact, you do your job very diligently, Andre," Carlson said.

Okay, so there is no problem but then what is all this about? I wondered.

"So the conclusion I came to was simple—instead of controlling a comparatively small inventory, you should concentrate and increase your focus on centralizing your purchases. Therefore, we have concluded that we need to refocus our efforts by creating a purchasing department. Mrs. Burnes and I have discussed this at length and we have agreed that, to put it in simple terms, the cost control function of the hotel will be reduced to a simple administrative part, with purchases charged directly to the receiving departments, and instead we will set up a proper purchasing function." Carlson smiled again, went back to his chair and sat down.

I looked at Mrs. Burnes and she smiled. "Thank you, Mr. Carlson, that was very brief and to the point. Now, what does that mean for you, Andre? Well, as Mr. Carlson has said, you are working very diligently and that's why we have decided to convert your function from cost control to purchasing and make you the hotel's purchasing agent."

Purchasing agent—what kind of title was that? James bloody Bond? I was not happy about this development and did not know what to say. It seemed that this whole meeting was about my position and me.

"Now because you don't have any purchasing experience, we will send you to the Sheldon Park Tower and the Sheldon Heathrow for a cross-training for one month. After that you will have to set up the purchasing department here at the hotel. Sheldon Grand has also scheduled a number of purchasing workshops which you will attend on behalf of the hotel." She looked at Clark. "We have asked Clark Keeves to put a training program together and make sure that you learn everything you need to become an effective purchasing agent." There was that silly title again—purchasing agent!

Everyone looked at me expecting me to say something, but all I knew was that they took away my "manager" title in exchange for a silly "agent" title. I remained quiet.

"I know this is a major change for you but don't worry, we are here to assist you. What do you say?" she asked. This was a very direct question and I knew I had to give her a straight answer.

"I think what Mr. Carlson said makes sense. It is true that we have never controlled our purchases and I am sure we could make a lot of savings," I said this without really meaning any of it.

"Good, that's what I thought. Gentlemen, we have an agreement. The training for Andre will start next week on Monday. Jerry will look after cost control during Andre's absence, which I am sure he will do well," she said. I was not so sure about that and thought, *Yeah, good luck to you people.*

After the meeting, Mrs. Burnes had a long chat with me about my new role. She was very honest and I trusted her for that. When we finally finished an hour later I felt much better, even though I was still not happy about the title. I decided that it was too early to mention this to her.

Things were going well at work but much less so with Tatiana. We were once again in a long distance relationship with Tatiana having holiday only every six months. Whenever her ship berthed in Southampton I would jump into our small Volkswagen Polo and drive down to see her. Most times, we had only enough time to sip a coffee and go for a walk before she had to return onboard and I drove back to London.

At that time, I pondered a lot about our relationship and the more I thought about it, the more I concluded that we seemed to be the happiest when we were apart. It was not that we were happy to be apart as such, but the fact that we could not see each other made us miss each other tremendously and this feeling we automatically translated into—love.

Such long distance relationships cannot and will not work. We both were in our prime, with Tatiana, attractive and outgoing, working on a world-famous cruise liner (and I knew how things worked onboard) and me in one of London's finest boutique hotels. And, if I may say so, at that time I was not too bad-looking either. Therefore, what happened next did not come as a surprise—we broke up. Having been together with Tatiana for a little over eight years, the breakup did of course affect me emotionally and I dealt with it the way I had always dealt with such emotional issues—I focused even more on my work.

The following Monday I reported for duty at the purchasing office of the Sheldon Park Tower Hotel, more determined than ever to make this new job work. Clark Keeves welcomed me to the purchasing department and showed me around. Clark Keeves was in his early forties and with his rather large belly and slight hunchback, it was clearly visible that he had done nothing but desk jobs all his life. Purchasing was his life; Clark Keeves was something like a legend within the Sheldon. He knew all the big suppliers and the big suppliers knew him. He knew how to negotiate and they always gave him their best prices. It was rumored that he had stakes in some companies and got incredible gifts from others. I do not know if this was true or not and I did not really care; fact was that I learned a lot from him.

Clark had five employees in his department and from what I could see there was precious little work he actually did himself. Over the coming days, he and his staff introduced me to the world of purchasing and although they showed me a lot, I had the distinct impression there was also a lot they did not show me. For the first time I was confronted with the concept of competitive quotes and the art of using leverage to get the best prices. They taught me when to walk out of a deal and when to accept. I watched and learned and I made notes. The more I saw during that one week the more I realized that we had been pretty naive and stupid at the Belgrano when it came to the pricing of products. There were many examples where I felt that suppliers simply overcharged us. Clark and his team showed me how to keep track of quotations and prices once they were agreed upon with a supplier. After that week I had a good idea what purchasing was all about. I had already many ideas of the cost savings I could make for the Belgrano once I got back.

The first thing I did when I was back in the office was to compile a list of common items used by two or more departments. When the list was completed, I worked out the annual consumption of each of these products. The result was amazing—the amount of computer paper we went through, for example, was staggering and we had never questioned the price. I was determined to change all that.

Armed with prices from Park Tower and Heathrow, I made appointments with suppliers. When I met the different suppliers and hit them with consumption figures and comparative prices, they were surprisingly humble and receptive to my demands. It took me more than two weeks just to complete this first initiative. I began to realize that the financial impact I made as cost controller compared to my first few days as purchasing agent—I still hated that title—was simply no comparison. My cost controller task had been a purely administrative function whereas as purchasing agent I actually made a real impact. Mrs. Burnes and Chris were utterly impressed with the headway we made. I established a database of suppliers and negotiated prices and deadlines when deals expired.

Three weeks later, I attended the first Sheldon Grand purchasing workshop in Surrey. This was my first workshop ever. To my surprise, there were purchasing managers from not only hotels but also other companies affiliated with Sheldon Grand. Amongst over fifteen purchasing *managers,* I was the only purchasing *agent.* Many of my colleagues questioned my strange title, which just made me more determined than ever to get rid of it as quickly as possible. I had to talk to Mrs. Burnes about it.

On the last day of our three-day workshop, we had to identify twenty products used by four or more different Sheldon Grand companies. Once the list was ready, each of us was assigned one or more products for which we had to negotiate prices based on the quantities required by the number of units identified as users. I had somehow naively not expected that I would be one of the chosen ones but I was. My project was called Hotel Linen. I was given the task of identifying one supplier who could supply all four Sheldon Hotels in London with hotel linen, from bed sheets and pillowcases to towels and bathrobes. We were given five weeks to complete our projects. In the evening, we all had dinner together and the next morning we returned to our hotels.

The next day Chris called for a meeting with him and Mrs. Burnes to brief them on the workshop. We met in the afternoon in the same boardroom where Mr. Carlson the auditor had presented the results of his audit. I briefed Mrs. Burnes and Chris on the workshop and of my assignment concerning the hotel linen. When I had finished my briefing Mrs. Burnes and Chris asked me how I intended to complete the assigned project. Up to that point, I had not really grasped the scale of the task nor did I have any clue where to begin.

"Ahm, I haven't thought of that yet," I answered.

Mrs. Burnes smiled. "Now, you have a lot of work to do. First you need to compile a master list of what linen is needed and then you have to find out from the other hotels what their requirements are in terms of quantity, linen quality, thread count and so on."

"You also need to find out what suppliers they use and what prices they pay. Once you have all that information you have to analyze all data on hand and prepare requests for quotations. Make sure that you know which suppliers to approach; this is a big job and they have to be able to handle it when it comes to timely delivery, quantity and different quality levels," Chris added.

All this sounded like a lot of work and I was not sure at all if I could handle all this. First, they had asked me to set up a purchasing department from scratch and now this. I was overwhelmed.

"I understand," I lied; the truth was, I was completely lost. I knew nothing about linen and much less about linen suppliers. I knew I would need a lot of help.

"Good, let's get started. If you need help, just shout," Mrs. Burnes said. "Mr. Carlson had informed us that he will be here in five weeks' time to review your proposal."

"No problem," I lied again.

We left the boardroom and on the way out Mrs. Burnes patted me on the shoulder. "You are doing a good job, Andre," she said and I forced a smile.

Back in my office, I sat down at my desk and took a deep breath. *Where do I start?* I asked myself. I looked at the files with suppliers and quotations I had begun to compile. Setting up a purchasing department seemed easy compared to this.

Overall it was a tiring task and more than once I worked 'til late at night. It was also a rewarding experience because in the process I learned a lot. My office was full of samples of bed sheets, pillowcases, towels and bathrobes. Mrs. Burnes had asked me to prepare a presentation of my findings to her, Chris, and Singh. For three days I sat in my office preparing overhead sheets with supplier information, cost comparisons and other data. I used different colored pens to make the presentation look as professional as possible. Then in the afternoon of the third day Mrs. Burnes, Chris and Singh joined me in the boardroom and I presented my findings. I was a little nervous at first but the more I talked about the subject of linen, the more I began to relax.

During the presentation, I kept on referring to samples which I had laid out on a side table. Mrs. Burnes and the others inspected them with interest. They asked several questions, all of which I answered with ease. By now, I was fully familiar with the linen specifications required by Sheldon. The airport hotels had slightly lower specs than the city hotels; therefore all guest-room linen I presented were made of 180TC, 100 percent cotton and 300TC, 100 percent cotton. The higher specs were for the city hotels.

Chris asked what type of cotton was used for bath towels. I confirmed that all towels were made of 100-percent combed cotton terry for the city hotels and a slightly lower quality for the airport hotels. Mrs. Burnes asked me what my weight and sizes of linen were before and after washing. I was prepared for that one because I had both figures ready for every piece of linen—before and after washing.

How many times were each item washed? Chris asked and I had to laugh at that one because despite protests of my housekeeper, I had insisted on fifty wash cycles. I finished the presentation with my recommendation for the supplier who had produced the best quality at the best price—Kenell Linen Ltd.

There were more questions regarding shipping times, delivery times, costs and some other details. Mrs. Burnes and Chris made some suggestions on how to fine-tune the presentation but overall they were pleased and finally they all clapped their hands and applauded.

"Well done, Andre," Mrs. Burnes said. "You have done a great job and I am sure Mr. Carlson will be pleased."

I was pleased too; I had put a lot of work and many hours into this project. At the end of the following week, I had my big day in front of an audience of fifteen which included Mr. Carlson, the purchasing managers of the other three hotels, their controllers, and several others. I did my presentation. I was far more nervous this time but again it all went well and after the final question and answer session, they all clapped. I was tremendously relieved that it all was over and I got many congratulatory comments.

Three months later Mrs. Burnes finally changed my title from the silly purchasing *agent* to purchasing *manager*. By the time I had completed twelve months as purchasing manager, I had settled well into my administrative routine and began to get bored with the daily nine-to-five office routine. I had been working in the accounting department of the Sheldon Belgrano now for a little over three years and was completely removed from the front-of-house operation. For several weeks already, I had felt restless but did not know exactly why. Then one day I realized that I missed the interaction with guests! I missed meeting all those weird and wonderful characters with their weird and wonderful little problems.

Those three years working in the back of house had been an interesting and educational experience and it had certainly expanded my knowledge of the hotel operation in terms of the financial aspect, but the daily nine-to-five routine had gotten plainly boring. To do something I had never done before like food and beverage control and then the task of setting up a purchasing department from scratch had been an exciting learning experience but now that all was up and running it had become boring, very boring indeed. For the past three months, I had already done voluntary duty manager shifts in the evenings but still, it was not enough. I missed the operation. Of course, I had no intention to ever work as a waiter again; no, I really could not stand the thought of spending eight hours or more in guests' presence ever again. I was looking for a job or position where I could choose when I wanted to see customers.

For days I pondered what I should do and how I could possibly get back into a guest-contact position. I concluded that the next logical step for me would be to become an assistant food and beverage manager and the only way to do that was for me to talk with Mrs. Burnes. One day I gathered all the bravery I had in me and asked for an appointment with her. That afternoon I entered her office with the magnificent view of Chesham Place. Mrs. Burnes sat behind her large teakwood desk and looked up from under her reading glasses as I came in.

"Oh, hello there, Andre, take a seat. I will be with you in a minute," she said and continued reading.

"Good afternoon, Mrs. Burnes," I said a little shyly.

When she heard that, she took off her glasses and took a deep breath. "How many times have I asked you to call me Michelle?" she asked in mock frustration. In fact, she had asked me many times to call her by her first name but for me, being German and from Black Forest, it was not something I was used to.

"I am sorry, Mrs. Bu…sorry, Michelle." Her first name was hardly audible.

"There you go, it's not that difficult now, is it?" she laughed.

"It is very difficult for me, Mrs...Michelle."

"Well, you have to get used to it if you want to continue working with me." She waved a finger at me and smiled. "Now what can I do for you?"

"I don't know how to start...Michelle...but I think it is time for me to move on in my career," I mumbled.

Mrs. Burnes'eyes went wide. "What do you mean? You want to leave?" She looked very serious now.

"No, no, I don't want to leave, not at all. You see, I had always wanted to become food and beverage manager eventually and I thought that after three years in cost control and purchasing I should now move on to another position," I said; the last words were again hardly audible. I had this strange sensation of doing something wrong.

Mrs. Burnes looked at me, obviously deep in thought. She remained quiet for a moment and then spoke. "So you eventually want to be a food and beverage manager. I see," she said.

"Ahm, yes."

"Hm, okay, why don't you let me think about it and see how we can move on from here? I have to talk with Chris of course and see what he has to say, okay?"

Now I looked up. I somehow had expected her to get angry but instead she was calm and collected. She got up and walked around the table.

"Leave it with me. We will meet again tomorrow, " she said and shook my hand. I smiled, thanked her and left her office.

The next day she called me in the afternoon and we met again in her office. To my surprise there was also Chris, Singh and out new executive assistant manager Terry Stanhope. Terry had joined us from the Sheldon Park Tower only three month earlier. He had held the position of food and beverage manager there and was rumored to be moving on to resident manager once he had successfully completed the opening of our renovated fine dining room. I hoped that this meeting with so many senior executives and managers was not called exclusively for me. It was.

"Andre come in and take a seat," Mrs. Burnes said.

I sat down next to Chris and Singh. "Hi Chris, hi Singh." The two accountants smiled. "Hello, Terry."

Chris talked first. "So I hear you've had enough of finance?" Chris said. For a moment I was not sure if he was joking or serious.

"No, I like my job, it's just…"

Chris interrupted. "Don't worry, I am only joking," he smiled. *So he is joking,* I thought, relieved.

"Andre, I have told Chris about your wish to become a food and beverage manager and we have discussed your wish at length. We fully understand and appreciate that you are ambitious and we want to help you reach your goal. You have been in finance now for over three years and we all have agreed that first you need to get back into the food and beverage operation." *So far so good,* I thought, and wondered what came next.

"Obviously your next move would be to become an assistant food and beverage manager but as you know, we are a small hotel and we don't have that position here," she paused and looked at me. "Although we don't have this position we had another idea, or rather Terry had the idea as to how you could move on.

Now since you are already working as part-time duty manager in addition to cost control and purchasing, we have decided to make you operations manager. As operations manager you will be reporting directly to me, and on a dotted line, to Chris on the finance side and to Terry on the operational side. Your responsibility will be to look after 20 Chesham Place, the bar, cost control, purchasing and you would be in charge of the hotel in the evenings. You would become an Excom member and your salary would be adjusted of course."

I was stunned; that was far more than I had hoped for—operations manager.

"You would work very closely with Terry here who would also coach you in regard to the food and beverage part. Overall you would be in charge of the hotel's operational departments."

All four of them looked at me expectantly and I did not know what to say. As far as I could see, I had not much choice. "Sounds good, Mrs. Burnes."

"Gentlemen, what do I have to do to make him call me Michelle—give him my job?" Everyone started laughing.

"Sorry, Michelle," I said.

"That's better. So I take it that you accept the position?"

"Ahm, yes," I mumbled and with that I had accepted the position of operations manager of the Sheldon Belgrano. We all got up and everyone shook my hand, congratulating me on my new position.

I started my new assignment as operations manager two weeks later, after having received a thorough briefing by Mrs. Burnes, Terry and Chris. The briefing had been quite an intimidating experience, especially the part where I was told that I had to chair a weekly operations meeting. I had attended plenty of meetings but I never had chaired one before. I was also asked to review the revenue and expense forecasts of the different departments and if we had VIP visitors, I was expected to organize these down to the last detail. I did not dare to ask any questions because I did not want them to think I didn't know. The only problem was that I didn't actually know. When Mrs. Burnes then informed me that she wanted me to chair the first such meeting two days later, I was slightly shocked because I had no clue as to what to say to all those people. After the briefing, I pretended to be confident that I could do the job and in return I was rewarded with a sleepless night.

I spent the next two days trying to figure out what to say in that meeting. It was a terrifying experience. I sat at my desk in my office trying to write a speech. I knew I had to make an impression if I wanted them to take me seriously; the last thing I wanted was for them to walk out of that meeting thinking, *The operations manager is a complete dork.* I wrote some words, crossed them out and began again and so it went on the whole day and in the end I had—nothing.

At the end of the second day I still had not progressed any farther and the piece of paper in front of me was still empty. That evening I went to bed doing what I always did before going to sleep—read a book. Since coming to England, I had developed an interest in books about the Second World War. One of the reasons was the super abundance of such books in English bookstores and also because to my surprise, the Brits seemed to look at this period of history in a much more objective manner than what I was used to back in Germany.

The book I was reading at the time was a biography of Winston Churchill. The part I was reading at that time talked about him justifying his confidence that England would win the war against Germany. I was surprised to read that he actually was not confident at all about the outcome of the war but he knew he simply could never show his concerns openly. *That is ironic,* I thought, because I was in just the same position as he with my meeting the next day. I continued reading with interest about how he was full of doubts but created one of his finest speeches—"We fight them on land…"—and the more I read, the more I realized that at the time, Winston Churchill faced the same problem as I—a severe lack of confidence. By the time I fell asleep a plan had formed in my mind—whatever happened in that meeting, I had to project confidence.

The next morning I was in tatters. The thought of that meeting occupied my mind completely when I was in the shower. When I got dressed and on the way to the hotel, I was terrified. Of course, there was no way I could admit or even show that to anyone. Outwardly, I projected calmness and confidence but inside I was a mess. Finally, at three in the afternoon, the big moment came and I went up to the boardroom. The moment I entered the room my heart stopped. There were more than fifteen people crowded around the boardroom table, including Mrs. Burnes, Chris and Terry. The moment I entered, the room fell quiet, and although I did not look at anyone's faces, I knew they all were staring at me.

Mrs. Burnes turned to me and smiled. "Ah, Andre, there you are. Here, take a seat," she said, pointing at the empty seat at the head of the table.

This gesture caused some instant murmuring around the table; obviously everybody was wondering why the purchasing manager cum cost controller was asked by the general manager to sit at the head of the table, a place which was normally occupied by her. I looked around the table; there was Tim, the chief concierge; Jean Pierre, the chef; Brian, the new restaurant manager of Chesham's; two front office supervisors and all the other operational managers. I could see that they all wondered what this meeting was all about. Looking at them I suddenly realized I was scared shitless.

"Good afternoon, ladies and gentlemen," Mrs. Burnes began.

"You are probably all wondering why we have summoned you here this afternoon. Well, I can assure you that nothing bad has happened but we have an important announcement to make."

The boardroom was dead quiet and not even the slightest whisper could be heard.

"As you all know, the hotel has undergone some substantial changes over the past year. We have completely renovated the lobby and the bar and we have created a new restaurant—our award-winning 20 Chesham Place," she said. There were several nods around the table.

"Besides the renovation, we have now an executive assistant manager, Terry, who has been a great help to me over the past month. And last but not least, you all know that we have converted our food and beverage control department into a purchasing department. This was a big task which would not have been possible without the efforts of Andre here." She looked at me, giving me one of her famous smiles.

"As part of all these changes we now need someone to assist Terry to look after the operation of the hotel. It did not take us long to find the right person to take on this responsibility, which brings me to the reason for our meeting this afternoon. We have decided to promote Andre Schwarz from purchasing manager to operations manager. Andre will be in charge of the operation of food and beverage, rooms and he still will be overseeing purchasing and cost control." It was still dead quiet in the room; nobody spoke.

"Andre has plenty of operational experience, having worked for several years in Michelin-rated restaurants, a cruise liner, banqueting and for the past three years here at the Sheldon Belgrano as food and beverage controller and purchasing manager. On top of this, Andre has done evening-duty manager for over three months and that was completely voluntary. Therefore, I feel that he is more than capable of handling this important position. I know that I can count on you to give Andre your fullest support in this challenging task," she said and began clapping her hands and everyone followed. Mrs. Burnes looked at me, nodded with a smile, and motioned for me to talk. I froze instantly; I had hoped at one point that I might get off without saying anything but that hope had evaporated in an instant. The clapping died down and I began to feel very hot. My heart was beating fast now. The room had turned quiet. I suddenly had to think of Winston Churchill and his pretending to be confident even when he was not. Everyone looked at me and I knew I had to say something.

"Ahm, good afternoon, everyone," I began rather lamely. Some of the guys started to smile. "Ahm, well, first of all I would like to thank Mrs. Burnes and Terry here for giving me this opportunity." *So far so good, I had thanked them and now what? I have to tell them a little about myself first.*

"I don't want to make this too long. As Mrs. Burnes has mentioned, I have worked in several hotels, restaurants and a cruise liner as demi chef de rang, chef de rang, headwaiter, food and beverage controller and most recently as purchasing manager." I looked around the quiet room; all eyes were on me. I had no idea what everyone was thinking. I glanced around the table and hardly dared to look in anyone's face. What were they thinking? I had to continue.

"I am not here to make big changes but to help you to achieve the goals set out by Mrs. Burnes." I had not dared to call her Michelle in front of the assembled managers. Mrs. Burnes remained quiet. I felt I had said all there was to say and decided to close. "That's really all I have to say at this point. I look forward to working with you all. Thank you."

Nobody said anything and then Mrs. Burnes started clapping her hands and everyone followed.

"Thank you, Andre, that was short and to the point—just like the way you work," she laughed. "I ask you all to give Andre your fullest support in his new and challenging position." And with that, the meeting ended.

I had no idea what impression I had made on the assembled managers and with trembling legs I got up. To my surprise, many of the managers walked up to me and congratulated me on my promotion and my "speech." Mrs. Burnes stood next to me and was smiling; she knew that despite my doubts, the meeting had been a success. I was still not sure what to make of all this and I was not sure at all whether they had accepted me or not but I knew I could not show what I felt. So I stood there with an artificially confident look on my face.

Over the coming weeks, I got a taste of what it was like to be operations manager. Whenever I did my rounds, managers confronted me with problems and requests for guidance. In the beginning, I was a little shy, especially when some of the older managers approached me, but I got the hang of it pretty fast.

For the first few evenings, things were relatively quiet and I leisurely did my rounds around the hotel checking on staff presence in the outlets, guest floors and other areas of the hotel. One evening the concierge called me to the hotel lobby. When I reached the lobby, the concierge clerk, Paul, pointed discreetly at a woman sitting on one of the tables in the lobby lounge. She was dressed in a short—very short—skirt with a sort of leopard-skin pattern, a very tight tank top of the same color and pattern.

"See that black lady over there?" he whispered. "That's Tina—she is a prostitute, mate, and she has AIDS."

"She has what?" I whispered in disbelief.

"AIDS, you know the disease which…" he tried to explain.

I interrupted him. "I know what AIDS is Paul, but how do you know that?" I wanted to know.

"Everybody knows she is certified with AIDS and whenever she comes to the hotel we ask her to leave," he said.

I looked at the woman seating there, not knowing what to do next. I knew I had to do something, especially because this was my first "case" as operations manager. I had only one choice—I had to go up to her and ask her to leave. I knew we did not allow prostitutes in the hotel and therefore I had enough reason to go up to her and ask her to leave the premises.

"Okay, let me handle it," I said as confidently as I could and walked off.

"Good evening," I said politely as I approached the table. From the corner of my eye I could see my fellow colleagues watching me, probably wondering what would happen next. I found out later that they did not actually *wonder* what *would* happen because they *knew* exactly what would happen and I did not.

She looked at me with an angry expression. "What do you want?" she hissed.

"Ahm, I am afraid I have to ask you to leave," I said rather lamely.

"May I ask why?" she said in an aggressive tone. That was a tricky question.

"Ahm, you should not be here."

"Why not? I am a guest."

Shit, what now? I thought there was no way I could leave this lobby without getting her out first. I was feeling annoyed now.

"Look, we both know why you are here and this is not the place for you." Although she was obviously aggressive, I felt bad talking to her like that.

"I will sit here as long as I want," she said and looked away.

"If you don't leave I'll have to call security," I challenged her.

"Try that and I'll scratch you!" she hissed.

540

That was unexpected and instinctively I answered, "In this case, I have to call the police." Of course, I had no intention of calling the police but somehow she must have gotten the message and, to my surprise, she got up.

"I will get you," she hissed. At the same moment, her outstretched right hand shot threateningly towards me with her long bony fingers and nails pretending to grab me.

She has AIDS! The thought shot through my head and I instinctively stepped back with my eyes wide open and adrenaline pumping. She missed me by an inch. I was scared now. "I will call the police," I barked angrily.

She began to laugh like a maniac and to my horror, she stepped towards me. I was about to run when she suddenly turned towards the door. At the door she stopped and turned. "I will see *you* again," she hissed and then she left. I just stood there looking at the door; it had been a scary experience.

"Well done, mate," the desk concierge suddenly said, standing behind me.

"Thanks," I muttered, trying to pull myself together. At least the woman had left. All the girls behind the front desk looked at me, smiling and nodding approvingly. My heart was still pumping from the experience. *Act confidently,* I said to myself and I forced a smile.

I turned to the concierge. "Let me know if she comes back," I said and walked off in the hope that she would never return.

The encounter with Tina was only the first of many to come but over time I learned to deal with her in the appropriate manner and after a while it was enough for me to walk towards her and she would get up and leave, not without some of her famous mock attacks. This first incident had earned me the respect of the people and, as I learned later, there had been cases before where security and even Mrs. Burnes had to get involved.

After this incident, the evening had all signs of becoming a quiet one when suddenly my pager started beeping—it was a fire alarm. As instructed during my induction, I rushed to the front desk where I found a nervous front desk supervisor.

"What happened?" I asked. Looking at the fire panel, I heard a beeping sound and noticed a red light flashing but I could not quite make out the location.

"I don't know, sir, it suddenly started. It seems the alarm was set off in the room-service office," he stuttered.

"In room service and not in the kitchen?" I asked, thinking that it may be a mistake and the alarm was set off in the kitchen.

"No, you see, here it says RS underneath the light—that's the room service office."

"Have you informed the emergency response team?"

"Yes, sir, they are on the way."

"Good," I said. I picked up my walkie-talkie. "ERT leader to ERT team, are you on location?" I shouted into the radio. I waited for an answer; it did not take long. The radio crackled.

"In room service, just a burned toast. Over."

"Okay, got that. Over," I said and hit the *silence* button on the fire panel. I was relieved to hear that it was a false alarm. The beeping sound stopped but the light kept on flashing.

"How do I switch off the light?" I asked.

"You can't, sir, the fire brigade will do that when they reset the panel."

The fire brigade! I had completely forgotten that part and suddenly I could hear the sirens of fire engines in the distance. *Shit.*

I dashed out of the front office into the hotel lobby where several guests, waiters, waitresses and concierge staff members were already assembled, wondering what was happening.

"Come on, guys, get back to your stations," I said nervously; the last thing I wanted was a crowd of people in the lobby. I went outside hoping to stop the firefighters from rushing inside my hotel lobby with all their gear and other stuff.

When I stepped outside, I could already see the fire engines turning onto Chesham Place. To my horror there were three of them, including one with a large ladder. Several passersby had stopped to see what was going on. The noise from the sirens was deafening as the three large red vehicles with their flashing lights pulled up in front of me. I wanted to scream, "Shut that off!" but I knew that that would not help much. The fire engines came to a screeching halt and before the vehicles had stopped completely, the doors opened and several firefighters jumped out.

Suddenly one of them, dressed in a dark red overall with bright orange stripes and a large red helmet stood right in front of me. "Are you the manager in charge?" he asked.

"Yes, that's me, it was a false alarm," I said immediately, hoping they would get back into their truck and leave.

"We don't know that yet. Show me the location of the alarm," he barked and moved forward. Behind him the men had opened some doors of the fire engine and had begun retrieving cylinders of some sort. There was shouting of instructions and I suddenly felt hot.

"Ahm, yes, of course, please follow me," I said and took the lead.

I entered the lobby where several guests began asking me at the same time what had happened. "Don't worry, it's just a false alarm," I kept on repeating. I turned around and suddenly my heart stopped—there were at least ten or twelve firefighters with heavy equipment in the lobby, dragging their heavy cylinders across our brand-new marble floor.

"Come on, come on, let's go. Where is the location of the alarm?" the firefighter said impatiently.

I led him via the back office to the staircase leading down to the basement. We reached the room-service office, which still smelled heavily of burned toast. The firefighter went over to the toaster and observed the blackened little machine. He looked at the ceiling at the smoke detector and then again at the toaster.

"This thing stood right here underneath?" he asked.

"Ahm, yes," a nervous room-service manager answered.

The fireman shook his head. "Wrong place. In the future you place it somewhere else. Do you understand?"

"Yes, sir."

The fireman picked up his walkie-talkie. "L1 to L2—false alarm, pack up. Over," he barked. To me, he ordered, "Bring me to the fire panel."

"Yes," I answered and led him back to the front office. At the fire panel, he hit the reset button and the red light stopped flashing. I was relieved; everything was back to normal.

When we came out into the lobby the twelve firefighters had settled on chairs and sofas and some were standing, leaning against the pillars. It was a nightmare. The fire team leader ordered them back to the fire trucks and then he turned to me.

"You make sure that toaster is removed from underneath that smoke detector."

"Yes, sir, I will" I answered. I went outside with him and mumbled "Thank you." He climbed back into his truck and then the three fire engines left. I took a deep breath, happy that this was over. The incidents with Tina the prostitute and the fire brigade were only the beginning of weird and wonderful encounters during my evening shifts.

Over the coming weeks I got involved in all aspects of the hotel operation, especially in food and beverage where I finally had the chance to do something about the service in our signature restaurant, Chesham's. With my Columbus Hotel days in mind, I began to organize service-training sessions, which I conducted personally. We introduced daily briefings with the chef and I taught the service staff what I had learned at the Columbus, from wine training and table management to up-selling. In the beginning the Irish restaurant manager was not too happy about that but after a while he began warm up to the idea, especially when he saw how much the chef participated.

I had not much experience when it came to rooms but I tried to be there when they needed me and that was mostly for guest complaints. I had no problem in handling our sometimes obnoxious guests because I learned a lot during those demanding times. I began to understand the difference in room types, the importance of accurate room assignments and maximizing revenues during full-house situations. I still looked after purchasing and cost control but that had become second nature by now.

One day our human resources director left the hotel and for three months I had to look after that department too. I conducted interviews and prepared the monthly HR reports for Mrs. Burnes. Soon I was fully familiar with staff turnover numbers and disciplinary procedures. After eight months, I had an impressive portfolio of departments to look after: human resources, food and beverage, culinary, rooms, cost control and the purchasing department. I enjoyed my new responsibilities and in particular the fact that I attended many workshops and seminars. I joined the Hotel Management Association, became a member of the Chaine de Rottiseur and was even sent to Lausanne in Switzerland for six months. Mrs. Burnes and the hotel invested some serious money in my ongoing education for which I am still grateful today.

It was during my time in Lausanne that I met a fellow student by the name of Bo Bennet Chang. Bo was Malaysian Chinese and soon the two of us became friends. We didn't actually get on in the beginning because I thought of him as pompous, extravagant and spoilt. Expensive brands and money were everything for him. He continuously had to show off his Armani suits and kept on bragging about his rich parents. One day, however, he did something truly amazing—he jumped into the air and landed on the floor in a split! As I found out, he held the black belt in tae kwon do. I asked him where he had learned that and he offered to teach me and we became friends. Bo had always wanted to move to England and when I returned to London, I recommended him for a captain's job in Chesham's restaurant. Bo got the job and started two weeks later and from that day we were inseparable.

It was through Bo that I met Nancy, the sister of one of his friends from Lausanne. Nancy was Hong Kong Chinese and I fell for her from the first moment I saw her. It did not take long and we started going out together. Nancy was beautiful and I simply could not stop looking into her amazing almond-shaped eyes. From that moment on, I was hooked on Asian girls for a long time to come.

I knew nothing about Chinese culture and the more time I spent with Nancy, the more I learnt. We had countless dinners in London's Chinatown in Soho and if we did not dine in Chinese restaurants, we bought Chinese take-a-way meals from one of the many shops in London. During my time on the ship, we went several times to Asia but there was of course never enough time to learn anything about the culture. I remember when we were in Singapore, Angelika took us to Newton Circus with its many hawker stalls. At the time, I had never eaten Chinese food and even the thought of it had turned me off. In any case, Nancy taught me much about Chinese food and it did not take long for me to like it. I learned that there was more to this cuisine than sweet and sour pork. One day Nancy had to go back to Hong Kong to visit her grandmother and when she came back, she brought with her a brochure from the Hong Kong Hotel Association. As we sat in her apartment and looked through the brochure, she told me all about the glamorous hotels in Hong Kong. So far the London hotels had been the most luxurious I had seen in my career and it was difficult for me to imagine how much more luxurious they could possibly get, but the way she described them, I was impressed. I had never before seen so much marble and glamour than on those pictures; it was truly amazing. Up to that point I had not known much about Hong Kong. I knew it was in the Far East but I had no idea whatsoever what this city was all about. If anything, I had thought of bamboo huts and rice fields when I heard the name Hong Kong.

Incidentally, soon after, our assistant financial controller Singh was transferred to China as financial controller in a place called Xian. The only thing I knew about China was that it was a huge country and very far away. Of course, more recently, there had been reports on TV about some violent demonstrations at Tiananmen Square in Beijing but again, the place was so far away and I knew so little about it that it did not really affect me. We had a leaving party for him at Mrs. Burnes' home where we drank and talked a lot.

At one point during the party Singh took me aside and told me that he might need some good people there and he would be in touch. I thought not much about it at the time and assured him if I heard from him, I would consider. The party finished in the early morning hours and as usual, I had a pretty bad hangover the next day.

Life in London was good, especially in summer. I enjoyed weekends in London in particular. I enjoyed the relaxed atmosphere on sunny Friday afternoons when all the businessmen and women gathered in local pubs celebrating their TGIFs with pints of foamless beers. When the pubs got full, the crowds spilled over onto the streets. It seemed to me as if the whole city of London turned into one big party on Saturday nights. I had just bought a second hand M-series BMW 325 and I truly loved that car. Such cars were expensive in London at that time and I enjoyed driving through Soho at night with Nancy and her friends at my side. He friends were of course all Chinese and I was the only European in our group. We had lots of fun and in the process, I learned a lot about them and their culture, which was dominated by Armani suits, Gucci bags and Prada shoes. They were a materialistic bunch but I liked them and we thoroughly enjoyed those weekends. Besides branded clothes, I learned about other aspects of their culture such as feng shui and the moon festival.

At the hotel things went well and I had long since established my daily routine. Although I had many responsibilities, I began to feel bored. I had been at the Belgrano in London now for nearly four years and knew the hotel inside out. Then one day I decided to ask Mrs. Burnes.

"You want a transfer?" she said, a little surprised. "You don't like it here?"

"Of course I like it here, Mrs. Burnes, but I have been here now for four years and I think I have to start thinking of my career."

"I understand. So what exactly do you want to do?" she wanted to know.

"Well, I always wanted to go back to food and beverage as assistant food and beverage manager."

"But you are doing that already here and more, Andre."

"I know, but the operation here is very small and I feel that I still have a lot to learn in order to work in a larger operation."

She looked at me and remained quiet.

"Don't get me wrong—I very much appreciate everything you have done for me and I like the Belgrano but I can't stay here forever." Despite what I had said, I felt bad and somewhat ungrateful.

"I understand. Look, let me think about it and I'll get back to you. Let me see what we can do."

I left her office and felt good that finally the subject was on the table. In the coming weeks, not much happened. I continued to look after the operation, had my encounters with Tina and two more fire alarms.

A few months earlier, I had applied for a placement at the Cornell University in New York. I had done this with the Karl-Duisberg-Gesellschaft in Cologne, Germany. They had accepted me and Mrs. Burnes had been very helpful in securing me a position at the St. Regis Hotel in New York for my practical training. Unfortunately, with the American invasion of Iraq a few months later, the United States cancelled all foreign visas and that had spelled the end of that. I was now determined more than ever to get a transfer abroad and if not with Sheldon then with another hotel company. Mrs. Burnes kept on telling me she was working on it.

I liked her a lot but I also knew that she wanted to delay my departure as much as possible but for the moment I waited. Chris, our financial controller, called me to his office one day and tried to persuade me towards a career in accounting. He told me that I was doing well in purchasing and cost control and I had the talent to go further in the accounting department.

"Why do you want to stop doing something you do so well?" he asked me.

My answer was simple—I missed the food and beverage operation and the contact with guests. He asked me to think about it; I did not have to think much. I would not consider a career in accounts and it was that simple. I was not the type to sit in an office day in day out crunching numbers; it just was not me. I was sure that Mrs. Burnes had spoken about this and it was her idea to have him talk to me. Nevertheless, I knew she was trying to help me.

One day she informed me of a possibility as purchasing manager at the Sheldon Hotel in Riyadh, Saudi Arabia, but I was not really inclined to work in that region considering the current political circumstances with the Americans fighting a war in Iraq. Besides, I wanted to go back to food and beverage. I declined and waited.

In the meantime, I enjoyed my time with Nancy. I had taken up tae kwon do classes with Bo and my skills were improving rapidly. I could not quite master the split yet but I was getting painfully close. Our training ground was Nancy's living room and more often than not, we broke vases or other sensitive furniture pieces in her apartment during our exercises, but it was fun nevertheless.

Then one day, I was just doing my evening shift when I received a call from Singh in China, which came as a total surprise for me. He called from the Golden Flower Hotel in Xian; I still had no idea where exactly that place was. He told me that he was looking for a purchasing manager for his hotel. Over the phone, he told me everything about the hotel, the city and the job. I did not know anything about China and I had never heard of a place called Xian, but the prospect of moving to Asia made me listen to him. He promised to send me more details by mail and asked me to call him as soon as I had received everything.

Two weeks later, I received the package. There was a letter from Singh and a brochure of the hotel. It was an amazing-looking property, just like one of those hotels in Nancy's brochure. The salary package was very attractive and to my amazement, the hotel would take care of tax, accommodation and all other costs. I had many sleepless nights trying to make up my mind as to whether to take the offer or not. The problem was the position—it was purchasing and not food and beverage. I was twenty-eight years old at the time and did not want to spend any more time in a department I was not really interested in and it was for that reason that I declined.

I called Singh and informed him of my decision, saying that if he had an assistant food and beverage manager position I would join him without hesitation. Although I was not a hundred percent sure whether I had done the right thing, I knew that if I ever wanted to get the job I wanted I had to stand firm. He tried to explain that this was a once-in-a-lifetime opportunity and tried to persuade me to take it but I stood my ground and in the end, he respected my decision and promised to be in touch if such an opportunity occurred. Once again, I felt bad and wondered for several days to come whether it had been the right choice to decline a chance to go to Asia. Of course, I had consulted Nancy but with her being from Hong Kong, she had advised me to wait for an opportunity to go to Hong Kong.

In the meantime, I had made contact again with my old friend Franz from the *Europa* and offered him a job as room-service manager at the Sheldon Belgrano. Franz accepted and a few weeks later, he joined us. The timing was perfect because my flatmate Christine had decided to move to Miami in the States and I had to look for a new place to live. Franz and I found a flat in Muswell Hill and moved in together. We got on well and in a way, it was again like in the good old days on the ship. Christmas came and went and we celebrated the new year at a restaurant called Barbarellas. It was a great party and we only left in the early hours of the next day. I did not know it at the time but it was to be my last New Year's Eve in London and Europe.

The new year started not much differently from the way the old one had ended. I worked long hours, had my challenges with Tina the prostitute, obnoxious guests, and the fire brigade. Even Franz was not able to stop his staff from burning toast and, in the process, setting off our highly sensitive fire alarm system. By now, I knew the commander of the fire brigade quite well and whenever we had such false alarms, I welcomed the fire brigade at the main entrance and everything thereafter—the inspection and the resetting of the system—went like clockwork.

During Christmas and New Year's there had also been increased activity by the infamous IRA with several bomb attacks in central London. Hotels such as ours were on high alert. Mrs. Burnes had us attend courses and workshops organized by the London bomb squad and soon we became very conscious about unattended briefcases and luggage which was left alone in the lobby. Much of this responsibility fell on my shoulders and in turn, very much to the annoyance of our concierge, I became very pushy keeping up the safety and security standards in the hotel. I did not tolerate any unattended luggage, briefcases or other items in the lobby and I inspected all back-of-house areas daily. I was ruthless when it came to boxes left in fire exits or unattended cardboard boxes in back-of-house corridors. Mrs. Burnes loved me for it.

Then, one fateful day, four months after his first call from Xian, Singh called again. He had moved from Xian to Beijing in the meantime and was now the financial controller at the Sheldon - Sara Hotel in Beijing and he was looking for an assistant food and beverage manager! Of course, I was very exited. He told me everything about the hotel and that the current management company, Sara, was in negotiations with the owners and Sheldon to convert the hotel into a Sheldon. He went on to explain that they were looking for people who were familiar with the Sheldon system and standards and that they were looking to transfer several staff from the four London hotels to accomplish this task. He wanted me to come as assistant food and beverage manager. I could hardly contain my excitement when I heard that. I knew right there and then, without knowing much about the salary package, that I would accept that job. The waiting had finally paid off; I had an offer to go to Asia as assistant food and beverage manager.

Singh explained in detail everything about the hotel—it had four hundred rooms, four restaurants, a nightclub and a lobby lounge and bar. I would get an expatriate's package, which at the time did not mean anything to me but it was very attractive nevertheless. He informed me that the food and beverage manager would call me for a telephone interview and we would take things further after that.

Two days later, the food and beverage manager called. His name was Emil Aver, he was Swiss, he grilled me for over two hours, and in the end—I had the job. He told me he would send the employment contract by courier and asked me not to do anything before I had it in my hands. I promised to do just that and waited.

When I told Nancy the news she was a little skeptical, telling me how backward Beijing and China in general was. There was of course the concern about the crackdown on Tiananmen Square a few years earlier but that did not dampen my excitement at all. There had been many reports in the media about China and its rapid development and I was overall very positive about the move. Emil had told me on the phone that Beijing was like Hong Kong twenty years ago and although I did not know what Hong Kong was like twenty years ago, it sounded exciting anyway. Nancy slowly warmed up to the idea, especially since she had planned to return to Hong Kong, where she had recently secured a position at the prestigious Mandarin Oriental Hotel. This of course meant that we would only be three hours apart by plane.

After that telephone call, I went to the concierge every day, checking if my package had arrived. I was trying to figure out how to break the news to Mrs. Burnes. Work was not the same again after my telephone interview; I could not stop thinking about China and my impending move there. I felt a strange sensation, or rather excitement, which I had not felt for a long time—the feeling of doing something completely new, like stepping into the unknown. I was also excited because I would not only travel to a completely new country very, very far away but I would do so in the position I had always wanted— assistant food and beverage manager.

The name "China" alone was already mysterious. Closed for centuries, not many people really knew much about it except that it was far away and had an incredibly ancient culture. The more recent happenings at Tiananmen Square didn't deter me at all. The way I saw it, it was just one of those occurrences which were bound to happen when a country underwent a major change, and for China to move from a centralized Communist-style economy to a more Western-style market economy was just such a change. The news about China since Tiananmen had been positive throughout and many people talked about the dawn of a new era for China and Asia as a whole. No, I was not scared at all. Quite the opposite, I was excited as never before in my life and I couldn't wait to start this new part of my life.

At last, the long-awaited package with my contract arrived. I grabbed the UPS envelope, went to my office, and retrieved two copies of the eight-page employment contract and an enclosed brochure of the hotel. I liked the hotel from the moment I laid my eyes on it; it was a large brand-new modern building with some distinct Chinese features such as the Chinese-style roofs. The lobby was very large with a wide marble staircase descending from the first floor gallery to the lobby.

I read the contract that covered everything from flight tickets, accommodation, and meals to laundry and hotel rules. The owner representative and the general manager of the hotel had signed it. Without further delay, I signed the last page of the document and then sat back. All that was left now for me to do was to write my resignation and see Mrs. Burnes. That was the hardest part. I decided to see her the following day.

That evening I went for dinner with Nancy. The mood was solemn even though I was very excited; only now did the prospect that I would be leaving sink in. So far, it had only been talk but now I had actually signed a contract and in my mind, there was no way back. We finished dinner and then went home, where we had another bottle of champagne to celebrate. Nancy took it all very bravely even though I knew she felt differently. The next day I saw Mrs. Burnes at three in the afternoon.

"What can I do for you?" she asked, looking at me suspiciously. Her eyes fell on the envelope, which contained my letter of resignation.

I wanted to get this finished as quickly as possible. "Ahm, Mrs. Bu..., Michele, I am here because I want to resign."

"Really?" she asked in obvious disbelief and sat up in her chair.

"Ahm, yes."

"Where are you going?"

"I am going to China."

"You are going to China?"

"Yes."

"I see. Are you joining Singh in Beijing?" she asked.

"Ahm, yes."

"You are going as assistant food and beverage manager?"

"Yes."

"I see."

I carefully placed the letter on the table. She picked it up and opened it. It had taken me the better part of three hours to write the letter and besides the resignation part, I had written a little about how much I thanked her for all she had done for me. When she finished reading, she folded it up and placed it on the table. I looked at her and for a moment, I had the impression as if she had watery eyes, but I was not sure.

"Well, Andre, this is the opportunity you have always been looking for and I guess there is little I can do to change your mind."

"Ahm, that is correct," I mumbled.

"Well..." She was just about to talk when her office door flung open and the chief concierge stormed in.

"Mrs. Burnes, there is a bomb alert on Chesham Square," he cried.

She looked at me, I looked at her, and we laughed. We got up and walked over to the window. What we saw made my heart stop. The entire square had been cordoned off and several members of the bomb squad had gathered near a lonely briefcase. They had brought in a remote-controlled bomb-retrieval robot and we watched as the little machine slowly rolled towards the suspected bomb. The whole incident lasted for little over two hours until finally the all clear was given; it had been a false alarm. We returned to her desk.

"Andre, all I can do is thank you for what you have done for the hotel over the past four years and I wish you good luck for the future." With that, she got up and shook my hand.

"Thank you, Michelle."

She laughed. "That's the first time that you've called me by my first name. At least I have taught you something."

"Oh no, Mrs. Burnes, you have taught me much more than that." We shook hands and I left her office.

Outside in the corridor I took a deep breath, thinking that this was the beginning of a new chapter in my life. I went to my office and collected the envelope with my contract. At the concierge desk I packed everything into a DHL envelope and asked the clerk to send it off to China. I had planned to take at least three weeks' leave back in Germany before departing for Beijing.

In the weeks to come, I was busy preparing for my imminent departure. I had to give notice to my landlord, cancel my bank account and other necessary chores. Mrs. Burnes had asked me to prepare a handover, which I did in as much detail as possible; I wanted to make it as easy as possible for my successor to take over. The final document contained no less than thirty-three pages. Then on my last day, I cleaned up my office and handed over my keys, hotel ID card and other documents.

Mrs. Burnes had organized a leaving party for me at her house the same night. The chef had prepared a selection of fine canapés and we had plenty of champagne. After the speeches, Mrs. Burnes handed me my leaving gift, a brand-new Delsey suitcase. Once again, we drank until the early hours of the next day and after some emotional goodbyes, I left Mrs. Burnes' house for the last time.

Three days earlier my brother Ralf and his girlfriend had arrived from Germany. We spent the remaining days with some sightseeing and a final dinner with Nancy. The next day we left London at five o'clock in the morning with my car loaded to the rim with luggage. As we drove through the deserted city of London, I said goodbye silently, taking with me many wonderful memories.

An unusually beautiful sunrise greeted us when we entered the M1 to Dover and I thought, *A fitting start to a new part of my life.*

To be continued in *Hotel—Untold Stories: Part II - Asia*

Printed in the United States
106690LV00003B/8/P